Memory and Writing

from Wordsworth to Lawrence

Memory and Writing

From Wordsworth to Lawrence

BY

PHILIP DAVIS

Lecturer in English Literature
in the University of Liverpool

BARNES & NOBLE BOOKS
TOTOWA, NEW JERSEY

First published in the USA 1983 by
BARNES & NOBLE BOOKS
81 ADAMS DRIVE
TOTOWA, NEW JERSEY, 07512

Copyright © 1983 by
Liverpool University Press

ISBN 0-389-20342-4

First published 1983

Library of Congress Cataloging in Publication Data
Davis, Philip.
  Memory and writing from Wordsworth to Lawrence.

  (Liverpool English texts and studies; 21)
  1. English literature—19th century—History and criticism.
2. Memory in literature. 3. Self in literature. 4. Fiction, Auto-
biographic. 5. English literature—20th century—History and
criticism.
I. Title. II. Series: Liverpool English texts and studies (Totowa,
N.J.); 21.
PR468.M45D38   1983   820'.9'353   83-12242
ISBN 0-389-20342-4

Text set in 11/12pt Baskerville
Printed and bound in Great Britain by
Biddles Ltd, Guildford and King's Lynn

*For Sheila and Sid Davis
and
Margaret and Stanley Middleton*

Contents

PART III
MEMORY AND WRITING

Acknowledgements

I am pleased to be able to put in print the names of people who have befriended and helped me in the years during which this book was written: Rita and Paul Acarnley, John Davies and Cynthia Lalli, Jean and Alan Hughes, Tim Langley, Juliet Lewis, Lyvia Morgan, Annette and Brian Mountford, Mary Ann Radzinowicz, Jenny Sanders, Graham Sutherland, Betty Wood and Malcolm Woodfield. Jean Gooder was concerned, helpful and supportive as the supervisor of my Ph.D. thesis. *Stand*, and Jon Silkin, published me at a time when I felt despondent about that possibility. I am grateful now to Liverpool University Press, where Rosalind Campbell and Anne Crowe have been most helpful; Cathy Rees gave me kind assistance in the preparation of the final manuscript.

I owe much to Philip Edwards for his kindness and support, encouraging me in both the final writing and the publishing of this work. Stanley Middleton and Wil Sanders have given me great help and backing, and the personal example of them both, in their different ways, has done me more good than I can say; I have also benefited greatly, if not sufficiently, from the challenges, as well as the kindnesses, offered by J. H. Prynne: I shall always be grateful for the example of serious understanding which he has provided. I am only rueful, when I think of the help of these people in particular, that the end-product is not more worthy. Even so, the only way I can express my most personal feelings of memory and gratitude is in the dedication of this book to Sheila and Sid Davis, my parents, and Margaret and Stanley Middleton, all four of whom have seen and helped me through.

PHILIP DAVIS

Liverpool,
September 1982

Source Acknowledgements

The author and the publishers are grateful to the following publishers and literary executors for permission to include copyright material:

Frank Cass & Co. Ltd. for extracts from *D. H. Lawrence: A Personal Record* by Jessie Chambers; Cornell University Press for extracts from *The Cornell Wordsworth*, General Editor: S. M. Parrish; Faber and Faber Publishers for extracts from *Joseph Conrad: The Three Lives* by Frederick R. Karl; Harvard University Press for extracts from *John Keats: Letters*, edited by H. E. Rollins; William Heinemann Ltd., Laurence Pollinger Limited, and the Estate of Frieda Lawrence Ravagli for extracts from *Phoenix: The Posthumous Papers, Phoenix ii: Uncollected, Unpublished, and other Prose Works, Studies in Classic American Literature, The Fantasia of the Unconscious, The Rainbow, Aaron's Rod, Sons and Lovers, Women in Love, The Complete Short Stories of D. H. Lawrence* by D. H. Lawrence, and *The Collected Letters of D. H. Lawrence*, edited by H. T. Moore; Macmillan, London and Basingstoke, for extracts from *The Life of Thomas Hardy* by F. E. Hardy, *Thomas Hardy, Complete Poems*, edited by James Gibson, *Thomas Hardy, New Wessex Edition of the Works*, and *Personal Notebooks*, edited by Richard H. Taylor; the University of Michigan Press for extracts from *Matthew Arnold, Complete Prose Works;* Oxford University Press for extracts from *Prose Works of William Wordsworth*, edited by W. J. B. Owen and Jane Worthington Smyser, *Poetical Works of William Wordsworth*, edited by E. de Selincourt and Helen Darbishire, *David Copperfield* by Charles Dickens, edited by Nina Burgis (The Clarendon Dickens), *An Autobiography* by Anthony Trollope, and *Autobiography* by John Stuart Mill, edited by Jack Stillinger; Princeton University Press and Routledge & Kegan Paul Ltd. for extracts from *The Notebooks of Samuel Taylor Coleridge*, edited by Kathleen Coburn, and *The Friend*, edited by Barbara Rooke (Volume 4 of *The Collected Works of Samuel Taylor Coleridge*, edited by Kathleen Coburn and Bart Winer); Viking Penguin Inc., New York, for extracts from *Phoenix: The Posthumous Papers of D. H. Lawrence*, edited and with an Introduction by Edward D. McDonald, copyright 1936 by Frieda Lawrence, renewed © 1964 by the Estate of the late Frieda Lawrence Ravagli, *Phoenix ii: Uncollected, Unpublished, and other Prose Works* by D. H. Lawrence, collected and edited with an Introduction and

Introduction

'He sits up there, enjoying writing his gloomy poems.' That, at any rate, was how his young second wife thought of him. She had some reason. As far as she could tell, he had been relieved when his first wife died. But then he had found her private diaries. The literary husband read this work by his dead wife: the early diaries were full of the love they had known together at first in their young days, but the later ones consisted only of anger and bitterness. These diaries struck him with violence. Although he had known his own misery well enough in that marriage, it was as if he had never really known her pain. It did not prevent his re-marrying, but his second wife did conclude later that what he had wanted from that was a house-keeper-companion who would read to him. She had feared the worst when she learnt of the diaries: 'All I hope is that I may not, for the rest of his life, have to sit and listen to an account of her virtues and graces'. But just when he might have been ensuring that his second marriage was not to be the failure that his first had been, he turned to writing poetry in memory of his dead wife. The only places he would holiday at were places he had visited with her, and then he might not take his new wife with him. On the anniversary of the woman's death he would wear an old black hat; the other woman whom he had married thought it was 'very pathetic—all the more when one remembers what their married life was like'. Surely he too remembered that. And his second wife was scared that the world 'must imagine', from reading his poetry, 'that his only wish is to die & be in the grave with the only woman who ever gave him any happiness', and she felt both bitter and resigned. The poems made her feel a failure, she said. So there was good reason for her to think angrily of him sitting up there, cheering himself up by writing gloomy poems, while she sat down below without spirit.[1]

Notes and Bibliography begin on page 491.

But was she right to accuse him of enjoying himself? What was going on inside the study, inside the mind of the man who sat down every day to write? If she did not really know what he was doing there, do we know today as we sit and read the poems of Thomas Hardy? Or is it just easier for us to sit there and be moved, when we do not have to pay the price that Hardy paid in suffering over the memory of his dead wife Emma, when we do not have to bear the cost that Florence Emily Hardy, the second wife, had to bear? It would take a George Eliot, narrator of marriages like that of Dorothea to Casaubon, to begin to tell us what it must really have been like for Hardy and for Florence Emily Hardy. When Leavis gave a lecture about his personal memories of the philosopher Wittgenstein, it struck me simply and forcibly when he made, almost in passing, what I took to be the greatest tribute to the realistic novel: 'I can't say several complementary and corrective things at once, and I haven't the opportunities that the scope and complexity of a novel would give for being just to Wittgenstein. I have to rely on the cumulative effect of "memories"—an effect dependent on the order of rendering as well as on my commentary'.[2] Yet I suppose that when you read a work of art, like Hardy's, you do not often read it as a novelist might, looking for the story behind the work. For it was Leavis among others who offered us the word 'impersonality', as if true art were above such things as anecdote, biography, and personality. And yet, Leavis thought, a novel was the best way one could do justice to the memory of a complex friend. It is all right, is it, for a novelist to make art out of recollected life, but not so all right for readers to find mundane life still in that work of art? It is not right to confuse a Hardy poem with the misery that poem may have caused his second wife; but why would it be all right for George Eliot to be interested in making art out of such things? If art is above ordinary things, why did *she* by and large make her art out of them? She did not write of Saint Theresa, she tells us in the prologue to *Middlemarch*, but of Dorothea Brooke. The poet Hardy, likewise, is no saint.

I do not know what my reader will think of this. But you might be objecting: look, it is impossible to know what was in the mind of the poet writing his poetry; all we have is the result, the poem. And not only is it impossible to know, it is right that we do not know; it is the sanity of art that it is separate from autobiography, that it is free, and that it exists apart from autobiography for the sake of readers as well as writers. I am not at all sure that this is true. Poems often seem to me to bear as part of their meaning signs of memory, of the difficulties and untidinesses behind them. When I first read Wordsworth's Lucy poem, 'Strange fits of passion have I known', for instance, I think I judged it to be honest but trivial and fanciful. A lover is on his way to his beloved's cottage:

> My horse moved on; hoof after hoof
> He raised, and never stopped:
> When down behind the cottage roof,
> At once, the bright moon dropped.

> What fond and wayward thoughts will slide
> Into a Lover's head!
> 'O mercy!' to myself I cried,
> 'If Lucy should be dead!'

Because the moon dropped, he thought something had happened to his beloved. . . . I think I thought more highly of the Wordsworth who dared to tell us this than of the Wordsworth who, I presumed, had actually experienced it. Only, there is a sequel: when something equivalent did happen to me years later, I thought, some time after the small experience, that *that* was the reality that Wordsworth wrote of, or at least analogous to it in my imagination. And so I concluded that initially I had taken Wordsworth's poem as 'literature' because I had not taken—or perhaps had not the experience to be able to take—it seriously. Surely this lesson, that the polished art must have been more real to its author than it was at first to the casual reader, is not uncommon? Wordsworth, at any rate, must have been thinking of this when within the poem he wrote that it was a poem to be told 'in the Lover's ear alone'. I do not see why we should believe that art is ashamed of life when it is dependent upon it.

But how would I feel if it were proved tomorrow that there was no Lucy and that no such thing ever happened to Wordsworth? A man who has read this book for me told me, casually, that he could hardly trust Wordsworth again when he found out that the poem, 'The Solitary Reaper', was not based upon Wordsworth's own experience but upon a manuscript account written by a friend. So much seems to depend upon our feeling it to be poetry made out of a real experience:

> Whate'er the theme, the Maiden sang
> As if her song could have no ending;
> I saw her singing at her work,
> And o'er the sickle bending;—
> I listened, motionless and still;
> And, as I mounted up the hill,
> The music in my heart I bore,
> Long after it was heard no more.

Yet Wordsworth in 1805 took the episode from a passage in Thomas Wilkinson's *Tours to the British Mountains* (finally published in 1824): 'Passed a female who was reaping alone: she sung in Erse as she bended over her sickle; the sweetest human voice I ever heard: her strains were tenderly melancholy, and felt delicious, long after they were heard no more'. If I am worried about the ironies amidst which Hardy wrote his poetry, how can I ignore the fact that what a reader, at Wordsworth's instigation, naturally assumes to be Wordsworth's memory, life redeemed in art, was in fact no memory, only artfulness, of his? The man who complained to me felt somehow cheated by, and vaguely uneasy at, the secrets of the poet's imagination. Is it better not to know them? 'The Solitary Reaper' appeared, with a note acknowledging the debt to Wilkinson, in 'Poems of Imagination' in 1815 and 1820; thereafter it appeared in 'Memorials of a Tour in Scotland, 1803'. If we probe into the memorials of poets and novelists, will we be disillusioned to find them turn out to be sheer imaginations?

I do not think that there are sheer imaginations. I want to argue that imagination is a function of memory and personality. But, also, I do not think that the man who talked to me was right to feel cheated. It is not hard to argue against him. For Wordsworth the experience of hearing the solitary reaper was a memory, even though actually it was not his memory. He felt the power of the memory keenly enough for it to stir his imagination and verbal skill on its behalf. It was the sort of thing *he* might have been moved to see and hear, he must have felt; he would put it into poetry in gratitude to and also on behalf of his friend; he would make a few words of prose into the last line of his own poetry, for he did not believe that the prose of the world was alien to its poetry. Freqﬗently event and (what often only seems afterwards to be) the right response and expression do not coincide; sometimes, accordingly, it is the task of the writer to try to make them do so. A great deal of Wordsworth's poetry is taken and transmuted from his own life—which is why Wordsworth is so important to a book about memory as a constituent in the creative act. But one of the joyous flexibilities of human nature and human experience is the capacity of a man to find in the power which he has gained from the life behind him a further power to mould the life before him. If for so long the poetry took its power from the past and the poet recognized this, at some stage, knowing what would fire his poetry, he could create what he depended upon. In time, the explicit becomes implicit, memories become forgotten, and memory itself becomes a store for ideas to strike upon as well as an originator of ideas out of itself. That is what is so compelling about the idea of a literary man who begins to write for the sake of his life until he also begins to find how much his life *is*, and is even determined by, his writing and the fact of his being a literary man.

Moreover, there is evidence to suggest that Wordsworth himself would have felt no qualms about reading 'The Solitary Reaper' for the sake of the feelings of the man presumed to be behind the poem. In his second 'Essay upon Epitaphs' Wordsworth goes to some trouble to give particular examples of how men, seduced by the idea of Poetry and its language as something higher than themselves, artificially strain their words into approved and flighty diction. Thereby they forget what would be superior to all that: their real feelings at the death of another. Of course art is not simply real feeling without any need for the aid of artificial convention; but all the art will be as nothing without the memory of a human heart. It was just such a memory that led Wordsworth to exempt from his criticism of mere artifice some undeniably elaborate lines composed by the Marquis of Montrose on the death of Charles

I. It was said that he wrote them, immediately upon hearing the news, with the point of his own sword:

> Great, good, and just, could I but rate
> My griefs, and thy so rigid fate;
> I'd weep the world to such a strain,
> As it should deluge once again.

This is how Wordsworth read it:

> These funereal verses would certainly be wholly out of place upon a tombstone; but who can doubt that the Writer was transported to the height of the occasion?—that he was moved as it became an heroic Soldier, holding those Principles and opinions, to be moved? His soul labours;—the most tremendous event in the history of the Planet, namely, the Deluge, is brought before his imagination by the physical image of tears,—a connection awful from its very remoteness and from the slender bond that unites the ideas. . . . Hyperbole in the language of Montrose is a mean instrument made mighty because wielded by an affected Soul, and strangeness is here the order of Nature. Montrose stretched after remote things but was at the same time propelled towards them.
>
> *Prose Works,* ii, pp. 71–3.

If it were proved that Montrose did not write those lines in those circumstances, would Wordsworth have withdrawn his interpretation? When he put to himself the criticism that if we believed all the epitaphs, there must have been no bad people, he would not accept that an epitaph is essentially a falsehood. 'It *is* truth . . . it is truth hallowed by love—the joint offspring of the worth of the dead and the affections of the living!' (ibid., p. 58). The poem by the Marquis of Montrose would always have convinced Wordsworth as to the truth of its feeling and origin, whatever the subsequent evidence of the actual circumstances of its composition. The poetry would tell the truth when too literal-minded a devotion to facts would be a falsehood. But Wordsworth would not have stuck to the poem because he saw it as an act of 'impersonal' imagination, whereby the tears, made over into an image of the Flood, were raised from personal emotion into aesthetic wit. On the contrary, what interested Wordsworth was not how large an act was this but how small a one: it is the *slenderness* of the bond connecting the tears and the Flood that is so moving to him. The small lyric poem finds its power precisely in measuring itself against the big idea which human thought, straining to do justice to its emotion, calls in. For that the poem is smaller than the means of its expression, that tears are not floods and cannot provoke or withstand them or have much effect in general, was just what moved Wordsworth hugely. What supports the bond that unites the ideas? Not anything factual but something emotional in the face of reality:

> But she is in her grave, and, oh,
> The difference to me!

What Wordsworth sees between the tears and the Flood is not only what made the man a poet—the difference in the quality of his wit, in his capacity for imaginative ideas, for expression of his feelings—but also what made the poet even in that a man—'The difference to me' causing the tears to seek expression that way. 'The language of the earliest Poets was felt to differ materially from ordinary language, because it was the language of extraordinary occasions,' wrote Wordsworth in the great 'Preface', 'but it was really spoken by men, language which the Poet himself had uttered when he had been affected by the events which he described' (*Prose Works*, i, p. 161). What Wordworth was doing as a critic was trying to *remember* the emotion of the man which the poet had had partly to set aside in order to create the imaginative thought that would bring it back to the reader's mind. That is to say, crucially, Wordsworth read a poet's formal techniques as signs and reminders of the interior life of the man behind them. It did not disturb him if those techniques required the use of calculation or detachment; that was their duty to, rather than their betrayal of, human feeling. The imagination of the poet was to serve the memory of the man. That memory itself can be imaginatively recollected in some measure by readers who can read poetic conventions and techniques as a form of human translation. The sort of reading I have given in this book is, I hope, the sort that Wordsworth here displays and commends.

I cannot at all accept that Wordsworth's view of poetry and poets is no more than sentimental. When finally in the later version of his 'Preface to *Lyrical Ballads*' Wordsworth put the question explicitly, 'What is a Poet?', it was not a question that he thought to be beyond him. If I may put it thus, it *was* him; he was 'a Poet'. He did not suppose that a Poet, his Poetry and the questions which a Poet asked were beyond or apart from the concerns and passions of the rest of mankind. The Poet 'is a man speaking to men', 'nothing differing in kind from other men, but only in degree' (*Prose Works*, i, pp. 138, 142). In answering his questions in this way, Wordsworth provided the terms by which more ordinary men could presume to ask them again for themselves. What does poetry do? we can dare to ask. Poetry, concluded Wordsworth, quoting from Milton, 'sheds no tears "such as Angels weep", but natural and human tears; she can boast of no celestial ichor that distinguishes her vital juices from those of prose; the same human blood circulates through the veins of them both' (ibid., p. 135): 'long after they were heard no more'. That is to say, poetry is a human activity long before and (if Wordsworth had his way) long after it had become a specialized one. Poets 'do not write for Poets alone, but for men' (ibid., p. 143).

However, as I shall try to show in this book, Wordsworth's belief in the human basis of art is neither simple nor untroubled. Nor is it the belief that has helped literary studies into their present difficulties. It was the literary critics who would now be looked upon as old-fashioned that did that, when they spoke too easily and too merely professionally of the poet's 'essential humanity'. That coin was thin to begin with and is now worn and devalued, while in France, America, and England there has been the inevitable, professional reaction among the critics and in the universities. I am not the person to tell the story, having no heart for it. But there is a recent reviewer in *The Times Literary Supplement*, himself a poet, who condemns those moralizing, old-fashioned critics who are 'hostile to pure art'—the purity being 'the eloquence of form', the joy of 'aesthetic redemption': 'This formal pleasure has nothing to do with naive realism or with the "accurate rendering" of experience'. Nothing? And another recent writer, a novelist as well as critic, speaks of the 'paradox that it is not so much man that speaks language as language that speaks man; not so much the writer who writes narrative as narrative that writes the writer'. We are through the looking-glass.

It seems a good time, then, to turn back to Wordsworth, but without nostalgia, to ask if and in what way he was right to speak as he did. In this book I ask, what did it mean to be a literary person in the period from Wordsworth to Lawrence? The question is not asked primarily with respect to the social and economic status and circumstances of writers and book production in the nineteenth century, although the importance of these determinants is recognized and, indeed, has been written about by other people. In this work the emphasis has been put upon the personal and autobiographical aspects of the question. I have asked of my chosen authors, what does it mean for his human nature that a man is an author? and, to what uses does he put his life and personality in writing of matters of passion and conscience? I have wanted to know more about the relation between the writer's formal and verbal techniques and the person's more informal thoughts and emotions before, during and after the act of writing.

So, experimentally, I have extended the question 'What is a Poet?' into the question, what does it mean for a man to be a poet? will he still be like another man? The Poet 'is a man speaking to men'; but I have not wanted to repeat that hollowly. What does it mean for his relation both to himself and to the people whom he writes for, as well as among, that he *is* a poet? Against the clichés of 'essential humanity' I have sometimes wondered, sceptically, whether the very act of writing does not affect a writer's relation to what, again, we call 'reality'. These do not seem to me to be merely extra-literary questions, things from which the purposes of writing are remote and safe. It is not alien to the spirit of the author of *The Prelude*–Wordsworth's long poem of memory on the growth of a poet's mind—to suppose that the extended question, as to what it means for a man to be a poet, has a profound and not incidental relation to the meaning of that man's very poetry. Similarly, it is at the very heart of *The Fall of Hyperion* that Keats had chosen, as far as he could choose, to be a literary, and not a medical, man. And, equally, it is, as it was meant to be, utterly damaging to a study of the significance of George

Eliot, if you come to believe with W. H. Mallock that the
novelist, sheerly by being a novelist, falsifies the world by
creating one:

> Not only will lonely thought and study necessitate in
> general a certain withdrawal from life, and a consequent
> ignorance of it; but devotion to any special pursuit, that is
> possible only for the few, will tend to distort the judgment,
> and will lead a man to put the personal *motive* of his own
> career in place of the ultimate and general *justification*. . . .
> Interests which absorb [intellectuals such as men of
> letters] and give their lives a meaning, they imagine will
> affect the world at large in a like way; unconscious that
> the world at large has other interests which they know of
> but by empty names.[3]

Can we not try to ask of the century that culminated in the
development of the realistic novel, in what way is literature
'real'?

The works with which I am mainly concerned in what
follows are those which, in complicated ways, derive from an
autobiographical impulse often not choosing to express itself
directly in conventional autobiography. This has enabled me
to think, I suppose beneath it all, in that crude way one does
not usually want to put into words: are these works somehow
like the men who wrote them? what was it really like to feel
things in the way this poem describes? did the man who wrote
it feel that way? what would it be like to be Hardy? how does
the work stand in the order of reality when compared with other
things that the writer did in his life? I do not say that these are
very intelligent or answerable questions; but they have been in
my mind throughout, searching for better expression or a convincing re-direction. I could not even get so far as to ask how
far this autobiographical impulse constituted an origin for the
art of the nineteenth century more than ever it did for the art
of other centuries; although there can be found in this book
some suggestions or hints as to why this might be so. At any
rate, I confess I have found no reason to doubt the orthodoxy
that Romanticism was something relatively new in supposing
the individual, drawing upon the interior store of his personal
life, to be at least the starting-point or front from which a

serious consideration about the problems of living might proceed. It is with the individual's written consideration of himself as his own starting-point that I am here principally concerned. This procedure, centering on matters of individual personality, is, of course, a procedure itself dependent for its own recognition on alternative procedures which, on this occasion, I have not chosen to adopt. But in the chapters which follow, certain theological, economic and political objections to the primacy of the personal are registered as incorporated *within* the tensions of those particular writers whom I try to describe. There are indeed often pointers within people which point to what is wrong outside, rather than just inside them; but in this work I have been content to stay inside for the time, where the reality impinges.

But let me return from explanation and apology to the man who complained to me about 'The Solitary Reaper'. Actually, I do not believe that he was altogether wrong to feel as he did. For at least his feeling does credit to an intuition that John Ruskin, another important figure in this book, took pains to articulate:

> What master of the pencil, or the style,
> Had traced the shades and lines that might have made
> The subtlest workman wonder? *Dead, the dead,*
> *The living seemed alive; with clearer view*
> *His eye beheld not, who beheld the truth,*
> Than mine what I did tread on, while I went,
> Low bending.

Dante has here clearly no other idea of the highest art than that it should bring back, as in a mirror or vision, the aspect of things passed or absent. The scenes of which he speaks are, on the pavement, for ever represented by angelic power, so that the souls which traverse this circle of the rock may see them, as if the years of the world had been rolled back, and they again stood beside the actors in the moment of action. Nor do I think that Dante's authority is absolutely necessary to compel us to admit that such art as this *might* indeed be the highest possible. Whatever delight we may have been in the habit of taking in pictures, if it were but truly offered to us, to remove at

our will the canvass from the frame, and in lieu of it to
behold, fixed for ever, the images of some of those mighty
scenes which it has been our way to make mere themes for
the artist's fancy; if, for instance, we could again behold
the Magdalene receiving her pardon at Christ's feet, or
the disciples sitting with Him at the table of Emmaus;
and this not feebly nor fancifully, but as if some silver
mirror, that had leaned against the wall of the chamber,
had been miraculously commanded to retain for ever the
colours that had flashed upon it for an instant—would we
not part with our picture—Titian's or Veronese's though
it might be?

Modern Painters, vol. iii, pt. iv, chap. ii, para. 5.

Our poet-reviewer insists that 'pure art' 'has nothing to do'
'with the "accurate rendering" of experience'. All I really want
to do in this book is to suggest that if a writer could simply
bring to life again his previous experience, as Ruskin puts it,
'such art as this *might* be the highest possible'. I do not actually
believe that a writer simply can do this. For one thing, when
you try to write about a past experience, you find that that
experience is not simply an event out there, something you can
pin down and write about at a distance; the experience carries
over into the attempt to think and write about it in order to try
to resolve the unfinished memory. Ruskin himself did not
believe that an artist could simply reproduce the past, the
dead, the living and the absent; but the impulse that would
want to do so is still alive in being driven into conventions that
approximate to the original. The question, would you prefer
the landscape that this picture depicts to the picture itself, was
still an important one to Ruskin and, he thought, to art and
artists. And if one was to answer 'no', that would be because
there was something in the inability to reproduce and replace
the scene that carried with it the painter's extra effort to
indicate why this scene mattered to him. That extra effort
would be a spiritual bonus, but, as far as Ruskin could see, it
would arise paradoxically out of the painter's own sense that
he cared more for the subject of the painting than for the
painting itself; that was how the painting might then become
for a spectator more important than the scene itself—as an

untutored eye might have witnessed it before help was offered by the thought embodied in the painting. 'Painting has its peculiar virtues, not only consistent with, but even resulting from, its shortcomings and weaknesses' (ibid., chap. x, para. 7). To 'the small, conceited and affected painter' Ruskin says: 'Stand aside from between that nature and me'; to 'the great imaginative painter', 'Come between this nature and me—this nature which is too great and too wonderful for me; temper it for me, interpret it to me' (ibid., para. 19). It is true that such a view had painful, self-denigrating consequences for the life of the man who held it, as I shall indicate in chapter 4. But what Ruskin describes does seem to me the effect of Wordsworth's coming between the solitary reaper and us. Moreover, this is not simply 'naive realism': it has, as is manifest in the use of Dante, a theological, virtually metaphysical sanction for its belief in life. The effort to bring back the absent, though necessarily flawed and incomplete since mimesis is impossible for man, nonetheless brings with it an expression of soul in the artist which could not be brought out by his seeking to express it *per se*. Nor does anyone paint a great picture simply by making painting great pictures his aim. That paradox was for Ruskin the guarantee of the serious greatness of art.

Thus, one kind of objection to the preconceptions at work in this book must here be confronted explicitly—not least because it is an objection with its historical roots in the very period under discussion. I mean that line of defence of literature which stretches, with whatever qualifications, from the Blakean belief that the work of genius arises *ex nihilo*, from Shelley's axiom that poetry is something divine, from a Keatsian relish of beauty as truth, and finds a dead-end in Pater's defence of art for art's sake at the close of the century. Of course, to speak of that line is unjustly to over-simplify what was a complex, shifting, and often individual reaction to aggressive questions as to the social use and scientific worth of poetic thinking and feeling. But, even if Blake, Shelley, and Keats are not themselves wholly of it, there is a developed school of belief in art's transcendence of the merely mundane. And its classic expression is perhaps to be found in T. S. Eliot's Impersonal theory of poetry in his essay 'Tradition and the Individual Talent'.

Eliot put it thus:

> the more perfect the artist, the more completely separate in him will be the man who suffers and the mind which creates.
>
> *Selected Essays*, p. 18.

There is in this a strenuous objection to making the question 'What is a Poet?' a personal question; for, that it is not a merely personal question, Eliot argues, is part of what learning to become a poet means. W. B. Yeats said that although a poet writes always of his personal life, he is never the bundle of accident and incoherence that sits down at breakfast.[4] Indeed, it is true (as I try to show in chapter 1) that some distinction has to be made between the writer and the man, not least in order to identify the increased formal control that writing affords, that sheer verbal technique allows. But Eliot went further in making that formal distinction a basis for his belief in art's essential impersonality. It was not the duty of the artist to pay back the release he received through writing in order to achieve another form of servitude: that, I take it, is how he would counter the view of John Ruskin or, in a different way, George Eliot. T. S. Eliot's was a belief that the reparative sanity, the redemptive dignity of art lay precisely in the potential separation between the memory of the man who suffers and the imagination of the artist who creates. Indeed the separation was the very essence of creativity. 'Poetry is not a turning loose of emotion, but an escape from emotion; it is not the expression of personality, but an escape from personality. But, of course, only those who have personality and emotions know what it means to want to escape from these things' (*Selected Essays*, p. 21). For an anti-Romantic statement, 'escape' is a powerfully Romantic word. It signals the desire of the so-called true artist to distinguish himself from the immature amateur's embarrassing and sentimental belief that he could simply make art out of autobiographical confession.

The self-sacrifice that Eliot, partly out of buried emotional reasons of his own, demanded of the true artist was the sacrifice of the personal self to that work which the artist precisely tried to make more valuable than himself. In trying to make the work more valuable than the man behind it, the man made himself an artist. His work aspired to preserve only that part of him which he wished to preserve—or, perhaps, mercifully, it was not something that was even part of what he felt to be his responsible identity; at any rate, the rest, the autobiographical dross, was (it was the wisdom of the artist to recognize) best forgotten. The life of the artist was the life of his *works*, and that was a life apart from his everyday life and from the more mundane difficulties of the writer off-duty. A biography of T. S. Eliot could not possibly explain his poems. His intellectual vision, his power through language, transcend what shabbinesses there might be in any personal life. It is not the shabbiness or the turning loose of emotion that make the artist, though shabby and emotional men might like to think so.

This belief in a Transcendent Art and an Impersonal Artist has, for all its now old-fashioned diction, still something of the force of an orthodoxy even today. There is the text alone. We very rarely think to 'explain' the thought of a great scientist by reference to his personality: why then presume to do so in the case of a great poet or novelist? Yet it seems to me to be utterly obvious that a writer uses his memory in his work in a way that a scientist does not. I have some sympathy with what Eliot was trying to make of his art, and the personal, social, and historical circumstances that forced him to argue in the way that he did strike me as profoundly interesting and even moving.[5] But, taking the argument *per se*, I question whether the value of art is its escape from the chaos of personality; whether the virtue of technique is to escape rather than re-enter a man's interior world; whether creativity and imagination are indeed so special and so pure as not to be in articulate service of a man's memory of his life and times. In this particular book, at any rate, I consider the ideal of an art standing to life in a way analogous to that in which an ordinary man's memory stands to some important experience which it both recalls and originates in. Although, as I have said, that ideal is an impossible ideal, it is not a nugatory one; for the impetus contained within it does seem to me to be something powerfully in practice among the writers I here choose to look at: Wordsworth, George Eliot, Thomas Hardy, and D. H. Lawrence. Thus I do *not* start from the proposition that the artist so far transcends his personal life as to create works of art whose value is related to their apparently having arisen *ex nihilo*, to stand above merely human weakness by dint of sheer genius. That does not seem to me to be the real dignity of art. Eschewing Eliot's view of a transcendent art, I try in this book to see how far I may take the relation of the 'man writing' to 'the man himself' (however problematic that latter notion)—without, I trust, falling into the other, opposite trap of reductivism. I take as my guide here Wordsworth on the poet Burns.

When Wordsworth read Burns, he seems to have felt the separation of the poet from the man to have been something of a paradox. The poet wrote with greatness; the man lived ruinously. Or as Florence Emily Hardy said of her husband, in words which, Robert Gittings thinks, may actually have been borrowed from the first Mrs Hardy: 'he is a great writer, but not a great man'. To Wordsworth this was a paradox in Burns because some of the greatness of the poet lay in the literary treating of his own ruin. His ruin was partly his poetic subject-matter. Why could not his own poetry, his own writing of it, make a difference in him? Was he something in his poetry that he could not be in himself? If so, is that the virtue of poetry, as an Eliot might suggest? Is that poetry's strength that in it a man can turn round upon himself? Or is it mute testimony to poetry's weakness as a form of human action? unable to cure what it describes and perhaps even taking the place of curing it by writing about it? 'The most attentive and sagacious reader cannot explain how a mind, so well established by knowledge fell—and continued to fall, without power to prevent or retard its own ruin' (Wordsworth: *Prose Works*, iii, pp. 119–20). There would be no problem here had it not been Burns's strength to bring the memory of his life into the thinking of his poetry. Others might say that the poetry was one thing, a formal system, the life another, where mistakes even when written about are still repeated. But to the poet at the moment of writing his poetry it was no such compartmentalizing: there was a mind thinking, within the memory, of both the connections and the separations between his life and the writing work which he was doing now in front of him. Wordsworth knew by heart Burns's 'A Bard's Epitaph':

> Is there a man, whose judgment clear
> Can others teach the course to steer,
> Yet runs, himself, life's mad career
>   Wild as a wave?—
> Here pause—and, thro' the starting tear,
>   Survey this grave.

A moralist might say, should not Burns have seen from his poetry how to mend his life? If he had seen the necessity forcibly enough, could not he have seen the means? To this I guess Wordsworth would reply, don't you think *he* knows that?—the words Biddy in *Great Expectations* speaks to Pip when Pip complains of Joe's unsuitable manners. Don't you think that in writing the above Burns *knew* that he ought to have been able to mend his life, and this knowledge of an irreducible responsibility makes this writing at once both his achievement and his failure? Here art is a holding-ground, where the poet is not satisfied that 'the difference to me' should make no difference, sees no compensation in art, and yet, knowing that the power of his emotion is, outside the poem, well nigh powerless, still writes as if there were no simple irony or tragedy about the use of writing. If we paid no attention to the feeling and thinking and remembering that we construe as lying behind Burns's own written record of them, then we should not see what is at stake in art's thus being a holding-ground for all the contradictions that go into its making. That Burns knew that he was a man who could teach others but not himself neither stopped him writing, through a sense of temerity, nor allowed him then to write too comfortably.

   Although I concentrate on a few authors, there is of course a broad historical context for the problems considered in this book. Whatever his doubts about Wordsworth's personal motivation, William Hazlitt was sure that Wordsworth's genius was an emanation of the Spirit of the Age. Hazlitt wrote of Wordsworth's poetry that it proceeded on a principle of equality. 'It partakes of, and is carried along with, the revolutionary movements of our age: the political changes of the day were the model on which he formed and conducted his poetical experiments'.[6] To be a poet who is 'a man speaking to men', who is concerned, above all, with common sights and

ordinary sorrows, was a democratic act. And it had to do not
only with the French Revolution but with the role of the poet
in a society which in England in the nineteenth century was
becoming increasingly secular and increasingly industrial. It is
clear and crucial that Wordsworth did not believe in poets as a
separate category or class or caste, precisely for seeing the
temptations to think like that. The 'Preface to *Lyrical Ballads*' is
written against the notion of the Poets as a self-justifying
Profession, wherein Poetry and Literature were established as
autonomous and self-generative. Writers were not merely to
write like writers. As Hugh Blair had put it, 'when Poetry
became a regular art, studied for reputation and for gain,
Authors began to affect what they did not feel'.[7] *Lyrical Ballads*
accordingly proposed, against an authorized poetic diction, to
bring the language of the poets back to being both really spoken
by men and closer to the language of men. Hazlitt thus
described Wordsworth's as a crusading poetry 'founded on
setting up an opposition (and pushing it to the utmost length)
between the natural and the artificial; between the spirit of
humanity, and the spirit of fashion and of the world!' (op. cit.).

When I started this work, I put it to myself that it was
'natural' books, as opposed to artificial ones, that interested
me. For example, I cared (and still do care) more for
Wordsworth's 'The Solitary Reaper' than for Keats's 'La Belle
Dame Sans Merci' or Tennyson's 'Mariana'. No doubt this
was alternately a crude and a naive view thus formulated;
although the aspiration behind it remains in chapters 3 and 4
of this book in relation to the *Memorials of Thomas Hood* and the
Autobiography of Mrs Margaret Oliphant, two books which do not
seem to me to be, in that pejorative sense, 'artificial'. Natural
books, I thought, had more to do with memory than with
invention.

Part of this youthful view was gained from Wordsworth. In
an early, fragmentary 'Essay on Morals' Wordsworth
condemns in a way I found helpful what he calls the 'juggler's
trick' in literature. The juggler's trick 'lies not in fitting words
to things (which would be a noble employment) but in fitting
things to words' (Wordsworth: *Prose Works,* i, p. 103). In the
'Preface to *Lyrical Ballads*' Wordsworth builds on this use of
initial oppositions to become, at moments, almost anti-literary:

'However exalted a notion we would wish to cherish of the character of a Poet, it is obvious, that while he describes and imitates passions, his employment is in some degree mechanical, compared with the freedom and power of real and substantial action and suffering' (ibid., i, p. 138). And Wordsworth precisely did not go on to argue that therefore poetry should not try to describe and imitate human passion. Such reminders about priorities and principles and about the responsibility of the poet to the memory of the external reality of his subject-matter are necessary and salutary. For Wordsworth to put certain matters starkly at a critical historical moment was to make clear some vital ethical priorities concerning the relation of art to the memory of that of which it treats. Seeing the development of this scruple in the nineteenth century, I try to take up this question in chapter 4 by putting the real failure of a second-rate Victorian novelist, Mrs Oliphant, up against George Eliot's literary treatment of failure, in this way to test the latter in its ambition to be a sustaining influence for those who have failed. Such a test is in the very spirit of George Eliot's own worries about the success of providing human comfort within the form of the realistic novel.

Eventually, however, I found the clarity of priorities and terms which I believed I had taken from Wordsworth to be my own embattled clarity: one, I came to realize, threatening to become over-dependent upon the simplifying creation of mutually weakening alternatives, like the natural versus the artificial or literature often as opposed to real life. When the idea of such priorities hardened into a rigid idea of necessary and exclusive choices, then historically a literary man like Coleridge could find himself burdened within a cultural situation into guiltily thinking thus: 'Poetry—excites us to artificial feelings—makes us callous to real ones'.[8] This present work is indeed concerned with the sort of problem of conscience that Coleridge describes: a problem accentuated where the art is felt to have autobiographical responsibilities and debts. But it also includes a recognition which came late to me, although I suppose it is obvious: that Wordsworth did care about his words as much as, and because of, his subject-matter; that no art delivers memory 'naturally', unaffected by the fact of the memory being written; that, accordingly, the so-called 'real' works of feeling are highly dependent upon the so-called 'artificial' disposition and language. Still obsessed by my first principles, but now almost equally obsessed by the objections which necessitated their reformulation, I have tried in this book to treat the problems in a way that does not admit as necessary the cruder, battling oppositions which yet sometimes give my concerns most dramatic if not most accurate expression. This book is still not an essentially historical study, although its locale lies in the historical development from Romanticism. I try to recognize that certain things in what Wordsworth calls 'the history of feeling' *did* happen; but I am partly ignorant, partly sceptical of historical explanations as to *why* things did happen. And what I am really interested in is whether in some sense it was right and good and instructive *that* certain things did happen in the human spirit of a few literary people whom I care about from Wordsworth to Lawrence. That the terms 'right and good and instructive', together with their referents, are all most questionable, does not worry me overmuch, for it is the questions that I am interested in. This is a literary study attempting to think about the relation of writing to living and (by implication) of reading to living.

Part 1 of this book, its first two chapters, deals more or less exclusively with Wordsworth. It is with Wordsworth that we must start if we wish to see why it is memory that provides the creative link between art's verbal signs and men's store of private experience. He is our necessary starting-point. First, because his aggressive, apparently anti-literary stance in the 'Preface to *Lyrical Ballads*' is also related to a more troubled autobiographical situation when he is actually writing his poetry. Memory in Wordsworth is personally central to his ambivalence concerning the status of writing. For memory, as emotion recollected in tranquillity, is at the source of the poetry's creation, while also serving as a conscientious reminder that the original experience was often more powerful than the subsequent literary transmutation of it. The poet 'should consider himself as in the situation of a translator, who does not scruple to substitute excellencies of another kind for those which are unattainable by him and endeavours occasionally to surpass his original, in order to make some amends for the general inferiority to which he feels he must submit' (Wordsworth: *Prose Works*, i, p. 139). As the revisions to the 'Preface' show, Wordsworth worried over these things throughout his life.

There is a second reason for concentrating upon Wordsworth. In no other great English poet is the auto-biographical process by which the man made himself, and learned to become, a poet so clearly discernible in the very poetry itself. This for the reason that Wordsworth seems to have felt that he could not have become a great poet without knowing within himself and expressing within his poetry all the secrets of the growth of a poet's mind. He learnt technique as a translation of human worries, and thus knew technique in its human aspect. Metre, for example, Wordsworth thus thought of as something which, even in being distinctively of poetry, was in that, as 'the co-presence of something regular, something to which the mind has been accustomed in various moods and in a less excited state', constitutive of 'an inter-texture of ordinary feeling' 'not strictly or necessarily connected with the passion' (ibid., i, p. 147). Metre as a neutral convention was made over into the sanity of a supportive base for the writer and as a sign of a constant for the reader.

Thus it is possible to have a clear view of the *early* Wordsworth seeing himself as a translator, fitting 'words to things'; a poet finding most of his initial power in being moved by his subject-matter; a mind first finding its own power in being moved by others, then trying with feelings mixed of piety and guilt, of exploitation and usefulness, to articulate that power on its own. Thus it is also possible to have an equally clear view of the *developing* Wordsworth's difficulties with his role of translator, involving the apparent sacrifice of words to things even as his verbal power was increasing through that very sacrifice. Wordsworth wrote to John Wilson in June 1802 of the necessity of the poet to travel before men as well as at their sides. He must have been suspecting a competence of language beyond its function as translation; he must have been asking himself whether there was almost within his possession a distinctly poetic form of thinking—a capacity to think and signal through poetry, through being a poet, that xxxiv

Introduction

which could not be articulated by almost any other means. If that were true and possible, then his power in poetry was struggling to increase at some threatened cost to his initial ethical beliefs about art's necessary subservience. How Wordsworth came to use his difficulties about the status of writing actually within his own writing is the subject of chapter 1. How he developed the flexibility to avoid entrenched self-division in all this, how he was able to see poetic thought not as the enemy of private emotion but as its representative without being its slave, is the subject of close and particular analyses in chapter 2. I ask my readers for their help and patience through these close readings. There are some authors or books one takes to be at the root of affairs. And I have looked hard between the lines of Wordsworth's poetry because it has seemed to me to be a root-work with respect to knowing what is a poet and what is poetry.

This brings me to a third and final reason. Wordsworth has been very important to my thinking about the question 'What is a Poet?' not least because his work seems to hold together possible answers and positions which I, initially, would have insisted upon as contradictory and which he maintains are not necessarily so. He can insist upon the subordination of words to things and yet insist upon words as things in their own right. He can write powerfully by tacitly suggesting that the writing itself is subordinate to its own subject-matter. He gains from a sense of what writing cannot do fresh impulses to write about that. And it is not simply the case that the worries about writing are early in his career while the belief in writing comes later. Memory itself is a witness that there is more to a man, than the notion of his using the past merely to supersede himself allows.

> It seems, as one becomes older,
> That the past has another pattern, and ceases to be a
> mere sequence—
> Or even development: the latter a partial fallacy
> Encouraged by superficial notions of evolution,
> Which becomes, in the popular mind, a means of
> disowning the past.
>
> T. S. Eliot: *Four Quartets*, 'The Dry Salvages', ii.

I have had more to try to learn from Wordsworth than from anyone. What is so important about him is that his anxieties about writing are not separate from an increasing commitment to poetic writing as the most serious record of human purpose. The memories were most seriously worked out on the page while knowing themselves to have their origin off the page and anterior to it.

It is this sense of an anterior or external reality to that of which writing treats which is the subject of Part II (chapters 3 and 4). We have no secure means of telling whether the exercise of memory by ordinary people is fundamentally the same as a writer's use of his memory through his being a writer. But instead, I have tried to ask, cannot there be found a text which, almost by chance, seems to embody the ordinary reality usually anterior to writing and thus simply uses the written form merely to pass that reality on? Is there not a text, a real text, a natural text, like life?

> . . . Is there not
> An art, a music, and a stream of words
> That shall be life, the acknowledged voice of life?[9]

Cannot the written word be of the same nature as a man's memory in dealing with what it recalls? I have taken these questions to the study of a biography of Thomas Hood (in chapter 3) and an autobiography by Mrs Oliphant (in chapter 4). I deal with them at length because I think that most people have not read them and they are, for not being elaborately artificial, unjustly forgotten, when the memory of such people ought not to be. I find in these chapters that the idea of a 'natural' text, a memory unaffected by its status as written, is a fallacy. The necessary place of the artificial within a man's nature, the more particularly when he is a writer, became clearer to me in considering the case of Thomas Hood and the almost accidental, authorless text assembled out of his letters called his *Memorials*. These lessons could have been learnt from Wordsworth; but to show that there are other ways than the way of Wordsworth was necessary. Not least for this purpose: to point to that other fallacy, that the worth of a book is dependent above all on its style and on its structure. That is not true: books can have a memory and a human heart more essentially behind them.

Nonetheless, writing of things does change them. How a man's memory stands to the changes of it in his writing is an important preoccupation in this work. What is at stake here may be briefly illustrated by use of Plato's myth concerning the invention of writing. The translation is by John Stuart Mill for the *Monthly Repository* 1834—incidentally, the form in which Freud first came upon the myth. The god Theuth is described as bringing his inventions to the king of Egypt, Thamus:

> Now when the art of writing came under consideration, Theuth said, 'This art will make the Egyptians wiser, and will aid their memory: for it is a help to memory and to wisdom.' The other answered, 'Most sage Theuth, it is one thing to be able to invent an art, and another to judge of its beneficial or hurtful effects: and now you, who are the inventor of writing, have ascribed to it, from partiality, an effect the exact opposite of its real one: this art will produce forgetfulness in those who learn it, by causing them to trust to written memoranda, and neglect their memory. What you have discovered, therefore, is an aid not to memory, but to recollection; and you will give to your scholars the *opinion* of wisdom, not the reality: for hearing much from you, without really learning it, they will appear men of great acquirements, though really for the most part ignorant and incapable.'[10]

This makes a general question about the disposition of writing: what happens to the nature of thought when it is transferred, if so indeed it be, from the mind in its life and living speech to commitment to external marks on paper? Writing, Plato seems to be suggesting, so far from embodying the faculties of memory and wisdom as they are within ourselves, re-embodies them externally, either, at best, as reminders on the page or, at worst, as semblances and surrogates. Now, as Wordsworth helps us to appreciate, it may indeed be no damning criticism of writing that it is in the nature of a substitution: in being that, it may constitute a sane place for thinking to be neither the dry residue of experience nor a mere mimesis of the chaos of living, because it works both as a reminder and as a holding-ground. Nonetheless, Part II of this work, while registering admiration for the memory of Hood and Mrs Oliphant, is also concerned

with a sense of disappointment, which I was rather shocked to
feel, when I found that the power of these recording documents
was not only different from but less than the power of a
so-called 'genuine' work of art. Again, perhaps this disappointment may seem naive to a reader: what else could I expect?
But it still does seem to me to be a paradox that a person could
write more powerfully about his or her own life when treating
it in a fiction as if it were someone else's, than he or she could
when treating it straight. If it is not possible to do justice to a
life, perhaps then fiction is a grace, perhaps George Eliot does
it *for* us as she hoped, perhaps that is the glory of the novel.
But, equally, I have also felt, while glad that Mrs Oliphant
managed in her autobiographical fiction 'Mr Sandford' what
she could not quite manage on her own account, that it was
fundamentally unjust that human beings found it so difficult
to stick up for themselves by writing. In Part II, then, I treat
of Hood in relation to Charles Dickens and Mrs Oliphant in
relation to George Eliot, to try to see the advantages of the
novel.

It was a general problem to literary men of the nineteenth
century, how far the mind embodied on the page is and ought
to be the mind they actually live with. Consider the evidence.
Coleridge, as we have seen, felt worry on this score: 'Poetry—
excites us to artificial feelings—makes us callous to real ones'.
Wordsworth, writing for the most part of events that did
actually happen within his experience, had to re-create those
life-memories by literary imagination of them: that the
technique and the words should, on this new written level,
stand in memory of his memories on the old interior level was
vital to his purposes. A novelist of realism as George Eliot was
could not but have been anxious about how the world she
wrote of stood in the relation of memory to the world she lived
in. A poet like Thomas Hardy was obsessed by the thought
that his sober, written words stood so steadily for his quite
desperate private memories: the poetry thus bringing his
memories to his mind in the very writing of them, yet bringing
them to mind as also still terrifyingly separate from the written
words which had seemed so solidly to embody them. A man
such as Lawrence could not bear to believe that the relation of
writing to living should be felt to be such an ironic or mad one.

There had to be something less suffering-like about writing than that. My point is, again, that not merely did these people think like that at that time—for reasons which, I fear, I can only partly conceive—but, more important, that, to the best of my belief, these people did right to concern themselves in that way. That is why we should read the work of the nineteenth century.

The story of memory and writing from Wordsworth to Lawrence is primarily the tracing of a certain attitude to literature which I think is not merely my own invention but has a history. The general question as to the *nature* of being a literary man became a question which was involved in the specific social and economic problems of the age of industrialism; it became the question what was the *use* of being a literary man. In this particular work (in chapter 3) I merely sketch how the rise of Utilitarianism in response to the problems in the towns required a questioning as to the use of being a Romantic poet, the use of literary emotion alongside less privileged forms of suffering in the streets, the use of an individual's writing about himself and his troubles. Sidgwick reviewing Arnold's *Culture and Anarchy* maintained that culture had essentially to do with attempts at individual—rather than social—perfection; only where the development of the individual became dependent upon the development of society did men of culture foster the social impulse in their still predominantly self-regarding concern. At the same time, I note, the literary man in the nineteenth century was increasingly likely to have to try to preserve a sense of the spirit of mind as opposed to the conception of mind as determined by physical laws and external circumstances. Those who, in what Carlyle characterized as the Age of Machinery, were oppressed by a sense that the world was ultimately no more than a vast, albeit complicated, machine, that the minds with which men tried to understand it were only a complex mechanism of a similar kind, found the operation of memory a welcome intimation, undermining the attritions of time by its power to revive experiences in the human consciousness. Yet to preserve the spirit of mind meant also having to preserve a conscience as to what that mind could actually *do* usefully within the present time. The story of literary men I here choose to tell is in part a history, but for the most part an attempt to think of things through thinking about writers who have written about them. This story of Thomas Hood and of Margaret Oliphant, as of George Eliot and Thomas Hardy, is often the tale of baulked individualism: of the replacement of lyric poetry by the novel, of the threat of failure mocking individual literary efforts as provincial, sentimental, self-regarding and socially ineffective. What good did *Middlemarch* do? is a real question. Or again: Hardy, through his use of memory, turned his life into works of art, but at the end of his life did not know whether that art had been worth living for. The end of this book is reached in Lawrence's doubting not only the good of George Eliot but also the pessimism of Thomas Hardy. Part III, comprising chapters 5 and 6, is thus concerned mainly with Hardy and with Lawrence. The quarrel which in his 'Study of Thomas Hardy' Lawrence had with the older writer seems to me partly to sum up, from a distinctive angle, the problems described in this book, partly even to result from them. I thought it right to close by leaving the reader with an implicit 'choice' between two opposed beliefs about memory and writing—even if it only drives the reader away to a re-consideration of Wordsworth or George Eliot instead. For thinking about literature does involve thinking through it to the beliefs about living that it offers and challenges.

Let me say, as a final word of apology or explanation, that I could have treated my story differently. For instance, I could have been more circumstantially concerned with the biographies of my chosen writers. It is emphatically an important moment in Goethe's *Autobiography* when he recalls asking himself what, if not nothing, he was going to do in the intervals between periods of poetic inspiration when (as Shelley put it in *A Defence of Poetry*) the poet becomes a man. Goethe's decision, after reading Spinoza, was not to make his literary gift a separate kingdom within nature's own kingdom but rather turn himself also towards the business of the world, leaving none of his faculties unused. Matthew Arnold was a school-inspector; but the position of Arnold's hero, Goethe, was such that he could feel the duty as well as the privilege of performing tasks of state in Weimar.

But the fact is that I reject the whole idea that the poet is a

man only in the intervals between writing. The literature which
I examine here has a thrust quite the opposite of that: the
writer is the way of the man's being articulately conscious of
his past and of the uses of understanding it. Accordingly, this
book is not one of biographical investigation. It is concerned,
rather, with the evidence of the man, and what happens to
him, actually *within* his literary work, when his life is held in
his memory to be worked out. My concern, through close
reading, is with what might be called the autobiography of
writing: the way in which writing (so very differently in the
poetry of Wordsworth and the poetry of Hardy, or in the
functions of prose in comparison with poetry) discloses within
itself the memory of its creator's own processes of thought-
composition, particularly in works of autobiographical origin.
I realise that this method is not foolproof or complete. But the
quotidian biography, the rest of the writer's life, while not, I
believe, a matter for silence, is always a matter of speculation;
and a matter more speculative in fact than an analysis of what
in a man went into the making of his works of literature. It is
literature's deep sense of meaning that Cardinal Newman
invoked when, in response to the criticisms made upon him by
Kingsley, he wrote his autobiography: 'He asks what I *mean*;
not about my words, not about my arguments, not about my
actions, as his ultimate point, but about that living intelligence,
by which I write, and argue, and act'.[11] It is in their texts that,
with the great writers of the nineteenth century, we may have
the closest, if still fallible, sense of another's interior life. This
book is only partly to do with the writer's use of his own
memory in his imaginative work; it is more particularly about
the memory that writers leave behind of themselves in their
writing. I do not say that I can or do answer all my questions.

William Wordsworth, George Eliot, Thomas Hardy, and
D. H. Lawrence did not write autobiographies as such but
used their memories in their writing as if they were not quite
familiar with themselves. In what follows I offer comparisons
in that respect with the work of Mrs Oliphant, John Ruskin,
and John Middleton Murry as autobiographers. There is in all
this what T. E. Hulme characterized as the weakness of
Romanticism: a confusion of categories, as here between a
man's life and his life as a writer. I describe that confusion but

actually I also respect it—as being appropriate to the power of overflowing resonance that works of literature have in the memories of their writers and their readers. The question of the relation of the thoughts of a writer to the words of his writing becomes doubly important when the subject of that writing is, in a broad sense, the writer's mind itself. The problem of the relation of a man's life to a man's work becomes doubly important when the subject of that work is not merely the work itself but the man's own life. It is within the memory of a writer that these important problems tangle, and it is in relation to this that I have tried to think, speculate and hesitate.

PART I

'WHAT IS A POET?'

1
'On the difference between writing and speaking'

If you think about life or your own life, what would be important about writing it down? Why do some people think that that is a good thing to do?

In a still famous poem, of which the first printed version we possess is dated 1508, William Dunbar recorded in verse the work of Death upon the Poets: 'Sparit is nocht ther faculte', he wrote. He set down the great names: Chaucer, Lydgate, Gower, the Gawain poet—their prowess, even, is not spared. Death, wrote Dunbar lamenting his evidence, dealt the same to one Mersar ('Merseir') for all his gifts as a poet of love:

> He hes reft Merseir his endite,
> That did in luf so lifly write,
> So schort, so quyk, of sentence hie;
> *Timor mortis conturbat me.*

Dunbar thus praises the sheer liveliness ('lifly', 'quyk') of the power that Death ironically stole from Mersar. And beneath the praise of the life in it all, he also marks, in Latin as in another hand, Death's own short, quick, high 'sentence' for poets, as for all other men. 'The fear of death throws me into confusion', this poet equivalently fears and writes, as he marks down the death of greater writers. Now, when Dunbar wrote *Timor mortis conturbat me* as his refrain, was that the poet's triumph over ordinary mortality, as if that is what writing can do for fear? or was it, still as ever, Death's triumph, as it were making even the poet's hand shake?

Then again, consider how, after the Easter rising of 1916, W. B. Yeats, almost despite himself, felt moved to make not

Notes and Bibliography begin on page 491.

the names of poets but the names of dead rebels into lines of
poetry:

> I write it out in verse—
> MacDonagh and MacBride
> And Connolly and Pearse

This time it is not Latin but the vernacular (though not Yeats
going so far for the Republicans as to make it Irish vernacular).
Even so, is it not here still essentially as it was with Dunbar:
that the act of naming seems at once both a strong and a frail
act? 'I write it out in verse' are words that seem to be at the
basis of writing's purpose as commemoration. They seem to
say: 'This is for a future which, if that future does recall at all,
will recall as *past* that which now is so much present. But a
past which will not cease even then to have been written in this
present tense'. These words were written in a present. As such,
their frailty and their strength are mutually reciprocal within
the act of writing.

Here, then, are Dunbar and Yeats alongside each other.
Contemplating these two pieces of really quite simple verse,
across four centuries of differing modes of language and conventions of writing, one feels impelled to ask, undismissively:
why should it be that one is moved by the mere idea of
centuries of men writing?

I write it out in verse—no more than that; and how much of
a thing *is* it? For perhaps there are people who will say that
that line, that act, has no more meaning, in itself or to its
writers, than simply to be the first person, present tense
indicative of the verb 'to write'; by the use of which the writer
just gets under way. But in what follows I shall be trying to
argue how being moved by the idea of writing constitutes one
of the 'primary sensations of the human heart'.

> If this be error and upon me proved,
> I never writ, nor no man ever loved.

Thus, in sonnet cxvi, Shakespeare himself bears witness:
putting his pressure on the pen to write 'I never writ', doing it.

But the phrase, 'primary sensation of the human heart', is
Wordsworth's.[1] Unsurprisingly so, for in the period from which
I have selected certain people for thought in this book—the
late eighteenth, the nineteenth and the early twentieth

centuries—I can think of no one more explicitly concerned with the idea of writing and the importance of that idea to his own ability to write than William Wordsworth. And nowhere is this made more manifest than in his 'Essays upon Epitaphs', to which it would seem wise for anyone, looking from Dunbar to Yeats, to turn for guidance.

Epitaphs, although a particular kind of writing, were also for Wordsworth as it were a model for the merest origins of the seriousness of the idea of men writing. Epitaphs: the last words formally managed, a few basic words engraved on stone, the human hope for permanence marked there between immortality above and remembrance below; yet, though lofty, accessible in simplicity to all men who can read them, while also bare and exposed not only to the eyes of men but to the day, to the elements and to time. 'An epitaph is not a proud writing shut up for the studious: it is exposed to all . . . the sun looks down upon the stone, and the rains of heaven beat against it' (Wordsworth: *Prose Works,* ii, p. 59). The bare words, on that boundary which Wordsworth so cherished between the factual and the spiritual ('Born: . . . Died: . . .'), partook of 'the conjunction in rural districts of the place of burial and place of worship' (ibid. p. 66). Epitaphs must have seemed to Wordsworth both strong, like worship, and frail, as mortality, at once. For it was the frailest possible example that gave Wordsworth the strongest imagination of what, from these mere origins, the existence of writing meant for the human heart:

> In an obscure corner of a Country Church-yard I once espied half-overgrown with Hemlock and Nettles, a very small Stone laid upon the ground, bearing nothing more than the name of the Deceased with the date of birth and death, importing that it was an Infant which had been born one day and died the following. I know not how far the Reader may be in sympathy with me, but more awful thoughts of rights conferred, of hopes awakened, of remembrances stealing away or vanishing were imparted to my mind by that Inscription there before my eyes than by any other that it has ever been my lot to meet with upon a Tomb-stone.
>
> *Prose Works,* ii, p. 93.

'Bearing nothing more than': for Wordsworth, had the epitaph borne more words, it would have carried less weight. For here was only the beginning of a life, and the words, equivalently, are only of a little more existence than silence. Half-overgrown with hemlock and nettles, 'a violet by a mossy stone',[2] here, born one day and died the next, is marked that minimal difference between something and nothing which is the very principle of life itself. The words commemorating it are themselves the difference between nothing and the smallest beginning to memory. What's the difference then? Feeling and Imagination rush in to that space between 'born one day' and 'died the following':

> But she is in her grave, and, oh,
> The difference to me!
>
> *P.W.,* ii, p. 30.

Yet, even in this Lucy poem, the big difference can be marked only by a little word of lyric disproportion. Writing moved Wordsworth not simply by being strong or proud but rather by bearing its own weakness. The words on a tombstone in a churchyard ideally must have seemed to the poet natural to man, and yet not natural to him as much as death was, nor natural in the same way as the surrounding landscape could be said obviously to be so. These distinctions lay about him poignantly, like a real image of the *place* of written words to a Wordsworth who, significantly, preferred to compose his own work in his head while walking up and down out of doors. If writing was in some sense 'natural' to man in relation to both his surroundings and his fate, then it was because man had made it so to himself.

But what did Wordsworth think the idea of writing, which he seems to have found so powerfully present in epitaphs, had to do with his art of poetry? For, surely, poetry is something more than mere writing, more even than writing in metre. And the epitaph on the child who lived only one day is surely not a poem. But, then, is the following a poem?

> Torquato Tasso rests within this Tomb:
> This Figure, weeping from her inmost heart,
> Is Poesy: from such impassioned grief
> Let every one conclude what this Man was.

It is Wordsworth's own translation, used in his third 'Essay upon Epitaphs' (*Prose Works*, ii, p. 91), of an epitaph by Chiabrera (1552–1638) on the death of the poet Tasso. It is on the face of it hard to see why this isn't prose. For suppose we do what Wordsworth himself recommended and test what is at stake in this verse by putting it into prose.[3] Do we lose so much? isn't prose what it really is?

> Torquato Tasso rests within this tomb. This statue, above it, weeping from her inmost heart, is (the Muse of) Poetry. Let everyone conclude from such impassioned grief what this man was.

Three sentences; and the answer to the riddle, likewise simple: the man whose death caused Poetry such grief must have been—a poet. Torquato Tasso. Arguably, Poetry, through sheer grief, banishes herself and her powers from the work of epitaphs.

For, although epitaphs were a sort of representative image for Wordsworth as to the place of writing, it still has to be admitted that they were also a distinct kind of case for the writer—one requiring an almost puritanical restraint upon the mind's linguistic power. In reply to Dr Johnson's criticism that most epitaphs lacked discrimination as to the individual character of the deceased thus recorded (because 'the greater part of mankind have no character at all'!), Wordsworth countered magnificently:

> To analyze the character of others, especially of those whom we love, is not a common or natural employment of men at any time. We are not anxious unerringly to understand the constitution of the minds of those who have soothed, who have cheered, who have supported us: with whom we have been long and daily pleased or delighted. The affections are their own justification . . . and, least of all, do we incline to these refinements when under the pressure of those feelings which incite men to prolong the memory of their friends and kindred, by records placed in the bosom of the all-uniting and equalising receptacle of the dead.
>
> *Prose Works*, ii, pp. 56–7.

These gentle writings have been subdued from an anxious duty minutely to measure light and shade, to a commonness induced by the thought of that universal End which puts by the smaller distinctions. But those who do not believe that Chiabrera's epitaph is really a poem may thus object: how, save by Romantic sentimentality, may this kind of writing stand as somehow representatively *primary*, when its minimalism is the result of a self-limitation of the strong, rich virtues of that special kind of language called Poetic? For indeed epitaphs may be written *to* the memory of the dead, keeping it by not disturbing it; with the epitaph it is enough to say that Poesy weeps from her inmost heart; this is conclusive if 'the affections are their own justification'. But the extra power that the language of poetry has over mere writing is that which will fight *for* the memory of the departed and the justification of affection, verbally seizing memory, lest what the language cannot cause to be remembered will remain unknown or become forgotten. Thus Johnson himself fought verbally for the memory of Dr Levet, to rescue decency and usefulness from the oblivion that both death and 'letter'd arrogance' would confine it to.

> Yet still he fills affection's eye,
>   Obscurely wise, and coarsely kind;
> Nor, letter'd arrogance, deny
>   Thy praise to merit unrefined.

Johnson's 'letters' make no such denial. 'Coarsely kind', for instance, is not two words anymore, meaning 'coarse but kind' almost ambivalently, but one memory, fought for out of the language, fusing words in the mould of its own complex recall and feel.

Now, Wordsworth does not deny the value of this extra force in poems which properly can be free of the decorum appropriate to epitaph. What he does deny is that that surplus resource of language is the essence, rather than the strong refinement and defence, of what is poetry. Rather, he seems to me to have believed that a thing like the epitaph on Tasso—to quote it again—was, in some way quite essential to him, a poem, and though indeed a poem under the rule of a certain genre, for all that something substratal.

> Torquato Tasso rests within this Tomb:
> This Figure, weeping from her inmost heart,
> Is Poesy: from such impassioned grief
> Let every one conclude what this Man was.

What was he? To answer prosaically, 'a Poet'. But, wrote Wordsworth:

> Taking up the subject, then, upon general grounds, let me ask, what is meant by the word Poet? What is a Poet?
>
> *Prose Works*, i, p. 138.

The answer to that is not merely 'what this Man was'. Rather, the poetry has its own answer lodged within the apparent prosaicness. This Man was a *Poet*, but *was* a Poet, past tense, death, and, as the poetry here discloses, his having been a poet meant, among other things, that he would have known what difference it made not to write 'what *that* Man was' but to put instead 'what *this* Man was'. For the difference between the two is a matter of the Man being a Poet, but also of the Poet having been a Man. The human heart lies in that difference; 'this' (here, close, for the last time on this stone) bespeaking a final, tacit resistance, which 'that' would cede, to the truth of 'was' as over-and-done-with; matters of humanity and mortality. It is a difference, albeit minimal and whispered, and one akin to the distinction between 'within' in the first line of the poem (which, like 'was', immures the poet) and 'inmost' in the second (which, like 'this', takes the burial to heart, instead of letting it go). Such verse is in defence of those who otherwise 'have been betrayed by a common notion that what was natural in prose would be out of place in verse' (ibid., ii, p. 74). For this verse makes poetry within its prose, proclaiming the mundane and the valuable not to be mutually exclusive. Tasso would have recognized what work went on within these tiny words and short lines; Chiabrera did; Wordsworth also; what these Men were.

For emphatically this, says Wordsworth, says the very syntax of his third line, 'Is Poesy'. The prose of this poem makes it clear that it is 'This Figure', presumably a statue above the grave, which betokens Poetry, and it is the duty of the poetry in this poem to support and stick to the letter of the prose. But, without ceasing to do so, what I may call the poetry's *second language* adds to the prose a meaning which is still the prose's own—as when 'Is Poesy' comes out, half-shaken, half-soberly recommitted, from somewhere, as it were, between the lines. Poetry's supportive second language for prose here makes 'Is Poesy', across the line-break, quietly defiant. But what is so remarkable is that that tacit, defiant affirmation (even this 'is poesy' now) is only induced by the syntatic enactment of something like Poesy's own sob for Tasso:

> . . . weeping from her inmost heart,
> Is Poesy

As if, at the end, Poesy still comes from these tears:

> the language of Prose may yet be well adapted to Poetry .
> . . a large portion of the language of every good poem can
> in no respect differ from that of good Prose. . . . Poetry
> sheds no tears 'such as Angels weep', but natural and
> human tears; she can boast of no celestial ichor that
> distinguishes her vital juices from those of prose; the same
> human blood circulates through the veins of them both.
> *Prose Works*, i, p. 135.

Wordsworth believed a poem like the epitaph to Tasso to be fundamental to poetry. It helps tell us why it is important that men write.

The so-called prosaic nature of the epitaph is in fact the human poetry of making emotion bear to speak with a control worthy of what is felt. 'Is Poesy' bespeaks what Wordsworth himself affirmed against those who argued that epitaphs were idealizing fictions ('Where are all the bad People buried?'): 'it *is* truth . . . it is truth hallowed by love' (ibid., ii, pp. 63, 58). The passion of this prose is its poetry, and that passion is felt as a presence between the lines. For what Coleridge noted of Shakespeare's short lines seems also true of Wordsworth's normal ones:

> His rhythm is so perfect that you may be almost sure that
> you do not understand the real force of a line if it does not
> run well as you read it. The necessary mental pause after
> every hemistich or imperfect line is always equal to the
> time that would have been taken in reading the complete
> verse.[4]

It is actually important that what could have been written as a line of prose is made into lines of verse, the mental pause letting in the idea of writing:

> . . . from such impassioned grief
> Let every one conclude what this Man was.

That mental breath seeking its own control at the end of the penultimate line is moving, as it stands between its own emotion ('grief') and the testimony which that emotion is trying to articulate by its very existence. For the last line is then both an achievement of the line previous and an achievement in its own line of right. That 'Let' is very different from the public call which it merely would have been had it opened the poem: though it retains that public authority, the slight hesitation as to how it manages to get itself out into a line of its own is enough to cause a mental pause, an escaped breath just before its saying: as if the line were slightly indented, if I hear it right, a fraction of a beat behind itself. There are such things that fall out in poetry as prosaic, as making sense and sentence almost by the delaying of the emotion behind them. When that emotion does speak, it then speaks the thing complete, as exactly, it seems, what the emotion had been waiting and wanting to say as a whole. Only then did Chiabrera, did Wordsworth, allow a full stop. I suppose that there are such moments of the grace of brevity, when every person who has struggled to write verse experiences an equivalent; inferior doubtless in degree but perhaps not in kind. For it is truly the idea of writing, when a simple sentence is achieved as the full form of the emotion's embodiment, all together, as if it were a breath. Wordsworth took words seriously and thought the *fact* of a poem a part of its achievement—that it has achieved sense and existence—rather than as a substratum merely prior to the professional evaluation of it. The words, individually taken, are not in this epitaph rich, complex, or even exploited; in seeming primary, without secondary meanings, it is their very closeness, as a minimum, to the possibility of a language *not* existing that constitutes an increased sense of the grateful relief that this does. This putting of feelings into words, like the putting of Chiabrera's words into his own, was moving to Wordsworth not least when the emotional was obliged *not* to be richly exhibited. That idea and this natural, human speech mattered most to Wordsworth: *'what this Man was'*. If poetry said that.

> . . . Is there not
> An art, a music, and a stream of words
> That shall be life, the acknowledged voice of life?
>
> *Home at Grasmere*, p. 76 (MS.B, 620–2).

Is there? It would seem that I, who am defending writing as in some sense 'primary' and in some difficult sense 'natural', am obliged to answer yes. But actually it is a more complicated affirmative that I have to make. Even after working through an epitaph like that on Tasso, we cannot hide from ourselves the suspicion that we have to *work* to acquire a feeling for epitaphs, a knowledge of their convention, and that, even so, later we may lapse back into neglecting them. At least, Wordsworth himself seems to have been aware of this:

> I began with noticing such [examples of epitaphs] as might be wholly uninteresting from the uniformity of language which they exhibit; because, without previously participating the truths upon which these general attestations are founded it is impossible to arrive at that state or disposition of mind necessary to make those Epitaphs thoroughly felt which have an especial recommendation.
>
> *Prose Works*, ii, p. 68.

If we need prior and repeated grounding ('previously participating', 'arrive at'), does not this cause us some hestitation in accepting as either natural or primary this kind of writing? Or, let us take the objection even further: if, as we have begun to see, writing takes up into itself some of the functions and patterns of speech, if poetry can be said to be a second language for prose, should not we be calling the place of writing in general and poetry in particular not 'primary' but, actually, secondary in the order of affairs? What I shall now argue is that this objection was itself very important to Wordsworth.

*   *   *   *   *

So much of Wordsworth's own writing seems prompted by the memory of the moment when speaking was unable to continue or unable even to begin. The thought that speaking on its own cannot answer the whole of human purpose and need is at the heart of his great early work—as thus in the face of sorrow:

> But, when I entered, Margaret looked at me
> A little while; then turned her head away
> Speechless,—and, sitting down upon a chair,
> Wept bitterly. I wist not what to do,
> Nor how to speak to her. Poor Wretch! at last
> She rose from off her seat, and then,—O Sir!
> I cannot *tell* how she pronounced my name:—
> With fervent love, and with a face of grief
> Unutterably helpless, and a look
> That seemed to cling upon me, she enquired
> If I had seen her husband.
>
> The Excursion, i, 648–58 (P.W., i, p. 30)

In this book, known as 'The Ruined Cottage', an old Wanderer (whose youth has been not unlike Wordsworth's own) is telling a young 'Sir' (also not unlike the young man Wordsworth still essentially was in 1797 when he wrote this) about the tragedy of Margaret, a deserted wife and mother. Wordsworth later admitted that Margaret was based on 'the character possessed in common by many women whom it has been my happiness to know in humble life', insisting indeed that 'several of the most touching things which she is represented as saying and doing are taken from actual observation of the distresses and trials under which different persons were suffering, some of them strangers to me and others daily under my notice' (P.W., v, p. 376). When he turned here from the level of his experience to the level of writing from it, it is as if Wordsworth split himself between the old man and the young man to make what he already knew fresh again to himself. At any rate, the narrative here offers itself as a tale told by memory, the diction suggesting that its sole achievement is that of honesty of representation. The postulated accuracy is cherished morally as a sign of feeling committed to recall, but too helpless to direct:

> . . . I wist not what to do,
> Nor how to speak to her.

And yet this apparently incidental recollection is at the heart of why 'The Ruined Cottage' had to be written: the poem is a form of 'doing' now, through narration, what before the protagonist could not do through more direct speech. It is indeed characteristic of Wordsworth to love thus to submerge and conceal the promptings of his imagination within the terms of his own and the Wanderer's memory. But it is more than simply characteristic that 'I wist not what to do'—the prime motive for doing now something that reclaims helplessness and speechlessness through writing—should still be returned here to no more than its temporal status as a mere part within the recollected whole. For it also testifies to what Wordsworth here thought poetry could properly *do*. What prompted the impulse to tell, in the case of the Wanderer, or to write, in the case of Wordsworth himself, is recorded not at the apex of events, in compensating control, but as still embedded within the narrative: this is not merely because it is characteristic of Wordsworth's style but because of his implied belief that he has no right to pretend, compensatingly through poetry, to more power in retrospect than he had at the time in life. Accordingly, the verse seems a thing that feels both sad *and* faithful in being as 'helpless' to save Margaret as the Wanderer and Margaret herself were. Certain phrases in the passage quoted above testify to this poetic integrity and restraint. 'Margaret looked at me', 'then turned her head away/Speechless', 'at last/She rose', 'with a face of grief', 'and a look': faithfully recorded in those pauses at the end of the line is that mute appeal which is but a second's hesitation within the continuing acts of her daily life. One line turns on into another because there is no one word to save her from her misery going on or to bring back her husband. The first half of each line seems to resolve too late and inadequately the struggle of the line previous:

> . . . Margaret looked at me
> A little while; then turned her head away
> Speechless

> . . . Poor Wretch! at last
> She rose from off her seat, and then—

Thus the beginning half lines—'A little while', 'Speechless',

'She rose'—being unable to provide the right words at the right time, themselves become the resistance Margaret has to get through in order to say what by the end of the line there seems hardly any time to say, or way of saying, or point in saying:

> Speechless,—and, sitting down upon a chair,
> Wept bitterly.

> . . . and a look
> That seemed to cling upon me, she enquired
> If I had seen her husband.

One feels constantly that the woman's spirit is trying to raise itself above the lines, as it were; but it is helplessly and vulnerably as if her words of suffering in silence hardly have strength to lift themselves from the lines in which, the more so for her efforts, she has to suffer. It is like the epitaph on the one-day-old child who had life enough only to die. The verse, through the eyes and memory of the Wanderer, can detect that minimal difference between the end of one line and the beginning of the next, between her physical situation and the hopes of her spirit, between her in herself and the grief that burdens her, between the 'look' she gives and the appearance she has, between description and sight of her sorrow *ab extra* and her immersedness in it. In short—those minimal differences which, almost in themselves unspeakable, are nonetheless here felt '*tell*ingly'. Inside these lines, we feel, 'The Poet thinks and feels in the spirit of human passions' (*Prose Works*, i, p. 142).

I conclude, therefore, this is writing reverentially conscious of *bespeaking* the trouble of which, at the time, neither Margaret nor the Wanderer could speak quite direct. It is written (by Wordsworth) as if spoken (by the Wanderer) through that justice in memory which requires that what could not be said before not only remains unforgotten but, through writing, gives itself back to speech again. Yet this *is* writing, nonetheless, and it is as if this poetry of memory (as Wordsworth admitted it to be) remains, with a mixture of fidelity, sadness and guilt, 'helpless'. Only, Margaret was 'unutterably helpless' and this, at least, is utterly so. If this writing can do no more than bespeak what trouble it is that cuts speech short, still it will do no less than that for the suffering, however much this too might seem inadequate. Hazlitt called Wordsworth's 'a levelling Muse' which, in the egalitarian spirit of the time, lowered the high and raised the low, till too little counted for all too much with him.[5] But, as we have seen, the real meaning of his 'levelling' lies in his keeping everything steadily within the lines of his verse and his temporal narrative: keeping suffering within its bodily situation, imagination within the act of memory, thinking within the particularity of feeling. For this is writing that does not transcend, although it re-enacts, the memory of the failure of action and of speech. Yet it would be hard to call this 'bespeaking' writing merely secondary.

*   *   *   *   *

But why this sadness at the failure of speech? Who ever thought that speaking (let alone writing) would successfully sort out human difficulties! Put that objection as a question and a reply lies in the work of a man who started from the belief that Wordsworth's Wanderer has to recognize when confronted with Margaret: that sympathy is finally no more than an inadequate substitute for justice.

William Godwin, whose *Enquiry Concerning Political Justice* was published in 1793, is known to have exerted a brief but powerful influence upon Wordsworth in the years 1794 and 1795.[6] Some of the central issues in that book and their relation to the man who wrote it are vital to my theme. For Godwin's is a strange and powerful story of the connections and distinctions between what a man writes and what a man is, and his case will help us.

William Hazlitt described Godwin as 'a writer who gives us *himself*' (Hazlitt: *Works*, xvi, p. 402), so powerful seemed the relation between what he wrote and what he was; yet Hazlitt also found that 'Mr Godwin in society is nothing' (ibid., p. 403), as if the man existed only in his writing. This apparently superficial contrast came to have for Hazlitt the force of a genuine contradiction: the writer who gives us himself, says Hazlitt, in the case of Godwin, also 'writes against himself':

He has written against matrimony, and has been twice married. He has scouted all the common-place duties, and yet is a good husband and a kind father. He is a strange composition of contraries. He is a cold formalist, and full of ardour and enthusiasm of mind.

Ibid., xi, p. 235.

Connected with this, in Hazlitt's mind, was the unreality of the *Enquiry Concerning Political Justice* in its argument that values such as family, sympathy and charity were not only substitutes for but replacements of disinterested principles of rational justice. 'Gratitude, promises, friendship, family affection give way,' complains Hazlitt, 'not that they may be merged in the opposite vices or in want of principle; but that the void may be filled up by the disinterested love of good, and the dictates of inflexible justice' (op. cit., xi, p. 18). Godwin's apparent raising of the standard of morality above the reach of humanity seemed to Hazlitt proportionate to the gap between the artificial level at which Godwin let his mind go in the act of writing and the correspondingly mundane level to which, vacantly, Godwin allowed himself to collapse when he had not a pen in his hand.

This is not how Godwin saw his own development. 'In my communications with others, in the endeavour to impart what I deemed to be truth,' he reported, 'I began with boldness' (*Thoughts on Man*, p. 335). But in the arena of dialogue, opposition threw him into confusion and objections of almost any quality took his breath and argument away. 'I therefore became cautious. As a human creature, I did not relish the being held up to others, or to myself, as rash, inconsiderate and headlong . . . I therefore often became less a speaker, than a listener' (ibid., p. 336). It was at this second stage, when verbal boldness gave way to silent diffidence, that a crucial, adult wound seems to have been inflicted upon Godwin's young sensitivity and presumption. In an autobiographical fragment written in 1800 it is as if Godwin were thinking of Hazlitt's complaint, 'Mr Godwin in society is nothing':

I am extremely modest. What is modesty? First I am tormented about the opinions others may entertain of me; fearful of intruding myself, and of co-operating to my own humiliation. For this reason I have been, in a certain

sense, unfortunate through life, making few acquaintances,
losing them *in limine,* and by my fear producing the thing
I fear. I am bold and adventurous in opinions, not in life.
                                Kegan Paul: *William Godwin,* i, p. 359.

It is as though the current of his own life had turned back
upon him, in reflections of himself from outside, in disappointment as to what living a social life might mean. 'I carry feelers
before me', 'I hate universally to speak to the man that is not
previously desirous to hear me', 'I can scarcely ever begin a
conversation where I have no preconceived subject to talk of'
(ibid., pp. 359–60). These are the stranded words of a man
who has retired behind the threshold between interior and
social life, with a fearful memory of confusion in the latter
sphere now transferred back into the former. Now, this is not
simply a matter of anecdote as to the life of a writer. For
actually this feeling of Godwin's that he was a man turned
round upon himself is the motive-source for what is perhaps
the heart of his *Enquiry Concerning Political Justice*—book iv,
chapter vi, 'Of Sincerity'. For there it is that Godwin sets
himself to write of the origins of that caution which wrecked
his own sensibility. Men in society, he argues, meet like
enemies, warily. What a man knows about another he often
feels obliged not to allude to in his hearing; if he speaks of him
in his absence, he speaks under the seal of secrecy like a spy,
fearing charges of indiscretion. Where youth cheerfully fits
into the manners of the world, middle age hardens in it,
becoming skilful in considering men as neutral instruments, in
playing the social game of indirection, while trying to forget
the disappointment of this collusive freezing of human warmth
in a world of strangers. There is not trust, there is guard; there
is not outspokenness but inference, implication, obliqueness.
'Every member of a polished and civilized community goes
armed' (*Enquiry Concerning Political Justice,* p. 316). If a man
complains of the defects of another, his are 'the sentiments of a
criminal, conscious that what he is saying he would be
unwilling to utter before the individual concerned' (ibid.).
Human speech does not do what it ought when it fails directly
to convey men's thought. Thus, in the social game, secrecy is
matched by curiosity, suspicion paired with hypocrisy, savoir-

faire in league with defensiveness, and there is no home out there for what a man truly has within him. Even that within becomes tainted with fear and cunning. For a man is essentially reduced and saddened by silence and indirection, it being the intrinsic nature of thoughts that they feel as if they belong to the reality outside a man as well as that within him and that they are meant to confirm that bond by their being *spoken*. When consistently a man could not speak thus, it was as though a justice had been denied him. He could not share and test with others a sense of truth that they might hold in common, that might hold them all in common. For Godwin believed that a true statement, by virtue of its justice, had an innate authority over men through the exercise of their reason. Men could trust that this would hold them together. But, inevitably, before there could be a society made up of individuals held together solely by the sharing of Truth, there had first to be an aggregate of individuals with the spaces between them filled only with candour. It was speaking, and plain speaking at that, which was for Godwin the essence not only of society but also of thinking: for the dialogues of reasoned conflict were to be the real scrutinizing and working-out of truth among men. Thus:

> The effects of sincerity upon others would be similar to its effects upon him that practised it. How great would be the benefit if every man were sure of meeting in his neighbour the ingenuous censor, who would tell him in person, and publish to the world, his virtues, his good deeds, his meannesses and his follies? We have never a strong feeling of these in our own case, except in so far as they are confirmed to us by the suffrage of our neighbours.
> *Enquiry Concerning Political Justice*, p. 313.

In such social confidence 'our character would expand' (ibid., p. 317). Godwin's own expansion from the first person singular to the first person plural is not rhetorical so much as political, a realigned recognition that the basis of living is social before ever it is personal.

And yet for Hazlitt it is clear that Godwin's work on the nature of society is transferred autobiography and evaded auto-biography, its idealism being a writer's refuge from his own psychology. 'He is ready only on reflection: dangerous only at the rebound' (Hazlitt: *Works*, xi, p. 27). The man's writing is on the rebound from his failures in speaking; his making the failure of speaking in part the subject-matter of his writing makes the compensation look more real and less surrogate. Indeed, Godwin's own, later account of the effect that writing *Political Justice* had upon him seems to reflect back powerfully upon his motives for undertaking it:

> A new epoch occurred in my character, when I published, and at the time I was writing, my Enquiry Concerning Political Justice. My mind was wrought up to a certain elevation of tone; the speculations in which I was engaged, tending to embrace all that was most important to man in society, and the frame to which I had assiduously bent myself, of giving quarter to nothing because it was startling and astounding, gave a new bias to my character. The habit which I had thus formed put me more on the alert even in the scenes of ordinary life, and gave me a boldness and an eloquence more than was natural to me. I then reverted to the principle which I stated in the beginning, of being ready to tell my neighbour whatever it might be of advantage to him to know, to shew myself the sincere and zealous advocate of absent merit and worth, and to contribute by every means in my power to the improvement of others and to the diffusions of salutary truths through the world.
>
> *Thoughts on Man*, pp. 336–7.

Did he know, a Hazlitt might say, that he wrote the book in order to recover that first boldness, the loss of which had made him turn from speaking to writing? 'I then reverted to the principle which I stated in the beginning': the man who felt himself turned back upon himself thus by writing turned himself back round towards his fellows. Isn't this what *Political Justice* really is: a 'rebound' from, a disguise for, autobiography, its real subject-matter? And weren't both the book and the consequent reversion to the principles for which the book had fought alike overstrained because of this disguise: 'a boldness and an eloquence *more than was natural* to me'? Writing out of memory cannot be simply having the time again or regaining the same original situation; there is always the artifice. Or, as Godwin added at the end of the above account: 'But, in pursuing this scheme of practice, I was acting a part somewhat foreign to my constitution' (ibid., p. 337).

Yet although Hazlitt came to see Godwin's book as not so much about society's troubles as about his own, to Godwin it had been no such thing. He wrote *Political Justice* rather than an autobiography, and did so because for Godwin auto-biography was not a primary base from which to proceed. Autobiography was secondary in the sense of being a substi-tution through loneliness for the really required basis of a man's life, namely social communication and social recognition in a community seeking to share Truth. Because he could not be sure of meeting sincerity in his neighbour, Godwin had not been able to be sure of or in himself. This was not primarily due to personal weakness but the strength of our social basis. Autobiographical thinking tends to annex to itself a responsi-bility for what also lies beyond the control of its protagonist; in this it is an unjust form. The problems as autobiographically perceived are not therefore autobiographically originating; writing has a license to use memory as well as merely follow it; and, in Godwin's analysis, the problems are political ones, to do with the structures of present social life, where privacy feels criminal and law feels tyrannical. *Political Justice*, Godwin might have replied to Hazlitt, was not written to straighten himself out, but to show why he, alone, couldn't—and why there was justice in that. For total concentration on the personal failure would be selfishly to fail to see, even in that, greater impulses both vulnerably dependent upon, and richer for aspiring towards, the wider human world for their reality. Writing can lend its strength to see this.

So, read *Political Justice* one way with Hazlitt, and it is a form of rebound, an excuse that memory wrought into writing. Read it through Godwin's eyes, and it is a form of reversal by which, through the instrument of writing, our chronological bases of perception—the autobiographical story of me, my family, my affections—are reinverted to show themselves as secondary to rational priorities and social involvements. Because I remain undecided between these two ways and because I am unsure how far Hazlitt's criticism detracts from, rather than adds to, the nobility of Godwin's achievement, I have found this case to be a powerful model of some of the problems of the relation of writing to memory. It leaves me wondering how far a man, by writing, can take his thinking out of his own experience and even, legitimately, extend it beyond that resource. For the moment, however, it may be concluded that, at least as far as Godwin was concerned, if *Political Justice* was in any sense a surrogate, it was so essentially because its writing was conceived as a necessary substitute for the failure of speech among men, that thus might be created the conditions thereafter for more primary interventions again: 'inestimable as is the benefit we derive from books, there is something more searching and soul-stirring in the impulse of oral communication. . . . Sudden and irresistible conviction is chiefly the offspring of living speech. We may arm ourselves against the arguments of an author' (*Thoughts on Man*, p. 251). We may wonder, if this is true, whether writing, along with reading, simply isn't an immediate and living experience. . . ?

                    *   *   *   *   *

Now, it is true that Wordsworth largely gave up Godwin after 1795, and the most obvious reason was that he came to find Godwin's ideal reason in writing too far removed from a recognition of the depth of men's real habits. Of writings such as Godwin's he concluded in 1798, 'They contain no picture of human life; they *describe* nothing' (*Prose Works*, i, p. 103). One can almost hear him thinking, 'but writing poetry shall be different'. That said, there is still a deeper reason that brought Wordsworth to Godwin and took him away again, and it extends further than the dropping of Godwin in 1795. It has to do with a deep-seated Wordsworthian ambivalence about the relation of writing poetry to failures of direct speech. Consider, for instance, an incident that befell Wordsworth in October 1800; he wrote of it in May 1802 in a poem entitled 'Resolution and Independence'. The poet puts a question to an old man whom he has met by chance: 'How is it that you live, and what is it you do?'. The reply—which Wordsworth in the Fenwick notes declared to be taken from the man's own mouth—was 'gathering leeches'.[7] It was a reply which silenced Wordsworth into asking himself, eventually and almost necessarily through writing, whether that was just something the old man said, a polite matter of fact but no return on the question of how he lived; or whether it was the only real answer. In a just society, a Godwinite would argue, a man like Wordsworth could learn, by speaking and by being told, whatever the leech-gatherer had to teach him, direct. For it was in that hope that the poet first put the question to him. But, on second thought and a second thought that had to do with putting it into writing, it must have seemed to Wordsworth that, pace Godwin, what the answer taught directly was less telling than the indirect inference from it of the necessity for a different sort of question to be asked of living (*P.W.*, ii, pp. 235–40).

Moreover, the earlier 'Adventures on Salisbury Plain', composed between 1795 and 1799, expresses something that remained with Wordsworth and must have been helped into articulation by reading Godwin. It is the feeling of a basic injustice in man's being unable to speak adequately of his troubles, as if the inability so to speak was related also to an incapacity to act on or resolve suffering. And, even if man was able to speak and be conscious of his trouble, still that ability, he knows, would provide him with scant relief. The version of this poem first published in *Lyrical Ballads* in 1798 as 'The Female Vagrant' ended on the conclusion of the widow's tale of sorrows:

> 'Three years a wanderer, often have I view'd,
> In tears, the sun towards that country tend
> Where my poor heart lost all its fortitude:
> And now across this moor my steps I bend—
> Oh! tell me whither—for no earthly friend
> Have I.'—She ceased, and weeping turned away,
> As if because her tale was at an end
> She wept;—because she had no more to say
> Of that perpetual weight which on her spirit lay.
> *The Salisbury Plain Poems*, p. 146, ll. 550–8.

Why did she weep at that moment? One who believed in plain 'sincerity', in the direct relation of words to that of which they speak, would answer that she wept in memory of the reality she spoke of: the losses—father, then husband and children—

of a past more real to her, yet more lost to her, than the present which is thereby left speechless. Another, who recognized the more indirect operations of speech, might say that she wept at the rehearsal of her own sorrow, at speaking it even more than at recalling it; for, telling it to a stranger, she found its effect on her in the present to be not quite simply the effect of the past. In *Things As They Are; or, The Adventures of Caleb Williams*, a novel first published in 1794, Godwin had written a counter-example of his own to *Political Justice* and in it it is clear how, at that present, direct speech had no mastery over the indirect operations of its meaning.[8] Yet Wordsworth, here going beyond these Godwinite alternatives of direct and indirect meaning, says the woman wept

> As if because her tale was at an end

Not as if she were weeping simply at the past as a discrete event; not as if she merely indulged in presenting to herself an external portrait of her internal sorrow; not as if she wept because she could get no more out of it or it out of her. But, encompassing all these, she wept as if because she could no longer put her grief into words and it has done no good that she even has. Her tale is at an end; its effect, her complex sorrow in having told it and in having still to live it, is not.

That is to say, to Wordsworth the reality of speech is not simply the desire to tell, as a relief of loneliness; it is here also the hope of being spoken to: of hearing from the person addressed a reply from human nature to human nature adequate to answer and console. In the act of writing, the writer thus can hear in the silence after recorded speech the echo of what hopes and fears the speaker had of being spoken to. It would not be so audible had Wordsworth written—'She wept/As if because her tale was at an end'. Rather, 'She ceased, and weeping turned away,/As if because her tale was at an end/She wept' releases the virtue of poetry by hearing, between the end of one line and the beginning of the next, how lost she was in her abandonment. While the facts are limited in time and in description, the meaning of them seems to her driftingly endless. This slight distance between the writing and the speech which it apparently records allows a gap not simply for hearing but for imaginatively recalling what went on beneath the words.

Such poetry is a promise that the meaning of a life, like that of the suffering woman, can be retrieved from the meaning of the words written in memory of it. Thus:

> . . .—because she had no more to say
> Of that perpetual weight which on her spirit lay.

To hear the inner voice or, as I have elsewhere called it, the second language of poetry is to recognize how 'no more' (used of saying) is played off against 'perpetual' (used of silent suffering), such that in the space between the two is lodged a recall of the predicament of her feeling. Such poetry not only *bespeaks* what can hardly be spoken, as in our earlier example from 'The Ruined Cottage'; it also holds its *memory*. That silence after 'she had no more to say' means 'The music in my heart I bore/Long after it was heard no more' (*P.W.*, iii, p. 77).

But now suppose we turn from 'Adventures on Salisbury Plain' to the rewritten version of it of 1841, nearly half a century later, entitled 'Guilt and Sorrow; or, Incidents upon Salisbury Plain'. And suppose, too, we turn, as a measure of possible shift within that time, from Godwin to another, later writer on sincerity.

The reality proposed by Godwin's sincerity involved the strenuous conflict of two or more minds opened out into a series of self-correcting arguments, giving to the human species as a whole the responsibility of being keeper of any one man's conscience. In 1840, J. H. Newman of the Oxford Movement, in contrast, published a volume containing among others his sermon 'Unreal Words'. Indiscriminate trade, he thought, in what a Victorian mass society all too readily thinks of as 'mere words' induces an individual to betray the meaning of his conscience through recourse to words no more than taken up by rote.

> To make professions is to play with edged tools, unless we attend to what we are saying. Words have a meaning, whether we mean that meaning or not; and they are imputed to us in their real meaning, when our not meaning it is our own fault.
>
> *Parochial and Plain Sermons*, v, p. 33.

When a man's profession of feeling outruns the real inward existence of that feeling, when he says all too easily or controversially what he does not understand, when he has no meaning adequate to his words, he is unreal.

In 1841, Wordsworth turned back to the point at which the sorrowing woman ended her tale, and this time he directed increased attention upon the response of her listener, a sailor unable to return to his wife and children after having committed a murder on the outskirts of their home:

> True sympathy the Sailor's looks expressed,
> His looks—for pondering he was mute the while.
> Of social Order's care for wretchedness,
> Of Time's sure help to calm and reconcile,
> Joy's second spring and Hope's long-treasured smile,
> 'Twas not for *him* to speak—a man so tried.
> Yet, to relieve her heart, in friendly style
> Proverbial words of comfort he applied,
> And not in vain, while they went pacing side by side.
>
> *The Salisbury Plain Poems*, p. 257, ll. 451–9.

The delay of the main verb in that second sentence—''Twas not for *him* to speak'—mimes how he is disabused of the thoughts of plausible comfort running through his mind; they sink, beneath his own 'perpetual weight' of misery, to a level from which the speaking of them would appear to be unreal. Newman wrote that

> many men, when they come near persons in distress and wish to show sympathy, often condole in a very unreal way. I am not altogether laying this to their fault; for it is very difficult to know what to do, when on the one hand we cannot realise to ourselves the sorrow, yet withal wish to be kind to those who feel it. A tone of grief seems necessary, yet (if so be) cannot under our circumstances be genuine. Yet even here surely there is a true way, if we could find it, by which pretence may be avoided, and yet respect and consideration shown.
>
> *Parochial and Plain Sermons*, v, p. 38.

The problem for the sailor-murderer is more complex still. Why could he not speak of real comfort? He could not speak precisely because, deeper than sympathy, he was a sufferer as she was and himself knew little of the comfort that he half felt she ought to hope for: '*him*' is a word with the grammatical structure and emotional authority of one who has suffered. But, worse, he of all men could not speak, though perhaps a more innocent sufferer could: '*him*' being also a word of guilt, in so far as he has caused an equivalent woman, his wife, to become a virtual widow as this woman in fact is. And yet, although it is not for '*him*' to offer or receive comfort, guilt also means that it is not for him *not* to utter 'proverbial words' of comfort—painfully unreal to himself, as if spoken by someone other than him, but really 'not in vain' as far as she is concerned. It is a mark of the difference between the directness of Sorrow and the indirectness of Guilt as emotions that the delayed verb in the passage of 1798—'She wept'—suffers in a way both more and less than the delayed verb in the example from 1841—''Twas not for *him* to speak'. Such poetry not only reveals what this speaker meant but also what it meant to be this speaker when speech failed or all too unsatisfactorily succeeded. It bequeaths his unspoken memory.

Between 1795 and 1841, what it meant to be Wordsworth came to include a further consciousness of the thoughts that lie too deep for tears, of secondary turnings and embargoes on meaning such as guilt. Through the years that separate what are now called *The Salisbury Plain Poems* not the least of Wordsworth's achievements was his capacity to make his own tacit difficulties his profoundest written subject-matter. But to do this required one fundamental acknowledgement. The more complex his consciousness with regard to matters like sorrow and guilt, the more Wordsworth (if he was not, like the Sailor, merely to mouth proverbs) had to accept that the most real words were written ones. This recognition—that the most real words (though not the only real feelings) were written ones— made writing something other than secondary to speaking. Thus, when in the revised version of the 'Preface to *Lyrical Ballads*' finally published in 1850, Wordsworth declared of the Poet:

> He is a man speaking to men.
> *Prose Works,* i, p. 138.

my guess is that he had come to mean by that two things,
albeit tacitly. One, that the poet is a man *writing as if* speaking
to men; as, for instance, a man writes in sympathy with sorrow.
Two, that the poet is a man making audible to himself realities
of which he could not speak to himself directly; as, for instance,
a man writes when in trouble with guilt. For, in summary, it is
considerations like these that have complicated the temptation
to think of writing as something as 'natural' to man as speaking
itself is. But we have seen that the more the idea of writing has
been deprived of an easy passage to the status 'natural' or
'primary', the more (not the less) important and necessary it
has seemed in saving human things from silence. We shall need
to explain this further, if we are not to consider Wordsworth's
prose-claims for the idea of writing to be over-simple or downright duplicitous.

                    *   *   *   *   *

For the remainder of this chapter I want to consider and
substantiate my two glosses as to the meaning of Wordsworth's
dictum, 'The Poet . . . is a man speaking to men'.

To take the first point again, The Poet is a man writing as if
speaking to men. It is obvious that if, as a writer, Wordsworth
was not some esoteric specialist but a man speaking to men,
still he was not as Godwin ideally would have had him be. His
communication was quite essentially by writing. Why this had
to be so is connected with what happened to the idea of
sincerity and real words between Godwin and the time of
Newman.

For the young Wordsworth the French Revolution was to
have established the true brotherhood of man with man. 'To
build Liberty'

> On firm foundations, making social life,
> Through knowledge spreading and imperishable,
> As just in regulation, and as pure
> As individual in the wise and good.
>
> *The Prelude*, 1805–6, ix, 366–70.

The ideal of the Revolution was to spread through society and
its institutions a knowledge and a humanity which each
generation could simply re-learn without the necessity of

having individually to re-experience it and suffer to attain it. Society, with its new institutions embodying corporate experience, could pass on to its members the lessons of the past without requiring them individually to go through them all again. Taking over what the function of memory was for the individual, the new world would ensure that any wisdom embodied in the old individual struggles of mankind was socially re-embodied without, and indeed in place of, the suffering which effected it.

The failure of the ideals of the French Revolution in Wordsworth's eyes destroyed this idea for him. In the second half of the nineteenth century, Matthew Arnold, a self-confessed heir to Wordsworth, offered in compensation for the unreformed ways of an increasingly secular society the belief that culture, handed on in writing, humanizes knowledge and touches morality with emotion. In works like *Culture and Anarchy* and *Literature and Dogma* Arnold was arguing that great writing expands the human family in so far as the experience of great men may be relearnt, without having to be entirely re-lived, by each subsequent generation. But, with the failure of the French Revolution, it was this sort of Hegelian view of the central stream of human tendency that Wordsworth had to reject, even ahead of its formally being made. Even thus he had also rejected Godwin on revolution by sincerity.

It is doubtful whether Wordsworth's Victorian readers, beguiled by the thought that here was a man speaking to men, realized how difficult it was to learn from Wordsworth or how difficult he himself believed the task of learning from writers to be. This Victorian position seems to me to find most dramatic expression in John Stuart Mill's famous account of how reading Wordsworth restored to him apparently primal human feelings repressed by his father's form of utilitarian education. In Wordsworth's poems, Mill testified in his *Autobiography* (first published in 1873):

> I seemed to draw from a source of inward joy, of sympathetic and imaginative pleasure, which could be shared in by all human beings; which had no connexion with struggle or imperfection, but would be made richer by every improvement in the physical or social condition of mankind.[9]

In this cultivation of the store of happier emotions, Wordsworth
became as a replacement father of the race and, in Arnold's
own words, 'laid us as we lay at birth/On the cool flowery lap
of earth,/Smiles broke from us and we had ease'.[10] To this
representative sense of Wordsworth as our replacement
memory, offering a basis of happiness reborn without struggle,
it was the litarary critic R. H. Hutton (1826–97), significantly
an admirer of Newman as well as of Wordsworth, who made
the devastating reply:[11]

> Now that does not strike me as by any means an accurate
> description of the influence of Wordsworth's poetry on
> the mind. Wordsworth does not restore us to the ease and
> freshness of our youth, he rather baptizes us in his strong
> and unique spirit. . . . Wordsworth is the last poet of
> whom I should say that he makes us children again. He
> gives us a new youth, not the old.
>
> Hutton: *Literary Essays*, pp. 323–4.

We have already seen, in relation to Godwin and Hazlitt on
Godwin, that questions of how a writer turns his past into
writing are complex. Does he turn to it or from it? does he turn
it or does it turn him? What Hutton is suggesting here is that
there is some strategy in Wordsworth's treatment of his own
memories by which when he seems to be taking us back, he is
in adult fact really bringing us forward. As if in those coinciding
distinctions between how it feels to remember and how it feels
at the time, and between writing of an experience and the
experience itself, Wordsworth found a sanction not merely to
go back in nostalgia but to go forward into new knowledge of
the past.

All this is not to say that Mill and Arnold completely
misunderstood the Wordsworthian belief that poetry's
education worked from and upon memory. For it is emphatically true that the sense of a *residue*—as from moments when
men find that speech cannot or has not articulated for them all
they are experiencing confusedly—constituted for Wordsworth
a vital store of resonance upon which a poet drew, not only in
himself but also for a response from his readers.

> O Reader! had you in your mind
> Such stores as silent thought can bring,
> O gentle Reader! you would find
> A tale in every thing.
>
>   *P. W.*, iv, p. 63.

No, the error of men like Arnold and Mill was to suppose that the memory that Wordsworth put into words could simply be transferred wholesale from poet to reader, becoming the reader's new memory of his life. Earlier in the history of the nineteenth century there had been, in contrast, a more strenuous sense of what was involved in trying to keep in real and living touch with Wordsworth while also being conscious of coming after him. John Keats in a letter to J. H. Reynolds, 3 May 1818, saw a dignity rather than a despair in the fact of a reader's being separate from the writer. On considering Wordsworth's genius, Keats writes:

> here I have nothing but surmises, from an uncertainty whether Milton's apparently less anxiety for Humanity proceeds from his seeing further or no than Wordsworth: And whether Wordsworth has in truth epic passion, and martyrs himself on the human heart, the main region of his song—In regard to his genius alone—we find what he says true as far as we have experienced and we can judge no further but by larger experiences—for axioms in philosophy are not axioms until they are proved upon our pulses: We read fine—things but never feel them to the full until we have gone the same steps as the Author.[12]

It is perhaps a weakness to be found elsewhere in Keats that 'proof upon the pulses' might be taken all too easily for the emotive aesthetic of the later nineteenth century. But what Keats is saying is that (to borrow Newman's term) 'real words' can only be recognized and in turn expressed by one whose true learning from culture is what at some level he has *already* experienced. So far from this being the diminishment of the worth of literature, that it cannot simply pass on the experience of another, it constitutes its dignity as a call upon the reader to see his literary experience not as a bonus to, but as a hard-won part of, his own experience. This is what

Newman in his *Essay in Aid of a Grammar of Assent* was to call knowledge in a real rather than a notional sense.

Now, in the stringency of his requirement to 'have gone the same steps as the Author', there is evidence that Keats could well have been the sort of reader whom Wordsworth himself wanted. For Wordsworth did not want mere followers; rather, it was his view that those who came after him could not follow but only independently arrive at his way. What is at stake in this belief of Wordsworth's may be illustrated.

In the issue of 14 December 1809 Coleridge printed in his periodical *The Friend* a letter from 'Mathetes', the pseudonym used by two young Scotsmen, John Wilson and Alexander Blair. It was a letter about the problems of youth, and in it 'Mathetes' argued that the problems, like that of delusion, sprang not from youth's worse but his better nature. This was worse than if the difficulties had been merely external to him: such as the plethora of bad influences or the models of pastiche seriousness. People might suppose that the internal strength of powerful young feelings ought to have acted to counteract the influence of the inauthentic. But it was precisely that strength which projected upon unworthy externals a value which not only did not belong to them but also betrayed the source to which it did belong. Disabused of the authority of his own emotions, frightened of what they might seize upon, 'Mathetes' called for 'a superior Mind', a 'living Teacher' to act as 'guiding hand' and 'protector' of youth. He proposed 'the name of WORDSWORTH'. And it was to Wordsworth himself that Coleridge sent the letter for answer. Surely, we might suppose, the man who believed that the poet was not a special case but a man and, what is more, a man speaking to men, would not hesitate to come into such immediate relation to his readership. Yet, when Wordsworth did reply, he did so virtually anonymously, at the last moment before printing inserting his own initials inverted. Moreover, he refused the role of fatherly teacher. 'The *Child* is Father of the Man' (*P. W.*,i, p. 226). Thus Wordsworth wrote to Mathetes of the dangers which discipleship introduces into the young mind:

> misgivings, a mistrust of its own evidence, dispositions to affect to feel where there can be no real feeling, indecisive

judgements, a superstructure of opinions that has no base to support it, and words uttered by rote with the impertinence of a Parrot or a Mocking-bird. . . .

These results I contend, whatever may be the benefit to be derived from such an enlightened Teacher, are in their degree inevitable. . . . Nature has irrevocably decreed that our prime dependence in all stages of life after Infancy and Childhood have been passed through . . . must be upon our own minds; and that the way to knowledge shall be long, difficult, winding, and often times returning upon itself.

Prose Works, ii, p. 23.

Wordsworth would never have written that had the French Revolution not failed. They are the words of a man who has learnt what cannot be taught, *and* learnt that it cannot be re-taught direct. It is this which is the force of Wordsworth's not speaking but writing. For it is Wordsworth's insistence on leaving 'Mathetes' alone without (by not replying at all) leaving him lonely that is here a paradigm of what human contact through the written word meant to Wordsworth. After the failure of the Revolution the human bond was not, for him, going to take immediate form; it was going to depend upon things like resonance: an invisible, indirect but not necessarily distorting communication between men.

I reassert then the claim that Wordsworth really meant that a poet was a man writing *as if speaking* to men. And I suppose he omitted the complication lest it unduly disturb the main sense of that double duty: to make the man a poet but to keep the poet a man. Yet, even in trying to be that sort of poet there seems to have been in Wordsworth at times a not quite logical fear: that the separation of writing from speaking might mean the separation of the poet from other men. It was this extra fear that his poetry could bespeak when in his prose he could but slide over it. And more than that, it was a fear which his poetry could use to raise itself above it. Consider two parts of *Home at Grasmere*. First, Wordsworth writes of 'an internal brightness' vouchsafed to him:

> Why does this inward lustre fondly seek
> And gladly blend with outward fellowship?

Why shine they round me thus, whom thus I love?
Why do they teach me, whom I thus revere?
Strange question, yet it answers not itself.
                    Home at Grasmere, p. 94 (MS.B, 888–92).

'Why shine they round me thus, whom thus I love?': a prosaic
man might answer, 'They shine because you love them
(emotional projection)'; or 'You love them because they shine
out (love is the way you connect with people whom you think
better than yourself)'. But in making that line one line,
stubbornly, the poet knew those answers and knew that they
were not answers. Though why they were not, he knew not.
'Strange question, yet it answers not itself.' Now, this awe in
Wordsworth that is surprised to find the brightness inside him
correspond to the brightness of people outside him actually
belongs with another side of Wordsworth. A side to which,
secondly, he turns within a few lines, when he claims to possess

Something within, which yet is shared by none—
Not even the nearest to me, and most dear.
                              Ibid., MS.B, 898–9.

It is just that 'something within' which was amazed to find
'this inward lustre fondly seek/And gladly blend with outward
fellowship'. When Wordsworth is most worthy of himself, that
is to say, it is 'something' that no more sets the poet apart from
men than it does so in the power with which it also draws him
back to them. It is that 'something within', other than
deviousness or formal difficulty, that distinguishes the consciousness of a man writing as if speaking to men; a man
separate in his own mind and in his own mind connected.

This leads me immediately to my second gloss, that the poet
is a man making audible to himself that of which he could not
have spoken directly. If writing is not to be dismissed as both
secondary and artificial in comparison with man's use of
speech, a case has to be made for what writing can do of itself
that communication by speaking cannot do.

For the purposes of reaching a conclusion, we may find the
outline for just such a case in an essay, 'On the Difference
between Writing and Speaking', published in *The Plain Speaker*
in 1826. Its author is William Hazlitt, the Hazlitt who found in

Godwin a specific, powerful example of the problematic status of writing. Here, dealing with the matter in more general terms, Hazlitt asserted more easily that:

> the writer and speaker have to do things essentially different . . . the distinction between those whose chief ambition is to shine by producing an immediate effect, or who are thrown back, by a natural bias, on the severer researches of thought and study.
>
> *Works*, xii, p. 263.

Those who seek to stand out, talk; those who are turned back, write. Now, it is important to note that Hazlitt further eases his task by treating 'speaking' here as both a political and a professionally political activity. Although this time he does not mention the peculiar case of Godwin, he offers comparisons between political orators and political writers. That said, however, the distinctions which he makes with respect to writing as the 'severer' test and testimony of human seriousness still stand. In writing, as in reading what is written, Hazlitt argues that 'we are by ourselves' (p. 267); writing is 'the habit of thinking aloud, but without the help of an echo' (p. 274), for there is no audience actually present. The echo, I might add, is rather within the writer: it is thus his making his thinking audible to himself.

> My own voice chear'd me, and, far more, the mind's
> Internal echo of the imperfect sound.
> *The Prelude*, 1805–6, i, 64–5.

—wrote Wordsworth of his experience of composing poetry in the open fields. There would not have been that extra dimension of 'internal echo', had Wordsworth been merely speaking, rather than speaking-as-if-writing.

'The great leading distinction between writing and speaking,' says Hazlitt, 'is that more time is allowed for the one than the other' (p. 267). Indeed, it is true, as we have already seen, that the pauses in writing, which poetry formalizes into line-endings, give time for a man's hesitations to become thought, as well as draw a reader gently into thinking in the writer's own time.[13] Coleridge himself said that it was not association of ideas, the semi-mechanical memory by which one thing led to another, that constituted thought; real thinking depended not upon association but upon interruption of ideas, as the mind intervened to pause or shift or contradict the initial movement. At any rate, the measured thinking involved in writing allows the writer, in Hazlitt's own account, to search for and weigh the right word. It finds time, it makes time. What then does a writer make of this extra time which he has won for himself? If he is Wordsworth, then he sees how his repetition and modification of words obey as well as provoke the 'internal echo' of them in the writer's own mind. And into these echoes of the words inside his mind, into the time which they give him for thought, he induces his own echoes of meaning and the time which is that of his own memory. For example, the mind of the poet finds time to open up in the following from Wordsworth's 'Ode: Intimations of Immortality from Recollections of Early Childhood', where he finds that he is most grateful to his childhood past not simply for its memory of delight and liberty but, on the contrary, for:

> . . . those obstinate questionings
> Of sense and outward things,
> Fallings from us, vanishings;
> Blank misgivings of a Creature
> Moving about in worlds not realized.
>
> *P.W.*, iv, p. 283.

The words in that list are not in frantic competition with each other, as if in a race to overtake a meaning ever vanishing ahead of them. Rather, the pace, the time, is slow for the sake of intimation; it is that of a man whose writing has enabled him to get into rhythm with himself. The words themselves are 'fallings' from him, rising out of the echoes of words before, then 'vanishing' into what arises out of their own resonance. It is a provisional diction, and the race to overtake the vanishing meaning is honestly lost, that the meaning might be recognized as transcending the words which, fast or slow, straggle after it. It is a considerable achievement—one inseparable from the support which writing gives to a man—that Wordsworth could have actually felt *grateful*, in respect of words, 'That whatsoever point they gain, they still/Have something to pursue' (*The Prelude*, 1805–6, ii, 340–1). Grateful and not merely appetitively anxious. Steadied by his own writing, Wordsworth came to find in it something analogous to and supportive of the way that memory itself slows down time into experience. He was a man who needed time of his own—for calm, for thought, for change, for repentance, for development, even for his own difficulties and 'blank misgivings'. His development in and through poetry is moreover not simply linear, better one year than the next; rather, it lies not least in his being gratefully unanxious about picking up again, with all the feelings of sameness and difference, what another man might have left behind for the sake of a merely apparent progress. The interchange between the time that writing allowed sheerly in itself and the sense of time which was the writer's own memory behind his words seems to have appeared to Wordsworth to be almost like grace.

But not all the while. It was a double-edged sword: for there was also serious anxiety for Wordsworth about writing; specifically at the point of getting into a sense of his own time through writing. He found it hard to begin, and this left him feeling stranded, outside his sense of inner time. And even when finally writing and within it, he could feel potentially separated from the world. The recurrent difficulty that Wordsworth had in the matter of beginning to write suggests a man who sometimes found himself unable to turn the supportive experience, which he felt behind him, round into the present, in order to write forwards from it. 'Each most obvious and particular thought/ . . . Hath no beginning', he lamented (*The Prelude*, 1805–6, ii, 234, 237). Thus lyrics like 'A Night-Piece' seem self-conscious as to the necessarily arbitrary convention of beginning, as they start halfway in:

————The sky is overcast
P.W., ii, p. 208.

In their quietly confessed abruptness, such lyrics seek not to disturb that of which they write: so they back into the work, negatively, as in 'Airey-Force Valley'

————Not a breath of air
P.W., ii, p. 209.

For it is as though the poet, composing in the open air, were not always quite sure of the place of poetry. There is even at times a guilty unease, occasionally unavoidable to a poet of memory, as to how writing could be separate from living *and* as to how it could not be. *Home at Grasmere*, for example, has a diction of specifically economic unease about how much the poet, freed to pursue his vocation by a lucky legacy, owes to the life he writes of and to the poorer inhabitants of that rich countryside from which his soul feeds.[14]

This ambivalence of Wordsworth's concerning writing's gift of time is not merely a matter of temperament. More than that, it is something formally embodied in the very nature of writing, and therefore all too likely to accentuate his difficulties as a writer. Towards the end of the eighteenth century the Scottish school of Common Sense philosophy had put the problem in unemotive terms. On one hand, James Beattie, himself a poet, could say, 'Our thoughts are fleeting, and the greater part of our words are forgotten as soon as uttered: but, by writing, we may give permanency to both'.[15] Yet, out of the same Scottish school, Dugald Stewart warned that writing, though on balance a good, is also a habit 'unfavourable, in some respects, to the faculty of memory, by superseding, to a certain degree, the necessity of its exertions'.[16] Likewise, Beattie himself notes that a man should own his own thoughts and experience sufficiently to be able to speak from Memory; it was lamentable if thought, when committed to paper, became estranged from the mind in which it had its origin. Yet it is also true that a preacher who has spent years getting apparently extempore sermons by heart has wasted the time for thought simply by not writing and correcting. Beattie adds:

> Why does a musician choose to play by book even the musick that he remembers? It is, because, by taking in, with one glance of his eye, a number of contiguous notes, his mind is always disengaged, and he is everywhere the better prepared for introducing the expressive touches, and other necessary ornaments.[17]

Clearly these philosophers mean by memory not something personal but the basic act of reminiscence, and that makes their problem more tractable than ours. Nonetheless they do show this: that writing, formally considered, is not only about the seriously weighed commitment of mind to paper; it also concerns the creation of the possibility of the mind's 'disengagement' from its own previous thoughts, noted now in verbal holdfasts and reminders. The mind may go on to change itself thus, raising itself above itself by means of its verbally noted basis. Thus although it may be feared that writing threatens to replace thinking and remembering as they are in their physical life within a man, it only threatens to do so as any habit threatens to replace spontaneity. When fully habituated, the spontaneity may exist again within the terms of the habit. It is a second chance, through writing, rising like improvises and harmonizes off the score beside him, leaning on improvises and harmonises off the score beside him, leaning on it, like a habit, so that he may support himself from it.

The capacity of writing to release imagination even within the very province of memory is a matter to which we shall turn again in chapter 2. For the present it is enough to say that this virtue derives from the temporal licence that writing affords. For James Beattie, as for Hartley and Hume before him, what distinguished imagination from memory was the capacity of the former to free itself from the temporally tied order of the latter: it is 'a peculiar property of the memory to preserve the original order and position of its ideas, while the imagination transposes and changes them, as it pleases'.[18]

But freedom was only one thing that Wordsworth wanted. He also wanted to use that freedom which he had won from his own past in order to preserve a fidelity to that past; in much the same way he wanted the man that he was to be a poet, but a poet who differed not in kind, only in degree from other men. This could not but be a struggle and one of which outside his poetry he could hardly speak without it seeming theoretical and unreal to himself. But we can see the difficulty in a sonnet which begins by quoting Cowper's lines 'There is a pleasure in poetic pains/Which only Poets know'. The poet's thought of an infelicitous word in a poem is described as isolating him socially and discomposing him temporally: it

Haunts him belated on the silent plains!
P.W., iii, p. 29.

It is both its terror and its freedom that the poet's memory is out of phase with external time and felt as disturbing time as he tries to create and sustain his own. Wordsworth persisted in the search for the right words because first to disturb the natural order was the only way, in his own mind, secondly to restore it. But the written restoration of affairs also inevitably changed them. And it is this that Wordsworth's best critic, R. H. Hutton sees as Wordsworth's greatest strength:

> He could detach his mind from the commonplace series of impressions which are generated by commonplace objects or events, resist and often reverse the current of emotion to which ordinary minds are liable . . . his best thoughts come from the steady resistance he opposes to the ebb and flow of ordinary desires and regrets . . . as he recalls how 'the wiser mind'
>
> > 'Mourns less for what age takes away
> > Than what it leaves behind.'
>
> *Literary Essays*, pp. 90–1.

Wordsworth's is thus not just a syntax of recall but a syntax of reappraisal within that recall: as he writes of life in 'Argument for Suicide'

> . . .—till we have learned
> To prize it less, we ne'er shall learn to prize
> The things worth living for.
>
> *P.W.*, i, p. 316.

or as he describes the old man in 'Animal Tranquillity and Decay':

> . . . one to whom
> Long patience hath such mild composure given,
> That patience now doth seem a thing of which
> He hath no need.
>
> *P.W.*, iv, p. 247.

To recall and yet even in so doing to think again is to employ writing as both on the rebound from one's own life (which was Hazlitt's criticism of Godwin) and in reappraisal of it (which was Godwin's own sense of what he was doing). Writing gave

Wordsworth time not only to think over his memories but also to rethink them; it not only recommitted him to them, it also detached him from them by the act of putting them into words external to himself. As Hutton says, 'no poet gives us so strong a feeling of the contrast between the inward and the outward as Wordsworth; he dives into himself between his respirations, that he may exclude for a little while the tyranny of the senses, and so not waste his life in the mere animal pleasure of breathing' (*Literary Essays*, p. 114). 'Tyranny' and 'mere' are an idealist's overstatement of his case there. But it is still true that a reader does feel in the respirations between lines Wordsworth pulling himself back inside himself to find what will carry him on again outside: 'The things worth living for'. The syntax of reversal bespeaks a man who remained behind his forehead, so to speak, able to find space there within which to turn round his ordinary impressions because he was able to put them out of himself into words. The distance—in both time and form, between writing and its subject-matter, between his inner thoughts and the external words representing them—was for Wordsworth only an initial defeat; it was also a second chance and a licence for second thought ('That patience now doth seem a thing of which/He hath no need'). 'He wrings from the temporary sadness fresh conviction that the ebbing away, both in spirit and in appearance, of the brightest past, sad as it must ever be, is not so sad a thing as the weak yearning which, in departing, it often leaves stranded on the soul, to cling to the appearance when the spirit is irrecoverably lost' (R. H. Hutton: ibid., p. 100). It is sad that poetry sometimes feels, not least to its writer, like a secondary imitation of that of which it treats:

> However exalted a notion we would wish to cherish of the character of a Poet, it is obvious, that while he describes and imitates passions, his employment is in some degree mechanical, compared with the freedom and power of real and substantial action and suffering.
>
> *Prose Works*, i, p. 138.

But it would be even sadder if poetry could not take advantage, as in the syntax of considered reversal, even of this.

* * * * *

In this chapter then, poetry to bespeak; poetry to remember; poetry to bequeath a memory of what it meant to be this man; and finally, poetry with the courage to alter things. The difficulties that Wordsworth could hardly speak about directly were not simply those concerning the writing of poetry; they concerned, largely speaking, the trouble that poetry had in knowing what to say about human sorrow. In that, poetry was not unique among human efforts—after all, what could one say, what could one do anyway?—but it was at a high and lonely pitch of considered consciousness representative of those failed efforts. I want to close by reviewing a few examples of what Wordsworth could make audible to himself only by the writing of poetry—with all those articulate silences wherein a man leaves his memory.

In 1798, what could the young man reply to the tears of Simon Lee, when that old man was so grateful to him for youth's being able to do, all too easily, what age's feebleness no longer could? The young man could easily uproot the old tree which the old man was struggling over. To save both of them, when the old man was so pathetically grateful, the younger might have tried the comfort of saying, 'I'll be a son to thee!'. Yet when, in 'The Fountain', he does say this to old Matthew, he has no answer to give to the reply in response:

> At this he grasped my hand, and said,
> 'Alas that cannot be.'
>
> *P.W.*, iv, p. 73.

There is, beyond words of speech, a sadness in the adult truth of what 'cannot be'—all that is not possible although so desirable. As the young man and the old man both have to find in this case, to be adult, at least outside the ties of family, cannot be other than to be unspeakably solitary.

In 1798, of course, it was fifteen years since Wordsworth had been anyone's son. If there was one thing that his youth taught him, perhaps from the death of his mother in 1778, it was a lesson akin to that shared between Matthew and the young man: the lesson of a mutually reflected loneliness, felt in each, felt for each, curable by neither. Their spoken words of sympathy are less telling than a deeper sympathy of structure:

that between the words of Matthew to the young man in 'The Fountain':

> 'My days, my Friend, are almost gone,
> My life has been approved,
> And many love me; but by none
> Am I enough beloved.'
>
> *P.W.*, iv, pp. 72–3.

and, written during the same few months, the words of the young poet to his absent readers in 'A Poet's Epitaph':

> He is retired as noontide dew,
> Or fountain in a noon-day grove;
> And you must love him, ere to you
> He will seem worthy of your love.
>
> *P.W.*, iv, p. 67.

Surely the structure of the thinking is similar, as of Hutton's syntax of reversal. As those two stanzas face each other, respectively too late and too early for love, they bespeak a nature in between them, implicitly Wordsworth's own, which has on its own personal side a want and lack to match the imaginative sympathy which, in vain, it gives to Matthew. At heart, however, that nature has to be silent in the midst of the difficulties of expressing itself. Yet the words speak: the word 'beloved' in the last line of Matthew's lament takes to its heart the word 'love' in the line preceding it but only to bury the hope of it inside the memory of its lack. And the syntax speaks too: in each example the turn of the then stranded fourth line out of the words of the third—'but by none/Am I enough beloved', 'ere to you/He will seem worthy of your love'— bespeaks a man who is conscious of feeling that things work in a way the reverse of that which the world commonly assumes. If only worthiness of being loved created the being loved and the being enough beloved, as well as being retrospectively created by them! Wordsworth was a man who felt the greater part of himself behind-hand or back-to-front. There is in those lines, 'And you *must* love him, ere to you/He will seem worthy of your love', something of the sort of man Godwin himself was ('fearful of intruding myself', 'making few acquaintances, losing them *in limine*'). That 'must' is not a merely egoistical

demand but an essentially social recognition of one's dependence upon what turns out to be the impossibility of the prior
understanding of oneself by others, if one is to become oneself
at all. Wordsworth came to find 'that every author, as far as he
is great and at the same time *original*, has had the task of
creating the taste by which he is to be enjoyed: so has it been, so
will it continue to be' (*Prose Works*, iii, p. 80). A great author
might just be able to do this by writing, by trying to establish
his own memory thus; a man sheerly by speaking could hardly
hope to make any such impression. Wordsworth, to use the
metaphor of a runner, had to come from behind. He liked the
slower pace of writing. The value of things seemed to come to
him through chastening or disappointment of the original
desire, or through waiting, or only finally afterwards in the
memory, on second thought, after reflection, as if the reality of
his experience always predated his articulate consciousness of .
it. He was the sort of man who had to learn, as from his sister
Dorothy, the love of beauty which he associated with her; the
sort of man who, Hunter Davies thinks, really fell in love with
his wife years *after* he had married her.[19] In lyrics like 'The
Fountain' and 'A Poet's Epitaph' even his act of writing as in
retrospect seems to come too late to remedy the sadness which
it discloses as cutting speech short. The stanzas we have seen
seem by their last lines deadlocked, becalmed:

> . . . but by none
> Am I enough beloved.

> . . . to prize
> The things worth living for.

—ideas arrived at too late here to save the life and effort of the
poem and thus left as something to be stored in Wordsworth's
memory as what was gained from the writing.

But in 1798 and 1799 Wordsworth also began a sustained
piece of sheer writing, an unforeshortened work, *The Prelude*,
and by the time of the 1805 version he was able to turn back to
perhaps the major figure behind the composite of old Matthew:
William Taylor, the Hawkshead schoolmaster who had died in
1786, aged thirty-two, when Wordsworth himself was only
sixteen.

'I thought of Chatterton, the marvellous Boy,/The sleepless Soul that perished in his pride' wrote Wordsworth in 'Resolution and Independence' in 1802 (*P. W.*, ii, p. 236). But in *The Prelude* he thought also of the schoolmaster who had first introduced him to poets like Chatterton, and had died when Wordsworth, then no Chatterton, was only just starting. Wordsworth recalls in the poem how in 1794 he had gone back and stood at Taylor's grave, its stone engraved for epitaph with 'a fragment from the Elegy of Gray':

> . . . And now,
> Thus travelling smoothly, o'er the level Sands,
> I thought with pleasure of the Verses, graven
> Upon his Tombstone, saying to myself
> He loved the Poets, and if now alive,
> Would have loved me.
>
> *The Prelude*, 1805–6, x, 507–12.

It is, as he writes, a moment of double memory; recalling his visit of 1794 and his memory at that time of Taylor's words to him less than a week before his death in 1786: '"my head will soon lie low"' (502). Not only is this writing which seems to hear again those spoken words, it is also clearly the form of 'saying to myself' and attesting now to it. As a form of simultaneous hearing and saying, hearing what the dead man said and saying it again, hearing again now in writing what one said to oneself, this poetry is sustained by the thought that Taylor chose Gray's verse for his epitaph: it spoke for him and to him. The man remembered the verse, and, on his tombstone, for another poet, the verse now recalls him. That is Wordsworth's profound pleasure, such as moved him to write those 'Essays upon Epitaphs'. And so here Wordsworth's own verse hears in itself what the poet said to himself as a man in 1794 and now speaks it again in echo, as if imagining itself as just short of Taylor's own hearing of it:

> He loved the Poets, and if now alive,
> Would have loved me.

The way that last half-line *comes back upon* the line before it is an advance upon the stranded relation to each other of the lines from 'A Poet's Epitaph': 'And you must love him, ere to you/He will seem worthy of your love'.[20] For memory here does not find the writing out of the past to be too late to be retrieved as well as reported. The way that 'would have loved' comes back upon 'loved' feels like the memory of one's own life coming back to that life to give a love to it which is not simply that of self-love. I end then with two questions. First, if writing can do that, will a reader not admit that it is rightly 'one of the primary sensations of the human heart', that what men write is one of the first things we should care about? And yet the scrupulousness of the mood there—'*would have* loved'—also admits within the writing of it a sadness which, had it been spoken outright, could not thus have been subsumed, included and transmuted: a double sadness that Taylor is not 'now alive' and that, when alive, he could not go so far as to *love* the parentless boy as a boy, let alone a poet. My second question is: do not such thoughts almost make the writing secondary to them?

But the writing itself helped to form these thoughts. I answer that, in adding his bit to Gray's, Wordsworth does not seem to me to need to apologize even to himself that such writing is not speaking, is only in retrospect. There are times when it must seem to us curious that grown men merely sit down and write; and, paradoxically, this writing finds part of its strength, not its weakness, in the recognition that to write about Taylor is nothing like bringing him back to life. Perhaps it is not even as good as if Taylor had loved him those years ago; though Taylor himself, who loved the Poets, might have argued otherwise, and not simply because he preferred poetry to schoolteaching. For when Wordsworth used writing to attest:

> But she is in her grave, and, oh,
> The difference to me!

he knew even as he wrote it that the 'difference to me' would make no difference. But it is because it will make no difference, Lucy being dead, that he feels so powerfully 'the difference to me'. In the words to Taylor, similarly, Wordsworth's memory heard, in writing, the echo of speech extended beyond the grave of silence: 'Would have loved me'. Such writing matters a great deal not because it can do a lot but because it can do only a little, and that precious little it does.

Wordsworth's old Wanderer recalls Margaret's response to the words of conventional comfort he had to find for her:

> She thanked me for my wish;—but for my hope
> It seemed she did not thank me.
> *The Excursion*, i, 812–3.

In the space between the lines, in that articulate silence, writing holds the memory of speech's failure. It is a deep question whether hope is the thing to offer to despair, and the dash in that sentence knows the burden of that after-thought. Such writing both requires and produces 'patience of soul, and a power increasing with the difficulties it has to master'. (Hazlitt: *Works*, xii, p. 262). The great difficulty was that Wordsworth was not one who could easily speak hope to an equivalent Margaret. And when he found that speech could not answer such a purpose, it confirmed his sense of himself as one who did not care for talk:

> Better than such discourse doth silence long,
> Long, barren silence, square with my desire;
> To sit without emotion, hope, or aim . . .
> *P.W.*, iv, p. 73.

Not to speak thus deepened his life and stored his memory for his poetry. It meant that he did not only produce a poetry whose virtue was that of being as helpless as life itself was. Through writing, rather, he could say to himself more about people like his late schoolmaster than he could quite have said to them direct. It was a loss and it was a gain. The memory of William Taylor, by the time that Wordsworth believed in writing so much as to write *The Prelude*, was redeemed as justice to the memory of how it ought to have been, as well as, equally, of how it was. The writing of such poetry is not merely a secondary activity for offering thus a second language and almost a second chance. And if it is not life's most important thing, it is very important for being a means of 'saying' what the important things are—and why they need written support and attestation. Somehow, if not directly then indirectly, if not for ever then at least as permanently as possible, what matters must be *said*. Writing is that form of saying. In the gap between what can hardly be said and what therefore must be written is life's unspoken residue. In drawing on that residue writing bears, more profoundly than does speech itself, the memory of the person who gives utterance.

2

Mnemosyne, the mother
of the muses

I introduce this second chapter on Wordsworth with these
lines from an epitaph on Bernardino Baldi of Urbino (1553–
1617), a scholar who in later life set aside his scholarship to
devote himself to the Gospels as the only source of truly
enduring knowledge. From his tomb Baldi is conceived as
speaking thus:

> Pause, courteous Spirit!—Baldi supplicates
> That Thou, with no reluctant voice, for him
> Here laid in mortal darkness, wouldst prefer
> A prayer to the Redeemer of the world.
> This to the dead by sacred right belongs;
> All else is nothing.
>
> > *P.W.*, iv, p. 253.

The author through whom Baldi supposedly speaks is
Wordsworth's admired Chiabrera, and the translation is
Wordsworth's own. '*All else* is nothing' the poem ends; but was
it a good idea that the poem did not end there but added
something else? Why did Chiabrera carry on thus in his own
voice?

> Pause, courteous Spirit!—Baldi supplicates
> That Thou, with no reluctant voice, for him
> Here laid in mortal darkness, wouldst prefer
> A prayer to the Redeemer of the world.
> This to the dead by sacred right belongs;
> All else is nothing.—Did occasion suit
> To tell his worth, the marble of this tomb
> Would ill suffice: for Plato's lore sublime,
> And all the wisdom of the Stagyrite,
> Enriched and beautified his studious mind:

Notes and Bibliography begin on page 493.

With Archimedes also he conversed
As with a chosen friend; nor did he leave
Those laureat wreaths ungathered which the Nymphs
Twine near their loved Permessus.—Finally,
Himself above each lower thought uplifting,
His ears he closed to listen to the songs
Which Sion's Kings did consecrate of old;
And his Permessus found on Lebanon.
A blessed Man! who of protracted days
Made not, as thousands do, a vulgar sleep;
But truly did *He* live his life. Urbino,
Take pride in him!—O Passenger, farewell!

(The Stagyrite is Aristotle; Permessus is a river in Boeotia that descends from Mount Helicon, home of the Muses; the songs are the Psalms.) Thus Chiabrera deliberately extended the epitaph beyond the 'sacred right' that Baldi alone invoked. In so doing, did Chiabrera contravene Baldi's will as to what was required to be said in his memory or did he give meaning to that will by disclosing the life that lay behind it?

Wordsworth's own answer to such questions is clear: he called this 'a perfect Epitaph . . . a perfect whole . . . an organized body of which the members are bound together by a common life and are justly proportioned' (*Prose Works*, ii, p. 89). The extra lines, as though spoken in Chiabrera's own voice, were found to be necessary. It is as if, for Wordsworth, the words of the first six lines, written by Chiabrera as if spoken by Baldi, would not have been quite enough; although, presumably, he could have only known this in retrospect when he saw what the later lines added to them. Yet Baldi is conceived of as stating that what he says and what he asks for are enough.

> This to the dead by sacred right belongs;
> All else is nothing.

And almost at once Chiabrera, as a survivor, picks up from the voice of the dead:

> All else is nothing.—Did occasion suit
> To tell his worth, the marble of this tomb
> Would ill suffice: for . . .

and so he opens up again both what Baldi has closed and what, Chiabrera himself says, cannot here be adequately said. It isn't a mere trick. It is, in view of what I have tried to establish in chapter 1, a tacit recognition:

All else is nothing.—Did occasion suit

a tacit recognition, at that moment of taking off again, that extra *support* has to be given from writing to speaking in order to establish more deeply the memory of the latter. Writing as if speaking in the person of Baldi, Chiabrera had then to write on as if speaking not only on Baldi's behalf but also in his memory. When Chiabrera says that Baldi set to one side all his learning for the Psalms ('His ears he closed to listen . . .'), Wordsworth notes that 'we are thrown back upon the introductory supplication and made to feel its especial propriety in this case' (ibid.): the supplication, that is, for a prayer because all else, including human knowledge, 'is nothing'. We have Baldi's opening sense of the general truth for all men, as well as, through Chiabrera, the story of Baldi's particular attainment of it, beautifully balanced.

In chapter 1 we began to ask, with Wordsworth, 'Is there not/An art . . . That shall be life, the acknowledged voice of life?'. There is; but it *is* an art and a thorough complication of natural speech. And that being so, our example from Chiabrera, which seems so naturally eloquent and even so needs artifice to make it so, may also now point us forward, if we question it a little further.—For instance, is it not odd that Wordsworth rests his case for epitaphs upon translations? This may plausibly be because Wordsworth felt that recent English poetry had betrayed its own language, deserting simplicity for artifice of an overwrought and unnatural kind that obscured and even prevented true feeling. But actually I also think it was because for Wordsworth such translations were a special metaphor for a more general belief. The belief that, whatever the words, provided they are not affected, the spirit of the meaning beneath them will come through. It was a good test, said Wordsworth, either to translate a poem of a foreign tongue or to paraphrase an English one. If there was in the original an 'under-current', 'skeleton' or 'stamina of appropriate feeling', then even in the translation could be seen 'the *heart* of the Writer' and by the comparison of original and translation a reader might see what in that heart 'had determined either the choice, the order, or the expression of ideas' in the words first chosen (*Prose Works*, ii, p. 98).

In Chiabrera's epitaph on Baldi translated by Wordsworth we recognize just such an under-current, something which would be disturbed if, for instance:

> His ears he closed to listen to the songs ·
> Which Sion's Kings did consecrate of old

had turned out metrically as '. . . His ears he closed/To listen to the songs etc.'. For it is part of the grace that Baldi closed his ears to nothing until, without ostentation, he found what was worth more than anything. This spirit or under-current makes the reason why the poem was written and the feeling with which the poem was written themselves a tacit, supportive and underlying part of the poem itself. In this case, the underlying feel of this poem—to which the words are subdued and to which the subdued words thus add—makes the language seem less a thing drawing attention to itself than something in quiet *accompaniment* to the memory of the subject-matter. Now, this chapter begins with the question whether such poetry of memory, such verse of accompaniment, is indeed the perfect model of how a writer should stand in relation to his own words; or whether Wordsworth, for example, required something more of the language of poetry. We have seen how writing attests to man's seriousness; we have begun to see how a man could run through a poem, without using exceptional language, and still surface at the end with a poem of which the whole was more than the sum of its simple parts—precisely because the parts were always mindful of the underlying memory of something or someone to which they themselves were only making a contribution. 'Did occasion suit/To tell his worth, the marble of this tomb/Would ill suffice.'—But, now, what if occasion did suit? can any form of writing or poetry do more than this? could Wordsworth not only create through subduing his words a tacit under-current to support his meaning, but actually articulate that under-current and use it to increase the power of his words? In what follows, that is to say, I shall be asking whether poetry can or need be more than a translation of memory; whether if it can be more, memory may still play an important part in it; whether there is a form of thinking, of relation to language, called poetic thinking—by which not only can things be expressed that could hardly have been articulated by speaking but also things learnt and known in the very act of writing which could have been realized by no other means.

Writing, I have said, is important, not least because thereby a man may find words to serve the deeper meanings of his inner life delivered through his memory. Wordsworth himself provides the terms of priorities here when, in an early and fragmentary 'Essay on Morals', he established his first principles in condemning the 'juggler's trick' in literature—a trick which

> lies not in fitting words to things (which would be a noble employment) but in fitting things to words.
>
> *Prose Works*, i, p. 103.

The noble employment is where words serve things and act in their memory, not vice versa.

But in this chapter I shall be looking to see whether written words may serve things and memories by not being in mere subordination to them. In chapter 1 I considered some of the problems of the relation of living to writing in terms of the more specific distinction between speaking and writing. In what follows I shall continue to try to think about the relation, in writing, of literary imagination and the creation of art to the experience of life, individual and social, which provides the anterior substance of naturalistic poetry and prose. And I shall continue to argue that the deep connection between these two realms is memory. But this time I shall put the case for memory not simply in terms of the implicit priority of a writer's life to his art; rather, I shall argue that memory also functions connectively as a discovery, *within* the inventedness of literary writing, of a truth to feeling and to personal experience.

Thinking of a work such as *The Prelude*, let me put it this way: if a man surrendered to the page before him his sense of the whole that was the subject of the poem, if he started to work himself out in verbal parts, making himself work for the language as well as letting the language carry him, and began to learn from his own words as well a sheerly direct and utter them, then would he be betrayed and lost? Would he have to keep remembering to keep the poem under control? Would he lose the support of an under-current of memory? Let us for a while entertain the idea that there may be a real thinking which, won out of the particular turns and choices of words, begins on the page and cannot rely solely on experience anterior to the act of writing. I shall argue that such an idea of writing still has a relation to tacit memory, to the anterior experience within a man's life, to beliefs that lay in him, searching for expression, before ever he picked up his pen. There is a relation between memory and revelation subtler than that of mere opposition. But the relation will be a complicated thing to describe and investigate and I shall have to look intently at Wordsworth's words, not content with that sort of moralistic paraphrase which passes all too easily for literary criticism. But to consider in detail the relation of memory to writing, of mind to language in practice, now that we have established the validity of writing at all, I must ask for both the tolerance and the collaboration of the reader. For I know Johnson's warning: 'It is very difficult to write on the minuter parts of literature without failing either to please or instruct. Too much nicety of detail disgusts the greater part of readers' (*The Rambler*, 90). Yet if these matters are left tacit, shall we really be sure of knowing and sharing what is hidden in the thinking of the poets? For my part I began serious reading in order to find in a writer's words those hidden things about reality which in reality somehow could hardly be spoken of. We shall not know that silent man, William Wordsworth, except through trying to articulate the form his thinking took in writing.

I. THE NATURAL MAN AND THE
SPIRITUAL MAN: TERMS OF REFERENCE

That a man such as Wordsworth could have learned to become an artist, Sir Joshua Reynolds would have affirmed, but William Blake, in the margins of his copy of Reynolds, denied.

Reynolds Thinks that Man Learns all that he knows. I
say on the Contrary that Man Brings All that he has or
can have Into the World with him.

Blake: Complete Writings, p. 471.

Using terms borrowed from the mystic Swedenborg, Blake
must have thought of Reynolds as the 'Natural Man' in
believing with Locke that all knowledge is acquired essentially
from sense experience: 'Thought from the Memory by the
Sight of the natural Mind'. Blake himself was to be the
'Spiritual Man', possessed not of the Thought from Memory
but of 'the Thought of Wisdom' which, *a priori*, transcends the
world of sense (ibid., pp. 89–90, 95). To Blake, Wordsworth
was a poet who was unable as it were to throw off Reynolds
and become as Blake:

> I see in Wordsworth the Natural Man rising up against
> the Spiritual Man Continually, & then he is No Poet but
> a Heathen Philosopher at Enmity against all true Poetry
> or Inspiration. . . . Imagination is the Divine Vision not of
> The World, or of Man, nor from Man as he is a Natural
> Man, but only as he is a Spiritual Man. Imagination has
> nothing to do with Memory.

Ibid., pp. 782–3.

It is these antipathetic terms of Blake's that will help us to ask
what is the thinking of the poets and what is its relation to
memory.

It is significant that, in the midst of his criticism of
Wordsworth, Blake notes in opposition to Wordsworth's belief
in the memories of childhood and the influence of natural
objects some lines from 'Michael Angelo's Sonnet'.[1] It is
significant because Blake knew what was at stake in Sir Joshua
Reynolds's preference, in his *Discourses on Art*, for Raphael over
Blake's beloved Michelangelo.

To Reynolds, Raphael embodied the purpose for which
Reynolds's own Royal Academy was formed: to study Raphael,
as Raphael had studied others, would be to learn how to paint.
For to Reynolds, art was 'imitation', in the sense of learning
how to follow on from other masters, rather than 'inspiration',
Blake's favourite, the gift arising out of nothing.[2] And to

Reynolds it was Raphael, above all, who belonged to a human tradition of art:

> it is from his having taken so many models, that he became himself a model for all succeeding painters; always imitating, and always original.
>
> Reynolds: *Discourses on Art*, p. 104 (Discourse vi).

The genius of a Raphael was the power of producing excellencies which at the time of their production could not then have been taught by known rules; but once the secret is discovered and revealed by a Raphael, it can be assimilated into rules of practice. In his thus maintaining a recognizable balance between imitation and originality, Raphael's genius was 'conformable' (p. 124). Knowing what is 'analogous to the mind' (p. 127) and to the general nature of men, Raphael could create work which had power within men's memories. Creating as he did figures not much 'disjoined from our own diminutive race of beings' (p. 83), Raphael produced art which stirred men but reminded men. Clearly, Reynolds's interpretation of Raphael's achievement—namely: 'to find something steady, substantial, and durable, on which the mind can lean as it were, and rest with safety' (ibid., p. 134, Discourse vii) emphatically belongs to the age of Samuel Johnson and his 'Preface to Shakespeare': 'the pleasures of sudden wonder are soon exhausted, and the mind can only repose on the stability of truth'.[3] To Blake, however, such accounts of wonder and originality were mediocrity's compromise.

But in Reynolds's account of the genius of Michelangelo Blake recognized not the old men but a new man. He saw himself. To Reynolds, Michelangelo's was a power 'capricious' (p. 124) and 'peculiar' (p. 83) rather than 'conformable'. It is the mechanical parts of painting which may 'expand themselves by a slow and progressive growth'–rather like the accumulated building up of eighteenth-century couplets; but of other parts Reynolds himself acknowledges: 'those which depend on a native vigour of imagination generally burst forth at once in fulness of beauty' (*Discourses on Art*, p. 272, Discourse xv). Such energy is that of a sublime mind, outraging the sensible grasp; a mind like that of Homer or Shakespeare exploring the unknown. There is, in contrast to Raphael's figures, nothing about Michelangelo's people 'that reminds us of their belonging to our own species' (p. 83). For the unteachable works of Michelangelo are not 'analogous', as of Memory, but unique, as of Imagination: in Reynolds's words they 'seem to proceed from his own mind entirely, and that mind so rich and abundant, that he never needed, or seemed to disdain, to look abroad for foreign help' (*Discourses on Art*, p. 84, Discourse v). It is as if the man were author of himself, and knew no other kin. As Blake delighted to put it 'Genius dies with its Possessor & comes not again till Another is Born with It'. (Blake: *Complete Writings*, p. 470). Reynolds virtually feared this kind of genius for being humanly unaccommodatable. But that fear was also as near as Reynolds could bring himself and his preferences to awe in the face of the sublime which contravenes measurement and judgement.[4] Reynolds thus has an almost predictive consciousness of what form of man would oppose him and his Raphael. 'Ages are all Equal,' wrote Blake, like a threat in the margins of Reynolds, 'But Genius is Always Above The Age' (ibid., p. 461).

How, then, shall we use the terms which we have established? Well, certainly, there is evidence which might support the Blakean case against Wordsworth: the case that Wordsworth was compromised between Memory and Imagination or, as it were, between the age of Reynolds and the age of Blake; between Raphael, a man speaking to men, and Michelangelo, travelling ahead of men rather than at their sides.[5] Did Wordsworth believe in Poetry or did he not? In terms of an adverse Blakean view, Wordsworth, on the failure of the French Revolution to build Liberty on firm foundations, found that he needed a base on which to support from then onwards the superstructure of his own life; he allowed his memory to be that basis and thereby he confused spiritual base with mundane and temporal origins. Nor thereby did Wordsworth even trust to himself alone: his 'originality' was not of that sheerly new which Blake proposed for himself, but was a matter of recalling the old anew 'with the freshness and clearness of an original intuition'—that is, a fresh intuition of the old original feel of things.[6]

In fact Wordsworth was not merely fudging and confusing

the issue. The more he developed as a poet, the more he was
thinking about the nature of his work: the two things went
together. He knew and troubled himself over the distinction
that John Dennis (1657–1734) had drawn between what he
called the two kinds of Poetic Passion: 'imaginative and
enthusiastic; and merely human and ordinary'.[7] As Dennis put
it:

> I call that ordinary passion, whose Cause is clearly
> comprehended by him who feels it, whether it be Admira-
> tion, Terror, or Joy; and I call the very same Passions
> Enthusiasms, when their Cause is not clearly compre-
> hended by him who feels them . . . the Reason why we
> know not the Causes of Enthusiastick, as well as of
> ordinary Passions, is, because we are not so us'd to them,
> and because they proceed from Thoughts, that latently,
> and unobserv'd by us, carry Passion along with them.[8]

The distinction is one between Vulgar Poetry, often preferable
'because all Men are capable of being moved by the Vulgar,
and a Poet writes to all', and Enthusiastick Poetry which is
'more subtle'.[9] In his 'Essay, Supplementary to the Preface',
Wordsworth took up this distinction between the familiar and
the strange forms of passion:

> There is also a meditative, as well as human, pathos; an
> enthusiastic, as well as ordinary, sorrow; a sadness that
> has its seat in the depths of reason, to which the mind
> cannot sink gently of itself—but to which it must descend
> by treading the steps of thought.

Prose Works, iii, pp. 82–3.

The issue revolves around that word 'gently'. There is a
Wordsworthian verse which appears to be no more than
gently accompanying a sense of its own subject-matter; but
there is also a verse that has to fight verbally for its subject and
its sense of it.

The verse of gentle accompaniment is that which is celebrated in the 'Essays upon Epitaphs'. At the very end of the
'Essays' Wordsworth quotes his own account from book seven
of *The Excursion* of the life and death of a Dalesman whose quiet
life and loneliness of soul derived from his life-long deafness.
To quote from his own poetry in his own criticism seems here

less an act of egotism than a demonstration in both verse and prose that one who has written a powerful poem learns a lot more about it than he has put explicitly into the lines. In the thinking of the poets Wordsworth concluded thus at the grave:

> And yon tall Pine-tree, whose composing sound
> Was wasted on the good Man's living ear,
> Hath now its own peculiar sanctity;
> And at the touch of every wandering breeze
> Murmurs not idly o'er his peaceful grave.
>
> *Prose Works*, ii, p. 96.

He took the circumstances from reading the following epitaph in Mardale churchyard: HERE LIETH THE BODY/OF THOMAS HOLME SON OF THE LATE HENRY/AND JANE HOLME OF CHAPEL HILL/HE WAS DEPRIVED OF THE SENSE OF HEARING/IN HIS YOUTH AND LIVED ABOUT 50 YEARS/WITHOUT THE COMFORT OF HEARING ONE WORD/HE RECONCILED HIMSELF TO HIS MISFORTUNE BY/ READING AND USEFUL EMPLOYMENT/WAS VERY TEMPERATE HONEST AND PEACEABLE/HE WAS WELL RESPECTED BY HIS NEIGHBOURS AND/RELATIONS AND DEPARTED THIS LIFE AFTER A SHORT/SICKNESS ON THE 22D OF MARCH 1773 AGED 67 YEARS.

Looking at the poetry and its origin together, one reflects that Wordsworth could not have missed the sense of the deep respect for culture held by the words of the epitaph ('reading and useful employment' going together; 'the comfort of hearing *one word*' making the luck of the not-disabled no longer a commonplace to be taken for granted but an original intuition; the sense of reading and writing as the silent, deep and inner communication when speaking and hearing fail). Part of his poetic passion comes from ordinary things like a refusal to scorn the simple mathematics of the story (died aged 67, deaf for about 50 years, deafened in youth, when only about 17: all this within the facts of an epitaph incites imagination of what 50 years involved in such a life might mean 'without the comfort of hearing'). So that when we turn to the poetry the silent thought with which, we infer, Wordsworth attended the spectacle of the epitaph is not left idle. On the contrary, the presiding Pine-tree

> . . . at the touch of every wandering breeze
> Murmurs not idly o'er his peaceful grave.

Not idly, as if we who are not deaf are now particularly mindful
in hearing it; as if there is the dead man's memory to hear it
now, even when, to match the grave, the sound has died down
to the Wordsworthian 'murmur' of a tribute of silent, poetic
thought. The cause of such thought, in Dennis's formulation,
is clearly comprehended by him who feels it. For in this human
poetry, the poetry of a man speaking to men, the emotion
which is of the familiar sort naturally finds its home, as well as
its source, in the memory. It can be stirred as by a wandering
breeze, a brush with words; there is no necessity noisily to fight
for its recall. This is the poetry of the Natural Man; with the
deaf Dalesman, as with Torquato Tasso, it easily bespeaks
'what this Man was'.

But there are also thoughts that lie too deep for tears and
stranger emotions which come from more difficult considerations. We have already seen the wiser mind of Matthew,
mourning 'less for what age takes away/Than what it leaves
behind'; there is also:

> To be a Prodigal's Favourite—then, worse truth,
> A miser's Pensioner—behold our lot!
> O Man, that from thy fair and shining youth
> Age might but take the things Youth needed not!
> 'The Small Celandine', *P.W.*, iv, p. 245.

> —I've heard of hearts unkind, kind deeds
> With coldness still returning;
> Alas! the gratitude of men
> Hath oftener left me mourning.
> 'Simon Lee', *P.W.*, iv, p. 64.

In this syntax of reappraisal, the more ordinary emotions of
regret sacrifice themselves to a thought which takes its stand
outside, as that subtler regret for the very necessity of the
implicated existence of such emotions. This passion of thought
is a different thing from ordinary emotion: it has used the
latter to raise itself up to think of it. These lyrics, whose wiser
thought thus goes against the gentler grain, unravel their own
sadness in their sentences only to find the cause of that sadness
too deep for anything but a matter for ending on. At the close
of such lyrics we feel:

'Tis done; and in the after-vacancy
We wonder at ourselves like men betrayed
P.W., iii, p. 283.

Lyric action is transitory, 'a step, a blow'. To work up from the memory, by further written thought, that wisdom which is enclosed in the lyrics' thoughtful pain would require from Wordsworth something more sustained and less gentle. It required a long poem of suffering to replace the action of the short lyric blows—'Action is transitory':

Suffering is permanent, obscure and dark,
And has the nature of infinity.
Yet through that darkness (infinite though it seem
And irremoveable) gracious openings lie,
By which the soul—with patient steps of thought
Now toiling, wafted now on wings of prayer—
May pass in hope, and, though from mortal bonds
Yet undelivered, rise with sure ascent
Even to the fountain-head of peace divine.
P.W., iii, p. 283.

Wordsworth, I think, came to prize his lyric poetry less as poems than the things worth writing poems for. The Wordsworth who came to write *The Prelude* had become a man who did not merely want to arrive at certain thoughts by the act of writing. He wanted to go on, rather than break off; he wanted to be able to continue to inhabit the form of thinking that had given rise to the particular thought-content. He wanted to know what was the thinking of the poets and to possess it not merely by the end of a poem, when the cause of a poem is given articulate punch only as a line or two concluding it; but to possess it in such a way as to think like that without a prompting lyric occasion, in a long poem whose form of continuous poetic thinking was also the feel of the rhythm of his own life. If, as I have tried to say in chapter 1, he turned to poetry in order to do what he could not do by other means, later he looked to poetry not just for relief of a prior reality but for the constitution of an abiding and future one.

The Prelude, 'treading the steps of thought', 'with patient steps of thought/Now toiling, wafted now', thus goes beyond a poetry satisfied to leave tacitly resonant 'what this Man was':

> . . . 'twas my chance
> Abruptly to be smitten with the view
> Of a blind Beggar, who, with upright face,
> Stood propp'd against a Wall, upon his Chest
> Wearing a written paper, to explain
> The story of the Man, and who he was.
> My mind did at this spectacle turn round
> As with the might of waters, and it seem'd
> To me that in this Label was a type,
> Or emblem, of the utmost that we know,
> Both of ourselves and of the universe;
> And, on the shape of the unmoving man,
> His fixèd face and sightless eyes, I look'd
> As if admonish'd from another world.
>
> *The Prelude*, 1805–6, vii, 609–22.

Such a thought, in Dennis's phrase, latently carries passion
with it. Seeing those sightless eyes, Wordsworth felt his mind,
likewise, turn round upon itself, as if the natural man were
admonished by the invisible world of a Blake. It turns round
almost as if to say, ungently but sublimely, that all the poetry
'on written paper, to explain/The story of the Man' is no more
than this really; the utmost that we know, equivalent blind
beggars.

There is indeed some growth in Wordsworth, not strictly
datable but connected with his writing of *The Prelude*. It is a
growth involving a developing belief that writing finds its
reality not simply by turning back to the past for its subject-
matter—(be the past that of its author or that of a tradition)—
but by the thinking done within it in its present. But this is not
to suggest that the spiritual man merely came to supersede the
natural man. Nor is it merely to suggest, as a Blakean might
from the example above, that the spiritual man came to feel
guilty that he was so early compromised within the natural
man as never to be able to grow imaginatively independent of
him. If the difference I perceive is not development in a crude
sense, I do not mean that Wordsworth simply remained
divided in his own mind.[10] If the spiritual and the natural
would not let go of each other in Wordsworth, it was not
division or regression so much as a refusal to ease his situation

by resorting once and for all to *either* Reynolds's Raphael *or* Blake's Michelangelo. The sort of growth of which I am thinking meant a capacity for both kinds of poetic passion and an increase in that difficult judgement as to their relative appropriateness in the course of time and even in the midst of poems. This was not an easy matter of compromise or the best of both worlds. Rather the difficulty lay in the fact that the natural man and the spiritual man, like Kant's phenomenon and noumenon, were neither entirely compatible nor completely disconnected; to state the paradox, they were reciprocally independent. What is humanly at stake in saying this may be shown, but not by Wordsworth's relationship to Blake so much as by his relationship to Robert Burns.

*   *   *   *   *

In 1815 Dr James Currie published a biography of Burns, containing disclosures of the poet's drunken ruin. In 1802 Wordsworth had written, with Burns as one whom he had in mind:

> We Poets in our youth begin in gladness
> But thereof in the end comes despondency and madness.
> *P.W.*, ii, p. 236.

So there was nothing essentially in Currie's account that Wordsworth could not already have imagined, if not wholly known. Yet in 1816, on hearing of a proposal to republish Currie's account, Wordsworth wrote a public letter regretting the work. Why was he so upset? Here he was deploring a book which did yield a more explicit sense of 'what this Man was' and, although not a very good book, did give some account of the personal trouble out of which, as well as besides which, the man wrote his poetry. It will not do to attribute this merely to conventions of social propriety that Wordsworth learnt to share. For Wordsworth valued Burns's poetry not despite the man whom he knew Burns to be but actually in memory of him.

It is significant that Wordsworth therefore did not condemn Currie in the terms that a Blake might have employed. Blake could have disposed of the biographer without difficulty. He

would have said that the biographer merely dealt in the natural
man. Blake was aware of the contrary view; he had read
Lavater's argument that the weaknesses of great men were
inseparable from their strengths: that to deduct, for instance,
the roughness of a Luther from the fiery courage of which his
roughness was the exuberance or excess would be like trying to
deduct the redness from a rose. But Blake denied this: 'if
Raphael,'—to take another example—'is hard & dry, it is not
his genius but an accident acquired, for how can Substance
and Accident be predicated of the same Essence?' (Blake:
Complete Writings, p. 81). Blake said to Genius, be what you
are: but what is not of the essence of genius in you is you no
more than accidentally. Biographers of poets deal merely with
such accidents of luck, guilt and personality. As another poet,
Keats testified, 'Shakspeare led a life of Allegory; his works are
the comments on it' (*Letters,* ii, p. 67). The real life is hidden in
the spiritual man who is the poet; it is only manifest in the
poems.

But Wordsworth did not choose this argument which seems
nowadays almost the norm. Wordsworth could find no simple
refuge from Currie's version of the natural man by embracing
Blake's spiritual one. This was because—a Blake might retort—
Wordsworth had too basically committed himself to his initial
error of confusing the natural with the spiritual, memory with
imagination. Yet now he was also committed to deplore the
fact that Currie was more interested in the man because he
had been a poet than in the poet because he had been a man.

There is evidence that Wordsworth was himself aware of the
sort of criticism that declared him to be, as it were, too natural.
At the close of *Home at Grasmere* he writes:

> . . . And if with this
> I mix more lowly matter—with the thing
> Contemplated describe the Mind and Man
> Contemplating, and who and what he was,
> The transitory Being that beheld
> This Vision, when and where and how he lived—
> Be not this labour useless.
>
> *Home at Grasmere,* p.107 (MS.D, 846–52).

Conversely, William Hazlitt, on reading Wordsworth's public

letter of protest, complained that Wordsworth had not sufficiently defended Burns. There was, he thought, too much of the spiritual man in Wordsworth for him to make out the relation between Burns's vices, as a moralist would call them, and the economic conditions that were the explanation of them.[11] Wordsworth seems to be in the situation of the classic fudger of issues, attacked from both sides.

But in positioning himself thus in between extremes Wordsworth was following the only form of thinking he could trust here—the thinking of the poet, of Burns himself. In his 'Letter to a Friend of Robert Burns' he quotes Burns himself on those who fall into sin:

> One point must still be greatly dark,
> The moving *why* they do it,
> And just as lamely can ye mark
> How far, perhaps, they rue it.

> Who made the heart, 'tis *he* alone
> Decidedly can try us;
> He knows each chord—its various tone,
> Each spring, its various bias.

> Then at the balance let's be mute,
> We never can adjust it;
> What's done we partly may compute,
> But know not what's *resisted*.

Beneath this Wordsworth wrote:

> How happened it that the recollection of this affecting passage did not check so amiable a man as Dr. Currie, while he was revealing to the world the infirmities of its author?
>
> *Prose Works,* iii, p. 119.

It happened because to Currie this was just a piece of poetry written by a man during, say, a day in his life. It was, if anything, supporting-evidence for the biography of ruin. And for Currie, if he even remembered the words, these lines spoke more of Burns than to him. What Wordsworth was pointing to was the fact that the biographer did not use either his memory or Burns's in a real way, in the way that, Wordsworth knew,

Burns had used his own. As to the real use of memory,
Wordsworth asks of the following lines from Burns's 'A Bard's
Epitaph'

> —Thoughtless follies laid him low,
> And stained his name.

'Whom did the poet intend should be thought of?' Wordsworth
answers his own question, 'Who but himself,—himself anticipating the too probable termination of his own course? . . . a
history in the shape of a prophecy!' (*Prose Works*, iii, p. 126).
This was really spoken by the man, the memory spoken
through the writing.

What did Currie think that poetry was, a few words to paper
over the deeper reality of biography? When Wordsworth asked
why the recollection of Burns's own words did not check Currie,
he must have been remembering how, for instance, on 18
August 1803 his sister and he had stood at the grave of Burns,
heeding, as Currie had not, the plea to be at the balance mute,
and breaking silence only to repeat to each other Burns's own
words in epitaph:

> Is there a man, whose judgment clear
> Can others teach the course to steer,
> Yet runs, himself, life's mad career
>   Wild as a wave?—
> Here pause—and, thro' the starting tear,
>   Survey this grave.

Such words were not merely the product of one moment among
many others in that life; they were, with pain, a lasting sum
and judgment of that life taken even from within it. Yet their
power also lay in the contrary recognition of the weakness as
well as the strength in them: although, by writing, the words
presided over the life in which also they were rooted, still part
of their power lay in the very acknowledgement of their helplessness to save the life to which they owed expression.

'Here pause,' wrote Burns of his own gravestone. And at
that moment 'here', quite simply, means both here in this
Scottish churchyard and, inevitably, here at this word, on this
page. It is a simple paradigm of literature's achievement: to set
out to cover by imagination the distance between the page and

the external world to which it refers, so that a reader may feel
the one to be in imaginative memory of the other. It is a bonus
that 'here' in writing was the only means by which Burns in
his 'mad career' could pause, through imagination. In 1803 at
that spot, in that pause they made, it must have seemed to the
Wordsworths that *history* in their memory of Burns's self-
prophecy and *prophecy* in his anticipation of what to them was
now history here met at that grave. 'My mind did at this
spectacle turn round': as if Burns's imagination had called to
the future and been answered by Wordsworth's memory as a
necessary counterpart. On that day and the day following
Wordsworth, a man with respect for guilt as well as sorrow,
wrote two poems to Burns, as if they were due, and as if to
affirm:

> Deep in the general heart of man
> His power survives.
>   *P.W.*, iii, p. 68.[12]

Both through his own imaginative treatment and through
Wordsworth's, Burns's memory of himself rises as the nearest
point, from below, to that from which a God above might
judge him. 'Who made the heart, 'tis he *alone*/Decidedly can
try us'. It is memory that is the god within the man:

> the momentous truth of the passage already quoted, 'One
> point must still be greatly dark,' &c. could not possibly
> have been conveyed with such pathetic force by any poet
> that ever lived, speaking in his own voice; unless it were
> felt that, like Burns, he was a man who preached from the
> text of his own errors; and whose wisdom, beautiful as a
> flower that might have risen from seed sown from above,
> was in fact a scion from the root of personal suffering.
>   *Prose Works*, iii, pp. 125–6.

That poetry's flower from above in fact grows from below was
for Wordsworth not something that lowered the status of poetry
but, on second thought, a memory that raised it.

What fascinated Wordsworth was not the dialectical
extremes of a Blake but the idea of that infinitely small gap
between the flower that grows as if from seed divinely sown
from above and the flower which rises from the root of personal

suffering here below. *There* was a poetry which occupied the
space which is the echo of both above and below, between
prayer and memory. It was a poetry of that spirit in which
Wordsworth would have the dead like Burns himself
remembered: 'something midway between what he was on
earth walking about with his living frailties, and what he may
be presumed to be as a Spirit in heaven' (*Prose Works*, ii, p. 58).
What to a Blake would have seemed mere compromise and
confusion was, in Wordsworth's eyes, Burns's memory raising
itself above itself and reaching, as the spiritual hope implicit in
memory, just beneath the level of prayer, as just above the
level of despair. That is the force of Wordsworth's position
'midway' between Blake's and Currie's.

The story of Wordsworth's relation to Burns is not merely
extra-literary information, irrelevant to art itself. For
Wordsworth's midway position on Burns was no simply
notional belief but the shape his thinking took in his own verse.
It was the very world in which he walked about thinking, with
his own living frailties. Above him, for example, was there not:

> . . . the voice
> Of lordly birds—an unexpected sound
> Heard now and then from morn to latest eve
> Admonishing the man who walks below
> Of solitude and silence in the sky?
> *Home at Grasmere*, pp. 46–7 (MS.B, 148–52; MS.D, 129–33).

Even as Wordsworth walked along the ground as if it were his
steadying base, his measure of serial time, his line of verse
composed while walking, the man

> . . . below

would be thinking

> Of solitude and silence in the sky

above; holding in mind the space between the two wherein
they were both two and one. There hearing is also a sublime
imagination of seeing as from above, thus admonishing the
man that the higher 'solitude' up there is something more than
the feeling of his loneliness beneath it. It is a perfect image of,
in all senses, Wordsworth's situation. What is more, in its

relation to the sky and in its finding from the check upon sense the sublime thought of what is above sense, the thought is a Kantian one:

> That he must represent and conceive himself in this double way rests, as regards the first side, on consciousness of himself as an object affected through the senses; as concerns the second side, on consciousness of himself as intelligence—that is, as independent of sensuous impression in his use of reason.[13]

What I called before the reciprocal independence of the natural man and the spiritual man is that which at once holds the two together in one man and, within his mind, also keeps the two apart.

> Why do they teach me, whom I thus revere?
> Strange question, yet it answers not itself.
> *Home at Grasmere*, pp. 94–5 (MS.B, 891–2; MS.D, 680–1)

They teach me not just because I revere them; I revere them not just by reason of what they teach me. Yet something both makes and forbids the direct connection between learning and reverence, and it is to that something that Wordsworth puts his questions. In the same way, Wordsworth cherished both the distinctions between writing and living *and* the memory which supported their relation through and beneath those distinctions. The poet Burns, we may conclude, was one of those who 'teach me, whom I thus revere', even though the relation between his life and his writing was a lesson taught from 'the text of his own errors'. Despite Blake, Wordsworth found in Burns that imagination did have to do with memory. And even though the spiritual man did not always exist in gentle or easy relation with the natural man, they simply did not exist apart from each other. It is their relation actually within the poet's language that I shall next consider. We must look for the big ideas within the small inner movements of the verse.

II. MEMORY: AN INTIMATION
OF IMMORTALITY

'With the Poems of Burns I became acquainted almost immediately upon their first appearance in the volume printed at Kilmarnock in 1786' (*P.W.,* iii, p. 441). In this part of the chapter we shall turn from the poets as men to the dependence, within the poetry, of their humanity upon their technique. The qualities which the poems of Burns impressed upon the young Wordsworth were those of simplicity, truth and vigour (*P.W.,* iii, p. 442): on these foundations verse, such as 'O my Luve's like a red, red rose', 'may build', thought Wordsworth, 'a princely throne' (*P.W.,* iii, p. 66).

> As fair as thou, my bonie lass
> So deep in luve am I
> And I will love thee still, my Dear,
> Till a' the seas gang dry.—
>
> Till a' the seas gang dry, my Dear,
> And the rocks melt wi' the sun:
> I will love thee still, my Dear,
> While the sands o' life shall run.—

If the throne of verse is raised like this on the basis of native simplicity, truth and vigour, it is, the verse suggests, because these qualities rest upon nothing but themselves. The repetitions admit this and are strengthened rather than weakened by the admission. For it is no accident that when the lyric is put to music, the repetition, between the end of the one stanza and the beginning of the next, causes the music to lift itself notes higher, as if the feeling of love now rejoices in itself and its confirmation, raised on nothing but its own support.

> Till a' the seas gang dry.—
> Till a' the seas gang dry, my Dear,

It is like love that there is nothing but its repetition of itself to guarantee its constancy. Men, in both life and verse, create that on which they depend.

The poetic ancestry from Burns to Wordsworth was, Wordsworth recognized, an ancestry that went further and deeper than that, into the secrets of the thinking of the poets.

When Wordsworth wrote on repetition as a clue to that form of thinking, he could almost have been writing about Burns's lyric rather than his own poem 'The Thorn':

> There is a numerous class of readers who imagine that the same words cannot be repeated without tautology: this is a great error: virtual tautology is much oftener produced by using different words when the meaning is exactly the same. Words, a Poet's words more particularly, ought to be weighed in the balance of feeling, and not measured by the space which they occupy upon paper. For the Reader cannot be too often reminded that Poetry is passion: it is the history or science of feelings; now every man must know that an attempt is rarely made to communicate impassioned feelings without something of an accompanying consciousness of the inadequateness of our own powers, or the deficiencies of language. During such efforts there will be a craving in the mind, and as long as it is unsatisfied the speaker will cling to the same words, or words of the same character. There are also various other reasons why repetition and apparent tautology are frequently beauties of the highest kind. Among the chief of these reasons is the interest which the mind attaches to words, not only as symbols of the passion, but as *things*, active and efficient, which are of themselves part of the passion. And further, from a spirit of fondness, exultation and gratitude, the mind luxuriates in the repetition of words which appear successfully to communicate its feelings. The truth of these remarks might be shown by innumerable passages from the Bible, and from the impassioned poetry of every nation.
>
> *P.W.*, ii, p. 513.

Repetition constitutes a challenge to the reader to infer what extra-verbal, human reality is hidden in its poetic thought. Repetition is a notation additional to language's sense, such that a reader asks of this aspect of poetry's second language, 'in saying no more than what he said before, what is it *thereby* that he is saying?' It is not that Burns, for example, is unable to think of any other words: 'I will love thee still, my Dear,'— but that there is 'no cause, no cause' to do so. The authority of such repetition is its faithful refusal to use verbal power in any way other than in its remaining true to itself in keeping its word—as Charity, in the Bible, 'Beareth all things, believeth all things, hopeth all things, endureth all things' (1 Corinthians 13.7). Burns's voice rises in the 'spirit of fondness, exultation, and gratitude'; the lover, finding a home in language for his feeling, can feel it again through the words repeatedly and rewardingly coming back to him only for him again to give them to her. It is what Keats, so often following on after Wordsworth, was to call 'happiness on Earth repeated in a finer tone' (*Letters*, i, p. 185).

In the finer tone, the words become reclaimed less as words than as '*things*, active and efficient' by which feeling thus takes heart from itself:

> Till a' the seas gang dry, my Dear,
>   And the rocks melt wi' the sun:
> I will love thee still, my Dear,

The techniques of poetry can become, through practice, so known to the mind that the mind can begin to know and distinguish itself within its use of them. The philosopher Hartley drew attention to the phenomenon of 'double trans-mutation', by which at various levels of a situation the voluntary may lapse back into the automatic or the automatic become again an act of fresh will.[14] In the same way techniques like repetition become a second language bespeaking what is involved either in re-affirming or in modifying the originating words. The poet's thinking thus goes on tacitly within the act of repetition, for 'The Poet thinks and feels in the spirit of human passions' (*Prose Works*, i, p. 142). By interchange between the sense of the words and the meaning of their repetition, the feeling 'I will love thee still, my Dear,' is more quietly assured for also being thought. It is emotion being thought.

This power of repetition was something Wordsworth knew and practised in poems as early as 'The Idiot Boy' and 'We are Seven'. But what he also used as a form of poetic thinking was modified repetition:

> So to her feet the Creature came,
>   And laid its head upon her knee,

And looked into the Lady's face,
A look of pure benignity,
And fond unclouded memory.
                              'The White Doe of Rylstone' *P.W.*, iii, pp. 333–4.

Those fields, those hills—what could they less? had laid
Strong hold on his affections, were to him
A pleasurable feeling of blind love,
The pleasure which there is in life itself.
                              'Michael', *P.W.*, ii, p. 83.

The way that the lines fall out, from 'looked' to 'a look', from 'pleasurable' into 'The pleasure', is like a release from within the language itself of the essential memory implicit in the passages. As we go down the lines, we seem to reach in lines like 'The pleasure which there is in life itself' a base to which we are pulled by 'our life's mysterious weight' (*The Prelude*, 1805–6, v, 442); a base as of memory gently submerged beneath time, now gently raised by language's spell. Repetition was a matter of depth to Wordsworth.

For Wordsworth had greater ambitions for thought than did Burns and, with them, faced greater complications of the relation of thinking to feeling. The matter of repetition widened, through the use of modified repetition binding a poem together, into the question of what use the poet, looking down as it were at what he had just written, could make of his own words, to bring him new thought, or uncover deeper memory, sustaining the verbal journey. If Burns was one of the first examples to help Wordsworth answer 'what is a Poet?', it was Coleridge who made Wordsworth think again, harder, as a Poet, actually within the processes of his own poetry:

What is poetry? is so nearly the same question with, what is a poet? that the answer to the one is involved in the solution of the other.
                              Coleridge: *Biographia Literaria*, ii, p. 12.

Likewise, what is a poet? could really be answered only within the poet's act of writing, finding out, as he wrote, what is poetry. This is a crucial point for us, who are seeking some account of the relation between a man's attitudes and feelings outside his writing and what he does inside it. Is there not some relation? is it no more than that of translation? need it only be a one-way, life-to-art movement? Questions like this are what we ask of poetic thinking.

So let us begin simply. As his own prose shows, Wordsworth eventually did have retrospective knowledge of how he had learnt to become a poet. For example, in his 'Preface to the Edition of 1815' he asked the question, what, without the accompaniment of a musical instrument, constituted the music of a poem? The answer provides a small but interesting illustration of Wordsworth's development of repetition and modified repetition. For the answer he at once gave was to quote from his own 'A Poet's Epitaph' written back in 1798 or 1799:

> 'He murmurs near the running brooks
> A music sweeter than their own.'
>
> *Prose Works,* iii, p. 30.

There is no explicit repetition here, but something implicit has gone on in the mind of the poet in order to omit it. A real poem, said Wordsworth, has an 'under current' (ibid., ii, p. 75), and the tacit under-current here is that by which 'murmurs' takes the first line through the 'running brooks', even as 'own' returns the second line back to the memory of the first. For the 'sweeter' music is not simply his own as opposed to that of the brook; it is the action and re-action between the poet's music and the water's that brings the water's music into the very channel of his own.

> These processes of imagination are carried on either by conferring additional properties upon an object, or abstracting from it some of those which it actually possesses, and thus enabling it to re-act upon the mind which hath performed the process like a new existence.
>
> *Prose Works,* iii, p. 32.

Through interchange, in this small but telling example from 'A Poet's Epitaph', nature is returned to her 'own' but returned as from a level of consciousness itself raised by the thinking of her. 'What then does the Poet?' asked Wordsworth: 'He considers man and the objects that surround him as acting and re-acting upon each other, so as to produce an infinite complexity of pain and pleasure (ibid., i, p. 140). By the action and re-action, in the poetry, of the man and the water upon each other, the man, in making poetry, learns how to make himself a poet.

The idea of 're-action' is not a simple one and is something that Wordsworth added to his ideas on repetition to make a form of poetic thinking. It seems likely that Wordsworth first got some idea of 're-action' from Coleridge. For at the age of twenty-three, Coleridge was an enthusiast for a book by Andrew Baxter published in 1733 under the title, *An Enquiry into the Nature of the Human Soul Wherein the Immateriality of the Soul is evinced from the Principles of Reason and Philosophy*.[15] The very opening of the book is concerned to show how matter might be said to act through inactivity, the action therein being that of resistance:

> And first, though this resistance in matter is real resistance, or certain and real force exerted, yet it is *no action* in matter, nor is matter active in exerting it: it is rather only *re action*, resistance in the properest sense; for it is never exerted till matter is first acted upon.
>
> Section i, ix.

It is matter's negative resistance to enforced change that effects positive movement outside it, the power being passed on as the easiest way out of change. To what must have been Coleridge's theological delight, Baxter concludes that it is only some immaterial Being that can initiate action.

How conscious Wordsworth was of his own process of receiving power from the resistances that confronted him both in nature and in language is clear from a letter written in reply to Sir George Beaumont in February 1808. A friend of Lady Beaumont had complained about a poem 'on Daffodils *reflected in the Water*'; pointing to the precision of his language, Wordsworth responded:

> —Beneath the trees,
> Ten thousand dancing in the *breeze*.
> The *waves beside* them danced, but they
> Outdid the *sparkling waves* in glee.

Can expression be more distinct? And let me ask your
Friend how it is possible for flowers to be *reflected* in water
where there are *waves*? They may indeed in still water—
but the very object of my poem is the trouble or agitation
both of the flowers and the Water.[16]

The mind finds that the waves are for the daffodils 'something
to be counteracted, and which, by its re-action, may aid the
force that is exerted to resist it' (*Biographia Literaria*, i, p. 85).
Thus, 'beside *them*' becomes 'but *they*', as the daffodils to
Wordsworth's mind outdo what the waves did. 'The waves
beside' is like 'He murmurs near' in 'A Poet's Epitaph'; but
'Outdid' is like 'A music sweeter', absorbing mere spatial
proximity into a qualitative mental distinction made on the
basis not of physical but of spiritual 'reflection'. Nor is this,
therefore, merely a matter of pushpin or of the sheer
exploitation of pressures. For, as it was in 'A Poet's Epitaph'
with its give-and-take, so here Wordsworth cannot help being
re-acted upon by the waves, which he is using, to add to them
what is gently re-admitted to be their *own* 'sparkling' even as
he goes on past them: 'Outdid the sparkling waves in glee'.
Part of the glee in that 'new existence' still comes from re-
finding that sparkling even in outdoing it. There is here a
knowledge 'in what manner language and the human mind act
and react on each other' (*Prose Works*, i, p. 120).

I know that these are small examples. But just such
processes, from the act of repeating to the mental re-action to
it, helped to constitute for Wordsworth the music of a poem.
They were the tools of his trade. And it is a moving thought
that the poem's continuum is maintained by this internal
reminiscence, this pick-up and retrieval of its own words,
because it is as if the mind of the poet thereby rescues the
meaning of the words of his poetry from neglect; and because
he does seem in that to be learning from the language and
from himself. In such ways, memory, triggered within the
words, becomes a form of discovery of truth to feeling. It may
appear to make sense to speak of the man outside his work and
the poet within it; but that formulation, while it contains an
idea that I do not want wholly to withdraw, creates mutually
weakening alternatives when expressed too crudely: man-
without-poet, poet-without-man. The model which we are at

present considering at a simple level—that of the action and reaction of the mind and language—has the distinct advantage of constituting an area within which the relation of man and poet is felt, known and tested by a man in his verbal efforts to be a poet.

In this effort Wordsworth picked up his own words, raising his thoughts by means of the thought contained within the language, lifting his language through the work of his thought in response to it. He worked not only through repetition and modification but also by means of recursion, as when a sentence turns back on the way it is going in order to pull more of its own meaning with it through to its destination: for example, 'with heart as calm as'

> . . . mountain rivers, where they creep
> Along a channel smooth and deep,
> To their own far-off murmurs listening.
> 'Memory', *P.W.*, iv, p. 102.

—or again in a line from his own 'Resolution and Independence' which he quotes in his 'Preface to the Edition of 1815': 'Over his own sweet voice the Stock-dove broods'. Wordsworth underlined the word 'broods': 'as if herself delighting to listen to [her own soft note], and participating of a still and quiet satisfaction, like that which may be supposed inseparable from the continuous process of incubation' (*Prose Works*, iii, p. 32). Like the bird and the river, Wordsworth wanted to hear from within himself. He wanted a syntax turning back to discover more from within itself, as if it were a linguistic analogue to memory itself.

Over his own sweet voice our poet broods. In no poet more than in Wordsworth does the formative mind seem, in the act of writing, so self-conscious of its own hidden powers of formation.[17] For instance, of the sun he writes:

> . . . I had seen him lay
> His beauty on the morning hills, had seen
> The western mountain touch his setting orb
> In many a thoughtless hour.
> *The Prelude*, 1805–6, ii, 188–91.

At the end of each line there is a pause as of something trying to make sense of things before they close up to make sense of themselves. 'The hiding places of my power/Seem open; I approach, and then they close' (*The Prelude*, 1805–6, xi, 336–7). There is a silent strangeness hidden in the interstices of the familiar: 'had seen him lay/His beauty'; a hestiating conscious-ness as of the form about to meet its content, the two only visible in the actual incarnation of thought:

> had seen him   had seen him lay/His beauty
> had seen/The western mountain touch

One feels beneath the repetitions and the parts an under-current or under-sense of what binds them together. The parts of nature come to make sense together, in harmony with an under-sense as of something spiritual in the poet by this means also composing itself. In Keats's words, 'The rise, the progress, the setting of imagery should, like the sun, come natural to him—shine over him' (*Letters*, i, p. 238). So here, with a consonance that is Wordsworth's final retort to Blake, Wordsworth's thoughts rose, in the act of writing, with the sun they thought of. At such moments, by action and reaction between the mind of the poet and the thought of objects like sun, water, waves or daffodils, we in Coleridge's words—

> find poetry, as it were substantiated and realized in nature: yea, nature itself disclosed to us . . . as at once the poet and the poem!
>
> *The Friend*, i, p. 471.

Nature's connection with the poet may be provided by the terms of his own mind, but the provision itself felt to Wordsworth as if it were sanctioned by nature. 'A balance, an ennobling interchange/Of action from within and from without' (*The Prelude*, 1805–6, xii, 376–7).

But that sense of interchange, be it between the human spirit and nature or between mind and language, was not something that Wordsworth found merely conveniently easy to achieve in his writing. If it had been that, Wordsworth could not have believed in what he had written. For when in writing he tried to think through his relation to nature or the past, it was very important to him that his problems were not merely solved there by some juggler's trickery in the mechanics of language. What he did admire, however, was the man who did not merely rest with an intuition of the meaning of his life but took that meaning into the resistances and influences of words, saying of that life:

> —till we have learned
> To prize it less, we ne'er shall learn to prize
> The things worth living for.—
> 'Argument for Suicide', *P.W.*, i, p. 316.

For the man who thus goes into the system of language works to find, by a species of re-action, the memory of his spiritual life come back upon him. By poetry he might restore from his own words the meaning of 'The things worth living for', working the thought of those things through and out of his language, as if they had always been there behind him, waiting to be won again consciously at this level. It is not easy: that of which a man has a memory outside his work, within it he must regain through both language and re-imagination, on a new but related level.

For confirmation of this sense of Wordsworth's honest struggle, let us take an important example. Compare with Burns's lyric, with its beautiful 'I will love thee still, my Dear', Wordsworth's justly famous sonnet, 'Surprised by joy'. The poet, for a minute forgetful of the death of his daughter Catherine (who died in June 1812 aged three years and nine months), finds himself turning to share a sudden joy with her. Being Wordsworth, he does not rest in the comfort of supposing that this instinctive memory of her is proof both that his care remains deep within him and that her loss, equally, remains unjust and unthinkable; on the contrary, going against that gentler grain, he is shamed as well as hurt by his own momentary forgetfulness:

> Surprised by joy—impatient as the wind—
> I turn'd to share the transport—O with whom
> But Thee—deep buried in the silent tomb,
> That spot which no vicissitude can find?
> Love, faithful love, recalled thee to my mind—
> But how could I forget thee? Through what power
> Even for the least division of an hour,

Have I been so beguiled as to be blind
To my most grievous loss!—That thought's return
Was the worst pang that ever sorrow bore,
Save one, one only, when I stood forlorn,
Knowing my heart's best treasure was no more;
That neither present time nor years unborn
Could to my sight that heavenly face restore.

P.W., iii, p. 16.

'Save one, one only' is at the heart of Wordsworth's note on 'The Thorn'; it is the passionate voice of memory, able to re-call but unable to 'restore'. The repetition, however, does make the writing ('one') passionate enough to *speak* itself back over ('one only'). Similarly, 'Love, faithful love' seems like Burns's repeated 'I will love thee still, my Dear'—except that it is not the affirmation that here concerns Wordsworth but the paradox. This is just the sort of place where Wordsworth thought harder, and harder against himself, than most men. Love it was, faithful love itself, which '*recalled* thee to my mind'—anyone might think that; *but*, Wordsworth then adds, 'how could I *forget* thee?'. That, the difference between recalled and forget, is 'That thought's return': not only the thought that she is dead but also the thought that he forgot it. And it is great and sober that those two thoughts together were still not as bad as the moment when he first knew she died, for that is the moment the two thoughts together most recall. It squares with Wordsworth's earliest literary beliefs when we have no doubt, on reading this poem, that it is essentially the nature and the situation of the man who composed the verse which are responsible for the thought and feeling that come through it. But that brings me to a second important, if obvious, point: that the qualities in the poem which seem to have their origin outside it and before it are only recognizable as such by their expression within the poem. Those qualities form that on which also they depend: the words and their position. That antithesis of remembering and forgetting is not an Augustan antithesis; it is not, for instance, phrased like

Though meek, magnanimous; though witty, wise.

Wordsworth would have rejected the feelings expressed in that line as only artificially and formally, rather than naturally, connected:

a perfect image of meekness, . . . when looked at by a
tender mind in its happiest mood, might easily lead on to
the thought of magnanimity: for assuredly there is nothing
incongruous in those virtues. . . . Whereas, when meekness
and magnanimity are represented antithetically, the
mind is not only carried from the main object, but is
compelled to turn to a subject in which the quality exists
divided from some other as noble, its natural ally:—a
painful feeling! that checks the course of love.

Prose Works, ii, p. 81.

'Surprised by joy' is not a work of formal antithesis or divided
attention, where the form of the writing dictates the form of
the thought. Its poetic form of thinking is quite other than
that. It is the work of a mind which knows it has done one
thing, for which it has a word: 'recalled'; and it knows that
that thing which it did was also somehow a mistake, which the
word 'recalled' itself helps to articulate by pointing to 'forget'—
the word implicit in the mind's sense of what recall means, not
only as a word but as a personal action. Such is 'interchange'
between word and mind, mind and word, naming recall and
feeling it. Moreover, the verbal opposition, 'recalled thee/forget
thee', emerges, but emerges only on second thought over two
lines: if there is going to be patterning, it is going to be found
rather than made. In such a way 'recalled thee/forget thee'
constitutes the shape of a feeling in time; an experience which
makes the mind that phrases it preside over a sense of its own
inadequacies, even in love. It is a mind which, in composition,
stands as a man's representative, looking back down upon its
own past. Part of Wordsworth's interest in repetition lay in its
connection with passion and with words becoming passionate
things; but part also lay, as I have said, with the mind's
struggle to find and cling to expression, and it is this effort to
give what is in oneself verbal and conscious existence that is so
important here. Behind the lines, like their originating
memory, is an articulating presence at once creating expression
and itself being re-created by it. The genius of Wordsworth's
syntactic 'course of love' lies in his bringing together both the
passionate repetitions of the natural man *along* the lines
('Love, faithful love', 'Save one, one only'), in a verse of

accompaniment, and the contrapuntal re-actions of the spiritual man *down* them ('recalled thee/forget thee'), in a verse of reappraisal. Formal antithesis is replaced by this freer movement of the spiritual within the terms of the natural. When the words have affinities, they seem the affinities not of wit or pointedness but of memory. Thus here the movement of the spiritual within the natural enables us to see in this poem a second side to what is truly love, what is faithful recollection, when he looked to his daughter at that time. And the mind, which can hold those two together in something less 'literary' than Augustan formalism, nonetheless only proves itself to exist by means of those lines of poetry; without them, before, it was only an emotionally unresolved memory. In Wordsworth's own phrase, 'the mind is to herself/Witness and judge' (*The Prelude*, 1805–6, xii, 367–8). 'Love, faithful love recalled thee to my mind'—the witness, the verse reporting upon and accompanying a prior memory; 'But how could I forget thee?'—by a species of reaction, the witness become judge. Only on the page could the mind have maintained itself as both, at virtually the same time, undivided precisely by working between itself and its words and back again. Yet the mind, working at the level of improvising among words, can still maintain contact with the level of tacit memory.

*   *   *   *   *

We have begun to see some of the linguistic techniques that Wordsworth found in order to be able to use poetry not only as a second language but also as a means of thinking in its own right. At the same time, we have been moving closer and closer to one of this book's major sticking-points. Namely, the question what, if anything, explains and bridges the gap between ordinary human ways of expressing or considering experience and the less usual way that we call poetry. No one, I suppose, can know more about this so-called gap than the man who is also a poet. And, as I have said, the firm nature of Wordsworth's nonetheless complex commitment to the humanity of poets and poetry makes Wordsworth the poet from whom we have most to learn. For no poet taught himself so much about all this as did Wordsworth.

One of the formal bases on which Wordsworth's art established and confirmed itself in his long education of himself as a poet was repetition. We have already noted this, but let us take one final, confirming look. Here Wordsworth, released from London and from financial anxiety, and knowing himself free to be a poet, with all that that meant for the quality and nature of his human life, remembers how he felt on returning home to Grasmere:

> To flit from field to rock, from rock to field,
> From shore to island, and from isle to shore,
> From open place to covert, from a bed
> Of meadow-flowers into a tuft of wood,
> From high to low, from low to high, yet still
> Within the bounds of this huge Concave; here
> Should be my home, this Valley be my World.
> *Home at Grasmere*, p. 40 (MS. B, 37–43).

What is important here is not simply that the phrases are repeated, but that each repetition, free to turn 'From high to low' and then 'from low to high', generates the next, as if they could never be exhausted. The effect is musical, as Coleridge might have described:

> If we listen to a Symphony of CIMAROSA, the present strain still seems not only to recal, but almost to *renew*, some past movement, another and yet the same! Each present moment bringing back, as it were, and embodying the spirit of some melody that had gone before, anticipates and seems trying to overtake something that is to come . . . retrospection blends with anticipation, and Hope and Memory (a female Janus) become one power with a double aspect.
>
> *The Friend*, i, pp. 129–30.

'Another and yet the same' is exactly the nature of the successive repetitions above. It is as if the past, phrased and rephrased, will always make for a verbal future. Burns may have been content within the ballad tradition to have in mind the support that music could give to words—unmeasured (as Wordsworth put it in his note to 'The Thorn') 'by the space which they occupy upon paper'. But Wordsworth and

Coleridge went further in seeking a 'Language of Music/the power of infinitely varying the expression, and individualizing it even as it is'. This potentially infinite and free—yet harmonious and related—variety is the music of repetition and modified repetition drawn out of one essential memory-source: Home at Grasmere. 'Each time—I feel differently, tho' children of one family' (Coleridge: *Notebooks*, ii, entry 2035). This kinship or affinity between words is a property of the poetry's music as much as its formal grammar. The music is another means, additional to that of grammar, by which (to coin a phrase to which I shall return) the words 'go together'.

Music as a form of thinking clearly fascinated Coleridge—as if it were an analogy. For the sounds, repeated and reformed, proposed a form of language and notation that invited the mind to try to shape the visible concept which they seemed designed to brush. It must have seemed to Coleridge like the ideal movement of thought in poetry but without the explicit sense to which words visibly tied and committed the movement.[18] 'For it is, as far as sight is concerned, formless, and yet contains the principles of form.'[19] Musical thinking, like the thinking of the poets implicit and incarnate within their repetitions, was that synthesis of imagination described by Kant as 'a blind but indispensable function of the soul'.[20] Yet tempting as it must have been to Coleridge to think of such music as pure, *a priori* thinking from which the principles of form, without the sense of content, proceeded, there was still in Wordsworth the realization that such thinking would be nothing in poetry without words. In Kant's own saying:

> Without sensibility no object would be given to us,
> without understanding no object would be thought.
> Thoughts without content are empty, intuitions
> without concepts are blind.[21]

Where the poet was a man speaking to men, the beauty for Wordsworth was that, unlike music, poetry, while likewise raising itself in terms of its own spirit, had also to preserve its human responsibility to common language and understanding as its base. He was committed to the two-in-one conjunction.

Now, in the passage which prompted all this, there is at least one point, if not two, at which the repetitions have arrived at the meaning in the past which, in Coleridge's phrase, they have been trying to overtake. Let the reader hear the verse again to catch the moment when the writing's way forward is the mind's way back:

> To flit from field to rock, from rock to field,
> From shore to island, and from isle to shore,
> From open place to covert, from a bed
> Of meadow-flowers into a tuft of wood,
> From high to low, from low to high, yet still
> Within the bounds of this huge Concave; here
> Should be my home, this Valley be my World.

There is in this a point when the reader can tell that such joyfully self-supporting language is grateful for being supported also by the memory of that to which it refers. The point at which the words of witness ('field, rock, shore, island, high, low') give way to a word that judges and includes them is at the word '*here*'. 'Here', memory is triggered by the verbal recapture of the prospect; 'here' it is that the movement of the poem's music and that of its sense joyfully meet and reach home. And the word that prompted 'here', that (in my terms) *goes with* or *is kindred to* it is the word in a similar position in the line preceding: '*still*'. For at those two moments at the end of the line the verse seems to encapsulate its own repetitive movement, to take it up and be raised by it into a single word which goes back over the way that has brought it into expression. The verse reaches the point that the repetitions were struggling cumulatively to attain from within the very impetus of the poetry: his sense of what it had meant for him to be 'here'. The repetitions 'here' reach the point of being the thought of a man's life, within it, yet, at the same time, presiding over it. And, likewise, 'still' in the passage above is the very name for what repetition signifies in the thinking of the poets—stationary yet persisting;[22] and it constitutes the moment when the thought, so variously repeated, becomes as it were the thinker of itself, knowing both 'the bounds' of this Valley and yet also the huge freedom of the World 'within' them. By a species of reaction on the part of the poet's mind in response to the momentum of its own repetitions, 'still' comes to mind as a memory word, the deep level of the memory from which all the repetitions ('From high to low, from low to high') were free variants. With a meaning beyond 'yet', 'still' pulls up the dance of joy

> From high to low, from low to high, yet still

—only to feel within itself the dance *still* whirl:

> Within the bounds of this huge Concave: here.

The words stop; but the meanings of them ('still', 'here') continue to revolve in the mind raised from memory within this verse—as Burke explains:

> Whenever we repeat any idea frequently, the mind by a sort of mechanism repeats it long after the first cause has ceased to operate. After whirling about; when we sit down, the objects about us still seem to whirl. After a long succession of noises, as the fall of waters, or the beating of forge hammers, the hammers beat and the water roars in the imagination long after the first sounds have ceased to affect it; and they die away at last by gradations which are scarcely perceptible.[23]

'The immeasurable height/Of woods decaying, never to be decayed,/The stationary blasts of waterfalls' (*P.W.*, ii, p. 213); 'Long after it was heard no more' (*P.W.*, iii, p. 77); 'seems to say that they can never die' (*P.W.*, v, p. 342); 'Behind me did they stretch in solemn train,/Feebler and feebler, and I stood and watched/Till all was tranquil as a dreamless sleep' (*The Prelude*, 1805–6, i, 461–3). Wordsworth's own poetry shows how far he believed in Burke's account. And the way that 'by a sort of mechanism' the words stop and the meanings paradoxically still revolve is felt analogically in the sensation recorded in the skating scene in *The Prelude*:

> . . . then at once
> Have I, reclining back upon my heels,
> Stopp'd short, yet still the solitary Cliffs
> Wheeled by me, even as if the earth had roll'd
> With visible motion her diurnal round.
> > *The Prelude*, 1805–6, i, 482–6.

The body, thus 'stopp'd short', feels its sensations of itself, like repetitions, steady their meaning into the memory. The idea of the movement of the earth itself, felt in and through the body, became a physical consciousness. It became (to use a phrase from Coleridge's beloved Spinoza) an idea of the body.[24] For the idea was stored seemingly in the body, 'Remembering how she felt, but what she felt/Remembering not' (*The Prelude*, 1805–6, ii, 335–6); thence to be restored to mind by memory. That is how writing not only raises memory but raises, even from body to mind by means of the subtle knot that unites them, the level of consciousness at which the thing is recalled.

Now, it is the word thrown up by the mechanism of repetition in *Home at Grasmere*—the word 'still'—that names the silent moment in *The Prelude* in between

> . . . as if the earth had roll'd

and

> With visible motion her diurnal round.

At that point Wordsworth felt 'a repetition in the finite mind of the eternal act of creation in the infinite I am' (Coleridge: *Biographia Literaria*, i, p. 202). At the moment of stillness when the meaning of 'the earth had roll'd' comes back upon the mind which formulates it, memory becomes an intimation of the immortality of what is recalled. It gives 'to universally received truths a pathos and a spirit which shall re-admit them into the soul like revelations of the moment' (*Prose Works*, ii, p. 83).

At the end of a line and at the end of an event, Wordsworth, keeping still, could hear at the bound a rebound of immortality:

> Such rebounds our inward ear
> Catches sometimes from afar—
> Listen, ponder, hold them dear;
> For of God—of God they are.
> *P.W.*, ii, p. 266.

In that space between the words 'of God—of God' the mind is to herself both witness and judge and the intuition that came to memory by the end of the experience seems confirmed in the imagination's being kindled by it. In that space between what grows from below and what is sown from above, memory and imagination seem not opposites but reflections or echoes of each other; they share the same words, the same events, the

same language, 'of God—of God'; they seem to belong to the
same basic framework of human being. Memory is not merely
a means of *repetition*, it takes the form of imagination to *re-echo*
events at a different but kindred level. Keats once described
how it felt for a man's work or words sometimes to come back
upon him, as if what he had surpassed himself to recognize or
create through imagination turns out to be simply worthy of
him and his memory:

> the simple imaginative Mind may have its rewards in the
> repetition of its own silent workings coming continually
> on the spirit with a fine suddenness—to compare great
> things with small—have you never by being surprised
> with an old Melody—in a delicious place—by a delicious
> voice, felt over again your very speculations and surmises
> at the time it first operated on your soul.
>
> *Letters,* i, p. 185.

'Of God—of God', 'even as if the earth had roll'd'. Not only
did his own sense of revelation come back upon Wordsworth
after he had finished a work but actually during it, as he, his
memory, his imagination and his words worked together, at
best like grace. The whole of the man was involved. 'Great is
the glory, for the strife is hard' (*P.W.*, iii, p. 21).

What this amounted to was a belief that the soul could be
dramatically revealed in and through the memory—a thing
that Blake would have believed to be heresy. But in a famous
formulation Wordsworth actually described the process by
which, from mundane beginnings, this could happen:

> the emotion is contemplated till, by a species of re-action,
> the tranquillity gradually disappears, and an emotion,
> kindred to that which was before the subject of contem-
> plation, is gradually produced, and does itself actually
> exist in the mind.
>
> *Prose Works,* i, p. 149.

'Actually exist' is clearly for us the crucial claim on behalf of
memory and writing. Can we tell from Wordsworth's poetry if
the claim is justified?

I think such re-actions actually did take place for
Wordsworth within his writing: they happened in such a way

as to be almost visibly preserved for us in the very experience of the verse as he worked to recapture truth to feeling and personal existence. For example, he begins a poem about his return to Tintern Abbey as follows:

> Five years have past; five summers, with the length
> Of five long winters! and again I hear
> These waters, rolling from their mountain-springs
> With a soft inland murmur.—Once again
> Do I behold these steep and lofty cliffs,
> That on a wild secluded scene impress
> Thoughts of more deep seclusion; and connect
> The landscape with the quiet of the sky.
>
> > *P.W.*, ii, p. 259.

'Emotion recollected in tranquillity': at first, the number of intervening years is contemplated as if it were tranquillity itself, as well as its cause: five, five, length, long. The repetitions work both to steady the poem and to summon the memory; for the twin aspects implicit in repetition—summation (that which ratifies the past) and relation (that which is changed even in recalling it) seem almost equally co-present. Here is the man who sees, summoning and summoned by the man who remembers. By the time 'again I hear' has become '—Once again/Do I behold' as at a fresh breath of the past, the tranquillity is gradually disappearing.

Re-action then takes over from repetition as the poet, in the terms used by Coleridge to describe Cimarosa, begins to 'renew' as well as 'recall' the past:

> . . .—Once again
> Do I behold these steep and lofty cliffs,
> That on a wild secluded scene impress
> Thoughts of more deep seclusion;

It is possible to trace through the words the movements of the poet's mind and spirit. What words go together or are kindred here as we read down as well as across the lines? Clearly, 'secluded' and 'seclusion'; but also 'steep and lofty' and 'more deep'. Between 'secluded' and 'seclusion', we may say, there is the tacit presence of a mind re-acting in their midst. 'Secluded' thus 'impresses' itself into 'seclusion', even as the seclusion

itself becomes 'more deep' through the thought of 'steep and
lofty' cliffs above it. From high to low, from low to high. Now,
at this point, it is by no means clear that the thoughts of more
deep seclusion are thoughts simply and naturally of the cliffs;
although it is impossible to say precisely what those thoughts
are *of*, apart from being thoughts *of more deep seclusion*. For these
are the thoughts in a poet's spirit which are secluded even
within the act of his writing poetry:

> Something within, which yet is shared by none—
> Not even the nearest to me and most dear—
> > *Home at Grasmere*, pp. 94–5 (MS.B, 898–9; MS.D, 687–8).

Of the man of creative soul Keats wrote, 'very few eyes can see
the Mystery of his life—a life like the scriptures, figurative'
(*Letters*, ii, p. 67). It is the Mystery of his life I am trying to see
through the turns and movements of the words he disposes.
As it was with the arrangement of words, so with the siting of
the landscape here, there seems to be present within it a tacit
thinking, the creator in the creation. In Wordsworth, the soul's
figures are inseparable from the terms of his life (his sister, his
memories, the landscape near Tintern Abbey), even while the
soul thinks on a level separate from them. Imagination, like
'Thoughts of more deep seclusion', is embedded within the
terms and landscapes of memory. It is imagination that thus
finds that the cliffs, in a sense,

> . . . connect/The landscape with the quiet of the sky.

For by the time that Wordsworth could write like that, eight
lines into his poem, a line of poetry was no longer something
flat upon the page but a thing now existing in three, not two,
dimensions; the line now conceived as a means

> . . . to take unto the height/The measure of ourselves.
> > *The Excursion*, i, 87–8 (*P.W.*, v, p. 11).

That height is the point at which a word takes the measure of
what the other words bear witness to: 'God', 'here', 'still'. But
in Wordsworth a poet attains this height, as memory and
words build up, rather than starts from it.

In chapter xii of *Biographia Literaria* there is accordingly a
disagreement central to our story. Coleridge there argued

against Wordsworth that imagination and fancy, for instance, were quite distinct faculties in the human disposition, the one higher, the other lower. In his thorough-going Idealism, Coleridge had also argued that, in the balance 'between our passive impressions and the mind's own re-action to the same', the reaction was not a secondary or mechanical event but a primary, spiritual act: 'a primary act *originating* in the mind itself, and prior to the object in order of nature, though co-instantaneous in its manifestation' (*The Friend*, i, p. 453). I doubt that the more flexible Wordsworth was so worried about establishing priorities in this rigidly hierarchical way. He believed that the 'higher' faculties in their essence, rather than their application, were not irreducibly different from the lower. And this was not an insult to our higher nature but a hope for and blessing upon our lower. The child was father to the man. There was one man not a system of distinct and hierarchical faculties. And one had to be flexible to see that often the things that turned out to be of the first importance came in reaction, late realization or on second thought. That too was part of their meaning.

I have been considering in *Home at Grasmere* and 'Tintern Abbey' Wordsworth's linguistic breakthroughs into re-achieved memory. Yet in the course of close verbal analysis one cannot help asking oneself how much the play of words really matters. In answer I want to look at the end of a very great poem, 'She dwelt among the untrodden ways'. Here it is make-or-break that the poet should move us:

> She lived unknown, and few could know
> 　　When Lucy ceased to be;
> But she is in her grave, and, oh,
> 　　The difference to me!
>
> 　　　　　　　*P.W.*, ii, p. 30.

We have already established within poetry's second language some guides to the notation; let us first use them within the terms of these lines to try to see how the music works within itself. What words go together, are kindred?

In answer to this question, '*unknown*' seems an important word because it is the word that makes for and is picked up by the modified repetition, '*few* could *know*'. But actually what the next line does ('few could know/When Lucy ceased to be') is to make us see that the most important word in the preceding line was not 'unknown' but, quietly resting beside it, 'lived'.[25] 'She lived' goes with 'Lucy ceased to be': we had not noticed at first that 'lived' was not a story but a portentously past tense. Nor is this mere verbal play or trickery. It strikes with serious violence, with the force of something forgotten and neglected. For Lucy lived generally unknown and died so. But the retrospective change that the verse carries out upon its own word 'lived', to make it matter more, this time saves Lucy from a *reader's* neglect.

Moreover the feeling that spans the difference between 'she lived' and 'she ceased to be' is itself expressed as 'But she is in her grave'. Looked at this way, we can see that the third line of the stanza is articulated because of the felt difference between the first and second; but it is articulating a feeling by which it was also precipitated into existence: 'creator and receiver both' (*The Prelude*, 1805–6, i, 273). This then, when you look back at it, seems to be self-generated, predestined verse: as you look back you can see in those three lines the inner, linking memory that effected them. 'But', for instance, is an inevitable word. Indeed, 'But she is in her grave' has words within it which mutually support and reflect each other's feelings: it is not 'But she is in *the* grave', for 'her' is as it were the victimized, past tense of 'she'—it is as if at *her* grave now the poet cannot but think that *she*, unbelievably, is in it; but the difference to me is that *she* was alive and *her grave* means that she no longer is. That is, if I may put it thus, the logic of feeling that unites this poem; but I think that Wordsworth did not plan it, so much as feel driven forward a certain way which he guessed would in retrospect show planning. Thus 'The difference to me' is exactly the difference between 'She lived' and 'Lucy (how much the name matters!) ceased to be'; and between 'she' and 'her grave'. It is the word 'difference' that is on a different hierarchical level from those words which precede it, for, by a species of re-action, it is lifted by them, to be mindful of them, onto a level above them which also in this poem gives them their final meaning. It is analogous to memory itself reaching down to the past to raise it, as well as be raised by it. What we have thus been looking at is what makes up the music or the mental family of a poem—the words that are kindred and go together, the pick-ups and recursions, levels and echoes, recompositions and reactions.

But I do not mean to say that that Lucy poem is a self-generating machine. For the word 'difference' not only clinches the poem in its own terms. If it points back inside the poem to the movement of an intelligent heart within words that it cares for, it also seems to point back outside towards the poet. Now, I think that around this sort of issue there are a number of kindred questions which of themselves seem mysteriously moving: questions like, how can one take the measure of oneself while still also being oneself? how can a man both consider himself and his past and yet not be other than the man who lived that past? how can someone write a poem and at the same time as working within it also think, outside it, of how it relates to what he knows of himself? For Wordsworth, I suspect, answers would have had to do with the mystery of 're-action' between levels of being. Certainly here, 'The difference to me' is moving not only because it says how Lucy's loss affected him but also because it itself names the *difference* between its own putting it into words and what the reality of those words feels like inside 'to me'. Of course we do not and cannot know that reality; but the lonely poem draws us towards it, knowing we cannot reach it. 'The difference to me' lays itself in the space left by the formal difference between writing and living; but it reclaims that formal distinction between the two realms by making it also the sign for or measure of the informal emotional difference that is so telling within me when I put into external words what I feel within. It is like the way the word 'here' seemed to have travelled the whole imaginative distance between itself as a word and the living external world which it recalls. In just such ways, then, thought of the relation between thinking off the page and the linguistic mechanisms of thinking on it *is itself* a constituent, in Wordsworth, of the very act of writing. 'The interchange of action from within and without' (*Prose Works*, ii, p. 75).

Reading the poem makes us think that the man writing of 'the difference to me' is both inside and outside the poem at once. I find this almost of itself moving.

To explain why, I turn to William Hazlitt who, five years

after the publication of this poem, surely remembered its phrasing when he wrote in his *Essay on the Principles of Human Action* (1805): 'I am not in reality more different from others than any one individual is from any other individual . . . What is it then that makes the difference greater to me? (*Works*, i, p. 5). What is it that makes the difference greater to me? Rousseau, at the celebrated opening of his *Confessions*, had already given the quintessential Romantic answer: me, I make the difference, 'moi seul', 'je suis autre'. Why do I care more about myself and my own concerns? Because it is me, because those concerns are mine. So it is with everyone; we all care more about what affects us. Yet to Hazlitt this self-authentication made epistemological nonsense: all of us are colluding incoherently in finding our own concerns more powerful to us than the very similar concerns of our neighbours. Rousseau's emotional individualism produced, by its own contradictions, the subsequent Romantic guilt of a Hazlitt. Now Wordsworth stood apart from that historical chain which bound Romantic pride to Romantic guilt. Rather than merely react within the current of Romanticism, he did his thinking inside his own terms. For where to the question 'What is it that makes the difference greater to me?' Rousseau retorted 'me', Wordsworth had in his poem answered, 'Lucy's death'. Wordsworth had a quite distinct sense of the meaning of emotion: the validity of emotion lay not simply with the proud subject of that emotion, the person who felt it, but in the action and reaction between the subject and the object. Not for Wordsworth the egotistical sublime of a Rousseau:—it matters because it matters to me; it matters because of the felt difference between Lucy alive and Lucy dead. Part of the reason why Wordsworth's is so often a verse of action and reaction is that the relation of the man to himself in the poetry cannot lie in that straightforward, auto-biographical, self-reliant strength that Rousseau presumes to possess. It lies rather in the sense of limitation and yet, within that, the paradoxical freedom of rebounding reflections upon his limitations. It is with Wordsworth rather as Mrs Gaskell describes in chapter 22 of *Mary Barton* when she retorts to those who tell us that our tears are no help: that is why we weep. That is the sort of rebound that Wordsworth felt between himself and his poetry: knowing that that powerful

feeling of the difference to me is nonetheless powerless to make
any difference after all, yet feeling that weakness too with great
strength. That is why there is justified emotion in thinking of
Wordsworth at once inside and outside his poem: for here is a
man working out a trouble by writing and yet knowing at the
same time that he will still be left afterwards with that trouble.
He justifies for us the rights and status of feeling.

Thus it is with Wordsworth as Andrew Baxter had put it
when summarizing the state of this material world: 'each agent
must suffer in acting and act in suffering' (*An Enquiry into the
Nature of the Human Soul*, i, xxiv). Wordsworth himself seems to
have recalled Baxter when he wrote, 'Passion, it must be
observed, is derived from a word which signifies *suffering*; but
the connection which suffering has with effort, with exertion,
and *action*, is immediate and inseparable' (*Prose Works*, iii, pp.
81–2).

It was one of the mysteries of man that acting and suffering
went together for Wordsworth. It was something that prevented
him from merely mourning the suffering, like Tennyson, or
being sure that it was simply tragic, like Hardy. 'See God in
small', said Lancelot Andrewes, 'or you shall never see Him in
large'. So, I say, see these big beliefs in the small, daily acts of
Wordsworth's poetic vocation. There is an important conclusion to make on Wordsworth's pick-up of his own words and
raising of their levels, as they act and suffer amongst themselves, and it has to do with this necessity to work big intuitions
through small words and spaces. My conclusion lies in the
mere way that the words, in the tacit presence of Wordsworth's
mind, work in and on themselves to signal the poet's hidden
effort to get through and beyond them:

> The waves beside them danced, but they
> Outdid the sparkling waves in glee.

> He murmurs near the running brooks
> A music sweeter than their own.

> . . . these steep and lofty cliffs
> That on a wild secluded scene impress
> Thoughts of more deep seclusion.

I conclude that it is as if the terms were limited—as are the bounds of Grasmere in space, as the past is in time—but within those terms the fresh variations and the levels of meaning are responsively free and almost unlimitable. Language seems to add to, as well as serve, the meaning of the past. By a species of reaction, what was suffered may now be acted upon; what is now acted upon has still also to be suffered. This is not heroic transcendentalism; it is greater than such escape. As the man who actually saw *Lyrical Ballads* through the press put it years later, in terms of his own profession, chemistry:

> The future is composed of images of the past, connected in new arrangements by analogy, and modified by the circumstances and feelings of the moment; our hopes are founded upon our experience.
>
> Sir Humphry Davy: '*A Discourse Introductory to a Course of Lectures on Chemistry*' 1802.[26]

That is how the future is composed and it is, I have tried to show, much as Wordsworth's poetry was composed: a hope not despite his past experience but founded upon it. And this felt like creativity rather than determinism. The verbal recombinations of his past with his present reflections upon it constituted for Wordsworth a recognition of the meaning and movement of his life. He was far from ashamed to think the basic elements of that life to be much the same, in kind, as those of another man; it was the chemistry of their composition that was his distinction, for the sake of seeing a future in the meaning of past human experience, a future for memory. For Wordsworth not only had memories, he also had access to a dynamic use of memory:

> Wittgenstein once observed in a lecture that there is a similarity between his conception of philosophy (e.g. 'the problems are solved, not by giving new information, but by arranging what we have always known', *Investigations*, para. 109 . . .) and the Socratic doctrine that knowledge is reminiscence: although he believed that there were also other things involved in the latter.
>
> Norman Malcolm: *Ludwig Wittgenstein: A Memoir* (Oxford, 1958), p. 51.

It is to this use of memory that I wish finally to turn in this section.

* * * * *

The use of memory to which I am referring is memory as a form of spiritual discovery: how it reveals the way that one went and, perhaps, the way in future one will have to go to be true to oneself. For Wordsworth this was a fact of his experience not only outside but inside the writing of poetry. In that sense, rather than in the sense that Blake criticized, knowledge for Wordsworth was reminiscence.

'The Ruined Cottage' and 'Michael' are two of Wordsworth's greatest poems. I want now to take some representative and telling moments from Wordsworth at his best to see how the way forward was for him related to the way back, dynamically as a principle of discovery rather than mere conservatism.

By asking what words 'go with' each other, we begin to see that the poetry of Wordsworth not only acts as witness along the line, as if in time with that which it describes, but also re-acts, as in memory of itself, down the lines, judging what is happening. Consider a fairly long section from 'The Ruined Cottage', an imaginative poem based on an amalgam of memories. First, we shall hear Margaret speaking to the Wanderer; then the Wanderer, in the narrative present, speaking of this forsaken woman to the young man who is, like us, the story's audience; third, the Wanderer's resumption of the tale told by his memory. For no reason other than pressure of space, I have somewhat cut the second section, the interlude.

1. . . .—"I perceive
2. You look at me, and you have cause; today
3. I have been travelling far; and many days
4. About the fields I wander, knowing this
5. Only, that what I seek I cannot find;
6. And so I waste my time: for I am changed;
7. And to myself," said she, "have done much wrong
8. And to this helpless infant. I have slept
9. Weeping, and weeping have I waked; my tears
10. Have flowed as if my body were not such
11. As others are; and I could never die.

12.   But I am now in mind and in my heart
13.   More easy; and I hope," said she, "that God
14.   Will give me patience to endure the things
15.   Which I behold at home."
16.   'It would have grieved
17.   Your very soul to see her. Sir, I feel
18.   The story linger in my heart; I fear
19.   'Tis long and tedious; but my spirit clings
20.   To that poor Woman . . .'
21.   "'Ere my departure, to her care I gave,
22.   For her son's use, some tokens of regard,
23.   Which with a look of welcome she received;
24.   And I exhorted her to place her trust
25.   In God's good love, and seek his help by prayer.
26.   I took my staff, and, when I kissed her babe,
27.   The tears stood in her eyes. I left her then
28.   With the best hope and comfort I could give:
29.   She thanked me for my wish;—but for my hope
30.   It seemed she did not thank me.'

               The Excursion, i, 762–76, 776–80, 804–13 (*P.W.*, v, pp. 34–5).

This may seem like linear narrative, but down these lines there
is a contrapuntal binding to the still, sad music of humanity:
all that 'I feel/The story linger in my heart' means. What flows
down the lines, like tears, are words which seem frail even to
themselves, words like:

2.   today
3.   many days
6.   waste my time
8.   helpless
9.   weeping, weeping, my tears
13.   I hope
14.   patience to endure
16.   grieved
21.   care
22.   regard
24.   trust
25.   love, help, prayer
26.   The tears
28.   hope and comfort
29.   my wish;—but . . . my hope.

The most repeated word is the narrative 'and'; to the deeper sense connecting these lines, that fact only serves to make the final 'but' (29) the more telling. Some of these words are thoughts ('patience' 14) about feeling ('weeping' 9); others feelings ('The tears stood in her eyes' 27) about thoughts; what binds them is that they are in their different ways in memory of the movement 'my tears/Have flowed', for that is the real meaning of the fluency down the lines. In between these words and binding them together, like children of one family, are what Wordsworth in 'Resolution and Independence' called 'blind thoughts I knew not, nor could name' (*P.W.*, ii, p. 236). Blind thoughts which have

> . . . among least things
> An under-sense of greatest; see the parts
> As parts, but with a feeling of the whole.
> *The Prelude*, 1805–6, vii, 710–2.

That feeling of the whole is that which lies in the interlude (16–20), where 'I perceive/You look at me' (1–2) becomes 'It would have grieved/Your very soul to see her' (16–17), before her 'look of welcome' (23) turns, with his departure, to 'tears' (27) fundamentally unaltered from those she shed (7–10) before his arrival. 'Helpless' (8) as these lines are, there is running down them cries, needs, offers of 'help' (25) as if in secular antiphon. Although the name of God is twice spoken (13, 25), what really hears the sounds is something helplessly in place of a God: an 'under-sense' which lets the words which it could have held up for emotion *go*, past and down as parts

> . . . I have slept
> Weeping, and weeping have I waked

—not out of neglect but out of a complex 'feeling of the whole'.[27] For the soul, remembering such things—'my spirit clings/To that poor Woman'—seems not to emphasize them, at the time so much as carry them on down through the narrative. Thus, ' "And I *hope*", said she, "that *God*" ' becomes, by the logic of feeling, 'She *thanked me* for my *wish*;—but for my *hope*/It seemed she did *not thank me*'. 'Each agent,' as Andrew Baxter said, 'must suffer in acting and act in suffering': that is what happens to hope in the poem. Whenever it is picked-up, it seems to take to heart despair; yet the soul of the poem remembers 'hope' as if waiting, still, for God to answer it. This memory down the lines, carrying the soul, was what the philosopher T. H. Green called 'the spiritual principle':

> In reading the sentence we see the words successively, we attend to them successively, we recall their meaning successively. But throughout that succession there must be present continuously the consciousness that the sentence has a meaning as a whole; otherwise the successive vision, attention and recollection would not end in comprehension of what the meaning is. This consciousness operates in them, rendering them what they are as organic to the intelligent reading of the sentence.[28]

Wordsworth's linear art highlights all the more, as by counterpoint, the necessity for the reader thus to make the mind of the writer his own by making a spiritual synthesis down the lines, even as he or she reads across them. It is surely unlikely that that movement down the lines is pre-planned or the result of minute association. Rather, it seems to be the working of something—call it the spiritual principle or imagination itself— whose going forward may be seen in retrospect as being the other side of that memory which it leaves behind binding the lines together. Imagination and memory are not separate faculties but share the same structure: only, in their application, imagination works forward as if into the future, while memory works backwards as if into the past. To go forward, in the passage from Wordsworth quoted above, we can see that what happened was that the process of memory was turned round, taken up into the process of imagination and, at the end, left embedded in the work of imagination as the trace of the way that the mind in composition worked. Imagination was an almost unconscious memory in the mind of the poet of the way he had to go in his writing; the conscious memory of women like Margaret, dilemmas like these, was taken up into that semi-unconscious form of itself.

Wordsworth would not have written a sentence like:

> . . . I made no vows,
> But vows were then made for me.

What he wrote was:

> . . . I made no vows, but vows
> Were then made for me;
> *The Prelude*, 1805–6, iv, 341–2.

It is too characteristically Wordsworth to be a mere accident of metrics. The lines are set within a memory, a recognition in retrospect of being a man who was chosen. Yet the verse does not work in the mere confidence of the settled meaning now assigned to the past—as 'But vows were then made for me' would breezily suggest. The memory is more mysterious than that: Wordsworth's positioning of 'I made *no vows, but vows*', letting the repetitions go together through a magnetism not solely determined by grammar, takes the vows on their second appearance back into the mind, ahead of their own explicit formulation, and even when the mind of itself has not made them. It is as if he even then had an intimation of the way he was going, a foreknowledge in youth only fully revealed as tacitly present when realized by memory afterwards. 'No vows, but vows'—that, by a species of re-action between acting and suffering, was his intuition at the time; in retrospect, that premonition is spelt out—'vows'

> Were then made for me.

When in *The Prelude* Wordsworth wrote from memory, the memory felt to him as the other side of, or the way back to, that sense of predestination that had brought him thus far. So, equivalently, the verse still went forward following memories as though they were intimations again ('No vows, but vows/ Were . . .'), leaving memory within and behind it in the lines to explain the way it had gone.

We can look down the lines and see traces of the way that they came into being; we can see within them the memory behind them. The whole work may be essentially a matter of memory: *The Prelude*, for instance, is. But even so it depends on the revitalizing and foreseeing work of imagination for its creation. The relation between these two, memory and imagination, is also one of memory binding the two; for by analysis we can see the memory tacitly and dynamically at work again as an under-presence to imagination.

This belief in an 'under-sense', an unconscious memory or intuited premonition of the way to be travelled, was to Wordsworth both wonderful and yet common. In the poem 'Michael' there comes a point when Michael is trying to decide whether his son should be sent out into the world to get money to enable his parents to stay on in their home; the wife and mother speaks to the boy as follows:

> . . . 'Thou must not go:
> We have no other Child but thee to lose,
> None to remember—do not go away,
> For if thou leave thy Father he will die.'
>
> *P.W.*, ii, p. 89, ll. 295–8.

Nobody seems to have thought that sentence out: it seems as natural as the familiar emotion precipitating it. Wordsworth admitted that the work was based both on a specific family and general family cares. Nonetheless, the mother does not say, more simply, 'You are our only child' or even 'You are our only child and we must be sure to *keep* you': the word she uses is 'lose', not keep; lose, a word of imagination and fear at the end of the line. Nor did she use the phrase 'only child'. For the pre-conscious substitution or anticipation of 'lose' for 'keep' was itself foreshadowed, as we see if we read *backwards* along the line:

> We have no other Child but thee to lose

—foreshadowed by the dark negatives 'but thee' and 'no other'. It is, as Wordsworth said of Burns's 'A Bard's Epitaph', 'a history in the shape of a prophecy!'. The line has what the future reveals to be an internal, unconscious memory of that word 'lose' which it fears that life, as well as it, is coming to. All of the mother seems to lie in and beneath those words, in spirit. And in the last line

> For if thou leave thy Father he will die.

'thy Father' stands present in the midst: on one side facing the threat 'If thou leave thy Father'; on the other faced by his wife's thought of what that will mean: 'he will die'. Moreover, what is thus visible back and forth along these lines can also be revealed up and down between them. Look again:

> if thou leave thy Father he will die.

Suppose we ask, why, for 'he' she naturally (as much as metrically) does not say 'my Husband' but 'thy Father'? The answer lies in the reason why also in

> We have no other Child but thee to lose

she said 'We' not 'I' or 'he'. It is 'we' because of the memory, already operative tacitly, of that word 'Child' ahead: a joint offspring. And accordingly, the wife shares with her husband the meaning of parental care, such that, poignantly, she knows that his being 'thy Father', bereft, will kill him just as surely as his also being 'my Husband' will not suffice under such circumstances to keep him alive. When Reynolds said that Genius also had Laws, Blake supposed that that was a denial of Genius and its true nature of being a law unto itself. He countered Reynolds by saying, 'What is now proved was once only imagin'd' (Blake: *Complete Writings*, p. 151). And Blake was not interested in the later proof. But Wordsworth's poetry reveals laws within it which express rather than harass its freedom and humanity: tacit laws of being, under-senses even for natural speech. In such poetry, by analysis we see that what was once imagined can now be recalled.[29] The memory of the mother is here evident, in all its deepest structures.

What is more, there is an under-current in memory of the way of imagination and the soul not only across and down the lines but also through different parts of the whole poem. Line 298 of 'Michael', *'If thou leave thy Father he will die'*, finds kindred in line 472, with reference to the wall that the father and son were to have built together; Wordsworth writes of Michael who always went to it:

> *And left the work unfinished when he died*

The structure is again fluently tripartite. Thus, applying the rule of what 'goes together', 'the work' here is left centrally in place of 'thy Father': he left it, however unwillingly or not, in response to some deep memory of his son's having 'left' him. 'Left *unfinished*' thus expresses the very stasis of loss; but it is able only to be honoured if '*left* unfinished', partly with deliberate reverence, partly with hopeless incapacity. In the very middle of the line, 'unfinished' is what both of the verbs on either side of it essentially come to. And in the meeting of those two lines in 'Michael', consummatum est: it is as if the imagination of line 298 were the other side of the memory in line 472. Even so, there is something in the quietness of the poem which foreknows the necessity of reaching that conclusion, while still in the making not being pre-emptively harassed or poetically debilitated by that shadow. That something, in both its patience and its sympathy, is deeply human; is Wordsworth's care for Michael.[30]

I propose, then, contrapuntal analysis of this kind as a fresh means of seeing into what is hidden in the thinking of the poets. It is not just applicable to Wordsworth; although, equally, in looking for a deeper, tacit freedom than can be found by means of linear antitheses and in putting presentiment before premeditation it is not, without modification, a technique suitable for the analysis of Augustan couplets.[31] But what I am concerned with here is that such an analysis reveals the deeper ways in which Wordsworth makes his connections, disclosing thus the deep connections of his own mind. There is a profound sense in which a man can be himself without needing to be conscious of himself: there is a memory beneath him and behind him, like the soul of a deeper self, even as he seems to himself to be exercising present powers of freedom, discovery or innovation. Wordsworth's verse reveals that sense in which a man's deep memory is his soul.

In the thinking of the poets Wordsworth himself believed that he could see beneath the work of imagination the deep memory of the characteristics of a man's mind. Here is Wordsworth on Milton:

> Hear again this mighty Poet,—speaking of the Messiah going forth to expel from heaven the rebellious angels,
>
> > 'Attended by ten thousand thousand Saints
> > He onward came: far off his coming shone,'—
>
> the retinue of Saints, and the Person of the Messiah himself, lost among and merged in the splendour of that indefinite abstraction 'His coming!'
>
> *Prose Works*, iii, p. 34.

'Attended' goes with or becomes taken up into 'his coming'. That avoidance of transition, where the mind in its speedy desire to grasp what it seeks has already taken up into itself what it is that connects one thing with another, is the work of poetic synthesis. The poetry's brevity is an index of the speed with which the mind, impatient of detailed interpretation, goes for its meaning as if to snatch it out of the future. This impatience means that the forces explicit in, for instance, the act of repetition are held in the mind without being formally set down on paper, so that by a species of reaction the mind feels in itself what it can move on from without explicit statement. This is vital to the thinking of the poets: that a line and a sentence get made not because the rules of grammar are run through uniformly, but because the mind will not stop thinking until it has reached on paper the verge of what it is really thinking of, the connectives of grammar being simply a bridge to that. For that reason, the poets think of what they seize without at the same time being able to have time formally to think out how they seized it. Or, when Wordsworth does so think it out, his verse becomes like Cimarosa's symphonies according to Coleridge: the calling back and repetition of a past phrase re-opening its meaning and carrying the poet forward through the long poem. Wordsworth is sometimes able to 'do' his thinking, on the page in the instant of the right word, and think about it as well. But that second, underlying thought is essentially something created in the space left by imagination in its own thinking:

He onward *came : far* off his coming shone.

—a memory of the mind left behind in that space as if it were imagination's other half. For the mind of Milton went to the right word so penetratively as to take its expression clean out of a future whose possibilities that mind itself had created. As Hazlitt said, the future is the domain of the imagination. And the future in its real form—the readership of posterity—feeling its breath taken away, will have to look back to the poetry as something waiting upon it to be spelt out.

That is the memory that the thinking of the poets as epitomized in Wordsworth sought to leave behind. An impression of his difference that a man made upon language: partly by registering it upon the words, making them register it; partly finding it from words, learning what his relation to language taught him about himself and about the shape of his feelings and thoughts when he felt he had got the expression 'right'. This, at any rate, was Wordsworth. For in Wordsworth the use of memory in writing becomes the movement of the man's spirit among and within his words; a spirit in part carrying those words forward, in part brought forward and left behind by them. If in the thinking of the poets repetition is ultimately a sign for what, it seems to the spirit of man, can never die; remembering finally has kindred inside ourselves with the hope of a sanctioned and an immortal life. Wordsworth's poetry leaves behind, within itself, the memory of his soul, that deep assurance that lay behind the mind even as the mind struggled to find a way for the soul through words. For Wordsworth, more than for any other man in the nineteenth century I shall be saying, writing was not ironic or secondary; it was the place to bring, think over and leave his memory of living.

III. 'HE LOOKS BEFORE AND AFTER'

I have argued that for Wordsworth memory is virtually a religious faculty, an underpresence in a person's life and in a writer's work which, further, supports the relation between writing and living. In this final section I want to suggest how Wordsworth could be temporal as well as spiritual, artistically inventive as well as commemorative, while still acknowledging his allegiance to the deeper permanencies. This book is about memory and writing: it is not only about what memory does for writing but also about what writing, as we saw in chapter 1, can do and must do for memory.

In the last section I was finally trying to suggest a means of following the verbal traces of himself that a poet leaves as he works forward through a poem. These are traces of his memory not only tacitly following but foreordaining the work of his words and his imagination, without, however, thereby pre-empting that work. As this is a book addressed to the memory of several great writers, I find myself asking, in this instance, what would Wordsworth have thought of this?

I make no claims for this present treatment, but it is in general the case that subsequent, discursive explanations of his poetry would not have disturbed Wordsworth. They would not have disturbed him, even (indeed, especially) if he were convinced as to their truth as insights into the working of a poet's mind. And that is not because he would simply have ignored them as belonging to a level irrelevant to his art. For the idea of levels—what I thought then, what I think now—is vital to his art. So:—what if a law determining the nature of the mind of a poet were discovered tomorrow? what would Wordsworth, a poet, have thought?

> wisdom forbids her children to antedate their knowledge, or to act and feel otherwise, or feel further than they know. But should that time arrive [when miracles can be resolved into laws], the sole difference, that could result from such an enlargement of our view, would be this: that what we now consider as miracles in opposition to ordinary experience, we should then reverence with a yet higher devotion as harmonious parts of one great complex miracle, when the antithesis between experience and belief would itself be taken up into the unity of intuitive reason.
>
> Coleridge: *The Friend*, i, p. 519.

If miracles were discovered to have laws, if poets were shown to be obeying tacit rules or transmuting their own autobiographies, why should we feel cheated or disillusioned? If the higher thing seems lowered by such thoughts, isn't it a signal to raise one's estimation of those thoughts? For Wordsworth the way that present discovery might reflect back upon past experience was never, as it was for Hardy, fundamentally disabusing. That memory in Wordsworth is not 'antedating' is the force of his saying that the Child is Father of the Man.[32] As Coleridge makes clear, memory is the means by which subsequent knowledge does not disauthenticate the past but, by a species of re-action, harmonizes and is harmonized by it. Yet for Wordsworth there was also something looser and freer than those Hardy/Coleridge alternatives: of the present either unmaking or remaking what was previous to it.

For Wordsworth does not write in order that a subsequent line should be merely the product of contradicting the one previous to it. Although he is drawn towards intimations of immortality, he does not let his presentiment of a final destination detract attention from the countryside en route. He addresses the lakes of Locarno and Como thus:

> . . . Like a breeze
> Or sunbeam over your domain I pass'd
> In motion without pause; but Ye have left
> Your beauty with me.
>
> *The Prelude*, 1805–6, vi, 605–8

The words that go together, 'I pass'd' and 'Ye left', are not in contradiction; nor is it the case that 'left' merely remakes what 'pass'd' unmade: rather, the two phrases are in counterpoint or mutual wonder and the emotion is located not simply at the *end* of the experience but, as it were, somewhere retrospectively sited *in between* his passing them by and their leaving themselves in mind. This emotion is not that of the original, light passing or that of the strangely resulting residue, but of the union of the two: a sort of emotion of memory as if memory itself can be an experience rather than merely being subordinate to the past.[33] In being thus innocent of the necessity of choosing *either* what is 'pass'd' *or* what is 'left', such memory is equivalent to the moment which Coleridge describes, as, travelling, he sat down with Europe on his left and Africa on his right:

> This is Africa! That is Europe!—There is *division*, sharp boundary, abrupt Change!—and what are they in Nature—two Mountain Banks that make a noble River of the interfluent Sea, existing and acting with distinctness and manifoldness indeed, but at once as one—no division, no Change, no Antithesis!
>
> *Notebooks*, ii, entry 2026.

It was, thought Coleridge, the kind of experience that he and Wordsworth, above all, were capable of having. Now certainly Wordsworth's emotion of memory—

> . . . How strange that all
> The terrors, pains, and early miseries,
> Regrets, vexations, lassitudes interfused
> Within my mind, should e'er have borne a part,

And that a needful part, in making up
The calm existence that is mine when I
Am worthy of myself![34]

—maintains a similar balance between contingencies and a retrospective sense of predestination. The emotion here knows that memory exists between being the product and the orchestrator of that which it recalls: between being, as it were, Coleridge's river and Coleridge's sea. Out of the terrors of the past had emerged a calmness, just as in between two confronting profiles emerges the shape of a grecian urn. But the resulting calmness also involved seeing its own strange unity with the past from which it had emerged; like the work of Nature creating the world by splitting-up land-masses with the water which also unites them.

In the second section of this chapter I was concerned to show how memory at a level below that of conscious manipulation predestined the way the poet's mind was going without harassing that mind on its route. I now want to go on to say that the use made *within* the man's life of its own over-arching calmness, of its own under-current of predestination, is in Wordsworth's case not simply in terms of finality of result, immortality of implication. The more certainty Wordsworth had of a deep presence in himself, the more freedom he felt to acquiesce in the contingent turns of life on earth. As miracles might have laws, predestination need not be incompatible with a profound sense of freedom and scope for serious diversion.

Consider the poem 'Stepping Westward', a classic of memory as Wordsworth himself describes it:

While my Fellow-traveller and I were walking by the side of Loch Ketterine, one fine evening after sunset, in our road to a Hut where, in the course of our Tour, we had been hospitably entertained some weeks before, we met, in one of the loneliest parts of that solitary region, two well-dressed Women, one of whom said to us, by way of greeting, 'What, you are stepping westward?'

The voice, in Wordsworth's memory, changes level and

becomes in his writing a higher echo of itself, repetition in a finer tone: '*What, you are stepping westward?*'—'*Yea.*':

> I liked the greeting; 'twas a sound
> Of something without place or bound;
> And seemed to give me spiritual right
> To travel through that region bright.

> The voice was soft, and she who spake
> Was walking by her native lake:
> The salutation had to me
> The very sound of courtesy:
> Its power was felt; and while my eye
> Was fixed upon the glowing Sky,
> The echo of the voice enwrought
> A human sweetness with the thought
> Of travelling through the world that lay
> Before me in my endless way.
>
> *P.W.*, iii, p. 76.

Such a poem calls to mind De Quincey's account of echo augury. Using Jewish precedents, De Quincey speaks of the direct meaning ('the greeting') as the *mother* meaning and of the secondary or mystical meaning ('a sound/Of something without place or bound') as the *daughter of a voice*, the kindred echo seemingly created for one chosen hearer. It is just such echoing and re-acting relations that we have been considering in contrapuntal analysis. Anyway, De Quincey concludes that the miracle of this is not obsolete even in an age of reason:

> viz., where a man, perplexed in judgment, and sighing for some determining counsel, suddenly heard from a stranger in some unlooked-for quarter words not meant for himself, but clamorously applying to the difficulty besetting him.[35]

This may seem like 'mysticism' in Wordsworth when we think of how the sound seems to carry him along his predestined way by 'spiritual right'. But, as is proper for the poet who conceived of poets as men speaking to men, the mysticism is grounded in a firm sense of the ordinary, the predestination is based on the incidentally contingent, the means spiritually to transcend memory is itself memory's own means—namely, echo. The revelation on the way not only knows that it owes its origin to 'human sweetness' but it itself in high praise, rather than oblivious transcendence, of its origin. The sound may be said to be carrying him along the lines of verse, but, simultaneously, it is also something that inside the verse Wordsworth locally works at bringing forward to his end.

In the previous section I used the model of the action and reaction of the mind and language to show how the man within the poetry could find the way bit by bit forwards and downwards—a route which, for all his local struggles and dependencies on words, he also felt on another level was assured, as the way his memory outside his work was leading him within it. In partial qualification of this view, I am now pointing to those actions and reactions not only in terms of what we now see that they led to but also in respect of them in their own right, as they felt to the poet in the middle of affairs.[36]

For in the composition of *The Prelude* there is an attitude whose freedom is its effortless resistance to the question that a man might well ask of the memory of his life: what does this finally come down to? Hardy's sort of question. But Wordsworth remembers things such as, when he was a boy, he saw the place where a murderer's gallows had been; and the subject-matter of the memory is not murder or death faced full on but something contingent that happened afterwards and yet was mysteriously kindred:

> . . . I left the spot,
> And, reascending the bare slope, I saw
> A naked pool that lay beneath the hills,
> The beacon on the summit, and more near
> A girl who bore a pitcher on her head
> And seemed with difficult steps to force her way
> Against the blowing wind. It was in truth
> An ordinary sight but I should need
> Colours and words that are unknown to man
> To paint the visionary dreariness
> Which, while I looked all round for my lost guide,
> Did, at that time, invest the naked pool,
> The beacon on the lonely eminence,
> The woman and her garments vexed and tossed
> By the strong wind.
>
> *The Prelude*, 1798–9, pp. 50–1 (ll. 313–27).

'The bare slope', 'A naked pool', 'The beacon on the summit', 'A girl who bore a pitcher on her head': the capacity to list as significant, sights which at the same time are admitted to be ordinary and neutral, rests not on syntax but on the memory of a life. Even so, so simple a retrospective shift as that from 'A naked pool' to 'the naked pool' emphasizes how the ability to repeat an account of such sights, without finding very much more in them, is also essentially dependent on the act of writing within the domain of memory. The action and re-action between the memory as it is in the mind and the deictic[37] function of words on the page gives Wordsworth a freedom in making the one form of retrospection into the other and back again. In Wordsworth wisdom does not scorn prudence, and high thoughts use basic tools on a page; there are

> tender and subtile ties by which these principles, that love to soar in the pure region, are connected with the ground-nest in which they were fostered and from which they take their flight. . . . The order of life does not require that the sublime and disinterested feelings should have to trust long to their own unassisted power. Nor would the attempt consist either with their dignity or their humility. They condescend, and they adopt: they know the time of their repose; and the qualities which are worthy of being admitted into their service—of being their inmates, their companions, or their substitutes.
>
> *Prose Works*, i, p. 340.

Words may substitute for memories, may become their notation. The mere verbal ability to repeat and to change what is repeated allows the mind to return to an abiding experience, now stationed, in differing relations to it. Improvization may be allowed within predestination.

> The beacon on the summit, and more near
> A girl who bore a pitcher on her head
> And seemed with difficult steps to force her way
> Against the blowing wind. . . .
> The beacon on the lonely eminence,
> The woman and her garments vexed and tossed
> By the strong wind.

None of these differing relations, running back and forth between ideas of what is recalled because important and what is important because recalled, has a final or supersessive authority. It is not that the second sounding is the first sounding now got right. For here

> . . . feeling comes in aid
> Of feeling, and diversity of strength
> Attends us, if but once we have been strong.
> *The Prelude*, 1805–6, xi, 326–8.

As well as be made by his own past, Wordsworth could help to make his own future, making through his poetry precedents and future memories for it. The 'diversity' by which 'A girl who bore a pitcher on her head' becomes 'The woman . . .' lies partly in an implicit recognition that what one now sees to have been a girl was to a six-year-old boy also a woman; partly in the present recognition that the fight of an anonymous girl against the elements made her worthy of being 'The woman', growing up in his memory by both her strength and his until she is almost as primal as the wind which she combatted.

All this is to say, as I have tried to suggest before, that Wordsworth, at the start of the nineteenth century, knew what in the history of feeling its blind alleys were to be. For mine is a book that could almost have been written backwards. It is impossible to think, for instance, that Wordsworth could have allowed himself to get into the situation of Richard Jefferies, inheritor of certain of the obsessive intensities of Shelley and of Keats.[38] Jefferies can write thus in memory of his life:

> The earth and the sun were to me like my flesh and blood, and the air of the sea life.
> With all the greater existence I drew from them I prayed for a bodily life equal to it, for a soul-life beyond my thought, for my inexpressible desire of more than I could shape even into idea. There was something higher than idea, invisible to thought as air to the eye; give me bodily life equal in fulness to the strength of earth, and sun, and sea; give me the soul-life of my desire.[39]

Even so short an excerpt serves to illustrate the self-destructive link, hinted at in *The Dictionary of National Biography*, between

Jefferies's 'constant preoccupation with his own thoughts' and 'his tenacious struggle for survival' (vol. x, p. 703). All too necessarily tenacious did he make it for himself; Wordsworth with his discretion could survive and live in a more real relation to himself and his world. There is hardly a full stop in Jefferies's insatiable syntax. No wonder he says that 'No thought which I ever had has satisfied my soul' (op. cit. p. 107). This prose has no pauses. No wonder, thus lured greedily on and on as if in terrible misunderstanding of Wordsworth's 'Whatsoever point they gain they still/Have something to pursue', he is left saying madly that 'In the conception of the idea that there are others, I lay claim to another idea' (p. 179). The idea that there are other ideas is as nugatory as its own content; the upping of levels has gone mad. Of this post-Romantic longing to merge in and yet spiritualize the ancestral mother-earth, Andrew Seth, the Scottish philosopher who sought a more sober conjunction between philosophical Idealism and human personality, concluded in 1885:

> we know not what we ask in such moments of dim craving in the blood. To be made one with nature would be to resign our knowledge and our consciousness, to merge in the dumb being of natural forces, to be no more as we have been, and to lose, therefore, the very penetrative sense of life and enjoyment that prompts the desire.[40]

To merge oneself in nature or nature in oneself: it makes very little difference to the essence of the mistake. Before ever such lunacies of desire—or melancholy at their untenability—took form and place in the history of nineteenth-century literary sensibility, Wordsworth seems to have seen, known and avoided the disasters of the inner life and its relation to the world. I do not mean to suggest that the whole of the literary nineteenth century was a write-off for not being able, somehow, to see what Wordsworth saw; although I do think that Wordsworth would have known what was at stake in Lawrence's rejection of Thomas Hardy, and I do think that if Hardy could have felt as Wordsworth had been able to feel, Lawrence's rejection of Hardy would not have been so necessary (and I wonder whether either Hardy or Lawrence had any inkling of this). Still, I see some force in the objection that, in age, Wordsworth's wisdom could hardly save himself, let alone the nineteenth century. And I shall be trying to raise this large question, as to what happened in the new century, later in the book. But for the moment, let us simply acknowledge the evidence. Over eighty years before Seth's warning, Wordsworth had learnt to accept as an adult that the fact of relation seems to bring with it experience of separation. But his prudence was not to lament that paradox; rather, as in those great lists of 'visionary dreariness' where the things remembered seem at once close to and yet independent of his heart, he wisely *used* the separation as evidence also of a stranger kind of relation. Wordsworth began, crudely but powerfully enough, with a solitary temperament which found a match for its emotions in the hard, the heroic and the sublime; a young boy inclined towards the non-human and strange, insecure disturbances of the safely human, like murder and the gallows, like guilt and suicide. Two factors— one a person, his sister Dorothy, the other a contour in his experience, the recurrence of a chastening spirit in his memory of what his own temperamental preferences came up against— taught him a gentleness and patience, love even for the small, the delayed, the hidden and the beautiful.[41] Although Dorothy may hardly have known it explicitly, her brother learnt what gentleness and human sweetness she could teach, and, by learning through her his deficiencies, taught himself both his temperamental preconceptions and his real needs (as well as the difference between the two) in ways strenuously *un*gentle to himself. One of the results of this powerfully adult flexibility was Wordsworth's unique contribution to the debate over the Beautiful and the Sublime; he, not Burke, not Kant, but he alone argued that the two could exist in the same object:

> If I may judge from my own experience, it is only very slowly that the mind is opened out to a perception of images of Beauty co-existing in the same object with those of sublimity.
>
> *Prose Works,* ii, p. 360.

'Love & gentleness accompany the one . . . exaltation or awe are created by the other' (ibid., p. 349); and we are reminded of Wordsworth's verse of natural accompaniment and his verse of spiritual reappraisal: the necessity to see their difference but the necessity to see that difference as not for ever irrevocable. Such learning, that the sublime could also be beautiful, that for gentle motives one might have to work ungently upon one's resources, goes against the grain of one's simpler desires and against the belief that one's nature and emotions are immutable. Such a lesson Richard Jefferies had worked himself into the position of being unable to consider. Although not dealing specifically with Jefferies, chapters 3 and 4 will help to ask, if not to answer, why?

The aspect of this Wordsworthian flexibility with which I wish to conclude is that which is embodied in the test of seriousness that writing makes a man undergo. As we, reading backwards as it were, can see how down the lines of verse one word made for or became another by a kind of undercurrent, we can also recognize how at almost any moment in his writing Wordsworth was not only pushed from behind but pulling the past in front of him and changing it and re-working it, contingently, without anxiety as to his final security. . . . But these words, I fear, are no more than summary. Instead, let us look at one final example of greatness, for the sake of reality not summary.

At Christmas 1783, Wordsworth recalls, he was waiting with his brothers to make the return journey from school to home. He was on the look-out for the horses to fetch him home:

> . . . 'twas a day
> Stormy, and rough, and wild, and on the grass
> I sate, half-sheltered by a naked wall;
> Upon my right hand was a single sheep,
> A whistling hawthorn on my left, and there,
> Those two companions at my side, I watched
> With eyes intensely straining as the mist
> Gave intermitting prospect of the wood
> And plain beneath.
>
> *The Prelude,* 1798–9, p. 51 (ll. 341–9).

Within ten days of the arrival home, Wordsworth's father, his sole remaining parent, was dead. Perhaps it was the thought that he had been over-anxiously waiting to go home even as at home a man, whether he knew it or not, was waiting for death, that made the young Wordsworth feel the outcome of his impatience to be a chastisement as if from God. But an equivalent youth might have taken his own eagerness to get home to be evidence of a love of home to which fate was to show itself indifferent. Yet Wordsworth did not think that (—perhaps because his thoughts of home had not been thoughts of his father?). Wordsworth the writer does not reflect back subsequent events, as in Hardyesque irony. For the sentence which recorded the feeling of chastisement still goes on, as if ignoring its own temptation to antedate its subsequent knowledge:

> And afterwards the wind, and sleety rain,
> And all the business of the elements,
> The single sheep, and the one blasted tree,
> And the bleak music of that old stone wall,
> The noise of wood and water, and the mist
> Which on the line of each of those two roads
> Advanced in such indisputable shapes,

—He can barely finish the sentence, not because he is permanently unsatisfied like Jefferies, but as if its song, like that of the Solitary Reaper, could have no ending; for when the sentence does approach the end that we seem to have been waiting for, it is as if the main verb does not make for a clinching finality but is written parenthetically for the mere sake of syntax, sense and the reader:

> All these were spectacles and sounds to which
> I often would repair, and thence would drink
> As at a fountain,
>
>   Ibid., p. 52, ll. 361–70.

Obviously enough in the repetitions and rewordings between line 341 and line 370 certain words and phrases 'go together', carried by an under-current of memory that seems as if it will never die. Thus the day, the elements, the sheep, the tree, the wall, the prospect. But what is so marvellous about the second account of the memory ('And afterwards . . .') is that one feels that even as the list is being written in a new order, still, in order to do so, it is being simultaneously remembered in the old one. Such is the easy relation between change and continuity in the midst of a writing which is also a remembering. The 'intermitting prospect of the wood' is remembered now as 'The noise of wood and water, and the mist'—for memory grants him his hearing now where before it was subsumed by his greater conscious concern to see. Such casual restoration, contingent within the act of writing, betokens a calm of memory, the steadiness of a rich life lived, acknowledged, rather than craved for. We do not find this in Richard Jefferies but it is there, at the opening of his autobiography, in W. H. Hudson, writing on recovering from a near fatal illness:

> It is easy to fall into the delusion that the few things thus distinctly remembered and visualized are precisely those which were most important in our life, and on that account were saved by memory while all the rest has been permanently blotted out. That is indeed how our memory serves and fools us; for at some period of a man's life—at all events of some lives—in some rare state of the mind, it is all at once revealed to him as by a miracle that nothing is ever blotted out. . . .
>
> On the second day of my illness, during an interval of comparative ease, I fell into recollections of my childhood . . . the entire wide prospect beneath me made clearly visible. Over it all my eyes could range at will, choosing this or that point to dwell upon, to examine it in all its details; or in the case of some person known to me as a child, to follow his life till it ended or passed from sight; then to return to the same point again to repeat the process with other lives and resume my rambles in the old familiar haunts.[42]

The choosing of parts is there unpressured by the thought of being final and irrevocable; it is good that it is only partial, that we are greater than we know. Such choice in memory and writing seems supported by the emotion of memory which, being more in itself than it specifically recalls, both sanctions the good sense of loving selectiveness and declares the resulting partiality to be not irretrievable. The mind at such times finds a freedom to be less than (impossibly) comprehensive of the whole of the man's past life; but it knows that the whole of that life lies beneath it even so. If this is how W. H. Hudson felt on coming back into his life after grave illness, it is, I think, how Wordsworth felt at best when he wrote *The Prelude*.

So Wordsworth's sentence in memory of Christmas 1783 eventually comes to its end as follows:

> I often would repair, and thence would drink
> As at a fountain, and I do not doubt
> That in this later time when storm and rain
> Beat on my roof at midnight, or by day
> When I am in the woods, unknown to me
> The workings of my spirit thence are brought.
> *The Prelude*, 1798–9, p. 52 (ll. 369–74).

In the turnings and returnings between the lines, there works a spirit as of one who can contemplate change or realignment without their throwing into peril the moment, memory, thought or habit previous. The poet, like Hudson, seems strangely free, as if he were the spirit of himself, to take up no one finally privileged or responsible position in relation to the meaning of his own past experience. It is as if memory declares that the past is never finished, never exhausted. Once, twice, a third time he goes over it, different and yet kindred, super-seding and yet confirming, as things

> . . . through the turnings intricate of Verse,
> Present themselves as objects recognis'd
> In flashes, and with a glory scarce their own.
> *The Prelude*, 1805–6, v. 627–9.

—the meaning not owned but revealed by the turn of words and available again through them. By the third time through, Wordsworth has earned the right to say of such flashes, 'I do not doubt'; just as surely as, even in so doing, the memory also came back beneath him in the writing, 'unknown to me'. Who else could make kindred 'I do not doubt' and 'unknown to me'?

'"He looks before and after"' (*Prose Works*, i, p. 141). Wordsworth could move freely forward within writing which he also knew would compose and contain itself behind him— 'All these were spectacles and sounds to which . . .' he says, looking back and moving forward, consolidating and sustained. Within the recollection of emotion, Wordsworth's thinking also

reappraises it; a thinking which neither betrays its emotional
ancestry:

> For our continued influxes of feeling are modified and
> directed by our thoughts, which are indeed the represen-
> tatives of all our past feelings
>
> P⸱ ⸱se Works, i, p. 126.

nor sacrifices to its origins the inheritance of an autonomous
relation to them:

> instead of being restlessly propelled towards others in
> admiration or too hasty love, he makes it his prime
> business to understand himself
>
> Ibid., ii, p. 18.

*   *   *   *   *

At the end of this chapter am I in contradiction with myself by
putting forward a case for a poetry both of retrospectively-
manifest predestination and of a freely forward-moving
diversity? of religious teleology and yet of secular wandering?
It is true that this final section has concentrated on the
freedoms, improvizations and virtues which arise out of the
secular impossibility of finality. But this is not for the sake of
concluding with Coleridge that 'Every man is born an
Aristotelian or a Platonist'.[43] It is possible to oppose memory
as an intimation of immortality with memory as a sign of the
want of finality. But the purpose of this section on
Wordsworth's discretion is not to set up an opposition but to
say, with Wordsworth, that there is a finer connection than
that of contrast. He says it himself in his parable of Simonides
and the Sage, his greatest piece of prose:

> Simonides, it is related, upon landing in a strange country,
> found the corse of an unknown person lying by the sea-
> side; he buried it, and was honoured throughout Greece
> for the piety of that act. Another ancient Philosopher,
> chancing to fix his eyes upon a dead body, regarded the
> same with slight, if not with contempt; saying, 'See the
> shell of the flown bird!' But it is not to be supposed that
> the moral and tender-hearted Simonides was incapable of

the lofty movements of thought, to which that other Sage gave way at the moment while his soul was intent only upon the indestructible being; nor, on the other hand, that he, in whose sight a lifeless human body was of no more value than the worthless shell from which the living fowl had departed, would not, in a different mood of mind, have been affected by those earthly considerations which had incited the philosophic Poet to the performance of that pious duty. And with regard to this latter we may be assured that, if he had been destitute of the capability of communing with the more exalted thoughts that appertain to human nature, he would have cared no more for the corse of the stranger than for the dead body of a seal or porpoise which might have been cast up by the waves. We respect the corporeal frame of Man, not merely because it is the habitation of a rational, but of an immortal Soul. Each of these Sages was in sympathy with the best feelings of our nature; feelings which, though they seem opposite to each other, have another and a finer connection than that of contrast.—It is a connection formed through the subtle process by which, both in the natural and the moral world, qualities pass insensibly into their contraries, and things revolve upon each other. As, in sailing upon the orb of this planet, a voyage towards the regions where the sun sets, conducts gradually to the quarter where we have been accustomed to behold it come forth at its rising; and, in like manner, a voyage towards the east, the birth-place in our imagination of the morning, leads finally to the quarter where the sun is last seen when he departs from our eyes; so the contemplative Soul, travelling in the direction of mortality, advances to the country of everlasting life; and, in like manner, may she continue to explore those cheerful tracts, till she is brought back, for her advantage and benefit, to the land of transitory things—of sorrow and of tears.

Prose Works, ii, pp. 52–3.

This is a greater piece of thinking and feeling than Matthew Arnold's splitting of life, in *Culture and Anarchy*, into the mutually weakening alternatives of Hebraic moralism and

Hellenistic spirituality—a split offered for the polemic purpose
of urging the latter on Victorian England. But in Wordsworth
no polemic purpose could urge him to break the tender ties
between Simonides and the Sage. When Wordsworth stared at
the proposed gap between them, what he saw was the necessity
to maintain them both. Between the natural and the spiritual
man there are connections finer (in both senses of the word)
than those of contrast. Not for him life versus literature but a
writing which was in memory of living. A predestination which
does not harass freedom within it; a freedom which does not
doubt that it has, unknown to itself, rules that are still its own
and the expression of itself; these are levels, not opposites;
these are things revolving both within themselves and upon
each other. That 'subtle process', I believe, could not have
been sustained had Wordsworth not been a writer and a
poetic writer within the terms of his memory. In the midst of
his tale of Margaret, the Wanderer pauses; reminding us that
he also exists in a time outside that of the tale and after its end
in the death of the poor woman who had spoken so sadly to
him beneath the trees:

> And, looking up to those enormous elms,
> He said, ''Tis now the hour of deepest noon.
> At this still season of repose and peace,
> This hour when all things which are not at rest
> Are cheerful; while this multitude of flies
> With tuneful hum is filling all the air;
> Why should a tear be on an old Man's cheek?'

Is this, in resistance to what the Wanderer calls 'the weakness
of humanity', 'slight, if not contempt'? Why should he weep?
The Hardy who wrote *Tess of the d'Urbervilles* would surely
have answered: because of Tragedy, because she is dead after
long suffering, because he too, old and ineffectual, will die
soon. But the Wanderer does not ask his question because he
does not *know* that answer; he asks it despite that answer:

> 'Why should we thus, with an untoward mind,
> And in the weakness of humanity,
> From natural wisdom turn our hearts away;

To natural comfort shut our eyes and ears;
And, feeding on disquiet, thus disturb
The calm of nature with our restless thoughts?'
                    The Excursion, i, 592–604 (*P.W.,* v, p. 28).

The word 'natural' runs down those lines in soothing counterpoint to the words of dissonance ('disquiet', 'disturb'). For a
multitude of flies? a Hardy might protest. As flies to wanton
boys. . . . But the Sage does have a counter here. Why should a
tear be on an old Man's cheek? No tears if he can help himself:
because, admit it or not, there is the comfort of time and of
survival; because in 'the land of transitory things' there are
pauses and natural calms to interrupt even the supposed
permanence of sorrow and tears; because, above all perhaps,
he is an *old* Man and has no more necessity, let alone strength,
to vex a mortality that, anyway, will soon be taken from him.
The old man asks, 'Why should a tear be on an old Man's
cheek?', and our obvious reply is, 'because you too will die'.
But we would never dare speak that to him direct; and
Wordsworth will not use writing to make art say what it was
our reverence for life not to dare to say. 'Because you too will
die': he finds in that unspoken thought an echo which makes
the terms of the protest at suffering also the grounds for a
refusal to suffer further at this time. He will die, soon enough.
But the old Man does not therefore shrug off old sorrow: he
resumes the unhappy tale and picks up the memory again—
because one way of reverencing life need not preclude another
in that vast area between the country of everlasting life and the
land of transitory things.

PART II

JUST PROSE

3
Prosaic accounts

When, as must sometimes happen to everyone, people tell me, in a quite adult and sober way, about their lives' shortcomings and their struggle with inadequacy or personal difficulty, I am usually moved; although, on occasions, often through trouble of my own, I know I have been bored, angry, or uncomfortable instead. I do not want this common experience to sound portentous or pompous or sentimental. Even when I am moved, I think I have learnt by now that that of itself does not do the person who is telling me the tale much good. If it does give the person some temporary relief, I suppose that that is fair enough; though actually in a rather perverse and over-fussy way I get a bit prickly if I suspect that it is a performance to that end. Fine conscience aside however, all this is to say that when I report that I am usually moved by such things, I do not mean that, as far as I can tell, I actually make an emotional habit out of it. On the contrary, each time that such a thing does happen, it comes, I recall, with the force of a surprise and an eye-opener. I feel as if there are for the moment almost two people before me: the person who has, and suffers from, his or her shortcomings, and the person who knows all about that, can manage to put the knowledge into words, rationally and powerfully even, and wants to do something about it all. But what then strikes me as so moving and so surprising about human beings talking about their own lives is that those two people are actually, of course, one person, existing somehow together. Where I merely saw the person behaving badly or foolishly or awkwardly, as if not in possession of him- or herself, something in that person must have known what was going on, what was going wrong, even as it still went on happening; otherwise, where did the person who can now talk to me about such things come from? I take it that the speaker comes from the memory of his or her life, and

Notes and Bibliography begin on page 497.

that what finally emerges as memory begins as a latent
consciousness within the events which can later be recalled.
Memory is a power. In taking you back to your past, it also
tends to raise you above the past, where before you were in it.
The real effort lies in not letting this raised power be untrue to
the past which supports it.

Although such occasions open my eyes a little and, I
suppose, provide the other person with some relief and some
temporary sense of sharing and coping, my experience is that
nothing much is changed as a result. I am sorry if this sounds
over-gloomy. But the following week, or day even, the person
is still in trouble, I find, and the consciousness of that trouble
seems to be again crushed down within it rather than
remaining some higher, potentially redeeming power. But
even thus gloomily I do wonder whether the final authority
upon the meaning of such experiences should be Time's—the
disprover of the power of articulate consciousness, the
disillusioner on the following day, the subsequent disabuser of
warm emotions. And I sometimes wonder, perhaps idly and
naively, what would have happened if the person who once
spoke to me so movingly had written it down instead, had
been able to write it down, under different conventions from
those of speech, doubtless, but with equivalent emotional
impact? Would not that have consolidated, at least, the
temporary achievement? Or would it just have made me, a
sort of literary man, happier?

Of course, since most people do not write even at such times
of acute self-awareness, one feels grateful to the people who
have written. I think of things like that autobiographical fragment of William Godwin's from which I quoted in chapter 1:

> I am tormented about the opinions others may entertain
> of me; fearful of intruding myself, and of co-operating to
> my own humiliation. For this reason I have been, in a
> certain sense, unfortunate through life, making few
> acquaintances, losing them *in limine,* and by my fear
> producing the thing I fear.
>
> Kegan Paul: *William Godwin*, i, p. 359.

In such writing there is something very moving about the use
of the *present* tense in memory. Godwin can think of what is

wrong but also he cannot *get away* from it; he can write of it soberly and analytically, but *at the same time* he is still that man, as the writing acknowledges. 'I am tormented about the opinions others may entertain of me.' I find myself supposing that there are almost two men here: the writer, given substantiality and courage by the form and power of language, and the fearful man he is thinking of. But where it is now chic to quote Roland Barthes—'who *speaks* is not who *writes*, and who *writes* is not who *is*'—I want to know who it is who writes. And I think that the two people, as in my experience of confessional talk, are linked by memory and are still one person. The present tense here may well be the means by which a man may make formal sense in language where, informally, he cannot make peace with life. He is working here in a different system, a system of language, and can borrow strength from words. And yet, I also feel, the present tense here seems to mark Godwin's refusal to allow his formal language to disown its relation to himself; and if the language seems diagnostically detached from the predicament, it is not least because all its analytic intelligence is in effect helpless to relieve it. The man seems to brood upon the relation between his clarity and the irrevocableness of the facts which he is able so clearly to state. For the more there is felt to be a distinction between the act of writing as act and the reality of its subject-matter anterior to writing, the more both the writer when he is writing and the reader when he is reading are liable to make thought of that distinction an actual part of their literary experience. Godwin writes, as it were, this is what I am, even if I can now say so. The ability to say so and to recognize limitations is swallowed up completely in the saying itself, is absorbed in the achieved sense of those limitations. This is prose, the matter of fact, the medium in which men minutely confess themselves. There are no substantial pauses en route, although there are ends to sentences and paragraphs; there are no formal allowances for brevity in lieu of having to spell things out; there are no end-of-the-line lodging places for the spirit which composed the sense as in Wordsworth's poetry of memory. One reads to the end and for the end of the sentence, and one takes from its completion of its little narrative the sense which it arrives at, far more than any sense of its achievement in so doing. And yet to make a sentence can be an achievement and enable a person to get somewhere: '. . . and by my fear producing the thing I fear.' It is this idea of the prosaic which interests me in this second part of the book.

To generalize for the sake of introduction, it does seem to me that prose tends to surrender that power of unspoken resonance from a few words and in between a few words that was the subject of chapters 1 and 2. At the end of *Psychoanalysis and the Unconscious* Lawrence refers to that utterance of words which is not the beginning or the director of life, but the end of life, 'that which falls shed' from a life. In his *Testimony* Shostakovich tells of a pianist who told him how much he wanted to find 'a fresh approach' to playing the old classics. Shostakovich thought finally that you can't find a fresh approach, it has to find you—not by inspiration and only partly by sheer hard work. It usually comes to those who have a fresh approach to something else, to other aspects of life, to life in general. It must, that is to say, fall shed.

I think that the idea of sentences falling shed was one of Charles Dickens's major emotional interests. He could see just how sentences can be, quite seriously and yet quite casually so it seems, the product of a mass of experience felt as far greater than themselves; how sentences can be simply shed, left behind, by their writer, as he writes on with a verbal power that seems to come more from how he lived his life than from how he composed a style. And, being a novelist, Dickens can also see, almost deviously, how the way that such sentences seem merely to fall from a writer, affects us, the readers, all the more powerfully when we pick them up. Here for example is Dickens almost palpably listening to the words which his own protagonist David Copperfield sheds, as he recalls the plea to consider her as a 'child-wife' once made to him by his own (now deceased) Dora:

> . . . this one little speech was constantly in my memory. I may not have used it to the best account; I was young and inexperienced; but I never turned a deaf ear to its artless pleading. . . .
>
> I was a boyish husband as to years. I had known the softening influence of no other sorrows or experiences than

those recorded in these leaves. If I did any wrong, as I may have done much, I did it in mistaken love, and in my want of wisdom. I write the exact truth. It would avail me nothing to extenuate it now.

David Copperfield, pp. 550, 552.

These sentences fall from David, and Dickens wrote them in the name of Copperfield because, I think, he admired the way that such eloquence can be the natural product of a powerfully experienced life. I say 'natural' although, of course, here it is also the product of Dickens's art; an art which takes advantage of our sensation at such moments that there are almost two people present (the one who write of himself as well as the self of whom he writes), in order to conceal two people, Dickens and Copperfield, in one.

To think further about the additional complication of this being a novel is to anticipate the argument of this chapter. For the present, let us simply register the idea of words prosaically falling shed, and let me add one modification. The examples I have given have concerned people in trouble, and I have used such examples because I think that people generally feel the need to try harder for articulation when they are troubled; we often let joy simply pass. But the case does hold for the recollection of joy: as, for example, when De Quincey recalls how he felt as a young man waiting to meet his admired Wordsworth:

Never before or since can I reproach myself with having trembled at the approaching presence of any creature that is born of woman, excepting only, for once or twice in my life, woman herself.

Recollections, p. 128.

In the midst of this literary man's praise of his famous literary god there falls from him, almost incidentally, more ordinary memories that matter, in fact, quite as much to him. One or two girls shook the young man as much as did the famous poet. It is not merely ironical, it is lovely, and not least because the means to achieve this quite extra-literary memory are still literary—the movement from 'born of woman' to 'woman herself', like a birth throe of memory.

One does, I think, feel grateful for such things in our literature. And it is a gratitude that sometimes wildly spurs one on to the ideal, if I may put it thus, of a non-literary literature: a writing that fell from the lives of ordinary people rather than a profession with a code of taste and practice. Over-sentimentally, I am sometimes tempted thus to think: if only people could put their experience of trouble and joy simply into words, that too would make a claim for being literature. To put memories into words is a thing that sounds both proper and easy. But of course it depends not only upon the quality of the memories but also upon the quality of the words, and some people's words fall shed so much more powerfully than others'. There is no easy, natural, innocent commerce between the interior world and language, even if it seems to be one of the reasons why language should exist, to make our purposes known. There are styles to be won and lost, ways of putting things that conceal as much as reveal, compromises of meaning that have to be made and signalled. And so on.

And, more even than this, it is one of the hardest problems about literature to know whether the people who do write treat of the same experience as those who, in similar circumstances, do *not* bring themselves to pen and paper. Take the case of the person who for some moments can realize himself in conversation: 'why does he not write it down?' I tend to think. There are obvious answering guesses available. Perhaps he knows that he would not be proficient, on his own, in the sheer craft of writing. People find it hard to remember through writing the particular context that gave an occasion so much of its unspoken meaning. Or perhaps the person in question thinks, against the tendency of this book, that writing is not about ordinary troubles and joys, that writing is to do with things more important than his own life has thrown up. Perhaps writing would not be appropriate, even if available as an option; for speaking and being overheard provide a supportive context and a mercifully temporary occasion for brief, unrecorded catharsis. Perhaps speaking seems more like getting rid of trouble, writing more like storing it. Perhaps writing seems too serious and unforgettable, or too formally important and committing for troubles that one is sick of or humiliated by anyway. Perhaps the trouble or the joy is best left as potentially evanescent and unfixed. Perhaps in the movement of time there never does seem to be quite the right time properly to stop the course of one's life and judge it. It always seems premature, until perhaps it seems too late; and even when the judgement is made in depression, it is a judgement that seems to hate itself. Whatever my guesses, what I am suggesting is the real possibility that writing is sometimes a *solution*; where part of the interest and meaning of the *problem* was that the person concerned could not or did not want to write about it.

It is thoughts such as these that I want to leave complicating the endeavour, while I say, otherwise naively, that in this and the following chapter I am looking for texts of natural eloquence, words that fall from men's lives, books that tell me, prosaically enough, about people and their ways of feeling and living. For two things concern me here: that people can put their experience into words and that people can't. In what follows, I go to my chosen authors tacitly thinking, tell me what it was like to live like that, tell me what it felt like to think such things—even though I also know that there may be things that writing cannot tell. In this chapter, I shall be asking—so to speak—Hazlitt, Hood, and Dickens 'what it was like', while trying to provide sufficient historical context for the period from 1810 to 1850 to make the personal question possible.

I. ROMANTIC LEGACIES

The period after the emergence of the first-generation Romantics and up to the beginning of the rise of the great Victorian novel is one whose disturbances may only in the confidence of historians' hindsight be described as transitional. To do justice to its complexity would require a fuller, separate study. But one may say that it is a period that almost went missing. The sheer chronological facts show the problem. In 1821, for instance, the year in which Keats died, the Utilitarian, James Mill published his *Elements of Political Economy*. In the following year, in which Matthew Arnold was born, Shelley died. In 1824 Byron died in Greece; while Hazlitt, in the midst of writing against him, cut short an invective 'which was intended to meet his eye, not to insult his memory' (Hazlitt: *Works*, xi, p. 78). Yet, Hazlitt went on, 'As it is, we think it better and more like himself, to let what we had written stand' (ibid.). Clearly, then, through the premature loss of the second-generation Romantics some strange things happened in cultural memory of what we have come to call 'Romanticism'. It is, for example, a chronological curiosity typical of this period that Keats's letters to Fanny Brawne should only have appeared publicly for the first time in 1878. Such time-lags are astonishing to anyone seeking a straightforward literary history. The literary men of the following generation convinced themselves that the immediately preceding major literary figures had died too soon, leaving them an incomplete model of sensibility; yet some of the works of such figures were either published or valued too late. It is the most incredible of facts that 1850 was a year which saw the publication of both *The Prelude,* posthumously, and *In Memoriam,* two long poems of memory essentially separated by almost fifty years and also by more than just time. Any explanation as to why, in my view, no literary man coming after Wordsworth fully understood or benefited from the secrets of his wisdom must take into account these strange facts of chronology.

Such considerations make it extremely difficult to appraise the justice of the claim that I am most interested in—the claim in essence made by Matthew Arnold, that Romanticism had failed his generation. For even if what Matthew Arnold, in the generation immediately following, thought of as a Romantic problem did indeed have its roots in the experience of that earlier generation, still the problem may have been considered by men who did not even think of themselves as collectively 'Romantic' to be no problem at the time, but, say, a major challenge (for the Shelley of *Prometheus Unbound*) or a productive uncertainty (for the Keats of 'La Belle Dame sans Merci').

Nonetheless, amidst such difficulties it constitutes an important and helpful moment for us when Arnold produces as a touchstone an example from the letters of Keats where Romanticism does not fail. In 1880 Arnold claimed to have located the sort of spirit he was looking for in a letter from Keats to Benjamin Bailey on 23 January 1818, concerning the quarrels between others of Keats's friendship, Reynolds and Haydon, and Haydon and Hunt. For Arnold the following is, he says, more than mere words or a profession of faith, it is a virtuous act of sheerly practical reasoning:

> . . . It is unfortunate; men should bear with each other; there lives not the man who may not be cut up, aye, lashed to pieces, on his weakest side. The best of men have but a portion of good in them. . . . the sure way, Bailey, is first to know a man's faults, and then be passive. If, after that, he insensibly draws you towards him, then you have no power to break the link. Before I felt interested in either Reynolds or Haydon, I was well read in their faults; yet, knowing them, I have been cementing gradually with both. I have an affection for them both, for reasons almost opposite; and to both must I of necessity cling, supported always by the hope that when a little time, a few years, shall have tried me more fully in their esteem, I may be able to bring them together.
>
> Arnold: *Prose Works*, ix, p. 208.

'Practical' is the word that Arnold uses to applaud this prose, and it is an important word for him if he is to resist the criticisms made of him by men like Frederic Harrison and Henry Sidgwick, that the apostle of culture was more fit to study beauty than to act usefully. We too, if we are to defend our sense of words found almost incidentally as expressions of a way of living, need to know in what sense Keats's words could be said to be more than just words, but a moral act in themselves. Because this is such a difficult period let us accordingly think of this letter by facing two ways: back from Keats to an earlier generation and forward from him to a later one. For I want to ask: in what way is this 'practical'? what did it do for Keats's life? is this a touchstone, a guide, for men of the nineteenth century if they sought to live their lives by Arnold's 'the best that has been thought and said'?

Keats's words spring from a problem felt in its living context and worked out there by letter. The problem is the dilemma of a man who both knows, and knows that he shares, human weakness, as if he were two people at once. And it was for Keats an act of tender conscience not to separate but to compromise these two men. The man in him who possessed the usual human weaknesses could not simply continue to practise those weaknesses, unaffected by the thought of them. Knowing what men are and do, seeing how they display their own faults in (even rightly) finding fault with others, a knower, by virtue of his knowledge, could not simply, personally follow suit. Yet could he change himself just because he saw himself? and if he could change himself with respect to increasing his own moral humanity, what would be the cost in terms of those other qualities apart from weaknesses that he shared with other men? The man in him who knew human nature must have felt himself disturbed by the compunction which knowledge of a friend's faults might well cause with respect to the supposedly 'natural' warmths and spontaneous motives and duties of human friendship. Did he not now know too much, have to think too morally and deliberately, to be able to retain the instincts of emotion? 'The sure way, Bailey,' wrote Keats, steering thus between one difficulty and another, 'is first to know a man's faults, and then be passive. If, after that, he insensibly draws you towards him . . .'. What Keats was doing in that was not theoretical, in the sense that Godwin was theoretical in *Political Justice* when he drew up a number of principles of conduct and, in thinking of a number of test cases, tried to see how one could decide upon those principles' relative priority. Rather, Keats's principles, like his knowledge, are here kept as it were behind his forehead, lest his seeing them too clearly should make his emotional life all too mechanical. It is a personal solution, the taking up within the outlook of his own mind of a certain position: namely, Keats at twenty-three keeping the thoughts of an old head back behind the offered innocence of his youth. For the double impossibilities of knowledge of weakness without sharing of weakness and of perfection of principle without austerity of practice constituted for Keats a sanction to compromise the spiritual man and the natural man in one.

To Blake this would have been a species of atheism. When Blake specified the categories of imagination as opposed to memory, or of the spiritual man as opposed to the natural man, he saw the truth of those terms as a thing dialectically maintained through their mutual antagonism. A man who said he was in two minds was trying to trap the big polar opposites of the universe within his little head, within his little autobiography. Men were not properly in two minds; they swung, rather, to and fro between two forces, like the force of innocence and the force of experience. To Lavater's aphorism 'that the great art to love your enemy consists in never losing sight of MAN in him', Blake had countered as he would have replied to Keats's domestications:

> None can see the man in the enemy; if he is ignorantly so, he is not truly my enemy; if maliciously, not a man. I cannot love my enemy, for my enemy is not man but beast or devil, if I have any.
> Blake: *Complete Writings*, p. 72.

Where Keats puts his words in the service of the sense of a living situation which he feels shapes them, Blake puts personal perplexities ('ignorantly'? 'maliciously'?) to the test of an uncompromised language, a language whose truth measures, rather than is fitted to, autobiography. Blake tore his life between the words that he thought would disclose the truth in it: friend or enemy, innocence or experience, spiritual or natural, see their fighting claims upon each other. But Keats does not write, 'even the best of men have a portion of bad in them'; he compromises the dialectic and confuses the categories for the sake of a more tolerant, intermediate idea of a natural spirituality: 'The best of men have but a portion of good in them'. It is thus practical in the sense that on that way of putting it, rather than on the other, he proceeds; albeit a way that I am sure Blake would have thought of as an emotional compromise of knowledge. In this sense, the century belonged to Keats far more than to Blake, through the personal accommodation or domestication of large ethical tensions. If I may put it thus, nineteenth-century solutions tended to be individual and autobiographical rather than absolute and radical.

But there is another side to the history of Romanticism in nineteenth-century England, and it is a side that is less kind to Keats. It is a side that demands of this Romanticism, for all the claims made of it that it *is* 'practical', that it should be tested. Did Keats's wise letter have a practical effect not only upon the quality and conduct of his life but also upon its outcomes? could a letter be expected to? what was the practical result of being a writer? When Keats's letters to Fanny Brawne became public in 1878, Victorian readers could actually see how the sort of test that some Victorian literary critics wanted to apply to the Romantics had come upon Keats in the very course of his life.[1] A soon famous letter of 13 October 1819 shows how Keats's love for Fanny Brawne committed and bound his diffident spirit to a personal, sexual selfhood where it could not, as when writing to Bailey, be so generously or freely content with the twists and turns of human nature:

> —Love is my religion—I could die for that—I could die for you. My Creed is Love and you are its only tenet— You have ravish'd me away by a Power I cannot resist: and yet I could resist till I saw you; and even since I have seen you I have endeavoured often 'to reason against the reason of my Love'. I can do that no more—the pain would be too great— My Love is selfish— I cannot breathe without you.
>
> *Letters*, ii, pp. 223–4.

It is a letter which belongs with many others on the theme of whether he, now a sickly man, has the right to love her, to tell her that he does, to try to make her think of him and his feelings. And it was just this really rather vulnerable letter which Arnold singled out with a mixture of regret, embarrassment and sheer dislike.[2] For however much its publication was a regretable intrusion, it was still a revealing confirmation to Arnold that what lay beneath the literary skill would not prove to be strong and healthy. It was an example of that part of the Keatsian temperament which Arnold saw and deplored in the work of Maurice de Guérin (1810–39)—the French poet from whose letters Arnold translated the following as a symptomatic failure in the tests that life made upon literary models for living:

> 'I return, as you see, to my old brooding over the world of Nature, that line which my thoughts irresistibly take; a sort of passion which gives me enthusiasm, tears, bursts of joy, and an eternal food for musing; and yet I am neither

philosopher nor naturalist, nor anything learned whatsoever. There is one word which is the God of my
imagination, the tyrant, I ought rather to say, that
fascinates it, lures it onward, gives it work to do without
ceasing, and will finally carry it I know not where; the
word *life*.'

Arnold: *Prose Works*, iii, p. 31.

I think it fascinated Arnold that it was this sort of self-
devouring restlessness, rather than anything bearing the calm
of a Wordsworth, which was the example so many literary-
minded people in this period seemed to follow. '*Life*' as used
by Maurice de Guérin was a word of desire rather than
description, a word usurped by quasi-religion and having as
much to do with the poet's reading of his contemporaries as
with his living among men. 'Life' here is, in a more exaggerated
way, like 'Love' in Keats's letter: the creation of a secular God
and a religion of the emotions. And the only way that this sort
of temperament could avoid the thought that this God was
actually its own creation was to find that its God was so
apparently powerful and autonomous as to become its Tyrant!
What Arnold saw—so forcibly that it made him rather cruel to
the memory of Keats—was the almost self-congratulatory
surrender of mind to emotional objects partly of its own
creation. It was not 'life'; it was suicide.[3] It was, to use Cardinal
Newman's word, 'unreal'.

Now this Arnoldian view, whereby the letter of 23 January
1818 is a proper criticism of life where the letter of 13 October
1819 is not, does not seem to me to be all that, in the name of
fairness to a private as well as literary life, needs to be said
about Keats. However, for the moment, it is not fairness but
(to use Wordsworth's phrase) the history of feeling that is here
the point, however ambivalent we may feel as to whether
Arnold's critical defence of standards is a defence of life or an
affront to it.

The point is rather that there is good evidence to suggest a
difficulty in coming to terms with the sensibility of Keats in the
generation that followed him; and also that there is some
evidence for conjecture that there would have been objections
to that sensibility among some of the generation that preceded
him. I am aware that this talk of generations is, at best,

approximate and probably not open to absolute verification; that the differences between writers of the same generation may well be more significant than those between writers of different generations. All I ask is room to make a speculation which will take a little time to unfold. It is a speculation concerning the rise of prose among writers of the 1820s and 1830s—prior to the great age of novel writing and prior too to the literary emergence of the men of Arnold's generation. And it has to do with how writing stands to life's practice.

Consider first the evidence that we have brought forward. In 1818 Keats already knew that

> the best of men have but a portion of good in them.

What he then knew essentially, with respect to the general disposition of human affairs, he, by his own rule, less than two years later, came to know again accidentally of himself—

> My Love is selfish—

This is not necessarily surprising, and one need not on the basis of that juxtaposition leap to the conclusion that Arnold offered as a generalization in 'The Function of Criticism at the Present Time': that the knowledge of the Romantics was 'premature'. Perhaps, if one does accept the procedure of testing a man's professions by placing one part of his life against another, then in this case it serves to confirm the wisdom of 1818. But there is a perspective wherein the juxtaposition looks in practical terms ironic. Blake, for example, had seen the problem of the selfless and the selfish in love in dialectical terms in 'The Clod & The Pebble'. Now my guess is that Blake would have thought that if you do not see it dialectically, then through a species of revenge you have to live through it temporally. Try to compromise and what happens? you live to find by the end the horror of being unable to: 1818, 1819. This, I think, Blake had virtually predicted for the emotional life of the nineteenth century. In his poem 'Infant Joy' the new-born hope cries innocently

> 'I happy am
> Joy is my name.'

and in response there is, amidst congratulation, a disturbing
echo from a voice of experience

> Sweet joy befall thee!
>
> Blake: *Complete Writings*, p. 118.

Hinting, after all, at a separation of levels between the name in
language and the reality of fate, between emotional predisposition and the work of time, that second voice, lowering 'Joy'
to 'joy' however apparently sweetly, seems to know, but not to
say, what innocence will come to. That voice of experience
is a much more disturbing use of prophetic memory than
Wordsworth's sense of personal predestination for a life. For it
is that voice which says, here is Keats trying to be old and
young at once, trying to see human life and be a part of it at
the same time; let him have his overall view and live and write
from it; but then see him, a little older, beneath it at the end,
looking very young in sexual experience when life comes down
from verbal generalizations to really 'practical' tests of intimate
human particulars. Blake would have been much more harsh
than the Arnold who needed to make a religion out of culture,
when it came to assessing the 'practical' effects of Keats's
writing and wisdom.

Only a man like Wordsworth, I still think, could defy Blake's
categories and yet not be broken by the ironies of time:
because, in thinking and writing about any particular part of
his life, he came to feel himself supported by the underpresence
or tacit memory of the whole of his life. The meaning of the
'Immortality Ode' lies in just such a resistance to the irony of
time, when the later part of a life appears to betray the earlier
part. But if a man like Keats did remember in 1819 his wisdom
of 1818 and what had become of it, he could not but have been
seriously embarrassed. I think he would have felt as if his own
life were saying to him what, in another sphere, Hegel said to
Kant's ambitious and critical insistence that the knowing
subject ascertain the conditions of knowledge of which it is
capable *before* trusting its particular cognitions:

> to seek to know before we know is as absurd as the wise
> resolution of Scholasticus, not to venture into the water
> until he had learned to swim.[4]

It is a real question, what could men do but throw themselves into the water all too recklessly?

It was a Romantic legacy that the personal was the foundational, that out of personal experience came the real, as opposed to the notional, foundations of knowledge. So throw yourself into the water, don't just stand upon the bank. Emotional commitment was a tempting possibility for remaining securely, if tempestuously, in the personal subject and its desires. The commitment in an increasingly secular world to a base from which to live could well seem a solution. But what Arnold diagnosed in Maurice de Guérin, for example, was something effectively artificial in his throwing himself into the water. Emotional commitment to 'life' was all too liable to know itself partial while pretending to be integral. Very few people could explain to themselves formally why this might be so, but one at least was Coleridge who set it out in terms of the subject-object relation. His Idealism taught him that inside the relation of a subject to an object, there was for the subject a self-consciousness involving both his distinction from and also his relation to the object. On the personal level, for example, behind the apparent primacy of feelings is the very self-consciousness that we have them, a self-consciousness which itself cannot be an emotion since, by it, in feeling, we distinguish ourselves from the feelings as their subject. And, in general, such consciousness of the reciprocal relation between self and other must be wider than consciousness of the mere individuality of the self. Coleridge spoke of this wider-than-personal self-consciousness as 'the spirit', saying it was neither the subject nor the object but 'the identity of both':

> it can be conceived neither as infinite nor finite exclusively, but as the most original union of both. In the existence, in the reconciling, and the recurrence of this contradiction consists the process and mystery of production and life.[5]

That is to say: it is in between these two aspects of the self—the one that claimed the right to be exclusively personal; the other that knew what extra consciousness had to be jettisoned to support the idea of a merely separate self—that the real and particular mysteries of a life lay.[6]

Now the first part of my speculation is no more than to

suggest that there was a recurrent possibility of difficulty in the post-Romantic age with this idea of being as it were two men at once. Simply in illustration of this, I cite R. H. Hutton's criticism of *Amiel's Journal*, a work which became popular in England in the 1880s through its translation by Mrs Humphry Ward. Hutton saw in the work a representative danger for his age. The Swiss philosopher (1821–81) was forced into isolation when the aristocratic party deprived him of his professorship. In enforced isolation he wrote an account of what he thought happened to many of his generation by a more voluntary self-withdrawal. Able to reclaim neither an overall spiritual sense of the human disposition nor a specific point of view within it, Amiel felt himself instead becoming alternately a spectator of and an actor in his own life drama:

> I feel myself forced to feign a particular interest in my individual part, while all the time I am living in the confidence of the poet who is playing with all these agents which seem so important, and knows all that they are ignorant of. It is a strange grief obliges me to betake myself once more to my own little rôle, binding me closely to it, and warning me that I am going too far in imagining myself, because of my conversations with the poet, dispensed from taking up again my modest part of valet in the piece. Shakespeare must have experienced this feeling often, and 'Hamlet', I think, must express it somewhere.[7]

When Keats had written in his letter to Bailey, 'there lives not the man who may not be cut up, aye, lashed to pieces, on his weakest side', he was working not only from a personal but from a literary memory—of Shakespeare and 'use every man after his desert, and who shall 'scape whipping'. The situation of the Keats who loved Shakespeare and the Keats who loved Fanny Brawne becomes a terrible travesty of itself in these words of Amiel. That a man should stand to his own experience 'with an impartial imagination, as he would look at another person's or as Shakespeare might have looked at one of the characters he had created', as in Amiel's case, struck Hutton as evidence of 'the timidity of an excessive moral sensitiveness which made it intolerable for him to enter into the very heart of practical affairs'.[8] Again that word 'practical' signals a literary man's anxiety in this period, as if writing threatened to allow a man to withdraw from his social responsibilities and real life rather than afford the means for him spiritually and intellectually to lay hold of his natural existence. And even when 'strange grief' comes and returns such a man to the bounds of his physical experience, it appears in this context as a form of compensation and reassurance: which makes the emotion of grief and melancholy a strangely exploitable one for which a man might be secretly grateful. Arnold himself knew the experience of pining at pining in his verse; a grieving at grief which, as in *In Memoriam*, seems to be felt more powerfully in a removed sort of way than the original sorrow ever could have when it came to expression. That in itself, in the vicious emotional circles of the 1840s and 1850s, is an additional cause for grief in the school of defeated Keatsianism that leads to Tennyson.[9] That is the dead end which the cultural memory of a certain strain of Romanticism reached in Arnold's self-lamenting generation.

But before we get to that, there is a second part to my speculation. It is that Keats's situation as we have seen it in his letters could only really have been understood in 1820, say, rather than in 1880. Because in the 1820s there emerged a peculiarly vulnerable form of prose.

*   *   *   *   *

It is prose that in the 1820s begins to replace a poetry of autobiography and the lyrics of single, memorable feelings. It is worth trying to find out why.

While in retrospect Arnold noted the psychological danger established in the 1820s and 1830s by behaviour such as de Guérin's 'old brooding over the world of Nature', at the time there seems to have been rather different trouble for young men a decade or two older than Arnold himself. I refer to men like Carlyle's friend, John Sterling (1806–44), Carlyle himself, in Edinburgh in 1826 and in London in 1834, the Lake poet Charles Lloyd, writing *Desultory Thoughts in London* in 1821, or Thomas De Quincey. Their careers took these men, with their neo-Wordsworthian model of childhood memories of the love of nature within the countryside of their home, into the cities for their living. Halfway through *Confessions of an English Opium Eater* (a work which itself appeared in the year of Keats's death), there is an account of the meaning of this geographical dislocation of memory. The book records how the young De Quincey, fleeing from his guardians in the year 1802, wandered London's Oxford Street, longing for what he, through his reading, took to be his spiritual home—Wordsworth's Grasmere. As he writes of this in 1821, De Quincey feels pain in recalling that when in fact he did escape north what awaited him there was not poetry but opium; the stuff of his present authorship. In 1821 De Quincey was again in London, unhappy this time for having had to leave his wife behind in the house which the De Quinceys had taken over from the Wordsworths. Constrained by financial worries, De Quincey can only repeat the words of his earlier homesickness: 'Oh, that I had the wings of a dove . . . And *that* way I would fly for comfort' (*Writings*, iii, p. 378). But what happened before? He went that way to opium and his ruin. His Wordsworthian echo of the past words can hardly redeem the earlier irony, even though he desperately wants that poetic redemption of a fallen memory. In cases like De Quincey's, the feeling was not simply the luxurious restlessness that possessed a Maurice de Guérin or an Amiel. It was more prosaic and far less literary than that. For it was the much more specifically physical, economic, and urbanized experience of restlessness and displacement within the hastening, crowded, insanitary industrial cities. Romanticism had now to live in towns.

With such experience of a vertiginously broken security, it was De Quincey who could best understand cultural phenomena such as Coleridge's apparently voluntary and temperamental decision to leave the Lakes in 1810:

> There are *positive* torments from which the agitated mind shrinks in fear; but there are others *negative* in their nature, that is blank mementos of power extinct, and of faculties burnt out within us. And from both forms of anguish— from this twofold scourge—poor Coleridge fled, perhaps, in flying from the beauty of external nature.
>
> *Recollections,* p. 92.

The man was fleeing his memory; the only difference for younger men was that they were being driven and drawn away from theirs. It is a symptom of the century's secularization that men lodged their memories in landscapes, partly to find a more permanent hold for them there, partly to seek assurance that their otherwise lonely lives belonged on the earth. Ruskin noted this with respect to the way that men projected their feelings upon neutral, natural things—the phenomenon he called 'the pathetic fallacy'. What De Quincey thus recognized through Coleridge was the loss for his generation of a tacitly supportive, natural background to memory, in the very serious sense of feeling at home. Wordsworth was no use here; a legacy had got *him* back from London to Grasmere for ever. What that loss meant for the verbal expression of memory now was the necessity for prose: for a stationing, circumstantial account of how one's feelings arose and changed and became confused in estranged and dizzy relation to one's surroundings. But this very necessity for prose also threatened to be a defeated acknowledgement of the loss of lyricism and its conversion into report.[10] Hence *Confessions of an English Opium Eater*, treating of not only 'positive torments' but 'others negative in their nature'. It might not have been so bad if the negative torments served a lyric feeling of loss; what was worse was a further sense of a lost power to presume even to feel adequately what was lost. In London, 'you become aware that you are no longer noticed; nobody sees you; nobody hears you; nobody regards you; you do not even regard yourself' (*Writings*, i, p. 181).

This double-negative feeling—of loss so great as to threaten even the positive emotional acknowledgement of loss—dogs the history of nineteenth-century English literature, as if the emotional aspirations of Romanticism were both denied by reality and also denied the right to lament the fact. We shall see this in works as diverse as Dickens's *David Copperfield*, Ruskin's *Praeterita*, Tennyson's *In Memoriam*, and Hardy's poems. Where desires are proved to be 'unrealistic', it is hard to find reality for protest at their failure. It is, I believe, in the new impetus to write prose in the 1820s that this recognition is most vulnerably experienced, and I now propose to try to show this in one particular case—the case of William Hazlitt.

For it is Hazlitt, for reasons historical as well as temperamental, who would have been able to understand much better
than did Matthew Arnold what was involved in the letters of
John Keats.

In the case of Hazlitt, the story of the unfolding of a life
based upon essentially Romantic preconceptions offers
sceptical post-Romantics much scope for the observation of
the work of irony upon the aspirations of the Romantic spirit
in the practical course of time.[11]

Hazlitt's first published work, *An Essay upon the Principles of
Human Action,* established his Romantic credentials philosophically. Significantly, it was William Godwin who managed to
get it published for him in 1805. For Godwin, committed to
the idea of man's innate belief in justice, could not but approve
of Hazlitt's idealistic argument on behalf of the natural
disinterestedness of the human mind, as opposed to eighteenth-
century views of the essential priority of self and self-interest in
human nature.

More than anything, the young Hazlitt passionately believed
that the first principle of human nature was not the construct of
a self but the power of free emotions, like desire and aversion,
and hope and fear. These emotions were free in the sense of
being primary and unfettered by the subsequent habits of
thinking in terms of the self. We learn how to think in terms of
self-interest and harness our emotions to that end, but that is
not our first principle of being. The notion of personal,
motivating, responsible, calculating identity was a later fiction
created by memory, because memory is a faculty of selfhood
and makes us think in terms of ourselves. By the time we come
to remember our actions, that which at the time of acting
constituted the idea of the future for which we were aiming has
become absorbed into the memory of a settled past. The idea
of the future, the imagination through which we acted towards
a future, the idealism, in that sense, no longer exist save in
terms of what actually became of them. So we read our lives
backwards and read them wrongly in retrospect by 'clothing
ideal motives with a borrowed reality' (Hazlitt: *Works,* i,
p. 31). The tacit ideals implicit in our actions before 'the final
absorption of the idea in the object' (ibid., p. 32) become
swallowed into the social reality of their outcome; we hardly

remember them. All we remember are plausible little reasons why at that moment we may have had personal interests in doing this or that: we transfer the emotions of interest excited by particular positive feelings to the idea of our own interest generally speaking; thus we neglect big, primal instincts that implicitly pre-date the story of our little autobiographies. In truth we live forwards, and at the time of acting there is a sheer, energetic innocence in the heart of man. Desire is not naturally a calculator of consequences, interests and minute collateral circumstances; rather, there is something big in the very idea of a possible good which naturally excites desire. Similarly, there is something big in the very idea of danger—however much one also wishes to add circumstances that explain why then it was socially prudent to be cautious. It is imagination, the faculty of the future, that leads us to act, that prompts the emotions towards an idea of their future fulfilment, and the impulses thus generated are stronger and earlier than consideration of who will benefit in particular or the specific circumstances in which the opportunity this time is clothed. As Godwin himself put it, with respect to the fiction of the interests and motives of the self:

> A mysterious philosophy taught men to suppose that, when an object was already felt to be desirable, there was need of some distinct power to put the body in motion. But reason finds no ground for this supposition. . . . What indeed is preference but a feeling of something that really inheres, or is supposed to inhere in the objects themselves?[12]

The fiction of the prime need for an intervening medium of conscious thought is—not surprisingly—consciousness's own, a persuasion backdated through memory. I paraphrase Hazlitt's argument, but it is clear that he thinks of imagination as the prime instrument of sheer action, not just fiction, and of autobiographical explanation as secondary, through seeing how things are in terms of how they turn out.

Even so, the sceptic might ask, what became of this philosophy of Hazlitt's? how did a life founded upon it feel or turn out? was the philosophy strong enough to allow him to resist the implications of autobiography as it recommends? I know that these look like epistemologically crude questions; but historically, as we shall see again later, Romanticism was under this sort of pressure from Utilitarians when once literary lyricism was physically located within the problems of the industrial towns. And they are also, as I indicated in chapter 1, the sorts of question that Hazlitt himself, in defence of practical political thinking, felt bound to ask of the relation of living practice to written principle in the case of William Godwin, as discussed in *The Spirit of the Age.*

It is here that the new prose of the 1820s bears witness to the pressure of such implicit questioning. In 1823 Hazlitt published *Liber Amoris; or The New Pygmalion,* an anonymous but apparently autobiographical prose account of the practical upshot of (what we may now think of as) a Keatsian religion of love. What is more, it concerns a love affair the very unhappiness of which is complicated by a sensitiveness to social distinctions which disabuses the sorrow of any easy access to lyricism. For it concerns the love between Hazlitt himself and Sarah Walker, the daughter of his own landlord; and doubts of her sexual integrity become involved in thoughts of her class-position as helper of other lodgers besides himself:

> 'You say your regard is merely friendship, and that you are sorry I have ever felt anything more for you. Yet the first time I ever asked you, you let me kiss you. . . . Now if you did all this with me, a perfect stranger to you, and without any particular liking to me, must I not conclude you do so as a matter of course with everyone?—Or, if you do not do so with others, it was because you took a liking to me for some reason or other.'
>
> *Works,* ix, p. 107.

Choose, he says to her in effect, between being the whore of the house or the pure lover of but one of its inmates. And those alternatives are not so much things that he puts to her for her calm choice as they are indications of the splitting of his own anxiety into extremes. If she is not the former, she must be the latter: 'Her hatred of me must be great since my love of her could not overcome it!' (ibid., p. 119). He can find no areas of neutrality, indifference, vague stirring, the preliminaries of liking and attraction. This is prose trying to enclose an area untouched by the earlier generation of the Lake Poets—the area of sexual knowledge as potentially disillusioning and subversive of cherished ideals. And in trying to enclose that area ('Now if you did all this with me . . . Or, if you do not do so with others'), he knows as he speaks to her that she herself, above all the real issue, is getting away.

The form of this work involves putting the thoughts about the situation actually within the situation itself. What he thinks about Sarah he either tries to say to her direct or puts into writing to a male friend. And this procedure does not seem to be either one thing or another but a mixture. The mixture, that is to say, of a helpless incapacity in the lover to stay within himself, keeping at least some of his thoughts and doubts to himself; and of an idealistically naive honesty, not unlike the sincerity that Godwin commended—such that what is thought must be spoken as a matter of conscience rather than merely indulgence, because of the innate duty that people have not to be solitary but to use their thinking to take a practical part in and try to affect the reality of its subject matter. It is a directness, but when we see it in the form of dialogue and letters it also seems that he is talking or writing to himself.

It is thus an extraordinary work, which does not seem to be authorially created so much as painfully transcribed. It appears as work which does not want to be precipitated out into merely eventual solutions or into the conventional world of Literature; rather, the more the anguished lover within it cries for alternatives and answers, the more the work seems to want to hold itself within that sense of remaining a mixture in the middle of life. For the dialogue form silently means that there is more than the needs of the protagonist involved. When the dialogue form breaks down through Sarah's silences, the man is left wildly unable to maintain the dialogue within himself; for that self feels merely like the relic of unconsummated dialogue outside:

> Shall I not love her for herself alone, in spite of fickleness and folly? To love her for her regard to me, is not to love her, but myself. She has robbed me of herself: shall she also rob me of my love of her?

Ibid., p. 133.

This is a man trying to double within his own head what does not have its true reality inside there. He cannot speak for both of them to himself, and when he tries to do so, what does that 'himself' reply? It tells him in the passage above that he must not lose his love twice over: once as a person, once again as an emotion. But the idea of love's constancy ought to lie in his seeing no such absolute separation between the two. 'To love her for her regard to me, is not to love her, but myself' is a powerful and moving thought but an almost irrelevant one. It wants the dialogue-retort: it is not loving her to think that love has absolutely nothing to do with your self, with how she treats you, or with the status in which she allows your emotion to stand in relation to her. The literary lover thinks of Shakespeare here, 'Love is not love that alters when it alteration finds'; but he might also have thought of Donne: 'it cannot be/Love, till I love her, that loves me'. As it is, the lover here faces the most terrifyingly prosaic thought that can confront an advocate of the primacy of the emotions: the thought that there is a possible distinction between the object of his love, Sarah, and the cause of his love. If the cause has also to do with him, how much then has he to do with her in his love? It is a simple thought, but its effect is utterly confusing. And in the speech above, under pressure, the lover too precisely fabricates his love's autonomy, for the sake of what is really his own servitude to it.

It is because this confusion of feeling within his mind is the result of a situation which originates from more than one mind, that Hazlitt took himself to prose for its capacity for dialogue. For dialogue was a model of his trouble, a formal recognition of the necessity for relativism in love, rather than an impossibly introspective monologue. As we have seen, when he is left doubling for her in his own head, the loss of dialogue and his own compensation for that loss betray him into an inner dialectic of verbal extremes: 'The sense I have of (her) beauty raises me for a moment above myself, but depresses me afterwards, when I recollect how it is thrown away in vain admiration' (p. 130).

Memory might conclude that this affair, as it proved to turn out, was much ado—rather sordidly and embarrassingly—about nothing: the literary man in love, or some such, with the more knowing working girl. He says to her, post hoc, 'the first time I ever asked you, you let me kiss you . . . if you did all this with me, a perfect stranger to you, and without any particular liking to me . . .'. But what was *he* thinking at the time? that he was a perfect stranger to the girl, that he was getting this far, that she was therefore easy meat? I think probably not, at any rate not explicitly, because it seems that Hazlitt needed to think of the episode as the beginning of the 'real thing'. His was a generation with increased expectations of love that had to wait too long for it apparently to come along: 'You are the only woman that ever made me think she loved me' (ibid., p. 109). Having waited too long, he feared both to test and to leave untested this chance of the real thing:

> After exciting her wayward desires . . . I did not proceed to gratify them, or follow up my advantage by any action which should declare, 'I think you a common adventurer, and will see whether you are so or not!' Yet any one but a credulous fool like me would have made the experiment, with whatever violence to himself, as a matter of life and death, for I had every reason to distrust appearances.
>
> Ibid., p. 128

But he made his hesitation a form of ardour, lest what might have been the beginning of love should become no more than sexual exploitation, lest an endeavour to follow an experience through its own natural course should precipitately degenerate into one person's violent experimentation upon life. This is an ideal, in resisting the absorption of big emotions into banal outcomes, the absorption 'of the idea of the object'; but it is also mixed with the thought of a shrinking from reality. For the source of fear, which dialogue tries to allay through bringing Sarah to verbal account, is that she has a separate mind, even as her body clings to him. In memory his idealistic impulses are thus betrayed into the following way of seeing it:

> Had I not reason to be jealous of every appearance of familiarity with others, knowing how easy she had been with me at first, and that she only grew shy when I did not take further liberties?
>
> P. 132.

His emotions over her have, as it were, dropped a class, towards sex and selfishness. Imagination becomes trapped within memory: if with me then, he suspects, why not with others before and later? This is what the young Hazlitt had warned about the growth of habits of self-interest in life: that memory would turn round, as by a species of jealousy, and annex the past to the emotional interests of the present. The older man's suspicion is that some pasts simply head towards their future death from the very beginning, having no way to go but to the vacuity of disappointment and the bitter confirmations of retrospective irony. There was no future in any of it. Are these the rules of the reality game then, that to delay the enticing danger of sex only allows the woman time to see the tameness of the man's desire for love? Better he should not hesitate than seek compassion for his flattering weakness by making his socially discomforting demands be taken seriously? A reader may find it over-harsh to think: this is what the young philosopher of the relation between the emotions and reality has come to! But the experience of high impersonal ideals too long held within a man in lieu of a personal life is part of the meaning of the debasement here. And however we may try to draw out of these examples a more gentle idea of the relation between what a man writes and how a man lives and the changes in the two, not necessarily synchronous, over the years, nonetheless it is true here that the spiritual man and the natural man seem to have taken revenge upon each other for mutual ignorance.

And yet, even so, *Liber Amoris* is still essentially in line with the youthful *Essay on the Principles of Human Action* with respect to the formal way that, despite the protagonist, dialogue keeps the memory of the affair out of the boundedness of one-sided selfhood. There is no doubt that the protagonist is Hazlitt, but there was also something in Hazlitt, to do with love but also to do with sheer extra-personal curiosity about ways of living, that wanted to know the other side. Thus when the lover puts to Sarah the question why she kissed him so freely the first time, if it was not that she really liked him, he gets the reply:

'It was gratitude, Sir, for different obligations'.
P. 107.

A prose which is a response to the dislocations of the 1820s is likely to be thus sensitive to the way love is 'socialised' on a secondary level into obligation and gratitude, humiliating the high Romantic principles of human nature. 'Sir'! But what is equally interesting here is the way that the form resists the self-enclosing conclusiveness of memory. For there is no way of checking whether Sarah's words are the truth, or the excuse of a common flirt—no way for us any more than for the man who first heard them. For that reply, locked into the ask-and-reply speech mechanisms of a present, is uncheckable with respect to the truth of the past; but even if it is not factual with respect to the past, the sickening thought is that it is present all too factually now, dissolving the question and the whole meaning of the past into the mere surface relativism of speech and counter-speech. That is how reality can simply leave you standing. Left stranded, the Hazlitt who stood there thus disabused and disillusioned, without even knowing whether he was disabused by truth or merely kept off with words, had no position left to take up but that of writer, looking to both sides of the story, although he has only known one.

Hazlitt was two men by the time he came to write *Liber Amoris*. One was the lover, who could not simply believe that it did not matter what the truth of the past was, when the present declared that, *whatever* it had been, the affair was now over. A Romantic, he still cared more, if I may put it thus, for the answers of Truth than for the upshots of Reality, if such a distinction could be sanely maintained. He is almost convinced that Sarah was indeed of a light character, however she thought of herself, but

> I strive to think she always was what I now know she is; but I have great difficulty in it, and can hardly believe but she still *is* what she so long *seemed*.
>
> P. 160.

Hazlitt found in such situations that the nature of his emotion indicated a relation to the external world in which the latter was something he was separated from and yet affected by. The problem is not only that what she 'seemed' to his loving eyes and what she 'is' are not at all the same; the problem is also that they are not quite separate either. Granted, the emotions may create what they are moved by, yet what they are moved by may nonetheless be independently true. Sometimes he sees how she who is the object of his emotion restricts the range of what he can think and feel as appropriately referring to her. At other times, he knows that his emotional beliefs about her nature are making 'her' affect him. He can neither cling to nor escape from his own point of view. He is a collusive victim of what I think is a Romantic contradiction: wanting emotion to be both a primary power within an individual and also a secondary sign of vulnerable dependence upon the object of its commitment. He feels himself pulled apart between these two forces. In his *Essay* Hazlitt had argued that 'we take the tablets of memory, reverse them, and stamp the image of self on that' (*Works,* i, p. 5). The sort of memory which demands that a newly discovered truth either abolishes or is abolished by the conviction previous to it, declares that the light character which she is, in so far as it is her character, is the light character she always was. But in the *Essay* he also said that there is an 'insurmountable barrier between the present, and the future' (p. 11); imagination cannot believe in the future that memory now declares to have been its fate. Imagination cannot imagine, still, but that she is as perfect as he always imagined her. He cannot bring the two faculties, their two versions, together. Memory attests to the reality of events, imagination to the truth of feeling; their criteria, like past and future, do not seem to touch. Hazlitt had set out those criteria at the very beginning of his reflective life, and I doubt that a man can commit himself thus in writing with impunity as to the effect upon the rest of his life. For certainly the memory of those principles and criteria remained with Hazlitt in his experience with Sarah Walker. And he could not bring together his expectations of experience with experience itself, however much he tried on for size convenient emotions like bitterness or disgust.

The other man, that second consciousness that seems to stay back critically behind the presented commitments and mistakes, is the one who, after all the furies of the emotional man, is left with a sensation of floating, unable to mediate between the faculties of memory and imagination or between internal feelings and the person to whom they are meant to refer. The other man, in part created by the very failure of personal commitment in the lover, is the writer here. For the book exists in the dimension of a floating present tense, holding its life as it were in a melting-pot. The beloved Sarah, for instance, at one point complains to Hazlitt:

> 'I own I have been guilty of improprieties, which you have gone and repeated, not only in the house, but out of it; so that it has come to my ears from various quarters, as if I was a light character.'
>
> P. 151.

This prose of the present offers itself as report, yet it is not only immediacy, apparently unmediated by authorship, that one feels. Try asking why Hazlitt did not only report this in writing but actually, albeit anonymously, published what he had 'gone and repeated' thus. One could try to find, from a series of collateral circumstances, plausible reasons.[13] But I think Hazlitt's *Essay* is right to suggest a more primal naivety before reasons and intentions. For the presence of dialogue in *Liber Amoris* means that the work itself is neither an act of self-love nor one of benevolence but an act prior to responsibility for itself, without an axe to grind. So much seems to be prior to the settling of memory; a present still in the act of stabilizing itself into language by recall, the real meaning of it still uncertain. Yet one does not feel simply immediacy, as if this were written very quickly and very soon after the events it refers to. It also seems to be a present which not only cannot yet realize itself as past but has not the resonance either to aspire to a future. There is something in these segments of the present which implicitly predicts its own failure to lead on. This work was written because the present which it describes felt unreal and unresolved, and such suspended animation feels paradoxical as if a man had to do something about it when there is nothing he can do. He writes accordingly like this:

> My esteem for her amounted to adoration. 'She did not want adoration.' It was only when anything happened to imply that I had been mistaken, that I committed any extravagance, because I could not bear to think her short of perfection. 'She was far from perfection' she replied, with an air and manner (oh, my God!) as near it as possible.
>
> P. 151.

That, coming near the end of the book, where the book is catching up finally with its own fruitlessness, corresponds most to the condition in which it was written: a condition of redundant consciousness. It is the consciousness which inhabits the space between

My esteem for her amounted to adoration

and

'She did not want adoration.'

For there the author, standing in memory of the lover's helplessness, sees the whole situation with the voices, now disembodied, set down before his eyes, and yet he knows that in that situation he could always have done very little more than had already been done. The gap between the sentences is unbridgeable, like the space between the protagonists. Only prose could be so flat and so resistant. For that sentence 'My esteem for her amounted to adoration' is, first, the report of a speech which she refused, and, second, despite that, a confirmation of a fact of the past which still survives her refusal. But that second point cannot in this sort of prose redeem the first; it is stuck in it with all this prose's fidelity to an intransigent reality. The author cannot rise above the spectacle of his own failure as here recorded without feeling merely apart from it; there is no position for the sort of wisdom that thinks 'I now see what was wrong; next time I could use this experience to get it right'. There is in this floating feeling no position of judicious first-person authority available. And he knows this, as is shown by the way that he does not write, for Sarah, 'I do not want adoration', but 'She did not want adoration'; the change of pronoun and tense indicating that he cannot get away from this fact, that it is something that he could never find an answer to but had to repeat, as if in shock that this was the end; it is the ever-present form of the past. And when he looks back in between 'My esteem for her amounted to adoration' and 'She did not want adoration', he sees behind the reality of what is what all the ideals and emotions that were lost in it. The prose puts it down, matter of fact, and goes on past it; time could not be held up so easily in the busier urban world. The pace and the facts of life had changed. And this suited prose, prose suited this, the medium commonly thought of as lower in status and in reference than the heights of divine poesy. It was everyday. And so in passing he can hardly get his sense of the transcendental out of its deflating embeddedness:

> 'She was far from perfection' she replied, with an air and manner (oh, my God!) as near it as possible.

—'(oh, my God)' leaves the man's emotion a parenthesis in nature, a lonely thing set apart in his own head, without anyone to hear it or respond to it, so that it is less a prayer or a revelation than an expletive in a London street. All the author can do is include it; he cannot save it. His sense of an overview is no right that he can assert; he floats rather, unable to remain in an implicated point of view, such as the lover's, because of its discredited humiliation; yet unable to get anywhere securely beyond that point of view because of the shock of its unresolved defeatedness. '"She was far from perfection" she replied': there is the fact of defeat in reality; 'she replied, with an air and manner . . . as near it as possible': there, still after that defeat, he cannot believe but that even in that he was also triumphantly right, without avail. In being an author under such circumstances there is, at best, a no more than temporary possibility to gain positive power from the memory of those defeats by battening upon them; even while, in their negative workings, the effects of those defeats are encroaching upon the man's very ability to *be* an author of the seriously personal. For Hazlitt here, to be an author is very close to being a victim; one whose higher consciousness can only find expression within the prosaic facts of its own entrapped ruin in the physical and social world. The anonymity of *Liber Amoris* at the time of its initial publication is all too appropriate, for it was not written by a man who could live in the restricted and defeated individualism of the book's protagonist, nor was it written by one who could yet live in any real sense outside that defeated self. A bigness had been lost in puny realizations, when what a man turned out to be was so much less than all that, within him, he had been able to imagine and to feel. His book challenges the mind to a view of a life in which mind itself, so far from being (even if only in writing) a controller, is no more than part of the reality within which it operated. This is the sober side to that excited setting up of the idea of a power called 'life' which men like Maurice de Guérin indulged in. However much the individual might want control of his own life, there was a strain of Romanticism which did not believe that its concepts did or indeed should have the power of sovereignty over what they were indeed enriched by describing and referring to. It was right, as well as dangerous, that the loved one was more than one's love for her.[14]

Liber Amoris was written, was managed, almost literally by no one. It is not that the book is simply written by 'life', a transcript of what actually happened, innocent of a shaping authority: that we cannot know and can hardly accept. But if it is not innocent of an author, it is almost in contempt of the possibility and presumption of one. No one and no one view has the right to stand over this text. Even its authorship was not achieved through sheer first-person authority. So much for Romanticism made prosaic.

* * * * *

So why did anyone think that he had the right, or had to find the right, to stand over and test authors like Keats and Hazlitt? Why did nineteenth-century men of letters, in the name of responsibility and practicality, have to do this to the so-called Romantics or to what they thought of as the legacy of Romanticism within themselves?

The way that Hazlitt or De Quincey gained literary power out of the defeat of uncertain feelings was not the mere matter of strategy that men of the subsequent generation suspected. For two reasons. First, writers like Hazlitt and De Quincey would not have recognized the word 'strategy' and, for the sake of the power for which they were already having to risk so much, could not have afforded perhaps to want to recognize it. Second, by the time that they could be described as strategies, by that very token they had become more explicitly post-Romantic problems. Leslie Stephen, born in 1832, complained about the strategies of 'the true Rousseau logic', as he called it:

> Everything must be right in some transcendental sense, because in an actual sense everything is wrong.[15]

The idea of justice, for instance, is created precisely by its own absence, precisely by being lamented over as wanting. What a man of Stephen's time was asking was whether such 'justice' was anything more than what a Romantic man wanted: what he merely desired, that is to say, where what he desired was merely what he lacked rather than what necessarily was owing to him. Emotions were beginning to be seen as strategical rather than natural. R. H. Hutton took the weight of what had happened. On one side of Romanticism there was Shelley:

> Other lyrical poets write of what they feel, but Shelley of what he *wants* to feel.[16]

On the other side, as a result of Romanticism's history, there was Clough:

> The effect on his poetry is to exercise his imagination in depicting not so much universal feeings as the craving of the cultivated mind for permission to surrender itself to them.[17]

It was as if the mind described as Clough's was determined by a Victorian reaction to the consciousness of inheriting the overwhelming desire attributed to Shelleyan Romanticism. What was it that was putting pressure on Hazlitt in the 1820s and put increased pressure on literary men throughout the remainder of the century? What was it that made Arnold's generation test and doubt, I say, the feelings which they believed had been passed on to them from the generation before?

A central answer lies in a memoir which looks back over the period 1810–40, and in keeping with that period's strange chronology, it is a work itself begun in 1853, not finally completed until 1870 and published posthumously in 1873. It is the *Autobiography* of John Stuart Mill.

Mill rightly identifies his father, James Mill (1773–1836), with that Benthamite Utilitarianism which was partly a product of and partly a response to the social and economic upheaval caused by rapid industrialization. What is more, Mill sees how that philosophy, with only a few absolute adherents, managed, on behalf of the aim of a wider social, material human happiness, to make a strong attack upon the

apparent luxury of Romantic lyric individualism. Thus of
James Mill:

> For passionate emotions of all sorts, and for everything
> which has been said or written in exaltation of them, he
> professed the greatest contempt. He regarded them as a
> form of madness. 'The intense' was with him a bye-word
> of scornful disapprobation. He regarded as an aberration
> of the moral standard of modern times, compared with
> that of the ancients, the great stress laid upon feeling.
> Feelings as such, he considered to be no proper subjects of
> praise or blame.
>
> John Stuart Mill: *Autobiography*, p. 31.

This was something more than merely prejudice. It was part of
a formal analysis which, through Bentham, revealed 'selfish
interest in the form of class-interest'.[18] Men could offer you
words like 'life' and 'nature', but beneath them you could see
the particular interests of a certain class and of a certain
culture. And this was indeed persuasive. For however much
Hazlitt might disagree with Bentham over the nature of
emotion, he was also deeply moved by the idea of testing the
use of political writing with respect to what it might suggest
could be practically done for the masses; indeed Bentham
himself failed the utility test on just these grounds, according
to Hazlitt. What had been the use of feeling? was a compelling
question in the new social conditions and in the new responsibilities devolving upon the intelligent middle-class for the
government of the country. What had been the practical effect
of Romantic feeling? 'As I proceeded farther,' writes John
Stuart Mill of his reading of Bentham, 'there seemed to be
added to this intellectual clearness, the most inspiring prospects
of practical improvement in human affairs' (*Autobiography*,
p. 42). Government, law, mutual interests, material welfare,
political economy: these were not, could not afford to be, 'left
in the dominion of vague feeling or inexplicable internal
conviction' but were to be 'made a matter of reason and
calculation'.[19] It was becoming increasingly difficult for men to
ignore the social changes and miseries of the nation; yet here,
it might be said, was a radical like Hazlitt occupying himself

by writing of love for his landlord's daughter—what James Mill would call 'a form of madness' indeed.

Literary men could try to line up against the Utilitarians in the way that Macaulay did against James Mill:

> Utility was denounced as cold calculation; political economy as hard-hearted; anti-population doctrines as repulsive to the natural feelings of mankind. We retorted by the word 'sentimentality' which, along with 'declamations' and 'vague generalities' served us as common terms of opprobrium.
>
> John Stuart Mill: *Autobiography*, p. 67.

And it is true that Carlyle, Hutton, and Arnold, among others, did speak powerfully for those who were not Utilitarians. In a review of J. S. Mill's *Utilitarianism* in *The Spectator* for 11 April 1863, Hutton, for instance, argued that without the work of conscience there was no bridge over the chasm between self interest and general human interest, there was no good reason for a man to be useful except to himself. In 1829 it had been Macaulay's case against James Mill that Utilitarianism, in this vital ethical respect, was itself 'useless'. And yet, increasingly, men could not guiltlessly resist the criticisms against feeling without themselves doubting feeling and needing to test it. Literary-minded people of the second and third quarters of the century had inherited a model of feeling which, if it could not be held directly responsible for the prevailing social conditions, was at any rate not easily suited to the present social changes. The effect upon Victorian intellectuals was profoundly destabilizing. Prose, the ordinary language of more people, the language in which to try to speak socially or in which to try to sort things out in relation to contingent circumstances, emerged powerfully as a complex response. John Stuart Mill himself wrote in articles such as 'The Spirit of the Age' in the *Examiner* of the new responsibilities that had to be taken up by the middle-classes for the sake of the life of the nation in a changing industrial world. And part of that responsibility, perhaps, was exercised in a rallying to the defence of so-called 'natural' feelings and pieties of family, creed, and country. This was not a Romantic reaction, these were not the same feelings as those of Keats or Hazlitt; more particularly,

they were not feelings that could be described as useless—
almost the contrary.

Utilitarianism was thus not defeated, it was compromised.
The story of John Stuart Mill's own nervous breakdown and
partial recantation is well known: it includes his turning to
poetry and his finding support from Coleridge in making
criticisms upon Utilitarianism's want of understanding of the
complexity of feeling. But Mill's defence of poetry is still a
relegated defence, containing a tacit admission that a powerful
lyricism had now no power to get near current political
realities. It was too 'high' for that. Poetry was a form of
compensation and repentance for Mill, but poetic feeling was
still never for him a form of thought or a form of action.
Reviewing Tennyson, he warned the poet not to depend upon
thoughts which appealed more to poetry than to reason. Even
Arnold ruled Wordsworth's 'philosophy' out of his selection of
the poems. The realm appropriate to poetry was shrinking; a
man could not bring his whole self there. Mill expresses
gratitude to Wordsworth because the poetry, Mill believed,
helped him over his breakdown; but when he comes to explain
what it was in Wordsworth that saved him, it really is the
expression of no more than sentimental nostalgia on Mill's
part. What Wordsworth stood for was Mill's miscalculation in
not giving more allowance to the necessary luxury of feeling
tucked within one's private life. But, as a Utilitarian might
ask, what had Shelley's emotive politics done for London?
what use was he even to his own family? Romanticism was
forced down from the heights of poetic isolation towards prose.[20]

Really, what was Wordsworth to most literary men in the
last twenty years of his life until his death in 1850? To De
Quincey and Hazlitt, a memory that they had left behind, a
mentor who withdrew his favour from them, damagingly. To
others, an old man, now grown merely conservative in politics
and religion; the socialized survivor of an age of false dawn,
still living on, remote in the Lake District. I have tried to
indicate the reasons why I think that Wordsworth, for all the
eventual obeisance paid by Arnold and by Mill, was not a real
force in the moral thinking that nineteenth-century literary
men drew from literature.

The reasons lie in the strange facts of chronology and in the sudden social, economic, and political changes in England. Where men did see a wisdom in past writers, it was a wisdom which either did not appear to be directly applicable to the new circumstances, or, for men under pressure from Utilitarianism, constituted a retreat into cultural nostalgia. The central Wordsworthian belief that love of Nature leads to love of Man was merely left behind by those whose memories were being physically uprooted and damaged by the subsequent resettlement. By the time men like Arnold did turn back to Wordsworth, it was a turn which, too late, had more to do with a conservative, literary defensiveness than with Wordsworth himself. Wordsworth's essential subject-matter was left behind through the accidents of time. Yet on the other hand, there were areas of human subject-matter that Wordsworth had not dealt in; in a later age, which needed to test high feelings in the force of physical circumstances, it was just such areas, such as the sexual one, that, like an uneasy bequest, seemed then to have to be treated of or disposed of more urgently. Only, the very urgency of the predicament precipitated writers such as Hazlitt into forms of thought and expression that Wordsworth himself would have recognized as signs of the pressure of defeat: as, for example, the splitting of experience into mutually incompatible extremes of high and low, imaginative and realistic, calculating and frenzied. Wordsworth saw the way that things in the human psyche could go, and he chose and worked hard not to go that way, as he watched the Hazlitts and the Charles Lloyds, victims of a cultural pressure that only greater men had been able to sustain.[21]

If it is true, why does it matter, even so, that Wordsworth for largely historical reasons was in essence forgotten? In itself perhaps it was not disastrous, for no one ever could simply have learnt from Wordsworth. But it does matter as a sign, as a major symptom—not only of a more general loss of faith in poetry, but of the trouble that, after 1820, many literary people felt in considering their own lives. Memory became a harder thing to live with, a harder thing to know what to do with, when people could no longer expect to stay in the home of their childhood. There was, literally then, a new adult world, full of tests, in which one had to find a way and make a home as well as a living.

One reaction to this increased pressure, internal and external, was that of the prose Romantics of the 1820s. If there was pressure, let it be used to pull life and identity apart; if there was a humiliation, disappointment and reduction of the possibilities of a life, let those forces make a man see what was left after them. They would live past and through their own losses. But this was a long road of Romantic disillusionment; a road that led, so to speak, to Thomas Hardy, to an end in pessimism and to a sense of life as barely adequate to the human spirit. And the journey could hardly be sustained by the thought of heroism, since that too was part of what was stripped away, if one survived.

It is a quite other reaction which, I would say, characterized the Victorian response, however diverse the personalities within that age. It is the reaction that the young Hazlitt both diagnosed and resented: throwing oneself upon the reality-principle. The idea of the inward springs of life—bigger than ideas of personal identity and self-interest—was surrendered to an alternative idea of adjustment to and accommodation within the force of external circumstances hypothesized as 'reality'. Private emotions were a secondary refuge. The most popular poem of Wordsworth's in the Victorian age was probably his 'Ode: Intimations of Immortality from Recollections of Early Childhood'; and I think that a Hazlitt might suggest, and suggest rightly, that it was read more for the end of one stanza, so to speak,

> Full soon thy Soul shall have her earthly freight,
> And custom lie upon thee with a weight,
> Heavy as frost, and deep almost as life!

than for the capacity to begin the next:

> O Joy! that in our embers
> Is something that doth live,
> That nature yet remembers
> What was so fugitive.

It was as if the Victorians were born into the second stage of Wordsworth's life with only an inherited memory of the 'visionary gleam' of the first. The big things, for the young Hazlitt, were being compromised and domesticated in a smaller, more prosaic world bound by external circumstances.

Approached from the anxieties of the 1820s and 1830s, the Victorian period seems to provoke, as well as itself ask, the question, 'Where is it now, the glory and the dream?'. It is virtually Arnold's question and the question of the voice of poetry more or less throughout the period. But it is in prose, a medium already responding to new conditions and freed from Romantic heights, that, as we shall see, the forces of emotion and imagination, forced to withdraw from a position of primacy in determining human action, on second thought went round the back of the powers of adjustment, compromise, accommodation and memory to do work again actually within them. The human reality involved in such a move is revealed, quintessentially, in Forster's description of the effect on Dickens of his being sent out by his family, in childhood, to a blacking warehouse, to earn his own way:

> What at once he brought out of the humiliation that had impressed him so deeply, though scarcely as yet quite consciously, was a natural dread of the hardships that might still be in store for him, sharpened by what he had gone through; and this though in its effects for the present imperfectly understood, became by degrees a passionate resolve, even while he was yielding to circumstances, *not to be* what circumstances were conspiring to make him.
>
> Forster: *The Life of Charles Dickens*, i, p. 34.

There is the emotional resolve, in reserve or on second thought.

It is an ironic fact (but one that makes this book a book rather than a series of essays) that far as this prose realism, yielding to circumstances without being what circumstances were conspiring to make it, was from Wordsworth, it was actually closer to him, who put the spiritual man within the natural man, who insisted that poetry should not be above the virtues and the subjects of good prose, than it was to Blake or Coleridge or even Keats.

II. A PROSE SENSE OF LIFE

It was the view of Matthew Arnold, apostle of high culture, that the lives of the Ancients were bigger and more essential that the lives of modern men. But if the young Hazlitt was indeed correct, that the life of the individual was getting even smaller and all too familiar, is Arnold's the only possible conclusion? Must we turn to Sophocles rather than to 'Dover Beach'? Is there nothing to be said—or to be written—for the reality of confessedly small, conventional lives?

Suppose, for the moment, we do not ask literature to enter and make those small lives bigger but leave them as they are. Suppose, therefore, we eschew Maurice de Guérin's rather literary use of the word 'life' and seek a more prosaic sense of what near the middle of the nineteenth century it meant for his life that a man of moderate ability was a writer. Will it make any difference, I wonder, that this small life is that of a literary man? What constitutes the nature and the use of a literary life? how does it affect a writer when he is, so to speak, off-duty, at home, with friends?

I propose to bring these questions to a close study of one book, a biography, and seek from it its sense of a life. There is a form of Victorian biography which offers itself as surrogate autobiography, compiled with little authorial intrusion from the subject's letters and diaries. Such biographies are usually written, or, rather, edited by a friend or relative of the deceased; they are thus familiar works, in the sense of revealing, with appropriate decorum, the private side of a public life, as if the private side, amidst friends and family, were at the heart of the subject's inner life. In memory of the dead, their pious ambition is to be in lieu of the autobiography which the dead man never wrote during his life. Their hope is that much of that life may be gathered and inferred through what falls from private writings like letters. There may be difficulties for us, now, as readers of these works: what, we may wonder, is being censored? how are we to place and correctly recognize what we thus over-hear as the voice coming from these books? For when that voice is not distorted by a literary framework telling us how to hear it, we feel even so the necessity for the rest of the context that seems to be tacitly carried along beneath the voice, supporting its meaning. Yet even with these difficulties, may we not at least try to see if these works deliver what they virtually promise: a real life delivered by writing which is not itself literary writing. For writing in such cases does not appear to be changing things but presenting things not meant for public, literary consideration: incidental letters put into place after the death of their writer. Surely this offers us a more neutral sense of life, for writing here is not art but the evidence of a life presented as apparently no more than the mere means of record by which we, as posterity, may still know the dead almost as his friends did. Surely here, as far as is possible, is the natural text we have been looking for, the thing itself, life delivered as by memory?

The book I have chosen in order to try out these thoughts is not Forster's *The Life of Charles Dickens* or Cross's *George Eliot's Life* but the biography of a smaller, more neglected figure short of genius and, plausibly perhaps, more ordinary for that. The book is *Memorials of Thomas Hood*. It is, I take it, largely unread today and forgotten.

The reaction of my reader to the idea of spending time on this book will, I guess, be rather like that of one of the first reviewers of it: an account which, incidentally, may serve us as a helpful introduction to it.

> Hood's daughter and son, who were left children at his death, and who have since grown up to cherish his memory, and to add, by their own deserts, to the respect they inherit by their relationship to him, have done but an act of duty in preparing and publishing these two volumes of *Memorials*. They do not form what could properly be called a biography of Hood. A single chapter carries over the first thirty-six years of his life, adding little or nothing to the information previously accessible; and the remaining chapters of the volumes consist of an account, year by year, of the last ten years of his life—the five years, from 1835 to 1840, which he spent at Coblenz and Ostend; and the five, from 1840 to 1845, which followed his return to England. This account does not take the form of a story regularly and connectedly told; but is made up chiefly of private letters by Hood himself

and by his wife, now first published, from which the reader is left to gather the incidents for himself, and to derive his own impression of Hood's habits and character. In what of connecting narrative there is, one notes a considerable vagueness, or thinness of particulars, and even an indecision respecting those that are given—owing, doubtless, to the fact that, while the writers retain a vivid recollection of their father personally, the external circumstances of his life, his literary connexions and companionships, the whole by-gone social milieu of London in which he moved, lie too far in the distance to be recovered by them without as much research as a stranger would have had to bestow. Taken for what they profess to be, however (and the critic, so considering them, will probably have no fault to find, unless he is finical enough to remark on the very incorrect pointing), the volumes are an interesting addition to our knowledge of Hood, and to his literary remains. They are written in a spirit of true affection, which communicates itself to the reader.

Macmillan's Magazine, vol ii, (May–October 1860), pp. 317–8.

The author of the review is the magazine's editor, later the editor of the works of De Quincey, David Masson. What is significant for our purposes, however, is the way that the dual thought of both the book's thinness and yet the loving commemorative purpose behind it prompts Masson into an uncomfortable consideration of what to make of the value of Hood's life itself. So what? this biography induces Masson to ask of the life it indicates. 'Hood does not rank in the first class among recent English poets', his seriousness consists 'in the vivid imagination and abrupt lyric representation of ghastly situations in physical nature and human life', but 'from a dark circumference of such thoughts, conceived with an almost reckless literality, we see the Humourist rebounding into the thick and bustle of ordinary social life' (ibid., p. 320). He was on the rebound a writer of lovely comic verse. Then Masson struggles with his own feelings of grateful tenderness towards Hood:

Well, but what is it all worth? In truth, '*I* don't know; nor *you* don't know; nor none of us don't know'; but this we all feel—that it *is* worth something. . . . As to the *use* of that or of any other kind of humour—this is not the only case in which it would be well once for all to adopt the principle, that the justification of the thing is to be sought, *a priori*, in the fact that it proceeds from obedience to an innate function, as well as, *a posteriori*, in an attempted appreciation of its calculable effects. But if an answer to the question, '*Cui bono?*' is still demanded, one may point out that, just as in reading a great poem or other serious work of imagination, two kinds of benefit are distinguishable— the benefit, on the one hand, of the actual matter of thought, the images, the expressions, delivered into the mind from it, and either remaining there to be recovered by the memory when wanted, or playing more occultly into the under-processes of the mind that lie beneath conscious memory; and the benefit, on the other hand, of the momentary stir, or wrench, or enthusiastic rouse, given to the mind in the act of reading—so, with a difference, is it with humorous writing too. First, there is the actual intellectual efficiency afterwards of the good things communicated . . . and, secondly, there is the twitch given to the mind, along with every good thing, in the act of receiving it.

                                                        Ibid., p. 323.

What is most noticeable in this is the felt pressure of the Utililitarian question and the consequent effort to find a way of thinking about a life and its works that will hold off the question, what did it *finally* come down to?

The editors of *Memorials of Thomas Hood*, Hood's own son and daughter, apologetically foresaw at least part of Masson's criticism when they acknowledged that the work was

> but a faint shadow of what he was, as he lives in our memories, and wanting in that light and colour, which would make it interesting to the general reader.
>
> *Memorials*, ii, p. 272.

Published in 1860, when Hood's children were old enough and steeled enough to perform the sad task, the work thus appeared fifteen years after Hood's death. This belatedness of memory which the editors acknowledge with respect to their enterprise is, we know, characteristic of the strange chronology of the period after the great Romantics. Hood's son writes that he fears that perhaps people will not be interested in this these days; but he hopes any lack of interest will be due to the inadequacy of the effort rather than be attributed to a deficiency in Hood himself. What is so moving about these vulnerable admissions, as to the possible failure of the well-intentioned act of piety, is that almost despite themselves the modest literary admissions carry within them quietly proud and tender claims about life and love and memory: 'A faint shadow of what he was, as he lives in our memories'. The editors are uncertain of the book's quality as a book, but that uncertainty as to the literary merit is related to the children's certainty of the reality which, perhaps only they can know, lay behind the compilation. This book, that is to say, offers itself as a 'natural' text: one descriptively anterior to the more literary forms of writing which Hood himself produced, and one in which, as readers, we seem either to know or not to know. If we know the essential truth of this life from this 'faint shadow', we know it through the imaginative and sympathetic power of the human heart; if we do not know it, it is lost and forgotten, beyond research. This is, if not explicitly or intentionally on the part of the editors, nonetheless the book's inviting presupposition. We shall have to consider and even test it. That is why I choose it for study here, as a test-case of the idea of a natural prose, the words falling shed from a life. This is important because it represents a different, possible way from the way of Wordsworth's development as it was discussed in chapters 1 and 2. For Wordsworth's story is first that of a commitment to the priority of humanly felt subject-matter over the high and artificial diction traditionally thought to be necessary to poetry; but, second, this human commitment is also followed by an increasing realization of the necessity for the creation of a language not secondary to its referents but actually living and thinking within their memory. Is it possible, instead, to carry on caring less about language: in terms of Masson's interesting distinction between the two benefits of reading, caring less about what one gets *in* the reading, in the parts, than what one gets *from* the reading, after having grasped the whole?

Moreover, there are at the same time good historical reasons for looking at Thomas Hood (1799–1845), sited chronologically as he is between what we have come to think of as the Romantics on one hand and the Victorians on the other. Masson himself was sceptical about Hood's historical importance:

> The most pertinacious zealot for the resolution of biography into history would hardly make anything feasible of such a notion as 'Hood and his Times', with whatever ingenuity he might select for his purpose this or that portion of the social history of Britain, or even of London, during the twenty years preceding 1845. The 'times' are of course there; but Hood's relation to them is that of a man of peculiar constitution, who sees them flitting by, has pensive, or humorous, or even wild and haggard thoughts about them, and makes the expression of such thoughts his business, but, on the whole, is so little incorporated with them, that, had he not existed, the 'times' would have been the same, and only his by-standing thoughts would have been lost.

Op. cit., p. 319.

Lacking the 'massiveness' to stand above his age, Hood merely stood by it. But Masson is wrong to think that even that is without its historical significance. Hood, after all, began his career as a poet and ended it by writing prose. He began moreover as a belated Romantic poet, using the model of Keats in poems like 'Ode to Melancholy' and 'Autumn' (1823) and of Wordsworth-with-Lamb in 'I remember, I remember' (1826). But these poems give way to a demotic comic poetry which hides the earlier melancholy, so that the melancholy either only tinges the humour or becomes split-off into the haunted relief of marginal work in the grotesque where nothing seems forbidden since nothing is condemned to be taken seriously. And with this lowering and socializing of Romanticism's serious passional elitism comes the development of a verse of emotional social concern nonetheless set warmly still at home within society:

'O! Men, with Sisters dear!
O! Men! with Mothers and Wives!

It is not linen you're wearing out,
But human creatures' lives!'
'The Song of the Shirt' (1843).

The appeal sung by the seamstress is made against social inhumanity in terms of the humane centre of society, the family: 'Sisters, Mothers, Wives!'. 'Certain classes at the poles of Society are already too far asunder; it should be the duty of our writers to draw them nearer by kindly attraction, not to aggravate the existing repulsion' (*Memorials*, ii, p. 257). The prose of the *Comic Annual* had by then already come into being, commencing in 1830. With *Hood's Monthly Magazine and Comic Miscellany*, which first appeared in 1844, Hood was offering in the prose work of the second half of his career 'harmless "Mirth for the Million"' to 'a public sorely oppressed . . . by hard times, heavy taxes, and [the characteristic demotic pun] "eating cares"'. An almost embarrassed, parodic, sentimental jocularity characterized the appearance of such productions, as the voice of ordinary speech sought to make England a family capable of recognizing, even in near cliché, hints of deep but homely feeling. It was a voice existing in that middle area between, on the one hand, the Victorian sentimentalizing of the family and a democratic concern with the uses of Romantic feeling and writing, on the other. The long poem, 'Miss Kilmansegg and Her Precious Leg' (1840–1) is an outstanding example of Hood's new compromising amalgam. It mixes with the grotesque story of a young lady, who loses a leg and insists upon the replacement being of gold not cork, a satire upon wealth. The high poetic style becomes associated with the commercial golden age:

She was one of those who by Fortune's boon
Are born, as they say, with a silver spoon
    In her mouth, not a wooden ladle:
To speak according to poet's wont,
Plutus as sponsor stood at her font,
    And Midas rock'd the cradle.

ll. 132–7.

—while this poetry becomes knowingly low, prosy, comic and satiric:

But the Coachman carried off the state,
With what was a Lancashire body of late
Turn'd into a Dresden Figure.

ll. 1591–3.

Low economic explanations undermine the high pretensions of the new commercial rich, while at the same time a humble and ordinary sentimentality is left untouched by the haughty rich who draw the comic-satiric fire. 'A double meaning shews double sense' (line 1882). The mixture of styles, classes and attitudes in this amalgam makes it a safe place in which to be dangerously playful on the margin of serious issues. It confirms Masson's observation, as if Hood himself recognized 'that, had he not existed, the "times" would have been the same, and only his by-standing thoughts would have been lost'; but had the 'times' not existed as they did, Hood would not have been the same, small comic by-stander. He had learnt the role.

He had learnt the role so well that he could play it in his own family. The *Memorials of Thomas Hood* covers the years from 1835 to 1845 when the abiding concern in the Hood household was the thought of Hood's death. Insolvency had forced the English comic to leave England with his family in 1834; five years, first in Coblenz and then in Ostend, saw the consumptive weakening of Hood's already weak and nervous constitution. But he had the trick of seeming a by-stander to his own trouble and the trouble of his wife and children:

> I one day overheard a dispute between Tom and Fanny as to what I was. 'Pa's a literary man,' said Fanny. 'He's not!' said Tom: 'I know what he is.' 'What is he then?' 'Why,' says Tom, 'he's not a literary man—he's an invalid.'
>
> *Memorials*, ii, p. 55.

The by-standing or over-hearing there is, beautifully, twofold. First, the comments of the children are overheard by their father who is Thomas Hood, writer but also debtor, exile from England yet author of comic annuals loved throughout the home country—a country which the comedy seemed to unite while the comic lived in sickness abroad, keeping friends and memories through writing letters like this one. Who could see

irony better than he? As it relieves the problems of his adulthood to write of what his children say of it, Hood becomes for
the moment not the invalid but the literary man, making it all
into anecdote. Second, this letter by the father is overheard
itself, years later, by the grown children, Tom and Fanny
Hood, who fifteen years after Hood's death assembled many of
his letters into a continuity. Tom junior writes:

> Looking back now on my own emotion, while reading
> over these memorials, I can scarcely think how I should
> be so moved after the lapse of fifteen years, and I can fully
> realise how intensely painful must the compilation have
> been to my sister, who, as the elder, was more intimately
> connected with, and has a clearer memory of the events
> chronicled, than I.
>
> Ibid., i, p. viii.

They must have felt that they saw, in his letters, their father
remembering their own childhood for them, through his eyes.
And because Tom 'can fully realize', he does not need, and
probably could not anyway give us, the full realization. Yet we
as readers feel unintentionally invited to share it, just as a
knowing recipient of the father's letter shared a pathos which
it was the literary skill of the letter-writer to skim over,
tactfully. Throughout this book, the reader then, at a third
level of overhearing, feels moved to imagine, through sympathetic trust, all that is remembered at the back of this
family's mind. It is like a serious version of what it felt like to
read Hood's *Comic Annual*. Yet what is this family trust into
which we are drawn? Family-feeling seems to be an important
part and prompt of memory in the nineteenth century. It
meant home and a background of feelings even when the home
itself shifted geographically.

When thus at the end of their collaboration Tom in the
preface looks across at his sister and feels for her, his words,
formally on living after their father, have become for the
moment as much those of a brother as those of a son. The book
incorporates through its levels of tacit overhearing precisely
this retrospective sense that the people involved in this family
had been, were, or were to be, also separate human beings.
From the first, Hood himself seems in this book to be a man

glad to have the responsibility of inhibiting certain forms of personal reaction without inhibiting those claims which make for close personal relations in a family: he writes to his wife 'I never was anything, dearest, till I knew you' (i, p. xv). Tom and Fanny Hood deal only with the years from 1835 in which they (being modest and filial enough to see how large a claim even this might be) knew him. It is the strange side of the familiar, the imaginative side of memory, that one's father is also, was also, a man in his own right, and this book seems to be compiled with this common form of awe by children with families of their own now. For his part, Hood, overhearing, might have been glad to be remembered thus as a husband and father. But that is also to say that there is, as it were dating from 1799 to his marriage in 1825, a hidden part within this man, something strange that within marriage and family he naturalized or conventionalized, just as he did when writing within the notion of the wider family of England.

It is clear that Hood came to have a sense of himself that was aptly biographical rather than autobiographical. He shrank, he said, from the egoism of autobiography, and seems to have felt that he existed as much in the mind of his family, whom he minded about, as in his own. He reports thus in a letter of a home-coming after a visit to his old home of England:

> He [Tom] was very delighted to see me back, but I suppose I did not romp with him quite equal to his expectations, for after a day or two, as I was sitting reading, he said with an arch look at his mother, 'I do wish my pa would come home.'
>
> ii, pp. 30–1.

If, impossibly, the children now wish they had never said such things, unwitting or arch, before a tired and sick man, still they preserve them; perhaps for the good *he* thought that they did him, at any rate not least because their father never seems to have allowed himself to feel hurt by them, but was ruefully jollied by their liveliness. Anyway it was recorded, as if—provided he could let a friend tacitly see it—Hood could make himself almost glad to think that nobody but he could ever really know how he felt deep within himself about such things. As it is, it feels more like shared trouble to us:

We have thought it best not to omit any of these frequent mentions of his children, as to those who knew him the letters would lack a characteristic, and to those who did not know him, would fail to show the warmth of his domestic affections, if those passages had been struck out.—T.H.

ii, p. 54.

This is all very publicly proper and scrupulous. But what is really nice in that little footnote is that, by calling themselves 'his children', they seem to follow in Hood's literary footsteps by becoming likewise biographical to themselves.

What are we to make of this biographical man? On the one hand he seems to be a person of conventional family piety; on the other, as Masson put it, 'a man of peculiar constitution' feeling within the conventions ironies of position and circumstance. The fact is, I think, that Hood sacrificed certain parts of his personality and of his talent for literary art in order to be the sort of husband, father, correspondent and man who wrote the *Comic Annual*. It cannot be clear how far this was unconscious, how far voluntary, how far compromising, how far reluctant; nor can one be sure whether hiding certain parts of himself was the best means, for a man of real but not outstanding gifts, of genuine but nervous sensibility, to find use and expression for them. But one may say that there is deep artifice in the way that Hood made himself what might otherwise unequivocally have been called a 'natural family man'. It was not only humour that helped Hood when he realized that he had not romped with young Tom 'quite equal to his expectations'. He was also helped by being a literary man, with artifice, as well as an invalid. He is able in that letter to show tacitly the literary possibility in 'I do wish my pa would come home' or 'he's not a literary man—he's an invalid' while at the same time, familiar and easy-going, not actually making it into literature itself. He used Tom's joke himself, as if the family had come to share a sense of the humour of misfortune among themselves:

The other night, when I came from Stratford, the cold shrivelled me up so, that when I got home, I thought I was my own child!

ii, p. 197.

While making his fate into his jokes, he was also seemingly amused to find his son an echo of his father's verbal ploys. Yet how easy was it to keep up this everyday surface style upon affairs? Its maintenance seems a sign of reassurance yet, equally, a sign of the necessity for reassurance.

It is not merely that we cannot answer the questions because the book is too 'thin' and what we overhear too remote and uncertain. It is as if the book is, rather, Hood's paradoxical bequest: a form which reduplicates the way that in his life he, in collusion with his friends, hid from them and partly from himself what he was up to when he had to write about his own affairs. The demotic and the childish were for Hood a form of still quite anxious relief, shifting at the very least the level at which that anxiety was registered. Thus he writes to the children of his doctor and friend, Elliot:

> Do you ever see such birds? We used to call them 'gulls',— but they didn't mind it!
>
> ii, p. 212.

By using language as a form of distraction, as a different level from the level of living, as a conscious gulling of oneself, Hood likewise 'didn't mind it'. In that capacity of language to be calm, to be innocent of its own meaning and the tricks that the mind can play within it, language is with Hood not mindless indeed but harmless. He writes, for example, to Samuel Phillips, recently widowed, a fellow-writer and, worse, fellow-lung-sufferer, on the poor man's being thrown from a horse— 'not content with expectorating blood—spitting mud', 'plague take you, all through trotting on an earthly roadster when you might have been soaring with Peguasus' (ii, p. 220). The use of language here is to force attention from the things they share— especially consumption—to words they may share with greater pleasure. Hood rides as long as he can on the pun that saddles a meaning, until he forces words back from their bizarre and painful task of representing and confronting reality to their more real task of expressing human feeling. Hood adds, however, soberly at the end:

> Seriously, I am glad you escaped . . .
> Write soon . . .
> Dear Phillips,
> Yours very truly, and hoping no offence,
> Thos. Hood
>
> ii, pp. 220–2.

Up until then the language was an attempt to avoid the burden of sharing verbally what they shared anyway all too painfully; yet an avoidance precisely by means of which there might be created a more real and affectionate, extra-linguistic acknowledgement of what was suffered and what could be said in response. To leave it a little unspoken, through a different strategy of speaking about it, was essential to Hood—up to the point when it then became a matter of felt duty to reclaim simplicity lest the purposes of the nervous, sensitive strategy be misunderstood. It seemed to Hood that he could not simply and solemnly say 'I understand', 'I am sorry for all your troubles' or 'I feel something of them too'; one had to do other things with words to show one understood while acknowledging that we do have to live with it all anyway. Hood made it necessary for mutual understanding to be felt performatively through this invitation to Phillips to read and translate, to know the game and why it has to be played, recognizing the intention in the act. Only thereafter, on second thought, could Hood turn round and sincerely enter into the conventional, direct use of words without feeling them to be merely easy. Hood had to work by indirect means in order to earn what we assume to be a primary, natural, direct tone. It was artificially won: a human tone, at the last, not disturbed by, but won through, the strategy of resolutely making over substantive meanings into accidents of language and mechanisms of writing. 'Dear Phillips' is here reclaimed as 'truly' meant. Yet, at the same time, for all the artifice, there is also an implicit claim that this is more like life, that people thus do not and cannot say directly all they mean to the person it at that moment most concerns. And Hood's way of keeping the writing indirect—rather than resort to the Wordsworthian sense of a responsibility to do on paper what speaking cannot do of itself in life—is, as shared with another literary man in a letter to him, a tacit admission that at this level at least writing should drop the pretension of being magical, for the sake of being convivial. Shostakovich, in the very different circumstances of living under Stalinist threats of ruin, put it more bitterly:

> I felt that they were killing me. But I don't want to be melodramatic at this point. It's only in fine literature that a person stops eating and sleeping because he's so over-wrought. In reality, life is much more simple. . . . I had to live and feed my family.[22]

Letters, in particular, are things of time and time it is, with its abrupt pressures, that takes people past moments of big, dramatic expression and questioning into smaller lives, thinner words, simpler starknesses.

'And hoping no offence', Hood signs off. These words are conscious that playing with experience by maintaining a discrete level of punning language may be construed as a betrayal of the subject-matter. In this afterthought Hood was trying apologetically to gesture towards the humanity of recognition that cuts short the necessity for further, particular thoughts upon thoughts. Language need not be a form of the necessarily explicit for all its usage in spelling things out. There is an authority of tone over words which acts as a governing memory upon their meaning; it makes the words *need* the man who uttered them in order to have their meaning fulfilled. Part of writing's reclamation of this human tone, which we normally associate with speaking, lies in the meaning becoming again implicit, opening the gap between words and sentiments in order to intimate an unspoken anterior link of personality and goodwill allowing such a gap to appear. Thus Hood wrote to his friend, Franck:

> What do you think, Tim! Dr Elliot says that my heart is rather lower hung than usual; but never mind, you shall always find it in the right place.
>
> ii, p. 16.

The humanity of 'never mind' in Hood lies in its not being able to be dismissed as obliviousness, cheapness or cavalier bravado. 'Never mind' is the sad name of the gap between what he says and what he feels, what his emotions are and what his physical condition is. The consciousness of the final

impossibility of never minding urges that the words do not
literally mean that, but use the final, literal impossibility to
make possible an interim discretion. A reader may not seek to
find the truth worked out here, because part of the tender joke
is at the expense of a language reduced by familiarity to occupy
only a small part of the ground across which personal relations
develop and subsist. Such meaning is dependent upon human
trust and pathos; the sense of life and of naturalness both
externally supporting, yet thereby also demanding the
weakening of, the language used.[23] 'Never mind' (gulls don't!)
saves Hood from the shudder of autobiography: 'who would
think of such a creaking, croaking, blood-spitting wretch being
the "Comic"?' (i, p. 298).

Hood was liable to use words crazily to make language as it
were foreign to itself, like a displaced person:

> My young landlady has paid me a smiling visit this
> morning, and we have had a little conversation in German
> and English which neither of us understood.
>
> i, p. 64.

By such means he provoked a deepening of understanding
onto a level of trust in the spirit of things beneath language,
while still retaining a comic gesture. He writes to Franck, a
fellow-fisherman, apologizing for not having written for so
long, on the grounds of a numbing depression: 'I have thought
of you, Johnny, if I have not thrown a line at you' (ii, p. 94).
Not wanting to seem to fish for friendship with emotional bait,
Hood takes up the fishing into a writing which even so does its
best to show itself merely secondary to such a real enjoyment.
Through what he calls 'the strength of my weakness' (i, p.
284), Hood was so much the professional writer as not to seem
one at all. It is this that makes *Memorials of Thomas Hood* seem
so 'natural'. That it is not merely natural makes one recognize
that Hood could not have made himself into so good a man,
had he not been the kind of writer who depended upon his
literary skill for a poise to make that skill itself apparently
secondary to his living. But it is a pathetic goodness.

The strength of Hood's weakness lies in the humane
authority of his not pressing language to achieve imaginative
recreations; setting a vulnerable tenderness of conscience

above the need to be explicit about his trials, which both tact
and fear prevent him from admitting at full strength. It made
him a good man, but what sort of writer did it make him? The
weakness of this strength lies in the way that, in this book and
in his other writings too, Hood's admirable comic seriousness
is yet disabling to any hope for him of a strong literary
creativeness. He replies as follows to criticism that his novel,
Tylney Hall, first published in 1834, was inadequate in its
treatment of love and courtship:

> In reality, the sentimental part of the passion was
> purposely shirked; not that I was exactly in the predica-
> ment of the innocent Adonis:
>   'Quoth he, I know not Love,
>   Unless it be a boar, and then I chase it;'
> but because that, to my taste, with very rare exceptions,
> Love reads as badly in prose as piety in verse. To be
> candid, the perusal of what is termed Religious Poetry
> always exercises a deadening influence, rather than other-
> wise, on my devotional feelings; and we all know the effect
> of reading even genuine love letters in a court of justice—
> that the tenderest expressions of the tenderest of passions,
> written in the softest of hours, with the softest of pens,
> seldom fail to elicit a roar of laughter from the Bar to the
> Bench. In short, rather than risk that my lovers should
> say too much, I have made them say too little—but it was
> erring on the safe side.[24]

Failures sometimes tell more, explicitly, about the obstacles,
problems and beliefs involved in writing than do those
successes which gain power from their own obstacles, seem to
overleap the problems and keep the beliefs implicit in what
they do. At times smaller men let in more room to see those
harder questions which a writer of greater genius absorbs. In
this section we are looking at a smaller man; in the next,
Dickens, a greater genius. For had Hood been born later in the
century, it is just possible, with the example of a genius like
Dickens before him, he might have written more lasting novels.
As it was, *Memorials of Thomas Hood* provided, through the
intervention of his children's love, a compensation to the
memory of Hood for what the choices of his life had meant,

with regard to their leaving so much of what was so valuable in him tacit. Yet even in the *Memorials* the compensation of disclosing that subdued human life also reveals the spiritual cost for the natural man that such a life had to bring down upon itself: 'purposely shirked', 'erring on the safe side', in writing of religion or of love.[25] With all the exaggeration of ersatz heroism, Yeats put it dramatically—perfection of the life or of the work. The harder question here is, could a better art have been achieved without a worse life? was Hood's balance and compromise the best he could do? 'what is it all worth?'.

Faced with severe questions about the 'use' of family life or the 'use' of second-rate writing, there is a creditable human wish to believe in the truth of apparently natural and good feelings, even at the cost of a complicit sentimentalism. Such a thought is important to the career of Dickens; there was purchase in it in his task of moving his audience. Now, a harsh, sceptical person would say that the situation in *Memorials of Thomas Hood*, edging, without Dickens's resources, towards a Victorian sentimentalizing of the family, is all too good to be true, or, if true, too small and limited in its range of feelings to be a test of the goodness. This, he would say, is the penalty for wanting to believe in the small men who make you feel better. Isn't reading the *Memorials* like going with Pip in *Great Expectations* to the Castle, home of Wemmick the clerk and his Aged Parent? A comically touching private world with its own drawbridge and customs; a deaf old man placated by nods, the bigger the better, what you actually say not being much to the point. Pip is moved by his visit, but he visits, he does not stay or live there, for all his emotion. As Arnold asked of Romanticism, it is enough, is it adequate? And out of that question comes the post-Romantic thought of the necessity for tests upon these so-called natural bases so beloved, also, of the Victorians. It is thus a disturbing thought that there is evidence, nowhere referred to in *Memorials of Thomas Hood*, that in June 1844, less than a year before his death, Thomas and Jane Hood were on the verge of separation as a result of the strains upon and within the household.[26] We do not know who was at fault, or why it happened then, or who instigated the idea of separation, or why it did not happen. All that can be said with certainty is that the separation did not take place. If it had, would that necessarily reflect back upon the way that they had found to live together for twenty years? That it did not, is it necessarily a testimony to the strength and resilience of the relationship? This mere external fact, or half-fact, cannot but make us ask how far we were doing right in trusting the family piety and pathos of this book as if it were a rock of human nature.

Does it ruin our experience of *Memorials of Thomas Hood* to have this tiny suspicion that towards the end all was not well? Is there a place for such a thing in the life of Thomas Hood as we know it? Or is the biography another form of literary cheating, of illusory comfort?

There is no doubt that the Hood we know from the *Memorials* could cope with some incongruities and ironies. '*You* shall always find it in the right place,' he wrote to Franck of his heart. But for Hood, as we have seen, writing, like humour, was a translation of his experience that in life the right thing was nearly always in the wrong place:

> Tom did his best at nursing, though it consisted in cuddling up one of my hands and keeping it warm with everything he could wrap round it.
>
> ii, p. 37.

—although the pain was actually in his foot. The things in the wrong place are tacitly kept there by the writing's refusal to be magical, showing the pathos of misplacement. Tom's heart was in the right place and that does. Or again, when Hood had not received a letter from Franck for some long time, he sent one to *him* in the form of a letter from Franck to Hood. To answer one's own desire for communication and then send it to the man who did not write is the very opposite of writing a letter to oneself and addressing it to someone else. Hood achieved normality in its right place by the double loops of turning inside-out and then outside-in, as a replacement for his feeling of the impossibility of straightforwardness. Normality is thus, as Masson suggested, achieved on the rebound, being as much a surprise as it is a joke. But he depended, even here, on goodwill to help him through.

It is thus true that Hood could cope with more serious

incongruities in marriage, only provided it was loving beneath them. Ill and stranded from his family on a brief return stay in England, he writes in reply to his wife's offer to come over:

> I do not know what to say; if I were merely selfish, it would instantly be 'Come'. I must leave it to your own resolve whether you can come comfortably, and can feel secure about the children, for I see you are fretting yourself ill about me.
>
> ii, p. 74.

This is a man who knows what a mutual decision is and how things have to turn inside-out (*'you* are fretting *yourself ill* about *me'*) before they can turn outside-in again (so, for reasons now more than mere selfishness, 'Come'). He seems to know what marriage is and that love also has to include, in quite practical ways, the consideration as well as the joy of being loved. Or, to take the opposite case, when Jane went away and Hood, at home with the children this time, found himself taken ill again:

> Your desire that I should wish for you, and *not* wish for you, literally came true. I missed the comfort, but was hardly sorry you were not present to be distressed by sufferings you could not relieve.
>
> ii, p. 36.

That was when young Tom tied up his hand for him. This sort of minding for her (*'hardly* sorry you were not present') is the other side of his wish that she should 'never mind' for him— still knowing as he does that even this attitude of his is dependent upon being sure of her love and needing it. It is further complicated by Hood's increasingly burdensome passivity under illness and his corresponding desire to be no extra burden even by saying that he did not want to be one. Yet this still did not and could not relieve the burden itself; none of Hood's strategies could alter reality or change his world, and the ways that he could help his family to bear with the troubles that were largely his troubles still very much depended, ironically, upon that family's support. In a quiet footnote, there is evidence between the lines that the children, inevitably, had to bear their share of the trouble that the husband and wife sought mutually to lighten:

> My mother was always careful to keep my father free from any anxiety and worry that she could, and we children were brought up in a sort of Spartan style of education, and taught the virtues of silence and low voices.—T.H.
>
> ii, p. 67.

The children, Hood must have known in his heart, were not simply echoes of his own joking; they bore also the marks of his trouble. Hood's death was the sadly central fact of those lives, yet it was, until near the last, apparently accommodated by a love adequate to fearfulness. In such practical living, often lost to human memory and hardly written of because so much of its work is subdued even at the time, what cannot be solved has to be shared, at various levels of mutual concern and mutual pain. There is also a kind of love whose very exercise is not to speak of, but as it were work on above, all that threatens to get uncomfortably in the way of loving. Hood's memoir, partly by accident, allows these silences to speak very quietly without the voice of a presiding novelist to trumpet them.

And yet, I say, the marriage nearly broke and has to be conceived of as breakable. This may only go to show that there is a reality of life too much for the persistance of any one feeling or defence. Or that such a reality, accommodated for so long, was staved off till the last, despite the increasing snags and abrasions that one still had not to mind. Nonetheless, what we now know must tend to make what this book stands for more shaky, less naturally and obviously strong than the book apparently grants. Perhaps Hood's pathos was finally a burden on his wife. This is a hard thing to think—as if we were on the road to Thomas Hardy.

Yet for all the editors' controlling selectiveness, this book lies open to us without firm direction. That is why it is so interesting and so difficult to think about it and its relation to the real past from which it selects and receives. Here it is; not indeed the whole story, yet not claiming to be; excerpts, remnants, hints, perhaps the most we can ever really know? So it is not quite as naive a book, in being virtually authorless, as one might fear. Hood himself, for example, must have had some notion, even before the threatened disaster of Jane's leaving him, of the frailty of trust. It was the very basis of his affectionate pathos. He wrote home to his wife 'As you cannot nurse me, take all good care of my other self' (ii, p. 69)—meaning, of course, herself. When he called her his other self, when he wrote to her words that he could almost see her reading, he acted with some consciousness of vulnerability, albeit vulnerability apparently and gratefully past. There is no means by which we can finally decide how far this is Hood's delicate tenderness, how far that essential childishness that contemporaries saw when they noted how thoroughly Jane Hood mothered and nursed her enfeebled husband and how glad he, seven years her junior, was to accept it. 'As you cannot nurse me, take all good care of my other self.' It is both the weakness and the strength of the *Memorials* that it cannot furnish us with the materials with which to make such a decision. Is it that experience itself, rather than experience in most books, will not admit of this sort of final man-made discrimination? Is it that, historically, weak feelings and humane ones had come to form an inextricable mixture by the middle of the nineteenth century, in the face of excessive demands for firmness and usefulness? Or is it that we have inherited from that century a diminished faith in decent, permanent feelings, all the more diminished by the experience of our own times?

One small thing, at any rate, is clear: that the sensibility implied in *Memorials of Thomas Hood* is temperamentally allied to the nature of letter-writing—and not merely, I think, because that is where the book has to gather its evidence. Letters were not only the obvious way for Hood to maintain friendships over the distance of exile; they seem also to have been the only way welcome to him of writing about himself, because in them he was writing about himself within a relationship where much could be left unsaid and taken for granted. Moreover, as we have seen in his letters to his wife, there is an inherent vulnerability about letters that struck a chord with Hood. For letters, all too vulnerable to what Hood called that 'roar of laughter from the Bar to the Bench', are at the moment of their being written unconsummated dialogue, personal yet waiting to be shared privately, existing on a boundary between the time of being written and the time of being read, poised between permanent writing and temporary saying. Witness Keats writing to George and Georgiana Keats on Friday, 12 March 1819, evening time:

> I hope you are both now in that sweet sleep which no two beings deserve more that [than] you do—I must fancy you so—and please myself in the fancy of speaking a prayer and a blessing over you and your lives—God bless you—I whisper good night in your ears and you will dream of me—
>
> *Letters,* ii, p. 74.

The solitary 'fancy' is played off against the desire for an honourably vicarious happiness in wishing truly for that of others; the 'prayer' displaces the playfulness, even as 'whisper' lightens the solemnity, by a species of reciprocal exorcism. This is an attempt to bring Blake's 'The Clod & The Pebble' into equilibrium ('Love seeketh not Itself to please'; 'Love seeketh only Self to please', Blake: *Complete Writings,* p. 211), and it is where we started our discussion of the relation of the natural man to the spiritual man after Wordsworth. The in-betweenness of the present tense in this unfulfilled dialogue with George and Georgiana floats trustingly in the space between the time of its composition and the thought of its reception. When they receive it on another day, they will think of him and of his thinking of them, but, Keats also knows, the letter will also belong to the recent past and the still distant; it will be out-of-date. There is a pathos in that which has to do with thoughts of loneliness, hopes of communication through writing, needs for memory and for patience; a secular thing that is writing's truest model of one's relation to others not merely in one's own mind. Hood must have known all this intuitively beneath his fun and tact: 'Your mama will show you on the map where I was when I wrote this' (i, p. 209). So much of the power of such writing is dependent upon the writer's lovingly imagining the feelings of the recipient. No other writing is quite like this; it deserves to be part of our literature. But where the recipient is adult, so much is also dependent upon the reader's being happy to fall in with that imagination of the reader which the writer has. And this is how Hood thought of all writing: as something which needed, as well as gave, support.

In our professional literature, the difficulties of secular trust and dependence, in which Hood was implicated, gain increased recognition in the prose of the century. Thomas Hardy finally was able to put in the professional terms of a practising novelist what was involved in the letter-form:

> The advantages of the letter-system of telling a story (passing over the disadvantages) are that, hearing what one side has to say, you are led constantly to the imagination of what the other side must be feeling, and at last are anxious to know if the other side does really feel what you imagine.
>
> Florence Emily Hardy: *The Life of Thomas Hardy,* p. 120.

In literary historical terms, the novel of sensibility is in origin epistolary. The movement from letters to the novel is part of the history of prose. In a novel, the intimacy of a letter, as it were from life, invites a reader to employ his vicariousness in the reconstruction, as well as the distanced testing, of what originally seemed to have no room for him or her. Novels responded to the need to place in context and to test circumstantially, seeing what could be retained after testing. In this way *Memorials of Thomas Hood* stands between letters and the novel, constituting the stage before a novelist steps in to guide and entice the reader.

Does this work only serve, then, to show us the necessity for the novel? No: it is precisely because a novel might well 'solve' some of the problems of interpretation that this surrogate autobiography, this ur-novel is indispensable. We can see what things might be like before a novelist could get his hands on them for his own purposes. Characteristically, Hood writes to his wife:

> I have rambled on to amuse you, and left little room to say all I could wish to yourself; but you will find in your heart the echo of all I have to say (rather an Irish one, but a truth-teller).
>
> i, p. 217.

We do not know all he might have said. And, at the risk of being unfeeling, it has been asked whether such an attitude could be equal to, adult enough for, a moment when Jane

Hood could not find in her own heart the echo of his feelings—
or whether that might be the moment of his come-uppance.
For it may indeed seem 'Irish' that Hood's selflessness was so
very dependent for its existence upon his own family. Actually,
I do not think that it is 'Irish', ironic or merely self-defeating.
Whatever its excesses, the honour in the Romantic usage of
the word 'life' was its reverence for existence as something at
least potentially strange to man. When Thomas Hood settled
down and absorbed himself in the familiar domestic affections
that succeeded the melancholy Romanticism of his bachelor
youth, he *knew* his new family life was a convention, a way of
living, an accommodation. That did not mean that it was a
mere act or a simple refuge, yet it also meant that it was
not naive and not a smooth development for him. He lived
himself into a convention of emotion, familiar and domestic,
to which his feelings then became both habitually and also
spontaneously committed. Near the end of his life, he turned
to his children as if to explain; making an effort, for the last
time, to re-expand his spiritual consciousness beyond the
good-humoured domestic man's usual bounds:

> He said once to us, 'It's a beautiful world, and since I
> have been lying here, I have thought of it more and more;
> it is not so bad, even humanly speaking, as most people
> would make it out'.
>
> ii, p. 264.

It is touching, but it does not regain a big sense of life. A
certain shrewdness, shown here, in being unfussy, in never
minding too much, how goodness was found in difficult and
diminished lives—'it is not so bad'— was precisely what made
his commitment to family conventions both admirably possible
and also sheerly necessary for him.

It is interesting that many post-Romantics were quite
devastatingly upset by the thought of emotional strategies, as
if to make a strategy out of an emotion was to threaten its
status as a natural recourse. Leslie Stephen's *Mausoleum Book*
is just one such account of the fear that re-marriage, after
bereavement and mourning, between a widow and a widower
was no more than a betrayal of memory and a means for them
to trade lonelinesses with each other on account of a similarity

of situation. William Cobbett says in a sensitively downright way in *Advice to Young Men* that he does not like to hear a man speak of his first wife in the presence of his second, and cannot bear it when a woman talks of her first husband. It is delicacy as much as dogma. Yet the spontaneous habituation of Hood's emotions—the way he learnt familiar and domestic emotions so well that they became both second nature and instinct—is a thing not to be upset by the implicit thought of strategy. For Hood there was no paradox in the thought of having to work, quite hard, for his naturalness with his family; but both as an invalid and as a literary man he could not have missed a consciousness of the slight gap therein involved. It would surely have killed him had Jane Hood left him. But even that consideration comports with his tacit belief that 'natural' feelings were a thing to work and to play for: emotions that could not be gained if they were not believed in, could not be believed in if they were not thoughtfully maintained. Hood's emotions, believed in as well as learnt, have a right to reclaim the word 'natural' for themselves, for having worked for the word. In small, this is how men make a home upon the earth. J. S. Mill's late essay, 'Nature', is flexibly helpful here. He distinguishes two meanings of 'nature': first, the sum of all the powers, human and inhuman, existing and everything which takes place by means of those powers; second, more narrowly, all that takes place without specifically human intervention. In the second case, the natural is opposed to the artificial, which tries to alter and improve it; in the first, art is part of nature as man is, having itself no independent powers but employing the powers of nature for a specific end. Hood intuitively exploited this ambiguity in order to use his artifice, the capacity for which was accentuated in him through his being a writer, to maintain a stable naturalness.

If these familiar emotions of Hood's could not but have broken down under the test of Jane's leaving him, that too is in *their* tacitly admitted nature. And if they would have broken down at that extreme, still they went so far as to bear this, as his son recalls:

> His presence of mind was remarkable; as his was, I
> think, naturally, and eventually from illness, a nervous

nature. One night I was sitting up with him, my mother having gone to rest for a few hours, worn out with fatigue. He was seized about twelve o'clock, with one of his alarming attacks of hemorrhage from the lungs. When it had momentarily ceased, he motioned for paper and pencil, and asked 'if I was too frightened to stay with him'. I was too used to it now, and on my replying 'No', he quietly and calmly wrote his wishes and directions on a slip of paper, as deliberately as if it were an ordinary matter. He forbade me to disturb my mother.

ii, pp. 262–3.

This—'as if it were an ordinary matter', 'forbade me to disturb my mother'—is the serious side of 'never mind'. The store of human feeling that rests in memory is manifest when we recognise that what he actually wrote was 'do not disturb your mother' and 'are you frightened to be with me?'. It must have meant much to him to ask in writing (his own steady trade) 'are you frightened to be with me?', when 'me' is also 'your father'. Yet Hood himself must have been resolutely oblivious to the cost of such writing (it being his only resource while bleeding), in his double consciousness of himself as the case to be watched and the father still to look out. It is of that seriousness which is kept beneath Hood's last letters, written to the children of Dr Elliot. The syntax there has a lovely equality:

> don't let the baby go in and swim away, although he *is* the shrimp of the family. . . . Have you been bathed yet in the sea, and were you afraid? I was, the first time, and the time before that.
>
> ii, p. 215.

'I hope you like the sea. I always did when I was a child, which was about two years ago' (ii, p. 212). The equality of 'were you afraid? I was' is that of a life enjoyed perhaps a little more the second time round, on the rebound and with gentle pretences, yet with a grown-up's sadness beneath it for that very reason. Yet, having set himself that habit of demotic, counter-Keatsian, child-like pun, having set himself that equality as a sympathetic distraction, Hood could live up to it and make 'were you afraid?' become, in mortal adulthood, 'if I was too frightened to stay with him'.

The son who was not too frightened says this of his father's work:

> Although Hood's 'Comic Annual', as he himself used to remark with pleasure, was in every house seized upon, and almost worn out by the frequent handling of little fingers, his own children did not enjoy it till the lapse of many years had mercifully softened down some of the sad recollections connected with it.
>
> ii, p. 249.

That is the other side of the boy who did not leave his father in the midst of seizure because he 'was too used to it now'. One is sure that Hood did not remark with pleasure, although he must have silently noted, that his own children could not enjoy his work. His last letters are to the children of Dr Elliot, but emphatically for reasons other than that bitterness which a Tolstoy felt when he found that his children did not read their father's books. This habit of silently noting things, behind the face of father, husband, friend, is the literary man's habit; in Hood's case it is exceptional in that it helped him to *remain* what he thought father naturally should be. And thus, for all the earlier smart, it is from his own children, after 'the lapse of many years', that *Memorials of Thomas Hood* came: the memory of the literature he did not write, of the pain beneath the literature he did write, now coming through again, like justice to him.

'His was a nervous *nature*':

> You know how my time is divided—first I am very ill, then very busy to make up for lost time,—and then in consequence very jaded and knocked-up, which ends generally in my being very ill again.
>
> ii, p. 3.

It is a tribute to Hood that only part of the reality of what his own life was is there described. He saw to it that his life was not just to do with literature and work, however great the financial pressure, however much he led the rest of his life, nonetheless, as a series of interludes and rests. Another part, just as true though more artifically made natural to him, is that illustrated in an anecdote which Thomas Hardy told of an acquaintance:

> Bos's brother Henry the invalid has what I fear to be a churchyard cough (he died not so very long after). His cough pleases the baby, so he coughs artificially much more than required by his disease, to go on pleasing the baby. Mrs. H.S. implores her husband not to do so; but he does, nevertheless, showing the extraordinary nonchalence about death that so many of his family show.
>
> *The Life of Thomas Hardy*, p. 127.

Hood's smiles are those artificial coughs; there are 'articulate sighs' (ii, p. 217) beneath them. It is as if one knows that Hood would have recognized Hardy, if he could have wanted to choose to, as surely as Hardy could have seen what Hood had been about, had his own memory not been so haunting to him. 'One of the most painful of the illustrations which accompany these *Memorials*,' noted Masson (op. cit., p. 320), 'is a sketch of himself lying in his shroud as a corpse, which he made while in bed during his last illness.'

> A man would never laugh were he not to forget his situation. . . . Laughter always means blindness—either from defect, choice, or accident.
>
> *The Life of Thomas Hardy*, p. 12.

I conclude thus: that the justice which memory, through his children, tries to do to Thomas Hood would have seemed to Hardy less substantial and enduring a thing than the want of justice which the art of a Hardy novel reveals with respect to human beings like Tess of the d'Urbervilles. As Wordsworth learnt, the natural man, the common man needs a strong art to speak for him. What Hood needed, he himself could not provide, and that is a mark of something inextricably valuable as well as pathetic in him. Other men in a later age could and did provide.

'Well, but what is it all worth?' Once a religious woman wrote in that vein to Hood. An Evangelist claiming to know what seriousness was, she felt it her duty to warn him that his comic writing would pall on his soul in his dying hour; she enclosed some religious verses for his better guidance. At first Hood seems just to answer in his own terms: sorry to disappoint her but 'if they be the Righteous, I am content to be the Lefteous of the species' (ii, p. 117). If this is evasive irony, well there are worse ironies in writing than that: one of the verses enclosed with her letter was 'unfortunately written by a minister, who, after being expelled in disgrace from a public foundation in London, went and robbed a Poor Savings Bank in the country' (ii, p. 116). And there, one feels, Hood would have left his retort—had it not been for one thing that touched him more nearly than any other: his family.

> your fanatical mother . . . interrupted with her jargon almost my very last interview with my dying parent. Such reminiscences warrant some severity; but, if more be wanting, know that my poor sister has been excited by a circle of Canters like yourself, into a religious frenzy, and is at this moment in a private mad-house.
>
> ii, pp. 119–20.

The authority is that of a family man, a secular man and a literary man, the three in his case being intimately connected:

> As for literature 'palling on my soul in my dying hour,'— on the contrary it has been my solace and comfort through the extremes of worldly trouble and sickness, and has maintained me in a cheerfulness, a perfect sunshine of the mind, seldom seen in the faces of the most prosperous and healthy of your sect. . . . My humble works have flowed from my heart, as well as my head, and, whatever their errors, are such as I have been able to contemplate with composure, when, more than once, the Destroyer assumed almost a visible presence.
>
> ii, pp. 116–7.

His, at any rate, 'is a beautiful world'. But it also leaves one wondering whether a man of harder, stronger literary powers, a Hardy, could have felt the same about his writing and his world. Why not? Partly because Hood compromised; partly because the more powerful have to go painfully too far, for their power if not for their own good.

How far then does Hood-after-Hazlitt, the early Victorian family resolution of post-Romantic problems, actually get us? Not quite far enough thought Charles Dickens.

III. DICKENS AND THE STRONG ART OF
THE AUTOBIOGRAPHICAL NOVEL

Commending the human warmth of Dickens's *A Christmas Carol*, Hood, quoting Wordsworth, lamented that 'ours is rather a selfish, luxurious age. "The world *is* too much with us"—there is a cold calculating utiliarianism'.[27] For Hood, Charles Dickens, thirteen years his junior, was coming to be one of such an age's saving graces. Touched by Hood's favourable reviews of his early work, Dickens maintained a correspondence and a friendship with, in effect, his comic predecessor. In turn he reviewed Hood, finding one of his books (with a Hood-like pun) 'rather poor, but I have not said so, because Hood is too, and ill besides' (Forster: *The Life of Dickens*, i, p. 106).

Now, it is fitting that Dickens's 'but I have not said so' embodies just the tender compunction before vulnerability which is at the heart of Hood's own life and best work. The unspoken pathos and the tacit resonance of not minding, of not saying so was what Hood was about in restraining the power of language: that is why *Memorials of Thomas Hood* is so much a book that is *left* to us. But the idea of not wasting but using such pathos, the idea of taking such a man and talking on behalf of that unspoken pathos without appearing to violate it, the idea of focussing on a person who on the inside minded very much and of finding in prose a sub-vocal means for him to indicate, even to himself, what he could not say aloud before his nearest and dearest—these were the things that Dickens seemed born to bring to the novelist's reawakening art at this time.

Hood himself had described how the young Dickens was able to warm the human heart:

> the drift is natural, along with the great human currents, and not against them.
>
> *Memorials*, ii, p. 41.

It is not hard to see how even the later Dickens followed this 'natural' rule. Take even the smallest piece of dialogue from the death-bed scene in *David Copperfield*:

> 'I have begun to think I was not fit to be a wife.'
>
> I try to stay my tears, and to reply, 'Oh, Dora, love, as fit as I to be a husband!'

P. 657

Of course it would have gone *against* the great human current had David replied, 'Yes Dora, I too began to fear that you were not fit'. But what David also knows, by a species of natural decorum which does not need to be and had no time to be consciously thought out, is that the reply 'Oh no Dora, you were most fit to be a wife, my wife' would not be any good either. He could not tell a lie at such a moment nor could he make a reply that was all too obviously a placebo. He answers instead not by trying, in a superior kind of way, to placate her side of things but by taking the trouble to heart from his own side: 'Oh, Dora, love, as fit as I to be a husband!' Neither party can, or needs to, say now just how fit that was. For David's words make the couple partners still in sharing doubts about themselves rather than about each other. It is, by these words, still a marriage, even though Dora can come back with: 'Perhaps! But, if I had been more fit to be married, I might have made you more so, too.' By this natural eloquence they share, at final parting, the memory that they had been too young, together. I call the eloquence natural rather than rhetorical because it seems to include a tacit knowledge of what in the Victorian age it would have been unnatural and inhuman for a man and wife to say to one another. We see the tenderness of the accommodation as well as the necessity for that tenderness.

Thomas Hood had been dead four years when in 1849 there had begun to appear in monthly parts Dickens's *The Personal History, Adventures, Experience, & Observation of David Copperfield The Younger of Blunderstone Rookery (Which He never meant to be Published on any Account)*. The title of the very first chapter, 'I am Born', seems to recall things like Hood's 'I remember, I remember,/The house where I was born': there is a tingling feeling in the thought that it cannot quite be 'I' who was born, that it cannot be the house where I was *born* that I actually

remember. Such writing, with its sense of the unremembered
basis upon which the trust in our lives is founded, knowingly
incorporates a strangeness into the heart of the familiar.
Accordingly, 'I' in *David Copperfield*, a novel which is offered as
if it were a private autobiography, goes on to include two
people in one: the young David who is remembered, the older
David who does the recalling. They are neither entirely the
same nor entirely different. 'I' am the product of the story of
my own life but at the same time 'I' have emotions about the
story of my own life, now, which are not merely the emotions
which I had at the time. My memory is a child, a product, of
this story, but through my memory I also preside over this
story and, as it were, father it, almost to my own amazement:

> What an idle time it was! What an unsubstantial,
> happy, foolish time it was!
> When I measured Dora's finger for a ring that was to
> be made of Forget-me-nots, and when the jeweller, to
> whom I took the measure, found me out, and laughed
> over his order-book, and charged me anything I liked, for
> the pretty little toy, with its blue stones—so associated in
> my remembrance with Dora's hand, that yesterday, when
> I saw such another, by chance, on the finger of my own
> daughter, there was a momentary stirring in my heart,
> like pain!
>
> Pp. 417–8.

It is not simply narrative that will give the meaning of this life
linearly from birth onwards. Memory, played-off against story,
saves the meaning from being merely speedily left behind, as
past, while the narrative goes on forward. Such moments as
that of the engagement to Dora enable us to see that there are
not even just two but three times involved in the work: the
time of David's youth, as of Dora's ring of yesteryear; the time
of David's adulthood, as of his daughter's ring seen yesterday
—a daughter, incidentally, not given him by Dora but by his
second wife as it turns out; and a third time, the extra time,
that writing affords, whereby today he can see how to bring
the thoughts of those times together through authorship.[28]
Moreover, as this is a novel and not simply an autobiography,
the novelist can help, articulately, the autobiographer to help

himself in both his younger and older appearances. Meanwhile, although this is thus a novel, it is a public work in the guise of being a private one never meant for anyone's eyes but the eyes of its author, and so the reader can enjoy overhearing a work which does not seem to demand a reader at all. Everything, through the pathos of the sort of trust that Hood had to rely upon, seems here to be working to Dickens's emotive advantage.

What the young married David could not say before his child-wife Dora, the older David can help him to admit now in writing, even while tacitly claiming his more mature under-standing to be nothing more than a product of the secret admission felt inwardly at the time:

> I had a great deal of work to do, and had many anxieties, but the same considerations made me keep them to myself. I am far from sure, now, that it was right to do this, but I did it for my child-wife's sake. I search my breast, and I commit its secrets, if I know them, without any reservation to this paper. The old unhappy loss or want of something had, I am conscious, some place in my heart; but not to the embitterment of my life. When I walked alone in the fine weather, and thought of the summer days when all the air had been filled with my boyish enchantment, I did miss something of the realisation of my dreams; but I thought it was a softened glory of the Past, which nothing could have thrown upon the present time. I did feel, sometimes, for a little while, that I could have wished my wife had been my counsellor; had had more character and purpose, to sustain me and improve me by; had been endowed with power to fill up the void which somewhere seemed to be about me; but I felt as if this were an unearthly consummation of my happiness, that never had been meant to be, and never could have been.
>
> Pp. 551–2.

These secrets a man can speak of to himself in memory when, earlier, he could speak of them to no one at all. On 'this paper', memory, as the witness that a man bears to his own life, replaces the lost 'counsellor', as if compared to a real soul-

mate it were second best. Memory is the descendant of the
unresolved anxieties he kept to himself and of the 'old unhappy
loss or want of something'. Here memory both speaks and
listens as the man writes. Moreover, in context this passage,
the product of the older David's writing, is interspersed
between forward narrative prose, apparently written from
memory, and the prose of dialogue. That is to say, it is not in a
separate compartment, chapter or form; the secrets are in the
middle of the world from which they are hidden, just as the
man's inwardness is; the writing has now the same status in
the book as the other forms of prose discourse, yet we also
know that at the time to which it refers it was both secret and
under-privileged, not to say ashamed. 'I had a great deal of
work to do, and had many anxieties, but the same considerations made me keep them to myself.' Prose is so various a
medium, so crowded, check-by-jowl and all-welcoming; it
offers no formal respect for divisions between inner and outer
worlds, no hierarchical sovereignty for the internal world, even
though it is from the inner sense that this autobiography must
be presumed to be written. And Dickens gained from this very
loss of a static position of authority over his own work. He
gained, for instance, pathos from the idea of a man able to
reclaim the past by now committing 'its secrets, if I know
them, without any reservation to this paper'—but a man not
able to change that past: so that Copperfield, older as well as
younger, is controlled by the narrative (which Dickens
controls), even as the older man saves the memory and internal
meaning of the younger man from being quite lost and
absorbed in the mere turn of external events. Dickens balances
so well these advantages and disadvantages, using his art not
to let his art seem to be doing more than life would allow.

   For the authority in this apparent autobiography lies not so
much with memory as with reality. That is to say, the book is,
to use an electrician's term, 'earthed', giving prominence to
events over dreams. 'I did miss something of the *realisation* of
my dreams; but I thought it was a softened glory of the Past,
which nothing could have thrown upon the present time. . . . I
felt as if this were an *unearthly* consummation of my happiness,
that never had been meant to be, and never could have been.'
All memory can do is intervene to save, from the charge of

being merely unrealistic, that old Romantic loss or want of something; but its main function in this book is to pose as the faculty that, above all, enables David to write his own story, a story largely made up of what externally became of him. What it means to say that the book is 'earthed' may be made clearer in considering the account of David's wedding to Dora in chapter 43. It is written in a floating dream of a present tense as if to mime the daze the young bridegroom was in all that day. Young David seems still to speak through his older narrator here: 'We have a delightful evening, and are supremely happy; but I don't believe it yet. I can't collect myself. I can't check off my happiness as it takes place' (p. 537). Checking off the emotions, finding their habitation, personal attachment or external location, finding them *not* to be too good or too bad also to be true: all this is the more usual 'earthing' which this book carries out. In such a book, memory is not a power in itself but has to surrender its power to create the spectacle of someone whose life and character, before the very eyes of his older self, from 'I am Born' onwards, emerged under and out of the force of circumstances. Dickens is less interested in the privileged strength a man may grow into than in that very strength having to see again the weakness from which it had to struggle to grow:

> I know enough of the world now, to have almost lost the capacity of being much surprised by anything; but it is a matter of some surprise to me, even now, that I can have been so easily thrown away at such an age. A child of excellent abilities, and with strong powers of obser-vation, quick, eager, delicate, and soon hurt bodily or mentally, it seems wonderful to me that nobody should have made any sign in my behalf.
>
> P. 132.

(Would the word 'wonderful' have been used so disappointedly seventy years previously at the height of Romanticism?). As Forster recognized, these words echoed Dickens's own experi-ence of being sent out to a blacking warehouse, an experience in which Dickens afterwards found 'the explanation of himself' (*The Life of Charles Dickens*, i, p. 34). The more Dickens could show that the power and status of a presiding memory was reduced from what, say, it had been to Wordsworth, the more he could find in that a pathos and a consequently compensating power. For, yielding to circumstances was, you may recall, a sign to Dickens at the same time not to yield to be what circumstances were conspiring to make him. In due course we shall have to consider how far he was exploiting, how far defending and redeeming, the more vulnerable and under-privileged parts of the human situation of his times and of his own history.

For the moment I want to suggest how memory in this novel is not a strong tool for self-investigation but, poignantly, a more secondary faculty. Quite simply, David Copperfield was always more concerned to find other people to know and love him than he was merely to know and find himself. What, more than anything, *David Copperfield* is about is a theme very close to the heart of this present chapter: the search for what David himself calls 'a natural home' (p. 419). That need is established from the first moment, when David tells us, 'My father's eyes had closed upon the light of this world six months, when mine opened on it. There is something strange to me, even now, in the reflection that he never saw me' (p. 2). The first thing with David was not to want to see his father but to want to be seen by him: the need for a witness, the witness of an older person, the person who was your life's begetter. A sense of insecurity, of having missed something from the very beginning of one's life, the feeling of being thrust into the middle of life without knowing whence, whither or why, a sense of anterior strange-ness always lurking behind the sense of the familiar to which one has grown accustomed, the need for a basis and an origin, the need for a person who knows your origin and instigated it, who guarded you and remembers you from a time earlier than the time you first recall, a person to be the embodiment of guardian memory to whom you can always turn to ask the future way: these are the things felt behind the image of posthumous birth. They are felt the more after the disastrous remarriage of the young girl of a mother to Murdstone, advocate of 'firmness' along with his interfering sister; with all the consequent disrupting of a sense of home to which one belonged and could be remembered as belonging. The Murdstones dismiss such things as weakness. 'My old dear bedroom was changed, and I was to lie a long way off' (p. 37):

they would not understand why he would use the word 'old' piously here, for instance. Or why he wanted a father to see him. Weak, passive, unfirm!

Yet, without first bases and with the memory only of their being wanting, all the subsequent action of David's life is to find second chances of finding a home and being seen with love. But it cannot simply be a matter of finding from the present mere surrogates for the sake of the past and 'the old unhappy loss or want of something'—although, indeed, this is a book of hardly conscious substitutions: the Peggotty family to substitute for his own, the familiarizing of ties to girls, like Little Em'ly and, later, Agnes, into ties with sisters, the opposing guides of his youth, Steerforth on the male side, Agnes on the female, the aunt who becomes a second mother, the young wife like the girl-bride his own mother had been, the meetings and reunions with people from the past until memory becomes a sort of family feeling—and so on. Even so, there is a powerful, earthing compunction against fantasy and the coarsening consequences of unhesitatingly making the future in the image of the past and human beings into models of replacement: 'From that night there grew up in my breast, a feeling for Peggotty, which I cannot well define. She did not replace my mother; no one could do that; but she came into a vacancy in my heart, which closed upon her, and I felt towards her something I have never felt for any other human being. It was a sort of comical affection too; and yet if she had died, I cannot think what I should have done, or how I should have acted out the tragedy as it would have been to me' (p. 53). As with Hood, something in the nature of the new, demotic, dislocated mixing-up of life, in the almost accidental relations out of which one tried to make a natural home, made for the instabilities of tragi-comedy in response, Moreover, as the young Hazlitt had suggested, people in times of confusion learn very quickly to find the reality of their inward emotions not in themselves but in what they can borrow from external circumstances, thus substituting what Hazlitt took to be first principles for secondary reflections. For example, the young David on returning home to find his mother remarried and the home quite altered: 'I was crying all the time, but, except that I was conscious of being cold and dejected, I am sure I never

thought why I cried. At last in my desolation I began to
consider I was dreadfully in love with little Em'ly, and had
been torn away from her to come here where no one seemed to
want me, or to care about me, half as much as she did' (p. 38).
If we ask, what would he have thought had there been no
Em'ly or if he realized that his feelings were not really to do
with her as such, we find an answer in an equivalent episode
later in the novel. It comes after David, sent out from the
family to work, finds funny-sad, childish-adult comfort in
lodging with the Micawber family, until they have to leave the
house through debt. Then he realizes: 'I had grown so
accustomed to the Micawbers, and had been so intimate with
them in their distresses, and was so utterly friendless without
them, that the prospect of being thrown upon some new shift
for a lodging, and going once more among unknown people,
was like being that moment turned adrift into my present life,
with such knowledge of it ready made, as experience had given
me' (p. 148). Beneath the narrative there may be sensed, from
time to time, a little apart from all that happens to involve
David, a sometimes frightened and lonely recognition of 'the
whole charge of my own existence'. The thing apart from
Em'ly or Dora or the Micawbers.

But never perhaps quite apart from Agnes—or at least
David's sense of Agnes as tacit support and witness. It is
Agnes, the 'sister' who for so long unbeknown to David loved
him more than as a brother, who holds the memory of everything in trust for the writer that David becomes—as, for
example, when the young man, in one of his assumed moods of
self-possession, dismisses the memory of the failure of his
adolescent loves:

> 'Whenever I fall into trouble, or fall in love, I shall always
> tell you, if you'll let me—even when I come to fall in love
> in earnest.'
> 'Why, you have always been in earnest!' said Agnes,
> laughing again.
> 'Oh! that was as a child, or a schoolboy,' said I,
> laughing in my turn, not without being a little shame-
> faced. 'Times are altering now, and I suppose I shall be in
> a terrible state of earnestness one day or other. My wonder

is, that you are not in earnest yourself, by this time, Agnes.'
Agnes laughed again, and shook her head.

Pp. 235–6.

The irony of Agnes's situation, since she never tells her earnest love, is precisely what saves this novel from being merely a linear story and makes a reader think back to how she must have felt in the background, as if it were indeed a memory. The tone of memory in the novel—sanely but poignantly between loving and laughing—is so often set or conditioned by her or the thought of her. 'Why, you have always been in earnest!' And in return the book often feels as if it were written for Agnes—so characteristic is it of this novel that memory should be not so much an independent power of mind as an association with a person. It is an art of association—which to Coleridge had been merely the lower function of the human mind. For Dickens it shows Hood's great human currents.

At any rate, the weight of a sense of the lonely responsibility for one's own existence is not in this book something that can be borne consciously over an extended period. It is, for David at least, something that has to follow the course of a story, being checked off against the impinging world outside him in which that existence of his makes its appearance with affection and with anxiety. Rescued from work, he goes back to school with memories that affect his outward behaviour precisely to the extent that, paradoxically, he feels them hidden behind it: 'troubled as I was, by my want of boyish skill, and of book-learning too, I was made infinitely more uncomfortable by the consideration that, in what I did know, I was much farther removed from my companions than in what I did not. My mind ran upon what they would think, if they knew of my familiar acquaintance with the King's Bench Prison?' (p. 195). This is not memory presiding over life but having to live beside it, in circumstances moreover where what is remembered is, virtually in terms of class, both low and lowering.

Yet for all the impossibility of carrying the weight of his own existence solely within his own private consciousness, only once, I think, does David turn to someone outside and ask explicitly what, for want of early security, he has always wanted to ask of a world that went on so indifferently before him. Namely, asking for help to live his own life and for knowledge of life's own hidden laws. It happens the once when, uncertain and newly-wed, he turns to his aunt, his 'second mother' (p. 296), after a row with Dora about the practicalities of home management. It is an important episode, and I wish to quote at length.

> It was two or three hours past midnight when I got home. I found my aunt, in our house, sitting up for me.
>
> 'Is anything the matter, aunt?' said I, alarmed.
>
> 'Nothing, Trot,' she replied. 'Sit down, sit down. Little Blossom has been rather out of spirits, and I have been keeping her company. That's all.'
>
> I leaned my head upon my hand; and felt more sorry and downcast, as I sat looking at the fire, than I could have supposed possible so soon after the fulfilment of my brightest hopes. As I sat thinking, I happened to meet my aunt's eyes, which were resting on my face. There was an anxious expression in them, but it cleared directly.
>
> 'I assure you, aunt,' said I, 'I have been quite unhappy myself all night, to think of Dora's being so. But I had no other intention than to speak to her tenderly and lovingly about our home-affairs.'
>
> My aunt nodded encouagement.
>
> 'You must have patience, Trot,' she said.
>
> 'Of course. Heaven knows I don't mean to be unreasonable, aunt!'
>
> 'No, no,' said my aunt. 'But Little Blossom is a very tender little blossom, and the wind must be gentle with her.'
>
> I thanked my good aunt, in my heart, for her tenderness towards my wife; and I was sure that she knew I did.

David here begins to feel relief and gratitude for the tenderness which his aunt shows to his wife, even though it means her being, very tactfully, just a little less tender towards him. It is a moment reminiscent of the time he needed his 'sister' Agnes to think well and speak well of Dora when she had just become his intended: 'Never, never, had I loved Dora so deeply and truly, as I loved her that night. . . . I told Agnes it was her doing' (p. 523). Other people, loved and trusted people, form the ratifying background that his own felt want of experience so much requires. When Agnes told him that it would not be like himself to be underhand in his courtship of Dora, he replied, 'Like myself, in the too high opinion you have of me, Agnes, I am afraid' (p. 485)—'Without her I was not, and I never had been, what she thought me' (p. 699). People, the memory of them and the consciousness of himself in their memories—these, not places, are his natural home. Dialogue is a form of family support here ('My aunt nodded encouragement') rather than, as in *Liber Amoris*, dialectical refutation. The drift is *with* the great human currents of tacit understanding: 'I thanked my good aunt, in my heart . . . and I was sure that she knew I did'. But on the strength of that David feels encouraged to ask a question which exactly shows what going *against* life's current might at that time consist in; ironically it is the very moment that he asks for outside help lest the two of them, Dora and he, totter and fall together:

> 'Don't you think, aunt,' said I, after some further contemplation of the fire, 'that you could advise and counsel Dora a little, for our mutual advantage, now and then?'
>
> 'Trot,' returned my aunt, with some emotion, 'no! Don't ask me such a thing!'
>
> Her tone was so very earnest that I raised my eyes in surprise.

What natural current, what tacit human law of this time, has he here transgressed? For once he is told; dialogue answers its purpose:

> 'estimate her (as you chose her) by the qualities she has, and not by the qualities she may not have. The latter you must develop in her, if you can. And if you cannot, child,' here my aunt rubbed her nose, 'you must just accustom yourself to do without 'em. But remember, my dear, your future is between you two. No one can assist you; you are to work it out for yourselves. . . .'
>
> . . . As she stood in her garden, holding up her little lantern to light me back, I thought her observation of me had an anxious air again; but I was too much occupied in pondering on what she had said, and too much impressed—for the first time, in reality—by the conviction

that Dora and I had indeed to work out our future for ourselves, and that no one could assist us, to take much notice of it.

Pp. 545–6.

It is a beautiful touch that even as she calls him 'child', she knows she is having to make him see his adulthood. She thinks, nonetheless, that she is refusing him. Actually, she is answering him in a bigger way than he had even hoped; the way which, once it is given, David to his credit knows to be not only what he needed but what he really wanted too. For what he wanted, beneath it all, was to be assured from without, appropriately enough, of what external circumstances had so long denied him: namely, the freedom to feel that his reality lay inside as well as outside him. Even Hood, it must be granted, had partially hidden from external hardnesses by pretending to be as a child. Not to hide yet not to remain a child, to be an adult yet not to lose in the outside world of strangers the earlier, familiar warmths and pieties, to grow up without merely growing to acquiesce in what circumstances were conspiring to make one: that was Dickens's fable for himself and for his times.

The idea that now he had a marriage and a home of his own seemed to David to offer a guarantee of inner security and an established life. It was virtually as if his emotions had touched and reached and created reality in this 'fulfilment of my brightest hopes'. And so as disappointment sets in during those early days of marriage it is only when his aunt puts it to him as a human duty, that he must live with his wife, if need be, on the same grounds as those on which he first chose and loved her, that he can bring himself to put aside the sense of a let-down. This means that he has to bear to think, within himself again, uncertain and unverifiable things about his child-wife that he must not tell her. Must not for the sake of the memory of his love and for the sake of her peace. This was hard, because for him this marriage was to be the one relation in which his innerness was not to be a vulnerable and ashamed necessity, the mere something upon which he had always to fall back upon after defeats. No, his innerness here was, rather, to have been literally at home for once, married with someone, given the discretion of socially recognized privacy. Thus even when he *can* bring himself to hold back these reservations about life with Dora from Dora herself, it leaves a memory of complex feelings of betrayal: 'I am far from sure, now, that it was right to do this, but I did it for my child-wife's sake.' No book of the time makes clearer to us, through the vulnerability of its protagonist and the openness of its memory of him, the sensitive human needs and tender contradictions that lay behind, and even lay in trouble within, what nowadays we are all too glibly tempted to think of as the stuffy Victorian institution of private behaviour in forms of marriage and family. For in this novel these very forms serve to highlight the more strange informalities, otherwise so difficult to see and to talk about, involved in transitions towards forms and accommodations within them.

'The drift is natural': but in following what seemed to offer themselves as the natural currents of what could and could not be said between people, the thing that the novel, over Hood, could do was also show the life that lay implicit or even immured within this contemporary sense of the natural. For example, 'impressed—for the first time, in reality—by the conviction that Dora and I had indeed to work out our future for ourselves'. 'Reality' here has now to do with two things. First, with realization, since it is on second thought, after his marriage, that David begins to see from within what the convention of getting and being married might mean. Second, it has to do with words, given to him, in this case, explicitly from outside through his aunt, in order that he might try to understand what has happened: 'Work out the future for ourselves . . . no one could assist us' he repeats to himself. To the young Hazlitt, I suppose, this would only be the way that people seem to think that they have to live their lives twice over before they are living 'in reality' at all. But for Copperfield and for his generation this was still a significant improvement upon his suffering the feeling that reality was always what was external to him. In the new world of urban and industrial post-Romanticism it is as though the writer had to begin again, through words, by giving up the claim to be adult and then working out from youth what it was he had grown into. Memory, more than he in himself, held in trust the meaning of what he was. For memory was both himself *and* the witness of himself.

The young husband who asked for a help that could not be given, and received from his aunt the help of words instead, is, for all the development, the same person as the little boy who, in the unwelcoming home of his mother's remarriage, tried to read his troubles away.

> My father had left in a little room up-stairs, to which I had access (for it adjoined my own) a small collection of books which nobody else in our house ever troubled. From that blessed little room, Roderick Ransom, Peregrine Pickle, Humphrey Clinker, Tom Jones, The Vicar of Wakefield, Don Quixote, Gil Blas, and Robinson Crusoe, came out, with a glorious host, to keep me company. . . . It is curious to me how I could ever have consoled myself under my small troubles (which were great troubles to me), by impersonating my favourite characters in them— as I did . . .
>
> This was my only and my constant comfort. When I think of it, the picture always rises in my mind, of a summer evening, the boys at play in the churchyard, and I sitting on my bed, reading as if for life.
>
> P. 48.

—Reading as if for life the books which, significantly, his father had left. 'It is,' notes Forster (*The Life of Charles Dickens*, i, p. 7), 'one of the many passages in Copperfield which are literally true'. This literary keeping up of his internal resources stems from the fact of a boy, in trouble, being incapable of living quite on his own. Yet, when it comes to the time of his mother's death, not long afterwards, he cannot quite bring himself to believe that the reading that has so vividly helped him to live is actually part of a real life:

> I can recollect, indeed, to have speculated, at odd times, on the possibility of my not being taught any more, or cared for any more; and growing up to be a shabby moody man, lounging an idle life away, about the village; as well as on the feasibility of my getting rid of this picture by going away somewhere, like the hero in a story, to seek my fortune: but these were transient visions, day dreams I sat looking at sometimes, as if they were faintly presented

or written on the wall of my room, and which, as they
melted away, left the wall blank again.

P. 116.

'Reading *as if* for life' is still very much the point, it being
another of David's half-unwilling attempts to find substitutes
and projections. 'Whether I shall turn out to be the hero of my
own life, . . . these pages must show' (p. 1) this novel itself
begins, as if in memory of that childish love of literary heroism,
but tempered by a sense of what literature must now be in an
adult age. What the pages do show, right up until to the end of
that crucial conversation with his aunt, is the picture of a boy
and a young man always prone to feel that the authority of
experience is something external to him, something to be
asked for and enquired of, something that he has to impersonate
if he cannot seize, a thing perhaps to be got, perhaps to be lost,
through words. It is as though the young David feels that he is
too weak in himself, for what *he* has, to constitute the real
thing, an equivalent authority. Yet what he cannot rely on in
himself in fact imaginatively built up the reality of books which
he felt supported him—and what he cannot rely on in himself
constitutes the subject-matter of this one, *David Copperfield*.
Strength and weakness look very much alike to the sort of
literary man that Dickens was, when, for example, he used his
own wounds to create David's. So it is with David, as the older
man is able to write his story out of the memory of the younger.

Equally then, the young boy who read as if for life is the
same person as the man who became a writer—particularly a
writer whose achievement is now to be able to write unapolo-
getically 'a Story, with its purpose growing, not remotely, out
of my experience' (p. 699). And it is virtually the completion of
the book when its protagonist becomes the sort of person
possessing his own experience sufficiently to have been able to
write of it. For by then David's experience is, what the young
man could hardly feel, his own. It is the story of how the want
of experience can be recognized, through writing, to have been
an experience and not just the want of one—and nothing
characterizes the writer for Dickens more than this capacity
for profiting the second time round, with all the mistakes as
grist to the literary mill. All the earnest pretences and pathetic
substitutes made by youth—for Hazlitt the borrowed life but

for Dickens the tenderly comic one—are not the absence of a real story nor at the other extreme a story to be taken upon youth's own extravagant terms: they are a story for memory to 'place' and tell. In short, *David Copperfield* is almost an allegory of the human importance of a man not only becoming a writer but also using his own memory in the act of becoming a writer. For those two things together, writing and memory, are the sign of David's rich adulthood. He can use his own words now, he can bear his loneliness.

Thus it is not simply a matter of artist's convenience that makes Copperfield become a writer, as if merely to explain how he could write his own autobiography so proficiently. Nor is it simply the case that Dickens wanted to cover his own professional tracks by making the supposed author of this apparently private document a professional likewise. For this novel is *The Prelude* of the age of prose, full of images like that of Dora, child-wife from whom David has to withhold his un-happiness, being allowed to hold the writer's pens for him on the edge of his activity. When David lets her copy out his writing neatly only that she should feel part of his work, is this as serious a thing as she childishly supposes? or is it just play and precisely because of its triviality no joke, as he suspects? is the writing he is actually doing at the time more serious than what is happening in his own home? is the writing of the memory of such a domestic scene itself now more important as writing than the very work which he did in spite of Dora?

Moreover when Dickens made Copperfield a writer (as, I suspect, something in the whole current of the novel gradually led him to), he was tacitly admitting that this fictional auto-biography by D.C. was the autobiographical fiction of C.D. : 'It is singular that it should never have occurred to him, while the name was thus strangely as by accident bringing itself together, that the initials were but his own reversed. He was much startled when I pointed this out'; 'Oh, my dear Forster, if I were to say half of what *Copperfield* makes me feel to-night, how strangely, even to you, I should be turned inside-out!' (*The Life of Charles Dickens*, ii, pp. 78, 98): Thus this from the near the end of the novel:

> We stood together in the same old-fashioned window at
> night, when the moon was shining; Agnes with her quiet

eyes raised up to it; I following her glance. Long miles of
road then opened out before my mind; and, toiling on, I
saw a ragged way-worn boy, forsaken and neglected, who
should come to call even the heart now beating against
mine, his own.

P. 739

—this, I say, is something like the following from Dickens's
own autobiographical notes 'turned inside-out':

> For many years, when I came near to Robert Warrens' in
> the Strand, I crossed over to the opposite side of the way,
> to avoid a certain smell of the cement they put upon the
> blacking-corks, which reminded me of what I was once. It
> was a long time before I liked to go up Chandos Street.
> My old way home by the Borough made me cry, after my
> eldest child could speak.
>
> *The Life of Charles Dickens*, i, p. 33.

And together they both remind us of David thinking of Dora's
ring while seeing just such another on the finger of his (and
Agnes's) own daughter. Clearly these accounts were written
by the same man, with the same emotional habits. But we
have to ask what is the relation between Charles Dickens and
David Copperfield, a relation not so open to us as that between
the writer of *The Prelude* and William Wordsworth.

As Forster notes, the piece about Chandos Road and the
blacking works comes from an autobiographical account which
'had all been written, as fact, before he thought of any other
use for it'. Forster goes on, significantly, 'and it was not until
several months later, when the fancy of David Copperfield,
itself suggested by what he had so written of his early troubles,
began to take shape in his mind, that he abandoned his first
intention of writing his own life' (*The Life of Charles Dickens*, i,
p. 20). Why didn't Dickens continue to write the autobiography, why did he turn inside-out, outside-in instead? For a
start, Dickens was not a steady man. The way he thought of
memory, found it acting upon him, could write from it, was
not the way of steady autobiography: memory was rather this
turning him at once back to his boyhood and forward to his
own son, back to his fiancee and forward, in the character of

David, to the daughter of his second marriage, as if in the midst of writing, his life sprang up before and behind him together: 'a boy . . . who should come to call even the heart now beating against mine, his own'. For Dickens, his inner thoughts were most real to him when they came to him, through that beloved power of his called coincidence, from outside; he could only find what was most permanently in him reflected in accidents and through chances. Prose with him was a contingent, associative medium; it offered him no hierarchies, no formal measure, but an overflowing jumble between youth and adulthood, joy and sorrow, held within a strong, external narrative line. By association and through contingency were the ways that Dickens the leveller felt his most important memories and ideas coming back at odd moments into his writing practice to help him, as, part by monthly part, he improvised his journey and took his chances through subject-matter that he fundamentally and emotionally trusted to give him his opportunities. Why did David Copperfield have to become a writer? Not just because Dickens 'wanted' him to; but because Dickens had put so much of himself, already, into Copperfield that he could not stop him. What could he not stop? The impulse, in David now, to find something on which to lean his life without his ceasing to feel through it the weight of his own existence; something to stand for his life without standing merely in place of it and without his life having to stand alone; an external assurance through words that at the same time had to be internally created and maintained. Dickens found this in the creation of David Copperfield, a version of himself that could come to him from outside; at a different but corresponding level David Copperfield himself found this in learning to become the man who could write his own life for the sake of Agnes, now his second wife and second chance. David is Dickens's second chance. Dickens saw himself as a father and an adult whose very length, depth and lowness of experience, when he compared it with that of his own children, seemed almost to unman him and partially disqualify him from roles of authority. The only position left him, to support his memory, his adulthood and his fatherhood, was that of author. Thus, through using his own experience through the fiction of its being young

David's, Dickens, as in Hood's joke, became his own child, as well as, through the control of the older David, father of that child:

> like many fond parents, I have in my heart of hearts a favourite child. And his name is DAVID COPPERFIELD.
>
> P. 752.

Dickens's imagination made real to him, made 'David' to him, memories of experiences which at the time had been too under-privileged to seem worthy of a status equivalent to the reality outside that was indifferent to them. David the auto-biographer was the way Dickens wanted to write of himself, the husband and father he thought he could have been. But the very creation of David is a tacit admission that Dickens could not write of himself in the way David did, even if, inevitably, David's style is Dickens's. This is very odd: we shall need to ask further what it means.

We are clearly at the heart of why and how *David Copperfield* had to be written when we read Dickens saying 'My old way home . . . made me cry, after my eldest child could speak'. When we acknowledge that it is characteristic of Dickens to make his sense of adult weakness emotionally powerful in that way, it is an acknowledgement that brings with it an ambivalent estimate. Part of that estimate finds release in harshness towards Dickens: one's suspicion of writer's oppor-tunism in the pathetic recourse which the memorialist, in the midst of thoughts of his own struggling youth, has to the thought of his own children. It is almost as if Hood had exploited his family and himself in publishing his own letters; or as if as soon as the old insecurity caught Dickens, he rushed to thoughts of his children for sentimental support and the gentle self-pity of contrasts. Arguably, in this mood of harsh-ness, it might be said that he used this part of him in writing *David Copperfield*, making that 'child' an innocent version of himself. Yet on the other hand, although we can spot this trick, calling it hypocrisy or exploitation, and although thereby we can cut off its effects by going against it, this in itself cuts us off from the great human currents that seem to flow from the thought of a man looking at both his own past and his own child at once. Who looked after *me* as I look after him? shall I

be able to look after *him* after such a childhood as mine? what
looks over me *now* as I look over him? my Past, perhaps? as I
look back at it? For us to see only the immaturity and sentimentality makes us not see big but vulnerable thoughts that
insist that their birthright lies in such things, while still claiming
to go beyond them. For Dickens there is a powerful connection
between the low—the sentimental, the popular, the vulgar,
even the devious—and the deep.[29]

Yet the fact is that the disclosure of Dickens's methods at
least threatens to harm Dickens's work of fiction in a way that
simply was not the case in our analysis of Wordsworth's poetic
art. In Wordsworth, on the contrary, the way he worked
through to his achievement was (in the work's own autobiography, so to speak) itself part of that achievement, confirming it. With Dickens there is always a question as to how
far the emotional effects are a reclamation of the rights of basic
human pieties, how far matters of opportunistic audience-
exploitation.

Nonetheless, when we turn to *David Copperfield* at its best
the novel seems to refuse to be reduced by these charges of
emotional deviousness. Consider a passage from chapter 48
where David again takes stock of his marriage to Dora. The
writing here seems to stand in memory of the failure of
speaking and sharing at the time:

> What I missed, I still regarded—I always regarded—as
> something that had been a dream of my youthful fancy;
> that was incapable of realisation; that I was now dis-
> covering to be so, with some natural pain, as all men did.
> But, that it would have been better for me if my wife
> could have helped me more, and shared the many thoughts
> in which I had no partner; and that this might have been;
> I knew.
>
> Between these two irreconcilable conclusions: the one,
> that what I felt was general and unavoidable; the other,
> that it was particular to me, and might have been different:
> I balanced curiously, with no distinct sense of their
> opposition to each other.
>
> P. 595.

The split between the Romantic man and the practical man,

between a sense of the general possibilities held within the spiritual man and a realization of the particular circumstances that the life of the natural man comes down to, is, as we have seen in this chapter, primarily historical—and equally post-Wordsworthian. But the recognition that it could not merely feel like a split, indeed that it was—without drama—worse in a way for being less certain a thing than that in a man's mind, we owe to writing such as this here by Dickens with its notion of 'curious balancing'. Such balancing meant that one could not be entirely satisfied with the particular realization of one's life, and one could find good, particular reasons for this ('better if my wife could have helped me more'—if *she* could have); but neither could one feel, as a so-called adult, the right to remain unsatisfied with that life for the mere sake of what now seemed proved to be a dream or fancy of simple youth. Neither satisfied nor dissatisfied, without a language in which to feel legitimate in expressing an unhappiness one nonetheless compromisingly suffered, this was a person's area of something-nothing that Thomas Hood would never have wanted to be able to refer to, that Charles Dickens desperately needed to. This writing is neither a generalization about the laws of life nor a commitment to telling simply a particular story: rather, in the area between the two there is here a man writing to discover if the disappointment he has found with 'some natural(?) pain' is the same 'as all men did'. Autobiographical fiction, pitched between the personal and the public, was the new form in which to ask: who are 'all' these men that each of us is meant to be like? is it a law of nature or the way we all at present hide our unhappinesses even from each other? The autobiographical novel takes its place in just such a middle distance between personal experience and the consensus view of experience for the sake of their mutual criticism in an increasingly uncertain world. All the evidence seems to suggest, moreover, that even in the years following the writing of *David Copperfield* Dickens himself felt as unresolved as David was here:

> Why is it, that as with poor David, a sense comes always crushing on me now, when I fall into low spirits, as of one happiness I missed in life, and one friend and companion I have never made?
>
> *The Life of Charles Dickens*, ii, p. 197.

Unable to know whether this trouble was due to him more than it was simply due to the nature of life, Dickens *had* to create David: it was his only means of thinking about his own trouble without the fact of its being perhaps merely his *own* pre-empting his thinking.

And yet when we think of Dickens's methods, we are troubled by suspicions. We sometimes suspect that Dickens made the narrator of the story the same person as its protagonist not to show the one growing out of the latter but in order to superimpose additional pathos intrinsic to the idea of an older human being able to make sense of his younger, confused self. Moreover, in the passage we have just been looking at, we have also to recognize that part of its basic function is to prepare the reader for the death of Dora being superseded by a marriage to Agnes. It is part of a plot, like it or not, and the plot does mean that, with the marriage to Agnes, the general problems of this life are resolved within the particular resolution, the something and the someone always missed being now found. Of course Dickens is a great enough novelist and a cunning enough improviser to resist the tendency of his plot long enough to create obstacles to that final happiness that, usefully, make his art work harder for what it could have won all too easily. David's hesitation over what the plot urges—namely, remarriage—is magnificently rendered. But it is only hesitation; it is not the reality of Dickens himself writing five or six years after publishing *David Copperfield*, in the midst of his unhappy marriage, that he has never found an Agnes. For beneath the final happiness that this novel leads towards, one senses a Dickensian demotic glee: 'No one was more intensely fond than Dickens of old nursery tales, and he had a secret delight in feeling that he was here only giving them a higher form' (*The Life of Charles Dickens*, i, p. 301): a higher form whose art lies in preventing us from dismissing it as fundamentally still childish. A secret delight, even if later he bemoaned the fact that his own life had no such happy ending. For the sort of concerns which bothered Dickens were precisely those that could be dismissed by the iron men in hard times as sentimental and childish. They were also those that, correspondingly, people struggling in hard times might well most want to believe in and see defended as inalienably 'natural'.

With this advantage and this disadvantage, Dickens tied his big thoughts to the sentimentalities in which they came most easily to him. In that way he could mime the pathetic situation of a particular life unhappily productive of more general aspirations which it could neither claim nor avoid. It is an art suffering from and thriving upon disproportion, high and low, big and small intervolved; the pathos a literary disguise for the unhappiness which it resembled; the thriving a disguise for the suffering. Our problem is not that Dickens *either* needed David *or* exploited him: the need was so great and various as to exist unstably between these two alternatives.

There is an example of this emotional fluidity in one of the beautiful, incidental little touches by which we come to register that David is a writer and a novelist:

> It is not my purpose, in this record, though in all other essentials it is my written memory, to pursue the history of my own fictions. They express themselves, and I leave them to themselves. When I refer to them, incidentally, it is only as a part of my progress.
>
> Pp. 588–9.

Yet just as David used reticence to support his marriage to Dora, so this quiet fact supports the whole of the book, morally as well as technically. For it is fluidly both an acknowledgement and a defence. It is a tacit acknowledgement that being a writer was a part as well as a consequence of this man's emotional quest and emotional life. It is a defence by which Dickens tries to hold off attention from the thoughts of fiction, from the professional manipulations that are also part of the writer's business—leave those to me, Dickens seems to be saying, and see instead the part of me on whose behalf I do the manipulation—David Copperfield, my favourite child. This is Dickens's signature, delicately indicating where he wanted us to stop: with the idea of all that goes into making the life of a writer thus recorded in the writer's own autobiography, yet without the fact of that writer being a novelist changing the humanity in him that led him to write. This is meant to be writing which is off-duty; Dickens asks us to accept it as such for the sake of what laws of life we may see with its help, as David did; but without that help getting in the way of what we see. The novel, of course, was still considered a low form of art and, accordingly, the whole business of the more cynically adult part of being a novelist, the artfulness even needed here to create and support the illusion of 'straight' and sincere autobiography, is lifted from David's shoulders. It is not of course as clear-cut as that, the art being too productively unstable to admit of the two levels of Dickens and of Copperfield remaining distinct and formalized in Dickens's mind. But what other explanation is there for Dickens's account of what *David Copperfield* meant to him?

> no one can ever believe this Narrative, in the reading, more than I have believed it in the writing.
>
> P. lxxi.

Of course, characteristically, this is a challenge as well as an acknowledgement to his readers: 'a stern and even cold isolation of self-reliance side by side with a susceptivity almost feminine and the most eager craving for sympathy' (*The Life of Charles Dickens*, i, p. 35). What could he expect? who could believe it more than he? Yet, when Forster mentioned to him that one simply could not believe in the reality of the courting David's love for Dora, that outside a book it would be over-done, Dickens, who chose not to write his autobiography, furiously wrote to Forster saying that the feeling was all true and was what he had felt in four hopeless years of courting Maria Beadnell: 'I don't quite apprehend what you mean by my over-rating the strength of the feeling of five-and-twenty-years ago . . . you are wrong, because nothing can exaggerate that' (*The Life of Charles Dickens*, i, p. 47). How could he have it both ways? was he or was he not writing his autobiography? And if it was only his autobiography at one remove, why did it move him so much that nobody could believe in this book as much as its own writer had?

Dickens may well have meant that books, and for him this particular book, had deeper meanings and firmer realities in the memories of their writers than readers could ever imagine from the words or feel within themselves. But within this general proposition there were, I think, particular considerations that complicate, as as well as enforce, it. It must have meant something more to him than it could to any other reader

that Dora was, I guess, not only Maria Beadnell but also his
own wife, the disappointment of living with whom led this
great novelist of the family to leave her in 1858 amidst public
rumour. He had already been married for thirteen years when
David Copperfield started to appear in 1849. Forster hints that
the separation came at a time when Dickens's books were no
longer the compensation for domestic difficulty that they might
have been and that the writing of *David Copperfield* had
something to do with this development: 'Up to the date of the
completion of *Copperfield* he had felt himself to be in possession
of an all-sufficient resource. Against whatever might befall he
had a set-off in his imaginative creations' (*The Life of Charles
Dickens*, ii, p. 194). In *David Copperfield*, however, he had used
himself and, he feared, exhausted himself and his resources of
experience. The ideals in his books were 'too exclusively made
up of sympathy for, and with, the real in its most intense form,
[for Dickens then] to be sufficiently provided against failure in
the realities around him' (ibid., p. 200). Where was his Agnes?
save in his own creation of her out of his own wants? She partly
had been, I guess, the sister-in-law who lived with Dickens
and wife during the early days of their marriage only to die
with them suddenly at the age of seventeen: 'an essential part
of my being' he called her memory, 'inseparable from my
existence as the beating of my heart is' (ibid., p. 402). He loved
her—what else can we conclude?—more than he loved his
wife, her elder sister. Mary died in 1837.

Like the necessities of his own fictional art, these were the
private thoughts that Dickens must have left behind his
writing of *David Copperfield*. These troubles were what he saw,
and only he, when he read his own book and was moved by the
purity which, through such thoughts as well as despite them,
he had created. He was moved not only by the innocence but
by the necessity of professionalism to restore it. The artistic
means were to dissolve into the artistic effect, the result
redeeming the memory of why Dickens, as insecure as Copperfield, had to disguise himself and his family troubles with art in
order to have a human life, to see the human life he had had.
He could not do this and admit he was doing it at the same
time: all he could was make his experience vigorously aesthetic
by making it young David's and making young David's

experience real by seeing it again through the older David's eyes; making David a writer was the nearest he could get to a sign and an admission. 'The more real the man,' he said 'the more genuine the actor': 'he seemed to be always the more himself for being somebody else' (*The Life of Charles Dickens*, ii, pp. 51, 399–400). A book like Forster's offers itself as a surrogate autobiography because its piety to the memory of its subject overcomes a disruptive questioning of why it was that the subject chose not to write an autobiography for himself: of what it was in him that was perhaps an important extension of not wanting to think or write that way. *Memorials of Thomas Hood* is another such book. But part of the modest usefulness of Forster's book is that it also gives answers to the questions which it cannot quite bring itself to ask. Dickens, it is clear from Forster's record, was the sort of man who needed to throw himself into his work by day, 'And I want a crowded street to plunge into at night' (*The Life of Charles Dickens*, i, p. 338): there was some analogy, as well as some straightforward relief, involved there, for a man whose earliest troubles were located in the streets of London. His writing was, as it were, a way of turning himself into the crowded streets: 'as if they supplied something to my brain, which it cannot bear, when busy, to lose' (ibid., pp. 419–20); he took the memory of the streets into his mind, into his writing, and poured his thoughts along them, animating cities. It is not conventional realism, in the sense of writing naively trying to reflect and serve the world outside; it was not conventional autobiography; it was subversive realism, the outside taken up into a means of expression for that which is within; it was autobiography that was both vulnerably hidden and not so vulnerably devious. For Dickens's own temperament suited his difficulties: this was precisely how in his writing he apparently yielded to outside circumstances without their making him what they wanted—on the contrary. He could not have been, and the age was hardly one to allow a literary man simply to be, a writer who without disguises and defences used words to bring out tender inner experience in the first person. Yet he needed recognition, readers to believe his work in the reading as much as he had done in its writing—in the same way as David himself needed witnesses to his life.

Nonetheless, what Dickens admired was the way David grew to be a man who could write simply in the first person. Dickens used his own toughness to reveal and protect his own weaknesses; he used his novelistic powers of deviousness, emotional cunning and manipulative artifice to defend and make strong immature experience, where the world of adults was all too likely to be cold and calculating. Hood did not have and did not want to have that self-defence; he could not, and would not, provide the strength for himself; as we have seen, that was both good and bad, for his work and for his family alike. But Dickens did use a strong art to protect an idea of natural feeling and natural writing, and that idea served to protect the writing which Dickens was actually carrying out. The novelist was still the lower idea of an artist, and Dickens, making his necessities his virtues in a way that Hood could not choose to do, defended emotion with one hand while he exploited it with the other, relishing the depths he could actually stoop to in order to try to move even the highest in taste, birth, and intellect: it was like subversive revenge upon Scrooges, reminding them of humanity. Yet it was David Copperfield who was the man and the writer that Dickens thought he really wanted to be, ironically his own creation. That is why reading the book meant more to Dickens, in his private heart, than it could, he felt, to almost anyone else. But what such an art forfeits to the idea of nature which it goes into supporting is the recognition, in full truth, of all the novelist is as a human being as well as a writer, and of all that writing involves. Perhaps that necessity for disguise involved in putting on a strong art is not a large price to pay to write a novel of such genius; perhaps this is the very best that Dickens's genius and the nature of the circumstances of his time could allow anyway; perhaps the cost is Dickens's business alone and it is proper that only he really knew how in his book his imagination had had secretly to give body to the excess of all that, trapped within him emotionally, still referred, looked and yearned for a natural home outside in expression and recognition. Certainly the book is movingly obsessed with what must be hidden that something right and good might be shown: as Ham says of his relation to the disgraced Little Em'ly to whom he was engaged, 'I could only be happy—by forgetting of her—and I'm afeered

I couldn't hardly bear as she should be told I done that. But if you, being so full of learning, Mas'r Davy, could think of anything to say as might bring her to believe I wasn't greatly hurt: still loving of her, and mourning for her . . .' (p. 631).

Dickens's would have been at the very least a more complicated story than Copperfield's, but even if Dickens could have wanted to be able to write it, it is probable that he would not have been able. As Forster said, he was most himself in being somebody else; he even needed disguises to show what was being disguised. It was because he could not wish to write his autobiography that he did write, and found he could only write, *David Copperfield,* his autobiographical fiction. And this shows in the novel itself. In this way: that we feel the real story of Dickens as it were in the interstices between the dialogue that flows with the great, natural currents. Dickens's story is buried there, like Blake's experience behind a song of innocence; except that it does not undercut the novel but urges powerfully the novel's necessity. His autobiography is buried there, in his middle age, not simply out of hypocrisy or deviousness—although, indeed, we have noted how Dickens used coercive methods to extract the pathos of his own and others' situation. But there is also a certain moral and emotional rightness in that burial of the autobiography within the life of the fiction. For I think it did feel to Dickens as if the primary shape of his life was the life of David Copperfield; his own corruptions of it struck him as departures from it, seen against that primary background of a good family life. And Dickens needed the *public* privacy of the novel in order to support this idea of primary values that he had within himself. That is to say, he could not simply look at himself, like David Copperfield the autobiographer; he needed a prior sense of readers looking at him in order that he could then look at himself through David. I attribute this in part to Dickens's temperament: David's weakness, his need for a witness, became Dickens's strength as he could work on himself by watching us watching him in the person of David. But I also attribute it to the public difficulties for private emotions at that time—as I have tried to indicate throughout this chapter. At any rate, David Copperfield was, I repeat, Dickens's second chance to say how, primarily, his life ought to have been. The novel came second in the order of time, after a good deal of his life and after a little go at autobiography. But he wrote it to try and show how it ought to have come first—for him as a writer and as a man.

'Though Dickens bore outwardly so little of the impress of his writings, they formed the whole of that inner life which essentially constituted the man' (*The Life of Charles Dickens*, ii, p. 376).—That is often quoted as evidence of 'impersonality', as if it were simply a sign of Dickens's achievement. Perhaps it is indeed. But it is also, I want to say, *not* a sign of a man's happiness or of a happy creativity that that should have had to be the case.

4

Autobiography and justice to a life

I. OF LIFE AND WORK

In the journals of a painter whose failure eventually drove him to suicide, Benjamin Robert Haydon (1786–1846), there is a haunting passage which may stand as an image of the subject of this chapter. Finding his own work rejected not least because of the animosity which his defences of historical painting and of the Elgin Marbles had aroused, Haydon persuaded himself that, notwithstanding external harassments, he still had his painting to do. He had already made a cast of a head of Niobe; the following day he would paint Niobe into his picture; for the moment he took himself off to bed, pleased with the thought of the artist's inner courage that he was trying to manufacture for himself. He knew, he thought over, what he had to do in the morning and he fell asleep. He awoke, he says, to find himself freezing cold and in his cast-room, staring at the head of Niobe at three o'clock in the morning. He went back to bed at once, but lay awake, anxious about his work, and waited for daylight. With the light, the painter got up, prayed in distrust and set his palette. What happened next?

> I could not paint, I felt sick. . . . All day I stood staring at the picture, longing to proceed, but utterly nerveless.
>
> Haydon: *Autobiography*, i, p. 99.

The subject of this chapter is failure and the writing which comes out of failure.[1]

I am interested in implicit thought, the thought, that is to say, which, unspoken, lies behind the way a person acts or writes, partly causing, partly determined by the behaviour and the articulations of that person's life. There are people who have themselves within themselves, the way that they act being in strong, implicit memory of what they are, without their having consciously to know it. Such people leave footprints, marks and memories of themselves. De Quincey, for example, thinking of Wordsworth's lines about the Boy of Winander hooting to the owls, until the visible scene—

> Was carried far into his heart,
> With all its pomp, and that uncertain heav'n received
> Into the bosom of the steady lake

—notes how the action of a single word created the intimation for him of an inner world with dimensions as real in their way as those of the external world: namely, the word 'far', 'Was carried *far* into his heart'.[2] Coleridge said that there was a voice which, even if he heard it in a desert, would set him crying 'Wordsworth!'.[3] What Wordsworth was to Coleridge or to De Quincey, J. M. W. Turner was to John Ruskin. There were men, said Ruskin, whose every sentence or brush-stroke 'as it has been thought out from the heart, opens for us a way back down to the heart', thus carrying us to what it has arisen out of: 'this inner secret spring of his power' (Ruskin: *Works*, iv, p. 252).[4]

Haydon, although befriended by Wordsworth and by Keats, was no such man. As he stood frightened and exhausted before his canvas, he knew he could not carry over his life from one realm to another; the fact that he feared there were two realms made his desire to bridge them, even while asleep, self-defeating and self-exhausting. He could not get across, he was left stranded before his own picture. For Haydon, this was a dramatic instance of a typical situation:

> At the moment of execution you suffer agony at your inability to complete the idea which the imagination shot forth at the moment of conception. . . .
> I was never satisfied with anything till I forgot what I wanted to do.
> *Autobiography*, i, p. 203.

The culmination was that when he most wanted and needed to paint, he found that he could not. This is Haydon's story. Only I am not sure how near it is to the truth. For it was very predictable that he was not going to be able to paint that day, and not merely because that is the unjust and ironic way that life works. He did not want to paint, he was frightened of painting: 'I got up, prayed in distrust and set my palette'— you can feel the edginess, the fingers setting the palette, wasting time. The drama of his walking in his sleep, assuming that it did really happen, was a dream-substitute for crossing the threshold of commitment; it belongs with his saving belief that his conception was always greater than his execution of it. Perhaps his conception *was* so much greater and Haydon lacked sheer technique; but eventually he also had indulgently to believe in the greatness of the conception if he was to salvage something from the disappointment of its execution and the discouragement of its reception; and, of course, the greater the conception had then heroically to be, the more impossible its realization on the canvas. There were objective factors involved here: not least Haydon's commitment to be a history painter at a time when history, in a less noble sense, ironically decreed that the genre was out of fashion and that its ambitiousness could not cover its expenses. Good souls, like Mary Mitford, who knew the way that the times were going towards domestic realism, warned Haydon to change course. It was sensible advice, and if the more noble course was not to take it, or not even to be able to take it, then what was required to accompany the nobility was a large talent. It seems, when one looks at Haydon's paintings today, that he did not have such a talent, that he could not leave his mark and memory. Instead, the life of a painter, what it meant to be an artist, the autobiography before, around and after the act of painting came to be more important to Haydon than the pictures themselves. The writing of his journal and auto-biography took over; it was not a fall-out from the life and the painting but their replacement. Haydon eventually did not have memories; he had only the present preparation of things to be remembered in the future. We, of course, do not think of this as a form of creativity; it is (since so obviously the result of failure) what we call self-deception. Yet what would we call it if he did have more talent, if he could have hidden his desire for compensation by a greater verbal skill, if, just once, he could even have painted a great Niobe? How far would we

have changed our tune? Or are we so confident that genius
and talent, talent and failure are recognizably different not
just in degree but actually in kind?

We can see Haydon trying to make us change our tune
when he began to write up his journals into an autobiography
for publication.

In the journals he drew verbal portraits of himself heroically
resisting the Academy in his debt-ridden defence of historical
painting, while meantime his rival David Wilkie compromised
politely and worked successfully in the Dutch tradition:

> Wilkie's system . . . was Wellington's; principle and
> prudence the groundworks of risk. Mine that of Napoleon:
> audacity, with a defiance of principle, if principle was in
> the way. I got into prison. Napoleon died at St Helena.
> Wellington is living and honoured, and Wilkie has had a
> public dinner given him at Rome, the seat of Art and
> Genius, and has secured a competence, while I am as
> poor and necessitous as ever.
>
> Ibid., i, p. 406.

Most of these journals of maddened failure were left behind
after Haydon's suicide, unwritten up into formal memoir.
Haydon's posthumous editor, Tom Taylor (1817–80),
dramatist and editor of *Punch,* treated such entries like a
biographer, trying to be fair by balancing the inside of
Haydon's mind with the life outside it:

> I cannot but think that at this time Haydon was spurred
> on by genuine noble aspiration—dashed, it is true, by
> that identification of his own glory with the glory of
> English Art, which seems to have been inseparable from
> his character. To many this identification will be
> repulsive. They will see in it a self-seeking and ignoble
> vanity. It undoubtedly sprung from a belief in his own
> powers, the manifestations of which it is difficult to
> distinguish from the workings of vanity. But it was at least
> the vanity of a powerful mind, bold in conception, vigorous
> in execution, impulsive, but warped by a suspicion that
> all the world of artists were leagued against him, and not

seeing that his perpetual and irritating self-assertion was, in the eyes of indifferent people, the best justification of the hostility which he complained of.

Ibid., i, p. 316.

In just the same way, decently judicious yet ineffectually so, 'it is difficult to distinguish' between what Haydon might have done had he worked on quietly; what he might have done if that work had been less intensely and unfashionably ambitious in scope and subject; and what, anyway, he was able to do while he suffered from, as well as continued to provoke, enmity. It is difficult to distinguish his public defence of his art from his private excuses for it, because failure collapses distinctions.

To his credit, however, when Haydon began to write up his voluminous, compulsive journals into an autobiography, it seems that he did try to weigh a sort of Tom Taylor balance of responsibility between the journals on the one hand and their potential readership on the other—thus acting as his own editor as well as on his own behalf. As a friend of Thomas Hood's put it at the beginning of his own autobiography, 'The consideration and reserve due to others, the candour and veracity due to the public, and the fairness and justice due to myself, formed a combination of elements not easily to be reconciled in a whole.'[5] Here is how Haydon tries to bring his journals into line with the requirements of a different genre, as he gives an account of his public railing against the Academy's really scandalous neglect of what was to be learnt from the Elgin Marbles:

All my youthful readers will say, 'You were right'. No, my young friends, I was not right; because I brought useless obstructions in my path, which though they did not entirely prevent the development of my genius, brought it out in such agonising distresses, as will make you wonder, as you proceed, that I did not go raving mad, though from the state of ignorance existing as to the value of High Art, I question whether if I had been as quiet as a kitten or more abject than Wilkie the result would not have been just the same; whereas by the eternal uproar I made I indisputably kept up the public attention.

Ibid., i, pp. 115–6.

That maturity is a thing borrowed from the thought of 'youthful readers' through whom Haydon can relieve himself of the mistakes of his own immaturity, while feeling the relief to be a matter of public duty. But the attitude of experienced prudence thus achieved in the first half of this passage begins to give way when Haydon also remembers again what it meant to be prudent at that time: it meant being like Wilkie. The jealousy shows; Haydon is still the young man he was, only grown older; the journals still show through the verbal dignity he gives to, and borrows from, the idea of autobiography. The idea was that autobiography, the account of what a man thought of and had learnt from his own life, should be educative, especially to those who, inexperienced, had still to travel the way that the author had been. This gave Haydon an authority; what it did not give him, with that, was a willingness to recognize that what he did in keeping alive interest in the Elgin Marbles was compromised by other truths which his self-interest still could hardly acknowledge, for all his stance as one who has learned from bitter exerience: truths such as his jealousy of Wilkie, his continued admiration for self-sacrificing display, his talent for publicity as much as for painting. It is tempting to think that the journals give us the anterior truth about Haydon, the autobiography itself only later falsifies them. But the journals themselves are the falsehood; it is in them, with all their talk of Napoleon, that writing succumbs to the temptation to manufacture a life, a life that did not feed his art but tried to feed off it. It was Turner who produced the Napoleonic picture of the period in *War. The Exile and the Rock Limpet* (1842). Haydon produced many portraits of Napoleon but spent most of his energy writing in Napoleon's image. Such writing stands charged with what all writers fear: the accusation of doing nothing but standing in place of doing something. He always meant his diaries to save his life and his art.

All his autobiography does is try to fill that place by re-writing the journals. But this is not an autobiography which can tell us how a man could go on, or how he could *not* go on, knowing the little truths about himself and his motives that might puncture his self-regard or his resentments. He carries on precisely by not acknowledging the possibility of these things, and whatever concessions he can make ('No, my young friends, I was not right') seem merely the result of writing a book on the part of one who has already betrayed the idea of writing into an idea of compensation. The failure of this auto-biography is its unwillingness to turn round on itself and think hard about failure. The book thus begins to do what so much later nineteenth-century autobiographical thinking tempted a person to do: go round the back of the past, under guise of remembering it, and make out of initial inabilities a secondary ability to write about them, thus, supposedly, to redeem them at a literary level. Here, for example, is J. A. Symonds, man of culture, on reading G. H. Lewes's *Life of Goethe*, that favourite Victorian hero:

> The reading is a continual process of self-comparison, how impotent and humiliating to myself. . . . Reading this life teaches me how much of a poet's soul a man may have without being a poet, what high yearnings may plague him without his ever satisfying them, what a vast appre-ciation and desire may exist where there is no expression or formative will.
>
> Brown: *John Addington Symonds*, pp. 114–5.

This hardens later into the critic's autobiographical apology, half-guiltily going round the back of his delicious weakness to find in it what is proposed as a strength:

> There is a passive and an active imagination. The one creates, the other sympathises. The one makes new things for the world, the other appropriates whatever has been made, informing the past with something of fresh life. To men who are not in the true sense artists, it is a solace thus to retrace the history of the world.
>
> Ibid., pp. 240–1.

Or again, here is Mrs Humphry Ward on the philosopher Amiel and 'la maladie de l'idéal':

> 'He awakened in us but one regret; *we could not understand how it was a man so richly gifted produced nothing, or only trivialities.*'
>
> In these last words of M. Scherer's we have come across

the determining fact of Amiel's life in its relation to the outer world—that 'sterility of genius', of which he was the victim. . . .

The whole *Journal Intime* is in some sense Amiel's explanation of these facts. In it he has made full and bitter confession of his weakness, his failure; he has endeavoured, with an acuteness of analysis no other hand can rival, to make the reasons of his failure and isolation clear both to himself and others.

Amiel's Journal, pp. xxii, xxviii.

Thus Mrs Ward can preface her translation with the paradox of compensation:

May it at least win a few more friends and readers here and there for one who lived alone, and died sadly persuaded that his life had been a barren mistake; whereas, all the while—such is the irony of things—he had been in reality working out the mission assigned him in the spiritual economy, and faithfully obeying the secret mandate which had impressed itself upon his youthful consciousness:— *'Let the living live; and you, gather together your thoughts, leave behind you a legacy of feeling and ideas; you will be most useful so.'*

Ibid., p. vi.

What is all this? Tom Taylor says that Haydon's defence of art was mixed up with the vanity of his defence of himself. Haydon says that, no matter what could be said against it even by himself, he did do something in an unpropitious age to keep up the Art. Symonds says that he suffered from feeling like a poet without being able to be a poet; but that that also made him a sensitive critic and cultural historian. Mrs Humphry Ward calls *Amiel's Diary* 'the reflection of a life' (p. xl), but Amiel himself leaves life to the living among whom he does not count himself; she admits that he felt himself to be a failure, but 'all the while' the very way in which he thought about his failure made for the achievement he thought he had missed. 'Irony of things' or fictions of compensation? Guesses posing as judgements, by editors quite outside the case in question—balanced merely against the delusions and excuses of 'cases' all too thoroughly inside themselves. Initial over-estimations of the greatness of being a painter, a poet or a thinker, followed all too readily by a welcoming of the failure to measure up, in order to *have* to rest more securely in one's own auto-biographical terms. Work to redeem life, accounts of life to redeem failures of work, attempts to redeem the failure serving only as its further symptoms. What are these accounts beside what Haydon, Symonds, and Amiel actually produced? Secondary, circular. I put all this assertively though I know my feelings of impatience here are not quite fair. But they spring from a belief that such accounts as Haydon's are, in the worst sense, just words, all words, the vilest little thing that human beings use language for—self-justification, compensation, rationalization, all that covering of tracks with words which usurp the meaning of a life and leave it open to analyses as well-meaning, intelligent and dead as Tom Taylor's. Yet, despite all this energy of covering up, Haydon committed suicide.

*   *   *   *   *

Autobiography in the nineteenth century is almost always essentially false. There is no position by which a Haydon can be just to himself while remaining himself; he cannot take a stand outside himself and he has falsified what is within himself by re-creating it in the image of an heroic past; it is a past whose heroism is itself created to stand in for present acknow-ledgement of something at once truer and lesser; but it is a lie which is hard to get rid of and hard to use creatively because it is the only, restricted expression of itself that the truth in Haydon can bear; it is not even a big, interesting, straight lie, as if Haydon merely defended art publicly or wrote an artist's journal because he knew in his heart of hearts that he could not paint a masterpiece—nothing so clear cut, everything more fudged, eroded through the years and lost, until there is no truth, no life left to argue about, only an autobiography safely in place of it all. No form of writing ever betrayed more men, because no form more explicitly asks them to tell the plain truth about themselves, to do justice to their estimation of the worth of their lives, while at the same time giving them no formal obstacles to prevent their succumbing to the most convenient and often transparent embellishments and defences. People were never more thus tempted and betrayed, perhaps, than in this secular century in which already they were struggling to prevent the meaning of their lives from being reduced to mere matters of fact, result, status, failure, or success. Ruskin, speaking with more truth of the present than of the past, compared modern Englishmen with ancient Greeks thus:

> They had indeed their sorrows, true and deep, but still, more like children's sorrows than ours, whether bursting into open cry of pain, or hid with shuddering under the veil, still passing over the soul as clouds do over heaven, not sullying it, not mingling with it;—darkening it perhaps long or utterly, but still not becoming one with it, and for the most part passing away in dashing rain of tears, and leaving the man unchanged; in nowise affecting, as our sorrow does, the whole tone of his thought and imagination thenceforward.[6]
>
> *Works*, v, p. 233.

There was distrust now of the sheerly physical and social circumstances of human life. A writerly retreat from that framework exacerbated the great nineteenth-century stress upon the permanence of feeling—inevitably mental feeling. Autobiography therefore could not simply be the telling of the story of a life, if a man was a feeling artist. Reviewers could hardly believe it when Trollope spent so much of his *Autobiography* detailing the money he made from writing as if it were just another form of work. It was an absurd reaction, as if to say their idea of artistic inspiration had nothing to do with such low realities; but it was also a reaction which contained a truth, in denying that the story of a man's outer life should be so cut off from his inner life as to be the story of wealth and leisure. There had to be feelings in an autobiography, decently subdued doubtless, for almost everyone in Victorian England felt that Rousseau had gone too far; but what was life without feelings? So, often, there were feelings without life, in place of it and hiding the want of it.

It is perhaps worth pointing to an exception in order to reveal the norm. In *Early Days* Samuel Bamford (1788–1872),

weaver, poet, and political radical, gives a sheerly narrative
account of what the *Dictionary of National Biography* dryly calls
the 'somewhat unsettled life' of his youth. He writes almost
like one of Ruskin's fictive ancient Greeks, more like a child, if
that is the correct alternative, than like a 'responsible' Victorian
adult. His feelings are treated merely as narrative facts, as he
records how the failure of his great early love, for Catherine
the daughter of a widow who kept a small farm in Crumpsall,
so affected him, then a young warehouseman in Manchester,
that he felt that his experience now required him to make a
change:

> In my intercourse with the fair sex, the emotions of the
> heart had hitherto been my only offering, and now the
> unworthy surmise first occurred that the offering had
> been too pure—that the heart and the imagination alone
> of man could not suffice for womankind—that the beings
> I had adored were not so entirely divine as my poetry had
> painted them,—and that, if I would be really loved with a
> womanly love, mine must be of a less ethereal nature than
> it had hitherto been. This notion I found to be the
> confirmed opinion of some of my more experienced
> acquaintance, who laughed at my simplicity.
>
> Bamford: *Autobiography*, i, pp. 215–6.

It is significant that this is the story of a young, literary
Romantic who is also (his 'more experienced acquaintance'
would not be slow to remind him) a working man in an
industrial town. To make himself a man worthy of woman, he
thinks he has to feel less in order to do more. Man and woman
come to be seen in basically sexual, rather than amatory,
terms. He resolves that neither his feelings nor his happiness in
general will be ever again at the disposal of woman. Yet, as we
see in the developing story, the consequence of this decision is
to make his now physically bound feelings all the more
unhappily dependent upon her: 'Hitherto "fond and sinless
love" had been my protection against many temptations, but
now that was gone I found myself beset with inducements to
vice which I had previously deemed not worth a thought.
There was a void in my existence, and it required to be filled
up by some means' (ibid., p. 217). There is an asymmetry

between decision and consequence of that decision; for the consequence is not a simple discarding of emotional idealism, but the creation of a felt void, almost as perverse compensation, in its place.

Yet before that void can be physically 'filled up' through temptation, there comes, almost as a relief to the young man, an exemplary corrective: 'One night as I was proceeding home, a woman of the town took hold of my arm, and desired me to go with her. . .'. In the preliminaries of conversation it emerges that they both come from the same town:

> Who could she be? I again asked, and she mentioned a name at the hearing of which I almost sank to the earth. She had been born and brought up at the house next door to that of my parents; she was the beloved child of their early friends and associates; she married when I was but an infant, and her husband, when I could run about, used to make whip-cord, and kites, and banding to fly them with for me. I knew the man well at that time, he was still living, and it not unfrequently happened that I was in his company when I went over to Middleton. I was disgusted with myself and her.
>
> Ibid., i, pp. 218–9.

This was how a man's memory could be torn not only between youth and maturity but also between home and city. In his trying to become a man who could 'suffice for womankind' and 'womanly love', the damage he has done in his memory is felt in 'when I was but an infant' and 'he was still living'. Repenting, Bamford acts by accordingly turning back to Mima, a childhood sweetheart, living in a place removed from this one. As thus he tries to find out what 'woman' is and means to him as an adult, his encounter with the woman of the town offers itself as a pivotal and decisive moment in his life-history.

It is not. The moment is not decisive, does not shape the literary narrative, because the physical life was not under control at that level. The young Bamford's relation to his own self-admonishments and decisions becomes just like his relation to his father's advice: 'My father, whom I frequently called to see, never failed to give me the best of advice, and I deferred to it for the moment, but seldom did its influence long remain after I had quitted his presence' (ibid., p. 217). He returns home from Manchester to Middleton and to Mima, but, torn between childhood and manhood, memory and sexuality as mutually damaging alternatives, he again falls in with a drunken crowd just as in Manchester. Dimly seeming to want life to teach him a lesson again, he flirts with disaster and gets a girl pregnant:

> I was somewhat relieved, however, by learning that she took the affair less to heart than many would have done, and that the obtainment of a handsome weekly allowance was with her as much a subject of consideration as any other. I say I was relieved, but I never hoped, never attempted to palliate the wrong I had done, or to evade the shame I had incurred.
>
> Ibid., i, p. 230.

The sheer story seems more important than the feelings which are part of it. The physical events seem, as it were, to forget the resolves made prior to them. The narrative, wherein what is said within or about the action is less decisive than the action itself, thus fulfils an urge deeper than the young man's will or self-recall, while also constituting the very contours of the older man's later memory. Neither the older man's regrets nor the young man's intentions stand as authorities above the narrative; through the reduced capacity of the physical man to think out his life, the mental and moral considerations lie side by side with the physical facts, unashamedly ashamed, relieved by let-offs but not cancelled out by them. Thus mental conclusions, either by the young or by the old Bamford, turn out to be no more and no less than sentences. 'I never hoped, never attempted to palliate the wrong'; yet, after getting the girl pregnant and paying his way out, the relieved young man goes back to his drifting and drinking ways. 'I was not so unreflective as not to perceive to what this course must inevitably tend,' he tells us in the penultimate chapter of *Early Days*, 'and with a view to put an end to it at once, I resolved to marry' (ibid., p. 291). Through whatever hidden resolves and impetuses, his physical life up to this point had had a presence strange to his own consciousness. Now, in desperation, he decides to accommodate that life within a marriage. He does marry, for the first time in this area of his life carrying out his resolve. Yet he seems unsurprised at the ease of the solution in comparison with the difficulties of the problem which it subdues. It is as if that form of solving had always been a purpose of marriage and now he has come to it like everyone else.

It is hard to decide upon Bamford's motivation in allowing his narrative to be so strangely honest; it is hard even to know whether, or how far, it is a thing that resulted from personal decision at all. I think it would be both condescending and wrong to attribute his inscrutable openness to a literary working man's naivety in the genre. For the accounts of his political action, which is the book's real subject and presumed to be the public's main interest, show no such resistance to mental control; on the contrary, Bamford offers himself as a model of reformist discipline and peaceableness in seeking justice. It is only with respect to sexual matters that he seems to have a life unattributable either simply to himself and his conscious resolves or to his economic masters and their laws. Speaking of the necessity of any action being the inferred result of some preceding event, physical or mental, David Hume describes the feeling of 'a certain looseness' in making the inference on one's own account rather than on behalf of others:

> we may observe, that tho' in reflecting on human actions we seldom feel such a looseness and indifference, yet it very commonly happens, that in performing the actions themselves we are sensible of something like it.[7]

It is that certain looseness within the course of the predictable which characterizes the sexual part of Bamford's narrative, the power of self-determination being regularly annulled in the course of time and circumstance. Curiously, this practical defeasibility, this looseness of the relation between resolve and action, seems a sign not of the bondage of the will but of the freedom of a life. In its 'indifference' to consciousness, the bodily life, in memory, seems free, when at the time it must have felt at the very mercy of the next set of tempting circumstances. This way of thinking about life does not seem to be something that is actually an admitted part of Bamford's own character; it seems to be an incidental result of the way that

working-class life and political autobiography together brought
sexual, literary Romanticism down to earth, if not into the
streets. A Chartist rebel, John James Bezer wrote thus of his
personal life in his political memoir:

> I *could*, I think, write a whole chapter on love—all
> about 'divine images' and 'angelic forms',—and how the
> sun shone when she smiled, and how all the stars looked
> dim when she didn't—for lovers can tell the weather by
> signs better than anybody else—but age, and reason, and
> the one object in writing this 'auto', call on me to stay;
> nor should I have mentioned this circumstance at all, had
> not the fact of her jilting me three separate times (the false
> Bloomer!) been one of the principal causes of my leaving
> my first love—my Sunday School—and having led me by
> degrees to the very confines of atheism.[8]

And atheism was an important step towards his political
activism. Now it is not the case that Bezer's rather demotic
breeziness here offers an instructive alternative to the language
of high Romanticism. What it does give is an embarrassed sign
of an ambiguous area—for Bamford, an area of ambiguous
freedom; for Bezer, an area leading to political life yet emphatically left at home, left behind by a political life: the area of
sexuality, privately so powerful, publicly so unplaced and
pointless within any contemporary scheme of human things.

However it be that this part of Bamford's autobiography is
so exceptional, the fact is that it is stunningly so, without his
seeming to notice. For there is no such temporal looseness in
most nineteenth-century autobiography; for in most of them
memory proposes itself as the end of time and therefore aptly
summative and conclusive of it. Everything falls into line,
becoming in the life's story what, with hindsight, it turned out
to be. Witness, for example, the words of Harriet Martineau
on the personal criticism which she received on her publication
of the anti-theological Atkinson letters on necessitarianism:

> I think I may sum up my experience of this sort by saying
> that this book has been an inestimable blessing to me by
> dissolving all false relations, and confirming all true ones.
> No one who would leave me on account of it is qualified to

be my friend; and all who, agreeing or disagreeing with my opinions, are faithful to me through a trial too severe for the weak are truly friends for life. I early felt this.

Harriet Martineau: *Autobiography*, ii, p. 357.

So this is what it is to be a necessitarian, this to be an adult! Yet as John Foster put it, of the settled form that the qualities of character seem to take, 'If the process has been so complex, how comes the result to be apparently so simple?'[9]. If they are not now friends, says Miss Martineau with the logic of retrospection, they never really were. Yet the real pain belongs to a sense of the defeasibility of life: that they were, but now are not any longer, my friends. There is no reality of the present left in between Harriet Martineau's 'it is what it will be' and 'it was what in retrospect it is'. When she was a young girl, she reports that she was amazed and frightened by the way that sights came to her in fractional advance of the sounds they made. She never seems to have appreciated how her *adult* life was a constant forcing of two or more aspects of reality into one solid outcome. Either they were friends or they were not; not for her the conditional tenses of a David Copperfield trying to tell himself that the way he had made Agnes a sister to him, the way that she perhaps had made herself a sister to him, precluded the possibility of her ever becoming his second wife:

> If she had ever loved me, then, I should hold her the more sacred; remembering the confidences I had reposed in her, her knowledge of my errant heart, the sacrifice she must have made to be my friend and sister, and the victory she had won. If she had never loved me, could I believe that she would love me now?
>
> . . . Whatever I might have been to her, or she to me, if I had been more worthy of her long ago, I was not now, and she was not. The time was past.
>
> . . . I had considered how the things that never happen, are often as much realities to us, in their effects, as those that are accomplished. . . . Thus, through the reflection that it might have been, I arrived at the conviction that it could never be.

David Copperfield, pp. 700–1.

In autobiography it was hardly possible to exercise that responsibility to bow to apparent necessity, while at the same time registering the self-weakening thought of the loneliness in having to do so. For loneliness is the only name I can think to give to the excess of emotion over the limiting facts of experience: nothing, no one, seems to want, to call for, to provide a home for the redundant conditionals of human need, 'if only' and 'it might have been'. It is hard for autobiography to do two things at once: give form to the course of one's own life, while expressing implicated reservations about the form one's self has taken. The novel can preserve the two in one, what might have been in what had to be; the writer of autobiographical fiction can work on two levels and save the meaning of 'the things that never happen' which are so real 'in their effects', because he can be the person who has thus suffered as well as another person who can freely feel and speak on his behalf. For the autobiographer, so aware of what the public will think adult on one hand and egoistic on the other, what never happened is all too vulnerable to being dismissed as the vanity of unreal regret—a mere tacked-on emotion afterwards, rather than a proper complication of the tense of thinking at the time. The autobiography as a form was thus liable to collapse Dickens's two, 'whatever I might have been . . . I was not now', into one; for it was under the double pressure not only of the apparent necessity of some situations of failure but also of their irrevocable pastness anyway. Through autobiography's matter-of-fact chronology and through the sheer age at which most men composed their memoirs, there was a tendency for the past to become inevitable just because 'the time was past' and had gone past the now-declared-redundant desire to have it otherwise. Reading his late first wife's love letters to himself, Leslie Stephen admitted, 'Partly as I read, I went back to the past; and partly, the past is remote enough to have become part of the inevitable. The desire to alter has been killed by the lapse of time' (*Sir Leslie Stephen's Mausoleum Book*, p. xi).

Miss Martineau's belief in the laws of necessity only reinforced this formal tendency. What is more, the dissolving effect that time's outcomes have over interim meanings like Copperfield's was the only protection that this single woman could find for her emotions. When she writes of the time when her own brother, James Martineau, an idealist, reviewed and criticized the atheism of her philosophical work, she concludes:

> Brothers are to sisters what sisters can never be to brothers as objects of engrossing and devoted affection. The law of their frames is answerable for this: and that other law—of equity—which sisters are bound to obey, requires that they should not render their account of their disappointments where there can be no fair reply. Under the same law, sisters are bound to remember that they cannot be certain of their own fitness to render an account of their own disappointments, or to form an estimate of the share of blame which may be due to themselves on the score of unreasonable expectations.
>
> *Autobiography*, i, p. 99.

Autobiography always suffered from appearing to be one-sided, from being unable to include a 'fair reply'; it was a monologue in an age increasingly adapted to dialogue—an assumption that Browning exploited in his collusive soliloquies. Here the power of the generalized expression means also that Harriet Martineau cannot trust *herself* to speak. She has literally no time for the expectations and disappointments of her emotions. Yet the way that her problems are thus cleared away does not clear away her problems. It is left to a novelist like Charlotte Bronte to risk expressing the suffering of a single woman without appearing, single-woman-like, to encourage the expression for its own sake. Miss Martineau, talent aside, could write no novel like *Villette* because she felt her emotions to be pre-empted by the laws of Necessity and silenced by the law of Justice. Autobiography became in her hands a life's acceptance of itself as no more than defined by what had happened to it; for what happened had to happen. Of the possibility of a husband she concedes only this:

> I can easily conceive how I might have been tempted—how some deep springs in my nature might have been touched, then as earlier; but as a matter of fact, they never were . . . If I had had a husband dependent on me for his happiness, the responsibility would have made me wretched. I had not faith enough in myself to endure

> avoidable responsibility. If my husband had not depended
> on me for his happiness, I should have been jealous . . .
> Thus, I am not only entirely satisfied with my lot, but
> think it the very best for me,—under my constitution and
> circumstances.
>
> Ibid., i, pp. 132–3.

'My work and I have been fitted to each other, as is proved by
the success of my work and my own happiness in it' (ibid., p.
133). But for Harriet Martineau the fact of her writing was a
form of proof which in her writing itself she never tested. 'As a
matter of fact, they never were,' she writes, characteristically,
of her deeper emotions and how they might have been touched.
All her grammar, through the apparent finality of its past
tense, aspires to a hardening condition analogous to that of the
past being settled into sense and fact at once. The formal
coincidence between the grammatical sense that the prose
makes and the matters of fact that the memory testifies to
makes this a prose committed to the reality principle of memory
rather than to the provisional nature of time. This is why
Harriet Martineau is a clear if exaggerated example of the
falseness of nineteenth-century autobiography, for inevitably
seeing as closed and settled events that plausibly were experienced as open and undetermined. No career more than a
literary career offered to such a woman independence in life
and compensation for life. It is almost a tribute to her resolute-
ness that she seems not to have recognized that what her work
did for her in saving her life cost the work itself dearly. There is
no *Villette*, but plenty of tales to popularize the necessities of
political economy, one of the public forms her personal rigour
took. Certainly she refused to use writing as the form of
compensation that Haydon tried for; but the very suppression
of that temptation deprives her writing of any other power. 'I
am not only entirely satisfied with my lot, but think it the very
best for me,—under my constitution and circumstances': that
last parenthesis sadly does not unleash her intelligence from
the first part of the sentence but reveals how all her intelligence
bound itself to accepting the terms of its own confinement.

'The limited folly of apparent common-sense' was the verdict
passed upon Harriet Martineau by another Victorian literary
woman, Mrs Margaret Oliphant.[10] But the sense of there

being something missing is also less specific than that. Autobiography during the Victorian age became, in general, recognizably less moving than the prose genre that dominated the
century, the novel. It is that second thing, a compassionate
background of understanding that supports the protagonist
by providing a mitigating context, a shared inwardness and
memory, which, above all, the novel added to the nineteenth-
century sense of a life. The memory of an autobiographer is,
from the start, something he or she knows we cannot share, in
the way that we can share the memory of David Copperfield.
It becomes lost history, not the memory, the resonance that
art can help to survive. If then autobiography at all survived
the encroachment of the novel, it may well be because the
autobiography, even when written to do justice to a life, was
actually read, rather, as expressing character. The autobiography was read, with a sense of relativism, by those predominantly used to reading novels:

> it is an instructive and somewhat sad pleasure for the
> student of human nature to watch those shadows as they
> appear before him, each anxious to give the best account
> of itself, some in serene human unconsciousness thrusting
> their own little tale of events between him and the history
> of the world.
>
> Mrs Oliphant: *Blackwood's Magazine*, January 1881, vol. cxxix, p. 2.

It is the word 'little' that is a key here. The little lives of
Haydon and Miss Martineau, written up into big books, leave
me worrying bleakly and rather guiltily about their scale: why
should I care about this life? why can't I place it as I might
place a simply mediocre novel? how do I connect with it as a
life? what criteria are there by which to try to work out whether
the author makes too little or too much of it all? It does not
seem, for instance, to do justice to a life to believe with Miss
Martineau that she could have been no more than she was,
than she had been. Yet it does no more justice to argue as J. A.
Symonds did from the other extreme:

> There are men who placidly believe that they could not
> have been better than they are—simply because they are
> themselves. But this egotism is vanity; vanity more ignoble
> even than the vanity of regretting misused opportunities

of enjoyment or abandoned paths of heroical ambition.

Who shall be contented with his life when he looks back upon it?

It is not possible upon this path or that to satisfy the insatiable within the mind. That is the frank-pledge of the soul's infinity—if not of personal immortality.

Brown: *John Addington Symonds*, pp. 464–5.

This is a man who has learnt too well the Idealist lesson, that the spirit is greater than the events of a life, to resist the equation that what we hope for is what we deserve. 'Not possible to satisfy' could as easily be Necessity's reproach to man as man's protest against Necessity, for to say a man's needs feel necessary is not to say that they are valid. To make satisfaction out of too little and accept that as justice, with Harriet Martineau, is hardly bettered by Symonds's making dissatisfaction into a spiritual philosophy. Without any reliable measure of justice I find myself thus thinking with bitter indifference of the disparity between what Mrs Oliphant calls these little tales and the history of the world. What does it matter what one makes of it, a bit more to be said of Miss Martineau, a bit less of J. A. Symonds, when the real measurements are so absurd? Now I think I recognize that my bitterness here is an anachronistic result of being a modern reader of the humanist novel of the nineteenth century which promised to save small lives from being dismissed merely as failures. And what I need to save these lives of Harriet Martineau and Benjamin Robert Haydon, which I cannot help thinking of as lives as well as autobiographies, is the sympathy Mrs Oliphant seems to have felt when she read equivalent memoirs. In some cases, of course, it was her own contemporaries she was reading—accounts which, to us now short-lived, were not yet for her lost words, books that were out of date, lives that had to be forgotten or under-rated. But she also had the sustaining interest and framework of a professional novelist; someone not looking to find in autobiographies truth or justice but specimens of human anxiety, vanity and pathos—the angle between the littleness of the lives and the big claims made for them lest they be seen to be worthless being a measure not for bitterness and disappointment on behalf of the race but for irony as well as sympathy.

This is a sane limitation on the part of Mrs Oliphant and has to do with the confidence that being a humane novelist at that time afforded. But I have put it to myself that it is worryingly likely that I would think more highly of Haydon when I read his *Autobiography* if I knew that he had been a great painter, or if a novelist like Charles Dickens had been able to make that autobiography into an autobiographical fiction. Now what I am presently wondering is almost the reverse: whether these autobiographies have not outlasted the sort of humanistic readership that protected them; whether, that is to say, the truth is that the failure and littleness of life in nineteenth-century autobiography is *not* simply a result of the limitation of a genre which seemed to promise to tell of a life but told only of a way of writing about it; nor simply the consequence of the essential evanescence of the full contemporary meaning; but something closer to a just estimate of nineteenth-century personal life than all the redemption of meaning offered by the nineteenth-century novel? Did the Victorian reader—if I may call up such a general ghost for such a general speculation—persist in reading sober autobiographies and biographies as well as novels for instruction because there was a tacit recognition that the human sympathy that a novel could produce was, still, a fictional emotion that indeed supported the reading of these other kinds of book but was also 'placed' by them? To put the question another way, did the failures of autobiography, did the failures of little lives themselves, *deserve* to be saved by the autobiographical novel and by humanistic fiction? Or was the salvation the only way that art could keep itself alive?

*   *   *   *   *

Of course a reader is right to object that the Victorian age was a boom-time for autobiography through an increasing interest in personality and fame, character and career. There were many thousands of autobiographies produced, and if many of them now seem to be a dull read, that is because the lives themselves may not have been very interesting, although at the time prestigious, or are not now very interesting to us. They were meant as accounts not as literature per se. It is proper to be interested in the way that Victorians thought they were leading their lives. But most of these books will not be about 'life' in some strenuously speculative sense; they will be about how people spent those parts of their lives that the public might be interested in, and the tone in which they are written will be familiar, in the sense of being written within a common, socially shared assumption of what is interesting. Moreover, whatever personal inwardness these books reveal will still tend to be that of people who, because of the very idea of writing autobiography near the end of one's life as its relaxed summation, will also be familiar with themselves. The autobiographer becomes as at home with his inferred readership as with his own memories, the two being blurred as he allows each to support the other. There is no reason for disappointment or bitterness about this, for it is the nature of this socially-personal exercise!

I think I appreciate this, and in order to try to find something deeper I have looked at autobiographies written by people who might be expected to look harder at their lives through a habitual responsibility to work harder over their language. These people obviously tend to be artists and, in particular, professional writers.

Yet one consequence is that the very thing which tends to make the life more accessible through the words—namely the skill of a practised writer even in dealing with himself—is just what prevents a reader being quite sure what it is that is being made accessible. The fact of these people being writers may have affected not only the way they lived their lives but also the way they remembered and wrote about them. The writing talent was indeed a part of their lives; what one cannot tell is how far it is being used in an autobiography, intentionally or unintentionally, to subordinate the other parts of the life to a style accepted as the writer's own. For the medium in which the life is written is the medium in which the work was done, and the writing of the life may be only another form of work. As Leslie Stephen wrote in his private testimony to the children of both his first and second marriages:

> I am so much of a professional author that I fear that what I am about to say may have the appearance of being

meant for a book than for a letter. That, however, will be accidental if it happens—at any rate, it will be unintentional.

Mausoleum Book, p. 3.

Such accidents may be a second nature with a professional writer that hardly allows us to see his first.

The unworthy thought that professional writers from the nineteenth century onwards are in defence of their position both privileged and devious seems to me to deserve some consideration. We have seen the different ways in which writing became a kind of cover for both Haydon and Harriet Martineau, and autobiography may be a special case, a special temptation, in this respect. But it may not. A writer like Dickens can make a bigger life in his fiction than it seems he could make in his own home: let those who think that it was merely his triumph to win the first out of the second also consider that the second was the concomitant, if not the consequence, of the first. Is that bigger life in the Victorian writer's mind a privileged fiction, a thing produced only through writing fiction, even when that fiction is supposed to concern a real life? Is it not even a fact of the writer's own life, let alone the lives of more ordinary people that autobiographical and realistic fiction purport to deal in? My reader will rightly answer with an appeal to the realm of imagination. But it is precisely and increasingly the role of imagination in the prosaic humanity of the nineteenth century that it did not offer itself as an extra existential dimension but as something in the moral service of memory and reality and human sympathy. I shall be considering these coarse questions in the second half of this chapter; for although they are coarse, if writers in the nineteenth century were bearing the responsibility of showing what in mundane life made life worth living, it is important to be sure if and how we can trust them. Measuring autobiographies against fictional autobiographies is one way to try to test what is happening. At the moment I am still endeavouring to find out what rightly may be expected of autobiography, before presuming to use it as a measure of any sort of basic truth about the life of its writer, like some stick with which to beat fiction if fiction does not beat it.

I keep thinking: surely it is not unreasonable to look in a writer's account of himself for something that writing, that his work, has added to his experience and something in himself that has needed and impelled his work; above all a *belief* that he can articulate for himself which *is* himself, holding together the two, the life and the work, in the last testimony he can make: his autobiography. The great nineteenth-century defenders of humanity: is it really too much to expect some sense that the greatness that went into the books was there, in their lives, without the books, the work not being only on the page a displaced result of compensation or suffering or social repression? Must we always hear that what they *did* was what they were, when what they did seems so dependent on the quality of life, as well as technique, behind it?

On the other hand, we have seen something of why, in a difficult time for the human spirit, Dickens could not write his own autobiography. And I recognize that there are indeed good reasons why, when a writer did manage to put his autobiography into straight prose, he might not do justice to himself or the deep life within him. In a secular age an autobiography is not the final word passed on a man's life by the God in him. In the age of the novel, prose-autobiography did not offer the novelist a challengingly different medium for expression. Trollope's *An Autobiography* (1883) is instructive here, being altogether different from Haydon's Romantic kind of memoir. An autobiography like Haydon's was a doomed attempt to save his work by rescuing through another medium the anterior context from which the work arose but which the work itself might not be sufficiently strong or sufficiently recognized to convey. Trollope's work, on the contrary, is something done after the real writing and resting upon it. It is not so much a life as the residue of one after all that had gone into the work.

> I then saw my father and my brother Henry for the last time. A sadder household never was held together. They were all dying,—except my mother, who would sit up night after night nursing the dying ones and writing novels the while,—so that there might be a decent roof for them to die under. Had she failed to write the novels, I do

not know where the roof would have been found. It is now more than forty years ago, and looking back over so long a lapse of time I can tell the story, though it be the story of my own father and mother, almost as coldly as I have often done some scene of intended pathos in fiction; but that scene was indeed full of pathos.

An Autobiography, p. 34.

At the time Trollope, lazy and young, had hardly been able to support himself, let alone help his family. As if in reparation now to his mother, in her example of 'writing novels the while', Trollope became so much the writer as to be able to carry on writing, no matter whose was the story or where his own feelings were. But this story is 'of my own father and mother', and he feels a scruple of dismay at the sheer professionalism with which he manages this story too. Yet the thought of his own professionalism conveys a coldness which is also a scrupulous refusal to be the tear-wringing novelist this time, this close to home. Trollope disapproved of what he took to be Dickens's exploitation of his own childhood misery, damaging his parents's memory. And he would rather write coldly than behave badly. The reduced power of the *Autobiography* stems from the fear felt by a manipulative, omniscient novelist, coolly controlling the lives and deaths of his characters, lest hubris awaits him when it comes to his own life, for his temerity. At the same time, as an incidental bonus, the way that his eschewing fictive pathos implies a real pathos, the way that he thus causes us to recognize that he is remembering rather than creating an effect, the way that he even uses his own professionalism to incorporate his own dismay at it, together constitute just what Leslie Stephen meant by the so-called 'accidents' of the practised author. Trollope could not have afforded to write his autobiography in this settled, professional way had he not been able to rely upon his being not only an accomplished writer but also a socially recognized and rewarded success. The fact of his being known to be a writer kept him, artfully enough, from being seen to be trying too hard for his own effect; while the fact of his knowing himself to be a success assured his not being obliged on his own account to fight too hard for his memory. What I offer, then, as a

measure of how to gauge nineteenth-century autobiography is
something in between the example of Haydon and the example
of Trollope: the work of John Ruskin, across the arts between
painting and writing, without assured personal success.

*   *   *   *   *

Ruskin's life lasted from 1819 to 1900; the main subject of his
work as a critic was the painter J. M. W. Turner, 1775–1851.
At once we have two of our earlier themes: the relation of the
so-called 'Victorian' to the so-called 'Romantic' generation;
the relation of the critic to the artist. A third theme lies in the
dates of the five volumes of *Modern Painters*, 1842–60; let Ruskin
himself, in his preface to the final volume, explain:

> It has not been written for praise. Had I wished to gain
> present reputation, by a little flattery adroitly used in
> some places, a sharp word or two withheld in others, and
> the substitution of verbiage generally for investigation, I
> could have made the circulation of these volumes tenfold
> what it has been in modern society. Had I wished for
> future fame, I should have written one volume, not five.
> Also, it has not been written for money. In this wealth-
> producing country, seventeen years' labour could hardly
> have been invested with less chance of equivalent return.
>
> Also, it has not been written for conscience-sake. I had
> no definite hope in writing it; still less any sense of its
> being required of me as a duty. It seems to me, and
> seemed always, probable, that I might have done much
> more good in some other way. But it has been written of
> necessity. I saw an injustice done, and tried to remedy it.
> I heard falsehood taught, and was compelled to deny it.
> Nothing else was possible to me. I knew not how little or
> how much might come of the business, or whether I was
> fit for it; but here was the lie full set in front of me, and
> there was no way round it, but only over it.[11]

Works, vii, p. 10.

It is the theme of a life-work. And the sense of proportion
between life and work.

The lie, the injustice, the falsehood to which Ruskin refers occured in 1836 when Turner was under real attack in the magazines for the paintings he submitted to the Royal Academy. Ruskin's immediate response was to write an essay in defence of Turner, against the claims of his critics, as a painter of real truth. Ruskin had the essay shown to Turner, but Turner said that he did not want it printed. Turner was then sixty-one, Ruskin seventeen.

Nonetheless, when the *Literary Gazette* violently attacked Turner seven years later in 1842, Ruskin, now twenty-three, wrote the furious first volume of *Modern Painters* in his hero's defence, whether he wanted it or not. It was in the very Ruskin home that Turner had expressed his contempt for the critics who had dismissed his *Snowstorm—steam-boat off a harbour's mouth* as 'soapsuds and whitewash': 'Soapsuds and whitewash? What would they have? I wonder what the sea's like? I wish they'd been in it'.[12] From that moment Ruskin committed himself to Turner's work, whatever Turner himself said.

'I knew not how little or how much might come of the business'. It was almost cruelly too soon for a young man to commit himself, even in the name of truth and justice, to a great, strange painter who was still painting and innovating. Ruskin had now always to be Turner's follower, trying, from a subsequent generation, to catch up in words with what his master did in paint. Ruskin doomed himself, already manic-depressive in temperament, to seventeen more years and four more volumes of *Modern Painters,* of massive and miniscule detail, in order to think out on paper during the best of his formative life grounds that would justify in maturity the first principles and preferences he had intuited in the passion of youth. He took Turner's rhetorical question seriously: 'I wonder what the sea's like?'. From 1835 to 1860 all Ruskin saw in nature and in paintings was bound to anxious processes of verbal translation, the eye now tied, as it were, to the expository, writing hand. Mere drudgery, he later called his writing up of his perceptions and investigations; work he read to his parents every day as a girl shows her handiwork. Nor was this a single-minded task: exhaustion and depression aside, the demands that a study of Turner made upon him called for a study of much more than Turner, while the life that was dedicated to this work called upon the work to develop with it.

His father, both anxious and ambitious for his son, worried for his health and, concerned about the distracting range of his study, 'piteously asks for the end of "Modern Painters", saying "he will be dead before it is done"' (*Works*, xxxv, p. 485). Even his own drawings had been used by Ruskin as academic experiments to try to find out what it felt like to see and paint as Turner did. This was the life of the critic who had to write down, he said, what Turner could merely remember. And it was to Ruskin of all people that Turner, thinking perhaps of his own batterings, had said, 'Criticism is useless'!

'But it has been written of necessity.' It was not the case that Ruskin was ruined by finding himself inferior to the great artist. On the contrary, it was precisely because he thought that Turner knew something big and important that he could not know that Ruskin chose Turner and not, say, the more conveniently realistic Norwich school. Nor was he going to commit himself to the painterly equivalents of what Dickens, for instance, meant to him:

> Dickens taught us nothing with which we were not familiar,—only painted it perfectly for us . . . he never became an educational element of my life, but only one of its chief comforts and restoratives.[13]
>
> *Works*, xxxv, p. 303.

It was for education, rather than restoration, that Ruskin turned to Turner, even though it meant the sacrifice of comfort. Speaking of a Titian, Ruskin commented, 'It is difficult to imagine anything more magnificently impossible than the blue of the distant landscape . . . Yet make this blue faint, aerial, and distant—make it in the slightest degree to resemble the truth of nature's colour—and all the tone of the picture, all its intensity and splendour, will vanish on the instant . . . Turner will not sacrifice the higher truths of his landscape to mere pitch of colour as Titian does. He infinitely prefers having the power of giving extension of space, and fulness of form, to that of giving deep melodies of tone . . . he becomes necessarily inferior in richness of effect to the old masters of tone . . . but gains by the sacrifice a thousand more essential truths' (*Works*, iii, pp. 268–9).[14] The old language of warm human colour is broken up by Turner's light: 'He paints in colour, but he thinks in light and shade' (ibid., p. 301). It is the thought, rather than any melody, that Ruskin, a puritan, was after. He wanted to grasp and spell out everything within a Turner picture. Here, for instance, is only the most part of one sentence, aiming at being a transcription of Turner's *Llanthony*, a storm dying over water and land:

> The shower is here half exhausted, half passed by, the last drops are rattling faintly through the glimmering hazel boughs, the white torrent, swelled by the sudden storm, flings up its hasty jets of springing spray to meet the returning light; and these, as if the heaven regretted what it had given, and were taking it back, pass as they leap, into vapour, and fall not again, but vanish in the shafts of the sunlight; hurrying, fitful, wind-woven sunlight, which glides through the thick leaves, and paces along the pale rocks like rain; half conquering, half quenched by the very mists which it summons itself from the lighted pastures as it passes. . . .[15]
>
> *Works*, iii, p. 402.

Turner's picture frames that sentence which has to be so long and so interconnected in order sympathetically to follow the 'paces' which Ruskin sees together as he writes of them in parts. Such syntax aims for a maximum of inclusiveness en route to a finality and conclusiveness that the grammar never gives up its search for. The painting is drawn along these lines; the lines turn back upon themselves, as if in obedience to the rhythm of thought in the paint that makes sunlight, after rain, still so much 'like rain'; half carrying the painting, half carried by it, the lines seek to bring the picture finally to spell out its point through Ruskin's tracing hand. The sentences Ruskin writes, he admitted whimsically, 'are all nothing but parentheses and bad grammar, and when I can't help coming to the end of a Parenthesis, I turn it outside in and put the bit of text nearest, inside it' (*Works*, xxxvi, p. 476). In fact, the sentences are a self-sacrificing means of becoming Turner: 'by the substitution of verbiage generally for investigation, I could have made the circulation of these volumes tenfold'. A word in one quasi-parenthesis

[the sunlight] half quenched by the very mists

recalls the other half of its own thought in the next

    which it summons *itself* from the lighted pastures

—so that '*quenched*', referring to the sunlight, goes with 'which it *summons* itself' in an ennobling interchange which is truly Wordsworthian. For it is Wordsworth who provides Ruskin with the nearest verbal analogies to Turner, and Ruskin quotes from Wordsworth in *Modern Painters* accordingly. But this is Wordsworth in prose: 'half quenched' goes with 'half conquering', with respect to the sunlight, just as 'half exhausted' went with 'half passed by', with regard to the shower. In such prose, one half has to prepare for, as well as hold off, the meaning of its countervailing half, and the stationing effect is only achieved through an almost anxiously tight intricacy, tying, untying, and tying up again the knot of the sentence. There are no rests for Ruskin, as there are for Wordsworth, only self-sacrifices to Turner's meaning. This is a syntax of ·local memory: the grammar stations in prose part of the argument for analysis, while the mind is also reminded to run on to ask why that part is but a part and so also a part of a whole. No mind could hold such thoughts on its own; Ruskin's mind needed the paper, the grammar, by which to hold itself open long and hard enough. No wonder then that *Modern Painters* is as long as a whole as this sentence on the *Llanthony* is as a part. No wonder, equally, that it was a life-work, a life and a mind put into it, but one which no mind, not even Ruskin's, can hold as a whole off the page and live with. Ruskin chose to write like a man who could not remember why Turner was important; he had to find out, he had to be surprised in being reminded, in the midst of the twists and turns of the syntax of local memory:

> . . . hasty jets of springing spray to meet the returning light; and these, as if the heaven regretted what it had given, and were taking it back, pass as they leap, into vapour.

Ruskin's mind here finds thoughts coming back upon it; by saturating the subject with his words Ruskin suddenly finds a message precipitated out of his own language: 'as if the heaven regretted what it had given'. This is his moment of discovery within the picture and of re-creation of it; but because he is a critic and because he must write in prose, the moment has to be registered en passant in the form of a shrewd guess rather than with the force of revelation. Ruskin's best life is buried in there, buried in and by his work.

Turner could do the subversive thing in one stroke, as it were: paint in colour but think in light. He made his paintings look unlike conventional paintings, not merely because conventional paintings did not look like nature, but because they looked too much as if they could simply be put in place of nature. 'No; he will make you understand and feel that art *cannot* imitate nature', 'Painting has its peculiar virtues, not only consistent with, but even resulting from, its short-comings and weaknesses' (*Works*, iii, p. 289; v, p. 176). Turner had himself lashed to the mast of a ship in the midst of a storm, not expecting to survive the experience, but feeling bound to record it if he did. He did survive and he recorded it by painting *Snowstorm—steam-boat off a harbour's mouth*. He did not expect to escape, he was not there for the sake of the painting; yet it is hard to believe that he would have been there had he not been a painter, had he not been the sort of painter he was. It is as if he wanted a reality stronger than his own paint, yet also desired by his own art; a reality in his painting whose fate was not merely to exist for the sake of his picture. Another man might have thought of these things as contradictions and duplicities; Ruskin did not think anything so envious of Turner. He came to attribute Turner's essential difficulty to the state of England and, particularly, to a boyhood spent in the squalor of London: he could not paint of the glory of man as the great Venetian painters had done, he could only paint of the solitude that man had left, the humiliation he had suffered. 'He must be a painter of the strength of nature, there was no beauty elsewhere than in that; he must paint also the labour and sorrow and passing away of men; this was the great human truth visible to him' (*Works*, vii, pp. 385–6).[16] To the critics who said of Durer, 'Yet is his strength labour and sorrow', Ruskin felt Durer reply in his work, 'Yes, but labour and sorrow are his strength' (*Works*, vii, p. 313).[17] Ruskin confessed he did not know how far the best work may be done with cheerfulness rather than this dark anger; but he did know that the strength that a Durer or a Turner found in labour and sorrow was not merely exploitative or compensatory. What Turner could do was work an area in between the world's negatives that were on each side of him, working neither for the sake of Art, Art for Art's sake, nor for the sake of Nature, which outshines the light of any painting.

It was not equivalently possible for a writer of discursive prose, as Ruskin was, to find such an area which held off negative alternatives for the sake of a space in which an artist might live through his work. It was desperately hard to open up space in which to find the real living bent and shape of one's thought when the medium was not paint but thoroughly explicit prose, trying half to lead what it was half led by. Ruskin was pulled between alternatives and found his way aggressively and particularly by knowing his enemies as they arose. He went along turning against one falsehood after another, only in retrospect beginning to see how he could reconcile all that he found he was opposed to with all that, consequently, he came to find that he must believe in. Receive my truths, he told his readers, before you try to look for their consistency (*Works*, vii, p. 358). On the one hand he was a puritan attacking the uselessness of aesthetes who were only nominally his allies; on the other he was a man of culture having almost simultaneously to defend serious art from the utilitarian, money-making philistines. On the one hand, to take a more technical instance, he defended the idea of 'finish', making the work of art an achievement in its own right; on the other hand, he did not believe in the idea of perfection that sacrificed passion and intuition for polish and rounding off. He had to say both these things and he said them in *Modern Painters* far apart from each other as they were prompted by different thoughts and objects of thought. But Turner could combine them, could implicitly see his way between them, by a single brushstroke.

What his prose could do, however, was try to recall through its own mimetic transcription of the painting the painting's deep meaning. The prose sank itself within the terms of that meaning until thought arose out of it through the sheer act of writing. The language packed itself into Turner's created spaces, half trapped in there by its own syntax, half enjoying its own crowding of co-operative meaning. Ruskin could write within the shape of rock crests in just the way that Turner had been able to paint himself out a space; it was a way—not Dickens's way— of finding a home upon the earth:

> while the main energy of the mountain mass tosses itself against the central chain of Mont Blanc (which is on the right hand), it is met by a group of counter-crests, like the recoil of a broken wave cast against it from the other side; and yet, as the recoiling water has a sympathy with the under swell of the very wave against which it clashes, the whole mass writhes together in a strange unity of mountain passion. . . .[18]

> *Works,* vi, p. 250.

The writhing unity of this writing is such as can only realize what it writes of via the 'sympathy' of structurally imitating it as comprehensively as possible. Devoted to all that is external to it, such prose, trying to do justice to the underpresence beneath that all, has not the brevity which, in the poetry of Wordsworth for example, is as sufficient grace. Ruskin risked losing his own mind in his words for the sake of finding such things emerge as that clinching word 'passion', as though forcing itself into mind out of deeply pre-established analogy. It constitutes the moment of intersection when, through a word, a man stands precisely between art and nature, with an irresistible language in him re-forming the bonds of sympathy between both. The world speaks to him and through him, just as in another medium it appeared to and through paint, as if nature were giving an assurance that it was part of man's world and man part of its. Here the critic stands, with all the pressure from both sides, acting thus as a verbal intermediary.[19] His language seems to uncover old memories of the world, ancient connections with the world, even as rocks carry memories of their own formation.

The word 'passion' there is something achieved and not merely projected. *Modern Painters* is not itself an example of what Ruskin diagnosed as a symptom of diseased seculariza-tion: pathetic fallacy, the projecting upon external objects feelings which belong, autobiographically, more to the people who behold them than to the objects themselves. For the advantage of his own work to Ruskin was precisely that it took him out of the confined space of being the grown-up son for ever at home with his parents. He did not consider himself second-rate when compared to Turner; he did not consider that he was in the running at all in writing *Modern Painters.* Young pseudo-poets say that they believe there is some good in their work so far and they hope they may do better in future; Ruskin, the puritan absolutist, replies, '*Some* good! If there is not *all* good, there is no good. If ever they hope to do better, why do they trouble us now?' (*Works,* v, p. 206). The great artist takes his mind beyond himself to 'the knowledge which is past his finding out' (ibid., iii, p. 23). Better to find out about these great men than try, uselessly, to become one oneself. The only autobiography Ruskin was then trying to write was that of the human world, the natural world in which humans found and made their home. Yet although this inter-pretative work seemed to Ruskin to take him beyond his own callow life, it also had something powerfully to do with what he was, to do with finding in work a second life and home. But this connection with himself was a thing to be *used* rather than simply known. More came of it that way.

> although to the small, conceited, and affected painter, displaying his narrow knowledge and tiny dexterities, our only word may be, 'Stand aside from between that nature and me': yet to the great imaginative painter—greater a million times in every faculty of soul than we—our word may wisely be, 'Come between this nature and me—this nature which is too great and too wonderful for me; temper it for me, interpret it to me. . . .'[20]
>
> *Works,* v, p. 187.

Turner was Ruskin's purchase upon the world, work on Turner his purchase upon life. Turner gave a name and a purpose to thinking in shapes which Ruskin as a boy fell back upon in lieu of the toys that his evangelical mother denied him: 'I could pass my days contentedly in tracing the squares and comparing the colours of my carpet;—examining the knots in the wood of the floor, or counting the bricks in the opposite houses'. Looking at clouds, water, forms made up of nothing more than the permanent changes of their own content:

this was Ruskin, whose life otherwise was empty. 'It was impossible to explain, either to myself or other people, why I liked staring at the sea' (*Works*, xxxv, pp. 21, 79). Yet with this, curiously, went something he took from the very philistinism and religious moralism of his upbringing: a predisposition staringly to ask, as if for the first time, what was the use of form or the point of painting, what was the purpose of painting landscapes. These two sides of him went into his work for relation. He dared to ask strange questions, imagining the challenge that earlier artists, painters of history, human portrait and religion, would put to modern painters: 'There is something strange in the mind of these modern people! . . . here are human beings spending the whole of their lives in making pictures of bits of stone and runlets of water, withered sticks and flying fogs, and actually not a picture of the gods or the heroes! . . . Trees and clouds indeed! . . . as if it mattered . . .' (*Works*, v, pp. 193–5). [21] He writes like a stranger to the idea of producing a picture because there is already established such a thing as 'Art', which this particular picture may enhance but to which it fundamentally surrenders its own justification. By the time he was writing the final volume of *Modern Painters* Ruskin had lost religious faith; there could be no appeal to God, through His works, for the purpose of painting landscape. Yet Turner's painting, which seemed almost as strange to mere professionalism as it might have seemed to the past masters of religious painting, was irreducibly 'there' as if challenging questions from every side as to how it belonged with nature.

And yet, for all this defence of a stranger life and belonging, it is profoundly disturbing that the work that was a life-work, in lieu of autobiography, *Modern Painters*, finally surrenders itself to an autobiography that acknowledges the defeat of Ruskin's life. *Modern Painters* had ended in 1860 on the note, 'I hear it said of me that I am hopeless. I am not hopeless, though my hope may be as Veronese's: the dark-veiled' (*Works*, vii, p. 457). By 1885, in writing his autobiography *Praeterita*, it is as though 'I hear it said of me that I am hopeless' came back upon him as something which, without Veronese or Turner or perhaps even *Modern Painters* itself, he could hardly reply to on his own account:

Many and many an hour of precious time and perfect sight was spent, during these years, in thus watching skies; much was written which would be useful—if I took a year to put it together,—to myself; but in the present smoky world, to no other creature: and much was learned, which is of no use now to anybody; for to me it is only sorrowful memory, and to others, an old man's fantasy.[22]

Works, xxxv, p. 330.

'Much was written which would be useful': 'would' there does not mean 'was to prove' but is the unfulfilled conditional, the mood of a man who is both no use to himself any more and, in a different sense, no use to others in the terms of a utilitarian society. His is a doubly felt redundancy: as the man turns round to look at the boy he was, with 'sorrowful memory', he also sees that he is simultaneously exposing his back to the charge of 'an old man's fantasy'. In *Unto This Last*, written in 1860, Ruskin showed how a man trained in the arts might presume to write of the state of economic life. Just as painting should not become a separate profession in which painters think the world exists for painting, not painting for the world, so money, argues Ruskin, should be subordinate to our values, rather than our values be at the mercy of money. But if that is the heroic presumption of the man of culture drawing radical political consequences out of his study of art, there is also the less heroic side of the coin: the demoralization of the man of culture, weakened in part by the society which he criticizes for having no use for him. That last consideration can only temporarily strengthen and must finally itself weaken the felt, personal right to make the criticism as though disinterestedly. The shrinkage of work and of rights into autobiography, carrying with it a consciousness also of a diminished chance therein to do justice to a life, must have seemed to Ruskin a final failure. For Ruskin was, in Arnold's terms, an Hebraic figure, charged with a concern for justice, truth, ends and judgments. Committed to the idea of finality, in a way that Wordsworth avoided, Ruskin wrote *Praeterita* more as a self-accusatory than as a self-pitying work, that it should be the mark of what finally he had come to. To those who prefer to think that this does not reflect back upon the worth of the life-work, *Modern Painters,* it must first of all be replied that *Praeterita* was written because Ruskin, at any rate, did not find that the worth of *Modern Painters* could save him. If autobiography is to have a status more than that of an old man's tiredness, it is worth asking whether in such a case a man does have the power of a uniquely authoritative judgement upon the value of his own life. *Praeterita* is Ruskin, the man who put himself second to his work and to Turner, speaking now in his own right. After all his life-work, what was left of the way he tried to live his life? what does his autobiography show of the implicit commitments and consequences of his way of living and working?

Certainly we may say that *Praeterita* is a work of disappointment, and, in its eschewing of any violent memories, many have found it to be also a disappointing work. In a way that last is a form of Ruskin's revenge upon autobiography and the expectations of compensation. Mark Rutherford writes, conventionally but seriously, of the use of autobiography:

> that the mere knowing that other people have been tried as we have been tried is a consolation to us, and that we are relieved by the assurance that our sufferings are not special and peculiar, but common to us with many others.[23]

Ruskin, on the other hand, reports:

> several letters from pleased acquaintances have announced to me, of late, that they have obtained quite new lights upon my character from these jottings, and like me much more than they ever did before. Which was not the least the effect I intended to produce on them; and which moreover is the exact opposite of the effect on my own mind of meeting myself, by turning back, face to face.[24]
>
> *Works,* xxxv, p. 279.

Although each of these accounts is a writing to others out of one's own isolation, where Rutherford supposes that the act of writing decreases the loneliness, Ruskin thinks that, if anything, it increases it. Whether Ruskin or his readership has authority over the meaning of *Praeterita* is, Ruskin himself seems to be saying wryly, almost nothing to Ruskin in view of what he does feel and has become. *Praeterita* is a work of giving up inseparable from Ruskin's sense of being finished, living on after the end of his reputation and, almost, of his wits.

Even when Ruskin does try to assert autobiographical authority over his own meaning and the meaning of himself, the effect is equivocal. He challenges the interpretation that the gift of Rogers's *Italy*, given to him as a boy by his father's business partner Henry Telford, had dictated, by virtue of its Turner illustrations, the subsequent direction of his life:

> it is a great error of thoughtless biographers to attribute to the accident which introduces some new phase of character, all the circumstances of character which give the accident importance. The essential point to be noted, and accounted for, was that I could understand Turner's work when I saw it.[25]
>
> *Works,* xxxv, p. 29.

Thus he seeks to rescue what Blake would call the substance of genius from the accidents of time, by making a distinction between power and the exercise or realization of it.[26] Yet what is so telling is that he can only do so assertively, by dissolving the Romantic sense of a decisive life-moment, of a pivotal, shaping turning-point in a life. Ruskin's narrative may describe the carrying out of his inner potential; but he knows that he cannot make a form or a space for that innerness to stand forth without, falsely to its spirit, dramatizing the mere circumstances that were no more than the occasion of its emergence. It is as though prose, the medium of empiricism, testified to Ruskin of the loss in the world of a notion of transcendence unaffected by time, of innerness undominated by force of circumstances; testifying instead to the defeasibility of the authority of personal emotion and belief in the mundane events and consequences which do so much to confuse and disillusion. We may recall Hazlitt's account: 'I could not bear to think her short of perfection. "She was far from perfection" she replied, with an air and manner (oh, my God!) as near it as possible'.[27] The God of emotion is trapped in parentheses. By acting as an indiscriminately merging medium along one level which seems to be that of time itself, prose seems here taken by surprise by the discriminations going on within itself, yet without belief in the power to lift the emotion out of the memory of subduing circumstances. Blake had warned the would-be Hazlitts: 'Never seek to tell thy love/Love that never told can be' (Blake: *Complete Writings*, p. 161): never try to cross or merge distinct levels of being. But prose mimed the way that distinctions did get lost and merged. *Praeterita* is thus part of the story of how emotions got lost in the sentences that life imposed. 'Man,' said the Coleridgean cleric, J. C. Hare, 'is a parenthesis in nature'.[28]

Yet *Praeterita* tells another story too. The prose of the critic in *Modern Painters* had frequently to store different levels of meaning within a single sentence, holding one level in a subordinate clause, while using it to follow up another implication via another clause: 'I am afraid this will be a difficult chapter; one of drawbacks, qualifications and exceptions. But the more I see of useful truths, the more I find that, like human beings, they are eminently biped; that, although, as far as apprehended by human intelligence, they are usually seen in a crane-like posture, standing on one leg, whenever they are to be stated so as to maintain themselves against all attack it is quite necessary they should stand on two, and have their complete balance on opposite fulcra' (*Works*, v, p. 169).[29] The tension of such defence has broken in *Praeterita*. For the autobiography marks the breaking of the man who previously could not write less than everything about his subject without his being haunted by the anxious shadow of what was excluded. What is left him is the memory of a past self whose uselessness now renders him unretrievable as an agent. The result is a writing far more trusting of itself in thinking as it goes along—more trusting if only because Ruskin is also more hopeless about expecting or even now wanting justice or completeness from himself to himself. Freed from aggressive concern by an admission of failure, the prose has about it an apparent casualness of present tense. Casual yet witnessing, Ruskin writes thus in memory of his father:

> I was particularly fond of watching him shave; and was always allowed to come into his room in the morning (under the one in which I am now writing), to be the motionless witness of that operation.[30]
>
> *Works*, xxxv, pp. 37—8.

and thus of his mother:

> I have just opened my oldest (in use) Bible,—a small, closely, and very neatly printed volume it is, printed in Edinburgh by Sir D. Hunter Blair and J. Bruce, Printers to the King's Most Excellent Majesty in 1816. . . . My mother's list of the chapters with which, thus learned, she established my soul in life, has just fallen out of it.[31]
>
> *Works*, xxxv, p. 42.

In that upper room of the erstwhile family house, his memories now all below as it were, Ruskin here writes like a man conscious of the fact that the son he was has now reached an age past that which his parents ever attained. The writing is on its own now, the writer is no longer writing between disciplines or between different media. The writing is slower, it has given up but it is Ruskin at last writing on his own account. As he transcribes the names of the Bible's printers, he seems to be at once reading and saying farewell. The whole book is written as if it were his means of reading and throwing away old diaries along with old photographs. As his mother's list of favourite chapters falls out of the Bible, Ruskin seems more prepared to accept, easily, that the most important things in his life can be left to, can now only be shown through, accidents, the chances of memory, chance words or present circumstances. To use a distinction made by Ruskin himself as critic, the autobiography is no longer tightly obeying the laws of nature and of grammar as in *Modern Painters*, but following, with a mind of its own, a personal commandment:

> The law is fixed and everlasting; uttered once, abiding for ever, as the sun, it may not be moved. . . . But the commandment is given momentarily to each man, according to the need. . . . The law is, 'Do this always'; the commandment, 'Do *thou* this *now*'.[32]
>
> *Works*, vii, p. 198.

The commandment to write *Praeterita* is a weakened and a disappointed self-commandment and it is also emphatically a secular one. *Praeterita* has a unique calmness amidst Ruskin's writings, a unique sense of the power of his own discretion, even though these things are also inseparable from Ruskin's sense of his being finished while yet having no religious end to his life. The frailty of the writing's permanence in *Praeterita* seems less important, however, than the act of writing itself, as if thus to be temporary were also for Ruskin by this time thus to be as close to oneself, at present, as possible, as bearable:

> I recollect that very evening bringing down my big geography book, still most precious to me; (I take it down now, and for the first time put my own initials under my father's name in it)—[33]
>
> *Works*, xxxv p. 79.

All this autobiography is thus Ruskin's putting his initials under his past and what he loved. The weakened secular commandment is that it has to be enough to write, this, now. Mrs Oliphant, writing of the autobiography of Benvenuto Cellini, considered how the majority of men take their cares to the grave or are cut-off before their old age; if they survive into age with a calm which is not despair, most lack the opportunity or means to give us the benefit of their memory; but

> Sometimes just enough is accomplished to make us feel the excellence of the method, when the pen drops from the feeble fingers, and has to be taken up by somebody who knows the subject only as others know it, from outside, seeing the mountains like molehills, and upsetting the perspective of events.
>
> *Blackwood's Magazine*, January 1881, vol. cxxix, p. 2.

Ruskin managed to write *Praeterita* alone in between fits of depression and virtual madness. Only in such trouble could he find, and have to be satisfied with, what was 'just enough', if not fully just or finally or permanently so. Only thus could he find a scale and a perspective for his own life. But the feeling that his own under-writing of his past is but temporary and parenthetical belongs to a consciousness that all these memories will die with death, his own initials left like the fading words he writes.

The story of *Praeterita* is thus not simply one of disappointment and the failure of a life and its work. In giving up striving towards the greatness of the past, towards Turner-violence, lashed to a mast, towards Romantic mystery, the book very

sadly succeeds at its own human level. *Praeterita* gives us a
scale by which to know and measure the genre of secular
autobiography in the nineteenth century. For it makes us
recognize something important and honourable in the reduced
capacity of a man like Ruskin to make the question 'has my life
been worthwhile or happy?' something more than futile. The
author sees only the shortcomings of himself and his books;
but in the book that is his autobiography, even so, there is an
intimation that the question is always too big, the answer
always premature. The Idealist philosopher F. H. Bradley
explains how such a question, asked in a world of successive, if
not supersessive, events in time, is an impossible one for
seeking to make a whole out of an open-ended life-series of
particulars:

> A series which has no beginning, or if a beginning, yet no
> end, can not be summed, there *is* no All, and yet the
> All is postulated and the series is to be summed. But
> it can not be summed till we are dead, and then, if
> we have realized it, we, I suppose, do not know it, and
> we are not happy; and before death we can not have
> realized it, because there is always more to come, the
> series is always incomplete.[34]

For the Idealist philosopher there could be no determination
of an indeterminate series. It was determinists like Harriet
Martineau who believed that life was not open but had its
conclusions. Ruskin was no formal Idealist, but he simply
could not believe that the impasse that his life had reached
was essential to the nature of things rather than personal: the
fact was just that 'all my chances of being anything but what I
am were thrown away, or broken short, one after another'
(*Works*, xxxv, p. 277). Unlike Miss Martineau he could not
comfort himself by disbelieving in the possibility of being
anything but what he had become. One alternative was to
believe that the judgments a person makes about his own life
are provisional and relative, often, for example, referring as
much to the time in which they are made as to the time to
which they are meant to refer back. Yet, equally, the sort of
failure that Ruskin felt his life had been induced him to feel
that *he* belonged to the judgment of his own past far more than

his past ever could come properly under his present jurisdiction: 'I have learned a few things, forgotten many; in the total of me, I am but the same youth, disappointed and rheumatic' (*Works*, xxxv, p. 220). He could not be conclusive; he did not feel free enough to be relative; yet he could not bear simply to give in to autobiography's formal encouragement of the difficulty that people have in raising themselves and their thoughts above the mere succession of their life-time: 'not only what happened to me . . . but what was *in* me' (*Works*, xxxv, p. 281). Something that was neither sullen conclusiveness nor unthinking acquiescence was given to Ruskin in *Praeterita* sheerly by the act of writing. Without writing, the present had for Ruskin no status over the past. For the knowledge that had come to him in time—'I never have known anything of what was most seriously happening to me till afterwards'—by that time meant nothing to him but dry residue, was no compensation or achievement so much as an irony—'But all this I have felt and learned, like so much else, too late' (*Works*, xxxv, pp. 442, 357). What is remarkable is that the act of writing did *not* give the present a final status over the past that might have been supposed as having led up to it; what it gave Ruskin was a means of expression by which correction of the past could not be imputed to a desire to reflect credit or hope upon the present. Writing for the moment lent Ruskin its own time.

What do I mean by that? Writing lent Leslie Stephen its time two weeks after the death of his second wife, Julia, herself a widow when he met her:

> 22 Hyde Park Gate, 21 May 1895
> I am about to try to write something for my darling Julia's children: George Herbert, Stella, and Gerald de l'Etang Duckworth; and Vanessa, Julian Thoby, Adeline Virginia and Adrian Leslie Stephen.
>
> *Mausoleum Book*, p. 3.

Writing thus to the children to whom he was a step-father together with those to whom he was a real father, all latterly united by the joining of his life to Julia Duckworth's, Stephen, in the trouble of a second bereavement in marriage, steadies himself by the act of writing and naming, as in testament. He manages to get writing to get him moving and starting: 'am about to', 'am about to try to write'. He puts it down and at the same time it moves him forward: that is the time felt by the writing hand.

Such support relieved Ruskin from the impossibility of protest. Humiliatingly, nothing much had ever happened to him outwardly; apart from the unmentioned and unconsummated marriage, it was a life of might-have-beens. The very fact of his self being defeated, without its ever really having been able to fight, disabused that self of any protesting reaction to that defeat—apart from that expression of feebleness which is the defeat's very own product. Thus he writes of his friends:

> I never expected that they should care much for *me*, but only that they should read my books; and looking back, I believe they liked and like me, nearly as well as if I hadn't written any.[35]
>
> Works, xxxv, p. 425.

It is not 'but looking back', it is 'and looking back', because this writing could carry him past his own contradictions. Those contradictions do nonetheless exist. Ruskin clearly needed the protection of his own gifts and felt himself less than they. Only when he thought that those gifts in every sense had failed, was he here 'nearly' writing as '*me*' rather than as the author of *Modern Painters* and *Unto This Last*. But then of course, as he knew, that was because it was too late. Still, 'I am about to try to write something'.

Because it transformed a limited genre into an experience of limitations, *Praeterita* is the greatest of nineteenth-century autobiographies, but—again the contradiction—its greatness is inseparable from its author's deeper sense of personal disappointment. This may leave us wondering whether this paradox is a sign of an ignored Victorian need for a redefinition of what is 'greatness' in art; even whether it unfairly pressurizes writers to claim great human importance for the role of art in society. For if *Praeterita* shows the real value of writing-in-memory being short of being justice, again its success at partiality is achieved at the cost of Ruskin's own feeling of total failure. Is not that paradox likewise a sign that Ruskin got his proportions wrong and only too late and too painfully found the right human scale and tone for himself?

Certainly there are contradictions. Ruskin believed in an art which could not let the Romantic spirit of Turner die, even if it could hardly live with it. Ruskin bought and owned what he took to be Turner's greatest painting, *Slavers throwing overboard the dead and dying—Typhoon coming on*, but eventually he sold it because he could not live with it. Because of himself? because of his times? He wrote *Modern Painters* on behalf of a moral view of art; he wrote *Unto This Last* for the sake of a moral view of economics. Yet how do these works stand beside a story he tells in *Praeterita*?—There he laments how he, a man of culture, turned round from looking at a favourite chapel at Pisa to humiliate his own father with a look of scorn. Because his father had interrupted him by asking him how much money, of all things, he should give the coachman!

In a word, has the story of Ruskin's life a final authority upon the meaning of his life-work? What art can do for humanity—but what did art do for him? It seems to have contributed to the felt disproportion between the narrow physical basis of his life and the mental achievement raised, with such strain, upon it. This was a man for whom the most important part of his life was an Art which would not permit itself to be self-justifying in terms of mere aesthetics. For all his love of form, form for Ruskin had to have a meaning, an articulatable meaning, for it to have inspired love. The importance of art for him was partly measured by the fact of its independence of the consideration whether, personally, it made him happy or not. Yet it was also partly measured by the dependence of the notion of its being important to him upon a moral, spiritual and political conviction that it ought likewise to be important to everyone else in a humane society. He believed in art which was committed to extend itself beyond art, but beyond art it was liable to find itself abused and ignored. Ruskin's sense of failure is inextricably bound up with his allegiance to the moral ambition of the most strenuous and uncomfortable nineteenth-century art, refusing to succeed by being anything other than committed on almost every front and caught on every front. This then is a story of complex failure, refusing to avoid contradictions as much as betraying itself in them.

And the precise point about *Praeterita* is that it is not the final word upon it all. The very way in which it had to be written—with adventitious fluency, with the sense of being temporary—teaches the big secular lesson to be learned from the disappointment of absolutes. That there are looser relations than those of cause and effect, act and consequence; loose, complex relations between life-work and the autobiography which reflects back upon it all. This, in the form of denial and irony, is what *Praeterita* is able to make of its own failure: a recognized incapacity to be the last word. What might seem the really big, testing question—the relation of Ruskin's work in art and love of art to the making and living of a life—becomes in the autobiography a relegated consideration. It is admission enough, perhaps, that the autobiography deals rather in the under-developed things that his life-work neglected. Yet the effect is that it leaves Ruskin's life, however poor and feeble it seemed to him, a thing intact, not merely culture's fault; a thing not just subordinate to, even when absorbed in, his work and his culture. And it also leaves the work intact, behind him now.

This sort of looseness, in belief, in style of writing, was a hard thing for puritanical Ruskin to achieve. But that is what makes it an educative, rather than merely commonplace, thing to behold. We may end with a final illustration of what is at stake here.

Leslie Stephen's first wife, Minny, died in November 1875. In the months that followed his bereavement the literary man found some help in reading Wordsworth: 'I used not to care for him specially; but now I love him'.[36] In 1876 and 1877, reports Stephen's biographer, he was writing as he had never written before: 'we may find in the work of this time a strong autobiographical element'.[37] In August 1876 Stephen published in *The Cornhill Magazine* an article entitled 'Wordsworth's Ethics'. It was an attempt to make explicit Wordsworth's implicit thought and thus find a form of practical thinking which could heal what Stephen called the divide between concrete experience and abstract reason. What Stephen had found in Wordsworth, above all, was the idea of the transmutation of suffering.

The other response that Stephen made to the death of his first wife is told in his *Mausoleum Book* written in 1895 when he was mourning the death of his second wife, Julia. It was in Julia, who had herself lost a spouse, that he found how a person transmuted grief; when he wrote of her he felt bound to quote from Wordsworth's 'She was a phantom of delight'; it was with her that he sought to live again and re-marry. His *Mausoleum Book* tells of the couple's hesitations and their final marriage.

The relation between the death of Minny and the effect on him of Wordsworth, the relation between the work on Wordsworth and the re-marriage to Julia, the relation between the second loss and the critic's necessity to write quietly and privately to the children on his own account—these are not causal things; they are loose, but they are related—in memory. In the same way, Julia and Leslie Stephen hesitated over marriage because they did not want their union to be 'caused' by their respective bereavements, though it was intimately and delicately related to them.

Nothing like so much actually happened to John Ruskin in his life as compared to Leslie Stephen in his. So perhaps it is all the greater achievement that in *Praeterita* he could show that his life was both more serious and less important than the work which had so often stood for it. More and less: this is the looser precision of which he finally found the necessity.

II. MARGARET OLIPHANT AND GEORGE ELIOT

When Mrs Oliphant praised autobiography for maintaining a perspective in which personal mountains could not easily be dismissed by outsiders as mere molehills, she was only telling half the story. The other half belongs with Ruskin who in his autobiography was not at all confident that his own mountains were anything more than molehills, when it came to his personal life; whereas in his professional life he was happy to draw the memory of a whole real mountain out of the structure of its smallest manageable part. This uncertainty about relations, proportions and scales of consideration is an important aspect of this age of secularization: what, for example, was the relation between the meaning of a person's own life and his belief in what life itself essentially had to offer? how was personal life measured on a different scale from published work, even when that work drew upon that life for power as well as subject-matter? how could one know how much to make of oneself? To the imagination of a Dickens this uncertainty about getting life into proportion was productive and invigorating. But as the century wore on anxiety was a more typical response. It is an anxiety that we may share. Large and authoritative prose works, from *Modern Painters* to *Middlemarch*, seemed to offer themselves as so complete. But if these works were not absolutes, making a world of their own—and, indeed, this was not their claim—how far, then, were they only relative to a personal viewpoint, massively and disproportionately expanded out of all recognition? How could these big works, if not world-views then in lieu of them, take their place, find their place in the world—a world which, in the age of realism that Ruskin and George Eliot in their different ways shared, these works were supposed to be dedicated to represent.[38] How could they be placed? what or whose reality was their reality? Did one need to believe in them, to know what made these sprawling, generous works wholes as totally as did Ruskin and George Eliot themselves? For these works seemed to contain the whole of their authors' secular beliefs. What claim were they making? were they overweening?

In this section, in wondering about such questions, I intend to focus upon one literary figure, a woman, in order to think about two related difficulties: the status of nineteenth-century realistic art with regard to the life outside it that it proposed to serve; the relation within one writer's life's work between two different forms of treating of her own life, namely autobiography and autobiographical fiction. As with Ruskin, I shall be looking for indications as to the place and the scale of the work in question. It will also become clear why it is important to have turned to the study of a woman at this point.

Born in 1828, died in 1897, Margaret Oliphant (whose thoughts on autobiography I have already mentioned) is remembered in the *Dictionary of National Biography* as a novelist of 'not the highest rank', 'but the probability is that she made the best possible use of her powers'. It is the judgment of herself that Mrs Oliphant had bitterly predicted but, indeed, half accepted. Beside George Eliot and George Sand, women novelists who were of the highest rank, she admitted that she did feel very small, very obscure; altogether a failure for never making the great critical impression: but 'why should I? I acknowledge frankly that there is nothing in me—a fat, little, commonplace woman, rather tongue-tied—to impress any one; and yet there is a sort of whimsical injury in it which makes me sorry for myself' (Mrs Oliphant: *Autobiography*, p. 4). But even in that she knew that there was not nothing in her, full stop. Although, as she recognized, there were good reasons why Leslie Stephen's pride and joy, the *Dictionary of National Biography*, should write her memory off, there was also enough in her to know that there were bad ones too. Reading Trollope's *An Autobiography*, Mrs Oliphant was amazed that he should want to talk so much about his own characters and creations: 'I feel that my carelessness of asserting my claim is very much against me with everybody. It is so natural to think that if the workman is indifferent about his work, there can't be much in it that is worth thinking about' (ibid., p. 1). Challenged by such a mixture of shrewdness and bitterness, it is worth our thinking again what might be justice to the memory of Mrs Oliphant.

Suppose we consult her own memory of her life. It is clear that it will not be the memory of her writings—so what use is it to us? Nor does she offer big, dramatic memories as Haydon did to offset the balance. But that's the point:

> When I look back on my life, among the happy moments which I can recollect is one which is so curiously common and homely, with nothing in it, that it is strange even to record such a recollection, and yet it embodied more happiness to me than almost any real occasion as might be supposed for happiness. It was the moment after dinner when I used to run up-stairs to see that all was well in the nursery, and then to turn into my room on the way down again to wash my hands, as I had a way of doing before I took up my evening work which was generally needlework, something to make for the children. . . . my heart full of joy and peace—for what?—for nothing—that there was no harm anywhere, the children well above stairs and their father below . . .
>
> I have always said it is in these unconsidered moments

that happiness is—not in things or events that may be supposed to cause it.

Ibid., pp. 44–5.

In between her children above and her husband below, the woman would hesitate, habitually, to feel her life, even when her time was hardly her own. This turning into her room has the suspended, temporary freedom that Ruskin, in such different domestic circumstances, felt when he wrote above the room his dead parents had inhabited. Only this is embedded at the centre of her busy domestic life rather than at its close: it is the point to which her life could constantly return for a sense of itself. 'There is nothing in me'—yet out of this admission and consonant with it is the authority of such a moment; a 'nothing' with 'nothing in it'. It seems as if she is writing of life rather than in novels; the event is a matter of casual habit rather than pivotal decisiveness. Yet in fact, even here in rejecting the Romantic and novelistic belief in unrepeatably happy life-moments, Mrs Oliphant is not merely opposing her experience of life to the way that some novels depict it.[39] Rather, her professional command shows how she has been able to write her autobiography precisely by *not* using her life and memory as she could have used them in writing fiction. With all the skill of a novelist herself, as well as with the prosaic ruefulness of a disappointed author, she writes autobiography as if it were an anti-novel:

> I was reading Charlotte Bronte the other day, and could not help comparing myself with the picture more or less as I read. I don't suppose my powers are equal to hers—my work to myself looks perfectly pale and colourless beside hers—but yet I have had far more experience and, I think, a fuller conception of life. I have learned to take perhaps more a man's view of mortal affairs,—to feel that the love between men and women, the marrying and giving in marriage, occupy in fact so small a portion of either existence or thought.

Ibid., p. 62.

Mrs Oliphant feels ambivalent about the thought that if Charlotte Bronte had believed in that perspective on love, a novel like *Villette*, the account of the sorrows of a single woman,

would never have been written. A great novel but a novel
whose power, Mrs Oliphant seems to have felt, came not
so much from a life as from the want of one. She was
not interested in power won that 'female' way. Mrs Oliphant's
Autobiography promises to be more about a 'real' life.

The key to understanding Mrs Oliphant's almost anti-
literary attitude lies in one fact: that it had always been her
practice to subdue beneath normal human purposes the tricks
of a writer's trade. For her, normal human purposes always
meant family purposes. As a young widow, she had to put her
own work second to the care of her children even though it was
her writing which economically fathered them. But even when
she was a girl at home, just beginning to write novels, she had
had to keep her talent subordinate to family needs and the life
around her. She was not allowed a separate room in which to
write, for that would have made the writing seem 'unnatural'
in the eyes of her parents, strict Scottish puritans:

> My mother, I believe, would have felt her pride and
> rapture much checked, almost humiliated, if she had
> conceived that I stood in need of any artificial aids.
>
> Ibid., p. 24.

Even so, these thoughts seem to be ones that she does not
allow herself to resent, but ones that she is at home in.
'I believe', for example, although grown-up, still plays a
supportive, subsidiary role in the sentence, as she by-passes
the possibility of humiliating her own mother—even as, years
later, she turned in and out of her own room of thoughts en
route to do her duty to her family. Mrs Oliphant notes how
even then her writing always ran through everything while still
also being subordinate to everything outside it (ibid., p. 23).
'Almost humiliated' she writes: 'almost' there saves the mother
(and the daughter) from the full force of a novelist's insight,
and that itself, the professional stylist must tacitly have known,
also makes the insight all the keener for being less sharp. The
parentheses thus seem better integrated—in the sentence, in
the ambience—than did poor, redundant John Ruskin's.

Mrs Oliphant's sentences of memory seem content to take
this sort of back-seat, reporting less of the past than almost
any moment in it could have experienced. 'I have always said

it is in these unconsidered moments that happiness is': that 'always' cannot literally be true but it sets the note for her autobiographical writing. She starts from the moment when consciousness has emerged not as tentative thought but as accumulated experience—experience accumulated sufficiently to be able to report itself as familiarly strange, '*curiously* common and homely', even in her own eyes. So it is in her description of what she understands by happiness; so too it is when she writes of her mother:

> How little one realises the character or individuality of those who are most near and dear. It is with difficulty even now that I can analyze or make a character of her. She herself is there, not any type of variety of mankind.
>
> Ibid., p. 12.

What she took for granted seemed wonderful and strange in retrospect, and all she wanted to do was to leave it as it was, as if the settledness, that her life had so assumed, was a matter for sober reverence. She was not going to write it all up into sharper, but less true, focus. The way Mrs Oliphant's life had become her memory was the result of a passionate and busy absorbedness, in the family of her childhood and of her marriage, so habitual to her as hardly to be distinctly available to her consciousness at all. She wrote of autobiography in *Blackwood's Magazine* for August 1881 in terms which contrast her own sense of memory with that of a Ruskin or even a Charlotte Bronte:

> It is curious to note how much more keen is the memory, how much more distinct all the personal details of recollection in the minds of those who have kept themselves intact, so to speak, and have never lost their childish individuality. The man, and more especially the woman, who has married, and confused the remembrance of early days with so many recollections more poignant—has a memory of a totally different quality from that of the virginal old age which has never replaced its first impressions with others more important. Gibbon and Cowper and Buckle are all of this stamp.
>
> *Blackwood's Magazine*, vol. 130, pp. 231–2.

This is why we have turned to Mrs Oliphant and her family-memory: it challenges greater and more solitary ways of remembering precisely on the grounds of her possessing ('more especially the woman') 'far more experience and a fuller conception of life'.

Thus she records with scrupulousness what the nature of 'replacement' of memories meant to her. She writes of her mother who died a few months before the loss of Marjorie, Mrs Oliphant's own, second, daughter: 'But at that moment her loss was nothing to me in comparison with the loss of my little child' (*Autobiography*, p. 33)—even though she also says that she misses her mother even now when she is at sixty almost as old as her mother was when she died. Such a sense of instinctive priorities at that time may have been no more than an 'animal instinct' (ibid.). Yet the child looked at her mother as she died, 'giving up her little soul in that look of consciousness, as it appeared to me. That was in 1855, thirty-six years ago, but I have never forgot the look with which that baby died' (ibid., p. 41). All this emotional replacement and relativism feels strange even to herself. Yet harder still is the fact that in 1859 her husband, a painter, died suddenly, leaving debts to a wife already expecting another child. That child, their second son, was born three months after the father's death.

The *Autobiography* was begun in 1864 but was mostly composed at odd, troubled times between 1885 and 1894. It was taken up again, for instance, on 18 January 1891, after the death of her first son in 1890. The stability of the work still survives the hiatus, but does so because it cannot bear, can hardly try, to touch it; she recalls:

> And, best of all, our delightful boy was born. Ah me! If I had continued this narrative at the time when I broke it in 1888, I should have told of this event and all its pleasantness, if not with a light heart, yet without the sudden tears that blind me now, so that I cannot see the page.
>
> Ibid., p. 42.

No wonder Mrs Oliphant treasured the memory of the mere happiness of 'no harm anywhere', that elder boy to whom she had given so much of her widowed life died aged only thirty-four. One recognizes so powerfully the defeasibility of meaning in time: had she written in 1888 her view of the past would have been so different from her view in 1891. Who knows which is the right time in which to put memories on paper, who knows what chances are won or lost by deciding to commit oneself at a particular time? And always we think writing is so final, so professional, so authoritative! This helps us see otherwise, as if the accidental death of the son broke open the smooth linear lie of conventional autobiography. For Mrs Oliphant at this point, the past feels so dependent upon the present and her recent loss; the surviving mother has now lost, with her son, access to the reality of the past which she could have written of before—even though that reality ought, somewhere, still, to be true. Moreover, the present now upon which that past depends itself feels only discontinuous, incidental and weightless rather than comprehensive and summative. The tears are more real for coming more like a surface reaction caught in the act of writing than like a deep conclusion. Even in this despair there is a necessary freedom, if so it may be called, from a responsibility to totality; writing cannot bear the weight of a whole life.

Mrs Oliphant is so sane and steady. Yet all the time, a reader waits for her to acknowledge the cost of that sanity, that sad, realistic control. It comes when she speaks of her novel-writing. Comparing herself again with Trollope, she says of the creatures of her imagination, the characters in her novels:

> perhaps my life has been too full of personal interests . . . to make me believe that they were more to me in writing than they might have been in reading—that is, my own stories in the making of them were very much what other people's stories (but these the best) were in the reading. . . . Perhaps people will say that is why they never laid any special hold upon the minds of others, though they might be agreeable reading enough. . . . It pleases me at this present moment, I may confess, that I seem to have found unawares an image that quite expresses what I mean— i.e. that I wrote as I read, with much the same sort of feeling. It seems to me that this is rather an original way

of putting it (to disclose the privatest thought in my mind) and this gives me an absurd little sense of pleasure.

Autobiography, p. 107.

Phrases like 'Perhaps people will say' and 'It seems to me' suggest her suspicion that even in writing in this sort of way she is carrying out what will be people's judgment of her—that she was a mediocrity. For her compromise as a writer lies in her taking up a sort of middle ground, writing with only the same sort of interest in her own conceptions as she felt in reading those of others. This was what Ruskin could hardly conceive: how people could live when their work had not its own justification but its justification in terms of what already had been done. Here too Mrs Oliphant still writes by siting herself between her own memory and her thought of her readers' lesser resonance therefrom.

And yet the distance between the shrewd guess—'Perhaps people will say that is why . . .'—and the really frightened sense of personal failure, facing the full responsibility, is actually the closest which this woman could get from one side to the realization of the other. It is the nearest she could get from the side of words to the feeling of their personal application: failure. It is almost the closest that a human being could get, in direct words which still allowed some dignity, to what conventional autobiography blindly supposes to be natural, easy and straightforward—the thought of what one is. Here, what is impossible—for Mrs Oliphant, this side of suicidal despair, fully to acknowledge failure—is what makes for the thing which, in being possible, is right for human beings—that she should leave it to others, probably fallibly, to judge. 'Perhaps people will say' may be her sane compromise in lieu of saying it herself, but it is also true that that is where her success or failure was to be given its name. Posterity settles it, as if the writing itself were a settled thing rather than something that rested upon living circumstances and depended, among other things, upon recognition and luck. There are so many buried stories and Mrs Oliphant's is one. Who reads even her *Autobiography* nowadays?

It seems right, that out of the very syntax of mediocrity—'It seems to me'—comes something from under her pen, in the act of writing, of which she can say, 'It pleases me'. It is good that even a thought, close to self-criticism at that, can so please her as to make her pause to toy with it. For all the self-sceptical whimsy, as if she had caught herself smiling at herself and gone fussy to hide it ('I may confess', 'quite expresses', 'rather an original way'), there is the serious power of writing here actually making a 'now' in which a woman treasures her sheer capacity to think through verbal images. If this was compensation for her, it was a compensation that she could hardly help: 'that curious kind of self-compassion which one cannot get clear of' (ibid., p. 4). For a second or two, as she verbally ponders that phrase 'I wrote as I read', the writing offers a serious distraction, opening up to her again the time she spent among phrases, the life that was hers sheerly by being a practising writer. The writing lets her into a writing life again. What is more, if she can see how she lived inside her writing, it is characteristic that, at another moment, she also recognizes how, still with the support of her writing, she also lived outside it; thus she writes of the first compliment paid to her by a boy: 'Perhaps if I were not a novelist addicted to describing such scenes, I might not remember if after—how long? Forty-one years' (ibid., p. 15). Her writing ran through everything but was subordinate to everything.

Yet if Mrs Oliphant felt that her writing supported her memory, she also almost believed that her personal concerns had weakened her artistic achievement. She recalls the way that economic circumstances forced her to say to herself:

> I must make up my mind . . . that to bring up the boys for the service of God was better than to write a fine novel, supposing even that it was in me to do so. . . . It seemed rather a fine thing to make that resolution (though in reality I had no choice); but now I think that if I had taken the other way, which seemed the less noble, it might have been better for all of us. . . . Who can tell? . . .
>
> In this my resolution which I did make, I was, after all, only following my instincts, it being in reality easier for me to keep on with a flowing sail, to keep my household and make a number of people comfortable, at the cost of incessant work, and an occasional great crisis of anxiety,

than to live the self-restrained life which the great artist
imposes upon himself.

Ibid., pp. 6–7.

It is a big question—the sort of question that might have
appealed to the Tolstoy who wrote *What is Art?* wondering
whether it was better to write tales for the peasants than *Anna
Karenina*—which Mrs Oliphant then decides not to ask: in
God's eyes, was it better to bring up the boys than to write a
great novel? The sentences, like the life, flow on past vital big
questions, not to answer, but to have to subsume the necessity
for them, as if the greatness of such questions was a tempting
over-simplification to which she, at any rate, had no right. It is
as if, by surviving rather than by asking or answering, she had
got past these questions, which nevertheless deeply concerned
her, in such a way as not to feel the right quite to approach
them. For she felt it was her failure that provoked such
questions, as tempting compensations, and it was the sanity of
modest compromise that made her refuse them. If she had
asked them, would she now be remembered, just as Matthew
Arnold is remembered for *Culture and Anarchy*, that large, brave
over-simplification? 'In reality', at any rate, the two things
that here prevented her—the failure and the sanity—were
complexly linked in her mind, like a double-bind which also
bound her to admit that insanity would not produce 'the great
artist' either. She wrote these words in 1885. After the death of
her second son in 1894 she was pushed even further from any
sense of the reality of these questions for her:

> At my most ambitious of times I would rather my children
> had remembered me as their mother than in any other
> way, and my friends as their friend. I never cared for
> anything else. And now that there are no children to
> whom to leave any memory, and the friends drop day by
> day, what is the reputation of a circulating library to me?
> Nothing and less than nothing.

Ibid., p. 130.

Yet there must have been something of her ambition left, as
she confined her memory here to writing.

If time made the question non-feasible, so did her Scottish
Nonconformist conscience which dissolves it into sceptical

syntax: 'Who can tell?', 'Perhaps', 'after all', 'only', 'in reality'. At the risk of leaving herself still small beside the George Eliots and Charlotte Brontes, she keeps herself in proportion. Yet her removing any excuse—'in reality I had no choice'—unwittingly provides for her, who cannot accept it, the only excuse that could be justifiable. She could not help making the choice she did; but if that is true she could hardly help her own failure. If it was justly only her own affair and not so big a thing at that ('only following my instincts'), the injustice is that it was her affair alone as a widow; while the dismissal of the possibility of heroism in that 'it being in reality easier for me' is actually, for us, its only possibility. Her sense of truth will not allow her the greatness to ask whether it was better to raise children than to write like George Eliot; because, either way, she still, she fears, might not have actually brought them up well for all that (she thought her indulgence of them made them ruinously careless with money when they grew up), and she might well not have had the genius or the discipline to write a great novel anyway. Truth thus abandons her 'in reality', into reality: she did bring them up, probably with inadequacy; she did not write a great novel. Perhaps only a woman, a woman in such circumstances who was yet a literary woman, could have known so intimately what was at stake in the reality that the nineteenth-century novel was dedicated to explore. Yet this woman did not write a great realistic novel and was possibly debarred from doing so by the very experience which seemed to make her so eligible for the work. But this was the very possibility that her sense of truth could hardly allow her to mention. Yet it is her sense of truth also that will not let the reality, in which her life is abandoned, make her say that that life was her desert and choice rather than her fate and trial. 'In reality I had no choice.' The words to which she entrusts her sense of truth do Mrs Oliphant more justice than she could do herself. Her words do not seem to be personal covers; on the contrary, they appear to take the shape and impression of her self, to fall from it in its hesitations as much as in its beliefs, and to make marks which suggest meanings extended beyond the point where she herself would have stopped speaking, without those extensions being out of line with the strong meaning of what she was. This is a real book, the language adding a reality that prevents her merely succumbing to external reality. Even-handed justice will not let Margaret Oliphant allow herself to become Harriet Martineau, for Mrs Oliphant's sceptical imagination struggles with and against her reality in the only partial freedom of the comparatives: 'better than to write a fine novel', 'it might have been better for all of us', 'it being in reality easier'. But if she does not entirely give in to the external facts in the way that Harriet Martineau made a virtue of doing, she likewise refuses to ignore them:

> I have been reading the life of Mr Symonds, and it makes me almost laugh (though little laughing is in my heart) to think of the strange difference between this prosaic little narrative, all about the facts of a life so simple as mine, and his elaborate self-discussions. I suppose that to many people the other will be the more interesting way—just as the movements of the mind are more interesting than those of the body, or rather of the external life. . . . any attempt at discussing myself like Mr Symonds, if I were likely to make it, only would end in outlines of trouble, in the deep, deep sorrow that covers me like a mantle. . . . Good Mr Symonds, a pleasant, frank, hearty man, as one saw him from outside! God bless him! for he was kindly to Cecco . . .
>
> Ibid., pp. 74–5.

Cecco, the younger son, was now dead along with his brother. Characteristically, it is his memory, rather than anything in Symonds's own autobiography, that for Mrs Oliphant saves Symonds's memory and makes her less self-pityingly bitter. It is a matter of lives not books that makes her own book and her own language so much more than merely something filling pages of self-explanation. It is a *real* book.

*   *   *   *   *

I argued in chapter 3 that autobiographical fiction as a strong art saved the meaning and memory of lives registered all too frailly in biography or autobiography. But, picking up on my ambivalence about Dickens, I have now to ask whether fiction saved lives only by distorting them. Isn't fiction unreal when compared with the reality of failure revealed in Mrs Oliphant's *Autobiography*?

It is at the heart of that *Autobiography* that Mrs Oliphant resumed work on it in earnest after reading J. W. Cross's *George Eliot's Life*. For a woman and a novelist at such a time, the questions of family versus literary achievement had to be asked with particular reference to George Eliot, who would be remembered when a Mrs Oliphant was forgotten. George Eliot lived as the common-law wife of George Henry Lewes. He protected her from the outside world. Was it, wonders Mrs Oliphant, 'in reality easier' for *her*?[40] 'Should I have done better if I had been kept, like her, in a mental greenhouse and taken care of?' (ibid., p. 5). But aware and sceptical of her own envy and power of self-delusion in putting such questions, Mrs Oliphant tried to say of her fear that she would leave behind her nothing that would live, 'What does it matter? Nothing at all now—never anything to speak of'. (ibid., p. 130). She uses the form of autobiography as merely postscript to carry her past her fear. Yet there is a bitterness in Mrs Oliphant's thought that nobody will mind, as there is not in Thomas Hood's thought that nobody should mind. Mrs Oliphant knew from Cross's book how George Eliot would have reacted to being in *her* position, as a novelist likely to be forgotten. Thus, Marian Evans, before ever beginning to write novels:

> My troubles are purely psychical—self dissatisfaction, and despair of achieving anything worth the doing.
>
> *George Eliot's Life*, i, p. 322.

—then George Eliot on finishing *Adam Bede*, receiving the applause, but having to start to write again:

> Yes, I *am* assured now that 'Adam Bede' was worth writing—worth living through long years to write. But now it seems impossible to me that I shall ever write anything so good and true again.
>
> Ibid., ii, pp. 107–8.

—on going on later to *Romola* after the success of *Mill on the Floss*:

> Will it ever be finished? Ever be worth anything?
>
> Ibid., ii, p. 336.

—and on struggling with *Middlemarch*:

> Sept. 11 [1869]—I do not feel very confident that I can make anything satisfactory out of 'Middlemarch'. I have need to remember that other things which have been accomplished by me were begun under the same cloud. G. has been reading 'Romola' again, and expresses profound admiration. This is encouraging.
>
> Ibid., iii, p. 99.

Mrs Oliphant's words were finally 'What does it matter?': even in that there was a consciousness for her of the sane failure of the second-rate artist to make too much of it. But in George Eliot's note to herself, 'Ever be worth anything?', it still does matter very much, for hers are journals written in the midst of the struggle to write—a struggle which Mrs Oliphant could not have borne to have felt or expressed so self-consciously. And what, I suppose, Mrs Oliphant must have seen in those remarks was the way that they spurred George Eliot on to make them things of the past, subjects of her own writing, even if that past was bound to recur almost every time the anxious woman picked up her pen to begin afresh. The fate of a second-rate artist was so feared by George Eliot, her fear was so used to motivate her, was so used to help her own subject-matter, until the culminating achievement was *Middlemarch*, making a success of writing about provincial failures: it must have seemed to Mrs Oliphant that the actual fate of second-rate failure was quite outside what was fully realized in the writing from the very fear of it. The reality of George Eliot's fear, that is to say, was someone like Mrs Oliphant who did not get away with it, who did not think that she could bear to frighten herself into so much; George Eliot's fears seemed to make for the success which left them as finally unfounded. Moreover, she made money, lived comfortably.

To George Eliot of course her fears could never be finally unfounded, for the sanity with which in her *Autobiography* Mrs Oliphant viewed her writing was a thing that George Eliot herself could only find and surpass in novel writing. 'I have need to remember', she writes in her journal, but it was her journal alone that could do the remembering for her; she seems to have put her fears compulsively into words, where

Mrs Oliphant with no time to write a journal leaves her fears beneath her words. Thus George Eliot writes on 25 December 1875 of *Daniel Deronda*:

> Each part as I see it before me *in werden* seems less likely to be anything else than a failure; but I see on looking back this morning—Christmas Day—that I really was in worse health and suffered equal depression about 'Romola'; and so far as I have recorded, the same thing seems to be true of 'Middlemarch'.
>
> *George Eliot's Life*, iii, p. 270.

It may simply be that this is how George Eliot happened to trouble herself in the fairly leisurely life she led before, around and after writing. But it is tempting to suppose that this factor, George Eliot's having evolved her existence to a psychical level at which writing became almost the only possible act of survival and reclamation, was what made her the potentially greater writer. The life was more essentially dedicated to, dependent upon, writing, for as George Eliot herself put it in chapter 13 of *Daniel Deronda*, she was 'a wordy thinker'. But nonetheless it clearly bothered George Eliot herself, that she had to consult her journal rather than her memory to see how she might pull through again, despite or because of herself. One day perhaps the trick would not work, the words of her novels or her journals would not take over her fears for her, the reality might not be helped by words and she might be left like Benjamin Robert Haydon. Speaking of her journal, she noted, 'I have often been helped in looking back in it, to compare former with actual states of despondency' (*George Eliot's Life*, iii, p. 324). Such comparisons Mrs Oliphant more usually had to do in her own head, getting her work into proportion. But George Eliot does not seem to have been able to hold encouragement or balance internally but rather to have been extraordinarily vulnerable to criticism, as she lent both on her pen and on the shoulders of others, when away from the pen. Lewes kept all adverse reviews out of her sight, soothing her along.

On the one hand, then, Mrs Oliphant does seem to be the realization of the failures that George Eliot only wrote of—for example Farebrother, who 'by dint of admitting to himself that he was too much as other men were, . . . had become remarkably unlike them in this' (*Middlemarch*, Bk ii, chap. xviii (i, p. 285)).[41] Justice is pre-empted by that being a matter not of compensation but of double-bind: only his (or her) pride could tell him how unlike them he was, and that would make him like them in that.

On the other hand, George Eliot in her journal seems closer to the fear, if not the failure, itself, unalloyed by the dignity of autobiography. Her knowledge that the creative process was for her *always* like this, always as bad, does right to recognize itself as a merely second-order sanity itself discontinuous with the fundamental sources of both her fear and her achievement. The habit of crisis, the recurrence of despondency are not things that can be owned or objectified in the way that Mrs Oliphant's family belonged to her or she to them. The family both subordinated and steadied Mrs Oliphant's writing, it was a visible sign of need and responsibility. George Eliot had no children of her own, kept her self-control not in her head so much as in her writing. If Yeats had chosen a word other than 'perfection', 'perfection of the life or of the work' would sum up the distinction we are witnessing.

A modern novelist gives expression to this sort of situation when he has one of his characters, a writer, say of another writer:

> 'He's the manners of a weasel; his breath reeks; two wives have left him, but he's written half a dozen poems that will be read when everything I've written has mouldered. It's odd, isn't it, that our age will be judged in a thousand years by what this pig-eyed paranoic has put down, but it will be right. Now and then his compulsions and inadequacies, his embarrassments and rebuffs, his scores and his talents have come together in such a way that people will envy us for having seen him, never mind spoken to him. And the likes of me will stand damned because we opposed him, bawled him out, and we'll be remembered, if at all, because of that and nothing else. It's an unfair world.'
>
> Stanley Middleton: *The Other Side* (London, 1980), p. 68.

Mrs Oliphant wondered to herself whether the difference between herself and George Eliot, excuses aside, was fundamentally no more, but no less, than the banal mystery that George Eliot, whatever else she was, had more sheer verbal talent than she:

> No one ever will mention me in the same breath with George Eliot. And that is just. It is a little justification to myself to think how much better off she was—no trouble in all her life as far as appears, but the natural one of her father's death—and perhaps coolnesses with her brothers and sisters, though that is not said. And though her marriage is not one that most of us would have ventured on, still it seems to have secured her a worshipper unrivalled. I think she must have been a dull woman with a great genius distinct from herself, something like the gift of the old prophets, which they sometimes exercised with only a dim sort of perception what is meant. But this is a thing to be said only with bated breath, and perhaps further thought on the subject may change even my mind.
>
> *Autobiography*, p. 7.

It is here, just when she resorts to the idea of a transcendental gift, that Mrs Oliphant's down-to-earthness betrays an element of reductivism. This reductivism was often an accompanying threat to what was admirable in a practical nature which both her experience demanded and the age as a whole encouraged and enforced. For George Eliot's achievement is precisely not that of a genius distinct from herself. It actually reduces her ('a dull woman', 'a dim sort of perception') to say so.

It is helpful to look more closely at George Eliot in the light of Mrs Oliphant's complaint that her art was separate from her self. Mrs Oliphant might well have read the following from Cross's *Life*; it more nearly shows the way things were with George Eliot:

> Lying awake early in the morning, according to a bad practice of mine, I was visited with much compunction and self-disgust that I had ever said a word to you about the faults of a friend whose good qualities are made the more sacred by the endurance his lot has in many ways demanded. I think you may fairly set down a full half of any alleged grievances to my own susceptibility, and other faults of mine which necessarily call forth less

agreeable manifestations from others than as many virtues would do if I had them. I trust to your good sense to have judged well in spite of my errors in the presentation of any matter. But I wish to protest against myself, that I may, as much as possible, cut off the temptation to what I should like utterly to purify myself from for the few remaining years of my life—the disposition to dwell for a moment on the faults of a friend.

George Eliot's Life, iii, pp. 123–4.

It is a letter from George Eliot to Madame Bodichon in November 1870. The syntax is that of a puritanism that George Eliot had only formally rejected: 'I was visited'. Perhaps a puritan like Mrs Oliphant might note, in turn, that here was George Eliot lying in bed worrying about the injustice of her remarks concerning a friend when, at this time, she ought to have been getting up to write more of *Middlemarch*. I put it perhaps bathetically, but was George Eliot, lying in bed worrying about what she had said, having a sort of practice of conscience for *Middlemarch*? Was she even really more worried about the writing than about the friend, thinking about whom staved off the moment of writing fiction, not letters, for the day? Or is it out of such self-troublings that the necessity to write *Middlemarch*, not just that day but at all, was found? When writers have attained a proficiency, when they have provided themselves with what Ruskin, discussing painters, calls 'a language', the task is then to see what thought comes from that language, what purpose that language serves. For the world is full of people, speakers or writers, who only use words in order to seem more than they really are. Some very skilled writers can make, more seriously now, a very great deal out of what they also know to be a very little; such, it seems to me, is the extraordinary interest to be found in Henry James. But an anecdote like this one does help to 'place' the work in question by giving us as it were the autobiography of its making. Of course this is a risky, potentially reductive procedure; questions like where does it come from? or what does it amount to? risk answers predetermined by just that sort of question. But somehow, at some point, one has got to try to decide what is important and how far it is important. Let us leave it for the moment an open question: would it diminish *Middlemarch* if it was true that it came from experiences like the one recounted above, if the great genius was not distinct from the worrying, dull woman, only the worrying goes on at a different level? A word of qualification here. The movement is not just from the life to the novel. The writing of *Middlemarch* may well have provoked a reciprocal conscientiousness outside the work: something in between a superstitious fear of hubris and a desire for an integrity of life and work. For there is obviously a relation between the way memory of a life fuels a work and the way that being a writer makes a person more interested and rather differently interested in certain aspects of life close to his or her subject-matter. At any rate, our anecdote does show us this. That the duty of George Eliot, as novelist, to describe fully and invent defects of character which in life we would admit to be part of our friends but would wish away, required of her extraordinary moral stamina, to judge, and susceptibility, to create and to extenuate, each raised by the other to levels beyond those of spontaneous conscience. 'If we had a keen vision and feeling of all ordinary human life, it would be like hearing the grass grow and the squirrel's heart beat, and we should die of that roar which lies on the other side of silence. As it is, the quickest of us walk about well wadded with stupidity' (*Middlemarch*, Bk ii, chap. xx, (i, pp. 297–8)). Spontaneous conscience had to be distorted and intensified, half-deliberately, in life, so as to strengthen the truth of art, without the conduct of the life being merely a matter of professional opportunism for the conscience's exercise. 'Perhaps our frames could hardly bear much of it' (ibid.). There is the life:

> I wish to protest against myself

and there is the work:

> But at present this caution against a too hasty judgement interests me more in relation to Mr Casaubon than to his young cousin. . . . I protest against any absolute conclusion.
>
> *Middlemarch*, Bk i, chap. x (i, pp. 124–5).

It is hard to know exactly what is the relation between the two. But whatever it is, that relation is obsessive.

Mrs Oliphant was wrong to see the author, George Eliot, as entirely distinct from the woman, Marian Evans. But her grounds seem to have been that the woman had not suffered or experienced enough to be such an author. For to Mrs Oliphant George Eliot seemed to be someone who profoundly understood failure—failure like Mrs Oliphant's own—despite her own apparently limited experience of it.

We have now to confront that paradox knowing that Mrs Oliphant's explanation of it is faulty. So we must ask, what did George Eliot really know about failure? and, how does her fictional account of failure stand in relation to the real thing?

George Eliot herself would not have disputed the necessity to ask such questions. It was a constant source of anxiety to her, whether her strenuous realism was, finally, unreal when compared to the story of a real life.[42] It was not hard to worry George Eliot in such matters, as Johnny Cross himself testifies:

> And I remember, many years ago, at the time of our first acquaintance, how deeply it pained her when, in reply to a direct question, I was obliged to admit that, with all my admiration for her books, I found them, on the whole, profoundly sad.
>
> *George Eliot's Life*, iii, pp. 430–1.

Why did it pain her so deeply? One would have thought that a novelist of relativism might have guessed that Cross's charge had at least as much to do with something in him (he was essentially a depressive) as with the work in question. Of course there are matters of temperament here with respect to George Eliot's great susceptibility to any criticism. Marian Evans did not become George Eliot, novelist, until she was thirty-eight years old. Earlier the young girl, after giving up her Evangelical faith, had been an ardent Rousseauist, looking for another human being to love and be loved by. She felt that she needed time: only bear with me for a few more years, she begged her friends, and I will repay, you will see the redeeming worth. She needed the time to make a part of herself the acquired compromises which, on second thought, she felt obliged by circumstances and by conscience to make upon her early emotional Rousseauism. She had said that it was worth learning French if only to read Rousseau's *Confessions*. But

'expecting disappointments' was the paradoxical formula she
came to prescribe for what she had to learn (*George Eliot's Life*,
ii, p. 278). It was no wonder, then, that she felt crushed, if after
all her efforts to make art's hope out of adult disappointment
Cross still found that the work pointed back to the profound
sadness which it was intended to relieve. It must have felt like
nemesis, back to square one, with all the rights to judge Cross
as she might have judged one of the characters in her own
books automatically forfeited.

Yet this was not only a matter of personal temperament.
There was a more formal, general difficulty at the heart of the
idea of writing a realistic novel. Realism had a double bond:
the thought of life contained in art and kept in art but kept
within art in such a way as to leave art conscientiously open to
the thought of the life outside it. The realistic novel, if not
actually in memory of reality, was at any rate a genre working
to analogous effect. Thus it was liable to make its author feel
vulnerably guilty in relation to the life which is its subject-
matter. The truth of such a novel has an apparently necessary
subservience to the authority of an externality conceived as
'real'. 'Humble and faithful' are George Eliot's words for this
art. If, say, the depiction of failure in such a novel is a travesty
of the real thing, a reader may reject with disgust its presumption on the grounds of his own experience. That is why George
Eliot was so vulnerable to criticism, why Johnny Cross's
reaction so upset her and why Mrs Oliphant's case would
have worried her. For *Middlemarch* was meant to do two things
at once: show the reality of provincial failure in little, ordinary
lives; help the reality of failure among her readership; help by
showing. For some, this view of art, so dominant throughout
the second half of the nineteenth century, was art's sell-out to
life. It was as if the deep reason why George Eliot could not trust
her imagination to work until she was thirty-eight was that she
suffered from the implicit suggestion of the age that imagination
could not be trusted until it was verified by, and subdued in,
experience and observation of the external world. Otherwise,
as the young evangelical Marian Evans must have been taught,
fiction was unreal, a toy. The view that this was how art was
sold out to so-called 'reality' was the view that most of the
poets of the Victorian period might have taken had they not

also been made to feel, morally as much as politically, on a backward footing in comparison with the relevance and popularity of contemporary fiction. In such a view the realistic novel, in trying conscientiously to make art what art was not, had to become a form of lying both about art and about life.

George Eliot seems to have had strong ethical reasons for denying that her art was a kind of magic separate from her ordinary self. Like Wordsworth in this, she lowered the idea of high art in order to raise the idea of the ordinary through art. The height of her own understanding of failure and loneliness was raised upon the memory of her own fears of these things. F. W. H. Myers gave an account of how, thus, George Eliot's genius, pace Mrs Oliphant, was not really distinct from herself:

> When a young friend put the question direct: 'But from whom, then, did you draw Casaubon?' George Eliot, with a humorous solemnity, which was quite in earnest, nevertheless, pointed to her own heart.[43]

That hand refuses to palm art off upon the external sources which contemporaries guessed at as the real-life model for Casaubon, *Middlemarch's* failed scholar. But equally the successful novelist, indicating her own weakness and fear of failure beneath it all, points imagination back to memory, back to her own heart. It is a matter neither of mere reportage nor of mere genius.

Yet at the same time, if George Eliot did not want it thought that her work had nothing to do with her, by the same token she did not want it believed that thus it had only to do with her. There was a use for memory in between those alternatives. For why, she seems to have thought, should it appear a damning criticism that an author writes disguised and transmuted autobiography? What else could people expect or do? where else could the knowledge of other people come from save from knowledge of oneself? True, it would have hurt George Eliot had Johnny Cross said at their first meeting that *Middlemarch* seemed to him to be a humanist novel written by George Eliot in order to forgive Marian Evans for her need for love and understanding: a form of self-compensation and self-consolation through which she made a strength of her weakness. Yet the novel itself understood how George Eliot was still, like Casaubon, even if dispersing her self more widely than he, 'the centre of [her] own world' (Bk i, chap. x (i, p. 126)). *Middlemarch* understood how even its own author, differing from her characters in degree rather than in kind, had to work out of human weakness, without that necessarily invalidating what was done. Mrs Oliphant thought Marian Evans had not suffered very much (compared with her); George Eliot would never have passed that judgment on a girl who felt desperately sorry for herself for having no one to love her. Because she had been that girl, true. But also because, having been that girl, she knew that the so-called maturity of judgment which 'placed' such experiences was the sort of thing that had come to her only later when, suspiciously, it was merely easier to be objective, the trouble being safely past.

The story of the effort undergone by Marian Evans to come to be, at the age of thirty-eight, George Eliot, novelist, becomes eventually the story of a struggle to express feeling and thought within an area which previously she had been able to define only by means of the opposite extremes on either side of it. Between those extremes she felt herself torn, for the extremes of her moods and opinions were only the expression of her need to inhabit what the extremes split between them. That was why the extremes were half-hearted and self-hating, ways of feeling and moaning rather than ways of really living. For example, above all Marian Evans wanted to be loved, but her moaning to her friends about this was also something like a refusal to make herself lovable; she wanted to be loved for what she was but she could not be what she really was until she was loved. She was suffering, but this recourse to extremes was not a sign simply of extreme suffering: it was a sign of that kind of suffering in early adulthood which is sick of the humiliation of personal life being too small—so small as to make worried consciousness of it admittedly and still desperately a fuss about nothing. Marian Evans seems to have been born an old head on young shoulders; she never liked children's company, she needed the support of adults. It is hardly a paradox that at the time when then she most needed her maturity—the time of the awakening of sexual adulthood— her young body would not allow her old head an authority of wisdom which the person as a whole had not lived fully enough to deserve. She had to retard herself, making herself mature and immature at once.

She was plagued by these mutually damaging extremes. As a young Evangelical, Marian Evans feared and detested fiction: 'For my part I am ready to sit down and weep at the impossibility of my understanding or barely knowing even a fraction of the sum of objects that present themselves for our contemplation in books and in life. Have I then any time to spend on things that never existed?'.[44] As Redinger says, imagination was for her at this time in her early twenties an admission of a dangerous dissatisfaction, involving exhibitionism and an evasion of reality. Yet when this puritan lost her faith and turned to translating one of the books influential upon the secularization of the nineteenth century, Strauss's *Das Leben Jesu*, she found herself complaining over her anxiety 'about a thing so trifling as a translation'. It was the 'very triviality of the thing' that was upsetting her, so she said: had it been a really grand undertaking the difficulties would have been worthwhile, 'but things should run smoothly and fast when they are not important enough to demand the sacrifice of one's whole soul'.[45] It was as if she wanted to take, in David Copperfield's phrase, the whole charge of her own existence, and writing was the only means she could find to do so, weighing herself seriously. But the puritan had ruled out the novel and the translator had ruled out not only the puritanism as a formal creed but the art of translation as a means of justifying one's existence in the secular world. She believed in writing, as far as I can see, because she could not bear to give in to the unhappiness and absolute despair she felt, any more than she could tolerate simply drifting on in her life wildly hiding from herself. Writing seemed to promise to offer something in between despair and evasion of despair, a place where she could face herself. Yet though during her thirties she was virtually the editor of the *Westminister Review*, Marian Evans could not be satisfied with the writings of intellectualism—it was as if such writings eschewed the broad and the specific physical problems of living. She edited the review alongside the failure of her relationship with John Chapman, its owner. We see, then, the last set of extremes into which her predicament drove her—extremes concerning the final thing that promised to free her from her splits, namely writing. Writing should have something to do with her, with the reality she possessed and cared for and felt trapped within and wanted to expand yet not evade. But writing should not only have to do with *her*, her troubles, her self-centredness which was a symptom of her troubles. It had nothing to do with her—that was no good; it had only to do with her—also no good; it was to extend herself beyond herself—but not as an evasion of reality or a transmutation of things physical into things mental; it was to let her into her life, rather than leave her suffering from her life—but her life had first to be more than her self. Although she knew as an intellectual that the substance of experience was dependent upon what we bring to what we see, she also knew that human beings, equally, were dependent upon what they saw and experienced, physically and emotionally dependent however much, also, they contributed. She herself felt both powerful and powerless, intelligent and feeble. The psychological and the philosophical concerns, her life and her ideas, seemed to enforce each other, but their very compatibility seemed to bring them together emotionally when intellectually she was obliged to keep them apart. In short, there were just so many ifs, ands, and buts in her requirement for a species of thinking, in writing, which was not to be utterly and unreally separate from living, yet not without an independent rigour either.

But even these strenuous requirements were suspended until she found George Henry Lewes, the nominally married man with whom she spent her life from 1854, when she was thirty-five, until his death in 1878. It was not only a matter of what he did for her in the way of encouragement and protection, talking over her work, hiding adverse reviews; it was also what he of himself meant to her in the sense of giving her a life worth writing from, if not of. He was the licence that enabled her to finish the personal struggle which she had had with life and find a new level from which to look back at that struggle, seeing in it elements that were not merely personal; she could afford to see that now. He allowed her creatively to remember; the race to get ahead of herself, to get to be neither too old nor too young for herself, began to be over; she ceased to live in a line of time, she found a new level; the balances of old and young, of mind and body, of self and others, could now be looked for more sanely. It was now that she turned to writing fiction.

Why fiction? For all her fears and reservations about it, she admitted that she had always thought of writing novels. She was less afraid of it now as an unreal solution of the real trouble which she had been almost ashamed to feel in her own self. For it was fiction that allowed a dispersal of self among characters which made art both something to do with her and yet not only to do with her. It released imagination but allowed a narrator, George Eliot, to 'earth' the imagination in terms of an analytic memory recalling through words what the reality of her characters' predicaments actually meant. Memory sometimes actually created these characters—most obviously, in the self-portraits Maggie Tulliver in *The Mill on the Floss* and Dorothea Brooke in *Middlemarch*, and in the portrayal of her own brother and father in *The Mill on the Floss* and *Adam Bede* respectively. But even more often George Eliot, at this new level of her existence, invented characters: then, memory working in analysis of them, alongside their creation, reminded her in her heart of the idea for them or the idea they stood for. She puts it thus, speaking of 'the severe effort of trying to make certain ideas thoroughly incarnate, as if they had revealed themselves to me first in the flesh and not in the spirit' (*George Eliot's Life*, ii, p. 441). That is not to say, with Henry James, that George Eliot's characters are only mental abstractions made flesh. But it is to say that her delay in putting her experience into words meant that what she knew and thought grew beyond specifically recallable relation to her self. For memory formed a large, implicit background that her ideas stood for and the characters, embodying her ideas, stirred into complex, imaginative life.

It seems almost incredible to us that the imaginative creation of Casaubon, the dry, scholarly failure, pointed back to George Eliot's own heart, reminding her of herself both as past translator and as present, still unconfident author. It would have seemed even more incredible to Marian Evans in her twenties and thirties. For she could not then believe that art was her, that art could be her in ways so apparently unlike herself; she could not trust the way that, in time, imagination became a function of lapsed memory. In many ways George Eliot was of course Marian Evans's second life, as David Copperfield was Dickens's second chance. But the difference was that George Eliot was not a character in the way that David Copperfield was. She stood not for the way that fiction may reclaim through secondary indirections the primary impulses of the human heart, as in *David Copperfield*. She stood, instead, in memory of the way that knowing so much about oneself eventually and mysteriously becomes assimilated into knowing so much about other people. As she puts it in *Impressions of Theophrastus Such*, 'the more intimately I seem to discern your weaknesses, the stronger to me is the proof that I share them. How otherwise could I get the discernment?'.[46] What this amounts to is a claim by George Eliot that fiction, for all her doubts about it and struggle against it, is not simply a secondary mode in lieu of autobiography, as it is so movingly as well as so deviously in Dickens. No, it is a primary mode: the first means by which Marian Evans had been able to find a form for all that was in her that was not simply her. There are works—life-works— which derive ultimately from a strong autobiographical impulse which it would have been quite inappropriate to channel narrowingly into autobiography. *Middlemarch* is one such, perhaps the greatest one such, not least because, as we shall see, it concerns the contradictions of a social life in which people are individually, autobiographically lonely but most primarily lonely when together, in conversations, in offers of help or needs for help, in marriages.

Still, Mrs Oliphant thought George Eliot or Marian Evans had not suffered much and was hardly a substantial person in her own right. George Eliot, however, actually seems to have used this thought of her own weakness in order to soften her judgment of other people and their less palpable, material or visible troubles. Yet for such softness of judgment to be ethically respectable rather than autobigraphically apologetic she had to produce it in work that was rigorously thought out. As Marian Evans had finally to find there was no alternative to the novel in order that she might willingly adopt it, so inside her novels her softness has to be seen to be a necessity not a luxury. I should like to dwell on just one magnificent sentence from *Middlemarch* in order to see how this softness of underlying memory found its place in the imaginative work of this novel. It is about Casaubon:

> His experience was of that pitiable kind which shrinks from pity, and fears most of all that it should be known.
>
> *Middlemarch,* Bk iii, chap. xxix (ii, p. 11).

Which word in that sentence, more than any other, is George Eliot's own? It is the word 'pitiable', for pitiable there is a word which has learnt to transform itself from 'pitiful':

> The last refuge of intolerance is in not tolerating the intolerant; and I am often in danger of secreting that sort of venom.
>
> *George Eliot's Life*, i, p. 471.

'Pitiable' is the word learnt during the years it took for Marian Evans to become George Eliot. It is sub-vocally expressed here for it belongs to the novelist's language of silence, the interpretation of 'the roar that lies on the other side of silence', when explicit talk and direct confrontation fail. Earlier in George Eliot's career these things did not fail, as when in *Adam Bede* Diana brought Hetty to the relief of confession; it is harder here, where confessions are silent or lost for opportunity. 'Pitiable', as a word of tacit experience and corrective memory in the background of affairs, has a quiet creative interrelation with 'shrinking from pity': it may stand almost as an image of George Eliot's whole work when once confession failed. For 'pitiable' stands prior to Casaubon's fear of pity for two main reasons.

First, it stands first because it is the fruit of the experience that George Eliot had to gain *before* she felt she deserved the authority involved in writing. Marian Evans had believed in the possibility of re-formation of one's life through the sheer 'quantity of existence' that time brought to memory and character (*George Eliot's Life*, i, p. 176). The phrase 'quantity of existence' was one she borrowed consciously from her reading of the radical Baptist John Foster during her evangelical days:

> *Quantity of existence* may perhaps be a proper phrase for that, the less or more of which causes the less or more of our interest in the individuals around us. The person who gives us most the idea of ample being, interests us the

> most. Something certainly depends on the *modification* of this being, and something on its comprising *each of the parts* requisite to completeness; but still perhaps the most depends on its quantity.[47]

It was quantity of experience that Mrs Oliphant felt that the dull woman lacked. But for Marian Evans quantity was as much time to think and modify as range to operate in; the sheer time seemed to make the difference between finding the shrinking from pity pitiable and finding it merely pitiful. These changes from within were what the novelist was able to make of her own autobiography: a word created out of her own experience now offered to something imaginatively other than just her own experience. Time enabled her own experience to start to become that of another person. That quality should come out of quantity was for Marian Evans the vital hope for humanity. That was why it was no shame if she differed from a Casaubon not in kind but only in degree. Inadequacy, such as the shrinking from pity, was something that George Eliot learnt from; but she did not then think that what she had learnt transcended the inadequacy so much as understood it. She did not transcend Casaubon; her memory pulled her back to him. But this is the first, the primary place, her memory could have shown itself.

What is more, George Eliot's pity for Casaubon includes a humbling recognition that he would shun her sympathy just as surely as he had had to run away from Dorothea's. Indeed, George Eliot's word stands in memory of Dorothea's almost inevitable failure here. Thus the second reason for 'pitiable' standing in front of 'shrinking from pity' does *not* lie in the former's transcendence of the fact of the latter. George Eliot is not a transcendent presence in her own novels: it is rather that the verbal quality of her presence is precipitated out of the sheer quantity of existence miserably unable to speak justly for itself within the novel. George Eliot knows that her pity has here to be kept quiet, helpless and in the background; but she also knows that it is still, thus forced back, a necessary *pre-condition* for seeing and interpreting Casaubon rightly. Hence the pity remains there, up front in 'pitiable', compromised into a covert adjectival form because Casaubon could not bear its open display, thus subordinate even while supportive; but still abiding there like an offer that knows that probably it cannot be accepted now but that it must not ever stop being made for humanity's sake. It tries to keep open, that is to say, an area of sensibility that might have been lost with the loss of formal Christianity. A Lancelot Andrewes, preaching at Easter 1620, can make the point with emphasis:

> Bring *Him* to the grave, and lay *Him* in the grave, and there leave him: but come no more at it, nor stand not long by it. Stand by *Him*, while *He* is alive, So did many, stand, and goe, and sit by *Him*. But, *stans juxta monumentum*, Stand by *Him* dead, *Marie Magdalen*, she did it, and she onely did it, and none but she. . . . But *Peter* is gone, and *John* too: all are gone, and we left alone; then to *stay* is love, and constant love. . . . Away we goe, with *Peter* and *John*; wee stay it not out with *Mary Magdalen*.[48]

Yet George Eliot has to stay it out in the interstices of sentences that describe quite well how she might not. For Lancelot Andrewes the act of a Mary Magdalene at the grave of Jesus was obviously a great thing. But George Eliot's is a world consciously existing after the end of the great things: if the spirit of them is to survive now, when there are no Saint Theresas but Dorotheas, it has to be worked through hard thought, imprisoning complications and small opportunities. George Eliot here stands to Casaubon as merciful Solitude stands to Dorothea, much later in the book, when after the death of Casaubon she fears she has lost Will Ladislaw for ever:

> In that hour she repeated what the merciful eyes of solitude have looked on for ages in the spiritual struggles of man—she besought hardness and coldness and aching weariness to bring her relief from the mysterious incorporeal might of her anguish: she lay on the bare floor and let the night grow cold around her . . .
>
> *Middlemarch*, Bk viii, chap. lxxx (iii, p. 388).

Why does she have solitude look upon her? Because the personification stands for the lost God, the no-help given when so much help was needed. And it also stands for the way that the omniscient author, so like a God but not one, sees that the loneliness that almost everyone at some time has, hardly anyone else at such a time can help. 'Merciful' is like 'pitiable', a verbal intervention for want of the ability to interfere. George Eliot's syntax consists in there being immanent in life's texture qualities which, so great as to be humanity's final greatness, are yet subordinate in circumstances, embedded in difficulties, so compromised as almost to be lost in failure or silence: close to remaining unrecognized accidents in a prosaic, unheroic world where principle is often forced into second place and interference is most difficult. Marian Evans was the translator of Feuerbach's *The Essence of Christianity*, a book whose aim was to retain the human content of Christianity even while discarding its form. 'The Greeks and Romans deified accidents as substances; virtues, states of mind, passions as independent beings'.[49] Similarly, the power and the virtue that men had projected upon God—His Mercy, Pity, Love, and Charity— were really their own powers and their own virtues and their own hopes and needs. The divine subject of a sentence had to be translated back into its human predicates; substances projected beyond earthly life had to be seen as undeified accidents actually trying to find a place for themselves within it. Hence the struggle in George Eliot's secular syntax of mundane realism, as people tried to find room to act for themselves and each other just as, before, they had prayed their God to do. Farebrother finds it so hard to interfere like a vicar to help the love between Fred and Mary when he already loves Mary himself: it is hardly possible to find the right balance between being Just and being oneself. Lygate feels that, as a doctor, he must support Bulstrode as he collapses at the public meeting that declares his ruin; even though this compromises Lydgate utterly. Some professional rules may thus aid a man to see trouble and do something about it. But without the support of professional ethics and often without the chance to be *able* to do something, to see trouble and not help trouble is for George Eliot a secular contradiction or paradox. Dorothea and Lydgate, two marriage-partners suffering equally from their marriages, are never able to say enough to help each others in the trouble which the merciful eyes of solitude knows they in many respects share. George Eliot, on second thought and as if in unredeeming reclamation, *can* say something: it is from that felt responsibility in the face of failures that words like 'pitiable' come. The placing of 'pitiable' in George Eliot's sentence is her saying 'What can I do?' in a tone which, as the following makes clear, is nearer to that which Dorothea would wish to use to Casaubon than Rosamond uses to Lydgate:

> 'What can *I* do, Tertius?' said Rosamond, turning her eyes on him again. That little speech of four words, like so many others in all languages, is capable by varied inflexions of expressing all states of mind from helpless dimness to exhaustive argumentative perception, from the completest self-devoting fellowship to the most neutral aloofness. Rosamond's thin utterance threw into the words 'What can *I* do!' as much neutrality as they could hold. They fell like a mortal chill on Lydgate's roused tenderness.
>
> *Middlemarch,* Bk vi, chap. lviii (iii, p. 93).

George Eliot's is a language which will not allow the silence of waste that follows upon seeing trouble without anything either being done or being able to be done in response. She cannot pass over in silence what seems to her the contradiction that the loneliness that people share in a tacit sense cannot be shared in any more real one. She speaks to make her book really shared with her readers, at any rate, to keep the possibility of human collaboration open. She uses her memory not for the sake of lonely autobiography, as does the defeated Mrs Oliphant, but in hope of a future social life in which private feelings, which now found loneliness a paradox, might find a home. And it is not as though she does the speaking because Marian Evans had grown up to be so much better than her own characters. On the contrary, she knows that this very novel proceeds out of her never having resolved the question, 'What can *I* do?'. 'She pointed to her own heart.' It is often said that George Eliot rules over her characters, God-like from above; it is a mistaken reading on the whole, for the creation of 'George Eliot' as an authorial presence is not that of some designing substance, some higher persona for Marian Evans; 'George Eliot' is, rather, the name Marian Evans chose for a humane language precipitated out of the novel's heart-felt protest at the misery which is being created within it. 'George Eliot' may have felt that beneath it all, where Marian Evans lay, she was like Casubon as well as, more obviously, also like the young, ardent Dorothea. But what makes this work *more* than autobiographical, *more* than just a way for Miss Evans to forgive herself, while still being *not* 'distinct from herself', is something in the nature of the form of dialogue in the novel. Splitting herself between Casaubon and Dorothea, for example, George Eliot had to find more than herself between the two, she had to find what she knew on another level now, in another form. For the formal necessities of dialogue, giving weight to two people, let her see that Dorothea's thought for Casaubon was entirely separate from him: 'George Eliot' as a result is that form of herself which has to occupy the space of misunderstanding between the two. All that dialogue implied as form and failed to convey in practice left 'George Eliot', raised from Marian Evans almost entirely by the responsibility of seeing and articulating the force of what was left unsaid between couples, working on a level where language tried to save the meaning of people whom it could hardly help directly. Through this humane responsibility, as well as through the formal obstacles that made her, as an intermediary between dialogue, lift her language beyond the language of daily failure, George Eliot came to exist.

But hers is a witnessing as well as an articulate presence. We feel it, tacitly, when we hear how little Dorothea and Casaubon really have to say to one another ' "What shall I do?" "Whatever you please, my dear".' (*Middlemarch*, Bk iii, chap. xxviii (ii, p. 3)). That tacit presence encourages us to hear in this, as by collaborative imagination, an echo of what, later, Rosamond says to Lygate: 'What can *I* do, Tertius?'. Or again as Lydgate has to help Bulstrode from the public meeting: 'What could he do? He could not see a man sink close to him for want of help' (ibid., Bk. vii, chap. lxxi, (iii, p. 301)).

Such echoes are not merely incidental, they are important. Lydgate's barely conscious tonal revenge upon Rosamond, for example, in response to her chiding him for refusing to borrow money from his family is 'Understand then, that it is what *I like to do*'. Moreover, his words are described as having the following effect upon Rosamond, 'There was a tone in the last sentence which was equivalent to the clutch of his strong hand on Rosamond's delicate arm' (ibid., Bk. vii, chap. lxiv (iii, p. 180)). And this in itself likewise recalls Casuabon's reaction to Dorothea after Lydgate had given him his medical death-sentence:

> His glance in reply to hers was so chill that she felt her timidity increased; yet she turned and passed her hand through his arm.
>
> Mr Casaubon kept his hands behind him and allowed her pliant arm to cling with difficulty against his rigid arm.
>
> Ibid., Bk. iv, chap. xlii (ii, p. 231).

Such moments, though small perhaps in themselves, form decisively in the memories of the people who suffer by them: 'But Dorothea remembered it to the last with the vividness with which we all remember epochs in our experience when dear expectation dies, or some new motive is born' (ibid., Bk. ii, chap. xxi (i, p. 323)). It is for George Eliot the modern tragedy that people drown in such apparent shallows. She knew, moreover, what a person could hardly do for him- or herself:

> is it not rather what we expect in men, that they should have numerous strands of experience living side by side and never compare them with each other?
>
> Ibid., Bk. vi, chap. lviii (iii, p. 84).

Yet, by bringing these echoes from so many different memories together as in one god-like memory, George Eliot succeeds in doing for the sake of the conscience of the race what individually we can hardly do for ourselves: she brings the numerous strands of experience, of experiences, side by side— even in their isolation and loneliness 'What can *I* do!' 'What shall I do?' 'What could he do?' 'what *I like to do*'. For the reader, memory works across the characters even as the characters' own memories work within them. The characters come to mind in various combinations in the reader's mind as well as in various dialogues within the book, and the effect of this accumulation of relationships, some acknowledged by the characters themselves but many not, is to give the book a reality which seems to go beyond the form of the book itself although it derives from it. One feels that one could keep turning the book around, seeing new relations and distinctions. This is of course only to follow the novel's very own procedure—as when Dorothea, for instance, felt in relation to Casaubon 'the waking of a presentiment that there might be a sad consciousness in his life which made as great a need on his side as on her own' (ibid., Bk. ii, chap. xxi, (i, p. 323)). Dorothea gets beyond her own view when in her own mind she thus sees that there is *one* world, with people with equivalent sadnesses hurting each other out of them. But as soon as she has to go back to her physical situation, she sees again the more isolating sense in which Casaubon is still the centre of his *own* world. 'The division between within and without in this sense seems to become every year a more subtle and bewildering problem' (*George Eliot's Life*, iii, p. 160).

One world and own worlds. This drawing together of people who still remain unfulfillingly apart is at once the hope and the resignation of *Middlemarch*. The problem is not merely one for the characters within a book. When Dorothea can see that Casaubon has as great a need on his side as she on her own, she has reached that apex of consciousness from which *Middlemarch* itself was written. But the writer also knew that even with such consciousness what Dorothea in her own person could do, just as what George Eliot in equivalent circumstances could do, was very little. That is the hardest thing, when people have to go back to, to carry on playing out, their restricted physical role even while on another level, mentally, they can see so much more than it. In writing *Middlemarch*, with full access to that less restricted consciousness, George Eliot herself nonetheless did not escape the dilemma of her own characters. When Dorothea felt herself rebuffed by Casaubon, she felt forced into asking herself the question which already supplied its own answer had she dared give it: 'Is he worth living for?' (Bk. iv, chap. xlii, (ii, p. 233)). Lydgate might have asked himself an equivalent question about his life with Rosamond, except that in his marriage 'the certainty, "She will never love me much," is easier to bear than the fear, "I shall love her no more"' (Bk. vii, chap. lxiv, (iii, p. 181)).

At another level, even while she was writing of such things, the novelist herself was asking: 'Will it ever be finished? Ever be worth anything?'. It is hard to say whether that is as important a question as Dorothea's. On the face of it, in order that George Eliot's own imagination should be worth anything, she would have to believe that the worth of the Casaubon marriage was more important than the worth of a book. But clearly the worth of this book depends on how far the author indeed can give a sense of how much it matters when marriages fail. Equally clearly, even while George Eliot's worry about the book must be kept out of the novel, on another level it obviously takes a transmuted part as the characters, equivalently, wonder about the worth of their own lives. That to save a marriage has a firmer relation to reality than to worry about writing a great book might just be the sort of belief Mrs Oliphant would have held. Yet the example of Mrs Oliphant herself shows that the failure to write a great book has a deep reality in the life of a writer, as if she had failed a supreme test of trying to make something worthwhile out of her own experience and self. The fact is, however different her own world as a writer from the world in which her characters lived, in the one world George Eliot felt herself an equivalent struggler:

> My book seems to me so unlikely to be finished in a way that will make it worth giving to the world, that it is a kind of glass in which I behold my infirmities.
>
> *George Eliot's Life*, iii, pp. 260–1.

But why then did Mrs Oliphant not see this in George Eliot? Because, I think, the thought of her own equivalence to these failures raised George Eliot to a power of language above them. Even so, as it was above them, it was also felt to be on their behalf, seeking justice of human expression for them. It is within that powerful paradox that George Eliot was trapped in uncertainty between success and failure; for her own success was beyond her. If Mrs Oliphant was a victim of injustice in her failure, George Eliot was a victim in her success. For in order to make sure that she was not making the worst kind of Dickensian exploitation of her Dorotheas and Casaubons, in order to make sure that she was not merely turning Farebrother's virtue, of thinking he was so like others as to be unlike them in that, into a strategy for herself, George Eliot had to make herself very unsure when she was already uncertain enough. She had also to create a work that would understand its author's own weaknesses and be no more and no less affected by them than if they were those of one of its own characters. That is how the work was more than an auto-biography. For just as Dorothea could include Casaubon's consciousness, as she began to see it, within her own and yet still find that consciousness of his in the outside world resisting her and autonomous to her; just so *Middlemarch* is a work that knows and shows how a person can hold a whole world in her head and still, in her own situation, be utterly frail again in the outside world which she had intended and largely succeeded in representing.

The anxiety and responsibility involved in art calling itself realistic are finally no less strenuous than that. What George Eliot's novels tried to create the conditions for being was a Dorothea, a Farebrother, a Mrs Oliphant, who could live, usefully, even if not be satisfied, within the limitations of the present. Yet because she herself could not live within her own limitations, or living within them, felt that she could not do justice to what was repressed within them, George Eliot was great in language. What did realism mean? It meant, in this context, that this greatness was not transcendent but was itself limited by the very life of which it treated. Only, the conscious-ness of these limits constituted a level of understanding which seemed to comprehend them. This level—the level at which 'George Eliot' came into existence with words like 'pitiable'—has the same status in relation to that over which it presides as memory has over the experiences it recalls: namely, a child of the sort of experience over which now it stands as father. In *David Copperfield* this was a matter of deep feeling—what David called 'the mind of the heart, if I may call it so' (p. 532). In George Eliot it becomes a matter of epistemology and ethics. Although she felt more like one of the failures portrayed in her books than the god-like author of them, George Eliot saw how one can use a sense of levels to be above oneself. But what she also recognized, even as she did this, was that the level of understanding of limitations was generically related to the limitations which are still at that understanding's physical basis. By self-reflection or second thought, clever people can seem to rise above their basic limitations, although only mentally. Books are often a result of that exercise of freed mentality. But not for George Eliot, who was no believer in such freedom for its own sake: for the mentality was related to its own physical origins and conditions, it owed itself to them; thus there was a moral obligation to use the increased consciousness gained from reflection upon the past to work back upon the past, to raise it as well as profit from it. Whatever the mind gained had to be ploughed back into that from which it had made its gains. She learnt this as much from her translation of Spinoza as from the help that Herbert Spencer gave her with the interpretation of Darwin. The Idealist philosopher, T. H. Green, waging war on Darwinism and empiricism, had asked increduously, 'Can the knowledge of nature be itself a part or product of nature?'. To him it made no sense if it were so: how could that which is a product of nature be the comprehender of nature? the mind cannot have a natural origin. But to George Eliot, secularist and empiricist, this seemed both plausible and just. It was the way her memory had taught her wisdom.

So, we have been asking whether the fact of Mrs Oliphant's living as she did, without all that George Eliot's language did to give meaning to the failure, was not a sign that George Eliot added to equivalent lives a significance that 'in reality' did not belong to them, but only to her. It was another aspect of George Eliot's realism, I have tried to answer, that such comfort as she could offer had to be no different in kind from Dorothea's in the face of Casaubon. A comfort which had to be recognized as often practically ineffectual. If a reader did recognize that—knew that the offer did not really help Casaubon, did not help George Eliot herself half the time, could not at any rate directly help the reader in his or her own life—if knowing and seeing that, the reader was still moved by it, then a point was justly and rigorously made. The point being much what Mrs Oliphant herself felt: that if a failure 'in reality' was denied the sense of significance that George Eliot fictively bestowed ('What does it matter?' Mrs Oliphant asked wearily of her own defeat)—then the truth was that it was just that sense of significance that life's failures 'in reality' most soberly needed. *Middlemarch* represents the power of external reality, the power that makes people compromise in their careers and marriages, demanding that they be 'realistic' and come to heel; but it also includes within it a claim and a language for the reality of people's suppressed internal natures, those thwarted desires and impulses that a sense of necessary failure commits to silence. In the final year of her life Mrs Oliphant felt bound to try to do for the meaning of her own existence what George Eliot had done for that of her characters. And that was perhaps, as we shall see, the greatest of implicit tributes to the author of *Middlemarch,* that most profound expression of the meaning of nineteenth-century realism. For Mrs Oliphant, consciously an artist of narrower talent, finally tried to do almost for herself what George Eliot had done for a variety of characters—save a life. I say 'almost' because, like George Eliot, she still needed fiction to be able to do so.

*   *   *   *   *

It was three years after she finished writing her *Autobiography,* which she left in manuscript, that Mrs Oliphant in 1897 published in a volume called *The Ways of Life* a long short story called 'Mr Sandford'. It is an account of what she calls the ebb tide when an artist reaches a time of life at which he finds he has outlived his reputation and his capacity. As an autobiographical fiction it is a work that stands between the autobiography of a small life, on the one hand, and a big, wide novel of life like *Middlemarch,* on the other. It is as if it is a work written, in the last year of Mrs Oliphant's life, in response to the problem of whether there might be a way for a consciously lesser artist like Mrs Oliphant to write something, on behalf of her own life, which might be, if not great, still, in her own words, 'somehow enough'.

Prose in the nineteenth century is often, of course, the prose of narrative. But it is a powerful realization when human beings discover that their lives do not only consist in following a line directed by time. As we have seen in *David Copperfield,* this discovery was not only important in the nineteenth century, its importance was still compatible with the idea of life as a story. The older David is as important a part of *David*

Copperfield, in the form of memory, as the life of the younger David is in the form of narrative. The memory that tells a person that he or she has to some extent lived a life which makes up an autobiographical narrative itself constitutes a faculty and a dimension which is not narrative, although it seems to have been produced by one's life-story and in turn is now productive of it. The things that Wordsworth knew had to be rediscovered in a different way and in a different medium throughout the rest of the century.

What is there if there is not simply a story? As we learn by reading from Dickens to George Eliot, there is a sense of levels in human experience, levels as well as linearity. You are not born with a sense of levels; they are formed on second thought at the moment when on looking back at yourself you are conscious of a capacity so to do which is not simply a part of that self. In writing 'Mr Sandford', accordingly, what Mrs Oliphant saw were her own limitations. As she looked at Sandford, the failed artist, she still saw herself; her authorship was being stared at by a sense of her own deficiencies even as it existed by virtue of a clear focus upon those deficiencies. Seeing these limitations, during the time in which writing enabled her to prolong the otherwise insupportable view, raised her above them, in so far as she became for the time the seeing author and Sandford became the embodiment of her inadequacies. When Sandford saw his own inadequacies he became almost more than his own author was in her life. Without that possibility of levels and of self-reflection writing would be impossible. But what the prose writers of the later nineteenth century did that Wordsworth, on the whole, did not do was to turn these thoughts in self-reflection into distinct characters: the character of the author, the character of the personal limitations of the author. Although the two were not simply split off from each other, it did threaten to mean that the writer used his memory fictively, as if for the sake of another person. This, of course, is good economy, not to use oneself up in one book. But I reject the view of those idealists who say that this is simply how art *should* be: impersonal, beyond self, beyond personal motives and interests, imaginatively free to be something or someone new and strange. For why did people hate and fear the autobiographical? Why do they equate it with the egoistical, splitting off the human qualities which they admire from the idea of self which is thus left impoverished and narrow? Why do they resent that earlier story of the deep memory in which imagination and its works have their origin? This book has been about those fears—where they are reasonable, where they are unreasonable—and I think we have inherited from the Victorians both a profound concern with personal life and an accompanying distrust of personal life, thinking it only a way of escaping from wider engagements. I am saying now that 'impersonal' is not how art should be but how, in the nineteenth century, art *had* to be—not because of its happy purity or innocent freedom but because it felt so difficult then to do what many people at the time seemed to want to do: write directly of themselves and their experience of the world. And that was a deep sadness—albeit a productive one for novelists. Mrs Oliphant's sign for this is to make the other person to whom she gives her memory in 'Mr Sandford' still a form of herself, at a different level and with a narrative line of his own. A second chance to reclaim not only the meaning of her own life but also the truthful purposes of writing fiction.

In 'Mr Sandford' Mrs Oliphant touches the sore point of her self-criticism that 'I wrote as I read'. She had read Trollope's complaint against the novelist who writes 'not because he has something which he burns to tell, but because he feels it incumbent on him to be telling something' (*An Autobiography*, p. 230). In the case of Mr Sandford the fact is that his particular genre (which was Haydon's), historical painting, is behind the times and becoming unsaleable:

> There was nothing to be said against the picture; except, perhaps, that, had not this been Mr Sandford's profession, there was no occasion for its existence at all.
>
> *The Ways of Life,* p. 40.

He is one of those men who, in Trollope's phrase, 'have gone on with their work till their work has become simply a trade with them' (*An Autobiography*, p. 230). And this work for work's sake is the subtlest variation here on the fashion that Sandford found was replacing history painting: art for art's sake, significant form, abstract, the late resistance to realism in the century. As Sandford's own son and his fashionable friends put it, 'the beauty of colour for itself and art for art'—to which Sandford's wife replies in defence of her husband and in his hearing, 'I always did think that there was a great deal in a good subject' (*The Ways of Life*, p. 43). In the midst of this family debate, Sandford stands tacitly accused of his profitable and accomplished painterly habit having forgotten, by its very skill, the primary impulses which art originates from and stands for. And it is here that Mrs Oliphant accordingly finds her own limitations to be something not, as even in her *Autobiography*, to be cunningly rested within. Her style here is not allowed to rest secure by falling confessedly short of being stretched to and beyond capacity. Her limitations here are, rather, something that through Mr Sandford she has to *be*, as well as the measure of what she could not attain. 'Mr Sandford' is not merely professional work, because the strengths and weaknesses of professional work are now used against themselves.

Shaken by a sudden failure to sell his work and irritated by the young around him, Sandford one night sketches what he calls an 'unreal scene' of strange moonlight (*The Ways of Life*, p. 58) and after he has finished it whimsically thinks of passing it off as an impressionist to fool the lot of them. In the light of the following day, typically of the sceptical and self-sceptical Mrs Oliphant, the bitter man sees that it is not even a good impressionist, though he had assumed the new thing was easy. His family go away on holiday; he plans to join them later; for the moment he stays behind at home to turn back to his old stuff:

> And that day his work did not advance so quickly or so satisfactorily. He listened for the swing of the door at the other end of the passage which connected the studio with the house, though he knew well enough there was no one who would come to disturb him. . . . There are days when it is so agreeable to be disturbed! And it was when he was painting in this languid way, and, as was natural, not at all pleasing himself with his work, that there suddenly and most distinctly came before him, as if some one had come in and said it, a thing—a fact—which strangely

enough he had not even thought of before. When it first occurred to him his hand suddenly stopped work with an action of its own before the mind had time to influence it, and there was a sudden rush of heat to the head.

The Ways of Life, pp. 58–9.

The thing, the fact, is that his work is 'finished'. He had wanted someone to disturb him, just as Mrs Oliphant needed her work to be subordinate to everything while running through everything. The intruder here is unfamiliar, the entrance of a strange thought, telling him that he is sixty and that this time, quite arbitrarily, his getting stuck over his work will be something quite other than temporary. This time, too, his wife is not there for him to turn to. And the economic and emotional life-line which, like the passageway itself, 'connected the studio with the house' is terribly threatened.

Mrs Oliphant said of her own profession:

I have written because it gave me pleasure, because it came natural to me, because it was like talking or breathing, besides the big fact that it was necessary for me to work for my children.

Autobiography, p. 4.

Now, although Mrs Oliphant wins a right to the word 'natural', as did Thomas Hood, to describe her writing, it is likewise a complex right in one who was so much and so necessarily a professional. Speaking of 'that which is known too well to admit of recognized self-analysis while the knowledge is being exercised', Samuel Butler noted that a professional and practised musician thus

remembers more than he remembers remembering . . . the more the familiarity or knowledge of the art, the less is there consciousness of such knowledge.[50]

If, to Mrs Oliphant's own inner ear, habituation and professionalism made writing over into a form as natural as talking, at the back of her mind, where one remembers remembering, she must have known that that was her way of redeeming talking as well as naturalizing writing. She had never been able to afford to make quite known, even to herself, that writing was not natural, for she had to make it normal and part of the family. Yet, without moving from its customary stance of being a style in which all that is written was already known to the writer beforehand, Mrs Oliphant's writing faces a challenge in the transmutation which it undergoes in 'Mr Sandford':

> . . . painting in this languid way, and, as was natural, not at all pleasing himself.

'As was natural' may seem simply part of the natural habit of her own writing style, the easy parenthesis of experience revealing through a glimpse in tone the authority of the mind of the author over what is written. But here that very natural- ness is implicated in the equally natural fate of professional habit: it is all described as naturally as if it were spoken, yet what is described is the way that it is also the nature of such habitual work to be habitually unpleasing to its compromising practitioner. It is as if the skilled familiarity of eloquence displayed even in the unhappiness of the *Autobiography* was itself now not only still in the writing but also being judged by it. It is a little image as of George Eliot reading her journals of past despair in order to try to urge her present writing on: 'I have need to remember that other things which have been accomplished by me were under the same cloud'. 'As was natural, not at all pleasing himself'. In thus getting at herself, Mrs Oliphant, I think, was not at all pleasing *herself* with this work, or, if pleasing herself, pleasing herself only with a sustaining incidentalness: 'It seems to me this is rather an original way of putting it . . .'. 'As was natural' is Mrs Oliphant's thought at the level of her art as it is Sandford's in his. There is something even more terrifying, for being profes- sional, about such fear and troubles; they lie beneath Sandford's hand as well as behind his forehead. And then it is that something more primarily 'natural' breaks in: 'his hand suddenly stopped work with an action of its own'. What habit and professionalism covered, allowing art to be done by circumventing the problems that might have prevented the doing at all, now uncovers itself to the painter in the vision of failure, poverty, family ruin, living death. Although Trollope despised the degeneration of 'work' into 'trade', it was his success that afforded him the distinction. But Mrs Oliphant's writing was necessary as well as natural to her: 'besides the big fact that it was necessary for me to work for my children'. Unlike Trollope, she had no other source of income. All too used to having her claims for herself made realistic by the big incidentalness of a prosaic thing like money, not conventionally accounted as a heroic motive for writing, Mrs Oliphant makes one of the first things that Sandford fears that of economic ruin. His children, brought up to be comfortable, have careers to find, marriages to provide for, and no training to help them now that money cannot see them clear. Sandford thinks he sees the walls of his home shake.

As Mrs Oliphant as a second-rate artist now forces herself to remember what she forgot in order to have the facility to be second-rate, the language, previously as natural as talking, has now to work harder; as George Eliot had to work harder in Mrs Humphry Ward's description of her:

> Impossible for her to 'talk' her books . . . She was too self-conscious, too desperately reflective, too rich in second thoughts for that.[51]

For the language, like the language of Ruskin as critic, has to work harder for translating what the painter physically embodies and sees. The words of the novelist work blindly, as it were, towards the feel of the painter, analogous yet different, and the difference between the two media becomes a mark of the movement from autobiography to autobiographical fiction. Take a minor instance:

> his hand suddenly stopped work

The language is physically committed here, but the effect this time is the opposite of the joy in mastery that Ruskin celebrates, when 'your hand obeys you thoroughly' (*Works*, xv, p. 97) The 'work' is both the work the hand does in painting and the painting, the art-work itself; the hand stops its work, stops the work itself, simultaneously, as if disclosing by failure the simply strange dependent relation between 'you', 'your hand' and the realization of all that is potential in your work. Behind this physical thinking of the painter is Mrs Oliphant's own fear:

Scarcely anybody who cares to speculate further will know what to say of my working power and my own conception of it.

Autobiography, p. 67.

The 'working power' disclosed in 'Mr Sandford' is such that the power of work and the power in work are realized together or not at all. If the hand fails, no one other than the artist will ever be able to see what lay behind the failure.

The strain on language to become here an imaginative medium of perception forces Mrs Oliphant to find again what, too often with resignation, she already knew, and to find it at a level where her already knowing could not save her. It is a different use of memory from that in the *Autobiography*. Sandford, after the shock of feeling he is finished, goes out for a walk, his usual procedure when stuck. As if using the painter's own technique, Mrs Oliphant writes, delicately, that there was 'shadow . . . over him' this 'summer evening' (*The Ways of Life*, p. 77). And he himself tries to use aesthetics to act, not really ironically, as a narcotic for his art's failure:

His heart was unaccustomed to anything tragical. It tried even now to beguile him and escape; to withdraw his attention to the long, streaming, level rays of the sinking sun; to get him out of himself to the aid of a child who had broken its toy and was crying with such passion—far more than a man can show for losses the most terrible— by the side of the road. And these expedients answered for the moment.

The Ways of Life, p. 78.

'To bring up the boys for the service of God was better than to write a fine novel'? Equivalently this scene seems, in the spirit of realism, to set art and the artist against a mere child crying in the street—as if to ask, like a provincial Tolstoy's *What is Art?*, how does art stand to that?[52] But no sooner does Mrs Oliphant hint at the big question than the very requirements of being an adult rather than a child forbid recourse to the sentimentality. 'A thing—a fact' is what Sandford has to cope with, and to be adult here means the incapacity to cry with passion over the 'fact' which all feeling has to go into accepting as such. This scene is thus a parable of reality's anti-tragic cheating a man of his own feelings—for without recourse to the big questions and complaints, expedients must serve for an answer. The realism of the scene, tinged with emotive symbolism, is a compromised reaction to the failure of a larger Romanticism. Yet, even at this moment, there comes to Sandford a revelation of how much, for all that, he passionately cares about his own fate, spiritually as well as practically, despite all his own efforts at self-distraction:

> Behind the sunset rays a strange vision of the unsold pictures came out into the very sky. They shaped themselves behind the child, whom it was so easy to pacify with a shilling, against the park palings.
>
> *The Ways of Life*, p. 78.

The shilling (which perhaps he still, distractedly, hands out in lieu of what he can give his own children) is now subordinate to an impressionism which Sandford before was not capable of without scepticism. The work here is both moving and canny: a child cries more easily over nothing than a man, whose fall may ruin his own children, can feel about everything; but the man also has to see that a child is just as easily soothed as an adult is not, adult life and memory being something other than simply defeasible in time. These second thoughts are typically Mrs Oliphant's, big because simple; yet here not, as in the *Autobiography*, so sceptically at her own expense. Here they take place as something bigger than the really not very rewarding self-compensation of shrewd self-checking. There is here a big living picture of the child against the whole sky, and although *he* is unaware, behind him stand, like a question, the paintings. Many of the themes with which we have been concerned in this second part of the book—such as the nature of adulthood, such as the place and size of art—are here powerfully gathered.

But perhaps it is worth mentioning a difference between this picture and a picture which is at the very centre of *Middlemarch*. In 'Mr Sandford' the pictured scene becomes bigger against the sunset when the vision of the unsold paintings looms large, signalling the setting and failure of the painter's life behind all that he sees and tries to see. If it is the sight of failure that enlarges the picture for Mrs Oliphant, for George Eliot it is something that challenges the whole idea of failure:

> She opened the curtains, and looked out towards the bit of road that lay in view, with fields beyond, outside the entrance-gates. On the road there was a man with a bundle on his back and a woman carrying her baby; in the field she could see figures moving—perhaps the shepherd with his dog. Far off in the bending sky was the pearly light; and she felt the largeness of the world and the manifold wakings of men to labour and endurance. She was a part of that involuntary, palpitating life, and could neither look out on it from her luxurious shelter as a mere spectator, nor hide her eyes in selfish complaining.
>
> *Middlemarch*, Bk viii, chap. lxxx (iii, p. 392).

It is as though George Eliot were here struggling to reclaim something of the spirit of Wordsworth, yet without falling into the trap of the pathetic fallacy of which Ruskin warned. Facing this 'largeness of the world', Dorothea, between two negative extremes ('neither as a mere spectator', 'nor in selfish complaining') manages to sustain a vision which is itself not negative. It is true that had Dorothea got closer to the 'man with a bundle on his back and a woman carrying her baby', all the old difficulties of intimacy and relatedness would begin again. She knows this and knows too that from such a distance she and Casaubon might have been seen by an equivalent viewer walking, apparently happily, arm in arm. But these are not ironic thoughts: there are, in Wordsworth's phrase, connections finer than those of contrast. That man and woman, seen beneath the sky, gave Dorothea hope, and although in fact they may have been in worse trouble than she was, still her hope is not merely self-delusion. For, as George Eliot makes clear, the sight of Dorothea, herself often unhappy, at other times gave other people hope. It is a fair return. Moreover, the hope comes not as a gift but almost as a rebuke. Part of what Dorothea is is what she thinks herself to be. But part of what she is is also to be only 'a part of that involuntary, palpitating life'. And this relativism, loosening the hold of ideas of solitude and failure, stands in place of the idea of a

God here and keeps human beings within this life for their meanings, their judgments and overviews of it.

Mrs Oliphant, absolute by temperament, has no such width to her tale; she has a narrative which goes forward personally rather than spreads outward socially. Accordingly, she has not George Eliot's defence against the charge of failure: that the disparity between the largeness we see and the tight smallness of our physical predicaments is a hope, since the one is won out of the other, as well as an injustice. It is not simply a failure—for Marian Evans or for Dorothea.

But Mrs Oliphant presses onwards. As if in memory of his pictures, Sandford turns back from his walk and returns to the studio and the work he gave up. There is now a second thought, to match his earlier disillusionment with the impressionistic sketch he had at first been pleased with:

> The first thing that caught his eye was the glow of that piece of drapery which he had painted under the keen stimulant of the first warning. It had been a stimulant then, and he was startled by the splendour of the colour he had put into that piece of stuff—the roundness of it, the clear transparence of the shadows. It stood out upon the picture like something by another hand, painted in another age. Had he done that only a few hours ago—he with the same brushes which had produced the rest of the picture which looked so pale and insignificant beside it? How had he done it? it made all the rest of the picture fade. He recognised in a moment the jogtrot, the ordinary course of life, and against it the flush of the sudden inspiration, the stronger handling, the glory and glow of the colour. He had never done anything better in his life.
>
> *The Ways of Life*, p. 82.

Mrs Oliphant's *Autobiography* was a place where she could never allow herself the chance of 'the flush of the sudden inspiration'. Like the child by the side of the road, for the introduction of whom Mrs Oliphant is of course ultimately responsible, the drapery here is a little touch, in this case Sandford's touch, which, if it were ever to be noticed, would be praised only for honesty, fidelity of details, craft:

When I die I know what people will say of me: they will
give me credit for courage (which I almost think is not
courage but insensibility) and for honesty and honourable
dealing; they will say I did my duty with a kind of
steadiness, not knowing how I have rebelled and groaned
under the rod.

Autobiography, p. 67.

In writing her own obituary in anticipation of what the
Dictionary of National Biography was to make of her, Mrs Oliphant
turned against the stinted praise of her natural, modest honesty
not because it was not superficially true but because what it
stood for, what lay concealed beneath its necessity, was so
much more than that. Typically there is a reciprocal relation
between Mrs Oliphant's self-criticism and her criticism of the
superficiality of the critics, as in this case too she rebels against
the rod beneath which she bows. Even so, there is a greater
writing than that in the *Autobiography* and it is the type of
writing wherein one tries to save oneself. Mrs Oliphant in 'Mr
Sandford' puts her power into that drapery for him, drapery
meant to be subordinate to the whole but lapsed into becoming
itself, an equivalent of that passionate adult containment and
redundance that cannot cry out as a child can.

Of draperies Ruskin wrote that originally they were painted
for the purpose of signifying past as well as present motion by
force of their resistance, but 'the drapery gradually came to
represent the spirit of repose as it before had that of motion,
repose saintly and severe. The wind had no power upon the
garment, as the passion none upon the soul' (*Works*, viii, p.
150). Sandford's drapery is lost subject-matter. As George
Eliot knew, the time for saints was past. The drapery lies
splendidly at peace in Sandford's painting but at the cost of
being too late, too far in the background. It reminds me of the
painter Mihailov in *Anna Karenina* showing his painting *Christ
before Pilate*:

Each face that, after so much searching, so many blunders
and alterations, had grown up within him with its own
character, each face that had caused him such torments
and such raptures, and all of them so often placed and
replaced to make a whole, all the shades of colour and

tone obtained with such effort—seen now with their eyes struck him as a series of commonplaces repeated over and over again. Even the face of Christ, which he most prized, the centre of the picture, that had sent him wild with joy as it unfolded itself to him, was lost when he glanced at the picture with their eyes. He saw a well-painted (and not so well-painted in places either—he noticed a multitude of defects)repetition of those innumerable Christs of Titian, Raphael, Rubens, with the same soldiers and the same Pilate. It was all hackneyed, poor, stale, and positively badly painted—weak and unequal.[53]

This is of course partly reaction, but after his visitors have gone, the painter begins to make some alterations to his Christ and finds the equivalent to Sandford's drapery in the background of affairs:

While he was correcting the foot he kept glancing at the figure of John in the background, which the visitors had not even noticed but which he knew was beyond perfection. . . . He was about to cover the picture, but stopped and, holding up the sheet, stood a long time with a blissful smile on his face gazing at the figure of John.[54]

For George Eliot the piece of unnoticed perfection in the background was the Vicar in Middlemarch, Farebrother who never told his love. When Mrs Oliphant gives Sandford his piece of drapery, it is as if, out of her own jogtrot, she were here trying to gather up the wisdom that came too late in her own autobiography and hand it on in another life as art. She could never have expected to be mentioned in the same breath with George Eliot. But George Eliot and Tolstoy precisely did see that they could be mentioned in the same breath with those who tried and failed.

But anyway is not this, the sheer colour of the drapery, just what in trying the moonlight scene, 'that unreal scene which was so undubitable a fact' (*The Ways of Life*, p. 58), the artist really needed to do? Even if it could not be done by Mr Sandford or by Mrs Oliphant without the support of natural, representational art, nonetheless it is arguably what their art really aspired to. Otherwise in anxious omnipotence of realism, the achievement is only incidental, a bonus, the substance of colour reduced to an accident amidst the narrative scheme of things, when the fact unreal to a conventional sense of reality is true to imagination. Here at the end of the century, Mrs Oliphant, conscious of doing what was both old-fashioned and better done by George Eliot, writes a parable of what the art of memory in the nineteenth century became increasingly committed to—realism. For it is necessary to Mr Sandford, as to Mrs Oliphant, that the inspiration should be seen as coming out of the jogtrot rather than as independent of it. You might say that this is the lesser artist making a virtue of necessity. But it leaves a question implicit in the parable: whether the greatest art is that which is apparently independent of the reality external to it or whether great art is George Eliot doing to the whole scene what a Mrs Oliphant could mostly only do with the drapery.

The moral value of the latter lies in its taking over autobiography's largely failed aspiration to speak justly and finally on one's own behalf. F. W. Bateson once registered a complaint against 'the hideous ultimate nature of the novel': 'the unreal masquerading as the real'. But realism offers itself as reclamation and retrieval of life, and behind that offer is not a masquerade so much as a hidden metaphysic. It is a belief that the power of the writer is to be found no more in the success of the painting—

> against it *the flush of the sudden inspiration*, the stronger handling

—than in the failure of the painter

> When it first occurred to him his hand suddenly stopped work with an action of its own before the mind had time to influence it, and *there was a sudden rush of heat to the head.*

This is not because the writer is indifferent to the difference between the two but rather as if the two were related. For to find what is too much for you is also to find, if your writing or painting can hold it, the creativity of surpassing yourself without the ease or freedom of merely shaking off that self. Realism is the sort of art where surpassing yourself must still include yourself. Music, I sometimes feel in my amateur way, surpasses sorrow, can make big and fine notes from it, in an harmonious language above it: that, at any rate, was what De Quincey felt when he listened to Handel, with the organ pulling together the notes of discord to make through its language a sorrow which it also triumphantly rises above.[55] But realism uses the representational power of prosaic language precisely *not* to transcend that to which it refers. Or rather—and this is what leaves us with that impression which we have been looking at throughout part II of there being almost two people or two levels involved in such work:— the ability to put inadequacy into adequate words and the inadequacy itself reciprocally raise and lower each other, in both senses of the word 'qualify' each other; so that the words do not transcend the predicament any more than the predicament devalues the words. It is something like the relation that Dorothea has to what she sees through and beyond her window: realism will not let art selfishly hide from the sight of life nor allow language to assume any detached mastery over that upon which it looks out. To *make* something from the meaning of one's life and yet that the making should be in terms of that life and not separate from it: that is realism's metaphysic of a secular and democratic kind. The strength gained from the language is ploughed back into the weakness that prompted the need for it. Commonsense lets time in, between the thought 'I am a writer/painter' and the recognition 'but I am not a great writer/painter'. There are times, as we have seen with Mr Sandford, when a person writes or paints with just that commonsense. But there are occasions when there is no such time—'before the mind had time to influence it'—when to creativity the fact that the artist is not a great artist feels more than a shock but like a *paradox*. As if, as a George Eliot seems to know, it ought to be possible for more people to do what great writers alone can do, rescue experience with what seems to be simple and is so desperately hard—the right use and choice of words. Great realism tries to make amends for this paradox, not out of the heights of genius but out of its fears that it is not genius—out of Mihailov's fear that his work is only presumption and repetition. The privilege of genius is abolished; the work has to be raised from acknowledgement of and responsibility towards low and mundane things; success becomes so final a thing after a series of failures and fear of failures as to become lost beyond the horizon; personal doubts and artistic scruples are utterly interfused in the struggle for an honourable reclamation of human purpose. Out of the energy of the paradox, that the source of creative work may still be, relatively, the source of creative failure, creativity in the nineteenth century struggled for, with and against itself: always left in between the impossibility of success (when you compare the power of art with the power of all that lies outside it which it tries to represent) and the unfaceableness of failure.

There is nothing I have said that Mrs Oliphant did not know and indeed did not suffer from the knowledge of. In a review of an autobiography by Giovanni Dupré, she records how the sculptor was forced by economic factors to give up stone and return to wood-carving for the sake of his family. She quotes Dupré thus:

> Not that I despised that art—I have already said the material is of no account; but I wanted to be a sculptor, and meantime I had nothing to do, and my family looked to me for support. . . . Sometimes returning home with the children, [my wife] would stop to see me, and would look at and praise my work, and perhaps, because it reminded her of our early years, would say—
> 'Beautiful, this work, is it not Nanni?'
> 'Yes; do you like it?'
> 'Yes.'
> But in the exchange of loving words there was a certain sadness; and although it did not appear on the surface, yet the ear and eye of him who loves, hears and sees what is hidden below.

—Then Mrs Oliphant comments, as though to say that that tie to the family is not a bondage to reality more than it is also a human bond:

> Whenever this gentle woman appears the scene brightens, and the husband's words glitter with a tender light. No doubt in her heart there was always a sincere conviction that the beautiful work which was within the reach of her

modest capacity was really the best, and that Nanni would
have been safer had he held fast by it, and eschewed those
big shining ghosts in marble, which no woman could be
expected to care for.

The woman loved the small things, the artist the big ones, and
the husband had to compromise the artist in him. Mrs Oliphant
was both a woman of more than modest capacity and a
compromised artist. Moreover her own husband had been an
unsuccessful painter, using their dining-room as his studio
while she used the little back drawing room for her own work,
both domestic and literary. To the anxieties of the age of
realism concerning the relation of art to life, she had had to
add her own personal difficulties about the relation of her life
to her work. Wordsworth, I have been implicitly arguing in
this book, was the last writer in the nineteenth century to be
able to get those balances right, using a special relation of
words to memory in order to hold himself in between what
would otherwise have been the mutually damaging alternatives
of life or literature. The story of Giovanni Dupré is only one
measure of the general difficulties of art in the nineteenth
century, with the pressures of economics and the demands of
realism operating in concert. But what Mrs Oliphant sees is
an achievement which, partly lying in the fact of its not being
freely chosen, is the product of those difficulties. What irritated
and frustrated the sculptor still made the autobiographer.
Whenever the wife appears in his autobiography, the husband's
words become art for her, whatever the sadness beneath them;
perhaps more art than his own art of sculpture, had he been
free to pursue it, might have achieved; but somehow related to
what his being an artist means. Art here is a matter neither of
freedom nor of genre; it is a human power defeated in one
place and re-emerging in another, as the sculptor turns to his
wife, as the novelist turns to her own past, as art turns back to
life to save itself by memory.

In the last years of her life the act of creation had to be felt
by Mrs Oliphant to be an act of re-creation—not because of
the mere fear of the demands of the real, but because of what
that fear brought out: a feeling that the real includes, if it will

only remember, a creative heart within it. The artist does that remembering. I have dealt only with the strengths of 'Mr Sandford'. The weaknesses of the tale are obvious and have a human source: the weakness of the dialogue as the painter lies dying derives from a thoroughly understandable wish finally 'to say everything'; while Mrs Oliphant apologized in the preface for shirking the hard edge of tragedy by killing the painter off, hoping she had done enough without leaving him to live a living death. But the strength of the tale lies in the power of remembering things that count more than the weakness that may surround them. The image of the purpose behind 'Mr Sandford' is realized when the dream of the dying painter is painted verbally for him; Sandford is thinking of his unsold works in the back room of Daniells's gallery:

> 'All against the wall—with the faces turned,' he said. 'Three—all the last ones: the one my wife liked so. In the inner room: Daniells is a good fellow. He spared me the sight of them outside. Three—that's one of the perfect numbers—that's—I could always see them: on the road, on the moor, and at the races: then—I wonder—all the way up—on the road to heaven? no, no. One of the angels—would come and turn them—turn them round. Nothing like that in presence of God. It would be disrespectful—disrespectful. Turn them round—with their faces—' He paused; his eyes were closed, an ineffable smile came over his mouth. 'He—will see what's best in them,' he said.
>
> *The Ways of Life*, p. 143.

Perhaps it helped Giovanni Dupré that he was not working in his own medium when he wrote his autobiography, but Mrs Oliphant, one feels, would have liked her own *Autobiography* to have been just such a work. And here she re-makes it by reworking her own medium, as well as her life, through the eyes of a painter, the profession of her debt-ridden husband who died young. Where George Eliot in *Middlemarch* goes for the width of life as the new secular dimension, Mrs Oliphant kept her faith and in 'Mr Sandford' is still concerned with the old direction towards finality, is still concerned with life's end. And it is here, at the end of the tale that virually marks the end of her own life, that she is turning her own work round, God's seeing being her doing. 'No one will ever mention me in the same breath with George Eliot'. Yet there is no greater tribute to either George Eliot or Mrs Oliphant than to say that Margaret Oliphant need not have turned her face from *her* who always tried to turn from outside estimates of her characters to see what was best in them.[56] We have looked at the best in 'Mr Sandford' and seen how the failures which autobiography has to accept as its author's responsibility need not be left at that. But 'Mr Sandford' is not merely a final, bitter attempt for the compensation of making a last success out of those failures. For all its neo-religious finality of structure and purpose, this marvellous tale by the end is not looking forward to anything, neither to the future nor to success. It ends not so much by transcending the past as by turning back to it. And there it wipes away the criteria of success and failure as the main determinants of the value of a life; for Sandford's life is not made better at the end, it is just that the best in it is then seen and known—as if it were enough to have (if not leave) a memory of the way one has been. And that is a matter not of finality so much as completion, as memory supersedes ambition.

We have seen prose works in memory of life in various forms, from autobiography to realism. If nineteenth-century fictional realism is more moving than the story of real life called autobiography, it is greater and more moving in the way that 'Mr Sandford' is greater than Mrs Oliphant's *Autobiography*: because it remembers it is greater, as art, and knows it has to be, for the sake of justice to the memory of a life. What 'Mr Sandford' turns round is the terrible close to the *Autobiography* when the professional writer, finding no readers, no family, sees finally no point in writing:

> And now here I am all alone.
> I cannot write any more.
> *Autobiography*, p. 150.

I think that it was because of the example of George Eliot that Mrs Oliphant, finally and in her own way, managed to help herself beyond that dead silence. She did it by the power of memory and by the help that writing gave to allow memory its power. If writing increasingly meant fiction in the nineteenth century, the good thing about fiction was that it was not ashamed, as a reputedly low and bastard form, to admit that its origins lay in quite personal needs and interests. At the end Mrs Oliphant, like George Eliot, pointed to her own heart.

The end of 'Mr Sandford' is a wonderful thing in our literature; in the nineteenth century probably the last image of hope in memory. It is enough that the best of us is seen and remembered somewhere, somehow, although unrecognized by the public or posterity. Her idea of God saved Mrs Oliphant in this way. George Eliot had no such idea, there was no God at the end of her novels, only human society. In a way, therefore, she was even more afraid of failing; in another way she was all the more impelled to re-define the idea of success and failure— as, say, Ruskin hardly managed to. But what above all she did was, so to speak, to take Mrs Oliphant's image of God finally seeing the best of us and say that it did not matter if it was untrue, if it was a fiction. That did not matter—not because it was of no importance that the best we thought or did, even *Middlemarch* itself, might well not last. But because there was, if nowhere else, always in us that human God that Mrs Oliphant for once had managed to draw out of herself into words. That human God, seeing the best of us, might die with us as individuals. But he lived in the race, in the consciousness and the memory that people always have of themselves. And just occasionally someone like George Eliot can tell the story that we often cannot tell for ourselves but equally often rehearse within ourselves. In the final part of this book I shall be asking whether that is enough for us, that there is consciousness, there is memory, there is writing and reading, where there is not God. It is a great Victorian question we inherit.

PART III

MEMORY AND WRITING

A sense of the meaning of life

5

Memory:
'One of the dubious gifts
of Prometheus'?[1]

I. 'IS LIFE WORTH LIVING?'

In 1879 W. H. Mallock published a book, dedicated to John
Ruskin, entitled *Is Life Worth Living?*. The book is an attack on
what Mallock calls 'Positivism', meaning by that term not
merely the specific followers of Comte (that apostle of moral
progress through the application of the methods of natural
science to the study of man in society) but the whole body of
modern, secular, scientific, humanist thinkers epitomized in the
names of T. H. Huxley, Darwinist, and George Eliot, post-
Christian moralist. Stiffened by Ruskin's conviction of the
necessity of religious belief for the survival of a meaningful
sense of ethics and value, Mallock's book is nonetheless, until
its closing proposition in favour of Catholicism, not merely a
reactionary work. For at its best it dares to pose, before it
ventures to answer, the question as to what decidedly secular
ethics and purposes will look like.

They will not look like ethics did before. Mallock argued that
it was George Eliot who was being reactionary in pretending
that they would. Marian Evans had translated Feuerbach in
1854 and found in his *The Essence of Christianity* a key to
translating Christian religion into humanist morality. The form
of religion had been created by human needs; God was man's
creation as well as his need; the best qualities of man, as well
as his greatest anxieties, had been projected into an alienated
objectivity. Men had found strength in their God. The task
now was to recognize that the strength that they found in their
God was really their own strength. Let them now recognize
and accept their own strength. The form of Christianity could

Notes and Bibliography begin on page 503.

be thrown away; its humane content and origin could be given back to men and retained at a now higher level of self-consciousness as the ethical wisdom of humanity over the course of its historical evolution. If men had acted ethically in obedience to a religion which they themselves had created, it was inconceivable that they should cease to act ethically merely because they found that the rules which they had obeyed were their own rules. Marian Evans, for example, in a moment of rebellion following her conversion to agnosticism, refused to go with her father to church anymore. When, however, she saw how much this grieved her father and ruined their family life, she resumed her going to church. It was of course a personal compromise, but as always with her the feelings on one level were tied to ideas on another, auto-biography and epistemology were intervolved. The compromise was in the spirit of Feuerbach; she went to church for human, rather than divine, considerations, no longer believing in the form of the faith but still believing in the human content which that form expressed.

To Mallock such a compromise could be no more than historically temporary, a hiatus between the old and the new. For Mallock the problem of the new self-dependence of values proposed by the 'Positivists'—duty for its own sake, goodness as its own reward, happiness as an end in itself—was that what these values presently mean to men derives from what they had meant when supported by Christianity. Secularist morality was 'a mutilated reproduction of the very thing it professes to be superseding' (*Is Life Worth Living?* p. 138). The meaning of Christian ethics cannot be simply translated into a post-Christian context, not least because Christian ethics were supported by the idea of another world than this one. The meaning of Christian ethics is one that the secularizers 'have already repudiated, and only do not recognize now, because they have so inadequately re-expressed it' (ibid., p. 135). Mallock's book thus marks the transition in the status of belief between, on the one hand, George Eliot, making a faith of human hope, and, on the other, Thomas Hardy, unable—by definition—to believe in what he saw he only hoped for. 'Positivists', Mallock argued, forget that the ideals that were once active in the world were active amongst people who thought that they were more than ideals, and who very certainly did mistake them for facts; and they forget how different their position will be, as soon as their true nature is recognised.

Ibid., p. 20.

I have been arguing that the nineteenth-century concern with personal memory is an aspect of, and a response to, secularization. The continuing need for a witness; the need for something to preside over one's life; a sense of something abiding and returning that will not let life become a matter of mere drifting or forsaking; an internal voice reminding one of the weight and seriousness of a life which otherwise one takes too easily as simply one's own affair—these are some of the post-religious functions of human memory by means of which the individual cannot escape considering his own life, at some distance from himself. 'How different their position will be,' says Mallock, above, and that, with respect to Thomas Hardy in this chapter and D. H. Lawrence in the next, is the subject of the final part of this book.

I shall argue that George Eliot attained, in a different medium and a different way, a moral equilibrium that had not been attained since Wordsworth. It was not to be reached again after George Eliot—unsurprisingly so, if one accepts Mallock's view of George Eliot's work as the last but temporary compromise that could be made, in god-like memory of human feelings that were now, in a consciously secular context, going to have to change. We have of course already seen, in Part II, the changes that the cultural movements from poetry to prose reflected and expressed: changes in national, social, and personal life which were marked in the memory of individuals or in their treatment of their own memories or in the work that was done in memory of the meaning of their lives. The type of change which we witnessed between the Ruskin of *Modern Painters*, Mallock's hero, and the Ruskin of *Praeterita*, a hero to nobody, results from an implicit loss of a belief in a finality of life other than the finality of exhaustion, decay and then death. If George Eliot or someone like George Eliot did not succeed in making that implication bearable, with respect to sustaining life as worth living despite it, then, George Eliot knew, the thought that there was no final goal or purpose for life would become increasingly terrible. We have asked, what happened after Wordsworth? We have now to ask, what happened after George Eliot?

On her own admission George Eliot found beginnings and endings difficult. Her novels emphatically belong to the middle of life, particularly by the time of *Middlemarch*. For Mallock this was a telling loss of a sense of a significant form for life. However much George Eliot may have wanted to be to people an equivalent of Bunyan, although without the final destination of the Heavenly City, the fact was that *Middlemarch* could offer no direction to purpose such as Bunyan offered in *The Pilgrim's Progress*. Where Bunyan gave his readers a narrative conviction that their faith and problems with faith were getting them somewhere, that they were not standing still but were all the time on a journey of life, George Eliot had to leave her readers in a provincial town amongst men and women who half suspected that their little lives had led nowhere. All moral systems, argues Mallock, must postulate some end of action, an end to which morality is the only road:

> Further, this end is the one thing in life that is really worth attaining; and since we have to do with no life other than this one, it must be found amongst the days and years of which this short life is the aggregate. On the adequacy of this universal end depends the whole question of the positive worth of life, and the essential dignity of man.
>
> *Is Life Worth Living?*, p. 27.

But the 'Positivists' had no definite teleology. Lives did not move forward to a goal or a prize, they were meant to be worth living for their own sake. We have seen how Mrs Oliphant managed at the end of 'Mr Sandford' to use her old-fashioned belief in God to make memory a proper end to life, as if our remembering the best we have done might be enough for us. But if looking back discloses a pattern hardly felt at the time it was presumably being made, such looking back is perhaps too late to provide for life an adequate substitute for a sense of journeying, struggling but moving forward. Certainly Mallock had in mind the example of John Stuart Mill during his nervous breakdown:

> From the winter of 1821 when I first read Bentham . . . I had what might truly be called an object in life, to be a reformer of the world. . . . But the time came when I awakened from this as from a dream. . . . It occurred to me to put the question directly to myself: 'Suppose that all your objects in life were realised; that all the changes in institutions and opinions which you were looking forward to, could be completely effected in this very instant, would this be a very great joy and happiness to you?' And an irrepressible self-consciousness distinctly answered 'No!' At this my heart sank within me: the whole foundation on which my life was constructed fell down.
>
> Quoted in Is Life Worth Living?, p. 27.

If all the Utilitarian improvements were made, still life would not of itself be worth living. The end of this life, according to its potential narrative-scheme, was not going to be adequate. The 'Positivists' might say that the end of life is to live life for the sake of each other, but to Mallock this was no end, it was a virtuous circle:

> There is no real escape in saying that we must all work for one another, and that our happiness is to be found in that. The question merely confronts us with two other facets of itself. What sort of happiness shall I secure for others? and what sort of happiness will others secure for me?
>
> Ibid., p. 52.

' "I am so glad that you are glad that I am glad" . . . But . . . all this gladness must be about something besides itself.' (ibid., p. 53). We all dance together in a circle, and if we are happy it is not because we are dancing but because we each rejoice in the sight of such a spectacle! That will not be enough, says Mallock, it is the individual that has to find happiness and he cannot find it in that deflected, social way. If he does not himself enjoy dancing, the dance will become a sham of happiness, with each looking out for the happiness of others. But who are these others that each is looking out for? A social fiction that each plays upon himself, whistling in the dark.

What Mallock says is true in a way. Writing novels did constitute for George Eliot an admission that life now took a different shape. By the time she came to write *Middlemarch*, stories no longer gave lives the relief of a rigidly external form. It was Lawrence who recognized that George Eliot was the first to put the action inside.[2] But before that one of her firmest admirers, James Sully, using almost Darwinian terms, had described her stories 'when regarded from one point of view as the outcome of her characters, from another point of view, as the formation of her characters' (*Mind*, vi, (1881), p. 385). Neither of these two points of view was allowed to precipitate out of the novel's solution: 'there in no species of art which is so free from rigid requirements. Like crystalline masses, it may take any form, and yet be beautiful'.[3] For this is a novel written by the translator of Feuerbach—Feuerbach who argued that all forms of the divine were made from human content and must now be translated back into that content. It is there, back in the human melting-pot, as it were, that George Eliot leaves her characters. Their situation often prompts her to give off abstract thoughts on their behalf and in their memory, as if the greatest sympathy was to say for people what they dare not say even in their heart of hearts to themselves. Lydgate, we recall, says to himself 'She will never love me much' because he cannot bear to think 'I shall love her no more'. But the precipitation of such thought by George Eliot is fundamentally only a testimony to how saturated is the solution of human affairs that the novel bears. It is not a matter of enabling us to find a direction for life; it is rather a matter of giving us such complexity of consideration that we are prevented from wanting to bring things *out* of life's solution at all. The honour involved in thus staying inside something that seems directionless and virtually hopeless is made clear to us at moments such as the fall of Bulstrode:

> It was eight o'clock in the evening before the door opened and his wife entered. He dared not look up at her. He sat with his eyes bent down, and as she went towards him she thought he looked smaller—he seemed so withered and shrunken. A movement of new compassion and old tenderness went through her like a great wave, and putting

one hand on his which rested on the arm of the chair, and
the other on his shoulder, she said, solemnly but kindly—

'Look up, Nicholas.'

He raised his eyes with a little start and looked at her
half amazed for a moment: her pale face, her changed,
mourning dress, the trembling about her mouth, all said,
'I know;' and her hands and eyes rested gently on him.
He burst out crying and they cried together, she sitting at
his side. They could not yet speak to each other of the
shame which she was bearing with him, or of the acts
which had brought it down on them. His confession was
silent, and her promise of faithfulness was silent. Open-
minded as she was, she nevertheless shrank from the
words which would have expressed their mutual consciousness, as she would have shrunk from flakes of
fire. She could not say, 'How much is only slander and
false suspicion?' and he did not say, 'I am innocent.'

Middlemarch, Bk viii, chap. lxxiv (iii, pp. 334–5).

There is no release here into something like 'And so Mrs
Bulstrode saved the world'. These are little unremembered
acts, and they are left here waiting for a recognition that,
without the reader's help, will probably never come. But their
memory abides, unlifted out into large celebration. We are
kept inside this incident and we are not allowed to take it any
further than this in any direction. She does not write of Mrs
Bulstrode: 'She *did* not say, "How much is only slander and
false suspicion?"', she writes, 'She *could* not say', for there is
fear in her pity. She does not write of Bulstrode: 'He could not
Bulstrode: 'She *did* not say, "How much is only slander and
false suspicion?"', she writes, 'She *could* not say', for there is
fear in her pity. She does not write of Bulstrede: 'He could not
say, "I am innocent"', for he is beyond being able to do
anything, the man has shrunk to being as hopeless as the fact
of his guilt. He simply did not say that he was innocent: that is
all Mrs Bulstrode knows and that is what she has to bear the
knowledge of.

To push this further—to know what happened next between
them, to break the silence on the other side of which lies the
great human roar of inner pain—all this would be to go to

extremity with Thomas Hardy. For it is Hardy who narrows the width of *Middlemarch* in his novels, forces it into single-mindedness and drives one big character to the end of death. Here is the Hardy version of the above passage, albeit in a quite different set of circumstances—Elizabeth-Jane has accused Henchard of deceiving both herself and her real father by his false claim to paternity and his lies to Newson about the death of his daughter:

> Henchard's lips half parted to begin an explanation. But he shut them up like a vice, and uttered not a sound. How should he, there and then, set before her with any effect the palliatives of his great faults—that, he had himself been deceived in her identity at first, till informed by her mother's letter that his own child had died; that, in the second accusation, his lie had been the last desperate throw of a gamester who loved her affection better than his own honour? Among the many hindrances to such a pleading not the least was this, that he did not sufficiently value himself to lessen his sufferings by strenuous appeal or elaborate argument.
>
> *The Mayor of Casterbridge*, chap. xliv (New Wessex Edition, p. 326).

For Hardy the silence of Henchard before the accusations of Elizabeth-Jane is meant as more terrible for its sheer finality of real isolation than the silence of Bulstrode before his wife. It is as if Hardy agreed with Mallock that George Eliot stopped short, compromised, tried to fill a terrible gap yawning before her with old values that no longer had a coherent religious context to make them a means to salvation. There were no rewards on earth for Mrs Bulstrode and there was no heaven. George Eliot might think that the spectacle of our all being in the same boat of troubles saves us from the loneliness of individual failure; that the sight of someone like Mrs Bulstrode struggling to help trouble makes life worth living—as if 'life has some deep inherent worth of its own beyond what it can acquire or lose by the caprice of circumstance' (*Is Life Worth Living?* p. 3). Wasn't this worth doing? isn't what humans do and believe something that makes life more than what it would otherwise be? Yet Hardy comes very close to suggesting that failure is failure; that nothing stops the final loneliness and very few people try to assuage it anyway; that everything, consolation included, is only a temporary distraction or compromise. 'He did not sufficiently value himself to lessen his sufferings.' In his novels Hardy will not accept George Eliot's belief in a necessary terminus. Between the Bulstrodes, there is so much waiting to be said that it is too much for each of them separately to bear: there is in that a terminus for George Eliot and in that terminus a licence for them to join together in supportive silence. 'He burst out crying and they cried together': George Eliot does not write 'and she cried too', because the separate reasons that she has for crying Mrs Bulstrode covers over, in her immediate decision to join tears with him. 'Together': both for him and because of him, hence with him. In going beyond that terminus and into loneliness, Hardy was eschewing the social width of *Middlemarch* and turning back to the old sense of linear narrative that we saw at the end of 'Mr Sandford', for example. Only with Mrs Oliphant that finality was supported by the idea of God; with Hardy, substituting telos for the compromise of terminus, the finality is simply that of death. Moreover, when he writes of what Henchard could not say—'the palliatives of his great faults'— his writing does not redeem injustice so much as express bitterness at it.

When George Eliot wrote of what could not be said by her characters to each other, it was with a very different sense from Hardy's of writing for the memory of the race. The difference was that the novel was not for her, as it was for Hardy, an ironic and belatedly secondary form, for writing of the failures to speak and the failures buried beneath the reach of dialogue. When we, as readers, see how Mrs Bulstrode did for her husband what, we recall, Dorothea could not do for Casaubon and Rosamond would not do for Lydgate, it is not as if we think that Mrs Bulstrode is actually helping Casaubon and Lydgate into the bargain. But she is helping our memory of the other two, she is saving us from the thought of irredeemable failure. There is a community in *Middlemarch* which in a sense shares the same trouble—trouble in marriage, trouble in vocation, trouble in loneliness, and a sense of failure. But all we see is how that sharing never really takes place at the level of speech or direct alleviation: for George Eliot, that is a paradox, a contradiction, an irony, a sadness close to tragedy. We can hardly admit the trouble we have, so separately, in common. But there is another community in *Middlemarch*, the community of readers, and the hope is that the sheer acknowledgement, that we mortal millions live alone, will keep open the chance of a future evolution of society where the sharing of troubles will mean relief and not isolation. In *Middlemarch* there is the writer, George Eliot, with her god-like memory drawing lonelinesses together as if caring for them, and there is the memory of Marian Evans, no better off than any of the other lonely, frightened souls in the book. In the same way, we are there, suffering individually in our lives outside the book rather as a Casaubon or a Lydgate or a Dorothea or a Bulstrode does inside it. We recognize that, George Eliot hopes. But on another level, a level corresponding not to that of Marian Evans but that of George Eliot, we also recognize through the convocation of a community of readers that this isolation is something that we share with others: not really share, but ironically share, yet may potentially share. Potentially, because of the covert hope that writing and reading afford the idea of human community—in that binding through sympathy and memory which individuals, who still remain private and separate as they read, acknowledge in their reading. George Eliot tells us that she knows this by addressing her readers directly, giving us a place. *Middlemarch* is written to leave a memory for the future and to consolidate readers at that level of consciousness whereby we see our own troubles, see that they are not simply our own individual troubles and become almost, if not yet, different people for seeing these things. In the same way as George Eliot became almost but not quite a different person from Marian Evans—or Casaubon. In this the novel for George Eliot had a primary role to play in maintaining human life. Not least, it sustained a conscious memory of powerfully felt inner emotions when their failure to initiate action or alleviate suffering otherwise threatened them with redundancy in the order of human affairs. Writing and reading were thus primary, not ironic, activities for George Eliot: they saved memories of lives, albeit through recasting them.

   In all this George Eliot was the novel's heir to the

Wordsworth of whom I spoke in the first two chapters of this book: the writer who through language learnt to raise himself to be more than he ordinarily was, precisely for the sake of the memory of what he had felt and been. As with Wordsworth, so with George Eliot the relation between living and writing was a complex and conscientious concern. By temperament George Eliot was primarily a believer in explicit communication and direct human interference. At the end of *Adam Bede*, for example, Dinah interferingly goes to the child-murderer Hetty in prison and virtually draws her confession out of her, for the sake of her peace. Yet George Eliot's development from *Adam Bede* onwards involves a recognized narrowing of the possibility of direct communication and interference. Correspondingly, writing, instead of seeming a merely secondary and indirect medium, came to be for her something more than merely in lieu of direct speech. By the time of *Middlemarch* George Eliot created a memory, above the characters, of all that the characters could not say to each other or do for each other. That memory is 'George Eliot' in that book, and it functions, on behalf of the race, in writing rather than in speaking. Yet it was to this memory—a memory whose sadness at the ways that life had become too small is itself a belief that life is and must be worth living—that Thomas Hardy, in my view, felt himself pushed and forced to say no. He almost hated himself for it. Because it amounted to the guilt of finding life hardly worth living. And Hardy barely knew whether to curse life or himself for that.

For George Eliot it had been so different. She had started her adult life as a Rousseauist, searching for individual happiness and freedom, treasuring her own emotions. But there had come a check, a big second thought that led to her second life, from the age of thirty-eight, as a writer. On second thought, she had come to find the isolation of the individual not a proud and noble thing but something mean and self-devouring. No one, short of the greatest geniuses, was going to do very well on his or her own in making the individual life worth living. The great medical discoverer Vesalius might manage it (although it is doubtful that it made his life actually happier); Lydgate would not. Mallock argued that the failure of the individual would not find compensation in that indivi-

dual's attempt to help other individuals instead. But for George
Eliot it was right and proper that the individual could not on
the one hand simply substitute love of others for the maintenance of his own life or on the other hand simply persist in
his own life without recourse to the thought of others. In
between those alternatives was the nature of life as it had to be
led. And this checking of Romantic individualism was not, as
it was for Hardy, a cause for profound disappointment. For
George Eliot or Marian Evans seems always to have lived on
two levels, both essential to her. There was not only her life,
there were also her ideas of life, and the two were to be mutual
witnesses, correctives, and supporters of each other without
either merely giving way to the other through rationalization
or through emotionalism. She needed her ideas to run along
the touchline of her life, explaining it in such a way that
disappointment became an occasion for learning as well as
lamenting. That is how and why she became a writer, even
while, on the other hand, she also became a writer of fiction in
order to keep her tendency to preach and intellectualize
embedded in life's physical inconclusiveness.

For Mallock, however, writers were suspect, it was they
who always entertained new ideas. Words, he seems to have
thought, were a defence, an evasion, an illusion: you think you
are coping with the things to which they refer, when in fact all
you are coping with or entertaining is words. Writers are
narrow and lonely people; their very activity leads towards a
certain intellectual withdrawal from the very life they propose
to make their subject-matter; it was easier for them to eschew
Christianity and still write that life was worth living for its own
sake because they had the support, through the use of words
and through a privileged role, which ordinary people in
practical daily life did not possess. To Mallock, what were
George Eliot's ideas? A way of making her physical life
aesthetic, as in her books; an aesthetic intellectualism that
gave her the illusion of universalizing what was really her
own limited, autobiographical experience. In earlier days the
religious moralist might well instruct the world, though he
knew little of its ways and passions, 'for the aim of this teaching
was to withdraw men from the world' (*Is Life Worth Living?*
p. 135). But the aim of the positivist, of the aesthetic moralist

was precisely opposite: 'it is to keep men in the world' (ibid.). The advantages that writers enjoyed were more dangerous now. And yet it was precisely this sort of objection that had induced George Eliot to turn to writing fiction: for there, at any rate, her thoughts could be tested against lives, the two parts of her mind could work with and against each other, it would not be just her life and it would not be simply thoughts without their physical origins. It was considerations like Mallock's that had prompted George Eliot, on second thought, to find neither autobiography nor didacticism to be the primary mode in which she could express herself. The very responsibilities of being a writer and finding meaning in a secular age led her towards fiction instead—the very medium which in her evangelical days she had thought to be least trustworthy or responsible. Now she made it responsible for the meanings of human life. George Eliot found in the novel an art which held within itself a sense of what was external to it: the life outside art and the objections that could be made against art from that life outside. For me this makes her the heir of Wordsworth. Part of the value of life lay in her belief that human procedures for handling life were not synonomous with it: the only procedure that simultaneously recognized this was, for George Eliot, the novel. That was the way realism became for her the most strenuous form of thinking about living, forming a testing ground between the otherwise mutually weakening alternatives of life and art.

Even so George Eliot thereby had increased the conscious responsibilities of being a writer. And it was that oppressive sense of responsibility, rather than George Eliot's means of shouldering it, that Thomas Hardy inherited. I know of no evidence that Hardy had read Mallock's book, but it is as though Hardy knew how George Eliot had anticipated and countered Mallock's objections ahead of their being made and yet he still found Mallock's objections all too painfully convincing. What is at stake here may be illustrated by an anecdote or parable which I take from a twentieth-century novel very much within the tradition of the nineteenth century of George Eliot and Thomas Hardy. The head of a College of Further Education, John Lindsay, is talking to his wife and daughter about a member of his staff:

'A little while back I was talking to a parson on my staff. He teaches philosophy. Dry little chap. We were just walking along the corridor together; we'd exchanged a word or two, when he said, "One of my students asked me what I'd do if I became convinced that there was neither a God nor an after-life, what I'd think of the way I'd spent my span, in churches, in prayer, in alleged communion with a non-existent being. And I said, 'Young man, I would not regret one minute, because man must be serious and this is the way I was taught. It's as if I'd spent my life working on some branch of mathematical physics, and then found my theories superseded. I could not help feeling disappointed. I'm human. But I would not regret it, because I had done my serious best.'" And with that he turned off into a room.'

The women smiled together, still holding on.

'For me,' John said, 'the belief would have been more important than my seriousness.'

'You're beyond us,' his wife answered.

'If I'd practised something all my life, and found it wrong, I'd be shattered never mind how serious I'd been.'

Stanley Middleton: *Still Waters* (London, 1976), p. 182.

It is a parable of one of our inheritances from the nineteenth century. For John Lindsay is here almost two people at once. First, he stares across the religious divide at the parson on his staff just as George Eliot in her seriousness might look at the Methodist in *Adam Bede*, Dinah Morris in her belief. By virtue of what Feuerbach meant to her, George Eliot could translate religious faith into her own faith in human seriousness, no matter what form of belief it took. And yet there is a second side to Lindsay's admiration: the side that looks across at the parson and, admiration notwithstanding, says no. No, because no matter how serious one's belief in Christianity or humanity, no matter what human good derives from that seriousness: if that belief is false, then a life led under that belief is a failure and a ruin. The part of Lindsay that thus refuses to go along with the parson, as George Eliot went along with her father to church for the sake of the human good it would do, is the very voice of Thomas Hardy. In his poem 'The Oxen' Hardy writes that, although no longer believing in God, he would still go, as in childhood, to see the oxen supposedly kneeling on Christmas Eve: 'Hoping it might be so'—yet, hoping against hope, knowing that it was not so and knowing that when he saw it was not so he'd be 'shattered never mind how serious I'd been'.

Sadness in George Eliot was a sign that life in itself was worth living: no one could be sad about the waste of his own life or anyone else's were it not so. Hardy's sadness was very different. W. H. Mallock had seized upon what Mill said about his breakdown, 'I felt that the flaw in my life must be a flaw in life itself' (*Is Life Worth Living?* p. 28). Going on from that, the question to be asked, said Mallock, was whether and where 'life has some deep inherent worth of its own, beyond what it can acquire or lose by the caprice of circumstance.' (ibid., p. 3). The question was whether, regardless of particular content, 'life is worth living, not accidentally but essentially' (ibid., p. 137). And Hardy, I shall be saying, could have no certainty that it was or was not so. What he had was rather a feeling of guilt about his sadness, about his emotional sense that it was hardly worth living. Was the flaw in his life a flaw in himself or in life itself? How was he to know? All he felt was a pessimistic conviction based on the authority of his own memory—and a mixture of bitterness and guilt that memory, personal memory, should go so close to condemning life, as itself to be condemned for presuming to do so. Memory was enough to blight a man's sense of life, but it wasn't enough to save him from the loneliness of the charge that that might be only his own affair, his own fault even. Personal memories and emotions could not remain privately contained and yet, at the same time, a private individual in this century was under pressure not to dare to extend the authority of his personal experience into wider generalizations. Even so, there was no entirely coherent religious or political belief that could subsume, relieve or place the personal difficulties: in the Prelude to *Middlemarch* George Eliot had mentioned explicitly the want of a coherent faith or social order. Yet personal emotions and memories did seem to mean something powerful, if unplaced, and did seem to have irresistible reference to things outside the self. Literature had to cope with that set of contradictions; it had to cope with problems of the status of personally felt experience in a secularized century. We have seen George Eliot's effort to hold these problems in solution, awaiting a better day; we must now turn to Thomas Hardy's trouble with these questions.

> 'After reading various philosophic systems, and being struck with their contradictions and futilities, I have come to this: *Let every man make a philosophy for himself out of his own experience.* He will not be able to escape using terms and phraseology from earlier philosophers, but let him avoid adopting their theories if he values his own mental life. Let him remember the fate of Coleridge, and save years of labour by working out his own views as given him by his surroundings.'
>
> Florence Emily Hardy: *The Life of Thomas Hardy*, p. 310.

In the new secular world described by Mallock as so fragmentary and transitional, how could a man live on his own by the authority of his own experience? For Hardy, even that authority was a form of uncertainty. How could the emotions presume to interpret a world within which, essentially, personal experience was vulnerable rather than judicious? They could do so because the memory of that vulnerability seemed productive of wisdom, albeit only in after-thought. They could do so because the pressure of feeling was so great that they could hardly be prevented from doing so anyway, even when some of the pressure was that of uncertainty and tension. For Hardy emotions and memories were too large and powerful to be contained within himself: he wrote out of them; yet they were also too slighted by, too vulnerably dependent upon, an indifferent or even scornful world to take a large, commanding place within it. They rested uneasily, therefore, on the uncertain boundary between himself and the world, and that boundary was his writing. I guess that it felt something like this:

> Naturally, without sparing colour and in broad strokes, I could describe my depressed condition, my mortal torment, my constant strong fear, not only for my own life but for the lives of my mother, sisters, wife and daughter,

and later my son. And so on. I don't want to deny that I
went through a bad period. Perhaps the careful reader
will understand that, or perhaps he'll just skip all this
rubbish and think, munching a chocolate, 'Whatever
made me read this book? It's just upsetting me before
bedtime.'

When I picture a fool like that, I don't even want to go
on reminiscing. I just sit with a feeling of guilt, when
there isn't anything really that I'm guilty of

Shostakovich: Testimony, p. 87.

Only, Hardy's additional problem within his personal life, out
of which he wrote, was that there *were* things he was guilty of,
also making him feel small. When he proposed then to make a
philosophy out of his own experience, he was not supposing
that he alone could offer the world an answer. But where
certain beliefs were no longer possible and where society
replaced those beliefs only with so much cant and lip-service, it
was the duty of every man to make as honest and coherent
account as he could of what his memory told him of the life he,
at least, had led and known. This manifest individualism was
not a mark of pride so much as a confession of near despairing
loneliness and uncertainty.

II. 'A STORY OF A MAN OF CHARACTER'

What is the memory of a man?

In Hardy's *The Mayor of Casterbridge*—a novel which, more
than any other of his, I take to be Hardy's statement about the
status of the individual within the world—memory is not
merely an internal function of mind or merely a nostalgia to
brood over in private. It is the memory of a man, rather, that
dynamically connects, in the following, passage i with passage
ii. Both passages treat of Michael Henchard's relation to the
girl whom he once thought to be his own daughter and has
since discovered to be the daughter of Richard Newson, a
sailor. In the first passage the girl, Elizabeth-Jane, is contemplating coming back to live with the man whom she still takes
to be her father; in the second she is about to marry Henchard's
erstwhile protégé and present successor, Farfrae.

i. 'You are very lonely, are you not?'

'Ay, child—to a degree that you know nothing of! It is my own fault. You are the only one who has been near me for weeks. And you will come no more.'

'Why do you say that? Indeed I will, if you would like to see me.'

Henchard signified dubiousness. Though he had so lately hoped that Elizabeth-Jane might again live in his house as daughter, he would not ask her to do so now. Newson might return at any moment, and what Elizabeth would think of him for his deception it were best to bear apart from her.

The Mayor of Casterbridge, chap. xli, p. 298.[4]

ii. The remembrance would continually revive in him now that it was not Elizabeth and Farfrae who had driven him away from them, but his own haughty sense that his presence was no longer desired. He had assumed the return of Newson without absolute proof that the Captain meant to return; still less that Elizabeth-Jane would welcome him; and with no proof whatever that if he did return he would stay. What if he had been mistaken in his views; if there had been no necessity that his own absolute separation from her he loved should be involved in these untoward incidents? To make one more attempt to be near her: to go back; to see her, to plead his cause before her, to ask forgiveness for his fraud, to endeavour strenuously to hold his own in her love; it was worth the risk of repulse, ay, of life itself.

Ibid., chap. xliv, p. 321.

Henchard had opposed the match to Farfrae until Newson turned up again to show that he had no real right to such opposition. Then Henchard had left Casterbridge before he could be charged directly with deceit. Now, as passage ii describes, on second thought he wishes to return for the wedding, the wedding which he had opposed as a father. On the face of it, therefore, what connects the two passages is nothing more than human inconsistency, inconsistency in his opposition to the marriage and in his desire to keep away from Elizabeth-Jane rather than be sent away by her. 'Though he had so lately hoped that Elizabeth-Jane might again live in his house as daughter, he would not ask her to do so now': from that moment of resolve, induced partly by the fear of being found out and partly by vulnerable pride, all Henchard's resulting actions were going to be in contradiction of his real desires. Passage ii, following from that, marks the irresistible return of those real desires, albeit now too late; that is to say, the desires that are really Henchard. What connects passage i with passage ii is not inconsistency, then, for there is a deeper logic to it than that superficial appearance. What connects them is the abiding power of the real Henchard—however much that power causes him external inconsistency and humiliation. For the real inner man, 'It was worth the risk of repulse, ay, of life itself'. 'The last desperate throw of a gamester who loved her affection better than his own honour' (ibid., p. 326). It is not as if he has consciously to remember what are his real, what his compromised desires. The real desires, the desires on which he has staked his existence, instinctively come through his behaviour and action. And it is this will to live which is the memory of the man in a dynamic sense. He carries it along with him, making certain acts the distinctive mark of his being, his traces on the earth, while leaving others as no more than things he felt he ought to do. ' "Character is Fate," said Novalis' (ibid., p. 137). That pre-conscious memory of himself that a man carries about and most really acts out of is his character, is his fate. The sort of thing, we say with the wisdom of hindsight, he *would* do. 'To make one more attempt to be near her'—at a time when, he had virtually predicted three chapters previously, such an attempt was bound to be too late and a failure.

So why did he make the attempt, eschewing that prudence which in the book is associated with Henchard's successor, in work and in love, Donald Farfrae? The answer lies, I think, in the way that passage ii seems to follow inevitably as well as inconsistently from passage i. For what that movement signifies is a refusal on Henchard's part to learn from experience: he sticks by the course of action which he recognizes is dictated by his sins and mistakes. The memory of the man, in the sense in which I have begun to define it, is more powerful to him than the memory of the world—by which last I mean that way in which the consequences of our deeds determine us quite as much as we in the first instance determine our actions. In that sense the furmity woman is wrong when she laments, 'The world's no memory' (ibid., p. 55)—indeed, she proves it to be quite otherwise when later in the book she reveals Henchard's youthful sin in selling his own wife. For Henchard the memory of himself is deeper and stronger than a consciousness of the circumstances into which it has led him. And that is not simply a matter of ignorant egoism, although clearly his proud naivety is not free of that taint. There is here a refusal as well as an incapacity to learn from life, to change resolvedly, rather than just moodily, with experience. And that refusal involves, as well as selfishness, a rejection of *internal* strategies for the purpose of physically avoiding and mentally subsuming external realities. For Henchard, to walk away from Elizabeth-Jane is a sort of substitute, induced by self-consciousness, for being rejected by her; it is for him more an emotion than an action and emotions cannot be stuck to. Mental subsumings, anticipations, substitutions of that order seem to Henchard to cheat both his guilty fears of being found out and, worse, his hidden hopes of still being loved—but, more than even that, they also seem unworthily to cheat life itself as an external and profoundly social affair. In the same way, memory for Henchard is an external not an internal thing: not a matter of internal consciousness so much as the characteristic moves, marks and effects of a man in the world. He deals kindly with his former mistress, Lucetta, Farfrae's first wife, in chapter 35 for instance, not through moral introspection on his part but because she has come to plead with him in the same outside place, the old Roman amphitheatre, in which he became reconciled with the wife he had sold in his drunkenness to Newson. It is as if Henchard intuitively believes that a man has no right to inner emotions that refer outwards, unless he acts outwardly on the basis of those emotions. He is an emotional man who does not believe that emotions of themselves are important: what is important are the actions appropriate to them and the persons referred to by them. What is inside the man exists for the world outside him: that is why loneliness is intuitively a terrible paradox for Henchard. *The Mayor of Casterbridge* is thus an almost mythic account of the fate of belief in the physical, external reference of emotion and memory: its strength and its weakness, its unself-conscious warmth and its subtle selfishness—a belief belonging to an earlier stage in the development of man. For Henchard does not believe in the emotion of guilt without the fact of punishment or the emotion of hope without the effort of attainment. That is why he goes back to Elizabeth-Jane's wedding. And that is how he exists at an earlier evolutionary stage than that of a George Eliot character—for whom, generally, the fear of external punishment has begun to be subsumed by the development of the inward scourge of conscience.[5] Henchard has no such concept of the self, for him the development of self-monitoring, later described more fully by Freud, has been instinctively denied and avoided as dishonourable. For Freud says that in man the fear of external authority gives way to the fear of internal authority; to cope with the anxietes of external punishment and the loss of outsiders' love, man brings the fear of such loss and punishment inside himself by the creation of a self-monitoring super-ego—thus anticipating and controlling the danger by internally sequestering it, but also thus increasing consciously the presence of that danger.

> Originally, renunciation of instinct was the result of fear of an external authority: one renounced one's satisfactions in order not to lose its love. If one has carried out this renunciation, one is, as it were, quits with the authority and no sense of guilt should remain. But with the fear of the super-ego the case is different. Here, instinctual renunciation is not enough, for the wish persists and cannot be concealed from the super-ego. Thus, in spite of the renunciation that has been made, a sense of guilt comes about. . . . A threatened external unhappiness—loss of love and punishment on the part of the external authority—has been exchanged for a permanent internal unhappiness, for the tension of a sense of guilt.[6]

The super-ego does not simply punish acts, as the external authority might; ever-vigilant, it can see from inside what the external authority could not see—the repressed but persistent desire to disobey—and it punishes that with guilt. It is this development, at the heart of the ethics of individualism, that

Henchard resists, often selfishly and always with blind instinct; as when he refuses to punish himself by anticipating Elizabeth-Jane's wish not to see him. It must be dealt with outside himself. And that, although selfishly motivated undoubtedly, is also somehow right too and more essential than the developments that the evolutionists describe.

It is not easy to say just how this thing is right when obviously so morally flawed, so contrary to the way of moral development. But it has to do with the subject-matter of section 1 of this chapter; it has to do with Mallock's suspicion that the values of evolved secularization—wherein the external religious framework is internally subsumed into individual self-consciousness—are flawed and incoherent. It is as if man is punished, by himself, for his evolution into secular autonomy. And the punishment is increased unhappiness.

At any rate, there is something primevally right in the following. Farfrae is having a bitter quarrel with Henchard over Henchard's dragging poor, unpunctual Abel Whittle out of his bed, without his breeches, to work, for punishment. Farfrae at this point is not only Henchard's new, modern manager and young protégé, Henchard has also made him a confidant of his betrayal of both the wife he sold and the mistress he deserted. Farfrae countermands Henchard's old-fashioned authority and sends Whittle home to get properly dressed.

> 'Come,' said Donald quietly, 'a man o' your position should ken better, sir! It is tyrannical and no worthy of you.'
>
> ''Tis not tyrannical!' murmured Henchard, like a sullen boy. 'It is to make him remember!' He presently added, in a tone of one bitterly hurt: 'Why did you speak to me before them like that, Farfrae? You might have stopped till we were alone. Ah—I know why! I've told ye the secret o' my life—fool that I was to do't—and you take advantage of me!'
>
> 'I had forgot it,' said Farfrae simply.
>
> Henchard looked on the ground, said nothing more, and turned away. During the day Farfrae learnt from the men that Henchard had kept Abel's old mother in coals

and snuff all the previous winter, which made him less
antagonistic to the corn-factor. But Henchard continued
moody and silent, and when one of the men inquired of
him if some oats should be hoisted to an upper floor or
not, he said shortly, 'Ask Mr Farfrae. He's master here!'
The Mayor of Casterbridge, chap. xv, p. 124.

There is no doubt that Henchard behaves both tyrannically
and then childishly here: the preservation in him of an earlier
stage of man can in a later context be charged with both those
forms of behaviour. Yet that is not what he essentially is—a
child or a tyrant. For there is something 'right' in the sequence
of events here, something that would be damaged if the order
were Henchard humiliating Whittle, being rebuked for it by a
younger man, and then in the winter sending coals to Whittle's
old mother—although the latter would be the conventionally
good moral order of making amends. He no more connects his
treatment of Abel Whittle with his kindness towards the man's
mother than he thinks to mention to the accusing Farfrae, as a
mitigating background to his harshness, his kind treatment of
the mother. If he has thought of Whittle's mother, that has
only made him, with all the speedy harshness of a self-made
man, the more angry with Whittle for not getting his life and
labour sorted out, if only for his mother's sake. But the main
thing is that Whittle has delayed the day's business. And,
actually, so far as we are told explicitly, Henchard has simply
lost his temper, after giving repeated warnings, in a rather Old
Testament way; despite the fact that the culprit is foolish and
simple rather than wicked or ill-intentioned. It is like Henchard
not to connect up the various parts of his behaviour into one
self-conscious memory but to act on the apparently appropriate
emotion at the particular time. Rather, connection by memory
is something the novel does for him, just as the world seems to
do so around him, sealing consequences from impulsive but
characteristic actions. And the sign that the kindness to the
mother matters much more than the harshness to the simple
son is given by Abel Whittle, in this case a finer moralist than
the measuring, calculating Donald Farfrae, when he goes after
the self-exiled Henchard towards the end of the novel:

'You see he was kind-like to mother when she wer here below, though 'a was rough to me. . . . I seed en go down street on the night of your worshipful's wedding to the lady at yer side, and I thought he looked low and faltering. And I followed en over Grey's Bridge, and he turned and zeed me, and said, "You go back!" But I followed, and he turned again, and said, "Do you hear, sir? Go back!" But I zeed that he was low, and I followed on still. Then a' said, "Whittle, what do ye follow for when I've told ye to go back all these times?" And I said, "Because, sir, I see things be bad with 'ee, and ye wer kind-like to mother if ye were rough to me, and I would fain be kind-like to you." Then he walked on, and I followed; and he never complained at me no more. . . . "What, Whittle," he said, "and can ye really be such a poor fond fool as to care for such a wretch as I!" Then I went on further . . .'

Ibid., chap. xlv, p. 331.

There, as in a parable of the good and faithful servant, the novel sends its memory and (what goes with it in Hardy) its heart out after its own exiled protagonist. Farfrae is a decent enough man, as his simple response to Henchard's charge that he has taken advantage of his confidentiality makes clear: 'I had forgot it'. Indeed, that response is something very close to the way Henchard himself forgets background considerations in the heat of his own impulses. Yet Farfrae, for all his modern methods of measuring and producing, is no adequate calculator of the worth, on balance, of his predecessor in Casterbridge society. Or something emotionally valuable has gone out of the calculation. It is Abel Whittle, on the contrary, who cannot make that sort of calculation and seems to be right in doing without it, as if Henchard is a bigger man than a computation of his faults as against his virtues can allow. Only when Henchard dies do they get 'a man to measure him' (ibid.).

What is this big thing, this essence in Henchard that demands acknowledgement and not simply rebuke or a placing judgment? It is something that Lawrence might well have recognized in his reading of Hardy, for it is with Henchard as it is with another flawed father-figure in Lawrence's *The Rainbow*. Will Brangwen turns on his little daughter Ursula when the charwoman complains to him of her playing in the church, but his wife, the child's mother, takes the daughter's part:

> His voice was harsh and cat-like, he was blind to the child. She shrank away in childish anguish and dread. What was it, what awful thing was it?
>
> The mother turned with her calm, almost superb manner.
>
> 'What has she done, then?'
>
> 'Done? She shall go in the church no more, pulling and littering and destroying.'
>
> The wife slowly rolled her eyes and lowered her eyelids.
>
> 'What has she destroyed, then?'
>
> He did not know.
>
> 'I've just had Mrs Wilkinson at me,' he cried, 'with a list of things she's done.'
>
> Ursula withered under the contempt and anger of the 'she', as he spoke of her.
>
> 'Send Mrs Wilkinson here to me with a list of the things she's done,' said Anna. '*I* am the one to hear that.'
>
> 'It's not the things the child has done,' continued the mother, 'that have put you out so much, it's because you can't bear being spoken to by that old woman. But you haven't the courage to turn on *her*, when she attacks you, you bring your rage here.'
>
> He relapsed into silence. Ursula knew that he was wrong. In the outside, upper world, he was wrong. Already came over the child the cold sense of the impersonal world. There she knew her mother was right. But still her heart clamoured after her father, for him to be right, in his dark, sensuous underworld. But he was angry, and went his way in blackness and brutal silence again.
>
> > *The Rainbow*, chap. viii (Phoenix Edition, pp. 215–6).

'"'Tis not tyrannical!" murmured Henchard, like a sullen boy', "Ask Mr Farfrae. He's master here!"': these are words 'in the outside, upper world' where the man is wrong and, in truth, feels himself uncomfortably to be so. But what goes wrong there, as his emotions flare up and become confused, is something that at a deeper level, in its origins, was right—as

Ursula feels with regard to her father. For there is something strong and warm and blindly powerful at the root of the mistakes, something at the very origin of emotions and prior to upper-world tactics, which is the deep principle of life and character in the man. This life-principle, of which his emotions are an expression, is a thing irreducibly earlier than the thought of social accommodation and it is this, rather than some merely underdeveloped primitivism, that Henchard is in memory of. His emotions are the memories of his deep character. Only, what Henchard has to decide, as his life-principle circumstantially surfaces through the flares of anger and passion, is whether this time, in this situation, at this level, his emotional life really is at stake. Primarily his emotions are in memory of himself and his deepest intuitions, they are the only way he can bear to remember, not only because that is his character but also because he is guilty of having sold his own wife and the whole of his subsequent life is founded in despite of that recollection. Only secondarily thus does he look around and about himself to see how appropriate his emotions then are to the contingencies that have apparently provoked them. When he finds, on second thought on cooling, that his emotional life is not so very much at stake in the circumstances, he can forgive or forget or apologize or make amends—as he does in this particular incident with Farfrae, managing to get over his pride as essentially a secondary manifestation of his primary selfhood. For Henchard, his life begins earlier than its social entanglings: it is that earlier deeper level, from which his energy proceeds blindly into the world, that cares little for memory or even grudges, when once it sees that it has been called up into the world unnecessarily or mistakenly. But it is genuinely hard and painful and disappointing for Henchard to recognize these mistakes of undue emotional self-commitment within the world—for he can hardly bear, as perhaps George Eliot would have him bear, the thought that the world does not need his wholeheartedness. Indeed, that is what finally kills Henchard: the realization that most of his manifestations of his real, deep self in the secular world have been unnecessary—as corn-factor, mayor, husband, lover, friend, and father. In each he has been substituted by another; none of his roles has lasted him, himself. Each time he has been forced to find, on second thought or in the consciousness of memory, that his emotions do not belong to the world but only to himself. There was not sufficient love, either granted or deserved, to make him in any of his manifestations entirely recognized or deeply understood, wholly at home or—in a word—necessary. Always his primary selfhood had surged up; almost always on second thought he had found himself mistaken or misplaced. And he had not learnt from that to live at a secondary, compromising level. So, we as readers stand to him partly as Ursula stood to her father, partly as Anna stood to her husband in that passage from *The Rainbow*. For in terms of the latter we also stand to Henchard, seeing through him, as the scoundrel Jepp positions himself to learn Henchard's weaknesses: he 'had regularly watched Henchard in the market-place, measured him and learnt him, by virtue of the power which the still man has in his stillness of knowing the busy one better than he knows himself' (*The Mayor of Casterbridge*, p. 198).

Now, it is the burden of Lawrence's own 'Study of Thomas Hardy' published in *Phoenix* that Hardy ought to have looked at Henchard more as Ursula looked at her father than as Anna considered her husband. The latter is a merely predatory prudence achieved by the sacrifice of such a man. To Lawrence a figure like Henchard is

> a man of distinct being, who must act in his own particular way to fulfil his own individual nature. He is a man who, being beyond the average, chooses to rule his own life to his own completion, and as such is an aristocrat.
>
> *Phoenix*, p. 439.

Henchard is the old Adam, the Old Testament father, the self in its supremacy: 'While a man remains a man, a true human individual, there is at the core of him a certain innocence or naiveté which defies all analysis, and which you cannot bargain with, you can only deal with it in good faith from your own corresponding innocence or naiveté. This does not mean that the human being is nothing but naive or innocent' ('John Galsworthy', *Phoenix*, p. 540). Henchard, for instance, says to Farfrae of the way the younger man has undercut his authority over Abel Whittle, 'Why did you speak to me before them like

that, Farfrae? You might have stopped till we were alone.'
Such words do seek a corresponding innocence or naiveté.

Lawrence's view of Hardy is not a mere distortion. After all,
the subtitle of *The Mayor of Casterbridge* is 'A Story of a Man of
Character', and Hardy had read in John Stuart Mill's *On
Liberty*, a book he claimed to know almost by heart, the
definition of character given in the chapter 'Of Individuality'
which Hardy in 1868 numbered as one of his 'cures for
despair':[7]

> A person whose desires and impulses are his own—are
> the expression of his own nature, as it has been developed
> and modified by his own culture—is said to have a
> character. One whose desires and impulses are not his
> own, has no character, no more than a steam-engine has a
> character.[8]

Such a definition is not so very far from Lawrence's account of
the natural aristocrat as his own man. It was a view which
gave Hardy courage to resist the pressures of social conformity
and optimism, through belief in the authority of his own
emotion, thought, memory and experience.

The subject-matter of Lawrence's 'Study of Thomas Hardy'
is how men struggle, after they have attained the primary task
of ensuring their survival, to make a life and a home upon the
earth. And it is Lawrence's major complaint against Hardy
that, having found the man who will live on his own terms,
Hardy will sympathize with him only to slay him: 'He sympa-
thizes only to slay' (*Phoenix*, p. 435). For example, we looked
above (pp. 342–3) at how Hardy spoke for Henchard when
Henchard could not and would not speak on his own behalf:
'Among the many hindrances to such a pleading not the least
was this, that he did not sufficiently value himself to lessen his
sufferings by strenuous appeal or elaborate argument'. These
words are Hardy's attempt to write what Henchard cannot
say, art's bitter rescue-work; but to Lawrence, I think, they
are the sympathy that slays—because if Henchard *had* been
able to say these things, Lawrence seems to suggest, Hardy,
for more than merely formal reasons, would not have been
able to say them. Hardy needed the man to fail in order that
the social community should not be threatened; but he also

needed the man to fail so that, by the sacrifice of the aristocrat, he could protest to the community against what the aristocrat had stood for in respect of a larger life. Hardy was neither courageous enough to be his own man nor resigned enough to be the community's. But if he was too frightened to let his aristocrat live, he was also too frightened not to mourn his dying. 'He must go against himself' (*Phoenix*, p. 439). He was able to create Henchard not out of the hope of his success but out of the despair at his failure; the book is, as it were, written backwards from its assured end in death to make the life one worth missing. If Hardy felt he was pushing George Eliot's compromise to extremes, to D. H. Lawrence Hardy himself was still compromised and compromising, using writing to hinder as much as help the liberation of the individual.

'Let every man make a philosophy for himself out of his own experience': at any rate, neither Hardy's experience nor his philosophy was Lawrence's. Across Lawrence's road to freedom there fell for Hardy in the person of Henchard two obstacles, as real as the road itself. One had to do with guilt, the other with need, both preventing the man being simply his own man. Firstly, Henchard had thrown himself into business and society in order to forget what he had done to his family; as soon as he was forced to remember, by the re-appearance of his wife and her child, he lost the race against his own past, slowed down, steadied down, and began to fall behind the days of his success. For the greater part of the book, the novel is saying to Henchard 'remember' while Henchard still resists becoming the memory of himself, 'living like a fangless lion about the back rooms of a house' (*The Mayor of Casterbridge*, p. 311). The business and prestige that he used to drive away the past fold under him, he turns back to love to try to hold himself up. Yet 'he experienced not only the bitterness of a man who finds, in looking back upon an ambitious course, that what he has sacrificed in sentiment was worth as much as what he has gained in substance; but the superadded bitterness of seeing his very recantation nullified' (ibid., p. 319). It is here that the second factor—need—comes in: the need of the man to be more than just his own man, to be loved. It is a terrible truth for Hardy that this necessity weakens Henchard as a strong man. Strong feelings about the need to be loved are not themselves strong or powerful in what they can do externally: their power is used against the man who holds them. His emotions were always either generous or violent, they had always precipitated relationship and action, they had always referred him to more than himself even when at the very heart of him. Now, in the final turn of the novel, as his emotions are turned back inwards through rejections, he is forced to see the equal truth of the converse: that emotions that refer to more than just the self are still liable to be, to be seen to be, or to be left alone to be, selfish. I have tried to indicate that the first movement of this novel may be characterized by Henchard's treatment of Abel Whittle: that is the early man. The second movement, the turn to the later man with whom time has caught up, is, as if by nemesis, insistent on memory not now as the mark of a man left in the world but as the scar made within him. One can almost point to the precise moment at which Henchard has to begin, so to speak, to swallow himself. Not long after trying to lure Farfrae into a fight to the death, Henchard, with characteristic inconsistency, goes after him to bring him back to his wife who, unbeknown to Farfrae, is dying. It is Henchard's last tribute to Lucetta, his former mistress, now his rival's wife; such that he can almost forget that the husband of the woman whom he wronged is also the enemy who has replaced and humbled him. Identities of that kind seem to be of later development and it is a mark of Henchard's being a man of character that he is essentially unconcerned with identity in the real heat of the moment. Only *he* knows where Farfrae is travelling, he learnt this at the end of their fight, and at this moment to himself he is the man who knows the vital piece of information far more than he is the man who tried to kill Farfrae—and could not bring himself to, anyway. Now his emotions are stronger as a form of instinctive memory, for Lucetta's sake, than that other form of memory which consists in the consciousness of other relations, other times and other contexts. But this time, crucially, that almost physical consciousness of Henchard's is halted and forced to become mental when Farfrae, suspecting another trap, refuses to believe this messenger who has so recently been his attacker. Henchard wants to say: messenger or attacker, it is just me and my feelings, nothing is fixed; take no notice of me, only take notice of what I say this time, go home to your wife.

> Farfrae was silent, and at his silence Henchard's soul sank within him. Why had he not, before this, thought of what was only too obvious? He who, four hours earlier, had enticed Farfrae into a deadly wrestle stood now in the darkness of late night-time on a lonely road, inviting him to come a particular way, where an assailant might have confederates, instead of going his purposed way, where there might be a better opportunity of guarding himself from attack. Henchard could almost feel this view of things in course of passage through Farfrae's mind.
>
> *The Mayor of Casterbridge*, chap. xl, p. 289.

Why had he not, before this, thought of what was only too obvious? 'There is at the core of him a certain innocence'—for all the evidence of his guilt before. But this incident is a culmination of a gradually appreciated sense of guilt encroaching upon Henchard—given most impetus perhaps when, in chapter xix, he discovered that Elizabeth-Jane was not, after all, his own daughter, as if too he were no longer his own man:

> His usual habit was not to consider whether destiny were hard upon him or not—the shape of his ideas in cases of affliction being simply a moody 'I am to suffer, I perceive.' 'This much scourging, then, is it for me?' But now through his passionate head there stormed this thought—that the blasting disclosure was what he had deserved.
>
> Ibid., chap. xix, p. 146.

Now he must feel this in his innocence before Farfrae. He deserved to be thought guilty. 'Character is Fate', the messenger is the erstwhile attacker, life's possibilities narrow to catch him out with responsibilities for his past.

As he began to lose ground in the later stages of the book, Henchard had found that he could behave warmly and well only when the bitterness in him at his downfall is destroyed along with his social position. The closeness to bankruptcy, to exhaustion, to zero was to him like the extinction of his guilt by punishment. Only at such moments when he is at his lowest, when most stripped of roles and appurtenances, is he free to be himself again, the emotions in memory of his trouble being overtaken by events. In the depths of his desire to kill Farfrae he finds, through the action of trying the desire out, no wish in the essential part of him really to murder a former friend. When once the feelings deep at the centre of him were degradingly soured and disappointed on the surface of the world and, rejected there, turned back upon him to poison him within with bitterness and loneliness, Henchard had tried instinctively to exhaust his violence and destroy his own destructiveness with acts such as his attack upon Farfrae. There he could work through his bitterness to find the memory of his own goodness the second time round, behind it. But this sort of emotional trial and error cannot go on and on, as Henchard damages others in trying at once to maintain and re-find himself. It is as if recurrence of action were the only sort of re-considered integrity he could grasp. It cannot go on and this meeting with Farfrae, with Lucetta dangerously ill, is the sign of its nemesis.

> Henchard could almost feel this view of things in course of passage through Farfrae's mind.

This is the moment when the current of the novel really begins to run backwards—the sort of moment, I guess, that led to Lawrence's quarrel with Hardy:

> the moment man became aware of himself he made a picture of himself, and began to live from the picture: that is, from without inwards. This is truly the reversal of life.
> *Phoenix*, p. 380.

It is as if for the first time Henchard were presented with a picture of himself in the eyes of another. It would not be so devastating if this view of things were felt to be merely in Farfrae's mind; it is now in Henchard's too as by infection. As though looking at his own reflection, Henchard has now found himself more tellingly in his own consequences than in his own self. This had hardly happened before. Instead of emotion, there is now thought and thought no longer at home in or even quite originating with its thinker. For it is not as if the reflection were merely a product of Henchard's own mind. This has come to him, as if from the consequences of himself, from outside. It is from himself but from himself outside, at once. He produced this and he now has to see, recognize, think this, in memory and consciousness of what he has done. And that is the other meaning to memory in this book. In this sense to recollect himself is the sign that he is finished; it is the death of him.

Yet the power that undoes Michael Henchard in the latter part of the book, for all that it does not allow him to be simply his own man, is nonetheless his own power. Even if it is now his own power used against himself.

> & that no man remember me.
> To this I put my name.
> MICHAEL HENCHARD
> Ibid., chap. xlv, p. 331.

It points us in the direction to which this concluding part of my book is moving if I say that to Hardy this was tragedy, to Lawrence mere self-punishment. And we shall see that what was at stake here was the very future of Romanticism: the issue of what a person could make of himself, could make in and from his life, against the background of the use of personal memory in the nineteenth century.

But for the moment I simply conclude as follows. *The Mayor of Casterbridge* is for Hardy a primal, dramatic fable of the tragically necessary shift from emotion to thought, from a large externally-orientated sense of life to a diminished, internally self-punishing one, narrowly personal yet sanely responsible.[9] The world had narrowed into smaller, discrete individuals. Each of these worlds, the earlier and the later, I have tried to suggest, has a quite different sense of memory: one dynamic and external, the other conscious and internal; one a memory despite the self, the other a memory of it; with radical differences between the two in the apportioning of innocence and guilt. For Hardy, to cross from one world to the other was, as we shall see, irrevocable and decisive, the act of a post-Romantic adult. He knew himself not to be a big man of action like Michael Henchard but, in Henry James's phrase, 'the good little Thomas Hardy'—if not good exactly, at any rate reduced by his own power (of emotion, guilt, conscience and memory) and less dramatically so than Henchard. For

Henchard is, as it were, Hardy's imaginative recall or recapitulation of a state from which he had felt obliged to fall: albeit a flawed and imperfect state of emotion, yet the state which his desires seemed to have descended from.

III. FROM NOVELIST TO POET

For Hardy, to be a thinking man in a post-Romantic age was to have to give up the idea of being Michael Henchard. Let us now see what that involved.

It involved his saying to himself, my character is my fate, but how far also can I help being me? He was caught in a double bind; on the one hand thinking, I am fated to be me; on the other, it is still by definition I who make my fate. And even if I only partly make it, even if Henchard by selling his wife was only partly responsible for the subsequent chain of events, still this leaves Henchard and me free only to know that we are not free—either from ourselves or from the force of circumstances. When a woman let him down, Hardy had to suspend his right to resentment, writing, in the poem 'A Broken Appointment', 'love alone can lend you loyalty'. He needed from her the love he wanted to demand *before* he could ever demand it as of right; and if he did have it, he did not need to demand it; and if he did not have it, he could not demand it. That was life's little irony. Hardy was trapped in it where Henchard was broken by it.

In a book which Hardy read as an introduction to the philosophy of Schopenhauer, James Sully, a disciple of George Eliot, had written of his age: 'We have resolved to measure the value of the world by human feeling' (*Pessimism*, p. 398). But implicit in such latter-day Romanticism were two assumptions: that the world exists for human emotional purpose or it has no purpose; that human feeling is a just and trustworthy measure of human concerns. The fallacies within this Romantic expectation, argued Sully, doomed post-Romanticism to end in depressed pessimism. For being relative, Sully said, emotions were unreliable measures of a man's essential condition:

> there is a constant tendency to measure the dimensions of any given feeling not from an absolute zero-point, but

from the point of our most frequent, customary and habitual emotional states.

Ibid., p. 276.

'Am I happier or unhappier now?' was a question more of mood than of knowledge since what a person took as the norm against which he measured the increase or decrease of happiness was itself idiosyncratic and temperamental. This worked against any simple notion of an individual being able to make a philosophy of life out of his own personal experience.

Although he had read the book, Hardy also came to recognize in himself how emotions tormented a person with apparently absolute messages which yet he knew to be only relative to himself. Emotion, moreover, was a fallen and unstable substitute for a lost absolute and suffered at its own hands accordingly:

> reminiscence is less an endowment than a disease, and . . . expectation in its only comfortable form—that of absolute faith—is practically an impossibility; whilst in the form of hope and the secondary compounds, patience, impatience, resolve, curiousity, it is a constant fluctuation between pleasure and pain.
>
> *Far from the Madding Crowd*, chap. xxv, p. 188.

This is a world of secular compounds—hoping against hope, expecting disappointment, pessimism trying to pay for the fear of still desiring happiness, remembering as a guilty debt for not foreseeing. In secondary compounds and second thoughts, a man lost himself compromisingly as Henchard never quite had.

Yet it is evident that Hardy as a young man had begun by resolving, like any Romantic, to measure the world by his feelings rather than be shamed into apologizing for his personal emotions.

> He constitutionally shrank from the business of social advancement, caring for life as an emotion rather than for life as a science of climbing.
>
> Florence Emily Hardy: *The Life of Thomas Hardy*, p. 53.

what happened was that Hardy applied himself to architectural work during the winter 1871–2 more steadily than he had ever done in his life before . . . determined to stifle his constitutional tendency to care for life only as an emotion and not as a scientific game.

Ibid., p. 87.

He perceived that he was 'up against' the position of having to carry on his life not as an emotion, but as a scientific game; that he was committed by circumstances to novel-writing as a regular trade, as much as he had formerly been to architecture.

Ibid., p. 104.

The social world, to which he was tied by the necessities of finance if nothing else, demanded prudence. Virtually from the beginning of his career Hardy believed that a person who wished to be above such prudential considerations and to live life as an emotion rather than as a scientific game would be a poet rather than a novelist. Why?

Partly because novel-writing was still conceived of as 'trade', while poetry was the voice of the solitary feeling soul. But partly also because the novelist's relativism involved recognizing how difficult it was to retain an uncompromised clarity of emotional life. This led Hardy to consider his own novel-writing as a bitterly scientific game. Consider, as illustrative explanation, the juxtaposition of two passages from *Far from the Madding Crowd* (1874).

At the end of chapter xxxv there is the following description of two unsuccessful lovers of Bathsheba Everdene:

Gabriel, for a minute, rose above his own grief in noticing Boldwood's. He saw the square figure sitting erect upon the horse, the head turned to neither side, the elbows steady by the hips, the brim of the hat level and undisturbed in its onward glide, until the keen edges of Boldwood's shape sank by degrees over the hill. To one who knew the man and his story there was something more striking in this immobility than in a collapse. The clash of discord between mood and matter here was forced painfully home to the heart; and, as in laughter

there are more dreadful phases than in tears, so was there
in the steadiness of the agonized man an expression deeper
than a cry.

Far from the Madding Crowd, chap. xxxv, p. 253.

There is in this an emotional convention of the nineteenth-
century humanist novel. Telescoping summary, making
Boldwood into 'this agonized man', constitutes the sort of
temporary definitiveness that pulls a book together at a chapter
end in sympathetic memory of the way its protagonists have
travelled.[10] Hardy's distinctive contribution to this convention
lies in his feeling for 'the clash between mood and matter',
such that the novel indeed opens up humanity here:

> If all hearts were open and all desires known—as they
> would be if people showed their souls—how many gapings,
> sighings, clenched fists, knotted brows, broad grins, and
> red eyes should we see in the market-place!

The Life of Thomas Hardy, pp. 342–3.

—but, as Gabriel Oak sees it, the opening of Boldwood's heart
is still enclosed within him. The novel is an art of inference
channelled from author to reader via Gabriel looking at his
own sorrow in another despised lover: 'one who knew the man
and his story'. Boldwood's powerful feeling is out of step with
the steady indifference of time, whose rhythm his horse seems
to follow: what the novel does is give that inner emotion, so out
of step with time, a moment of its own out of the novel's
artistic time. Yet the key phrase in our passage is the hidden
warning against the hope of redemption: 'Gabriel, for a minute'.
For juxtaposed against that single minute of indirect insight is
another, later minute seemingly incapable of learning from
what was previous to it. Chapter xxxviii shows in Hardy's
sense of the novel a realistic, sceptical capacity to forget as well
as remember:

> 'I thought my mistress would have married you,' said
> Gabriel, not knowing enough of the full depths of
> Boldwood's love to keep silence on the farmer's account,
> and determined not to evade discipline by doing so on his
> own.

Far from the Madding Crowd, chap. xxxviii, p. 270.

'Experience *un*teaches' said Hardy (*The Life of Thomas Hardy*, p. 176); time's defeasibility rules over all the human resolves, insights and hopes that we should prefer to think of as permanent. Gabriel Oak had an idea of the trouble but even in having an idea, as well as a similar trouble, knew it not. Such a situation in the novel creates an ironic point of view just outside or above the situation itself—creates it from the spectacle of hearts open in this novelistic market-place yet in the world which the novel describes closed to each other. With the author, the reader's memory has the privilege and pain of seeing how, within the inadvertent partialities of human relativism, the one scene, from chapter xxxv, is *paid out* by the other, three chapters later.

> human existence, far from bearing the character of a *gift*, has entirely the character of a *debt* that has been contracted. The calling in of this debt appears in the form of the pressing wants, tormenting desires, and endless misery established through this existence. As a rule, the whole lifetime is devoted to the paying off of this debt; but this only meets the interest. The payment of the capital takes place through death. And when was this debt contracted? At the begetting.[11]

These are the words of that great German pessimist, read by Hardy, Schopenhauer. There can be no doubt that Hardy gained artistic power from the formal coincidence between the pessimist's feeling that a person has to pay for his life and the craftsman's view that a scene in a novel has to pay, then and later, for the space which it takes up. The craftsman even allowed the pessimist to revenge himself covertly upon life, including hurting his own readers. Yet what finally worried Hardy about this arrangement of scenes for the sake of a bitter scientific game was, I think, the problem of who paid for the novelist's power. The characters in the novel paid, the readers of the novel paid, but something in the partial detachment of the novelist did not pay. As a novelist writing ostensibly about another person, Hardy seemed able to convince himself of a humanist duty to bring out the emotions that the world tended to keep in hiding within a person. Yet at the same time, that duty was exercised by creating the character's loneliness and thus leaning on the reader's sympathy. For all the satisfactions of revenge, there was in this procedure something that was for Hardy a form of evasion. The novel did not really tell what it felt like to be Boldwood or to be Gabriel Oak; at the expense of these characters' failure to know each other or to acknowledge themselves, the novel created vicarious emotion in between the characters. The novelist wrote out of self-dispersal, splitting himself between the characters, and the reader read to find a vicarious emotion and an overall, if ironic, understanding which he, no more than any one of the characters, could not really embody in his own physical, rather than aesthetic, life. For this reason, angry with his readers and with the George Eliot idea of the novel, even as he wrote, Hardy had finally to turn from novel writing to confront through some form of autobiography the problems which he had evaded through the novelist's self-dispersal.

Although Hardy wrote poetry throughout his life, he was primarily a novelist until 1895 and after *Jude the Obscure* was exclusively a poet. I do not believe that the change was merely circumstantial, dictated by the harsh reception of *Jude*. For the dates are significant when on 6 January 1917 Hardy noted, as a poet now, as follows: 'I find I wrote in 1888 that "Art is concerned with seemings only", which is true' (*The Life of Thomas Hardy*, p. 374). The novels of the seventies, eighties and nineties, that is to say, had trafficked in 'seemings', like Gabriel's inference about Boldwood, and had profited from the balance of feeling that arose even from the incompleteness of such inferences. What, in the name of responsibility and guilt, Hardy required of himself after 1895 was an art which went on to bear the consequences which the novelist laid upon and between his characters, an art which paid directly and autobiographically for what the novel had gained from self-dispersal and displacement. Thus on the death of Emma, Hardy's first wife:

> It was your way, my dear,
> To vanish without a word
> When callers, friends, or kin
> Had left, and I hastened in
> To rejoin you as I inferrred. . . .

So, now that you disappear
For ever in that swift style,
Your meaning seems to me
Just as it used to be:
'Good-bye is not worth while!'
'Without Ceremony', CP 282.[12]

The poet here takes over on his own account the position of
'seeming' which the detachedly implicated novelist witnessed
between Oak and Boldwood. 'Your meaning seems to me': on
the one hand, it hurts loneliness that her 'meaning' is only
'seeming' and, 'without a word', can never now be verified; on
the other hand, the unverifiable meaning, 'not worth while', if
extended seriously to the whole meaning of their marriage,
would hurt, he knows, even more if it could be verified as truly
her view. Compromised between these two forms of painful
emotion, Hardy could not know whether his wife's habitual
and final omission of the demonstration of domestic affection
really covered a marital tragedy; or was itself too small to be
worth bothering over; or was even a way of hers to be
remembered affectionately as merely characteristic. Hardy was
a man who made over the years a series of mental accommodations of his powerful emotions, 'dying, so to speak, before
one is out of the flesh' (*The Life of Thomas Hardy*, p. 209): thus

. . . is it that, though whiling
The time somehow
In walking, talking, smiling,
I live not now.
'The Dead Man Walking', CP 166.

He covered over his Henchard-like emotions until his emotions
became buried in, and only revived by, his memory. 'To think
of life as passing away is a sadness; to think of it as past is
at least tolerable' (*The Life of Thomas Hardy*, p. 210). Hardy
was a man who had to make tolerable the thought that his
wife, from life even to death, seemed to suppose 'Good-bye is
not worth while'. Equivalently, taking his part from hers,
Hardy, by 'whiling' the time, had given up or forfeited the
little touches of a wife's affection without his being able—or

willing—to know whether that absence 'seemed' more like
casualness than deliberate withdrawal. He learned to shrug
and play the game, 'not worth while'. The game was the one
that human beings were obliged to play in order to become
resilient about the emotional goals they desire but cannot
expect to attain— Goethe explained it thus in his *Autobiography*:

> So much which belongs to us inwardly we must not
> develop outwardly; what we require from outside for the
> completion of our being is withdrawn from us; on the
> other hand, so much is forced upon us which is as foreign
> as it is burdensome to us. . . .
>
> To solve this problem, however, Nature has endowed
> man with rich power, activity, and toughness. But
> especially does lightheartedness come to his aid, for this is
> given to him inalienably; by means of this he is capable of
> renouncing the particular thing every moment, if only at
> the next moment he can reach out to something new: and
> so, unconsciously, we keep restoring our whole life. We
> put one passion in the place of another; occupation,
> inclination, tastes and hobbies, we try them all, only to
> exclaim at last, 'All is Vanity'.[13]

Hardy had shown that he knew all about that sequence of
linear replacement in his novels—Henchard

> experienced not only the bitterness of a man who finds, in
> looking back upon an ambitious course, that what he has
> sacrificed in sentiment was worth as much as what he had
> gained in substance; but the superadded bitterness of
> seeing his very recantation nullified. He had been sorry
> for all this long ago; but his attempts to replace ambition
> by love had been as fully foiled as his ambition itself.
>
> *The Mayor of Casterbridge*, chap. xliv, p. 319.

Ambition, turning on second thought to love only for love to
turn away from ambition, was left at the end in limbo,
redundant—'All is Vanity'.

Hardy had in many ways put his own troubles, imaginatively
made larger and clearer, into his tragic novels. A critic, his
own friend Edmund Gosse, had in 1896 made explicit the
protest of a whole section of the Victorian public, in wondering

aloud at the hidden autobiographical impulse that seemingly could alone account for Hardy's writing thus tragically:

> What has Providence done to Mr Hardy that he should rise up in the arable land of Wessex and shake his fist at his Creator?[14]

In his poetry, half in outward aggression but half in inner, depressive uncertainty, he virtually replied to such criticism:

> And nothing is much the matter; there are many
>   smiles to a tear;
> Then what is the matter is I, I say. Why should
>   such an one be here?
>   'In Tenebris ii', CP 137.

If they were going to try to pull his imagination and philosophy down to a matter of his own circumstances and memory, all right he would follow and lead them down there: the consequence was his personal poetry. When he reflected on the possibility that his novel work had been a compensation for his troubles, Hardy knew that sooner or later he would come to think of himself in relation to his writing even as Henchard, in the passage above, had finally to think of what he had made of himself in his marriage and work. I am not saying that the novels are no more than autobiographical images, objective correlatives; on the contrary, I shall be arguing that after writing the tragic novels Hardy became in his life and work almost an image of *them*. To Hardy, I think his novel work became an act not so much of justice in an unjust world as hubris. If the circumstantial consideration of human troubles tended to belittle their essential elements, it was justice to lift these troubles imaginatively into the larger person of a Michael Henchard. Yet, even so, Hardy also felt that what the work had gained in substance from his own troubles would have to be paid for, just as Henchard's ambition had had to come to a final reckoning. His poetry would now be his personal payment for his tragic presumption—even at the risk of that effort, if not recantation, proving finally to be vain too. For there was no compensation that would not have to be paid back, there was no final exorcism for those who tried even by writing to restore or replace their lives. 'We try them all,' Goethe had said of such expedients, 'only to exclaim at last, "All is Vanity"':

All was, alas, worse than vanity—injustice, punishment, exaction, death. The wife of Angel Clare put her hand to her brow, and felt its curve, and the edges of her eye-sockets, perceptible under the soft skin, and thought as she did so that a time would come when the bone would be bare.

Tess of the d'Urbervilles, Phase the Fifth, chap. xli, p. 301.

This is an image of what the tragic novels, in Hardy's imagination, think of themselves. Even this, the tragic writing about life, is fiction, just like 'Justice' is for Tess. Their plots fleshed out with realism, the novels are still stripped bare by the reality which says that what is imagined in these pages will come to dust, even as they themselves describe. The tragic presumption, Hardy's response to his nineteenth-century inheritance, had itself to be paid for, personally, by Hardy not only in his life but also in his later, more acknowledgedly personal writing.

For, notoriously, Hardy was not what Goethe said human beings almost had to be if they had not faith—light-hearted, for the sake of emotional survival. And it was when he took his alternative tactic of 'whiling' into his verse that he had most to recognize that 'whiling', though temporarily sane, was finally intolerable. For him the composition of poetry had enough traditional authority in defence of the human soul to forbid writing being yet another form of distraction. 'It bridges over the years to think that Gray might have seen Wordsworth in his cradle, and Wordsworth might have seen me in mine' (*The Life of Thomas Hardy*, p. 386). Wordsworth knew it was vital for a person to remain in touch with his own inner, forgotten world, otherwise he lived in fragments of himself from one moment to the next. Probably only writing enabled a person sustainedly to remind him of himself, to remind him 'that we are greater than we know'. For Hardy, however, it was also true that such access to himself was going to hurt in uncovering all that he had felt obliged to bury within himself. He could not through writing live in his memory in the way that Wordsworth had, as we saw in Part I. Indeed, as we shall see, it is a mark of the movement of the nineteenth century recorded in this book that Hardy, unable to live easily in his memory,

had to write a poetry that made that feared memory spring out
at him—making writing and memory an enemy necessary for
the sake of one's real life, yet still not that life's support and
friend.

For Hardy his emotions had been forced back into his
memory, he only felt after the event. Can the poetry of memory
tell us what had made him write tragically and, more, why he
had given up writing tragedy in prose for autobiography in
verse? On the face of it when we put to the verse Gosse's
question, what had happened to Hardy, what was the matter
with him, the answer seems to be nothing, nothing unusual,
nothing in particular:

> And nothing is much the matter . . .
> > 'In Tenebris ii', CP 137.
>
> I lightly: 'There's nothing in it. For you anyhow!'
> > 'Near Lanivet, 1872', CP 366.
>
> And nothing was left . . .
> —Well; she knew nothing thereof did she survive,
> And suffered nothing if numbered among the dead.
> > 'The Photograph', CP 405.
>
> . . . to keep down grief
> I would not turn my head to discover
> > That there was nothing in my belief.
> > > 'The Shadow on the Stone', CP 483.

The first thought, the depressively reticent front, that Hardy
offered to the world out of evasiveness as well as depression
was—nothing, nothing uncommon, nothing worth mentioning.
He would point to nothing to explain himself. Yet, even in
that, forced to the back of his mind was the fear that he could
point to nothing, at his most serious. Tess had asked Angel
Clare whether they would meet again after death: 'Like a
greater man than himself, to the critical question at the critical
time he did not answer; and they were again silent' (*Tess of the
d'Urbervilles*, Phase the Seventh, chap. lviii, p. 417). That a
man of words will at his own final summing up be speechless,
for all his literary life, was Hardy's fear as surely as, through
Marlow, it was Conrad's in *The Heart of Darkness*:

'I have wrestled with death. It is the most unexciting contest you can imagine. It takes place in an impalpable greyness, with nothing underfoot, with nothing around, without spectators, without clamour, without glory, without the great fear of defeat, in a sickly atmosphere of tepid scepticism, without much belief in your own right, and still less in that of your adversary. . . . I was within a hair's breadth of the last opportunity for pronouncement, and I found with humiliation that probably I would have nothing to say. This is the reason why I affirm that Kurtz was a remarkable man. He had something to say. He said it. . . . He had summed up—he had judged. "The horror!"'[15]

Hardy feared that he would not be Henchard at the end but someone greyer, and the poetry embodies this realization. The last cry will not manage a cry of tragedy—'The horror' of Nothing—but will have been diminished long beforehand into a sense of nothing without speech, rights or past feelings. And this will be the consequence of learning Henchard's lesson and accommodating one's individuality to the reality principle— or, in Hardy's terms, pessimism:

Pessimism (or rather what is called such) is, in brief, playing the sure game. You cannot lose at it; you may gain. It is the only view of life in which you can never be disappointed. Having reckoned what to do in the worst possible circumstances, when better arise, as they may, life becomes child's play.

The Life of Thomas Hardy, p. 311.

Hardy could see how, having been made to learn to expect disappointment, he had almost deliberately turned himself, as it were, back to front. In tackling the question of what he was if he was not Kurtz or Henchard, the poetry took his back-to-front stance and still found the old emotional front, that he had ceased to present to the world, in memory behind his words:

> Your meaning seems to me
> Just as it used to be:
> 'Good-bye is not worth while!'

On the face of it, 'just as it used to be' is her casualness and his acceptance of it. And yet to the memory behind the face, there is also the saddening recognition that things from now on can never be just as they used to be—a recognition that gives Emma's voice an echo in Hardy's lonely mind. 'Just as it used to be,' the widower hears himself writing: an echo charged equally with real bitterness (just as it used to be, even at the last you couldn't say it, couldn't, wouldn't leave me with anything) and with guilty grief (even at the end it was just as it used to be, the unhappy marriage, not enough love, given to me or deserved by me, to make it 'worth while' for you). That echo is poetry's taking seriously the casual word 'just' in deeper memory of justice. Thus, if in Hardy's dying before he was out of the flesh, the game had been to take a novelist's back-seat to his own experience, as if it were that of another person whom the novelist observed, the self-revenging seriousness was:

> 'that I have a faculty (possibly not uncommon) for burying an emotion in my heart or brain for forty years, and exhuming it at the end of that time as fresh as when interred.'

> *The Life of Thomas Hardy*, p. 378.

'Not worth while': in life he had buried the inference, distracted himself from it; in poetry the echo of its meaning had been revived behind his own words; finally the memory would have to be paid for and the echo surface again in life—just over a month before his death:

> 'Speaking about ambition T. said to-day that he had done all that he meant to do, but he did not know whether it had been worth doing.'

> Ibid., p. 444.

'Not worth while'. Memory came back upon him as if, in defence of permanence and fidelity, to atone for the game by which his emotions had replaced each other in the interests of temporising survival. Echo, the deeper meaning of the outward sound, the haunting ghost, did not work for Hardy as it did for Wordsworth, as an intimation of immortality; on the contrary, it was in memory of mortality's fears, as Tolstoy shows in his account of the dying lawyer Ivan Ilyich:

'What is it you want?' was the first clear conception capable of expressive words that he heard. 'What is it you want? What is it you want?' he repeated to himself.

'What do I want? Not to suffer. To live,' he answered. And again he listened with such concentrated attention that even his pain did not distract him.

'To live. Live how?' asked his inner voice . . . 'Live as you lived in court when the usher boomed out: "The Court sits! The Court sits!" . . .'

'The Court sits, the Court sits!' he repeated to himself. 'Here's my sentence. But I am not guilty!' he shrieked in fury. 'What is it for?' And he left off crying but, turning his face to the wall, fell to pondering one and the same question: Why, and wherefore, all this horror?

But however much he pondered he could find no answer. And when the thought occurred to him, as it often did, that it all came of his not having lived as he ought to have lived, he at once recalled the orderliness of his life and dismissed so strange an idea.[16]

'He did not know whether it had been worth doing.' At eighty-seven Hardy was not only still uncertain; the uncertainty, like a form of judgment, was drawing closer.

You might think that if a man spends his life not as a lawyer but as a writer, writing to a large extent in memory of his own living, the questions has my writing been worth doing? and has my life been worth living? double the intensity of the final question, have I lived as I ought to have lived? And yet if the writer guiltily fears that his writing about his living gained a power more in memory of its mistakes and pains than in reclamation of them, then plausibly he might feel only half a right to question a life that his writing already profited from by questioning. Somewhere between these two possibilities—his questions both doubled and halved by his writing—Thomas Hardy was stuck. On the face of it a literary man to whom a tragedy happens—what we commonly call a 'tragedy', say the death of a wife—ought, if he can survive it as a person, to have more ready-made means than another to treat his tragedy as a tragedy in writing. For a tragedy is not just the occurrence of something terrible and fatal; it is also a literary genre—yet the genre in which literature tries most seriously to close the gap between itself and the terrible reality of what can happen outside. But suppose that the wife who dies is a woman whom the man once loved, has ceased to love and now remembers both loving and not loving. And suppose too that the man most eligible to make literary tragedy feels precisely on those grounds of professional eligibility, of all life being potential grist to his literary mill, a massive, hubristic compunction. Then we have Thomas Hardy, the poet.

For the poetry, in taking tragedy out of Hardy's writing, also stored tragedy up for his life. For example, Hardy stood lonely, supported only by the discipline of being a poet, at the entrance of Max Gate at eighty-four:

> A car comes up, with lamps full-glare
> > That flash upon a tree:
> > It has nothing to do with me,
> And whangs along in a world of its own,
> > Leaving a blacker air;
> And mute by the gate I stand again alone,
> > And nobody pulls up there.
>
> 'Nobody Comes', CP 715.

'It has nothing to do with me': on the habitual, professional face of it, that line accepts the quotidian necessity and teaches his disappointment not to think of indifference necessarily as neglect. It is the self-corrective of one who has been a novelist, for we have seen in her *Autobiography* how, likewise, Mrs Oliphant exercised prosaic second thoughts against her own emotional Romanticism and sense of heroism. Yet, as with Tess feeling beneath her skin the bone, this line still has beneath it a poetic echo of the words of resigned sadness. 'Nothing to do with me':

> 'January (1899). No man's poetry can be truly judged till its last line is written. What is the last line? The death of the poet.'
>
> *The Life of Thomas Hardy*, p. 302.

The last line of Hardy's poetry was this, its final echo which, just before publication, Florence Emily Hardy, the second wife, decided to cut from *The Life:*—

Hardy remained unconscious until a few minutes before the end. Shortly after nine he died, when a few broken sentences, one of them heartrending in its poignancy, showed that his mind had reverted to a sorrow of the past.

The Personal Notebooks of Thomas Hardy, p. 287.

In memory of a sorrow of the past, I think one of Hardy's broken sentences was 'Not worth while' and another was that people, including his wives, really had 'nothing to do with me'. As if Kurtz had broken through Marlow at the end. If I am right, was not this the final emotional revenge of that part of him that earlier had written tragedy upon the poet who wrote pretending 'He Never Expected Much'?

If that is so, does not this consequence of the locked impotence of the poetry of memory for the very life of Thomas Hardy show why we need a strong, impersonal art, a big seriousness like tragedy defended by imagination from the personal implications of memory? I tried to show in Part I how Wordsworth made strenuous poetic efforts in order that memory and imagination should be related by something more than antithesis. But we have already seen how, partly for historical partly for temperamental reasons, Hardy's situation was far more embattled in his writing than Wordsworth's had been. Now at any rate, far on in the nineteenth-century post-Romantic tradition, was it not the case that Hardy needed something—like the art of *The Mayor of Casterbridge*—or someone—like the imagination of a figure like Michael Henchard—to speak *for* him and not leave him immersed in his silenced littleness?

Something like this, for instance: the journey of Fanny Robin in chapter xl of *Far from the Madding Crowd*, where she drags herself from pillar to post towards that Union-House which, at journey's end, gives her only the ironic rest of death, that last line of all which the poetry could not articulate.

> Holding to the rails, she advanced, thrusting one hand forward upon the rail, then the other, then leaning over it whilst she dragged her feet on beneath.
>
> This woman was not given to soliloquy; but extremity of feeling lessens the individuality of the weak, as it increases that of the strong. She said again in the same

tone, 'I'll believe that the end lies five posts forward, and no further, and so get strength to pass them.'

This was a practical application of the principle that a half-feigned and fictitious faith is better than no faith at all.

She passed five posts and held on to the fifth.

'I'll pass five more by believing my longed-for spot is at the next fifth. I can do it.'

She passed five more.

'It lies only five further.'

She passed five more.

'But it is five further.'

She passed them.

'That stone bridge is the end of my journey,' she said, when the bridge over the Froom was in view.

She crawled to the bridge. During the effort each breath of the woman went into the air as if never to return again.

'Now for the truth of the matter,' she said, sitting down. 'The truth is, that I have less than half a mile.'

Far from the Madding Crowd, chap. xl, p. 278.

'Less': how much more that seems than less. For in those repetitions what Fanny Robin is counting on to help her make her way is at the self-same time what Hardy the novelist counts as the blows that helped kill her. 'Five further . . . five further'. The novel was for Hardy *his* form of 'fictitious faith' that enabled him to get trouble moving, to make trouble moving, to journey towards a catharsis that life itself hardly allowed, to tell 'the truth of the matter'. By a fictive sense of progress Hardy himself, alongside Fanny Robin imaginatively, could squeeze the last ounce of strength out of his own weaknesses, both hammering himself and taking his own blows.

And yet, I say, this writing came to seem to Hardy not to be 'the truth of he matter'. The truth was this, as he stood before his own mirror:

> I look into my glass,
> And view my wasting skin,
> And say, 'Would God it came to pass
> My heart had shrunk as thin!'
> 'I Look Into My Glass', CP 52.

'Pass' there is not allowed to have its way at the line-ending. It was not only that life and the life in his own heart would not let him pass:

> . . . O! let him pass; he hates him
> That would upon the rack of this tough world
> Stretch him out longer.
>
> *King Lear,* Act v, scene iii, 312–4.

But life too would not allow him to push on, like Fanny Robin, as though there were some physical journey to make, some destination to aim one's life towards. All the personal meaning lodged in that desire to 'pass' at the line-ending is thrown back off the prison wall of rhymes and rebounds back inside the poem to what is confined within it, namely Hardy's own heart:

> . . . 'Would God it came to PASS
> My HEART had shrunk as thin!'

That is how on the rebound Hardy took to heart the meaning of himself that, in writing, he now saw again before his eyes. That indeed was how Hardy was able to disinter himself within his poetry: he needed obstacles, like the resistance of rhyme, like the resistance of life itself, in order to find the countervailing strength that was himself, though so long buried at the back of his mind. As life would not let him pass, so his own memory could not let his life go easily past. He could not but recall how life had always baulked and frustrated him by obstacles (mimed by the placing of 'pass') set at a point earlier than the end-point to which he, or his sentences, were looking forward:

> Oct 30 1870 Mother's notion, & also mine: That a figure stands in our van with arm uplifted, to knock us back from any pleasant prospect we indulge in as probable.
>
> *The Personal Notebooks of Thomas Hardy,* p. 6.

—even the not customarily pleasant prospect of death. 'Five further . . . five further' he wrote of Fanny Robin in the 1870s; but it must have felt to Hardy in the 1890s, looking into his glass, that he passed his own life throbbing like that, five further in his own heart. To 'get strength to pass', Hardy in his own mind felt not much better off than his own imagination of Fanny Robin on her way. His own mind is where the novels *came from,* but is what the poems, more, were to *express.* His own poems became to him like Fanny Robin's five posts: the merely temporary support that got him through his time. For his mind had to hang on to mental rails, like rhyme, in order to get by; the poetry acting as support only in so far as also acting as obstacle, his words steadying him enough to enable their meanings to shake his heart. This was the reality behind the metaphor of Fanny Robin's journey, this was that reality brought home, taken to heart, this was how Hardy became an image of his own earlier tragic writings, in the reality of his own life. Hardy found that what it cost him, in small, to 'pass' from one line of his poem to the next and drag articulation out was not so very different from what had been seen in large in the extremes of his novels. And if you counter by saying that at the turn of the century Hardy's situation was actually much safer than that of his past, fictional characters, my reply is that such safety had its own terrors—in bearing the more extended and lonely reality of sorrow being much less heroic and cathartic than the tragic novels suggest.—

> Thus I; faltering forward,
> Leaves around me falling,
> Wind oozing thin through the thorn from norward
> And the woman calling.
>
> 'The Voice', CP 285.

In those words which hang together with the ghost of a syntax, there is something very like the staggering steps of Fanny Robin. These are Hardy's 'broken sentences', the pains of memory that would surface again at his death when he was finally free of the day-to-day necessity to work them into acceptable sentence and form. For it is not that the poems are really smaller than the large, imaginative tragedies; rather, they pull those large tragedies down into physically small, intimately tested and personally felt tight-spots; the poems deliberately decreasing the space available for expression in order to increase the pressure that releases large meanings. The poems, though emphatically not able to enjoy the freedom to make up a long poem of memory like *The Prelude,* are nonetheless not really small because, as creative prisons, they include within them the memory of the man who wrote them. That is to say, the memory of how it felt to write and take seriously one's own words: that feeling of writing them when they embodied the meaning of a man's life suffered and stored over years. True, these poems, nagging rather than cathartic, could not exorcise the ghosts that haunted Hardy finally on his death-bed. But Hardy had virtually accepted that as the cost of more directly shaking his memory and his heart by writing poetry. For all his work of imagination, Hardy finally wanted a work of memory—not Henchard but himself and less space, less freedom even, for the sake of more, personally witnessed, truth. In my view, for the first time since Wordsworth (albeit in a way less free, more painful and more religiously fallen than Wordsworth's), Hardy brought back into English poetry an intimate connection between the poet's technique and the man's human heart. A connection made through memory, as I have here described it.

The way that Hardy's poetry could pull out of itself buried echoes is entirely distinctive. If for Hardy it was finally poetry that mattered and not fiction, it was a poetry that had come through the novel whose predominance had forced it back. Out of being forced back in status, out of finding emotional thoughts also forced back in the unpoetic post-Romantic age that Matthew Arnold complained of, Hardy's poetry found a power on second thought to bring personally-held emotion forward again. I believe that this was the only way for emotion to be won back by poetry without evading the demands of nineteenth-century realism. For that is why I have turned to Hardy as poet in this book rather than to Browning or Arnold or Tennyson; and that is why the shape of this book had to be from poetry in part I to prose in part II before Hardy used prose to win back poetry.

But perhaps I may briefly summarize my reasons for thinking Tennyson's poetic effort a failure which would side-track my present purposes. It is clear from the writings of J. S. Mill and G. H. Lewes on the nature of poetry that many Victorians conceived of poetry in the age of the realistic novel as a defence of feeling and the soul within the solitude of the individual. Poetry threatened to retreat into solitude, if not solipsism, to become a rural and religious backwater in the world of the 1830s and 1840s. Tennyson's own closest friend, Arthur Hallam, reviewing Tennyson's poetry in 1831 in terms of the general state of modern poetry, noted the predominance of poetry of sensation, after Keats and Shelley, rather than poetry of reflection, after Wordsworth: tears, idle tears, one might say, rather than thoughts that lay too deep for them. The concentration on the sensuously beautiful, lamented Hallam, was no longer one part of the whole poetic disposition; it had become a part that now had to stand in defence of the whole in an age where poetry itself was not in harmony with the general movement of society. Hence, said Hallam, the melancholy of modern poetry: melancholy, that the part now has to stand for the whole, itself becomes the strategic, substitutive whole in such poetry, and it is even more self-collusively depressed for not being fooled by its own device. Victorian poetry is filled by these vicious circles of pining at pining, with all those contradictions of a half pleasurable, half unbearable sadness.[17]

Now what is almost shocking to record is that the problems in Tennyson's verse diagnosed as characteristic of the age by Hallam could only reach successful expression, in a fully human way, in the poem that Tennyson wrote on Hallam's death. For in *In Memoriam* the melancholy has a real, but absent, subject to fill a sense of absence which Tennyson's poetry already had before Hallam's death. Weeping in solitude, the unpoetic age might say, was of no use; but now the poetry of Tennyson could weep at the knowledge that tears did not avail: 'O sorrow, then can sorrow wane?/O grief, can grief be changed to less?' (*In Memoriam*, lxxviii, 15–16). These echoes are emphatically Tennysonian, they are quite unlike Hardy's. 'O last regret, regret can die!' (ibid., 17): the last regret now has to come first, a replacement presiding over the memory of what it has been; the secondary thing—grief over the ways of grief—is shocked to find itself become primary, like a dead echo mourning in front of what, it recalls, used to be a living word, and wondering whether its very mourning helped to kill it. Hardy's echoes, you recall, were forced backwards in an utterly opposite way. But the diction here is (what Hallam called rhyme) 'the recurrence of termination', echo on echo, making up not a genuine long poem of memory like *The Prelude* but a self-enclosed continuity of lyrics which protect themselves in a way that Hardy's poetry does not, in admitting its broken-ness. To summarize my reasons thus is, I realize, to be less than just to Tennyson in particular and Victorian poetry in general. But this verse of aesthetic as well as anaesthetic last regret is at the end of an emotional line, is a dead-end for Keatsianism.

In my view, it is neither Clough nor Browning who are the poets to avoid that dead-end and find a new form for the expression of moral and emotional language; it is Hardy, not least for his having gone through all that the novel meant for poetry in the nineteenth century. Yet not only for that reason. For Hardy's poetic forms were borrowed of course from the Wessex dialect poet William Barnes and a whole provincial tradition of ballad. And in that provincialism Hardy was offering a challenge to Arnold's notion of a high, European art:

> Arnold is wrong about provincialism, if he means anything more than a provincialism of style and manner in exposition. A certain provincialism of feeling is invaluable. It is of the essence of individuality, and is largely made up of that crude enthusiasm without which no great thoughts are thought, no great deeds done.
>
> *The Life of Thomas Hardy*, pp. 146–7.

Hardy's provincialism of feeling amounted to an attack on what this book takes to be Arnold's quite false notions of 'centrality' as established within *Culture and Anarchy*: sweetness and light, freedom, disinterestedness, a detachment from practical life and from the puritan rigours of conscience. Hardy, even more perhaps than George Eliot, was a puritan in Arnold's sense, a Hebrew to whom the world was a struggle or a prison, rather than an Arnoldian Greek, a noble being freely at home in the whole of a spiritually nourishing world. And what Hardy set against Arnold's theory of culture—a theory which anticipates so much of T. S. Eliot's view of impersonality and the classic—is an art of personal memory rooted in his life and geography. This, from Wordsworth to Lawrence, is the alternative view with which I am here concerned in all its variations.

But for the present we must consider further Hardy's distinctive poetry of memory, in our next section, in order to see if this poetry, the nearest to his own heart that the man could get, can answer Gosse's question, what was the matter with Hardy?

IV. THOMAS HARDY AS POET:
'THE OTHER SIDE OF COMMON EMOTIONS'

On 17 July 1868 Hardy, looking forward, had written in his notebook

> 'Perhaps I can do a volume of poems consisting of the *other side* of common emotions.'
>
> Florence Emily Hardy: The Life of Thomas Hardy, p. 58.

After this note, another hand, perhaps Florence Emily's but more likely Hardy's own in his role as his own editor, added, 'What this means is not quite clear'. If these were Hardy's own words, it is hard to know how to take them: are they deviously reticent? are they wryly and ironically amused? Whatever they are, it is still possible to make clearer what he had meant in 1868.

Hardy stood before the strong, rhymed frames of his verse even as he stood before a mirror, in that sense on the other side of common emotions:

> I look into my glass,
> And view my wasting skin,
> And say, 'Would God it came to pass
> My heart had shrunk as thin!'
>
> For then, I, undistrest
> By hearts grown cold to me,
> Could lonely wait my endless rest
> With equanimity.
>
> But Time, to make me grieve,
> Part steals, lets part abide;
> And shakes this fragile frame at eve
> With throbbings of noontide.
>
> 'I Look Into My Glass', CP 52.

It is as if Hardy had to work at himself from 'the other side' of invention, not freely invoking words so much as forcing himself

to discover them with a release of meaning equivalent to that
of uncovering the repressions of memory.[18] The empirical
Scottish philosopher admired by Mill, Thomas Brown, had
written thus of rhymes:

> from the accidental agreement of their mere verbal signs,
> conceptions arise which otherwise would not have arisen,
> and consequently, trains of reflection altogether different.
> Our *thoughts*, which usually govern our language, are
> themselves also in a great measure *governed* in this way,
> by the very language over which they seem to exercise
> unlimited command.[19]

Words are sounds as well as meanings. The accidents of
rhymes, indifferent in themselves to what they mean, were
almost like accidents of fate to Hardy, if he could manoeuvre
them right against himself: they brought out of a poet, who
had so much to hide, thoughts, tied to words, which, had life
been easier, he would never have admitted. Wordsworth's
balanced action and re-action between language and the
human mind has here given way to something less co-operative,
more combative, in the struggle between technical advent-
itiousness and the essence of a man's life. A Hardy poem is a
provincial craftsman's adventitious siting for what he nonetheless commits himself to as essentially of himself, the right
word coming as the moment of recognition, of remembrance,
when the accidents of sound are made over into the substance
of personal meaning. So, for once, 'With equanimity' fell into
place for Hardy, like grace filling the space left for it. On the
whole rhymes, like 'pass', took power from him rather than
gave him peace. It was only from the other side, in that second
stanza of 'I look into my glass', that he could envisage through
his own sense of being 'distrest' what it might mean to feel
'undistrest'. In a notebook Hardy had written down what
Matthew Arnold had marked out as Goethe's great note of
Romantic freedom:

> 'Through me the German poets have become aware that,
> as man must live from within outwards, so the artist must
> work from within outwards, seeing that make what
> contortions he will, he can only bring to light his own
> individuality.'[20]

But, on the other side of Romanticism, writing, like emotion, was for Hardy achieved on the rebound, a matter for reflection as in a glass: that is to say, proceeding, necessarily for a start, from within outwards, the real work came at the moment of reversal when the thought he owned, on second thought, owned him and could be seen and felt working from without back inwards, shaking him with a reminder of his own power of feeling:

> And shakes this fragile frame at eve
> With throbbings of noontide.

Even by 1898, thirty years before his eventual death, Hardy felt this paradox: an old man shaken but kept alive by the power of a young heart within him. It was typical of Hardy's emotional defensiveness that he wanted the reverse of what most people might want in that position: not a young body to go with that young heart but an older, thinner heart. But the verse kept turning this reversal round, to the other, vulnerable side of himself his pessimism had tried to protect. And characteristically what must have felt to Hardy so much the right word upon his finding it—'throbbings'—dominates the poem no more than, in completing it, it is enclosed still within it, like a heart trapped powerfully within a bodily frame:

> 'I look in my glass. . . . Why should a man's mind have been thrown into such close, sad, sensational, inexplicable relations with such a precarious object as his own body!'
> *The Life of Thomas Hardy*, p. 251.

Yet his verse persists in that relation in a way that his self-dispersing novels did not. Hardy's mind, which reflected back upon the relection of his face in that glass, was amazed to see what Hardy appeared to be to the outside world. Equivalently, in his poetry, his mind positions itself between the words his hand puts down on the paper and the meaning of them that returns upon him to shake his memory-throbbing heart. So when Hardy wrote the word 'lonely', trying rationally to put the case in which he would be 'undistrest' by his own loneliness

> Could lonely wait my endless rest
> With equanimity.—

he must have felt the word turning back emotionally to what he was now—lonely; the word must have spoken, beneath the writing, to his own heart, en passant, even as the rhymed, disciplined writing had to go on past. 'Lonely' now, on 'the other side' of writing, was what he was, without equanimity, in endless unrest; for, unable either to rest or to pass, waiting was, horribly, what he was now doing. The poetry thus has a second, tacitly emotive language beneath its language of reason, a language of second thought and echo personal to its writer. It is that extra dimension, the experiential reality to the writer of the mere words he writes in memory of his condition, that I ask to be taken as part of the meaning of such poetry. For such meaning hangs about the words like a ghost, the other side of what we otherwise take to be merely common emotion; that mere loneliness that otherwise does not seem sufficient warrant to think tragically.

Circumstantially, it seems that nothing happened to Hardy save an unhappy marriage. Yet only the poems written after Emma's death disclose what that might really mean, revealed in retrospect.

> Well, well! All's past amend,
> Unchangeable. It must go.
> I seem but a dead man held on end
> To sink down soon. . . . O you could not know
> That such swift fleeing
> No soul foreseeing—
> Not even I—would undo me so!
>
> 'The Going', CP 277.

'O you could not know . . .' he says of his wife and her desertion by death (had she always meant to leave him?). Suppose we ask his poetry *why* she could not know how badly it would affect him. The first answer is because he could not bear (at a level where it cannot be distinguished whether it is for her sake or for his memory of her) to think of her as one who would want revenge in that way. 'Good-bye is not worth while.' But beneath this common emotion is an echo, a guilty second thought about his own emotion now: she could not know what her death would do to him because he had shown no evidence of love for her or concern about her for years. This *he* could know. Her memory, the memory of her he had, turned him both ways within himself: out towards her, in towards himself; yet the words, both ways, are the same. It is as though Hardy wrote the first with intent, read the second, with shocked acknowledgement, from his own words. 'Not even I—' could have said this—until 'undone' to 'me' by remembering, by writing, and by seeing writing recall even more deeply than a man on his own could bear. We can see in Hardy's verse more than a mere image as it were in a glass—if only because we can also see him looking at it.

This strange relation that Hardy had to his own written words may be illustrated further. Hardy had read something of the work of W. K. Clifford (1845–79), a young Cambridge mathematician who tried to reconcile Hume's empiricism with Kant's Idealism, through the use of Darwin who had demonstrated how empirically acquired characteristics became innate through evolution. The mental world which has emerged out of the material world, argued Clifford, is actually made out of the same stuff as the physical world, only existing, through consciousness, at a different level of being. 'The actions that take place in the brain differ in no way from other material actions, except in their complexity', 'When matter takes the complex form of a living human brain, the corresponding mind-stuff takes the form of a human consciousness, having intelligence and volition' (*Lectures and Essays,* pp. 209, 284). Hardy seems to have been deeply attracted by the idea that there is a parallelism between matter and mind, between mind and body, between brain and mind, made up of the same common stuff existing at different levels of organization. Clifford had offered an analogy for these parallelisms:

> A spoken sentence and the same sentence written are two utterly unlike things, but each of them consists of elements; the spoken sentence of the elementary sounds of the language, the written sentence of its alphabet. Now the relation between the spoken sentence and its elements is very nearly the same as the relation between the written sentence and its elements. There is a correspondence of element to element; although an elementary sound is quite a different thing from a letter of the alphabet, yet each

elementary sound belongs to a certain letter or letters. And the sounds being built up together to form a spoken sentence, the letters are built up together, *in nearly the same way*, to form the written sentence. The two complex products are as wholly unlike as the elements are, but the manner of their complication is the same.

W. K. Clifford: *Lectures and Essays*, pp. 279–80.

The words made out of sounds and the words made out of letters are, moreover, meant to mean 'nearly' the same thing, by definition. What did this mean to Hardy? To Hardy there was just such an analogy, parallelism, isomorphism, between what his hand wrote before his eyes and what, thereby, his memory heard calling behind his forehead: 'O you could not know . . .'. Hardy stared at his hand writing formal words, near yet far,

> And he looks at his hand, and the sun glows through
> > his fingers,
> While he's thinking thoughts
> > 'She Who Saw Not', CP 623.

—and he felt his rhymes begin to lay hold of his mind from outside, from on the page, in a way as strange as that in which the hand seems to feel out the memory in 'Under the Waterfall' (CP 276):

> 'Whenever I plunge my arm, like this,
> In a basin of water, I never miss
> The sweet sharp sense of a fugitive day
> Fetched back from its thickening shroud of gray.'

The words which he put out, for the sake of clarity, came back upon the mind, in its dark memory, like brail. The lines 'Went on inside' his mind ('The Musical Box', CP 425), as well as outside on the page, by no simple correspondence of words to feelings, one to one, but by the sort of strange correspondence that Clifford described, the same stuff at quite different levels. Hardy did sense some primordial matching between nature and man, a common origin for both mind and matter in what Clifford had called 'mind-stuff', and this common basis seemed to bring with it an almost physiologically determined sympathy between not only man and man but also man and animal. For

Hardy could be moved by the suffering of a starving bird—
even when he could not bear to be moved, less mystically, by
the suffering of his own wife. As he sat warm by a Christmas
fire, he glanced outside and saw a thrush struggling for a
rotting berry in the freezing cold:

> Why, O starving bird, when I
> One day's joy would justify,
> And put misery out of view,
> Do you make me notice you!
>   'The Reminder', CP 220.

It is of course true that 'you make me' is simply a projection,
perhaps even of the misery he was guilty of ignoring and
resenting in his wife. Still, it is also true that Hardy would
have felt more comfortable had he been sure that it was only
projection—had he been sure that when his nerves screamed
for the bird, they were only really screaming for himself. His
situation was more paradoxical than that: so powerful were his
feelings for others that he had an almost primitive intuition
that the world was still, even in misery, homogeneous. We
have seen that some such intuition lay at the heart of Michael
Henchard who could hardly bring himself to believe that the
emotions inside him referred more to himself, narrowly and
personally, than to their external objects.

   At the same time Hardy was neither Henchard nor a neo-
mystic like Clifford, he was a realistic, a guilty and a frightened
man. Thus, so powerful was his wincing, nagging sensitiveness,
as illustrated in 'The Reminder', that he feared that, even thus,
the feelings of others would rob him of his own precariously
coherent heterogeneity, his own sanity of identity. In protecting
this narrow sense of self, he had to repress these emotions,
force them back into the enclosing privacy of his memory. In
this later individuality of common sense, which prevented his
being a Henchard, he concluded thus of theories of correspondence like Clifford's in a letter to Roden Noel, 3 April
1892:

> You may call the whole human race a single *ego* if you
> like; & in that view a man's consciousness may be said to
> pervade the world; but nothing is gained. Each is, to all
> knowledge, limited to his own frame. Or with Spinoza, &

the late W. K. Clifford, you may call all matter mind-stuff (a very attractive idea this, to me) but you cannot find the link (at least I can't) of one form of consciousness with another.[21]

The heart, which seemed to refer outwards, was still trapped within the man's own fragile frame. For all the feelings that seemed to be common to mankind, mutual misery could constitute a divorce within a marriage: a little point, perhaps, made by a sceptical realist against more sophisticated philosophers, but enough to have massive implications for Hardy. For the physical and then moral separation of one body from another seemed to Hardy both sheerly banal as fact and painfully paradoxical to the intuitions of emotion. George Eliot had talked of sympathy, but 'you cannot find the link': George Eliot had split herself between Casaubon and Dorothea but her sympathy for both was, for Hardy, less important than her knowledge that Dorothea's sympathetic thoughts for Casaubon were still in reality quite separate from him. That is why he gave up the self-splitting technique of the novel and became, as a matter of tragic knowledge, more *apparently* limited and subjective than George Eliot had been. Limited, that is to say, to the paradoxes of personal emotion, referring outward yet trapped within one person's make-up. Hardy had said that he wanted to be 'undistrest/By hearts grown cold to me', but actually what he had to take to heart, the heart that swelled with trouble, was the thought of those 'hearts grown cold to me'—he had to have within him the memory of hearts that had forgotten him, to admit within his heart the memory of hearts that would not admit him. 'Hearts' go together in the basic homogeneity of mankind but they do not go with 'my heart' except ironically. There is no link, other than that of baulked emotional instinct, between one heart and another in Hardy's world. Similarly, writing and living, words and feelings may run parallel to each other but, again, 'you cannot find the link'. For Hardy's greatest poetry became that of a man writing words which, he now guiltily thought even as he wrote, he ought to have been *saying* long before that:

> Why then, latterly did we not *speak*,
> Did we not think of those days long dead?
>
> 'The Going', CP 277.

This he asks Emma, while Emma in 'The Haunter' (CP 284) says that she now stands, as a ghost, still near him:

> Just as I used to do
> But cannot answer the words he lifts me—
>   Only listen thereto!
>
> When I could answer he did not say them . . .

He had not spoken and he now wrote—instead. And it did not make up for it, however much, like Wordsworth, Hardy knew that writing could be more than speaking. But in this context the art was written precisely so that art, in retrospect, should recognize itself as *not* more than life: its prime purpose being as writing consciously secondary in the writer's mind to the memory of its not having been speaking. Had not the writing earlier encouraged his unwillingness to speak, storing it all up? Now he heard an echo of his written words speaking but only in his head, too late and to him alone, hardly able to bring himself to the thought that his memory of her was not her memory or herself. What obsessed Hardy was the thought that things which at one level could be said—by someone like Clifford—to be structurally alike, at another level, usually the most immediately important one, did not agree with each other for all that. At one level Hardy wrote as a literary man what at another level he heard as a ruined man: 'Woman, much missed, how you call to me, call to me' ('The Voice', CP 285). And although the literary and the personal levels were made out of the same stuff and ran parallel, as speaking and writing do in Clifford's analysis, yet even as they connected they felt confusingly separate, *discordia concors*.

This was Hardy's idea of art:—something whose own terms were at once powerfully strengthened and powerfully weakened by the memory of the life outside them—life which, internally within the poems, was of course their subject-matter. This paradox of memory turning inside and outside the poem at once corresponded for Hardy to the paradoxical dilemma of the individual and his emotions in the modern world: that so much within him which referred outwardly was not wanted or needed out there. Hardy took to heart 'hearts grown cold to me'; he felt actually *inside* his emotion the presence of everything that did not care for him outside, that would not care even for this emotion about that. Now he put that emotion inside a poetic frame which contained him when he could hardly contain himself, his inner emotions feeling as if they would burst outward. But even while he worked himself inside the tight spaces of his own poetry, he also knew that by the time he had finished, the poem would be outside him and he would have to live on with its feelings still inside him, having to be paid for in life and by death. Take that great poem 'The Photograph' (CP 405). When Hardy looked at a photograph of some one he had loved, he could hardly tell whether what he saw was inside him or outside; when he remembered his love, he hardly knew whether he possessed her or was possessed by her. Often he felt that *he* had become no more than one thought among many in the minds of those whom he had cared for:

> As for one rare fair woman, I am now but a thought of
> hers
> 'Wessex Heights', CP 261.

even while inside himself he felt his memory of her to be her memory. Now, a photograph, on the boundary between a thought and the reality that thought thinks of, was to Hardy like his own internal memory-image made non-humanly external; it confused utterly his already confused sense of boundaries. And a photograph stood to his memory even as a poem did, borrowing reality from him to the amazement of his sense of reality. Hardy burnt the photograph of his former love and in the following four lines the memory of the event is given out in rationalizing words:

> She was a woman long hid amid packs of years,
> She might have been living or dead; she was lost to my sight,
>   And the deed that had nigh drawn tears
> Was done in a casual clearance of life's arrears;

—yet what is there given out rebounds off the rhymes to resound further down

> But I felt as if I had put her to death that night! ...

The outside, the photograph, the poem by that fifth line turns back, like revenge, inside, and that fifth line seems to be read even as it is written, for this is writing 'on the other side' of its customary dictatorial relation to words. That line seems to have come to the surface of the poem from further back than the others, on second thought from the deeper meaning of the past, a ghost. W. H. Mallock had warned modern man:

> Conscience, if it still remains with him, will remain not as a living thing—a severe but kindly guide—but as the menacing ghost of the religion he has murdered.
>
> *Is Life Worth Living?* p. 156.

The inconstancy of love was for Hardy the fallen substitute of faith: the memory of that inconstancy haunted him as if he had in such acts also killed his own soul. Emotions without religion were for Hardy, despite all that Feuerbach had promised, a torture, as if his own memory had now an unexercisable responsibility which, before, men had looked for in their God.[22]

So often in his poetry Hardy is now confessedly his own character Boldwood who

> was now living outside his defences for the first time, and with a fearful sense of exposure.
>
> *Far from the Madding Crowd,* chap. xviii, p. 148.

—although living outside one's defences is still something that is felt internally. In the poetry the threat of living outside his defences is registered at the line-endings—as here, for example, when Hardy hopes and fears that the shadow cast on the stone in front of him is thrown by his dead wife behind him:

> . . . and to keep down grief
> I would not turn my head to discover
> That there was nothing in my belief.
>
> 'The Shadow on the Stone', CP 483.

Hardy looked at his own words as he looked at that stone, feeling the presence behind him of his own memory casting its shadow, and hardly daring to face it. At 'grief' and at 'discover', his shoulders, as it were, wince, the emotions cry out from within him, and, as if in answer, the memory of it all within his verse 'dis-covers' that last line, bringing it up from the depths like 'But I felt as if I had put her to death that night'. THERE almost palpably WAS—NOTHING. As the lines turn outwards and inwards, as the diction looks out, turns back or rises from a deeper level, it may be concluded that memory in Hardy's poetry pulls the man in and out of himself, forward and back; stretching and contracting him across those boundaries that mark his confusion as to where he ends and how he stands to what, outside himself, he cares about; uncovering layers of the past and changing the levels of reference to it. This was Hardy's torture: that the consciousness of what was internal, what external to him was still, for all that, a naggingly internal consciousness of his own; that this consciousness still suffered from knowing inside what remained denyingly outside for all that.

And this may be put in more formal terms and placed in historical ones. In 1883 there was published a collection of essays edited by Andrew Seth and R. B. Haldane intended to extend and consolidate the place of Idealist philosophy in England. The ninth essay, written by T. B. Kilpatrick, was entitled, significantly for our purposes, 'Pessimism and the Religious Consciousness'. Its opening proposition is that the individualism that emerged near the end of the eighteenth century is 'at once an axiom and a problem':

> The self claims infinite satisfaction; but, by the very terms of its claim, it shows itself to be merely finite, and therefore incapable of the satisfaction which it demands.
> *Essays in Philosophical Criticism,* p. 247.

The vulgar Romantic emotional desire had been that empirical individualism should find, on earth, transcendent satisfaction. Meanwhile, in philosophy, Kant had been concerned with the self not as a principle of being and feeling but as a principle of knowledge, a unifying consciousness. Succeeding Idealist thinkers, having also to battle against opposing Darwinists, were thus left with the problem how this self-consciousness as a formal principle in the Kantian theory of knowledge related to real individuality in the way of daily living. As one of Kilpatrick's own English Idealist mentors had put it,

> The union in one person of a consciousness of the self as a universal subject and of the same self as one particular object is for Kant *the* difficulty of difficulties which no theory can cope with.[23]

It is consequently not hard to see how Kilpatrick might almost have thought of Hardy as a symptom of this frustration—the frustration between Idealism's larger idea of man, whose consciousness, like all men's, made fundamental sense of the world in terms of seeing it aright temporally, spatially and morally, and Romanticism's personal man who could make no emotionally satisfying sense of his own life within it. Lawrence himself in the ninth chapter of his *Studies in Classic American Literature* had called Hardy the last of the Idealists, bitter at Idealism's failure to help the personal life whose enlargement it had seemed to encourage. In his poem 'In the Seventies', for instance, Hardy speaks 'Of the vision . . . Of the vision' that he had within him then, unknown to those around him, when he was under thirty. 'In the seventies nought could darken or destroy it': it was securely 'Locked in me . . . Locked in me'. But what happened as the century wore on, Hardy sees, is that he became locked in *it*, imprisoning himself within himself while the vision itself, meanwhile, faded. Was it a punishment for thinking that the vision was his alone? The Kantian principle of consciousness of man, which all men shared, constituted the meaning of the human world, giving form and significance and shape to the world and implicating man in relation to it accordingly. But for Hardy this, even if it were true, became for him in personal terms a redundant and ironic consciousness, setting up our world in the first place but leaving us suffering from what has been set up in the second. Hardy's predicament here is in mute contrast to Wordsworth's use of Kant in balancing the natural and the spiritual man: in consequence the 'interchange of within and without' is in Hardy's poetry the opposite of 'ennobling' as it was in Wordsworth's.[24] At any rate, Kilpatrick would argue, I think, that this pessimism in Hardy was characteristic of that of the later nineteenth century, the age of Schopenhauer: its cause lay in thus confining self-consciousness to consciousness of the narrowly personal self encouraged by certain strands in popularly received Romanticism:

> It is only because in self-conscioiusness the self is not confined to its mere individuality that it can be aware of anything confronting it. . . . the consciousness which is

aware of the self and the object cannot be identical merely with the individual self; but is dependent upon and identical with a principle of synthesis which comprehends both in one grasp, and bestows upon both organic relations to one another.

Essays in Philosophical Criticism, p. 261.

To put it in the terms of this book, what Philosophy, developing from Coleridge's Idealism, is here urging upon Thomas Hardy, ironically too late, is something very like the attitude of William Wordsworth. Something by which Wordsworth could write the tragedy of Margaret in a way very different from that in which Hardy wrote the tragedy of Tess.

The world, Kilpatrick was concluding, took form from our own primary consciousness of it. Even the evil and the pain in that world are relative to our own consciousness of them. Of evil in relation to our consciousness, Kilpatrick summed up,

the principle which makes it a significant conception is superior to it, and involves its conquest.

Ibid., p. 274.

It was precisely there, however, that Hardy would protest. A man's consciousness of his predicament may indeed be 'superior' to it, in the sense of being worthy of a better return than it, or, at least, knowing why it may not have better returns; but that ideal superiority of consciousness and human knowledge can do no more in Hardy than still feel itself bound and tied to the predicament. Consider one such predicament in Hardy, the death of Emma:

> Never to bid me good-bye,
> Or lip me the softest call,
> Or utter a wish for a word, while I
> Saw morning harden upon the wall,
> Unmoved, unknowing
> That your great going
> Had place that moment, and altered all.
> 'The Going', CP 277.

Hanging at the line-end, pausing and stressed in memory, 'going' there for a second brings into line the time that the poem takes in itself with the life-time tracking its meaning behind it. The nominally presiding consciousness of the author is thus actually wedged tightly down within and behind the word. It is prevented by guilt from feeling now 'superior' to the predicament it recalls: because now that he *is*, beneath his words, both 'moved' and 'knowing', it is nonetheless too late for that to make any difference. When Hardy set his past moving again in verse it knocked him over as if it were now again present. So, in that penultimate line, 'going' *has place*, through the holdfast of rhyme, *before* in the last line it is actually said to have done so. That is to say, Hardy is absolutely unlike Wordsworth with his innocent sense of a life's and a verse's predestination which remains true even in retrospect; in contrast to that, which we witnessed in chapter 2, Hardy's is a poetry guilty of 'If you had known'; Hardy finds writing from memory to be a species of fallen foreknowledge which cannot prevent, even the second time round in writing, what it cannot help again see coming. The 'going' has shocking place again. And worse, this verse as of a fallen Prometheus not only cannot prevent the going this time but also cannot help strengthening the power of its second coming.

All this bespeaks a man to whom the status of mind had not much more than the status of memory. The power of consciousness, like the power of memory, was always something that comes second in the order, in the chronology of life: if 'superior', superior only in retrospect, in making back over internally facts and events that were external. For to Hardy, as I mentioned in the last chapter in relation to George Eliot,[25] there was against Idealism the countervailing influence of Darwinism. And for Hardy this meant, among other things, that man's mind was not created as it were in the beginning to preside over the rest of creation; rather, it rose, it evolved, in subordinate place, finally to reflect upon all that had given it its origin. And for Hardy, unlike George Eliot, this superior consciousness was not a mark of possible freedom: it became the way that one was all the more ironically bound to recognize one's own determinism.[26] Mind was in memory of its own physical origins: the more memory was released above them, the more it was released to remember them, rather than escape them. A prison and a consciousness of prison which itself was still not freeing. It was thus that Hardy felt his situation was too small for his soul without a belief in how to enlarge it.

I wish to consider finally 'The Shadow on the Stone' (CP 483) where Hardy thinks his dead wife to be behind his back, yet she will not answer his cry. To keep down grief, he writes,

> I would not turn my head to discover
>   That there was nothing in my belief.
>
>   Yet I wanted to look and see
>   That nobody stood at the back of me;
> But I thought once more: 'Nay, I'll not unvision
>   A shape which, somehow, there may be.'
>   So I went on softly from the glade,
>   And left her behind me throwing her shade,
> As she were indeed an apparition—
>   My head unturned lest my dream should fade.

At the beginning of that last stanza Hardy first wrote, 'I felt I must look to see/That nobody stood at the back of me'.[27] A lesser man would have stuck at that, or, if re-writing at all, would have started with 'I wanted to' and covered his tracks with 'I felt I must'. But for Hardy poetry was meant to uncover him and his past, and here he produces just sufficient honest courage to enable his verse to turn back upon him on second thought. For pushed by that confessed 'I wanted to look and see', the verse really discloses a buried wish, hoping against hope, 'that *somebody* stood at the back of me', Emma. When Hardy turned his back on what his Romanticism wanted, it still appeared at the back of his mind. This then is a poetry of post-Romantic second thought, redeeming the emotion pushed back and qualified by thought, making it rise again, bringing it forward again, from the memory. Look how far the short, apparently negative lines—'That there was nothing in my belief', 'That nobody stood at the back of me'—look how far forward they seem to have come as if their deeper meaning rose before Hardy's own eyes, in the act of writing, like the ghost of his real self! That second thought should redeem the past is an idea we have already seen working in Dickens' writing of *David Copperfield*.[28] But there is another, less positive side to this question of the status of second thought and it may be presented by the Idealist tradition. Here is the negative view of a Coleridgean cleric, J. C. Hare:

Second thoughts are best, says every second person you meet; fitly enough; for second thoughts are always second-rate ones. A second thought is only a half-thought . . .

No second thought ever lead a man to do anything generous, anything kind, anything great, anything good. By its very nature it can suggest nothing; except difficulties and hinderances. It objects, it demurs, it pares off, it cuts down. . . .

Second thoughts, I have said, are only fragments of thoughts; that is, they are thought by a mere fragment of the mind, by a single faculty, the prudential understanding . . . Our first thoughts . . . are much likelier to be just: for they are the expression of our whole being; or at least, if the feelings have a somewhat undue prominence, they still act in unison with the intellect; and moreover they have been fashioned by the intellect, and trained by the experience of our whole lives . . .

Are we then always to halt at our first thoughts? Yes: if we cannot go beyond our second thoughts. These are only good as a half-way house to bait at in the progress of our third thoughts; which . . . are mostly found to chime in with the first, like the third line in the *Divina Commedia*, that magnificent spiritualization of all sensuous things, the very title of which declares the harmony between earth and heaven.[29]

Like his own heroes, for reasons discussed in the first two sections of this chapter, Hardy was 'in a chaos of principles—groping in the dark' (*Jude the Obscure,* pt. vi, chap. i, p. 336). It is true that in his poetry Hardy had managed to turn round through art's second thought his own depressive tendency in life to hide his primary nature behind a secondary, protective front. In this respect Hardy could reply to a critic such as Kilpatrick just as Ruskin had Durer replying to critics of *his* melancholy:

'Yet is his strength labour and sorrow.'
        'Yes,' he replies, 'but labour and sorrow are his strength.'[30]

Hardy was forced into courage by having to see his own fear. Yet, for all that, Hardy still remained uncertain that the art of second thought could have a primary status rather than an ironic and apologetic one; his autobiographical poetry, after the writing of his novels, is a tacit admission that he could not be sure with George Eliot that art had a primary role to play in life. It was as if he was haunted by Hare's intuition—that his own way of thinking was fundamentally fallen and self-divisive, that it was a form of thinking that kept him, by its pressure upon him, meaner and smaller than he felt he ought to have been. As with Henchard in the second movement of *The Mayor of Casterbridge*, the man was no longer thinking thoughts, the thoughts were thinking him, had him at their mercy. Hardy's rhymes, in contast to Hare's account of Dante's, fall rather than chime, trap or lower rather than spiritually regenerate. In this tightly reduced life, by definition Hardy the poet felt he could have no recourse to a larger, tragically gestural language. He gave up writing tragedy in order to have to live it, while simultaneously unsure whether his life was important enough for the word tragedy. The marks of that life are left in his poetry: forced to store his sorrow, because he trusted himself to no gesture that could purge it and found no means to cure it, Hardy stored it in the silent memory buried behind his verse. What was the matter with Thomas Hardy? The thought that our consciousness and our emotions at one level do make the meaning of our world, yet at another level suffer from that meaning, feel utterly dependent upon, vulnerable to, the world they have helped to make. This was such an implicating thought that what Hardy had learnt in his life he felt almost too frightened, ashamed and compromised to work into clear expression out of his life. Moreover, what he had learnt felt more in the nature of illusions unlearnt: the power of emotion is also powerless; 'feeling most what most cannot be' makes one ashamed of feeling; memory which seems to fill a person with buried feelings and thoughts of other people is nonetheless even thus a self-isolating mode. Hardy did manage to say these ironic things but only in the memory hidden behind his verse, only in the vulnerably individual sense of life within which the world seemed to oblige him to bury his sense of the truth of life.

In Hardy there is thus a connection between the problem of the status of the individual and his sense of experience and the problem of the status of art itself. We have been concerned throughout this book with whether the individual's art has a primary or secondary status in relation to living—from the moment when at the beginning we saw Wordsworth working out a balance or interchange between the two possibilities. All Hardy finally could do was make the problem in his poetry of memory an autobiographical one—the relation of his writing to his living. And Hardy is Wordsworth's ironic counterpart: not balanced but torn between a sense of writing as primary and writing as secondary. For example, the impulse that made Hardy not want to turn round in his poetry and find the truth of life behind it threatening to destroy it:

> I would not turn my head to discover
> That there was nothing in my belief.

—in fact does turn him round there in spite of itself—yet equally making itself greater. And it is thus much the same impulse, in not turning round, as that which at another time led Hardy as an adult actually to turn round, to go and check out the childish superstition that the oxen themselves kneel at Christmas eve:

> I would go with him through the gloom,
> Hoping it might be so.
> 'The Oxen', CP 403.

A poetry that lowered its own status by the thought of real life, yet simultaneously raised its own power precisely by that lowering—and without a hint of compensation in that. Hardy as poet is like Wordsworth through the looking glass. . . .

> So I went on softly from the glade,
> And left her behind me throwing her shade . . .

'So I went on softly' is a marvellous touch there. 'Thus I; faltering forward' but for her memory's sake softly. For it maintains, through literature, the memory of belief: ·

> So they went on and looked before them, and behold, they saw, as they thought, *a Man upon his Knees*, with Hands

and Eyes lift up, and speaking, as they thought, earnestly to one that was above. They drew nigh, but could not tell what he said; so they went on softly till he had done.[31]

This is, of course, a moment from John Bunyan's *The Pilgrim's Progress*. As Hardy must have known, it is Stand-fast who is there down on his knees praying.[32] Hardy, on his knees in his poem, could not pray, was often down, knew no progress or direction, but did stand fast. Yet this echo of the soul in 'The Shadow on the Stone' is preserved alongside another of the memory, more fallen than it and recorded now in the Dorset County Museum:—an annotation by Miss Irene Cooper Willis to page 306 of what was first published as the *Early Life of Thomas Hardy*, in the copy owned by Florence Emily Hardy herself:

> Mrs Hardy, the second, walking round the garden with me, the first time I stayed at Max Gate (1933) on coming to the erected stone, remarked:— 'Hardy found his first wife burning all his love-letters to her behind that stone, one day'.

The same stone by which his words of love had been burnt when she was alive! If Hardy said nothing of this explicitly in his poem, not the least of his reasons was one secularly analogous to the way that while Stand-fast was praying, 'they could not tell what he said'. Hardy had to hurt himself with that memory even while he wrote his poem over the pain. Even thus, the extension of consciousness beyond the mere ego, for the want of which nineteenth-century Idealists were blaming pessimists like Hardy, was in fact being maintained through Hardy-like efforts to hold together such painfully contrasting memories of his soul and of his marriage. Yet it was only within himself, paradoxically, that Hardy could maintain that extension of consciousness beyond self; no wonder it felt like being haunted and tortured.

By an historical accident then we know a little more, explicitly, about the life and the memory behind the poem, with regard to 'The Shadow on the Stone', than we do in the case of most of Hardy's other poems. Yet Irene Cooper Willis' revelation should come as no surprise to a close reader of the poems: the way that most of the poetry is written signifies, implicitly, the buried presence of memories like that one. Incidents not anecdotally or biographically irrelevant to 'pure' art, to art in itself, but actually at its heart. In one sense, the sheer fact, that a man had to watch his own wife burning his old love-letters to her, matters to one interested in the history of human feeling *almost* as much as does the resulting poem 'The Shadow on the Stone' which surfaces later. To be so interested in art as to neglect as irrelevant what art comes out of is not to be intelligently interested in art and in its moral and human purposes, particularly in the nineteenth century. Yet in another sense, it is also true that it would hardly matter if we did not possess this extra piece of information from Irene Cooper Willis—not because we care only about the poetry but because the poetry itself cares so much about such things as tacitly to embody them in the memory of a man that his words may leave.

Here, then, was Thomas Hardy echoing Bunyan even while also recalling his own wife's betrayal. It is as though high classic art and low mundane truth had intimate connection in the man's memory; as though the recognition of a relation between culture and personal trouble was part of what it meant to be a literary man. Similarly, the mind which creates is not here separate from the man who suffers: for to its maker the apparently finished and external art is no such sanctified thing saying 'touch me not'. Such connections and implications, so far from being reductive, seem to me to increase the importance of literature in the life of human beings.

6

D. H. Lawrence:
'Physician, heal thyself'

When they said to Lawrence Art for Art's sake, he retorted, Art for *my* sake.[1] He wanted none of that 'touch me not' art—or life for that matter—with its accounts of purity:

> Loerke snorted with rage.
>
> 'A picture of myself!' he repeated in derision. . . . 'It is a work of art, it is a picture of nothing, of absolutely nothing. It has nothing to do with anything but itself, it has no relation with the everyday world of this and other, there is no connexion between them, absolutely none, they are two different and distinct planes of existence, and to translate one into the other is worse than foolish, it is a darkening of all counsel, a making confusion everywhere. Do you see, you *must not* confuse the relative work of action with the absolute world of art. That you *must not do*.'
>
> 'That is quite true,' cried Gudrun, let loose in a sort of rhapsody. 'The two things are quite and permanently apart, they have nothing to do with one another. *I* and my art, they have *nothing* to do with each other. My art stands in another world, I am in this world.'

To this Ursula retorts that 'it isn't a word of it true':

> 'As for your world of art and your world of reality,' she replied, 'you have to separate the two, because you can't bear to know what you are. . . . The world of art is only the truth about the real world, that's all—but you are too far gone to see it.'
>
> *Women in Love*, chap. xxix, pp. 421–2.[2]

While opposing views similar to those of Loerke and Gudrun,

Notes and Bibliography begin on page 503.

we have found nonetheless some reason to be a little less confident than Ursula about the relation of the world of art to the real world. That is to say, we have witnessed Thomas Hardy's guilt and worry about himself and his poetry registered, notwithstanding, within his poetry.

In the last chapter I was ultimately concerned with Hardy as a poet, in tacit contrast to what we learnt of Wordsworth and the art of poetry in part I of this book. Continuing, however, the concern of part III—the endeavour of the individual to make sense of life through his own experience and through writing out of that experience—I want now to bring Hardy forward towards a consideration of D. H. Lawrence. For if, in looking for help from books, one of our most serious concerns, in my view, ought to be a reckoning of what is at stake between Wordsworth and Hardy, another serious piece of thinking, Lawrence himself insists, lies between Hardy and him. On his deathbed, Hardy was unsure whether his work had been worth doing and was tormented by old sorrows which that work had borrowed and used but not exorcised. As we shall see, to this idea of the writer paying life his final debt Lawrence offered a challenge. 'Physician, heal thyself.'

I. LAWRENCE AND THE WRITERS AMONG THE RUINS

Watching Lawrence reading Conrad one day, Catherine Carswell remarked that reading for Lawrence was an act that involved so much more than merely reading.

Trying to find a life worth living, Lawrence wrote to Edward Garnett on 30 October 1912 thanking him for sending on to Italy some books:

> The Conrad, after months of Europe, makes me furious— and the stories are *so* good. But why this giving in before you start, that pervades all Conrad and such folks—the Writers among the Ruins. I can't forgive Conrad for being so sad and for giving in.

Collected Letters, i, p. 152.

It may help us to understand Lawrence's quarrel with another of those whom he accused of giving in—Thomas Hardy—if we first try to make out why he was furious with Conrad. On the face of it, it is not altogether easy to see why he should have picked on Joseph Conrad for the role of despairing coward. Is it, for example, a coward who has Captain MacWhirr say at last to his young mate in the middle of the storm in 'Typhoon':

> 'Keep her facing it. They may say what they like, but the heaviest seas run with the wind. Facing it—always facing it—that's the way to get through. You are a young sailor. Face it. That's enough for any man.'
>
> U.E., p. 89.³

Ironically, in terms of the story, 'facing it' was precisely the nature of MacWhirr's folly in thinking he could get through the storm intact when he might merely have avoided it instead. But let those who suppose that Conrad's view of courage was simply ironical consider that those words, published in 1903, have on the other side of them the private memory of moments like that upon Good Friday 1899 when Conrad wrote, as Lawrence was to, to Edward Garnett:

> The more I write the less substance do I see in my work. The scales are falling off my eyes. It is tolerably awful. And I face it, I face it but the fright is growing on me.
>
> Quoted in Frederick R. Karl: *Joseph Conrad*, p. 485.

In 'The Shadow Line' the protagonist writes in his diary that he was always frightened of shirking it and here he was, shirking his responsibilities at the testing moment: my guess is that the diary was Conrad's own virtually transcribed. And what MacWhirr says to Jukes in the world of action, Conrad is saying to himself as he struggled to write. At the same time as writing his tale he was writing a note to himself, a note by which the hand, so to speak, tries through language to steady the mind directing it. That is what Hardy meant by working on 'the other side' of oneself, I believe. 'Our thoughts are fleeting,' wrote the philosopher James Beattie, 'and the greater part of our words are forgotten as soon as uttered: but, by writing, we may give permanency to both'.⁴ But that permanency is itself relative: behind MacWhirr's solid 'Keep facing it' is the memory of something more temporary and informal, what at that moment Conrad was saying to himself in writing that. I am not saying that that private note matters *more* than the imaginative account of MacWhirr in relation to Jukes. But against the assumption that books have nothing to do with reality, it is worth stressing that the private resonance that Conrad took from his own work in writing it was just the sort of personal meaning that, he hoped, his readers would take from it in reading: 'That's enough for any man'. Those private echoes *are* part of the meaning of 'Typhoon', part of its human significance, where otherwise it is just a grown man writing fiction.[5]

Yet clearly there is a difference between Conrad writing a note for himself in his diary and Conrad putting that note into a story. For Conrad himself there was a difference between MacWhirr in the storm and himself in trouble with his writing, even though the former came out of the latter, the latter out of the former. Conrad knew the reality, as well as the metaphor, of being at sea; of the strain of writing he wrote in *A Personal Record* that it was

> something for which a material parallel can only be found in the everlasting sombre stress of the westward winter passage round Cape Horn. For that too is the wrestling of men with the might of their Creator, in a great isolation from the world, without the amenities and consolations of life, a lonely struggle under a sense of over-matched littleness, for no reward that could be adequate, but for the mere winning of a longitude. Yet a certain longitude, once won, cannot be disputed. The sun and the stars and the shape of your earth are the witnesses of your gain; whereas a handful of pages, no matter how much you have made them your own, are at best but an obscure and questionable spoil.
>
> U.E., pp. 98—9.

Conrad's own autobiograhy of the sea is just such a 'material parallel': it serves as a metaphor for his deeper psychology which itself is involved in his writing. The realism of 'Typhoon' is sustained in its sea-violence not only by memory of equivalent storms but also by something as correspondingly

immaterial as the storms of Conrad's mind. He used his
memory of the sea to realize himself metaphorically within the
literalness of his own life-experience. Yet Conrad will not
flatter himself that writing is itself a heroic journey into the
unknown: it is more uncertain, more frighteningly impalpable
than its own metaphor—and less certainly heroic. When the
storm is as powerful as it is in 'Typhoon', Conrad's storminess
of mind becomes its own metaphor; he serves it as its memory
overwhelms him. And of this mental danger Conrad wrote,
'the danger lies in the writer becoming the victim of his own
exaggeration' (*A Personal Record*, U.E., p. xx).

Thus, even while recognizing the distinction, Conrad did, in
Loerke's terms, 'confuse the relative work of action with the
absolute world of art'. In 'Amy Foster', the tale of a foreigner
washed up on an English shore and unable to speak the
language, it is as if Conrad's own life as a Pole here served as a
literal metaphor for his psychological feeling of strangeness. A
country doctor recounts how the suspicious native villagers
locked the stranger in a barn:

> Before his excitement collapsed and he became uncon-
> scious he was throwing himself violently about in the
> dark, rolling on some dirty sacks, and biting his fists with
> rage, cold, hunger, amazement, and despair.
>
> U.E., p. 121.

And behind that, with the words biting as the stranger bit his
fists, is Conrad, as he wrote to Edward Noble, a young writer:

> You must squeeze out of yourself every sensation, every
> thought, every image,—mercilessly, without reserve and
> without remorse: you must search the darkest corners of
> your heart . . .[6]

That dark barn was in Conrad's imagination his own brain.
Behind the achievement of the stranger

> with his forehead against the trunk of one of [the old
> Norway pines], sobbing, and talking to himself.
>
> U.E., p. 129.

is the cost for the writer incorporated, there almost holding his
head in his hands for being unable to get hold in his mind of its
contents:

> Well I feel my brain. I am distinctly conscious of the
> contents of my head. My story is there in a fluid—in an
> evading shape. I can't get hold of it.[7]

When he could get hold of it, he could do so only by seeing it
get hold of him: a self-destroying imagination. The confirmation of the life in the work thus turns in what Conrad described
as a 'vicious circle . . . like the work in a treadmill' (Frederick
R. Karl, *Joseph Conrad*, p. 944). Conrad felt like the stranger he
also had been in fact: 'I suppose there is something in me that
is unsympathetic to the general public—because the novels of
Hardy, for instance, are generally tragic enough and gloomily
written too and yet they have sold in their time and are selling
to the present day' (ibid., p. 634). What it was in him that had
gone further than even Hardy was this: a two-edged self-
absorption in the work by which the realism of 'Amy Foster'
was so strangely itself as both to swallow completely, and yet
therein still leave estranged behind it, Conrad's own felt
strangeness.

The foreigner marries Amy Foster, the first person to show
him kindness in a strange land. The simple girl bears him a
child to whom he longs to teach his native tongue. But one day
he falls into a fever, begging his wife's help as he had begged
on the day he was first washed up:

> Suddenly coming to himself, parched, he demanded a
> drink of water. She did not move. She had not understood,
> though he may have thought he was speaking in English.
> He waited, looking at her, burning with fever, amazed
> at her silence and immobility, and then he shouted
> impatiently, "Water! Give me water!" . . .
> He sat up and called out terribly one word—some
> word. Then he got up as though he hadn't been ill at all,
> she says. And as in fevered dismay, indignation, and
> wonder he tried to get to her round the table, she simply
> opened the door and ran out with the child in her arms.
>
> U.E., p. 140.

Now, of his collaboration with Conrad over *Romance* Ford
Madox Ford wrote: 'Conrad had been perpetually crying:
"Give! Give!"'. The writing was to give one more, and more,

and again one more turn of the screw.'[8] That is to say, when the man cried 'Water! Give me water!', Conrad had *given* so much of himself that the creator was so close to his creation as only to feel how much it was also his antagonist. Such a thing can only end in death, and the man dies face down in a puddle in the road, only able to give out a few last, broken words in English—'Gone! . . . Why? . . . Merciful!' (pp. 140–1). Like Conrad, he chokes on his own words.

Yet perhaps the worst is that moment when 'he may have thought he was speaking in English' and that she was ignoring her own husband's cries for help. For we hear these cries in English, while knowing that Amy Foster did not. The tale is absorbed into the foreigner's fevered thought of speaking English while also, in the same language, simultaneously aware of itself as translation outside the sick man's head. It is worse than the fear of a novelist towards his readers, lest the words do not get across; and the narrating doctor ironically can heal nothing. 'Physician heal thyself!' 'Amy Foster' only actualizes the strangeness of verbal translation from the medium of life. 'He sat up and called out terribly one word— some word.' Conrad had said that you must write till 'there is nothing—nothing left in you'.[9] And the key-words, 'one word—some word', end up as almost palpably that 'nothing— nothing'; rather like in 'The Heart of Darkness' Kurtz's 'The horror! The horror!'.[10] It was profoundly hard for Conrad to see, despite human language, that anything in itself could *mean* much. The critics would say of his work, '"Failure"— "Astonishing": take your choice; or perhaps both, or neither' (*A Personal Record*, p. 99). Yet even Conrad's consciousness of his own failure meant nothing to him. How could 'Failure' mean anything if failure meant nothing by definition? That is why Marlow admired Kurtz's having something to say about the nothingness and why Conrad needed his own writing, equivalently. Even though like a foreigner he hardly believed in words, human knowledge, the redeeming power of art. But he had to keep on writing, facing it habitually.

There is then a terrifying logic by which, just as the words of courage in 'Typhoon' echo words written four years before in private, so 'Amy Foster', likewise published in 1903, became this in 1910, as Conrad's own wife attests:

> He spoke all the time in Polish, but for a few fierce
> sentences against poor J. B. Pinker. That day seemed
> endless. I could get no one to help me but the old
> maid. . . . Day and Night I watched over him, fearful that
> if I turned my back he would escape from the room. . . .
> More than once I opened my eyes to find him tottering
> towards me in search of something he had dreamed of.
>
> Karl: *Joseph Conrad*, p. 680.

Before, he had turned himself inside-out in imaginative
memory of his foreignness. Now, at this breakdown of health,
he found himself turned back outside-in, living in memory of
what he had dreamed of in 'Amy Foster'. If it is what Lawrence
meant by 'giving in', it is not so in the sense of mere surrender,
but, worse, in the cracking sense of giving inward, going
under, giving way. 'Give! Give!' It is a terrible way of keeping
facing it, like Hardy on his death-bed; perhaps worse.

It was Lawrence's instinct to have nothing to do with
Conrad. Had he had anything more to do with him, he would
have concluded, on the basis of evidence like that above, as he
did with respect to another later nineteenth-century figure
Van Gogh. In a letter to Lady Ottoline Morrell, Lawrence
said of Van Gogh's madness that it was a result of neither
resisting the artistic life and going for something else nor
resigning himself to it and sticking to it as his good angel. He
ought to have chosen rather than have been torn between art
and the need for a life outside art. Best of all, however, if he
could have helped himself through his art so that his art could
be

> the final expression of the created animal or man—not
> the be-all and being of man—but the end, the climax!
>
> Lawrence: *Collected Letters*, i, p. 327.

That last was to be Lawrence's way to work in memory of
himself—because of his belief, concerning the relation of life to
work, that work must not be what he called the putting of 'the
tail in his mouth' (*Phoenix ii*, p. 427); rather it must be 'the
extension of human consciousness' (*Phoenix*, p. 431). The
extension of life into art, not the throttling of life within it.
Lawrence would have said to Conrad, then, what Birkin said
to Gerald Crich about his 'seeing this job through' to its bitter

end: 'You force yourself into horrors, and put a mill-stone of beastly memories round your neck' (*Women in Love*, chap. xiv, pp. 180–1). Always facing it in memory of purposes of goal and courage that in these later, secular days were inappropriate.

*   *   *   *   *

Nonetheless, I am *not* claiming that Lawrence 'understood' Conrad. Unless it was in his own terms, in terms of Gerald Crich, it has to be said that Lawrence never truly realized all that was at stake there. But then it must also be said that to realize that in Conrad's own terms would have been to have to succumb to it: 'No human being could bear a steady view of moral solitude without going mad' (*Under Western Eyes*, Pt 1, chap. ii, U.E., p. 39). Yet Lawrence steered clear of Conrad not merely because of his contrary beliefs about the relation of life and work; rather, he was not going to succumb to Conrad because his own battles, when measured against Conrad's, were sanely, obviously and luckily for himself nothing like so irrevocably authentic. To her son's claim that he did not care about happiness in life, Mrs Morel had cried:

> 'But it does matter! . . . And you *ought* to be happy, you ought to try to be happy, to live to be happy.'
> *Sons and Lovers*, Pt ii, chap. x, p. 257.

Yet Jessie Chambers recalls the young Lawrence of 1907 when torn between her and Louie Burrows in a search, apparently, for happiness in love:

> The deadlock thus complete he would turn his face to the dark fields and exclaim with the vehemence of despair, '*Nothing* matters'.
> Jessie Chambers: *D. H. Lawrence: A Personal Record*, p. 143.

Jessie herself had said, when he said he had to break with her, 'Never mind . . . it doesn't matter' (ibid., p. 150). And nearly four years later she felt the memory of their failure was still with him when he said again to her, now that his mother had died, '*Nothing* matters' (ibid., p. 213). Emphatically this is not the voice of Conrad: in Conrad the despair would have absorbed the vehemence into 'nothing'. The tone here is indeed bitter but bitter in a way that is reactive rather than final; for it is, above all, a young voice still. A voice, moreover, that, unlike Conrad's, did not finally mean it. For in some way he still wanted to believe the words of his dead mother as they are recorded in *Sons and Lovers*: 'Then suddenly all her passion of grief over him broke out. "But it does matter!"' (p. 258). Yet she is dead. And what she had wanted for him while she was alive was, if true, all too humiliatingly and over-simplifyingly true: 'But if you could meet some *good* woman who would *make* you happy . . .' (p. 257). It is, that is to say, a second-generation voice, almost consciously; the voice of a son who has lost parental moorings.

Moreover, there was another, less personal way in which Lawrence was, if I may put it thus, a secondary man. I mean it neutrally not pejoratively. For what Lawrence inherited from nineteenth-century pessimism was its continuing Romantic distinction between, first, the sheer form of life and, second, its personal content. He had read Schopenhauer:

> The striving after existence is what occupies all living things and maintains them in motion. But when existence is assured, then they know not what to do with it; thus the *second* thing that sets them in motion is the effort to get free from the burden of existence, to make it cease to be felt, 'to kill time', i.e., to escape from ennui. Accordingly we see that almost all men who are secure from want and care, now that at last they have thrown off all other burdens, become a burden to themselves.[11]

The first task of man is survival; the second task to find something that makes that survival worthwhile—or, as Schopenhauer cynically thought, something to help distraction and forgetfulness of our burden. It is often thought that Lawrence's 'Study of Thomas Hardy' has very little to do with Hardy himself: in fact it can be seen that Lawrence went beneath his memory of Hardy to the very heart of the issue that Hardy posed for him—

> Man has made such a mightly struggle to feel at home on the face of the earth, without even yet succeeding. Ever since he first discovered himself exposed naked betwixt

sky and land, belonging to neither, he has gone on fighting
for more food, more clothing, more shelter; and though he
has roofed-in the world with houses and though the
ground has heaved up massive abundance and excess of
nutriment to his hand, still he cannot be appeased,
satisfied. He goes on and on. . . .

Phoenix, p. 398.

But on and on for what purpose? The first-order task of self-
preservation was secured; it was the second-order problem of
living the preserved life that was the essence of his concern,
even as Hardy's protagonists cared little for 'immediate self-
preservation' (p. 410). In the name of personal urgency,
Lawrence gave that second-order level the first-order priority
now in his work: that is what he meant by the word 'life' in his
writing. Conrad was willing this problem of 'life' into the old
first-order problem of life and death; he killed the new
problem by making it a physical issue in his extremist fiction.
And even when Hardy gave up such extremism in fiction, he
found himself, as we have seen, nearly ashamed of his status as
an individual, for being secondary, for being a matter of
second thoughts under cover of the loss of first principles by
which to live life.

As we saw at the beginning of chapter 5, W. H. Mallock's
analysis of the incoherence of the secular world of ethics and
purposes indicated that either men must go back to religion or
forward to a complete re-thinking of the basis of living. In
between was the state that led to Schopenhauer: Mallock
thought so, Kilpatrick agreed. Yet it was, above all, Nietzsche
who said, all right then let us not go back but go forward.[12]
Nietzsche's Zarathustra came to men of decadence that they

> might become weary of the old words which ye have
> learned from the fools and liars:
> That ye might become weary of the words 'reward',
> 'retribution', 'punishment', 'righteous vengeance'.—
> That ye might become weary of saying: 'That an action
> is good is because it is unselfish'.
>
> *Thus Spake Zarathustra*, p. 112.[13]

Like Mallock in this at any rate, Nietzsche had turned on the
compromisers: 'G. Eliot.—They are rid of the Christian God

and therefore think it all the more incumbent upon them to hold tight to Christian morality' (*The Twilight of the Idols*, p. 63).[14]

Lawrence himself was not only a reader of Nietzsche but one whose own work is both of and by a young man who has grown 'weary of the old words':

> *connu, connu*! the endless chance of known cause and effect, the infinite web of the hated cliché which nets us all down in utter boredom.
>
> *Phoenix*, p. 579.

'But damn your happiness!' Paul Morel shouts at his mother, 'So long as life's full, it doesn't matter whether it's happy or not. I'm afraid your happiness would bore me' (*Sons and Lovers*, p. 257). Lawrence knew that this weariness, like 'nothing matters', was in large part reaction against the old values; how else could Paul be so foolish as to say 'your happiness' when he knew that her trouble was that she had hardly had any. Lawrence's public sayings are likewise bitter for their knowledge that they are both the upshot of the post-Romantic tradition and a reaction against its very endlessness. The cure hardly knows itself from a symptom of the Romantic disease— as Hermione says of Birkin:

> He is so uncertain, so unstable—he wearies, and then reacts. . . . That which he affirms and loves one day—a little later he turns on it in a fury of destruction. He is never constant, always this awful, dreadful reaction.
>
> *Women in Love*, chap. xxii, p. 287.

Sometimes in sheer secondary reaction against such old, parental words as 'love' Lawrence 'in a fury of destruction' wanted to pommel and erase their memory for dominating his sense of his own life:

> I say feelings, not emotions. Emotions are things we more or less recognize. We see love, like a woolly lamb . . .
> Convenience! Convenience! There are convenient emotions and inconvenient ones. The inconvenient ones we chain up . . . The convenient ones are our pets. Love is our pet favourite.
>
> *Phoenix*, pp. 756–7.

'Connu, connu!'—he said it both to his mother and to his sense of the past behind this present. Yet there was also in that the risk that he who pays less than full attention to the whole consciousness of meaning available may then bear the cost of his partiality appearing merely cheap or perverse—as Birkin seemed to Hermione. For Lawrence may well have been sick 'of the idea of the "good man"' (*Phoenix*, p. 751)—the man whose being is covered by his knowing, who substitutes for the passion of his own life, on second thought, the reasonable social virtues, the good emotions that compromise and accommodate. And for all his admiration of her as a novelist, I think Lawrence may even have been sick of the good physician, George Eliot, who cannot cure the disease by a compromising tolerance which is its main symptom. Yet nonetheless, for all that, there was also in Lawrence something puritanically, even nostalgically, committed to what Birkin calls 'the old effort at serious living' (*Women in Love*, chap xxiii, p. 294)—so that, suffering from his own reactions to the incoherence of values behind and around him, on another day he again 'affirms and loves':

> 'You love me?' she said, rather faltering.
> 'Yes.' The word cost him a painful effort. Not because it wasn't true. But because it was too newly true, the *saying* seemed to tear open his newly-torn heart. And he hardly wanted it to be true, even now.
> 'The Horse Dealer's Daughter', *The Collected Short Stories*, ii, p. 454.

Yet, in reaction, Lawrence would still be saying even of moments like this,

> Why, I never yet met a man who was anything but what he had been *told* to be.
> *Phoenix ii*, p. 415.

—speaking, that is, like a man horrified at the oppressive conjunction between the race's old words and the individual's *new* feelings on his own account at any rate:

> This is our true bondage. This is the agony of our human existence, that we can only feel things in conventional feeling-patterns.
> *Phoenix*, p. 753.

Yet in 'The Horse Dealer's Daughter' the man knew that it was not 'because it wasn't true' that he did not want to admit love. Lawrence needed the felt circumstantiality of art against that opinionatedness in him which was itself the memory-product of circumstances, but outside art was delivered too absolutely free of any context.

For let us acknowledge frankly the possibility of absurdity and cheapness in an individual's attempt to throw off the past, personal and impersonal, and establish his own values. It was a possibility that Lawrence, in turn so personal and yet so tired of the merely personal, must have known, as he tried to struggle on his own to find what was essential, what personally accidental to his own life. How did his life stand to what life itself might offer? how could he know what life itself could offer save through what his own life meant and he wanted? what he wanted, was life itself no more than a fictive expression for that?

With such questions Lawrence had turned Hardy inside out again—no longer keeping his desires and the doubted right to them 'Locked in me' but turning them out, at the risk of humiliation, to test them out. Consequently Lawrence's essential mode of writing lay not in the poetry of Hardyesque confinement but in the prose of testing dialogue. Lawrence had given up on Hardy as soon as he had completed the major novels, but it was Lawrence's need for prose as much as his despair at Hardy that made him refuse to enter Hardy's prison of poetry. And, once again as with Conrad, the refusal to understand all that was at stake in Hardy's predicament was itself a measure of living understanding by dint of antipathy. To establish this, let us now try to see a Hardy poem this time, as far as we possibly can, as if through Lawrence's eyes:

> You did not come,
> And marching Time drew on, and wore me numb.—
> Yet less for loss of your dear presence there
> Than that I thus found lacking in your make
> That high compassion which can overbear
> Reluctance for pure lovingkindness' sake
> Grieved I, when, as the hope-hour stroked its sum,
> You did not come.

> You love not me,
> And love alone can lend you loyalty;
> —I know and knew it. But, unto the store
> Of human deeds divine in all but name,
> Was it not worth a little hour or more
> To add yet this: Once you, a woman, came
> To soothe a time-torn man; even though it be
> You love not me?
> 'A Broken Appointment', CP 99.[15]

Those two stanzas have the same, apparently oblivious, pre-established shape to which the content of Hardy's emotional life has to adjust itself—though, as we have seen, it works both ways since the very force of adjustment can strengthen as much as weaken the power of what has to lie within it. Hardy, Lawrence might say, in some sense needed his difficulties, waited for trouble, looked for circumstance to fasten upon the otherwise unoccasioned and apparently unwarranted pain within him. Beside this, we know also of Hardy's technical interest in fitting different meanings into the same body of outward words, sounds and forms. He experimented in triolets, splitting the elements of one line ('For long the cruel wish I knew') into three different compounds:

> For long the cruel wish I knew
> That your free heart should ache for me
> While mine should bear no ache for you;
> For long—the cruel wish!—I knew
> How men can feel, and craved to view
> My triumph—fated not to be
> For long! . . . The cruel wish I knew
> That your free heart should ache for me!
> 'The Coquette, and After' CP 103.

Hardy could not be a different sort of person: all he could feel were transformations made, yet remaining, within the terms of a set structure, of life as of poetry. In life all the elements are known, it is the unknown factor of their individual, personal combination that makes the difference. Outwardly we, like the words in 'For long the cruel wish I knew' in each of the line's appearances, are the same; but within, in the different meaning of the same events to individual emotions and memories, there lies heterogeneity. It is like the novelist's distinction of the dancers from the dance in 'The Ballet' (CP 438):

> Links in one-pulsed chain, all showing one smile,
>   Yet severed so many a mile!

—for the dancers still have each their separate inner thoughts 'Of lover, rival, friend', even in dancing so similarly together. It was even so, Hardy knew, within a marriage partnership. And it was so too of the words that made up the pulsed chain of a sentence of pain, that they held beneath their public faces private, though not quite separate, meanings for their penner. So in 'A Broken Appointment' the repetitions of the same words and the gap between the two stanzas marked out by those repetitions have a formal function on the face of it:

> You did not come . . .
> You did not come.
>
> You love not me . . .
> You love not me?

—yet the ratification that a repetition provides in the first stanza ends up being questioned in the second because of the informal difficulty felt in allowing the full personal meaning to sink in, to sink home, *between* the two stanzas. We also read, as in triolets:

> You did not come.
>
> You love not me . . .

—so that in between the stanzas is not simply a formal silence but the tacit memory of what it felt like to wait for and have finally to make the inference. For in that space of inference it can be felt that it is a terrible thing when a man arrives to find that the future he put his hope in and the woman he offered his love to alike fail to turn up; a terrible thing to find emotion to be not a reality but a loneliness; to see that the hope of the future was only the emotional delusion of the present.

And all this is felt 'on the other side' of the 'common emotion' of being stood up—on the other, private side of the public, formal meaning of reality, 'You did not come'. Hardy cannot say like Wordsworth 'and, oh,/The difference to me!';

he has to feel it against a sense that the world is indifferent to the difference to me. It is that alien closeness of a *private* meaning to a *public* one that creates in Hardy the undercover consciousness which, distinguishing the former from the formal indifference of the latter, also fulfils the meaning of the latter thereby. The effect is like that described by Adrian Stokes in his account of Agostino's low relief carving in the Tempi Malatestiano, Rimini. In *The Stones of Rimini* Stokes notes that it is the very closeness of the inch-and-a-half raised figures to the stone frame from which they are carved that paradoxically makes them seem all the more literally out-standing:

> Carving is an articulation of something that already exists in the block. The carved form should never, in any profound imaginative sense, be entirely free from its matrix. In the case of reliefs, the matrix does actually remain: hence the heightened carving appeal of which this technique is capable.[16]

Hardy had always been alive to this as a craftsman. Jude, near the end, comes back to a milestone on which as a youth he had carved a hand pointing towards Christminster and its university, in mark of his ambition. The stone-mason felt for the carving of his youthful meaning against the permanent yet impervious stone: 'It was still there; but nearly obliterated by moss'.[17] In the poems there are similarly verbal marks partly rising, partly struggling through the poetry's capacity to remember the man who wrote it, like hope raised only just above the surface of the hard form: 'You love not me?'. The key to Hardy's art is the closeness of what arises out of the matrix of rhyme to that matrix or set block; the closeness of memorable emotion, which is personal, to the grammatical matrix which, like the ways things fall out in the world, seems impersonal. In writing with and against his rhymes Hardy just managed to get something out of the world in his time, so close is memory to oblivion. Indeed it is the closeness of the individual to the world and the landscape which, dust to dust, will absorb him, that makes in Hardy the individual's frailty the more telling for appearing to be the less so.

And we can now say, from Lawrence's own words in his 'Study of Thomas Hardy', how Lawrence intuitively knew what Hardy was up to and how he would have read 'A Broken Appointment' accordingly:

> It would seem as if each soul, detaching itself from the mass, the matrix, should achieve its own knowledge. Yet this is not so. Many a soul which we feel should have detached itself and become distinct, remains embedded, and struggles with knowledge that does not pertain to it. It reached a point of distinctness and a degree of personal knowledge, and then became confused, lost itself.
>
> *Phoenix*, p. 433.

Hardy was one such soul who became embedded and then lost in the matrix he should have detached himself from; for all that, he knew the advantages to his art, in terms of the power of pessimism, in sitting tight. This, I believe, is the objection that Lawrence would have made against the ending of 'A Broken Appointment':

> Was it not worth a little hour or more
> To add yet this: Once you, a woman, came
> To soothe a time-torn man; even though it be
> You love not me?

Hardy had kept a note of Goethe's translation of Spinoza: 'He who truly loves God must not require God to love him in return'.[18] And similarly here in the world of 'human deeds divine in all but name', where a person's wants are always liable to be merely self-perpetuated by a person's lacks, there was for Hardy no position invulnerable to second thoughts questioning the justice of the claim that one deserves what one desires. Goethe himself explained that Spinoza's thought lay behind his own: 'If I love thee what is that to thee?'.[19] Yet Hardy, while seeing as clearly as Goethe that matrix of the human disposition, still cannot but ask inside it, 'what *is* that to thee?', 'even though it be you love not me?'. For beneath the apparent question in the last stanza—'even though it be the case that you love not me, was it not worth coming just once more for the sake of human decency?'—and struggling against the omnipotence that grammar in Hardy seems to bear as a form of common sense, is that echoing question which he asks obliquely, frightened, hardly bearing to ask it straight or hear it denied:

> You love not me?

It is the insecurity beneath the tenacity that makes the questioning so frighteningly great. For what Hardy is doing is making one question come through under cover of another, playing off, as he put it, 'logical reason' against 'emotional reason' in a form of contrapuntal verse far more self-imprisoned than Wordsworth's.[20] For it is in the name of a complex sense of justice, to and against himself, that the admission that he cannot claim this love and the felt necessity still to ask for it emerge out of the self-same structure. Yet to Lawrence what could this seem but asking on second thought for what one had not the courage more directly to ask in the first place:

> It is an absurd fallacy this, that a small man wants a woman bigger and finer than he is himself. A man is as big as his real desires.
>
> *Phoenix*, p. 489, 'Study of Thomas Hardy'.

—whereas in Hardy a man was reduced by his desires. Another remark of which Hardy had made a note was one by John Morley: 'Success is only the last term of what looked like a series of failures'.[21] And at the very end of 'A Broken Appointment' he had so managed his poem that he might find in the space left by the memory of his failure room for the successful expression of his own resistance to it. That was just about the space that life allowed an individual to find his own thought, if not his own happiness. Yet for Lawrence this was pitifully a man who found room in his despair for hope but could this seem but asking on second thought for what one had

> Have we achieved to true individuality and to a sufficient completeness in ourselves? Because, if not—then, physician, heal thyself.
>
> That is no taunt, but the finest and most damning criticism ever passed: 'Physician, heal thyself'. No amount of pity can blind us to the inexorable reality of the challenge.
>
> *Phoenix*, p. 405, 'Study of Thomas Hardy'.

Thus, Lawrence's 'Study of Thomas Hardy' *is* about Hardy as well as Lawrence for it is the work of one who has so strong a memory of Hardy that he can hardly articulate what it means to him at the same time as providing explicit documentary evidence for that personal meaning. And, indeed, it is a view that seems related to Hardy's own self-doubts. On the eve of the new century, in the gloom, he heard, he says in 'The Darkling Thrush' (CP 119), a little storm-beaten bird managing a frail note of hope—

> That I could think there trembled through
> His happy good-night air
> Some blessed Hope, whereof he knew
> And I was unaware.

As a supporter of George Eliot had put it, most people live with a permanent conviction that there is some basis for hope in life, and when something happens to put that in doubt, they still manage to recognize that the lasting conviction, being better and more salutary than the fugitive one, is worth the risk of being retained:

> If, however, as was the case with Schopenhauer, the temporary belief is cheering while the permanent one is depressing, the mind has, in addition to the dejection which results from its dominant conviction, the painful sting of the suspicion that after all the depressing view of things may be a foolish and unnecessary piece of self-affliction.
>
> James Sully: *Pessimism*, p. 81.

To Hardy, the fact that he, with his temperament and views, was implicated in the creation of his own tragedy was itself his tragedy—but a tragedy which, for that reason, he was debarred from writing about as such. To Lawrence precisely that double-bind offered hope that the tragedy was not necessary: 'Physician, heal thyself'. Hardy, Lawrence seems to have thought, was living with the ghost of conceptions of human purpose no longer at home in the twentieth century. The emotions that Hardy suffered from were really memories; hope, for example, being a Darwinian relic of past certainty and faith:

Certain states of the mind lead to certain habitual actions, which are of service . . . Now when a directly opposite state of mind is induced, there is a strong and involuntary tendency to the performance of movements of a directly opposite nature, though these are of no use.

Charles Darwin: *The Expression of the Emotions in Man and Animals*, (London, 1893), p. 28.

Certain emotions, like fear, have a survival value. Yet as Lawrence knew, we were now past the stage of fundamental self-preservation, and emotions ceasing to be useful became merely triggers of a lost memory. The gloom one night at the end of the century mixed with Hardy's own sense of gloom; there was something heard in the gloom which seemed the opposite of gloomy; this triggered an involuntary accession of hope.

But we have had things like Emerson's real old courage, said Lawrence, and what we need now is something new to take account of our new differences: 'We've got to have a different sort of sardonic courage' (*Phoenix*, p. 318). And one of the things that 'sardonic courage' meant to Lawrence was his reply to a wretched hanger-on begging him for *another* favour—all of which meant Lawrence's again looking after *his* life:

'I don't *want* to,' said I.

'But you will! You will! You will go to the monastery for me, won't you? Everything else is no good if you won't. . . .'

I decided in the day I would *not* go. Without reasoning it out, I knew I *really* didn't want to go. I plainly didn't want it. So I wouldn't go.

Phoenix ii, p. 336.

—'So' there, utterly characteristic, being the mask of sardonic courage. 'I don't want to': it is as if there is now no answer to the question, why should I? So I didn't: the new fluid inconsequentiality, not seeing everything through to its end.

My wife chafed, crying: 'What have you done! We shall have him on our hands all our life. We can't let him starve. It is degrading, degrading, to have him hanging on to us.'

> 'Yes,' I said. 'He must starve or work or something. I am not God who is responsible for him.'
>
> *Phoenix ii*, p. 388.

In this sense of inconsequentiality, hardly anything could be further from the moral world of George Eliot who would have us stand in for God.

For what then, it might be asked, was Hardy's prison of memory thrown off? Answer: for another, open, more irresponsible kind of memory, unwalled in by the body; something like Henchard's in the first major movement of *The Mayor of Casterbridge*. A memory, that is, carried along with the man through the variety of his life and work, too deep for the more superficial distinctions between the two. For the memory of the questions that he kept asking from within his own life of Life itself—where was it? did he have it? what was accidental to him, what essential to it, in the life he did have?—is a thing we can trace, as a matter not of Hardy's inner confinement but, more naively, of Lawrentian outward recurrence. Lawrence's past seemed to be pushing him to the desire to be a married man, with a new established life of his own; but even while pushed from the past he openly questioned that impetus within the present. For Lawrence was a driven man, driven from behind, ambivalently, by his past, even thus—from his mother's words:

> 'if you could meet some *good* woman who would *make* you happy—and you began to think of settling your life—'

through the closed question of Will Brangwen:

> For how can a man stand, unless he have something sure under his feet.
> And upon what could he stand, save upon a woman?
>
> *The Rainbow*, chap. vi, p. 184.

to the question re-opened by Birkin:

> But after all, what did it matter? . . . Really, what a mistake he had made, thinking he wanted people, thinking he wanted a woman. He did not want a woman—not in the least.
>
> *Women in Love*, chap. viii, p. 100.

In the mingled memory of it all, from woman to woman, from living to writing and back again, there is a note like the cry of Tom Brangwen at his daughter's wedding:

> He was still as unsure and unfixed as when he had married himself. His wife and he! With a pang of anguish he realized what uncertainties they both were. . . . When did it come to an end?
>
> *The Rainbow*, chap. v, p. 131.

—while there is also the voice of Nietzsche saying that a man *has* thus continually to have to try to come through and go back and come through again:

> And this secret spake Life herself unto me. 'Behold,' said she, 'I am that *which must ever surpass itself.*'
>
> *Thus Spake Zarathustra*, p. 136.

—yet all the time, Lawrence saw, under threat of such individualism seeming wilful and cheap and self-aggrandizing:

> He feels full of blood, he walks the earth like a Lord. And it is to this state Nietzsche aspires in his *Wille zur Macht*. . . . The *Wille zur Macht* is a spurious feeling.
>
> *Phoenix*, p. 491.

Even with these complications however, the recurrence, action and reaction, may still be felt from the inside as part of Birkin's struggle:

> it infuriates me that I can't get right, at the really growing part of me. I feel all tangled and messed up . . .
>
> *Women in Love*, chap. xi, p. 117.

Yet from the outside Jessie Chambers made a necessary point when she commented thus on his fury as a young man at college when an experimental essay he had handed in for marking got the predictable hammer:

> 'I know it isn't an ordinary essay,' he said; 'it wasn't meant to be, and I thought she'd have the wit to perceive it. But I'll give her the kid's stuff she evidently wants,' he concluded in chagrin. I was surprised to see him so hurt at this reception of his essay—after all, what else could he expect?
>
> *D. H. Lawrence: A Personal Record*, p. 79.

That is to say, surely there must come a point when situations recur so often that consciousness, induced by their familiarity, has to bring itself to ask whether you yourself are not implicated in such situations as their creator as much as their victim. And this goes with another question that Lawrence had at times to face and at times to avoid, as he struggled to throw off 'convenient' expectation. It was this: how could a person throw off a sense of responsible duty, learned from the past, without at the same time suffering a reactive cheapening of his power of thought—a cheapening so scarring as to prevent the achievement of a sort of self-limitation ('I don't want to') which was still the maximum one could be? For that was what Lawrence wanted: to be free to be 'at the really growing part of me' without the cost of that freedom being a reduction of what he could be through life. He let the recurrences of his troubles show outwardly precisely because it was not some merely inner man that he was struggling for.

Yet, in that mess which Lawrence both held together and still kept messy, the one thing perhaps that he could hardly have borne was the thought that, beneath all these voices, a Thomas Hardy could still have spoken back to him in the words of Mrs Morel, pronouncing it all spurious:

> Battle—battle—and suffer. It's about all you do, as far as I can see.'
>
> *Sons and Lovers*, Pt ii, chap. x, p. 258.

For that is all, said Birkin, that Gerald could do; all, thought Lawrence, that Conrad, in his own way, had done. Indeed, when he had challenged Hardy's self-confinement, Lawrence knew deep inside that merely breaking out of it in that way was not sufficient. 'Have we achieved to true individuality and to a sufficient completeness in ourselves?' If not, a Wordsworth could have said of Lawrence as much as of Hardy, is man no more than this?

*   *   *   *   *

Lawrence was turning Hardy inside out. If a man sat inside himself wondering whether his emotions belonged more to himself than to the world they seemed to refer to, let him go out and test his worry, see how much his life belonged to life, and not merely by adapting himself to the world's convenient expectations either. It was a tough balance between that course and the course of sheer individualistic arrogance, but the novel existed for the sake of feeling the movement around the point of ideal balance: 'morality is that delicate, for ever trembling and changing *balance* between me and my circumambient universe, which precedes and accompanies a true relatedness' (*Phoenix*, p. 528). For the novel was not a prison, it measured 'the trembling instability of the balance' in the life it charted, it was the fluid means by which we see why and how 'we must balance as we go' (*Phoenix*, p. 529).

Yet this openness in the novels was related to Lawrence's own youthful vulnerability; the sensitivity about the trembling of the balance was itself a product of Lawrence's early insecurity and fearful sense of personal weakness. He said to Jessie Chambers, 'Most writers write out of their own personality . . . Wells does, of course. But I'm not sure that I've got a big enough personality to write out of' (*Lawrence: A Personal Record*, p. 121). It was that uncertainty that in *Sons and Lovers* was powerfully responsible for moments in dialogue like this one:

> Then the next time he saw Miriam he said to her:
> 'Don't let me be late to-night—not later than ten o'clock. My mother gets so upset.'
> Miriam dropped her head, brooding.
>
> *Sons and Lovers*, Pt ii, chap. vii, p. 176.

You can feel, through Lawrence, how that second sentence of Paul's speech has crossed a boundary on the ether, crossing from his intention in speaking to the effect on Miriam on hearing. This is so different from Hardy in his poetry. There a wall of flesh meant that all of him which referred outside or was pulled outside himself was kept all too controlledly inside, so that his emotions did not rest easily inside him as if they were at home there but seemed to be on the rejected rebound, thrown back from the outer world to be stored in memory of that outer world within. With Lawrence, however, life, particularly through speech, leaked vibrations: even as he spoke, the young Lawrence could feel that the words coming from little him were trespassing across lines and bounds which did not belong to him and yet had profoundly to do with his life, outside his control of effect. It is these tremulations on the ether that the writer could feel between two people, and that is what makes *Sons and Lovers* as sensitive to atmosphere as human litmus paper and a more just book than the mere autobiography of Paul Morel, written from the first person, could ever be. It was as if Lawrence did not believe in the first person he was sometimes obliged to be, as if his sense of life was bigger than that small youth he also often felt like. A reader of *Sons and Lovers* often feels that a sentence is written electrically from between the poles of both people involved in dialogue and relationship:

> Their two hands lay on the rough stone parapet of the Castle wall.
>
> Chap. x, p. 291.

> Sometimes they looked in each other's eyes. Then they almost seemed to make an agreement. It was almost as if he were agreeing to die also. But she did not consent to die; she would not.
>
> Chap. xiv, p. 417.

And it is so too in *The Rainbow*:

> The hand that touched her shoulder, hurt him, as if she were sending it away.
>
> Chap. vi, p. 151.

There are invisible feelings that percolate through and are absorbed by the walls of flesh. In owing this sensitive recognition to his own self-doubts, Lawrence virtually made *Sons and Lovers* a second version of *David Copperfield*:

> Scott was succeeded in our affections by Dickens, with *David Copperfield* pre-eminent. I was aware even then that Lawrence felt an affinity with the hero of that story— 'the nicest young man in the world', he would quote mischievously.
>
> *Lawrence: A Personal Record*, pp. 95–6.

But this time the young man did not find his way through to the personal authority that made him a writer or to the right woman after much searching. Lawrence in many ways always wanted authority, always wanted to be the son who grew up into his own man. And he was not going to sacrifice himself in order to trade as a writer upon his own weakness as a source of sensitivity. But the writing also made him see that his own authority and strength were not really what he wanted. He wanted a bigger, more open life than those proud things would admit, and that forced him to be more modest and yet less self-contained. The struggle was always there: to let life happen without making himself merely aesthetically passive; to let the writing part of him make him not try to take over life, and yet himself still participate in his own life as a man rather than as an experiment for a writer. Jessie Chambers and Catherine Carswell both describe the knots this tied him in; and the rows, the sulks, the need for a little chaos are undeniably signs of a desperate, lonely foolishness. But the endeavour itself, that does seem to be a large and great thing which illuminates those women's memoirs. For Lawrence refused to say of his life and his writing that one was primary, the other secondary and, as we shall see, refused to think of them as two things rather than one. In this, of course, he was challenging Hardy; even while the tension of maintaining the two together—without living for writing or writing for living—caused him as much a sense of pain as a sense of wholeness. And it has to be said that Hardy and Conrad might well be invoked here in the name of scepticism—as if to say that Lawrence's was in fact not the life of a man who had successfully balanced writing and living. Sometimes it looks like that of one suffering hubris in his presumption at aiming to work the two together. But isn't that precisely *why* he wrote? And is the endeavour to be scorned if it is incomplete? Is it to be scorned if, more seriously, it is misconceived rather than simply, heroically impossible? I need hardly say that such is precisely the quarrel which is at the basis of this present work, even if not resolved by it. All I can do is to try to put the case for Lawrence and the case for Hardy, while also wondering whether the case for Wordsworth might not have already transcended their opposition. For the rest, for the final moral decision, I must leave it to my readers; for my own feelings are often all too forced towards Hardy's side, from which, I fear, without thoughts of

Wordsworth and of Lawrence, there is anyway hardly any escape. And no relief: for even to see Lawrence as wrong is still to wish to be right in that sort of area and to find oneself unable so to be.

In that sense mine is a preliminary work, prior to choices one may not anyway be free to make. So, needing help, not least by temperament, I have been saying that Lawrence was turning Hardy inside-out. I also want to repeat now that Lawrence was also subverting Joseph Conrad by fighting in a quite different way from his, for a quite different notion in a writer's mind of the relation between art and life. And this is best illustrated in the light of that very sensible complaint made by Jessie Chambers about Lawrence's demands upon life and people: 'after all, what else could he expect?'.

Lawrence was clear in his own mind about what Conrad expected. His accusation with respect to Conrad was of 'giving in before you start'. As in the case of Hardy, there is truth in the criticism.

In Conrad's tale 'The End of the Tether' a naive old stoical sea-captain called Whalley has to visit a remote part of the coast to bring mail to a sceptical young recluse, Van Wyk. The young man, as if deserving Lawrence's judgment, tells his elder that, for all his old-fashioned hope, he will die of disgust when he finally sees that there is no improvement for modern man. Such prophecies Lawrence, at his cheapest, dismissed as the work of 'little Jesuses' (*Phoenix ii*, p. 419).

What happens to Whalley on his last command, however, is not that he finally sees, as Van Wyk predicted, but that he finally goes blind. On the one hand, Whalley in his blindness becomes a literal metaphor for and victim of Conrad's own sceptical pessimism in the heart of darkness:

> It is as if the light were ebbing out of the world.
>
> U.E., p. 304.[22]

Yet, on the other hand, Conrad also feels bound to turn round on himself in the person of the pessimistic Van Wyk, to shake him with the fulfilment of his own prophecy:

> as if the fact of Captain Whalley's blindness had opened his eyes to his own.
>
> U.E., p. 315.

For the sake of the money to be given to his daughter, Whalley tried on his final trip to steer blind: the sight of the predictably broken old man breaks the youth. For the young man cannot for long bear presiding with easy prophecy over the fate of the old one. For Conrad, the authority of experience cannot for long abide in knowing life without collapsing into the old, old suffering from it. It is the only way he could escape and punish Van Wyk's contradiction of living by a disbelief in life. Conrad's self-enclosed short stories, bitter successors to the Romantic lyric, sacrifice the accumulated familiarity of humanist memory built up within the sense of a world created by a nineteenth-century novel like *Middlemarch*. They put in place of that an isolated, self-insulated form of memorable adventure both alien to humanist accommodations and self-avenging for being so. This was why Lawrence called Conrad a Writer among the Ruins.

What Lawrence offers is a brand of memory which is not prophecy or experienced expectation. It is like that revealed in a sort of parable in *The Rainbow* where Anna, the Polish woman, tells the young Ursula, her English granddaughter, the (so to speak) anti-Conrad short story of her life with her first, sickened husband:

> 'He was bitter, and he never gave way. He lay beating his brains, to see what he could do. "I don't know what you will do," he said. "I am no good, I am a failure from beginning to end. I cannot even provide for my wife and child!"'
>
> 'But you see, it was not for him to provide for us. My life went on, though his stopped, and I married your grandfather.
>
> 'I ought to have known, I ought to have been able to say to him: "Don't be so bitter, don't die because this has failed. You are not the beginning and the end." But I was too young, he had never let me become myself, I thought he was truly the beginning and the end. So I let him take all upon himself. Yet all did not depend on him. . . .'
>
> 'Will somebody love me, grandmother?'
>
> 'Many people love you, child. We all love you.'
>
> 'But when I am grown up, will somebody love me?'

'Yes, some man will love you, child, because it's your nature. And I hope it will be somebody who will love you for what you are, and not for what he wants of you. But we have a right to what we want.'

The Rainbow, chap. ix, p. 257.

The child's question there, from within the heart of the family, points beyond it—'But when I am grown up, will somebody love me?'—to the time of the first great individual step for Lawrence:

The father and mother bonds now relax, though they never break. The family love wanes, though it never dies.

It is the hour of the stranger. Let the stranger now enter the soul.

And it is the first hour of true individuality, the first hour of genuine, responsible solitariness.

The Unconscious, pp. 102–3.[23]

In a similar way, only looking back, Anna sees the strange within the terms of the familiar: she says, 'I married your grandfather', although it was not of course 'your grandfather' she married. The past was innocent of what it would produce in the same way as the 'you' loved by all the family will become, both predictably as well as incredibly, the 'you' who is loved as a woman, sexually. 'In all this change,' wrote Lawrence, 'I maintain a certain integrity. But woe betide me if I try to put my finger on it' (*Phoenix*, p. 537). So the words of grandmother and child are not like Conrad's, foreign to the life of which they treat, but, as with the Polish woman herself in the first movement of *The Rainbow*, as strange as life is. 'My life went on, though his stopped' is just such a strange saying, made without her putting her finger, as it were, on that comma between her life and his. It is the human feeling of the meaning of Lawrence's otherwise apparently callous or opaque remark, 'Nothing is important but life' (*Phoenix*, p. 534). For memory here opens up the island of decisive failure upon which that other Pole, Conrad, landed his tales; it opens it up by an appeal to the life beyond and outside her husband's life and terms. 'You are not the beginning and the end': it is not simply harsh obliviousness for being a memory which, through time, brings with it feelings wider than the emotion which it recalls.

It says now what 'I *ought* to have been able to say', as well as what she did say, and what she ought to have been able to say was, in a strange way, for his sake too. For 'I let him take all upon himself', and 'the greatest conceit of all is the cry of loneliness' (*Phoenix ii*, p. 391).

And because of this past, Anna Lensky-Brangwen feels she can predict something of the future for her grandchild. Though, equally, because of the lesson of that past, she also knows it is right that what she is saying to Ursula she cannot thereby teach her. For Ursula's life too will go on, though her grandmother's stops. And Anna can live with her words as that other prophet, Van Wyk, could not. And the further implication is this: that Lawrence, unlike Conrad, could make his sentence on life without making it his own life-sentence.

Yet he could still write of his own life. For Lawrence had a stranger sense of memory—common both to the connection between past and future in his books and to the relation in his own mind between living and writing. Compared with Conrad, connections are more open and unexpected than closed. Let me show what I mean by juxtaposing two passages from 'Daughters of the Vicar' which are central to the tale's purpose and in their joint effect close to Anna's wisdom in that parable from *The Rainbow*. Here, first, is Lawrence's portrait of the young miner's mother dying:

> 'Mother!' he whispered.
> 'Yes,' was the reply.
> There was a hesitation.
> 'Should I go to work?'
> He waited, his heart was beating heavily.
> 'I think I'd go, my lad.'
> His heart went down in a kind of despair.
> 'You want me to?' . . .
> 'Yes, go to work, my boy,' said the mother.
> 'All right,' replied he, kissing her. His heart was down at despair, and bitter. He went away.
> 'Alfred!' cried his mother faintly.
> He came back with beating heart.
> 'What, mother?'

'You'll always do what's right, Alfred?' the mother asked, beside herself in terror now he was leaving her. He was too terrified and bewildered to know what she meant.

'Yes,' he said.

She turned her cheek to him. He kissed her, then went away in bitter despair. He went to work.

Collected Short Stories, i, p. 175.

The influence and the death of a mother are a strong autobiographical theme in Lawrence's work. And the syntax of those sentences has an authority of brevity based upon an imaginative memory of the life in between the moments of utterance—as if Lawrence could almost hear what lay behind it. At any rate, the passage thus works by something other than Conrad's turning of the verbal screw, squeezing the words out of himself; rather, it goes: 1. 'Mother!' . . . 'Yes' . . . 'Should I go . . .' 'I think I'd go'; 2. 'Alfred!' . . . 'What, mother?' . . . 'You'll always do what's right, Alfred?' . . . 'Yes'. In those two ebbing and flowing movements it works by something analogous to this:

That the LORD called Samuel: and he answered, Here *am* I.

And he ran unto Ē-́lī, and said, Here *am* I; for thou calledst me. And he said, I called not; lie down again. And he went and lay down.

And the LORD called yet again, Samuel. And Samuel arose and went to Ē-́lī, and said, Here am I; for thou didst call me. And he answered, I called not, my son; lie down again.

Now Samuel did not yet know the LORD, neither was the word of the LORD yet revealed unto him.

And the LORD called Samuel again the third time.

And he arose and went to Ē-́lī, and said, Here am I; for thou didst call me. And Ē-́lī perceived that the LORD had called the child.

1 Samuel 3. 4–8.

That is, in each narrative the short sentences are held in the middle of the page by an underlying faith which emerges at the end as obedience to an old law: 'He went away', 'And he arose and went'. We know that Lawrence admired the Book of Samuel as one of the great novels he had read at the prompting of his mother's own religiosity:

> Genesis, Exodus, Samuel, Kings, by authors whose purpose was so big, it didn't quarrel with their passionate inspiration. The purpose and the inspiration were almost one. Why, in the name of everything bad, the two ever should have got separated is a mystery.
>
> *Phoenix ii,* p. 418.

In *Son of Woman* John Middleton Murry sneered that Lawrence had made his mother the voice of his God. And indeed the big purpose of 'Daughters of the Vicar' does seem to lie in obedience to the memory she feels she must call him back to receive: 'You'll always do what's right'. Only, the way he keeps his promise is in open not closed relation to her words—as we see in our second passage where the purpose is big enough to prevent the tale quarrelling with itself.

His life went on, though hers stopped. There is now Louisa and a strange moment of decision as he kisses her in his pit dirt:

> 'What shall you do?' he asked.
> 'How?' she said.
> He was awkward at a reply.
> 'About me,' he said.
> 'What do you want me to do?' she laughed.
> He put his hand out slowly to her. What did it matter!
> 'But make yourself clean,' she said.
>
> *Collected Short Stories,* i, p. 182.

The saying of Lawrence's reactively disappointed youth, '*Nothing* matters', is here reclaimed, made right and clean this time as what he *ought* to have said and thought. 'What did it matter!'—this is 'making yourself clean'. For even thus the turn from Hardy or from Conrad to Lawrence is constituted by the capacity to find 'what did it matter!' as not cheating life but being it. What a parent might here call their carelessness or irresponsibility about decision is rather something which, between the pair of them, is grateful and amused that such things as earnest caution and portentous responsibility have been immersed into a situation innocent of—not merely

reactive against—their necessity. The relation of her laugh—
'What do you want me to do?'—to what she had earlier heard
him say at his mother's deathbed—'Should I go? . . . You want
me to?'—is complex and necessary, to make a sane new life.
And in this way, in doing what's right, the son both breaks
and keeps the hold of his promise to his mother and her
presiding memory. 'What did it matter!' is his only apparently
inconsequential way of responding to

> 'But it does matter!' she cried. 'And you *ought* to be
> happy, you ought to try to be happy, to live to be happy.
> How could I bear to think your life wouldn't be a happy
> one!'
>
> *Sons and Lovers*, Pt ii, chap. x, p. 258.

From life to work, from life to work, that continuous life-work,
trying to get it right, is quite different from Hardy's or
Conrad's. It is bigger than their sense of the fundamental
irony of being a writer about life. For here it is not merely
ironic that the woman who wishes him to marry and be happy
is also the person who has, in some measure, contributed to his
sense of unhappiness and his difficulty with women. Bigger
than that, it is because she knows this unhappiness and
something of her own role in it that she precisely does now
wish and beg him for his happiness. There is in Lawrence's
fiction a purpose big enough to do more than quarrel with
ironies. A life's 'big purpose', whereby the relation of the
words of Alfred's mother to what subsequently happens to her
son is also more than just ironic. For Alfred's was indeed his
way of doing what was right, not turning back in memory of
her way, but still going forward from that memory, like a son
towards being a husband—in all that change maintaining a
certain integrity, 'but woe betide me if I try to put my finger
on it'. So Lawrence leaves the connections open and untouched.
As if to say of the mother's 'You'll always do what's right' both

> We should ask for no absolutes, or absolute. Once and for
> all and for ever, let us have done with the ugly imperialism
> of any absolute. There is no absolute good, there is
> nothing absolutely right.
>
> *Phoenix*, p. 536.

and

> this is the beauty of the novel; everything is true in its own
> relationship, and no further.
>
> *Phoenix ii*, p. 422.

—everything:—'what does it matter!' and 'but it does matter!',
the mother and the wife—everything relatively true rather
than bitterly ironic.

It is not only, then, that the memory of the mother does not
simply stand over the work as Conrad's pessimism continues
to cast its shadow over his books, even though Conrad also
punishes it for doing so. Rather, it is also that the memory
from which Lawrence starts out in writing stands to the future
book as the words of Alfred's mother stood to their future
fulfilment. Lawrence did not preside over his own writing as
Conrad did until the moment of burying himself in it. So it is
this different *relation* of the writer to his work to which we must
now turn, if we are to understand what it meant for Lawrence
to be a writer not among the ruins but in the midst of his own
life. His was not to be writing merely in backward memory of
his life and his mistakes; for in it the writer was to move
forwards, the physician heal himself.

II. 'IN THE THICK OF THE SCRIMMAGE'

Like Paul Morel in his work as a painter, Lawrence as a writer
'worked a great deal from memory' (*Sons and Lovers*, Pt ii, chap.
xii, p. 301). Yet he also wrote, 'Memory is not truth. . . . It is
no good living on memory' (*Phoenix ii*, p. 414). He thought of
himself as a deeply personal writer, telling Ernest Collings in a
letter of 24 December 1912 that his motto was 'Art for *my*
sake'. Yet he also coined the famous aphorism, 'Never trust
the teller, trust the tale' which on the face of it seems closer to
T. S. Eliot's notion of impersonality. He was so personal, yet
at times seemed sick of personality, humanity, the vanity of
little autobiographies. He said he was tired of emotions and
the predominance we give to the idea that love is the greatest
thing. But no one was more emotional than Lawrence and no
one wrote more about love. He told Jessie Chambers that often
he felt like two men in one skin. Yet he could not abide the

thought of a split between the physical and the spiritual and hated the idea that the writer and the man were entirely separate.

John Middleton Murry was one who, both as friend and as critic, tried to make sense of what appeared to be Lawrence's contradictions. Another was Catherine Carswell who set herself the task of trying to think out why Lawrence gave up writing of the common people in work as warm as that of *Sons and Lovers* in order to dedicate himself to the hardness and coldness of *Women in Love*:

> I had always noticed that he took for granted the common virtues, and even many of what we call the Christian virtues. He built on a solid foundation.
>
> Carswell: *The Savage Pilgrimage*, p. 43.

That was what *Women in Love* was doing in following on from *Sons and Lovers*: it was taking it for granted. A risk which Lawrence took on trust that it was no risk; for really there could be no risk of what, if it remained, remained because it was essential. Although Catherine Carswell wrote her book to counter what she considered to be Murry's unjust betrayal of Lawrence, they were at least both agreed that 'he built on a solid foundation'. Murry said that Lawrence had been given, despite all the trouble between his mother and his father, a deep memory of common emotional warmths and pieties so familiar as to be beyond the necessity of explicit recollection. In contrast Murry thought that he himself was left with an almost pathological individualism: 'I did not know that I was seeking in personal affection the sense of "belonging" that was denied me' (Murry: *Between Two Worlds*, p. 329) and he felt he could take nothing for granted.

If only Lawrence had not turned his back on this deep memory! That was the charge that Jessie Chambers made not against the work after *Sons and Lovers* but versus *Sons and Lovers* itself, in which she thought herself travestied as Miriam. In her view, his writing from the first had a free and natural gift for not only remembering the common life but immediately giving value to the memory, adding to it a brilliance which, the writing convinced her, belonged to it: 'It was his power to transmute the common experience into significance that I always felt to be Lawrence's greatest gift.' (*Lawrence: A Personal Record*, p. 198). He gave her her memory, she felt, and 'in the passing of Lawrence,' she admits for all the pain he gave her, 'I saw also the extinction of my greater self' (ibid., p. 217). That power of making memorable common experience of life, rather than leaving it in the realm of the merely to be expected and taken for granted, is manifest even in the description of a miner in his bath, towelled by a wife who, though long embittered towards him, suddenly begins telling their son what a man he was whom she had married. That son was Lawrence and he writes of his father, almost as if he were Michael Henchard:

> Moral watched her shyly. He ṣaw again the passion she had had for him. It blazed upon her for a moment. He was shy, rather scared, and humble. Yet again he felt his old glow. And then immediately he felt the ruin he had made during these years. He wanted to bustle about, to run away from it.
>
> *Sons and Lovers*, Pt ii, chap. viii, p. 197.

Lawrence was praised by Jessie Chambers for finding the memory of the 'old glow', even the old glow that made his mother tell him that to be happy did matter. 'That's what one *must have*, I think,' Paul tells Miriam

> the real, real flame of feeling through another person—once, only once, if it only lasts three months. See, my mother looks as if she'd *had* everything that was necessary for her living and developing. . . . And with my father, at first, I'm sure she had the real thing. She knows; she has been there. You can feel it about her, and about him, and about hundreds of people you meet every day.
>
> *Sons and Lovers*, Pt ii, chap. xii, p. 317.

Yet, Jessie-Miriam thought, partly through that very mother and partly through the son's growing into a tense sexuality, there had come into this most natural writer an unnatural hardness that ruined his gift and betrayed the past and what he was:

It was difficult to see in the introspective young man of twenty-two the youth we had first known, brimming with delight in life and all it had to offer.

Lawrence: A Personal Record, p. 106.

I was aware of a deep tenderness within, that he held in check with an iron will.

Ibid., p. 128.

I could see so well the wonderful man he might be if only the deep reserves in his nature could be truly liberated.

Ibid., p. 173.

So, Jessie Chambers places earlier what critics such as Murry said later: that sexuality had ruined Lawrence, making him feel the sense of a strong discontinuity between family life and sexual life such that it was hard for an insecure mother's boy quite to see what meaning of the word 'life' the two shared. The familiar turned strange, the warmth grew cold, the emotions sanctified by a blood relationship found no equivalent home in the larger world. And all this, Lawrence's friends and critics seem to suggest, was at least partly due to a personal failure—to adapt, to grow up beyond adolescence, to keep his present in touch with his past. 'They all seem determined to make a freak of me,' he wrote, adding in characteristic reaction,'—to save their own short-failings, and make them "normal"' (*Collected Letters*, ii, p. 1124).

Yet was it merely a personal freak? W. H. Mallock had warned that, with their difference often signalled by the crux implicit in the sexual initiative, the social and the personal levels of life were becoming secretly 'incommensurate'. A man might sacrifice something for the social good but, at a testing point beneath that, would he give up the chance of winning his friend's wife for the sake of his friend and the principle of marriage? If in the seduction of a man's daughter, the matter were hushed up or seemed to give her no concern whatever, would the harm still be there?[24] Lawrence himself recognized just such confusions surrounding the relation between what one felt and what one was. To Hermione Rupert Birkin says, 'What do you want to feel unbounded for? . . . You don't want to *be* unbounded' (*Women in Love*, chap. viii, p. 78). Nor could one trust society to overrule what your emotions said and tell

you what you really were. For example, people say that love is
the greatest thing, notes Birkin of our social norms, and yet
they don't do anything like what they say and what they do
feel is really nothing like what they think they are meant to
feel. Ursula, however, fearing from Birkin that reaction that
refuses to reclaim the old ideal only because others have
betrayed it, replies that all that still does not alter the fact
which, she suspects, Birkin somewhere takes for granted, that
love is indeed the greatest. She argues with him:

> 'What they do doesn't alter the truth of what they say,
> does it?'
>   'Completely, . . .'

Ibid., chap. xi, p. 119.

Saying and doing, feeling and being seemed out of step with
each other as if the personal and the social were not mutual
aids towards a person's definition but different forms of self-
deception and cant.[25] It was like the problem that Tolstoy
when, confronted in *Anna Karenina*, the dogged Levin tries to
understand how Sviyazhsky can believe like a Liberal and yet
continue to act as a Conservative (Pt iii, chaps. 26–8). What,
asks Levin, is the connection between this man's life and his
thoughts? Indeed, at another level, that is precisely the question
which in this book I have been trying to ask of people who
write books about life. For writing, as Lawrence began to see,
is the only considered way of being able to test the relation
between what one feels and what one is, between what one
says and what one does—for in writing, especially for Lawrence
in the writing of novels, the saying, the putting down of words,
became a form of doing; the words being imaginatively in
memory of real life, whose memory now both tested and was
tested by its verbal treatment. When Lawrence wrote, 'never
trust the teller, trust the tale', he did not mean that the tale
was, as art, a thing magically separate from its creator; so far
from being separate, it was in the tale that the teller tested
himself not least in relation to things he did not *want* to believe
outside the book.

Yet writing could not do everything. Even if there was a
more-than-personal justification of, or basis for, Lawrence's
intensely personal troubles, as a reading of Mallock indeed
suggests, still for Lawrence these troubles could only be

registered most palpably by being registered personally. Any other way was open to a distrust that could not be personally tested by the act of writing it out. This indeed was the problem of individualism that Lawrence had so to speak inherited from Hardy. All he could do was not to write in the first but in the third person, not in poetic monologue but in prosaic dialogue in order that writing might test whether his personal experience was merely personal.

For Lawrence could not otherwise give up the personal; it was his basis, it was his evidence. The old words, like love and duty, were what he called the Word made Flesh, the old idea imposed upon every new life: 'The Word cannot be the beginning of life. It is the *end* of life, that which falls shed' (*The Unconscious*, p. 246). On the contrary, to use the shorthand employed in the original Foreword to *Sons and Lovers*, 'The Flesh was made Word'.[26] There was a deep wonder in Lawrence that the reality of many words was flesh, people, memories—as when Mrs Morel turned on her eldest son for nearly coming to blows with his father:

> 'A nice thing—your own father,' she replied.
> ' "*Father!*" ' repeated William. 'Call *him my* father!'
>
> *Sons and Lovers*, Pt i, chap. iv, p. 59.

And when he did, it went like this, on a return trip home from success in London:

> 'Well, dad!'
> The two men shook hands.
> 'Well my lad!'
>
> Ibid., Pt i, chap. iv, p. 81.

In the same way Paul is forced to take to him news of a success that he feels to belong really to the articulate, ambitious mother:

> 'I've won a prize in a competition, dad,' he said.
> Morel turned round to him.
> 'Have you, my boy? What sort of a competition?'
> 'Oh, nothing—about famous women.'
> 'And how much is the prize, then, as you've got?'

'It's a book.'
'Oh, indeed!'
'About birds.'
'Hm—hm!'

Ibid., Pt i, chap. iv, p. 73.

Yet while the young Paul hears only the mumbles of a father who understands money, not books, and has no place in this home, the older Lawrence can hear through memory something more, as when Walter Morel tries to comfront his sick son:

> 'Are ter asleep, my darlin'?' Morel asked softly.
>
> 'No; is my mother comin'?'
>
> 'She's just finishin' foldin' the clothes. Do you want anything?' Morel rarely 'thee'd' his son.
>
> 'I don't want nothing. But how long will she be?'
>
> 'Not long, my duckie.'
>
> The father waited undecidedly on the hearth-rug for a moment or two. He felt his son did not want him. Then he went to the top of the stairs and said to his wife:
>
> 'This child's axin' for thee; how long art goin' to be?'
>
> 'Until I've finished, good gracious! Tell him to go to sleep.'
>
> 'She says you're to go to sleep,' the father repeated gently to Paul.
>
> 'Well, I want *her* to come,' insisted the boy.
>
> 'He says he can't get off till you come,' Morel called downstairs.

Ibid., Pt i, chap. iv, p. 77.

From the point of view of the two sons, the words may seem no more than counters of the sort used by their mother against their inarticulate father; substitutes by which to hold him off. 'Well, dad!', 'Well, I want *her* to come'. The dialogue seems like cruel chess or a game of devalued exchange played with worn counters—the very opposite of the use of language admired by the devotees of high poetry where things *are* in virtue of their definitions:

> In prose as in algebra concrete things are embodied in signs or counters which are moved about according to rules, without being visualised at all in the process. . . .

> Poetry, in one aspect at any rate, may be considered as an effort to avoid this characteristic of prose. It is not a counter language but a visual concrete one.
>
> T. E. Hulme: *Speculations*, p. 134.

But if it is not the Word made Flesh, as prescribed by Hulme or T. S. Eliot, Lawrence can feel how for his father it was not merely a matter of counters but the Flesh made Word: 'Morel rarely "thee'd" his son . . . "Are ter asleep, my darlin?" . . . He felt his son did not want him'. For within working class Eastwood, as 'Miriam's' younger brother explains, this was not algebra but a passion and a culture of meaning:

> My mother had been brought up in a household in which the Christian injunctions of love and duty were literally rules of life, extending even to forgiving your enemies and turning the other cheek. Grievances must be silently borne, and frayed tempers must not give rise to hard words. In my father's family, on the other hand, frayed tempers and hard words were part of the currency of living. Life was a fight in which moods of anger, elation, love and hate alternated according to the swaying fortunes of the struggle. Words were counters of exchange, not symbols of eternal verities.
>
> J. D. Chambers, in Edward Nehls: *D. H. Lawrence*, iii, p. 535.

Lawrence in time found himself railing against the Christian injunctions of love and duty offered by the women: 'A cliché is just a worn-out memory that has no more emotional or intuitional root, and has become a habit' (*Phoenix*, p. 576). But the memory offered by those passages above is not worn-out. For although the words are not the eternal verities of writing but the transmuted memories of exchange through speaking, they gain their power through being written by Lawrence over the deep tacit memories which he can still hear beneath them. He hears and feels physically through this language how the father is a man stranded between his wife and his children unwanted on every side: 'He says he can't go off till you come'. He feels through the movement of dialogue, from father to son, from son to father, that the father is not merely the begetter of the son's general distress and the one bound to speak first, for he is on the receiving end of pain too; that the son is not merely the succeeding answer to and bearer of his father's ruined life, for he can hurt too from his own position of hurt vulnerability: 'I don't want nothing. But how long will she be?'. Both hurt each other, even with their pain, and it is the profound justice of dialogue to hear this. However 'unfair' Lawrence later felt he had been to his father in *Sons and Lovers*, there was still this deeper justice in the book:

> Even the dead ask only for *justice*: not for praise or exoneration. Who dares humiliate the dead with excuses for their living
>
> *Phoenix ii*, p. 359.

It was justice, above all, that Lawrence felt he needed in order to live properly, to die in peace. And he could feel, physically, in the act of writing a sense of justice to his father through his spoken words that hardly needed to come via Lawrence's own mental consciousness.

That what Lawrence gained in writing about himself as Paul is the same as what in the book Paul gains from his own past is shown quite un-self-consciously later in the book. The gain has to do with the deep memory of his father. For when Paul and his married woman, Clara, rise from their love-making, he, her younger man, tries to steady himself in this now strange world by instinctively borrowing his father's language to ease pain. Just as Lawrence felt for his father in writing of the young life of Paul, Paul himself, older now, finds something of his father's feeling in him like a physical memory. It is the inevitable justice of this sort of writing that the relation of father to son and of author to protagonist should come through; for this was an act of memory not in order to be as realistic but as true as possible.

> 'But tha shouldna worrit!' he said softly, pleading.
> 'No, I don't worry!' she laughed tenderly and resigned.
> 'Yea, tha does! Dunna thee worrit,' he implored, caressing.
> 'No!' she consoled him, kissing him.
>
> *Sons and Lovers*, Pt ii, chap. xii, p. 311.

Yet, as she consoles his consolation, Clara must know its inherent defensiveness—as described in a book Lawrence admired and reviewed:

> It is interesting how the folk mind betrays its need of this underlying subjective unity in its effort to offset the objective tendencies of differentiation. In its desire to express its feeling of unity, its sense of mutual understanding, the habitual mind automatically employs the phrase, 'It makes no difference'. For example, if one has been unintentionally thoughtless of another, he is at once put at his ease with the reassurance that 'it makes no difference'—it being obviously felt that the difference is the essential condition against which the social mind must preserve itself. Similarly we say 'It is no matter' or 'It is immaterial'—a material or objective basis of relationship being evidently likewise sensed as an impediment to unity.
>
> Trigant Burrow: *The Social Basis of Consciousness*, p. 122.

Dialect offers the protection of provincial unity against personal trouble, giving Lawrance an alternative, social coherence to offer against the decay and sham he felt men had inherited from the nineteenth century. The tone has about it the same dark, warm atmosphere as the cattleshed into which Tom Brangwen carries his step-daughter to soothe her cries— as if in memory of Walter Morel who could not help his own poorly son. The memory became a sense that Lawrence called his blood-consciousness:

> I cannot make the transfer from my own class into the middle class. I cannot, not for anything in the world, forfeit my passional consciousness and my old blood-affinity with my fellow-men and the animals and the land, for that other thin, spurious mental conceit which is all that is left to the mental consciousness once it has made itself exclusive.
>
> *Phoenix ii*, p. 596.

—Yet his own class had said, 'A collier's son a poet!' (Jessie Chambers: *Lawrence: A Personal Record*, p. 57). And if Lawrence was able to know a lot by personalizing the past, personalizing too what he read in Hardy or in Conrad, still the very presence of the personalities of his father and his mother in his mind was a pain as well as a strength to him. For the almost suffocating warmth and inclusiveness of the family world not only offered emotional violence as well as emotional support; it also had to confront the thought that there were, as Trigant Burrow said, differences in the outside world and even in the sexual world that could not be simply unmade. Clara saw that Paul could only lean on the words of his father's tongue; Lawrence had to fight his own way through to the freedom from fear that expressed itself not as 'Dunna thee worrit' but as 'what did it matter!'. Lawrence had to forget the idea of an alternative, coherent society, to which was attached other memories of his own pain and disgust within the miners' world. And putting all those memories behind him after *Sons and Lovers,* he had to go on with whatever was left of them tacitly in him. It was in this ambivalent relation to his past, a man anxious to change himself while fearful thereby of also betraying himself, that Murry and Carswell found him.

*   *   *   *   *

It is at this stage of the argument that it becomes important to consider again Lawrence's sometime friend, the literary critic, John Middleton Murry. In this context there are two important points to be made about Murry.

First, if there is one theme in his literary criticism, it is that of a felt necessity to keep a living memory of Romanticism. It was Murry who took up the Romantic, personal position against T. S. Eliot and his notions of impersonality in their rather nostalgically outdated and polarized debate over Classicism versus Romanticism: 'a comparison of Outside Authority with the Inner Voice'.[27] Murry as a critic tried to speak in memory of the inner voice of the artist's soul. For the artist's work was an allegory of his soul and it was for the critic to make explicit the life implicitly expressed through the work.

> The truly great man cannot be judged by our standards, he must be judged by his own. The inward compulsion which we feel to judge a man by himself, in relation to his

own being and the ideals which his being drives upwards
into his consciousness, is the surest evidence that we are
confronted with a great man.

Murry: *Keats and Shakespeare*, p. 209.

A person of real feeling had often to protect himself from other
people's words for feeling, if he was to think through his
emotions and make his own sense of his own life. The ideal
here was a person who through his writing revealed the
distinctiveness of his own being through his own terms. To
Murry that was 'a significant variation', someone out of the
normal run of words, expectations and formulae, who could
say what something meant to him.[28] It might almost have
been—indeed, Murry felt that it ought to have been—Lawrence
himself whom he was describing. Only Lawrence, Murry felt,
had gone wrong and become perverse.

Thus, although this present work owes a debt to the first
chapter of *Keats and Shakespeare*, a brave and wonderful book, it
is a debt to what Murry *said*, with reservations about what
Murry *did*. And this brings me to my second point. If there is
one obsession in Murry's life, it is the thought of Lawrence
cutting across and seeming to throw out in disgust this very
Romantic idealism from *Keats and Shakespeare* onwards. At one
moment in their friendship Lawrence seemed to be offering
Murry a way to change himself; at the next, declaring him
hopeless, he wanted him out of his sight. It would have been
better for Murry had he been able to give up the thought of
Lawrence, forget him and go his own way, but it was as if
Lawrence hung in Murry's mind over the thought of his own
weaknesses, and Murry was able neither to face nor to ignore
the challenge that Lawrence was to him. Thus he offers the
following account, testily, as from Lawrence's point of view
when really it may have been, more vulnerably, from his own:

Precisely because I was the person who could *not* understand Lawrence, I was called to be the person who must
understand him.

Murry: *Reminiscences of D. H. Lawrence*, p. 15.

But Lawrence who, here blamed, had died three years
previously, in life might have countered by saying, equally,

that Murry had offered himself to Lawrence as the person who
'*must* understand' but, alas so far, 'could not'. We shall come
shortly to what these inversions mean. At any rate it can be
shown that Murry was indeed good at being the sort of man
who could not help but helplessly find things turning his way:

> the terrible thing was that I *could* not submit to Lawrence.
> I could in a moment of impulse believe that I could do it,
> promise that I would do it; but there, lurking all the while
> in my secret depths, was the utter determination not to
> submit, not to follow.
>
> Ibid., p. 23.

'Terrible' there offers itself for the portrait of a man frightened
to think of the awesome, inexorable power of his individual
soul. But the 'secret' is perhaps more terrible than that depth:
what really frightened him was the thought that his failure
with Lawrence meant that he had 'lurking' nothing but the
shallows of a self-justifying, self-recalling mental consciousness.
And there is no way that one can test the language Murry uses
to see whether or not this is true. For he had put his words,
safely he thinks, into the realm and tone of opinionatedness.
He uses memory in his *Reminiscences* as a substitute for soul:

> We have made the idea supplant both impulse and
> tradition. . . . there is a substitute for everything—life-
> substitute—just as we have butter-substitute, and meat-
> substitute, and sugar-substitute.
>
> Lawrence: *The Unconscious*, p. 140.

To Lawrence it must have seemed that Murry's literary
criticism was a substitute for a more strenuous, frightening
and first-hand encounter with the meaning of his own life.
Certainly after Lawrence's death Murry had this to say to
those, like Catherine Carswell, who called him a Judas:

> They do not see that, so surely as Lawrence is destroyed
> in *Son of Woman*, so surely am I destroyed. The book is its
> own reply, and it will never have another. All that is
> impure in it, is to my everlasting discredit; all that is pure
> in it—and I know that most of it is pure—is to Lawrence's
> everlasting fame.
>
> *Reminiscences of D. H. Lawrence*, pp. 24–5.

It is deeply disturbing that no one would think of expressing himself like that without the idea of writing as offering authority even in self-justification. Indeed, a book so anxious to be its own closed-in reply is what autobiography, like Murry's own *Between Two Worlds*, was to Lawrence: evidence of the self-contained self-confirmed corruption of a soul who knows too much about itself to want to know how to get out of its predicament. 'Physician, heal thyself!' But Murry was only healing himself by justifying himself:

> Whether Lawrence was right or wrong, it came to the same thing in the end. Either I knew nothing about myself, or he knew nothing about me: and it didn't matter which it was. Whether the gulf was between me and myself, or between me and him, the gulf was there.
>
> *Between Two Worlds*, p. 331.

But at any level other than that of the circumstantial, it does matter. Yet to avoid facing the fact that it does matter, Murry set up in his mind a Murry and a Lawrence. There was a Lawrence's Murry who admits, in pre-emptive fear of Lawrence's criticism, everything to himself or, rather, to the Lawrence within him:

> All that is impure in it, is to my everlasting discredit.

And there was a Murry's Lawrence, really the Murry who is vain about himself but, uncertain of that self too and certain of Lawrence's criticisms of it, needs to call himself 'Lawrence':

> all that is pure in it—and I know that most of it is pure— is to Lawrence's everlasting fame.

This was the way that writing helped a man to take-over his own living.

And Lawrence had already diagnosed this tendency, long before Murry disappeared completely inside it. It was the creation of a substitute-unconscious, a substitute-memory:

> spawn produced by secondary propagation from the mental consciousness itself.
>
> *The Unconscious*, p. 204.

Murry looked into the past as if into a mirror; the image he saw there was not coming to him, he brought it back with him.

And he could not admit this mental substitution, he could only obsessively repeat it. This explains the inversions of which I spoke earlier. For Murry's syntax can be reversed against him so easily because it is so obviously the syntax of a man who carried out an initial reversal in order to get himself into words at all. Murry writes that he did not (—understand Lawrence, follow Lawrence), because he could not; we see that it is at least equally likely that he says he could not sheerly because he did not. He 'could not' is 'spawn produced by secondary propagation', called writing.

The autobiographical ruin of the critic who himself believed in the importance of the relation between the writer and his life becomes all too horribly clear an irony in Murry's treatment of Lawrence. For what Middleton Murry urged upon (a deceased) Lawrence with respect to his relation to woman:

> If Lawrence could have accepted his own intrinsic dependence, then he would, by that very act, have become independent.
>
> *Son of Woman*, p. 137.

—was also just what Murry was to condemn in himself in his relation to Katherine Mansfield:

> I had used the very freedom of my declaration of total dependence upon her to retain my practical independence. . . . I wanted the security of love and I wanted the security of myself; I wanted to be safe in both worlds.
>
> *Between Two Worlds*, p. 391.

In thus substituting personal and sexual affection for the want of a sense of belonging in the world, Murry had to be and to remain a confused man. He could not afford to ask himself whether that wish for both worlds created or followed from his intellectual claim that the existence of two worlds is a fact. A fact that, for Murry, created and excused his own sense of felt division of which the wish for both worlds was an expression. It was a fact, wrote Murry of *Aaron's Rod*, which Lawrence had neglected:

> Lilly is confusing the orders of human experience. He is asking for the final detachment of spirit, and for the warmth of human relation, at the same moment, and in

the same order. . . . There is no real contradiction between the acceptance of one's own isolation in the spiritual order, and the avoidance of isolation in the personal order. To be alone in spirit, and not to be alone in person are perfectly compatible; but to maintain that not to be alone in person is the condition of being alone in spirit is quite false. Lawrence is always pretending that there is this essential connection.

Son of Woman, pp. 217–8.

Yet that is to see Lawrence through the looking glass. For Birkin's apparently absurd hesitation over Ursula and his otherwise ridiculous attempt to talk out a basis for a relationship that has no familiar origin in blood are actually a form of ardour that refuses to accept relationship as no more than 'the avoidance of isolation in the personal order'. The mere trading of lonelinesses and failures was a travesty of what marriage ought to mean—that is why Birkin is so toughly sensitive:

'My life is unfulfilled,' she said.
'Yes,' he answered briefly, not wanting to hear this.
'And I feel as if nobody could ever really love me,' she said.
But he did not answer.

Women in Love, chap. xix, p. 241.

Lawrence precisely made it difficult for himself by refusing to hide spiritual inadequacy within a cosy marital union; yet at the same time as one was not meant to go to someone else merely out of the failure of one's own life, one was not meant to keep quite apart from a union in which one honourably could make the inner separateness that was also needed for commitment there. Lawrence feared as well as loathed what Trigant Burrow had called 'marital neurosis' (op. cit. pp. 93–4), whereby a husband and wife can cease to be themselves in becoming two mutually compensating halves of one couple. It was on the private level the equivalent of Mallock's account of what George Eliot's sympathy came down to: 'I am so glad that you are glad that I am glad'—those convenient old emotions of love and sympathy that Lawrence ridiculed in his depiction of the father of Gerald Crich who 'had substituted pity for all his hostility' and 'before the armour of his pity really broke, he would die . . . This was his final resource' (*Women in Love*, chap. xvii, pp. 206–7).

So, here was Murry using himself as a seesaw between the independence born out of dependence and the dependence which retains independence behind its own back. His mind seems to have watched his experience as if it were that of another person. Moreover, it is not as if Murry's being fearful both of being alone and of being love-trapped is the same as Lawrence's desire to be himself and to be married and to maintain a connection between those two states. Yet Murry, I think, suspected that the latter ideal in Lawrence was really the product of something analogous to Murry's own auto-biographical weaknesses; and that Lawrence became himself out of his anger with people like Murry who reminded him of his own past—became himself, that is, Lawrence the physician, precisely at the expense of the Murrys, by willing himself, even in verbally lashing them, *not* to be like them. That was why Murry would not believe that there was a real difference revealed between the fates of Birkin, whom Lawrence clearly made himself, and Gerald Crich, whom Lawrence admitted to be partly a portrait of Murry, from the time when the Lawrences lived next door to Murry and Mansfield. 'To our consciousness,' wrote Murry of the two men's relationships with women in *Women in Love*, 'they are indistinguishable', even if they are supposed to be somehow separated on 'a plane of consciousness other than ours'—namely, Lawrence's (*Reminiscences of D. H. Lawrence*, p. 229). Yet, in fact, when we look back at *Between Two Worlds* it is not hard to see that Lawrence had indeed got something right about Murry in his depiction of Gerald in relation to Gudrun:

> 'Strangers,' she said, 'we can never be. But if you *want* to make any movement apart from me, then I wish you to know you are perfectly free to do so. Do not consider me in the slightest.'
> Even so slight an implication that she needed him and was depending on him still was sufficient to rouse his passion. As he sat a change came over his body, the hot, molten stream mounted involuntarily through his veins.

> He groaned inwardly, under its bondage, but he loved it.
> He looked at her with clear eyes, waiting for her.
>
> *Women in Love*, chap. xxx, p. 447.

'He *loved* it', that menacing dependence of his; and never is the word love used with such anger and disgust by Lawrence as here, imaginatively fascinated as well as appalled by the death in the man. Where Lawrence had a strangeness of *feeling*, Murry adopted a *convenience* of *emotion*, as if in safer imitation. But that very corruption of convenience itself provoked in Lawrence a strange imagination related to the doubts that Lawrence did feel when Murry reminded him of something equivalent in himself, in his past and in his general human nature.

And this is what made Lawrence's art so dangerous. It was not as if his books, after *Sons and Lovers*, appealed to projective sympathy, so that Murry or someone like Murry could say comfortably of Gerald Crich as George Eliot had said of herself in relation to Casaubon: '"That's me! That's exactly it! I'm just finding myself in this book!"' (*Phoenix*, p. 518). Lawrence did not want his art on a shelf of distanced impersonality either:

> I can't bear art that you can walk round and admire. A book should be either a bandit or a rebel or a man in a crowd. . . . An author should be in among the crowd, kicking their shins or cheering on to some mischief or merriment. . . . And art, especially novels, are not little theatres where the reader sits aloft and watches—like a god with a twenty-lira ticket—and sighs, commiserates, condones and smiles.—That's what you want a book to be: because it leaves you so safe and superior, with your two-dollar ticket to the show. And that's what my works are not and never will be. . . . whoever reads me will be in the thick of the scrimmage, and if he doesn't like it—if he wants a safe seat in the audience—let him read somebody else.
>
> *Collected Letters*, ii, p. 821.

And that is what is involved in comparing Lawrence's use of memory and writing with Middleton Murry's: a fight to find and kill in a reader's imaginative memory the rotten bits, the 'connu! connu!', that do the dirt on life. Because for Lawrence relativism did not mean seeing and respecting differences; it meant bringing to one's own life and to the lives of those around the question, how to live? was this the right way? or this? or this? is life in this? And Lawrence is so busy testing himself as well as others in his novels that, unless the novel is an outright failure, there is no time to tell, only to test, and be tested by, the reader. This is what breaking out of the hold of Hardy and of Conrad had to mean for Lawrence, together with a stringent sense of the temporary and the changing.

The writing did not exist for the sake of his memory as it did for Murry in his autobiographical criticism. The memory existed for the writing, the writing for the sake of justice, if possible, to the life otherwise too 'conveniently' recalled. Lawrence did not seek mere control through his art. And though he cares very much in one sense, in another he does not mind laying himself open through the help of writing to most damaging criticism. His was a hardened art, involving above all the uncovering of lies:

> The curious thing about art-speech is that it prevaricates so terribly. I mean it tells such lies. I suppose because we always all the time tell ourselves lies. . . .
> Truly art is a sort of subterfuge. But thank God for it, we can see through the subterfuge if we choose.[29]

For in the novel the novelist cannot really preside. Saying and doing are tested in a way just ahead of the controlling responsibility of the novelist, in and in between the dialogue. Lawrence's art is to 'do' the saying and then see what the saying does. For example—when Birkin grudgingly says to Ursula:

> 'I must believe in you, or else I shouldn't be here saying this.'
>
> *Women in Love*, chap. xiii, p. 138.

—there is much wrong with him, much fear of responsibility. But in his reluctance to say the word that will make them lovers, there is one, so to speak, evasion of responsibility which is sheerly admirable: the avoidance of saying the last word on himself and what he feels in their mutual relationship.

For of course there is a great fascination in a completely effected idealism. Man is then undisputed master of his own fate, and captain of his own soul. But better say engine-driver, for in truth he is no more than the little god in his machine, this master of fate.

The Unconscious, pp. 207–8.

Murry was a great one for 'saying this' as a means of 'being this' in his writing. But here it is not that Birkin, 'here saying this', *is* what he is saying and no more than his own final word. Rather, what counts is the relation between saying 'this' and also being 'here': that is 'art-speech' with its imagination of physical context and human relationship. Dialogue physically complicated Lawrence's memory, forced him into a wider physical, rather than self-centredly mental consciousness, making it harder for him simply to tell lies just because one had the words to cover oneself with. For 'saying this' was not the only thing Lawrence's language had here to do. It had to do at least enough to enable a reader to feel Birkin's churlishness, know through that feeling the reason for it in that context *and* the more major honesty he was able to release through its exaggeration.

Jesus' question to His mother, 'Woman, what have I to do with thee!'—while expressing a major truth, still has an exaggerated sound, which comes from its denial of a minor truth.

Ibid., p. 68.

In the 'big purpose' of reclaiming a sense of the meaning of serious living, the cost was this taking for granted of smaller minor truths, the very room for which was left to the reader to fight for, as the more major truth tried to struggle free. Indeed often Lawrence in a sort of arrogant humility felt that the individual had no right, as well as little time, to hedge his utterance around with the protection of the other things to be said or the things other people, in response, would have to say. In a deeply social sense, one replied upon people recognizing and helping with the incompleteness. Thus in *Women in Love* there is this insistence that this man Birkin, so like Lawrence himself, is still only a part of what Lawrence describes and Birkin himself is involved in, 'here'. For Birkin's is a consciousness itself quite conscious of being *constituted* by the reality of which it is conscious. For Hardy this circle meant a hellish imprisonment. For Birkin the very relativism licences and places his presumption in speaking first only for himself— refusing to conjugate the whole verb for other people as Gerald's father does. For beneath that arrogance, which in itself is a minor truth and risk, is its dependence on trying to make others do likewise. The fundamental humility in Birkin's knowing that he cannot and will not master the life of which he is but part still involves integrity's necessity to be that part to the personal maximum of itself. Nonetheless, in that acknowledgement by consciousness that it is not captain or master but part, indeed part of one part, there is an end to what Lawrence called idealism and its concomitant disappointments in men such as Hardy and Conrad, who had wanted to be captains of their fate.

For Lawrence, if consciousness does dominate the reality of which it is conscious, then all we have is a monologue of memory, just words for flesh. And that is where we find Murry; writing thus, apparently impersonally and covering all a reader's objections, of his resistance to marriage in an early love affair:

> He dimly felt that the responsibility for this strained situation was being placed on him: that Marguéritte was asking him why he did not put an end to it by marrying her . . .
>
> He did not think or argue these things. He was not even conscious of his reluctance. His resistance was unaware of itself; it was expressed in its own non-expression. . . . and the form of his evasion of the simple serious question which Marguéritte was putting to him was a feeling that there was something on his side of the situation that she could not understand.
>
> *Between Two Worlds*, pp. 162–4.

How should a man know so much about himself in retrospect? How can the man here remember in such a way as to leave no resonance? 'He' here is written by 'I' as much in disguise as impersonal. For it is an I still between two worlds in wanting room both to confess himself apparently disinterestedly and to suggest that that past self no longer quite belongs to him, even as it was never quite controlled by him at the time. It is not the 'he' of an even-handed novel. For it creates the image of a person remembering as a form of controlling; a person whose memory actually shields from the reader, pre-emptively, any feeling of the reality of *what* it is he is recalling. This is what happens when a person tries to substitute personal relations for an understanding of his own relation to life; and that person was Murry rather than Lawrence. It is Murry who uses people in order to understand himself, but even then only safely understanding himself in retrospect. And it is Murry who thought one could get away with substituting love affairs for the want of moral coherence and purposive belonging in the modern social world. In fact of course, for all his attempts at control through memory, Murry's autobiography does give its man away—even as he seeks credit for its doing so. This is the justice, or hubris, revealed through writing. For if there is, as Murry wants to think, a courage in his own retrospective sense of cowardice, still that courage is, recognizably to us, spurious and secondary, of memory rather than of life. As if to know one did not know could itself claim to be knowledge! It is still a courage immersed in its own cowardice—'as surely as Lawrence is destroyed in *Son of Woman*, so surely am I destroyed'—the sneaky, unknowingly self-destructive courage of a coward. Now, Murry's autobiography is in this sense an achievement, albeit a corrupt one. For the spectacle of this partly inadvertent display of lying is indeed compelling, in the way that Maurice Magnus or Gerald Crich were fascinating to Lawrence. This autobiography is so truly a lie that we can see in it the same old Murry whose truth behind his lies had no form of expression save in 'its own non-expression'. To see through his account only requires the subtle knowledge that throws off Murry's rationalizing verbalizations in coming from equivalent experience of one's own lying. It is not, as Lawrence might say, life. There is no glowing heart to memory in Murry's expressions as there is in *Sons and Lovers* or *The Rainbow*. And to be just to Murry would be to know how much closer Murry was to Gerald Crich than he, out of mere fairness to himself, could have said. The Gerald who in chapter xvii of *Women in Love* is described as looking in the mirror and seeing, with fear, only a mask; who in chapter xxix is caught by Gudrun in reflection in her mirror, as if unconsciously he gave himself away to her. 'For the greatest of all misery is a lie' (*Phoenix*, p. 674) and Lawrence actually took Murry deadly seriously. Knowledge of Murry's real misery might make us, on our terms, sorrier for that man who wants us to be sorry for him than he in fact could dream or bear. Yet it is precisely to that point that he seems, half-deliberately, in *Between Two Worlds*, to have to tempt us, 'expressed in its own non-expression'.

Murry inadvertently teaches us what Lawrence learnt from people like him: that the retrospectively created sense of self is a fiction, a rationalizing lie, a secondary effect. In Trigant Burrow's phrase, Murry breaches 'the double negative of all unconsciousness' (*The Social Basis of Consciousness*, p. 183). That is to say, in such secondarily constructed memories as 'he did not think or argue these things' and 'His resistance was unaware of itself', Murry thinks that, through memory now, he knows compensatingly that then he did not know. Yet, really, he had before half-deliberately to *make* himself not know what he was up to. The present is not wiser than the past simply because the past puts off the day of wisdom. And the person who hides from himself in the first place will not find himself in the second; all he will find there is his own hiding. True unconsciousness, says Burrow, is not only unconscious in itself but unconscious of itself and its own existence: that is its double negative; that is why it is not susceptible to conscious, recalling summons but has to be recognized emerging through art and art-speech. Thus the unconscious to which Murry refers, with his sense of what he could and could not do whatever he willed or said, is what Lawrence called 'the inverted reflection of our ideal consciousness', 'a shadow cast from the mind' (*The Unconscious*, p. 208). His was a mind '*deliberately unconscious*' (ibid., p. 203):

> My instinctive presupposition has always been that if I like a woman, the woman will not like me. It is just the same today, even though I have to confess that my uniform experience has been that whenever I liked a woman it has always turned out that she has liked me.
>
> *Between Two Worlds*, p. 138.

'Instinctive' there is not what Lawrence meant by instinct, it does not surface, like an implicit or dynamic memory, from the nature of the human race:

> Queer little breaks of consciousness seemed to rise and burst like bubbles out of the depths of his stillness.
>
> *The Rainbow*, chap. i, p. 36.

Murry's instinct is conscious of itself as a personal deflection, 'all reflected downwards from the mind' (*Phoenix ii*, p. 493). But for Lawrence 'breaks of consciousness' are not merely the breaks that interrupt consciousness, as if consciousness were man's primary mode of being, but the breaks that form consciousness coming up from below it. That last signals that distinctive view of life which Murry the critic called the great man's 'significant variation'. Which shows that in Murry the critic was wiser than the autobiographer; he was able to use his own experience of life more fruitfully in criticism.

For otherwise Murry's notion of instinct as mental consciousness as a result of his own insecure past makes for autobiographical imprisonment. That's the sort of person I am and must be—enjoying having first things only second, instincts as substitutes, unions degraded into luck. Instinctively in the first place I think the woman will not like me; 'even though I have to confess' in the second that they always do. His difficulties are not those which consciousness inherits through unconscious memory; rather, they are reflected back into instincts by consciousness itself—'the woman will not like me'—'like' there being merely a social word fearfully substituting for 'love'. Murry, then, exemplifies after Lawrence's death all the faults that Lawrence had found with that Freudian psychoanalysis which he thought was beginning to dominate men's minds in the twentieth century. The faults of conscious creation of an unconscious.

'We must discover, if we can,' wrote Lawrence in consequence, 'the true unconscious, where our life bubbles up in us, prior to any mentality' (*The Unconscious*, p. 208). What Lawrence has always to ask himself is whether what he got from his memory was no more than what he had put into it, an idea, like Murry's; or whether it was 'the interpretation of a profound yearning': it is Birkin's question about his own self-generated philosophy of love—'Was it really only an idea, or was it the interpretation of a profound yearning? (*Women in Love*, chap. xix, p. 245). For Hardy it had been the irony of the place of man and human mind that they had both arisen from below in the course of evolution, rather than been pre-ordained from above. But it is another of the massive differences between Hardy and Lawrence, as between the end of one age and the beginning of another, that below, for Lawrence, was not ironically but dynamically where life started. And when Lawrence says 'only an idea', or only a word, or only in retrospect, he is challenging received notions of human dignity as in fact condescendingly belittling. In this, to my mind, Lawrence belongs with Tolstoy, in respect of Tolstoy's challenging the idea that art is a matter of pure, high beauty, raising man above himself. Tolstoy argued:

> Speech transmitting the thoughts and experiences of men serves as a means of union among them, and art serves a similar purpose. The peculiarity of this latter means of intercourse, distinguishing it from intercourse by means of words, consists in this, that whereas by words a man transmits his thoughts to another, by art he transmits his feelings.[30]

It is in that way, according to which Tolstoy wrote 'feelings' rather than 'ideas', that Lawrence found himself thinking 'only an idea'. And Lawrence also said, 'feelings, not emotions', in the wide sense of what it *feels* like to be, to think like, to inhabit the real life of this man or that woman. For there feeling is a physical, rather than simply mental, consciousness: a physical consciousness upwards from which the conscious life emerges. Now as far as I can judge, it is quite properly the role of a critic, such as Middleton Murry, to try to make explicit what was implicit in whatsoever of his life a writer was able to convey within words—in the deepest sense of 'his life'. For too much goes and has to go unsaid in the everyday world, men do not transmit through speech their thoughts to each other, too much is left secret or in dignified reserve. Lawrence, for example, was the sort of boy and the sort of young man who kept asking, particularly of his elders as if they already might know from their own experience what lay before him, 'what do you think life is?', 'what are we?' (Nehls: *D. H. Lawrence*, iii, pp. 593, 595). And though art can write what can hardly be said, it still cannot be utterly explicit, it still has to put out signals as much as statements. For to make explicit statements is certainly to try to say what life is, but at the grave cost of losing the felt context, the life, the memory in which it has, from which it derives, its meaning. Art cannot be the repetition of experience and it must not be the dry residue of experience. Tolstoy's sense of art as 'feeling' lies in between those alternatives. But where a man can be as explicit about himself as can Middleton Murry—'I have to confess that my uniform experience has been that whenever I have liked a woman it has always turned out that she has liked me'—he becomes unreal, his own idea of himself. Lawrence himself would not surrender the importance of the explicit in art and through art; for that was one of the aims of art for 'my sake' rather than for the sake of its own implicit success, that it should help the man who wrote it to know his own past and live his own future:

> Any man of real individuality tries to know and to understand what is happening, even in himself, as he goes along. This struggle for verbal consciousness should not be left out in art. It is a very great part of life. It is not superimposition of a theory. It is the passionate struggle into conscious being.[31]

But if he was not to be that mere residuum of himself that Murry was in his autobiography, Lawrence had to try for this explicit understanding within a realm that kept *alive* the difficulties of experience stored up in his unconscious.

Here, then, is a representative example of how Lawrence found in the 'feeling' of writing that life 'prior to any mentality' that his own mentality needed to think about yet not to distort. Aaron is urging the Marchesa to sing as he plays; likewise, as he writes, the reader can feel Lawrence listening to his imagination of what is happening, thus accompanying himself in a very different way from Murry's:

> 'I can't sing,' she said, shaking her head rather bitterly.
> 'But let us try,' said he, disappointed.

'I know I can't,' she said. But she rose.

He remained sitting at the little table, the book propped up under the reading-lamp. She stood at a little distance, unhappy.

'I've always been like that,' she said. 'I could never sing music, unless I had a thing drilled into me, and then it wasn't singing any more.'

But Aaron wasn't heeding. His flute was at his mouth, he was watching her. He sounded the note, but she did not begin. She was twisting her handkerchief. So he played the melody alone. At the end of the verse, he looked up at her again, and a half-mocking smile played in his eyes. Again he sounded the note, a challenge. And this time, at his bidding, she began to sing. The flute instantly swung with a lovely soft firmness into the song, and she wavered only for a minute or two. Then her soul and her voice got free, and she sang—she sang as she wanted to sing, as she had always wanted to sing, without that awful scotch, that impediment inside her own soul, which prevented her.

She sang free . . . For the first time!

Aaron's Rod, chap. xviii, p. 248.

Clearly this is in memory of those women, from Helen Corke to his own Frieda, to whom Lawrence riskily said, in his post-Hardy way, 'Suffering bores me' (*Women in Love*, chap. xiii, p. 145). Murry said that he 'could *not* understand Lawrence', '*could* not submit' to him. With something both related to, but redemptive of the principle involved in, the bullying that Lawrence risked in such situations, the Novel here takes on the Autobiography involved in the Marchesa's 'I can't'. The 'sardonic courage' of Aaron's refusal sympathetically to accept on her terms the fact that she can't sing is deliberately, aggressively but at least uncondescendingly, straightforward: if you can sing a song, you can sing—here's the song. Or as Nietzsche said, 'Your virtue is your self, and not an outward thing' (*Thus Spake Zarathustra*, p. 110). He dismisses 'the idea' she has, in her 'I know I can't', the idea 'which is at once so all-powerful and so nothing' (*The Unconscious*, p. 226). And the Marchesa before the song is also rather like Lawrence faced with a novel to write, feeling, he said, like praying, worrying that he was not big enough, but knowing it is no use merely thinking about it now:

> A character in a novel has got to live, or it is nothing. We, likewise, in life have got to live, or we are nothing.
>
> *Phoenix*, p. 537.

As she pitches in, there is no gap between the singer and the song and yet there is a sense of her having passed over, one knew not when, one knew not how, something she now knows to have been there by her not having been prevented by it. 'She sang free' gives us the two, the singer and the song, not as two (such as in Hardy's art of poet and poetry struggling together in a tight space) but in one:

> And just exactly as the people separate the lightning from its flash, and interpret the latter as a thing done, as the working of a subject which is called lightning, so also does the popular morality separate strength from the expression of strength, as though behind the strong man there existed some indifferent neutral *substratum*, which enjoyed a *caprice and option* as to whether or not it should express strength. But there is no such *substratum*, there is no 'being' behind doing, working, becoming; 'the doer' is a mere appendage to the action. The action is everything. In point of fact, the people duplicate the doing, when they make the lightning lighten, that is a 'doing-doing': they make the same phenomenon first a cause, and then, secondly, the effect of that cause.
>
> Nietzsche: *The Genealogy of Morals*, pp. 45–6.[32]

It is, likewise, the autobiographical memory of a Middleton Murry which 'duplicates the doing', needing to tell himself that he is the subject as well as the object of his own act of memory, needing to put what he has learnt from the memory of his actions back in front of those actions in the person of a motivated agent. But with Lawrence, we can do no better than quote Virginia Woolf's brilliant description of how his words

> flow as fast and direct as if he merely traced them with a rapid hand on sheet after sheet. Not a sentence seems thought about twice.
>
> Woolf: *Collected Essays*, i, p. 353.

—'and she sang—she sang as she wanted to sing, as she had always wanted to sing'. The sentence comes through itself: 'Look, we have come through!'. For Lawrence used his memory even as the Marchesa felt hers in her singing: in that deepening of tenses (to '*had* always wanted' finally), she moves forward in proportion to the movement of her past away from her, removing the block or 'scotch'. In Lawrence, unlike in Hardy, there is not a time of memory and a time of writing; there is not an agent with a memory as 'substratum' and, quite separately, the action of his words on paper. There is one thing: the action with the agent implicit in it, the movement forward leaving the memory beneath it behind after it. Lawrence was not going to be held back by a Hardyesque belatedness of retrospect. The very quickness of his insight into feeling comprised an inner memory of what might be subsequently recognized as already known at a deep level.

With Lawrence, that is to say, even in writing in retrospect, he thinks 'We cannot know beforehand. We are driven from behind' (*Phoenix ii*, p. 374). Take an example that Lawrence could only have known of before he started writing. It is an incident described by Jessie Chambers:

> It was on one of these walks . . . that I had a sudden flash of insight which made me see Lawrence in a totally new light. We were walking along anyhow, singly, or in twos and threes. I happened to be alone, admiring the bronze tips of the maple in the hedge. Suddenly I turned and saw Lawrence in the middle of the road, bending over an umbrella. There was something in his attitude that arrested me. His stooping figure had a look of intensity, almost of anguish. For a moment I saw him as a symbolic figure. I was deeply moved and walked back to him.
>
> 'What's the matter?' I asked.
>
> 'It was Ern's umbrella, and mother will be wild if I take it home broken,' he replied.
>
> We walked on together, but I did not tell him what I had seen. This was perhaps the beginning of our awareness of sympathy for one another.
>
> *Lawrence: A Personal Record*, pp. 41–2.

Yet she must have told him at some stage before the writing of *Sons and Lovers* in which the incident appears as this:

> Suddenly she realized she was alone in a strange road, and she hurried forward. Turning a corner in the lane, she came upon Paul, who stood bent over something, his mind fixed on it, working away steadily, patiently, a little hopelessly. She hesitated in her approach, to watch.
>
> He remained concentrated in the middle of the road. Beyond, one rift of rich gold in that colourless grey evening seemed to make him stand out in dark relief. She saw him, slender and firm, as if the setting sun had given him to her. A deep pain took hold of her, and she knew she must love him. And she had discovered him, discovered in him a rare potentiality, discovered his loneliness. Quivering as at some 'annunciation', she went slowly forward.
>
> At last he looked up.
>
> 'Why,' he exclaimed gratefully, 'have you waited for me!'
>
> She saw a deep shadow in his eyes.
>
> 'What is it?' she asked.
>
> 'The spring broken here'; and he showed her where his umbrella was injured.
>
> Instantly, with some shame, she knew he had not done the damage himself, but that Geoffrey was responsible.
>
> 'It is only an old umbrella, isn't it?' she asked.
>
> She wondered why he, who did not usually trouble over such trifles, made such a mountain of this molehill.
>
> 'But it was William's, an' my mother can't help but know,' he said quietly, still patiently working the umbrella.
>
> The words went through Miriam like a blade. This, then, was the confirmation of her vision of him! She looked at him. But there was about him a certain reserve, and she dared not comfort him, not even speak softly to him.
>
> 'Come on,' he said, 'I can't do it'; and they went in silence along the road.
>
> *Sons and Lovers*, Pt ii, chap. vii, pp. 166–7.

It is of course a comparison complicated by the fact that, although Jessie's experience pre-dates Lawrence's description of it, her own account was probably completed some time after she had read *Sons and Lovers*. Still it is possible to imagine how, as she read the novel, she might think that Lawrence had loaded the dice against her. For instance, in the passage above, the ironic confirmation of her *vision* results in 'She *looked at* him', just as the Romanticism of her seeing him 'stand out in dark relief' is brought down to earth in 'a deep shadow in his eyes'. She makes too much of things, she who accuses him of making a mountain out of a molehill. And Lawrence makes it worse for Miriam by making it her brother Geoffrey who has damaged his late brother's umbrella. This girl wanted an annunciation, she got family problems; she thought she had a new love, standing out from the rest of the world, she had a mother's son implicated in the family past. It seems extraordinary that Lawrence actually showed Jessie the manuscript and Miriam. 'What else could he expect?' as Jessie said about his college essay and its reception, what else could he expect but her pain? He could not pretend, could he, that he was not writing about living and that he was not a dangerous man, accordingly, to be living with? Yet Lawrence seemed willing to use any life as an instrument to find out about life, as if it were not ironic or devious to write about the secrets of his women and his friends: 'How can there be secrecy, when everything is known to all of us?' (*Women in Love*, chap. xix, p. 238). And the reason why Lawrence showed his manuscript to Jessie Chambers and the reason why at least some of the people who loved Lawrence, like Jessie Chambers, like Catherine Carswell, could write the one great book of their lives in memory of him are related, deeply related. Related, moreover, in a way similar to that in which Lawrence's own memory of the umbrella incident embodied in the oblivious Paul has connections with his recall of Jessie's account of it from her point of view: for the playing off of one against the other fired Lawrence's imagination on behalf of Jessie in the person of a Miriam about whom Paul knows so little. When people have a powerful memory of you, it makes you feel how much your own memory of them matters and not just to you. That is what Lawrence realized over Jessie, just as, later in writing, Jessie or Catherine

Carswell, rather than Middleton Murry, realized it with respect to Lawrence. For I do think that the umbrella passage in *Sons and Lovers* does Jessie Chambers fundamental justice, making a reader deeply sorry that young visions are so immediately disabused by, and bound up in, confusingly painful realities; realities so confusing and so impinging for the immature as to prevent the disappointment of expectation the confident luxury of loud suffering. 'They went in silence along the road'.

The justice with which, I believe, Lawrence here writes is something he could not have planned in himself 'beforehand'. It emerges most particularly from that sentence: 'A deep pain took hold of her, and she knew she must love him'—where Lawrence is drawn into the quickness of the moment without time to think yet what became of that moment subsequently (as a Conrad or Hardy might) or what he, as Paul, would make of it. For Lawrence's writing is—to use his own word—too 'quick' to be, like Murry's, too self-conscious (*Phoenix ii*, p. 420). So, that quick word 'must'—'and she knew she must love him'—has no controlling author as such, yet does more justice to Miriam's sudden feeling than even the words of Jessie Chambers herself, on her own behalf. For in the instant of feeling, that word 'must' is at once, characteristically with Lawrence, past and present. It seems to come—like life in Lawrence—'from behind' (*Phoenix ii*, p. 429): 'We know, really, that we cannot have life for the asking, nor find it by seeking, nor get it by striving'. It comes from behind Miriam as a past tense wherein she realizes that she *must* have loved him before she *knew* she did—'so, I must love him then!'; yet simultaneously, what she must do is what she is also now doing—'and this must be love I am feeling'. The Flesh made Word; the Ought and Is at one. Now, at the same moment, she sees and has seen, sees that she has seen in a complex physical consciousness. Writing, even from hindsight, could not pre-plan that moment; it has to be innocent of memory until it finds it under the pen—a fact that Murry, ironically enough, could see yet not implement:

The only memory which belongs to life is the unconscious memory, the memory that forgets, whose incessant task it is to change consciousness into instinct, and to remind us that only when we have forgotten have we remembered indeed.

Between Two Worlds, pp. 480–1.

It is a deep tenderness, the sort that Jessie Chambers thought Lawrence had betrayed in writing *Sons and Lovers*, which Lawrence here feels for Miriam through Miriam.

For as Miriam sees, has seen, sees she has seen all at once, so Lawrence, with that fast hand, equivalently writes and has recalled the past in the present, in one, producing the content of memory free of its form. Mrs Morel visits her husband in hospital after a pit-accident:

> And he looked at me when I came away! I said: 'I s'll have to go now, Walter, because of the train—and the children.' And he looked at me. It seems hard.

Sons and Lovers, Pt i, chap. v, p. 86.

Lawrence is so good at leaving spaces between sentences rather than cluttering them with verbal connectives. At the end of a paragraph, he can write of Miriam 'She hesitated in her approach, to watch' and the words seem written over a strong sense of the presence of the scene. At such moments imagination, in the act of writing, is a dynamic form of memory in the service of re-creating life on the page. And the writing leaves, for consciousness afterwards, the testimony of memory in the space in between the sentences:

> And he looked at me. It seems hard.

Probably the young Lawrence never went or wanted to go to visit in that hospital. But here, for an instant, through the speaking memory of his mother, I think the writer almost remembers his father's face, as the mother does her husband's. It is only an instant, one in which imagination, working through the feel of language, becomes a physical consciousness arising from more or less unconscious memory. And after that instant the writing hand keeps itself driven in fractional advance of the writer's own consciousness which it leaves behind in the writing. The man writes on, through writing still looking to make a future out of his past. 'And this time . . . she began to sing', 'and she knew she must love him', 'And he looked at

me': 'And' in Lawrence is equally a word remembering the
force of the words and sentences behind it, which precipitate
it, and one constructing a meaning ahead. It signals a connection with the words preceding it; but it is not so much another,
this time linking, word. It is a sign that the writer has thought,
quickly, of something that follows from the physical situation
that the preceding words stand for; and partly fuelled by the
impetus of those words' meaning, partly rescuing that meaning
from the words that only temporarily convey it, it is a signal
that although everything has to go on within language in a
novel, what goes on within language is a matter not simply of
words following words in linear prose but of a writer, immersed
in his work, continually coming to and going off from language,
touching down and taking off, yet with hardly a conscious
pause. The reader feels this in between sentences, in between
paragraphs, in those little introductory words within words—
'And', 'But', 'So', 'Only'—telling in language that the language
is not merely made of words but is articulating the silence
between sentences that constitutes the other presence of their
underlying referent. For instance, when the young Ursula
wants to join in her father's work in planting potatoes but fears
that joining in with the impatient man will only expose the
difference between a child's world and an adult's:

> When he came by he said to her:
> 'You didn't help me much.'
> The child looked at him dumbly. Already her heart was
> heavy because of her own disappointment. Her mouth
> was dumb and pathetic. But he did not notice, he went
> his way.
> And she played on, because of her disappointment
> persisting even the more in her play.
>
> *The Rainbow*, chap. viii, p. 220.

Levels change in life, as from work to play, but there are
connections between levels and those connections are felt in
the way that words like 'And' physically mark this continuity
of re-entry through words into a feeling which is pre-verbal.
'But' this, 'And' so that: yet this is not Conrad's or Hardy's
sense of consequentialism, the strange shapes that life turns
round upon itself and turns into a retrospect. The movement is

still forward, as if all this too were life, a bigger thing than irony or even mistakes. As Virginia Woolf said, the characters, the scenes, the words

> are not there—as in Proust—for themselves. . . . We must not look for more than a second; we must hurry on. But to what?
>
> *Collected Essays*, i, pp. 353–4.

Forward is the direction of life says Lawrence, in his criticism of Hardy in whom writing ironically turns back upon living:

> Man is himself the vivid body of life . . . In his fullest living he does not know what he does, his mind, his consciousness, unacquaint, hovers behind, full of extraneous gleams and glances, and altogether devoid of knowledge. Altogether devoid of knowledge and conscious motive is he when he is heaving into uncreated space, when he is actually living, becoming himself.
>
> *Phoenix*, p. 431.

And so, for his writing to have life, his sentences too must go 'heaving into uncreated space' without foreknowledge even when writing out of his own memory. It seems clear, for instance, from poetry written about the same time, that the first terrible row between Will and Anna is in memory of that between Lawrence and Frieda on their difficult honeymoon:

> If she would kiss him! He bent his mouth down. And her mouth, soft and moist, received him.
>
> *The Rainbow*, chap. vi, p. 152.

Lawrence, one feels, as it were lifted the pen at the end of that second sentence, but not long enough consciously to remember only to feel the uncreated space waiting ahead of him:

> And her mouth, soft and moist, received him.

To Will this comes as relief, grace, and hope that in the midst of her withdrawal from him he could hardly dare hope for. The future rests on a chance; it makes a young husband feel so insecure. Yet just as that possible future becomes present in the response from her lips, it is not chancy; there is a deep connection signalled in 'And', 'and she knew she must love

him'; and the future is only just now present and the present
has not yet any of the surety of a past; yet it is that underlying
sense of connection and continuity beneath him, here
momentarily surfacing, that enabled Lawrence to write on and
on, without time to register the feelings of relief and gratitude
for it that nonetheless were implicit there. Now he writes on
and on

> My hand, as it writes these words, slips gaily along, jumps
> like a grasshopper to dot an *i*, feels the table rather cold,
> gets a little bored if I write too long, has its own rudiments
> of thought, and is just as much *me* as is my brain, my
> mind, or my soul.
>
> *Phoenix*, p. 533.

—he writes on and on, as if writing physically embodied his
purpose without itself merely being it. For even in memory
within the books, let alone memory behind the books, the way
is still forward:

> At evening, towards six o'clock, Anna very often went
> across the lane to the stile, lifted Ursula over into the
> field, with a 'Go and meet Daddy.' . . . Once she fell as
> she came flying to him, he saw her pitch forward suddenly
> as she was running with her hands lifted to him; and
> when he picked her up, her mouth was bleeding. He
> could never bear to think of it, he always wanted to cry,
> even when he was an old man and she had become a
> stranger to him. How he loved that little Ursula!—his
> heart had been sharply seared for her, when he was a
> youth, first married.
>   When she was a little older, he would see her recklessly
> climbing over the bars of the stile, in her red pinafore,
> swinging in peril and tumbling over, picking herself up
> and flitting towards him. Sometimes she liked to ride on
> his shoulders, sometimes she preferred to walk with his
> hand, sometimes she would fling her arms around his legs
> for a moment, then race free again, whilst he went
> shouting and calling to her, a child along with her. He
> was still only a tall, thin, unsettled lad of twenty-two.
>
> *The Rainbow*, chap. viii, p. 211.

Look at the penultimate sentence in that first paragraph: it would never have occurred to another writer to put 'even when' rather than 'especially when'; as if there were something in this pain that nonetheless discounts the suffering that followed, rather than simply anticipating it ironically. The world let the little girl fall within sight of her father, for the love of whom she ran too trustingly; later she as a grown woman does not even come near him, she seems to him to have let him down; yet Lawrence keeps the two distinct as well as connected. Distinct as well as connected in the novel that often comes out of memory yet is not governed by memory. Look at that last sentence of all: it pulls back from the old man and even from the young father to another centre of gravity in the man's life, another truth that he lives with, deeper than knowingly, for he *is* it. A truth side by side with others rather than put into perspective by them. Lawrence recognizes that there are no longer coherent roles by which to lead life—as in *Middlemarch* George Eliot lamented. But to Lawrence this truth *is* life, life itself, now: father, husband, young lad, in exciting relativism. It is not perspective, proportion, hindsight, or irony that makes for form here. It is, rather, a feeling that the writer, physically immersed in the way his sentences lead him, has for what Trigant Burrow called 'the organic grammar of life' (*The Social Basis of Consciousness*, p. 183). That is to say, a grammar quite the opposite of Middleton Murry's auto-biographical syntax; a language that seems to be thrown up out of the solution of life it describes. It is not that Lawrence does not know what he is doing, but there are levels at which he cannot know what he is doing unless he becomes like Murry. And although as he writes he is inevitably not his protagonist who 'in his fullest living does not know what he does', still doing what he does in creating that sense of the fullest living is in fractional advance of what he knows and what he learns in doing it. And that is to say this: that Lawrence is not only unlike Hardy in refusing to turn the present that was lived into the past that is remembered; he is also unlike Wordsworth, because, unlike Wordsworth who also eschewed what were to become Hardyesque ironies, Lawrence had no interest in showing the effect of the writing and the sense of the past registered in it upon the writer in the writing present. He would not allow himself to catch up with himself in that way. He was not going to be held back, like Hardy, through the belatedness of retrospect.

So we must hurry on, as Virginia Woolf recognized: '*But to what?*' The very quickness of Lawrence's insight into feeling consists of an inner memory of what nonetheless may be recognized to be *already* known. Where was the new way? the new life? The question tortured him. Is it, then, as Catherine Carswell suggests:

> though each new book, *as a book*, came to me as a disappointment there was not only a curiously cumulative effect, but there was in each book that which had the power to enter into the texture of one's life and to work there like leaven. Who else was writing books which even partially possessed this power? . . . I began to understand how far from his aims was the production of 'masterpieces'.
>
> *The Savage Pilgrimage*, p. 72.

This brings us back to the beginning of the third and last part of this book. To Mallock and his question, is life worth living? For Mallock had argued that if the religion that was at the basis of our morality was displaced, then ethics would become a massive philosophical problem to be thought out again quite from scratch. And while in that book Mallock turned back to the old faith, Nietzsche, whom not only Mallock but also Lawrence had read, was turning forward, to try to begin again, yet with all the dangers of that fresh start also threatening to seem another old reaction. To Lawrence at any rate it seemed as impossible as it was necessary to begin again, free of the past both personal and historical. What he could do, however, was mix it all up, work tightly in amongst his own confusions and tensions, challenge utterly the notion of art as a calm 'masterpiece' existing on its own self-enclosed level—the notion offered by T. E. Hulme when he attacked Romanticism thus:

> You don't believe in a God, so you begin to believe that man is a god. You don't believe in Heaven, so you begin to believe in a heaven on earth. In other words, you get romanticism. . . . Romanticism then, and this is the best definition I can give of it, is spilt religion.
>
> *Speculations*, p. 118.

Romanticism, Hulme was arguing against men such as Lawrence, confused categories, always mixing up levels of existence as discontinuous as the human and the divine, the ethical and the biological, the language of literature and the practice of daily life. Yet to Lawrence these were Words made Flesh, categories created by language for life to fall into, words offering themselves as things. What he needed, as far as was possible, was the raw material of life on which to try out these words, to see if they were necessary. Yet one never had the thing itself, the raw material. 'Where was life, in that which he knew or all outside him?' (*The Rainbow*, chap. i, p. 19). And what one did have was clothed with inheritances and accretions that one could hardly know to be accidental or essential. Yet there was memory to offer some material from which to start, whatever the status of that material. And there was writing to bring what memory offered into an area where it might stand as evidence—even if one would have to wait and see of *what* it was evidence. For the greatness of memory was that it had no criterion, it was just the life that had made an impression; or, if it did have a criterion, that criterion was implicit, and to find what was implicit was a way of finding out what one had lived by as well as what one now thought of that. That was the experiment, the adventure for Lawrence, at a time when, as Mallock suggests, there was increasing consciousness of a want of coherent criteria for living life. Writing provided a language by which to begin to recognize experience, otherwise held silent in unconscious memory. And that is how Lawrence worked in the melting-pot of his novels, never coming out on top of his own solutions, as did George Eliot or even William Wordsworth, but working onward, forward, linearly sentence by sentence, within them. But to what? for what? There was no end, no goal in a life without religion said Mallock, and only Romantics, said Hulme, pretended that religion could be spilt into a merely mundane sense of life. Yet the forward movement of writing a prose embedded in the feeling of life, sentence after sentence from quite different levels of being, yet all working together in a sense of meaning, must have seemed to Lawrence a sign of implicit purposiveness as he went along. For it was that which kept Lawrence going, gave him a stamina for life and for not counting the suffering—in a way quite other than Conrad's way of keeping going by stoicism. So implicit is that purposiveness as to be available in no other language more explicit than Lawrence's sense of his life. For Lawrence did not know his goal, and yet this created not despairing aimlessness, as Mallock had supposed, but a sense of celebratory buoyancy, for still the process of Lawrence's life, as he wrote in pace with it, seemed to him a thing drawn onwards. The ultimate end could not be seen; our beginnings were pre-empted by the life, the family, the history into which we were born; moral principles seemed to be established not to stand at the head of our lives, generated out of them in order thereafter to guide them: they seemed to be things inherited, received, left over from past lives to burden ours, means apparently for living well having now become moribund ends in themselves. Thus set loose in the middle of life, in the confusion of categories, Lawrence could not see a clear way but in the dark could feel one. After *Sons and Lovers* the experience on which he drew for his writing grew nearer and nearer to him in time and often was more coldly bitter, more physically and sexually wounding, accordingly. But even then the writing was to him, I suspect, what the memory of Gerald was to Birkin at the end of *Women in Love*: the sign of something else and something necessary, apart from his marriage and his life with his wife. Above all, something social, an appeal to others on their own lives' way. Finally perhaps those others, even in the form of a readership, were bitterly despaired of, as before they had been ferociously sought and harangued. But for all that, it is remarkable that in no other work apart from Lawrence's does a reader feel both so free and so attacked at once—at once, as if in Lawrence, that most open and unashamed man, to attack and to free were mutually rewarding as well as mutually checking activities.

In a way, if I may put it thus, this book has been the story of how Thomas Hardy destroyed William Wordsworth, of how Hardy suffered from the loss of something in himself which, I believe, Wordsworth pre-eminently had been able to maintain. For Hardy could not maintain what Wordsworth had: an overall sense of the human disposition, as a spiritual man, together with his own point of view as a natural man within that disposition; the spiritual memory leading him down the lines and the years, even as the natural man worked his thoughts and feelings along them. With Hardy that larger spiritual man is contained within the body of the natural man and is imprisoned in there; all he knows and feels being still contained within the memory of the person he is or has been forced to become. Wordsworth was composed by·time, Hardy was shaken by his own memory of it within him. This story of how Hardy destroyed Wordsworth is just one way, my particular way, of saying what was the predicament in which Lawrence then found himself. As we have seen, he did break out of Hardy's impasse, he did open out life again as if a man had a right to be more than his reduced self. I have done no more than indicate how Lawrence began that breaking out. But I have wanted to end this book untidily, not with Hardy's finality but with the doubts and possibilities intrinsic to Lawrence's incompleteness and stamina amidst that incompleteness. What is at stake here is the difference between Karenin, as described in Part two, chapter eight of *Anna Karenina* as being always relieved

> at having found the formal category to which the newly-arisen circumstances rightly belonged

and Lawrence himself trying, as he says,

> to know and to understand what is happening, even in himself, as he goes along.

If anything marks out what it is to be a writer who has let the novel help him learn what life is, or what it is to be Lawrence and not Murry, it is that world of a difference.

And yet, and yet, there is something else to say. For, nonetheless, Lawrence's prose, even in its deep, implicit, forward purposiveness, still represents a very different sense of living from Wordsworth's poetry and suffers through having had to get through the Hardy that somewhere Lawrence must have felt he had within him, in writing his 'Study of Thomas Hardy'. Lawrence is like Wordsworth in refusing to use memory to make experiences retrospectively familiar to himself and in using memory in a more profoundly strange way. But in Lawrence an overall intuition of the human disposition has to be kept in the rear of the forward movement of his personal sense of purpose. This makes Lawrence often seem smaller-minded, more certain and aggressive than he is, for so much of him lies *behind* his first appearances and emotional starting-points, as if needing, among other things, a more trustworthy moral society in which to show itself. Indeed, the memory of himself was something about which Lawrence, for his purpose, had to be careless. For the alternatives seemed to be a Hardy or a Murry even. What Lawrence was careful about, instead, was this: that with a pen in his hand he was able to do what he wanted to do—'end at his finger-tips', without perversely limiting himself. And although by his writing he extended his life, both socially and philosophically, into his sense of life, nonetheless it was still a sense of life that was inevitably his own—confessedly his own, defiantly his own, physically his own, but, above all, inevitably his own. In that sense art for Lawrence was rightly and inevitably personal. He believed in art's owning up and also that owning up was more than merely a concession. It's me in that unresolved struggle that keeps life alive.

*   *   *   *   *

CONCLUDING

In her wonderful book of memory Jessie Chambers gives an account of Lawrence's literary formation, particularly mentioning at one point George Borrow and *Lavengro*:

> He said that Borrow had mingled autobiography and fiction so inextricably in Lavengro that the most astute critics could not be sure where the one ended and the other began. From his subtle smile I felt he was wondering whether he might not do something in the same fashion himself.
>
> *D. H. Lawrence: A Personal Record*, p. 110.

Now, isn't what Lawrence means by that writerly smile a warning against the sort of book I have here written? For what is Lawrence saying? Ah, those readers, they would like to think that books are just their authors' lives, as if they too could simply write one! Ah, readers, they so much want to know where they are, they cannot bear to think of the tricks that writers get up to with their material! What they think is memory was really imagination. With my imagination so concealed within my apparent memory, they'll never catch me out—or if they do think they have caught me out (there's Lawrence really giving himself away!), it will really be me catching them out with their literal-mindedness and their vulnerable hearts! I make them imagine it is me.

But I think the smile is subtler than that. As if Lawrence smiles at the thought that there *could* be a point where autobiography ended and the novel began, supposing memory to be truth and imagination to be fiction! Those who suppose art is no more than transcribed autobiography and those who believe that a writer's imagination transcends the life he has had are alike in one essential respect: the narrow idea they have of memory.

And still Lawrence smiles. Yet surely it ought not to please a writer that the critics might take his writing to be no more than memory? I think that finally and on his own terms it did please Lawrence. For to see the work of imagination as, if not a trick and a tactic, at any rate a signal, to see it all as finally in memory of the man, is to take literature very seriously indeed. 'Whereas by words a man transmits his thoughts to another, by art he transmits his feelings.' Lawrence's really subtle smile is at the thought that some apparent reductions of art are really celebrations of the life in art. Finally, I think, Lawrence would not only admit but be glad to say of his work, you are right, it is me.

This book has proposed memory—memory arising out of writing, writing emerging from memory—as the intermediate, human meaning between what would otherwise be the mutually weakening alternatives of literature and life. The writers with whom I have been concerned do not stand merely on one side or the other: through memory their work takes up the question of the two together, optimistically in cases even as different as those of Wordsworth and Lawrence, pessimistically in the case of Hardy. Indeed, although I end on Lawrence, I do not mean by that that Hardy's doubts can be simply superseded. At any rate, as a book on the writer and his memory, this work has been particularly concerned with the relation between literature and personal life, and I want my final word to be in defence of that emphasis which to some may seem narrow or bourgeois or sentimental. I do think that the personal is precisely the realm in which to ask, how to live? Not because there are not other realms of life; not because I think a person is particularly free or privileged in personal life; not because how people behave in or think of their close relations is the only measure of what they are. But because our personal life is often the only realm left to us where we cannot merely have an opinion. For there our language is involved in a serious, testing area to which we, on whom it makes a claim, also have a right. I hope in saying this I cannot be accused of ignoring the lesson of George Eliot: that in personal life a little counts for a lot these days because lives that are only personal lives are forced to be so small. That seems to me to be the way things are for us, still. Nor am I ignoring the pain that can accompany that confinement. Hardy could hardly bear it when anything outside him threatened to correspond with anything inside him—say, a photograph outside with his memory of love inside—because what was inside him above all was the memory of having given up, almost, the hope of a life outside. So I am not saying that our personal life is our best life; I am saying that writing about it forces us to be more truthful—or to risk being caught lying—in a more dangerous area than that of external opinion.

It is to their personal lives that the writers of memory go for the test of seriousness and truthfulness. So that writing may be in memory, in embodied memory, of what Tolstoy calls the 'feeling' of one's life. For the feeling of how one lives, most nearly and most intimately, is, when put into words, the basic meaning, from within, of what else one believes in. And writing allows this personal feel for life its expression, when otherwise it might be all too frustratingly, inarticulately and unrecognizably one's own. Writing is in memory of writers, writers are in memory of the people they are: so that we, as readers, may ask with some hope of success, 'what does it feel like to be the person who wrote this?' and 'what does this feeling mean in terms of a life worth living?'. For mostly we are all so immersed in peremptory life as to be unable to say or hear what it feels like; and when we do say, it is too late, too distanced from its context, too out of touch with the past that prompted the experience. But a particularly creative use of memory, I have been arguing, can heal that breach.

For this is what I think my chosen writers, from Wordsworth to Lawrence, do: on behalf of the creative depth in memory, they refuse to let the written word lose, as it does for most of us, the life which it names and fixes. For in these writers memory is not a dull, reportorial faculty far inferior to the creative power of imagination; rather, it is the very ground of imagination and its soul. We have seen the deep presence of memory behind these writers' work, both nourishing the imagination and needing it. It nourishes the imagination because memory, so far from being a secondary, dying or deathly faculty, has a profound and dynamic priority in human life. It bears all that residue of experience—what we did, what we did not do, what we ought to have done—which makes experience itself so much more than a series of merely external events. But as well as being the reservoir of our experience, it is also in its visitations a revelation of the heart-shaking seriousness of a person's life, preserved within. It is not only a base from which to write but also, inside the act of writing itself, a discovery within the inventedness of literature of a truth to feeling and to personal experience. And yet it is also true that memory needs invention, needs imagination and the arts of writing, for purposes of support, revitalization, freedom, and justice. Another person, perhaps, might stress this side of the issue even more than I have urged it in this book. Clearly, there are other ways than mine to an appreciation of the importance of literature, or language, or imagination— approaches favouring more autonomy for the texts themselves or arguing for more freedom in the act of invention—and my own view, notwithstanding a wish to test it here as strenuously as possible, is not settled for perpetuity. But at this time I have wanted to put forward the idea of memory, making and seeking relations between the ordinary and literary worlds, in order to challenge those who believe that writing and reading are essentially separate from living.

Notes and Bibliographies

Notes and Bibliography to pages xiii–10.

INTRODUCTION

1. See Robert Gittings and Jo Manton, *The Second Mrs Hardy* (London, 1979), especially pp. 80–3, 68–72, 104–6.

2. *The Human World*, no. 10, February 1973, p. 71.

3. *The Nineteenth Century*, vol. ii, p. 263 (September 1877).

4. W. B. Yeats, *Essays and Introductions* (London, 1961), p. 509.

5. See Brian Lee, *Theory and Personality: The Significance of T. S. Eliot's Criticism* (London, 1979).

6. *The Complete Works of William Hazlitt*, The Centenary Edition, P. P. Howe (ed.), 21 vols (London and Toronto, 1932), xi, p. 87.

7. Hugh Blair, *Lectures on Rhetoric and Belles Lettres* (London, 1783), ii, p. 323.

8. Samuel Taylor Coleridge, *The Notebooks*, Kathleen Coburn (ed.), 3 vols so far (London, 1957–), i, entry 87.

9. William Wordsworth, *Home at Grasmere*, Beth Darlington (ed.), The Cornell Wordsworth, iii (Ithaca, N.Y., and Hassocks, Sussex, 1977), p. 76 (MS.B, 620–2).

10. John Stuart Mill, *Collected Works*, F. E. L. Priestley (general editor), J. M. Robson (associate editor), 17 vols so far (Toronto, 1963–), Volume xi, J. M. Robson (ed.) (1978), p. 90.

11. *Apologia Pro Vita Sua: Being a History of His Religious Opinions*, Martin J. Svaglic (ed.) (Oxford, 1967), pp. 405–6.

BIBLIOGRAPHY (of works continuously cited)

ELIOT, T. S., *Selected Essays*, 1932, reprinted edition (London, 1972).

RUSKIN, JOHN, *Works*, The Library Edition, E T. Cook and Alexander Wedderburn (eds.), 39 vols (London, 1903)—of which *Modern Painters* comprises vols iii–vii.

WORDSWORTH, WILLIAM, *Prose Works*, W. J. B. Owen and Jane Worthington Smyser (eds.), 3 vols (Oxford, 1974).

CHAPTER 1

1. Wordsworth, *Prose Works*, ii, p. 70.

2. Wordsworth, *Poetical Words*, ii, p. 90: hereafter cited as P.W. throughout.

3. The principle is explained in Wordsworth, *Prose Works*, ii, p. 98 and practised ibid., pp. 73–4.

4. Samuel Taylor Coleridge, *Specimens of the Table Talk*, H. N. Coleridge (ed.), second edition (London, 1836), p. 71.

5. Hazlitt, *Works*, xi, p. 87.

6. See Mary Moorman, *William Wordsworth: A Biography*, 2 vols (Oxford, 1957, 1965), i, pp. 261–5; M. L. Reed, *Wordsworth: The Chronology of the Early Years, 1770–1799* (Cambridge, Mass., 1967), pp. 163–6.

7. For a further account of this memory see *Journals of Dorothy Wordsworth* E. de Selincourt (ed.), 2 vols (London, 1941), i, p. 63.

8. See, for instance, volume i, chapter iv of *Caleb Williams*, David McCracken (ed.), Oxford English Novels (London, 1970), pp. 28–31.

9. John Stuart Mill, *Autobiography*, 1873, Jack Stillinger (ed.) (London, 1971), p. 89.

10. 'Memorial Verses': *The Poems of Matthew Arnold*, Kenneth Allott (ed.) (London, 1965), p. 228.

11. For evidence of Hutton's belief in Newman's doctrine of 'real words' see Hutton's *Essays on some of the Modern Guides to English Thought in Matters of Faith*, first edition 1887 (new edition, London, 1888), especially pp. 94–6; also his *Cardinal Newman* (London, 1891). I am grateful to Malcolm Woodfield for talking to me about this unjustly neglected Victorian critic.

12. John Keats, *Letters*, H. E. Rollins (ed.), 2 vols (Cambridge, Mass., 1958), i, pp. 278–9.

13. On reading Wordsworth 'by taking his time', see Christopher Ricks, 'Wordsworth "A Pure Organic Pleasure from the Lines"', *Essays in Criticism*, 21 (1971), pp. 1–32. Also Geoffrey Hill, 'Redeeming the Time', *Agenda*, 10 (1972–3), pp. 87–111 and my own 'Trying to Compose Oneself', *Stand*, 18 no. 2, pp. 4–15.

14. For instance, Wordsworth recalls peeping in at the poor through their windows, an act he admits to be one of 'feeding by stealth', but he says in parenthesis: '(who could help it?)' (*Home at Grasmere*, p. 74 MS.B, 595–7). Ten years earlier that question would not have been either in brackets or rhetorical. 'Who *could* help it?' Beaupuy had said to Wordsworth in France: '"'Tis against *that*/Which we are fighting"' (*The Prelude*, 1805–6, ix, 518–9). The diction of *Home at Grasmere* both evokes and evades that memory at once.

On Wordsworth's nervousness about writing and fear of being pre-empted see, for instance, *Journals of Dorothy Wordsworth*, i, p. 123.

15. James Beattie, *Dissertations, Moral and Critical*, 2 vols (London, 1783), i, p. 41.

16. Dugald Stewart, *Elements of the Philosophy of the Human Mind*, 3 vols (London, 1792–1827), i, p. 441.

17. Beattie, op. cit., i, p. 55.

18. David Hume, *A Treatise of Human Nature* (first published 1739–40), L. A. Selby-Bigge (ed.) (Oxford, 1888, reprinted edition 1951), p. 85 (Book 1, Part III, Section V). Also see David Hartley, *Observations on Man*, first published 1749 (facsimile: Gainesville, Florida, 1966), p. 383 (The First Part, Chapter III, Section V); James Beattie, *Dissertations Moral and Critical*, i, pp. 78–80. On the general influence of Hobbes and Locke, see Beatrice Edgell, *Theories of Memory* (Oxford, 1924), pp. 52–63.

19. Hunter Davies, *William Wordsworth: A Biography* (London, 1980), pp. 249–52.

20. The phrase 'came back upon me' occurs within this incident at line 506.

BIBLIOGRAPHY

GODWIN, WILLIAM, *Enquiry Concerning Political Justice, and its Influence on General Virtue and Happiness*, 1793, Isaac Kramnick (ed.), (Harmondsworth, Middlesex, 1976).

——, *Thoughts on Man, His Nature, Productions and Discoveries* (London, 1831).

HAZLITT, WILLIAM, *Complete Works*, The Centenary Edition, P. P. Howe (ed.), 21 vols (London and Toronto, 1932).

HUTTON, RICHARD HOLT, *Literary Essays*, 1871, revised third edition 1888, reprinted edition (London, 1896).

NEWMAN, JOHN HENRY, *Parochial and Plain Sermons*, 8 vols (London, 1868).

PAUL, C. KEGAN, *William Godwin: His Friends and Contemporaries*, 2 vols (London, 1876).

WORDSWORTH, WILLIAM, *Home at Grasmere*, Beth Darlington (ed.), The Cornell Wordsworth, iii (Ithaca, N.Y., and Hassocks, Sussex, 1977).

——, *Poetical Works*, E. de Selincourt and Helen Darbishire (eds.), 5 vols (Oxford, 1940–9)—cited as 'P.W.'.

——, *The Prelude*, E. de Selincourt (ed.), second edition revised by Helen Darbishire (Oxford, 1959).

——, *Prose Works*, W. J. B. Owen and Jane Worthington Smyser (eds.), 3 vols (Oxford, 1974).

——, *The Salisbury Plain Poems*, Stephen Gill (ed.), The Cornell Wordsworth, i (Ithaca, N.Y., and Hassocks, Sussex, 1975).

CHAPTER 2

1. *Blake: Complete Writings*, p. 783: 'Heaven-born, The Soul a heaven-ward course must hold;/Beyond the visible world She soars to seek/(For what delights the sense is false and weak)/ Ideal Form, the universal mould.'

2. See *Discourses on Art* (cited below), pp. 94, 99. For Blake's Annotations see *Blake: Complete Writings*, pp. 470–1. I am much indebted in this Reynolds-Blake discussion to T. R. Langley.

3. *The Yale Edition of the Works of Samuel Johnson*, vol. vii, *Johnson on Shakespeare* (i), Arthur Sherbo (ed.) (New Haven and London, 1968), pp. 61–2.

4. On making the ground of Johnsonian prejudice the ground of Romantic admiration, see *Discourses on Art*, pp. 281–2 (Discourse xv). Blake, it appears, did not scruple to be as painfully fair to Reynolds as Reynolds had been to Michelangelo, not least because when Blake did recognize the fairness, he attributed it to compromised self-contradiction (*Blake: Complete Writings*, p. 449).

5. See Wordsworth's letter to John Wilson, 7 June 1802: *The Letters of William and Dorothy Wordsworth: The Early Years*, Ernest de Selincourt (ed.), second edition, revised by Chester L. Shaver (Oxford, 1967), p. 355.

6. The remark is made in the context of a discussion of epitaphs (*The Prose Works of William Wordsworth*, ii, p. 78); for evidence of Wordsworth's general equivocation over the question of originality see *The Prose Works of William Wordsworth*, iii, p. 82 ('Essay, Supplementary to the Preface').

7. *Letters of William and Dorothy Wordsworth: The Middle Years*, Ernest de Selincourt (ed.), second edition, revised by Mary Moorman and Alan G. Hill, 2 vols (Oxford, 1969–70), ii, p. 190.

8. *The Critical Works of John Dennis*, Edward Niles Hooker (ed.), 2 vols (Baltimore, 1939, 1943), i, pp. 216–7.

9. ibid., i, p. 339.

10. On the general critical problem posed by the relation of Wordsworth's 'sense' to his 'mysticism' see John Beer, *Wordsworth in Time* (London, 1979), pp. 26–8.

11. See Hazlitt, *Works*, v, pp. 129–30.

12. But in J. P. Muirhead, 'A Day with Wordsworth' (1841), *Blackwood's Magazine*, 1927, vol. ccxxi, especially pp. 735–6, the aged Wordsworth now wonders how far and for what the licentious Burns deserves the name 'poet'.

13. *The Moral Law; or, Kant's Groundwork of the Metaphysic of Morals*, translated by H. J. Paton, second edition (London, 1951), p. 125 (117).

14. David Hartley, *Observations on Man, His Frame, His Duty and His Expectations*, 1749 (Facsimile: Gainesville, Florida, 1966), p. 104.

15. See H. W. Piper, *The Active Universe* (London, 1962), pp. 33–5 in particular. I am also personally indebted to John Beer here.

16. *The Letters of William and Dorothy Wordsworth: The Middle Years*, i, p. 194.

17. For Hazlitt's borrowing of Kant's phrase, 'The mind alone is formative', see Hazlitt, *Works*, ii, pp. 153, 280.

18. See the opening to Book vi of William Cowper's *The Task* for the analogy between soul and music of which Wordsworth wrote in *The Prelude*, 1805–6, i, 351–61. Wordsworth's own musical experiments with repetitive verse of memory are included P.W., v, p. 342 (III, beginning 'The strains are passed').

19. *The Philosophical Lectures of Samuel Taylor Coleridge*, Kathleen Coburn (ed.) (London, 1949), p. 168.

20. Quoted in Andrew Seth, *Scottish Philosophy* (Edinburgh and London, 1885), p. 136.

21. *Immanuel Kant's Critique of Pure Reason*, translated by Norman Kemp Smith, reprint of 1933 revised edition (London, 1950), p. 93.

22. This binding of continuity with change is best illustrated in the motif in praise of sublimity: 'to which/With *growing* faculties she (the soul) doth aspire,/With faculties *still growing*, feeling *still*,/That whatsoever point they gain, they *still*/Have something to pursue' *The Prelude*, 1805–6, ii, 337–41.

23. Edmund Burke, *A Philosophical Enquiry into the Origin of our Ideas of the Sublime and Beautiful*, J. T. Boulton (ed.) (London, 1958), p. 73.

24. Baruch Spinoza, *Ethics* and *On the Correction of the Understanding*, translated by A. Boyle, 1910, Everyman Library reprint of corrected edition (London, 1977), p. 47. An idea of the body is both an idea which belongs to the body and an idea concerning the body; an idea which the body knows and by which also it is known.

25. In its first appearance in print in 1800, however, the poem read 'She *liv'd* unknown, and few could know . . .' (*Lyrical Ballads*, R. L. Brett and A. R. Jones (eds.) (London, 1963), p. 154). It seems that Wordsworth originally thought that he ought to italicise 'liv'd' in order to make clear that it, rather

than 'unknown' or 'know', was the key word. However in all subsequent printings the italics were dropped (see *Lyrical Ballads*, 1805, D. Roper (ed.) (London, 1968), p. 369). I think this was because Wordsworth became more confident that the poem might be allowed to work its own effect, as it had in the writing.

26. In Sir Humphry Davy, *Collected Works*, J. Davy (ed.), 9 vols (London, 1839–40), ii, p. 320.

27. This subduing of a rhetoric is discussed in Jonathan Wordsworth, *The Music of Humanity: A Critical Study of Wordsworth's Ruined Cottage* (London, 1969), pp. 136–7.

28. T. H. Green, *Prolegomena to Ethics*, A. C. Bradley (ed.) (Oxford, 1883), pp. 75–6 (Book i, chapter ii, para. 71).

29. Compare Reynolds, *Discourses on Art*, p. 275: 'Our art in consequence, now assumes a rank to which it could never have dared to aspire if Michelangelo had not discovered to the world the hidden powers which it possessed'.

30. In his *An Essay on the Principles of Human Action* (1805) Hazlitt hints that memory and imagination may be, respectively, the backward and forward referring modes of the same faculty. But he also argues against the trustworthiness of retrospective analysis: when the future is past, he says, we cannot remember as real the ideals of the imagination at the time, but reconstruct recalled actions in terms of personal identity and calculated self-interest. 'We take the tablets of memory, reverse them, and stamp the image of self on that' (Hazlitt: *Works*, i, p. 41). This refusal to see that there is a memory belonging to the soul as well as to the ego has damaging consequences in Hazlitt's later essay, 'Whether Genius is Conscious of its Powers?' (ibid., xii, pp. 117–27). Hazlitt answers negatively and Romantically; whereas Wordsworth *was* conscious of an under-sense in himself, itself deeper than consciousness, which knew the way that poetically he was going to have to fight for, word by word.

31. An article on the applications and limits of this technique, with respect to not only Romantic but Elizabethan and Augustan poetry, is currently in preparation.

32. The poem 'My heart leaps up' in which this dictum is given is quoted in *The Friend*, i, p. 40, as supporting evidence in a discussion of the right use of parental memory; part of Wordsworth's 'Ode: Intimations of Immortality' is quoted ibid., i, p. 510 for support in a discussion of method which concludes as above on the question of miracles.

33. For an account of how, for Wordsworth, fundamental priorities were often realized through wise passiveness, on second thought, at the moment of relaxation after disappointed expectation, see Thomas De Quincey, *Recollections of the Lake Poets*, edited by David Wright (Harmondsworth, Middlesex, 1970), pp. 159–61. This emotion of sublime realization is a more violent version of the emotion of memory as described by R. H. Hutton: 'the retrospect with which we revert to what we have previously seen without seeing it', *Brief Literary Criticisms*, edited by Elizabeth M. Roscoe, 1906 (Port Washington, N.Y. and London, 1970), p. 113—where Hutton gives an

excellent account (pp. 111–8) of why it would not be damaging to see Wordsworth's mysticism as also good sense.

34. The text is that of *The Prelude*, 1850 (i, 344–50), the later version being chosen this time chiefly for the sake of pointing to a reaffirmed continuity even so late. Some early drafts of *The Prelude* are discussed later in this section for precisely that reason of continuity, early or late.

35. *The Collected Writings of Thomas de Quincey*, David Masson (ed.), 14 vols (Edinburgh, 1889–90), i, (1889) p. 123.

36. In the terms used by modern linguistics, the distinction germane to sections II and III is generally that between forward-looking, or anticipatory, reference (e.g. where the pronoun precedes the expression with which it is correlated: sometimes called 'cataphora') and the more usual, backward-looking reference of 'stitching up' rather than 'counterpointing' (e.g. where the pronoun follows the expression to which it is related: called 'anaphora', although 'anaphora' is sometimes used to cover both functions). See John Robert Ross, 'On the Cyclic Nature of English Pronominalization', in *Modern Studies in English: Reading in Transformational Grammar*, David A. Reibel and Sanford A. Shane (eds.) (Englewood Cliffs, New Jersey, 1969), pp. 187–200.

37. 'The term "deixis" (which comes from the Greek word meaning "pointing" or "indicating") is now used in linguistics to refer to the function of personal and demonstrative pronouns, of tense and of a variety of other grammatical and lexical features which relate utterances to the spatio-temporal co-ordinates of the act of utterance', John Lyons, *Semantics*, 2 vols (Cambridge, 1977), ii, p. 636. R. H. Hutton recalls how 'Wordsworth was much excited on one occasion at being told he had written a poem "on *a* daisy". "No", he said, "it was on *the* daisy—a very different thing." There *was* a difference, and it was a difference characteristic of his best poetry' (*Literary Essays*, p. 124).

38. Matthew Arnold's criticism of Keatsianism in the nineteenth century is discussed in chapter three, section one. The effect of the Cockney school upon Tennyson's *In Memoriam* is briefly discussed near the end of chapter five, section three, pp. 387–9. The reader may gain insight into Keats's situation by comparing his 'After dark vapours have oppressed our plains' (*Poems*, edited by Jack Stillinger (London, 1978)) with Wordsworth's lists of recalled objects quoted above: by dint of the association of thoughts across the page in an act of writing too exclusively committing the poet's existence to that page alone, Keats's poem can only end in the finality of 'a poet's death', no memory being able to hold him back from that finality as memory can in Wordsworth. I have no room in this present study to consider fully other Romantic poets in order to substantiate all my claims about Wordsworth; I hope to deal with this more in future work, particularly on Byron.

39. Richard Jefferies, *The Story of My Heart* (London, 1883), p. 104.

40. Andrew Seth, *Scottish Philosophy*, p. 187.

41. The evidence is extensive: for example see *Home at Grasmere*, pp. 96, 98 (MS.B, 928–55), pp. 42, 44 (MS.B, 104–16); *The Prelude*, 1805–6, xiii, 224–46.

42. W. H. Hudson, *Far Away and Long Ago* (London and Toronto, 1918), pp. 2–3.

43. Samuel Taylor Coleridge, *Specimens of the Table Talk*, H. N. Coleridge (ed.), second edition (London, 1836), p. 95.

BIBLIOGRAPHY

BAXTER, ANDREW, *An Enquiry into the Nature of the Human Soul Wherein the Immateriality of the Soul is evinced from the Principles of Reason and Philosophy* (London, 1733).

BLAKE, WILLIAM, *Complete Writings*, Geoffrey Keynes (ed.), Oxford Standard Authors, 1966, corrected edition (London, 1976).

COLERIDGE, SAMUEL TAYLOR, *Biographia Literaria*, J. Shawcross (ed.), 2 vols (Oxford, 1907).

——, *The Friend*, Barbara Rooke (ed.), 2 vols (Princeton, 1969) (*The Collected Works of Samuel Taylor Coleridge*, Bollingen Series, lxxv, volume iv).

——, *The Notebooks*, Kathleen Coburn (ed.), 3 vols so far (London, 1957–).

HAZLITT, WILLIAM, *Complete Works*, The Centenary Edition, P. P. Howe (ed.), 21 vols (London and Toronto, 1932).

KEATS, JOHN, *Letters*, H. E. Rollins (ed.), 2 vols (Cambridge, Mass., 1958).

REYNOLDS, SIR JOSHUA, *Discourses on Art*, 1769–1790, Robert R. Wark (ed.), revised second edition (New Haven and London, 1975).

WORDSWORTH, WILLIAM, *Home at Grasmere*, Beth Darlington (ed.), The Cornell Wordsworth, iii (Ithaca, N.Y., and Hassocks, Sussex, 1977).

——, *Poetical Works*, E. de Selincourt and Helen Darbishire (eds.), 5 vols (Oxford, 1940–9)—cited as 'P.W.'.

——, *The Prelude*, E. de Selincourt (ed.), second edition revised by Helen Darbishire (Oxford, 1959).

——, *The Prelude*, 1789–1799, Stephen Parrish (ed.), The Cornell Wordsworth, ii (Ithaca, N.Y., and Hassocks, Sussex, 1977).

CHAPTER 3

1. See, for example, Hutton on Keats's writing where he was not actually tried, *Brief Literary Criticisms*, pp. 90–1, and on Shelley's comfortable 'deficiency of the power to hate what is hideous in those whom he supposed himself to love', *Brief Literary Criticisms*, p. 38. In general, the idea of a subsequent test which may shift the perspective of memory is part of that Romantic aggression of point of view against accepted truths which is characterized in Goethe's 'But *is* it so? is it so to *me*?' (on which, see Arnold, *Prose Works*, iii, p. 110).

2. See Arnold, *Prose Works*, ix, p. 206.

3. On the suicidal cultivation of the idea of happiness as the end of life see Leslie Stephen on J. S. Mill in *Hours in a Library*, new edition, 3 vols (London, 1892), iii, pp. 259–66. Also R. H. Hutton, 'Life in Poetry', *Brief Literary Criticisms*, Elizabeth M. Rosoe (ed.), 1906, reissued edition (Washington, N.Y., and London, 1970), pp. 405–10.

4. *The Logic of Hegel*, translated from the *Encyclopaedia of the Philosophical Sciences* by William Wallace (Oxford, 1874), p. 13.

5. Samuel Taylor Coleridge, *Biographia Literaria*, J. Shawcross (ed.), 2 vols (Oxford, 1907), i, p. 185.

6. See Geoffrey H. Hartman's essay 'Romanticism and Anti-Self-Consciousness' in his *Beyond Formalism: Literary Essays 1958–1970* (New Haven and London, 1970), pp. 298–310.

7. Quoted in R. H. Hutton, *Brief Literary Criticisms*, p. 320.

8. Ibid., pp. 321–2, 318.

9. See pp. 387–9.

10. For an interesting account of the relation of De Quincey's *Autobiographical Sketches* and his *Suspira de Profundis* as rival treatments of memory in prose, see Elizabeth W. Bruss *Autobiographical Acts* (Baltimore and London, 1976), pp. 93–126.

11. For a contemporary, if hostile, account of the accepted meaning of Romantic aspirations see John Foster, *Essays in a Series of Letters to a Friend*, second edition, 2 vols (London, 1806), ii, p. 50ff. Foster, a Radical Baptist, sees the Romantic, with its love of the big and mighty, as impractical and unthinking.

12. William Godwin, *Enquiry Concerning Political Justice*, Isaac Kramnick (ed.) (Harmondsworth, Middlesex, 1976), p. 349.

13. For De Quincey's and Haydon's guesses as to the motives of writing and publishing being to do with 'relief' in this case, see Herschel Baker, *William Hazlitt* (Cambridge, Massachusetts, and London, 1962), pp. 417, 427.

14. John Foster once set up a definition of Romanticism as eschewing practical definitions: 'the romantic mind vaults from one last day of December to another, and seizes at once the whole product of all the intermediate days' (*Essays in a Series of Letters to a Friend*, ii, p. 50). But Kierkegaard, writing in his journal for 1836, is wise to that sort of attempt to define Romanticism through its own reluctance to be defined, 'I must first protest against the notion that romanticism can be enclosed within a concept; for romantic precisely means that it oversteps all bounds' (quoted in Anthony K. Thorlby (ed.), *The Romantic Movement: Problems and Perspectives in History* (London, 1966), p. 146). In Kierkegaard, you cannot define Romanticism through creating the concept that it cannot or will not be defined; that is just words and they cannot trap real lives; the most interesting words and concepts are precisely those that refer to what is more than themselves.

15. Leslie Stephen, *Hours in a Library*, iii, p. 246.

16. R. H. Hutton, *Literary Essays*, reprint of revised third edition (London, 1896), p. 156.

17. Ibid., p. 303.

18. *Mill on Bentham and Coleridge* F. R. Leavis (ed.), fifth impression (London, 1971), p. 89.

19. Ibid., p. 92.

20. On poetic aesthetics in the later nineteenth century see chapter 5, section III, pp. 387–8. For the early story of Utilitarianism see, for example, Hazlitt on Bentham and on Malthus in *The Complete Works of William Hazlitt*, vol. xi, *The Spirit of the Age*, especially pp. 10–12, 105–11. For the later story see J. B. Schneewind, *Sidgwick's Ethics and Victorian Moral Philosophy* (Oxford, 1977), especially pp. 383–411. For a particular analysis of the general issues

here raised see Marilyn Butler, *Peacock Displayed: A Satirist in his Context* (London, 1979), pp. 102–39, 272–313.

21. For De Quincey's significant interest in Lloyd see *Recollections of the Lakes and the Lake Poets*, pp. 313–33.

22. *Testimony: The Memoirs of Dmitri Shostakovich*, as related to and edited by Solomon Volkov, translated by Antonia W. Bouis (London, 1979), p. 87.

23. This way of reading is very different from, say, Blake's. Blake sat himself, as it were, at the circumference of a book and waited there to find what spoke irrefutably even despite the personality of its writer: 'The Contradictions in Reynolds's Discourses are Strong Presumption that they are the Work of Several Hands. But this is no Proof that Reynolds did not Write them. The Man, Either Painter or Philosopher, who Learns or Acquires all he knows from Others, Must be full of Contradictions' (*Blake: Complete Writings*, p. 449). The subsequent nineteenth century tended not to follow this example of an aggressive search for a book's impersonal truth but to follow Keats's compromise, as it were, rather than Blake's levels. On trying to find the personal belief held in a book see the whole argument of Newman's *Grammar of Assent*; on the personal, extra-linguistic trust involved in the recognition of meaning see J. S. Mill's letter to d'Eichthal on communication as an act of confidence (7 November 1829): 'Words, or anything that can be stated in words, benefit none but those minds to whom the words suggest an ample store of correct and clear ideas, & sound & accurate knowledge previously acquired concerning the things which are meant by the words' (*The Collected Works of John Stuart Mill*, vol. xii, *The Earlier Letters of John Stuart Mill*, edited by Francis E. Mineka (Toronto, 1963), p. 42).

24. Thomas Hood, *Tylney Hall*, new edition (London, 1840), pp. 5–6 (Preface to the New Edition).

25. See Hood's article 'Diabolical Suggestions' in *The New Monthly Magazine*, July 1842, vol. lxv, no. cclix, for an attack on that 'German' Romanticism which made a man a slave of his own imagination: '"The wise only," says Coleridge, "possess ideas: the greater part of mankind are possessed by them"' (p. 291). Compare Charles Lamb's essay 'Sanity of True Genius', *The Works of Charles and Mary Lamb*, E. V. Lucas (ed.), 7 vols (London, 1903), ii, pp. 187–8 in particular.

26. See John Clubbe, *Victorian Forerunner: the later career of Thomas Hood* (Durham, N.C., 1968), pp. 177–8 for Hood's despairing letter to Ward, his assistant editor.

27. *The Works of Thomas Hood*, edited by his son and daughter, 11 vols (London, 1882–4), ix, p. 103.

28. I wish to express a debt here to Carol Preston in thinking this over.

29. It was of course this aspect of Dickens that came under attack from G. H. Lewes, George Eliot, and Henry James and has affected all subsequent reading of him. I have been helped by Frederick Busch's excellent Dickens-based novel *The Mutual Friend* (Hassocks, Sussex, 1978).

BIBLIOGRAPHY

ARNOLD, MATTHEW, *The Complete Prose Works*, R. H. Super (ed.), 11 vols (Ann Arbor, Michigan, 1960–77).

BLAKE, WILLIAM, *Complete Writings*, Geoffrey Keynes (ed.), Oxford Standard Authors, 1966, corrected edition (London, 1976).

DE QUINCEY, THOMAS, *Collected Writings*, David Masson (ed.), 14 vols (Edinburgh, 1889–90).

——, *Recollections of the Lakes and the Lake Poets*, David Wright (ed.), (Harmondsworth, Middlesex, 1970).

DICKENS, CHARLES, *David Copperfield*, Nina Burgis (ed.), The Clarendon Dickens (Oxford, 1981).

FORSTER, JOHN, *The Life of Charles Dickens*, 1872–4, A. J. Hoppé (ed.), revised edition, 2 vols (London, 1969).

HARDY, FLORENCE EMILY, *The Life of Thomas Hardy, 1840–1928*, first published 1962 to bring together *The Early Years of Thomas Hardy 1840–1891* (1928) and *The Later Years of Thomas Hardy, 1892–1928* (1930), corrected edition (London, 1972).

HAZLITT, WILLIAM, *Complete Works*, The Centenary Edition, P. P. Howe (ed.), 21 vols (London and Toronto, 1932).

HOOD, THOMAS, *Memorials of Thomas Hood*, collected, arranged, and edited by his daughter, with a preface and notes by his son, 2 vols (London, 1860).

KEATS, JOHN, *Letters*, H. E. Rollins (ed.), 2 vols (Cambridge, Mass., 1958).

MILL, JOHN STUART, *Autobiography*, 1873, Jack Stillinger (ed.) (London, 1971).

CHAPTER 4

1. Haydon's *Diaries* are now published in full, B. Willard (ed.) (Harvard, 1960–77). It is, however, Taylor's early editorship which is part of my present concern.

2. *Recollections of the Lakes and the Lake Poets*, David Wright (ed.) (Harmondsworth, Middlesex, 1970), p. 161.

3. *Collected Letters of Samuel Taylor Coleridge*, E. L. Griggs (ed.), 6 vols (Oxford, 1956–71), i, pp. 266–7.

4. i.e. *Modern Painters*, vol. ii, part iii, section ii, para. 4. In cases where it has seemed helpful to do so, I put this alternative long form of reference in the footnotes.

5. William Jerdan, *Autobiography*, 2 vols (London, 1852–3), i, pp. 1–2.

6. *Modern Painters*, vol. iii, part iv, chapter xiii, para. 14.

7. David Hume, *A Treatise of Human Nature*, 1739–40, L. A. Selby-Bigge (ed.), 1888, reprinted edition (Oxford, 1951), p. 408.

8. David Vincent (ed.), *Testaments of Radicalism: Memoirs of Working Class Politicians 1790–1815* (London, 1977), p. 177.

9. John Foster, *Essays in a Series of Letters to a Friend*, 1805, revised second edition, 2 vols (London, 1806), i, p. 47 ('On a Man's writing Memoirs of Himself').

10. *The Autobiography and Letters of Mrs M. O. W. Oliphant*, p. 263.

11. *Modern Painters*, vol. v, Preface.

12. Quoted in Graham Reynolds, *Turner* (London, 1969), p. 190.

13. *Praeterita*, book ii, chapter iv.

14. *Modern Painters*, vol. i, part ii, section ii, chapter i, paras. 15–16.

15. Ibid., vol. i, part ii, section iii, chapter iv, para. 13.

16. Ibid., vol. v, part ix, chapter ix, para. 20.

17. Ibid., vol. v, part ix, chapter iv, para. 18.

18. Ibid., vol. vi, part v, chapter xv, para. 11.

19. Ruskin speaks of the interaction between verbal knowledge and visual knowledge in *Modern Painters*, vol. ii, part iii, section ii, para. 2 (*Works*, iv, p. 23).

20. *Modern Painters*, vol. iii, part iv, chapter x, para. 19.

21. Ibid., vol. iii, part iv, chapter xi, paras. 3–4.

22. *Praeterita*, book ii, chapter v.

23. *The Autobiography of Mark Rutherford (and Mark Rutherford's Deliverance)*, The Victorian Library Series (Leicester, 1969), p. 2.

24. *Praeterita*, book ii, chapter iii.

25. Ibid., book i, chapter i.

26. Ruskin may have read Thomas Brown on the role of accident in the development of genius (*Lectures on the Philosophy of Human Mind*, 4 vols (Edinburgh, 1820), ii, pp. 437–8). See W. G. Collingwood, *The Life and Work of John Ruskin*, 2 vols (London, 1893), i, p. 98.

27. Hazlitt, *Works*, P. P. Howe (ed.), ix, p. 151.

28. *Guesses at Truth*, by Two Brothers, 2 vols (London, 1827), ii, p. 322.

29. *Modern Painters*, vol. iii, part iv, chapter x, para. 1.

30. *Praeterita*, book i, chapter ii.

31. Ibid.

32. *Modern Painters*, vol v, part vii, chapter iv, para. 32.

33. *Praeterita*, book i, chapter iv.

34. F. H. Bradley, *Ethical Studies*, second edition (Oxford, 1927), p. 97.

35. *Praeterita*, book ii, chapter x.

36. F. W. Maitland, *The Life and Letters of Leslie Stephen* (London, 1906), p. 286.

37. Ibid., p. 280.

38. For Marian Evans's review of *Modern Painters* iii as one of the great defences of realism see the *Westminster and Foreign Quarterly Review*, April 1 1856, New Series ix, p. 625ff.

39. For a belated summary of the significance of the pivotal moment in carrying out the Romantic ideal of art as 'rescue-work', see Joseph Conrad's 'Preface to *The Nigger of the "Narcissus"*'.

40. In the Zodiac Press edition of Mrs Oliphant's *Miss Marjoribanks*, Q. D. Leavis argues in her introduction that the novel influenced George Eliot in *Middlemarch*. But we should notice that the merit of *Miss Marjoribanks* lies in the strength of not making too much of things—a strength that was also Mrs Oliphant's sane weakness.

41. For *Middlemarch* all references in brackets are to *The Works of George Eliot*, Cabinet Edition, 20 vols (Edinburgh and London, 1878–80).

42. R. H. Hutton attacks the idea that it is the novel that has a monopoly of the word 'real' in an essay in which he praises Tennyson for including a certain idealism as an irreducible part of reality (*Brief Literary Essays*, pp. 184–6); for his complaint that poetry had become pessimistic and melancholy for being too realistic and not sufficiently romantic see his argument against Professor Courthope's view concerning 'life in poetry' (ibid., p. 408). Hutton used Newman's sense of the word 'real' (discussed above in chapter 1) to deplore the novel's reduction of matters of faith to agnostic mundanity (e.g. *Essays on Some of the Modern Guides to English Thought in Matters of Faith*, 1888 edition, pp. 289–302, where he accuses George Eliot of substituting human memory for the 'real' after-life).

43. Quoted in Gordon S. Haight, *George Eliot: A Biography*, corrected edition (Oxford, 1969), p. 450.

44. Quoted in Ruby V. Redinger, *George Eliot: The Emergent Self* (London, 1975), pp. 84–5.

45. Ibid., p. 141.

46. *Impressions of Theophrastus Such*, Cabinet Edition, p. 18 ('Looking Inward').

47. *The Life and Correspondence of John Foster (1779–1843)*, J. E. Ryland (ed.), 2 vols (London, 1846), i, p. 208.

48. Lancelot Andrewes, *Sermons*, G. M. Story (ed.) (Oxford, 1967), pp. 197–9.

49. Feuerbach, *The Essence of Christianity*, translated from the second German edition by Marian Evans, Chapman's Quarterly Series, no. vi (London, 1854), p. 21.

50. Samuel Butler, *Life and Habit* (London, 1910), pp. 5–6.

51. Mrs Humphry Ward, *A Writer's Recollections* (London, 1918), p. 108.

52. Cf. Edith Simcox at the funeral of George Eliot: 'Then I drifted towards the chapel, standing first for a while under the colonnade where a child asked me, "Was it the late George Eliot's wife was going to be buried?" I think I said Yes' (Gordon S. Haight, *George Eliot: A Biography*, p. 550). Even so the children around the death-bed in chapter eight of 'Amos Barton', 'cried because mama was ill and papa looked so unhappy; but they thought, perhaps next week things will be as they used to be again' (*Scenes of Clerical Life*, Cabinet Edition, 2 vols, i, p. 110).

53. L. N. Tolstoy, *Anna Karenina*, translated by Rosemary Edmonds (Harmondsworth, Middlesex, 1972), p. 498 (part five, chapter eleven).

54. Ibid., pp. 502–3 (part five, chapter twelve).

55. De Quincey, *Collected Writings*, David Masson (ed.), 14 vols (Edinburgh, 1889–90), i, pp. 47–8.

56. *Middlemarch*, book 1, chapter x (i, p. 125).

BIBLIOGRAPHY

AMIEL, HENRI FRÉDRIC, *The Journal Intime*, translated by Mrs Humphry Ward (London, 1885).

BAMFORD, SAMUEL, *Autobiography*, W. H. Challoner (ed.), 2 vols (vol. i, 'Early Days' first published 1848–9; vol. ii, 'Passages in the Life of a Radical', first published in 2 vols 1841–3), (London, 1967).

BROWN, HORATIO, F., *John Addington Symonds: A Biography*, 1895, second edition (London, 1903).

CROSS, J. W., *George Eliot's Life*, 3 vols (Edinburgh and London, 1885).

ELIOT, GEORGE, *Works*, Cabinet Edition, 20 vols (Edinburgh and London, 1878–80).

HAYDON, BENJAMIN ROBERT, *Autobiography and Memoirs*, Tom Taylor (ed.), 1853, new edition with introduction by Aldous Huxley, 2 vols (London, 1926).

MARTINEAU, HARRIET, *Autobiography*, with Memorials by Maria Weston Chapman, 3 vols, vols i and ii 1885 (London, 1877).

OLIPHANT, MRS MARGARET, *Autobiography and Letters of Mrs M. O. W. Oliphant*, Mrs Harry Coghill (ed.) (Edinburgh and London, 1899).

——, *The Ways of Life* (London, 1897).

RUSKIN, JOHN, *Works*, The Library Edition, E. T. Cook and Alexander Wedderburn (eds.), 39 vols (London, 1903).

STEPHEN, LESLIE, *Mausoleum Book*, Alan Bell (ed.) (Oxford, 1977).

TROLLOPE, ANTHONY, *An Autobiography*, 1883 (Oxford, 1980).

CHAPTER 5

1. 'Hope was one of the dubious gifts of Prometheus; instead of giving men the foreknowledge of the immortals, he gave them hope', Soren Kierkegaard, *Either/Or*, 2 vols (London, 1944), vol. 1 (translated by David F. Swenson and Lilliam M. Swenson), p. 240.

2. Jessie Chambers, *D. H. Lawrence: A Personal Record by E.T.*, second edition, J. D. Chambers (ed.) (London, 1965), p. 105.

3. *Essays of George Eliot*, Thomas Pinney (ed.) (London, 1963), p. 324.

4. All page references are to the *New Wessex Edition of the Novels*, general editor P. N. Furbank, 14 vols (London, 1975).

5. See G. H. Lewes, *Problems of Life and Mind, Third Series, Problem the First: The Study of Psychology* (London, 1879), p. 150.

6. Sigmund Freud, *Civilization and its Discontents*, translated by Joan Riviere, revised and edited by James Strachey (London, 1963), pp. 64–5.

7. Florence Emily Hardy, *The Life of Thomas Hardy*, pp. 330, 58.

8. John Stuart Mill, *Three Essays* (Oxford, 1975), pp. 74–5.

9. The question as to whether the principle of action is the self or the emotions has been discussed above with respect to Hazlitt's Romanticism. Similarly, the theme of Greek as compared to modern emotion was touched on in chapter four: Hardy of course took an intense interest in the large, unself-consciously tragic emotions of the Greeks. Also v. Nietzsche, *The Genealogy of Morals*, ii, xvi.

10. See the last two paragraphs of chapter xix of George Eliot's *Adam Bede* ('this rough man' with his secret which we now share) or the end of chapter xx of Trollope's *The Warden* for a secular obituary of Bunce, 'an old man'. In such cases, the names give way to the general humanism underlying such novels, as these 'men' confront common sorts of fate, whatever their individual differences and provocations.

11. Arthur Schopenhauer, *The World as Will and Idea*, translated by R. B. Haldane and J. Kemp, 3 vols (London, 1886), iii, p. 391.

12. The abbreviation CP is here used for *The Complete Poems of Thomas Hardy*, James Gibson (ed.), New Wessex Edition (London 1976); the number is that of the poem rather than the page in this edition.

13. *Goethe's Autobiography*, translated by R. O. Moon (London, 1932), p. 592.

14. *Thomas Hardy: The Critical Heritage*, R. G. Cox (ed.) (London, 1970), p. 269.

15. *Uniform Edition of the Works of Joseph Conrad* (London and Toronto, 1923–8), *Youth: A Narrative and Two Other Stories*, pp. 150–1.

16. *The Death of Ivan Ilyich* in *The Cossacks and Other Stories*, translated by Rosemary Edmonds (Harmondsworth, Middlesex, 1960), pp. 152–4.

17. *The Writings of Arthur Hallam*, T. H. Vail Motter (ed.) (New York and London, 1943), pp. 186–90.

18. In contrast, words, for Yeats, are said to 'obey my call' ('Words', *The Collected Poems of W. B. Yeats*, second edition (reprinted, London, 1969), pp. 100–1). In a comparison between poets of memory, Yeats's verbal jettisoning of emotion may be contrasted with Hardy's repression of it.

19. Thomas Brown M.D., *Lectures on the Philosophy of the Human Mind*, 4 vols (Edinburgh, 1820), ii, p. 241.

20. *The Literary Notes of Thomas Hardy*, Lennart A. Björk (ed.) (Göteborg, Sweden, 1974), vol. i, part i, p. 109 (no. 1017).

21. *The Collected Letters of Thomas Hardy*, Richard Little Purdy and Michael Millgate (eds.), vol 1 (1840–92), (Oxford, 1978), p. 262.

22. I have published an extended account of 'The Photograph' in *Stand*, vol. 9, no. 1.

23. Edward Caird, *The Critical Philosophy of Immanuel Kant*, 2 vols (Glasgow, 1889), ii, p. 251.

24. See pp. 76–93.

25. See p. 312.

26. The importance of Darwin to a study of Hardy is no more than touched on here. For evidence of Hardy's sense of the redundant over-evolution of man's feelings and consciousness, however, see *The Life of Thomas Hardy*, pp. 149, 163, 218.

27. *The Variorum Edition of the Complete Poems of Thomas Hardy*, James Gibson (ed.) (London, 1979), p. 530.

28. See pp. 224–5.

29. J. C. Hare, *Guesses at Truth by Two Brothers* (with A. W. Hare), 2 vols (London, 1827), ii, pp. 94–8.

30. Ruskin, *Works* (Library Edition), vii, p. 313 (*Modern Painters*, vol. v, part ix, chapter iv, para. 18).

31. John Bunyan, *The Pilgrim's Progress from this World to that which is to come* (1678), Roger Sharrock (ed.), Oxford Standard Authors (London, 1966), p. 389.

32. On Hardy's reading of *The Pilgrim's Progress* see *The Life of Thomas Hardy*, pp. 441–2.

BIBLIOGRAPHY

CLIFFORD, W. K., *Lectures and Essays*, Leslie Stephen and Frederick Pollock (eds.), 1879, second edition (London, 1896).

HARDY, FLORENCE EMILY, *The Life of Thomas Hardy, 1840–1928*, first published 1962 to bring together *The Early Years of Thomas Hardy 1840–91* (1928) and *The Later Years of Thomas Hardy, 1892–1928* (1930), corrected edition (London, 1972).

HARDY, THOMAS, *Complete Poems*, James Gibson (ed.), New Wessex Edition (London, 1976)—cited as 'CP'.

——, *New Wessex Edition of the Novels*, P. N. Furbank (general editor), 14 vols (London, 1975).

——, *Personal Notebooks*, Richard H. Taylor (ed.) (London, 1978).

LAWRENCE, D. H., *Phoenix: The Posthumous Papers*, Edward D. MacDonald (ed.), 1936, reprinted edition (London, 1970).

MALLOCK, W. H., *Is Life Worth Living?* (London, 1879).

SETH, ANDREW and R. B. HALDANE, (eds.), *Essays in Philosophical Criticism* (London, 1883).

SULLY, JAMES, *Pessimism* (London, 1877).

CHAPTER 6

1. *Collected Letters*, i, p. 171.

2. All such page references are to *The Phoenix Edition* of Lawrence's works, 26 vols (London, 1954–72).

3. All references to the works of Conrad are taken from the *Uniform Edition* (U.E.), 22 vols (London and Toronto, 1923–8). The pagination of 'Typhoon' and 'Amy Foster' (both to be found in the volume entitled *The Nigger of the 'Narcissus' and Typhoon and Other Stories*) and A Personal Record (in *The Mirror of The Sea/A Personal Record*) starts from the second half of the volume in which they severally appear.

4. James Beattie, *Dissertations Moral and Critical*, 2 vols (London, 1783), i, p. 50.

5. See Hardy's essay 'The Profitable Reading of Fiction' in *Thomas Hardy's Personal Writings*, Harold Orel (ed.) (London, 1967), especially p. 112.

6. G. Jean-Aubry, *Joseph Conrad, Life and Letters*, 2 vols (London, 1927), i, p. 183.

7. *Letters from Joseph Conrad 1895–1924*, Edward Garnett (ed.) (Bloomsbury, W.C., 1928), p. 127.

8. Ford Madox Ford, *Joseph Conrad: A Personal Remembrance* (London, 1924), p. 46.

9. *Letters from Joseph Conrad*, Garnett (ed.), p. 135.

10. On key-words and conventional words see *Under Western Eyes*, part first, chapter three, U.E., p. 67 and chapter two, p. 39, respectively.

11. Arthur Schopenhauer, *The World as Will and Idea*, translated by R. B. Haldane and J. Kemp, 3 vols (London, 1886), i, p. 404 (my italics).

12. On Lawrence's discovery of Nietzsche during his time in Croydon see Emile Delavenay, *D. H. Lawrence: The Man and His Work, The Formative Years:*

1885–1919, translated by Katharine M. Delavenay (London, 1972), p. 58, and Jessie Chambers, *D. H. Lawrence: A Personal Record*, p. 120. I have been helped, particularly in part three and in relation to Nietzsche, by Alasdair MacIntyre's *After Virtue: a study in moral theory* (London, 1981).

13. *The Complete Works of Friedrich Nietzsche*, Dr Oscar Levy (ed.), 18 vols (Edinburgh and London, 1909–11), vol. iv, *Thus Spake Zarathustra*, translated by Thomas Common (1909), p. 112.

14. Ibid., vol xvi, *The Twilight of the Idols; Or, How to Philosophise with the Hammer*, translated by Anthony M. Ludovici (1911), p. 63.

15. CP: Hardy, *Complete Poems*, James Gibson (ed.) (London, 1976).

16. *The Critical Writings of Adrian Stokes*, Lawrence Gowing (ed.), 3 vols (London, 1978), i, (1930–37), p. 232.

17. *Jude the Obscure*, part sixth, chapter eight, New Wessex Edition, p. 396.

18. *The Literary Notes of Thomas Hardy*, Lennart A. Björk (ed.), vol. i (Göteborg, Sweden, 1974), text, p. 14, entry 112.

19. *Goethe's Autobiography*, translated by R. O. Moon (London, 1932), p. 554.

20. On emotional versus logical reason see *Thomas Hardy's Personal Writings*, Harold Orel (ed.) (London, 1967), p. 115.

21. *The Literary Notes of Thomas Hardy*, i, text, p. 86, entry 839.

22. 'The End of the Tether' appears in the volume of the *Uniform Edition* entitled *Youth: A Narrative and Two Other Stories*.

23. I have used the abbreviation *The Unconscious* for Lawrence's volume *The Fantasia of the Unconscious* and *Psychoanalysis and the Unconscious* (Phoenix Edition).

24. W. H. Mallock, *Is Life Worth Living?* (London, 1879), pp. 49–50, 69.

25. 'It is true that a person has the last word on what his intentions are if by this we mean that it is *his* behaviour which is the criterion of what his intentions are and not *our* beliefs about the possibility of his success. But he has not the last word on what his intentions are if by this we mean that what he *says* is to outweigh what he *does* as evidence for his true intentions' Anthony Kenny, *Will, Freedom and Power* (Oxford, 1975), p. 100. In George Eliot *'his'* behaviour was just such a balance between what his life effected and what, within, he might say of himself and to himself in his heart of hearts. This balance goes awry in Lawrence for whom relativism did not necessarily mean sympathy.

26. *D. H. Lawrence, Sons and Lovers: A Casebook*, Gamini Salgado (ed.) (London, 1973), p. 30.

27. T. S. Eliot, *Selected Essays*, first published 1932 (London, 1972 edition), p. 29. For further background see Rayner Heppenstall, *Middleton Murry: A Study in Excellent Normality* (London, 1934), especially pp. 43–59.

28. See John Middleton Murry, *God—Being an Introduction to the Science of Metabiology* (London, 1929), pp. 45, 242; and for a particular example, significantly for us, Murry's analysis of Hardy's 'A Broken Appointment', *The Problem of Style*, 1922 (London, 1960 edition), pp. 21–6.

29. Lawrence, *Studies in Classic American Literature* (Phoenix Edition), p. 2.

30. *What is Art?* translated by Aylmer Maude, 1930 (London, 1969 edition), p. 121.

31. (unused) Foreword to *Women in Love*, reprinted in H. Coombes (ed.), *D. H. Lawrence: A Critical Anthology* (Harmondsworth, Middlesex, 1973), p. 124.

32. *The Complete Works of Friedrich Nietzsche:* vol. xiii, *The Genealogy of Morals*, translated by Horace B. Samuel (1910), pp. 45–6.

BIBLIOGRAPHY

BURROW, TRIGANT, *The Social Basis of Consciousness* (London, 1927).

CARSWELL, CATHERINE, *The Savage Pilgrimage: A Narrative of D. H. Lawrence*, revised edition (London, 1932).

CHAMBERS, JESSIE, *D. H. Lawrence: A Personal Record by E.T.*, 1935, second edition, J. D. Chambers (ed.) (London, 1965).

CONRAD, JOSEPH, *Works*, Uniform Edition, 22 vols (London and Toronto, 1923–8)—cited as 'U.E.'.

HULME, T. E., *Speculations* (London, 1924).

KARL, FREDERICK R., *Joseph Conrad: The Three Lives* (London, 1979).

LAWRENCE, D. H., *Collected Letters*, Harry T. Moore (ed.), 2 vols (London, 1962).

——, *Phoenix Edition of the* [*Prose*] *Works*, 26 vols (London, 1954–72).

——, *Phoenix: The Posthumous Papers*, Edward D. McDonald (ed.), 1936, reprinted edition (London, 1970).

——, *Phoenix ii: Uncollected, Unpublished and Other Prose Works*, Warren Roberts and Harry T. Moore (eds.) (London, 1968).

MURRY, JOHN MIDDLETON, *Between Two Worlds: An Autobiography* (London, 1935).

——, *Keats and Shakespeare: A Study of Keats's Poetic from 1816 to 1820* (London, 1925).

——, *Reminiscences of D. H. Lawrence* (London, 1933).

——, *Son of Woman: The Story of D. H. Lawrence*, 1931 (London, 1954).

NEHLS, EDWARD, *D. H. Lawrence: A Composite Biography*, 3 vols (Madison, Wisconsin, 1957–9).

WOOLF, VIRGINIA, *Collected Essays*, 4 vols (London, 1966–7).

Index